AN ECONOMIC
HISTORY OF RUSSIA

AN ECONOMIC HISTORY *of* RUSSIA

BY

JAMES MAVOR

VOLUME TWO

SECOND EDITION
REVISED AND ENLARGED

NEW YORK
RUSSELL & RUSSELL · INC
1965

FIRST PUBLISHED IN 1914
REISSUED, 1965, BY RUSSELL & RUSSELL, INC.
FROM THE REVISED AND CORRECTED EDITION OF 1925
BY ARRANGEMENT WITH J. M. DENT & SONS LIMITED, LONDON
AND E. P. DUTTON & CO., NEW YORK
L. C. CATALOG CARD NO: 64-66397

PRINTED IN THE UNITED STATES OF AMERICA

CONTENTS

BOOK IV

MODERN POLITICAL AND SOCIAL REVOLUTIONARY MOVEMENTS IN RUSSIA PRIOR TO 1903

Absolutism the outcome of the unification of disparate nationalities— Foundation of the autocracy—Destruction of traditional democratic elements—Byzantism—Causes of " the anarchy "—Conditional sovereignty—Power of the Patriarch—The principle of unity —Imperial ambitions—Absolutism and peace—Anti-revolutionary rôle of the autocracy—Stein's view of German unity—Metternich's view of Alexander I—Fluctuations of mental attitude of Alexander I —Nicholas I as anti-revolutionist—The Crimean War—Psychology of Russian absolutism—Effect of absolutism upon the duration of life and upon the character of the Tsars—Peasant views upon the autocracy—Relation of the autocracy and the gentry—The revolutionary " state of mind "—Revolutionary propagandas.

CHAPTER II

The origin of the Cossacks—Cossack communities—Effect of flights of peasants upon the peasant mass—Stenka Razën—Ground of the hostility of the Cossack towards the peasant—Effect of changes in administration—Mutual suspicion of the peasants—Grievances of the Cossacks—Origin of the disturbances—The Cossacks of the Yaëk or Ural River—Changes in the military position of the Cossacks— Obligations to render military service—Grievances about arrears of pay, &c.—Deputation to St. Petersburg—Conciliatory attitude of

CHAPTER III

CHAPTER IV

CHAPTER VIII

CHAPTER IX

CONTENTS

CHAPTER X

CHAPTER XI

CHAPTER XII

CHAPTER XIII

CHAPTER XIV

BOOK V

THE AGRARIAN QUESTION AND ITS REVOLUTIONARY PHASES

CHAPTER I

CHAPTER II

CHAPTER III

CHAPTER IV

CHAPTER V

CHAPTER VI

CHAPTER VII

CHAPTER VIII

CONTENTS

BOOK VI

INDUSTRIAL DEVELOPMENT UNDER CAPITALISM

CHAPTER I

CHAPTER II

The machine as a " separator " between land and factory—Proportions of temporary absentees in different industries—Workmen's contracts—Anomalous position of peasant workmen—Gradual emergence of a proletariat—Vicious circle in factory-land economics —Schulze-Gävernitz's scheme of the process of factory-land evolution.

CONTENTS

CHAPTER VI

BOOK VII

THE REVOLUTIONARY MOVEMENT IN RUSSIA, 1903-1907

CHAPTER I

CHAPTER IV

Moscow engine-drivers initiate strike—Rapid progress of strike all over Russia—Complete cessation of movement of population and goods and stagnation of life in towns—Government and bank officials join the strike movement—Its political character—Effect on local administration in Estland—Civil servants, financiers, and manufacturers make representations to the Government—Effect of the strike upon foreign trade—Business reduced to confusion—Extension of the terms of obligations—Destruction of credit—Significance of the strike—Organization of the striking mass—The Council of Working Men's Deputies—Its Manifesto—Its demands upon the Government—Arming of the working men—Relations of the Council of Working Men's Deputies with the St. Petersburg Duma or City Council—Relations of the Social Democratic Party with the Council of Working Men's Deputies—The Socialist Revolutionary Party—The dilemma of the retail shopkeepers—Incidents of the strike—Imitation of the St. Petersburg Council of Working Men's Deputies throughout the country—The question of publicity —The printers and the general strike—Antagonistic interests—The zenith of the strike—The Tsar's Manifesto of 17th October 1905— The reception of the Manifesto—Difficulty of securing publicity for it—Attacks by troops on the 18th October—Social Democratic views upon the Manifesto—Amnesty demanded—Demonstration for amnesty—Capitulation by the Government—The amnesty signed on the same evening—Ebb and flow in the intensity of popular feeling—Conclusion of the political strike ; continuance of economic strikes—Reopening of factories, &c.—Funerals of the victims of 18th October—Fear of counter-revolutionary movement.

CHAPTER V

The Union of Russian People—The Black Hundreds—Counter-revolutionary " underground " printing office—The *pogrom*—Attempt to excite the Russian against the non-Russian elements—Prince Uruzov's exposure of *pogrom* tactics—Constituents of the Union of Russian People and of the Black Hundreds—Assaults upon working men's deputies in St. Petersburg—Determination to form militant *drujini* for defensive purposes, not carried into effect— " Party " *drujini* employed to guard deputies—General arming of working men—Open sale of arms and open purchases by general

CHAPTER IX

CHAPTER X

CHAPTER XI

PAGE

Police shot by revolutionaries—The disarming of "reservists" —The revolt begins to subside—Presnya Quarter—Heavy bombardment—Surrender—The toll of the "uprising"—Shares of the revolutionary parties—Conclusions about the uprising.

CHAPTER XII

Bogoslovsky Mountain Foundry—Terror and "expropriations"—Lvov —Guerilla warfare—Communications interrupted—Reaction against Lvov—The "Syetch" in the mountains—Capture of Lvov and cessation of disturbances.

CHAPTER XIII

Ambiguous rôle of the police in political and revolutionary movements —The system of espionage and provocation—The political police— The case of Sudeikin—Russian police abroad—The spy Azef— Details of his career—His varied activity—Catalogue of his alleged crimes—Official *communiqué*—Lopukhin—Bakaya—Burtsev—Discovery of the treachery of Azef—Net results of the episode—Admissions and denials of M. Stolypin—General conclusions upon the revolutionary movement

CHAPTER XIV

Ambiguity of the expression *intelligentsia*—Constituents of the group— The *intelligentsia* in the Zemstvo—The "righting of the Zemstvos" —Failure of the *intelligentsia* to effect reforms—Social reasons for this failure—Views of Tugan-Baranovsky—Contrast between Russian and Western European society—Reasons for the adoption of socialist views by the *intelligentsia*—Detachment of the intellectual Russian—Self-criticism by *intelligentsia*—*Vyekhé*—Future of socialism.

BOOK IV

MODERN POLITICAL AND SOCIAL REVOLU-
TIONARY MOVEMENTS IN RUSSIA PRIOR
TO 1903

INTRODUCTION

WHILE terroristic phases, or phases during which the political or social order is sought to be overturned by violent means, are frequent, if not invariable concomitants of revolution, Russian revolutionary and counter-revolutionary movements throughout their history have been peculiarly characterized by violence. This circumstance may be attributed largely to the racial antagonisms which have excited or have contributed to the revolutionary movements; but it appears also to be due to certain characteristics of the Slavic peoples. Conspicuous among these characteristics is the combination of immense patience and of impulsiveness.[1] The Russian is capable of endurance of wrong to an extreme degree; but when accumulated grievances reach a certain point, they become unbearable to him, and, yielding to impulses normally foreign to his kind and amiable disposition, he may exact immediate and sometimes dreadful reckoning.[2] This characteristic is supplemented by another which makes its appearance in the most ordinary affairs of life, and on acute occasion becomes most impressive, namely the habit of pursuing an object with remorseless logic, regardless of consequences, without delay and without compromise. Disregard of consequences has indeed been elevated in Russia to the dignity of a principle of morals. The habit of disregarding consequences may not inappropriately be considered as a sign of youthfulness, feminism, or optimism in the people who practise it.

Mature life is a series of compromises, primitive life in societies and juvenile life in the individual are remorselessly logical. Thus whenever the mature minds in a society become inactive, and the

---

[1] The characteristic of impulsiveness is attributed by the Russian anthropologist Ivanovsky to the weakness of the controlling centres. He considers that the Russian temperament is more impulsive than that of Western Europeans. See article in *Psychological and Philosophical Questions* (Moscow Psychological Society).

[2] Also noticed by Ivanovsky (*op. cit.*). Russian peasants still torture horse thieves; and in the Caucasus they sometimes obliterate the Kurdish villages.

3

youth of society alone represents vigour, recrudescence of violence is likely to occur.[1] Intellectual decay in aristocracy and bourgeoisie is the almost invariable precursor of reform and of revolutionary movements.[2]

The primitive attitude of mind, partly habitual and partly reverted to at intervals, on occasion leads under the stress of widespread emotion to the execution in primitive forms of what is regarded as justice. For example, the adoption by the Novgorodians in the fifteenth century of the earlier form of punishment by " flood and pillage," [3] was a reversion of this kind, and it is permissible to regard the pillaging of estates by the peasants in 1902, in 1905, and in 1917, as well as the *pogroms* against the Jews in 1903, as being the outcome of the same attitude.

The social disintegration of which in these historical examples the peasants were in some measure made the victims, appears to have induced them to fall back upon primitive methods of punishing alleged wrong-doers, a usual result of individual or social psychological tempests.[4] These orgasms, though sometimes terrible in their intensity, have usually, in the case of Russian revolutionary move-

[1] This appears to apply to all societies, of whatever kind and magnitude, and to all races. In France, *e.g.*, those who played a leading part in the Revolution and its consequences were, for the most part, young men. In 1789 Danton, Robespierre, Desmoulins, Tallien, and many other conspicuous figures were under thirty years of age ; Napoleon was twenty-seven when he received the command of the army in Italy. Nearly all the leaders of the revolutionary movements in Paris in 1830, in 1848, and in 1871 were also young men of from twenty-five to thirty years of age.   Within the revolutionary ranks even, youth counts for much, partly because the fundamental idea of revolution involves rebellion against authority, and the " old men " of revolutions soon lose their prestige. (Louis Blanc, *e.g.*, was in his prime in 1848 ; he was an " old man " in 1871.) For an interesting account of this characteristic in Russian revolutionary ranks, see Debogoriy-Mokrievich (*Reminiscences*, St. Petersburg, 1906, p. 584). That the peasant revolts in Russia in 1902–1903 and in 1905–1906, as well as the risings in the cities, were led or chiefly participated in by young men, is shown *infra*, p. 331. In China the Boxer movement, which was essentially revolutionary, was characterized by the extreme youth of many of its adherents (*cf.* Smith, A. H., *China in Convulsion* (Edinburgh, 1901), i. p. 172). The apparent connection between increase in the influence of youth and the recrudescence of violence in recent years throughout Western Europe and in America is acutely discussed by M. Paul de Rousiers in " Les Solutions Violentes " in *La Science Sociale* (Paris, September 1909).

[2] *Cf.* Sorel, Georges, on the decadence of the bourgeoisie in *Réflexions sur la Violence* (Paris, 1910), pp. 91 *et seq.*

[3] *Cf. supra*, vol. i. p. 32.

[4] So also the feminist terrorism in England in 1912–1913.

ments, been brief in their duration. It is indeed impossible for the nervous system to sustain a long-continued strain of this kind. Thus among the peasants, after the storm of passion was exhausted, the results of the pillage were, in frequent cases, returned, the peasants calmly awaiting the decision of the Duma on the whole question of their grievances, and reverting to their habitual mode of life although their relations with the landowners had changed sharply. After the Jewish *pogroms*, when the fury of the moment had spent itself, Christian and Jew alike settled into their normal state of quiescence. So also after a period of terror and subsequent disillusion, the peasants relapsed into sullen passiveness under the rule of the Moscow Soviet.

The conduct of the Government at various epochs is not dissimilar. Reduced to panic by widespread disaffection, the functionaries resort to measures of great severity, suspend or neglect all processes of law, and, reverting like the peasants to a primitive attitude of mind, commit needlessly acts of indiscriminate cruelty; and then, when the passion of the moment has been expended, they sometimes offer unprecedented concessions.[1] The history of the early Slavs, of the later Russians, as well as that of the non-Russian elements, is a history of frequent clashing of economical and political interests, with intermittent outbreaks of violence among peoples racially widely divergent and very prolific, and frequent antagonism between the rulers and their immediate entourage, the mass of the people being drawn only from time to time directly into the latter conflicts, although they were at all times implicated in the larger issues which these conflicts involved. Warfare for centuries, urged with determined bitterness, and often accompanied by unrestrained cruelty, has left deep traces in the character of the people.

The revolutionary spirit has not only frequently been inspired or intensified, it has often been distracted, by racial antagonisms.[2] Even autocracy has been more considerate of Russian than of non-Russian elements.

---

[1] Although such concessions were absolutely necessary to prevent recurrence of peasant violence, the fact that the concessions were made after the disaffection was subdued is the important point.

[2] Particularism has been a source of weakness in all the revolutionary movements. There were, *e.g.*, separate Polish, Little Russian, Finnish, and other oppositional parties.

The tendency on the part of individuals and of governmental authorities alike to proceed rapidly to violent action, without thought of ulterior reactions, seems to be due to these fundamental characteristics, deepened and strengthened as they have been by centuries of conflict.

On these grounds, therefore, it is not surprising that dislike of governmental policy, after long endurance of its arbitrary character, should lead to immediate and summary violence towards the instruments of it, and that such violence should in turn lead to violent action by the authorities, and this again to reprisals, and so on. Count Leo Tolstoy's propaganda against all violence, though impossible of complete success, partly because of the incompatibility of meekness and government, and partly because of the struggles incident to increase of population and to contact of different races, is, nevertheless, based upon a profound appreciation of the character of the Russian people, and of the source at once of their strength and of their weakness.

While the growth of the autocratic power in Russia has been very gradual, and while that power has been greatly intensified in comparatively recent times, it is evident that at no period of its history could that power have been overthrown without violence. It is also evident that the autocracy owed its existence primarily to the numerousness of the races by which its seat of power was surrounded, and secondarily to the numerousness of the races over which it ruled. It has owed its historical justification to the circumstance that contemporary conditions made it appear as though only through the autocracy could the political unity of the heterogeneous groups be secured. So long as there was in progress the process of welding, for the most part by violent means, these different elements into a political whole, it was impossible to permit the controlled groups to share in the task of government ; at all events it was impossible within the limits of the political insight of the autocratic rulers, or even of their contemporary critics, such as they were. The revolutionary ideas which from about the sixteenth century began to affect Europe were thus late in affecting Russia. The Protestant Revolution of the sixteenth and seventeenth centuries, which deeply affected Western Europe, affected Russia not at all ; and the revolutionary ideas and events of the eighteenth century touched her somewhat tardily. Antagonism to the ruling order, with occasional outbursts of violence,[1] had been chronic; but the spirit of revolt against absolutism was not really aroused in Russia until more than thirty years after the French Revolution. Katherine II had coquetted with liberal ideas, and had initiated discussion and investigation of the " condition of the people question "; but she had abandoned liberalism with characteristic decision whenever she found that its progress might impair her own power. Alexander I in the beginning of his reign had been influenced by liberal ideas; but he also speedily turned his back upon them. Up till the period of the Napoleonic wars, even the most highly educated of the Russian upper class had little contact with Western Europe, while the mass of the people had none. The revolutionary movement in Russia towards the political and social ideas of Western Europe is thus a distinctively modern phenomenon. It is coincident with the rise of capitalistic industry. The emphasis of the social as distinguished from the political features separates it in a certain measure from all previous revolutions. Social disintegration has no doubt preceded or accompanied all outbreaks against authority; but political changes have frequently satisfied the demand for change, and the social relations have in effect remained undisturbed. The revolutionary movement in Russia during recent years has been otherwise characterized. It is true, as the following details disclose, that the industrial and social movement has exhibited a tendency to " pass over " into a political movement; but it has also been very evident that no political change which was not accompanied by profound social readjustments would be likely to produce any serious effect. The reason for this lies deep in the history and in the character of the Russian people.

[1] For early revolutionary movements, see, *e.g.*, Kluchevsky, *Course of Russian History* (Moscow, 1908); for the period 1584–1614, see Waliszewski, *La Crise Révolutionnaire* (Paris, 1906); for the rebellion of Pugachev (1773), see *infra*, chap. ii. The Cossack and peasant revolts of 1773–1775 were revolutionary movements, but they were not revolts against absolutism.

CHAPTER I

ABSOLUTISM *VERSUS* REVOLUTION

IVAN III (the Great, 1462–1505) is regarded as the founder of Russian autocracy,[1] because during his reign what remained of the primitive democracy of medieval Russia was destroyed. The " free towns " were drawn or forced into the imperial sphere through abolition of their privileges and the subordination of their princely houses ; and the princes of the appanages were subjected to the Moscow State. Moreover, the Tsar, on his marriage to Sophia, grand-daughter of Manuel (II) Palæologus, Emperor of the East, advanced the pretension of succession to the Roman Emperors in the leadership of Greek orthodoxy,[2] and in the defence of Christian Europe against pagan Asia.[3] The subjection of the appanage princes and the rule which compelled them to reside within the limits of Moscow,[4] brought the *boyars* to court, but did not necessarily bring them to council. Ivan III did not in fact habitually consult his *boyars ;* he acted on his own initiative, taking advice from " self-made men " [5] who surrounded the throne. The old *Boyarskaya Duma* was altered in its character,[6] and after the accession of Ivan IV a new council—the *Sobor*—came into existence, composed of those Moscow groups which were disposed to aid in the aggrandisement of the power of the Tsar, including a considerable number of the clergy.[7] Many of the ancient noble families refused to attend the Moscow court and to reside

[1] Kovalevsky, M., *Russian Political Institutions* (Chicago, 1902), p. 40.
[2] *Ibid.*
[3] On the rôle of the later Roman Emperors as defenders of Europe against Asia, see the suggestive remarks of Professor Bury, *History of the Later Roman Empire*, vol. ii. p. 536. The tribal groups of early Russia had, centuries earlier, played a considerable part in this struggle. During the period when the Roman Empire was immune from their attacks, they were themselves engaged in formidable conflicts with Asiatic hordes. Cf. *supra*, vol. i. pp. 8–9.
[4] As the Shoguns compelled the Daimios of Japan to reside in Tokyo.
[5] Kovalevsky, *op. cit.*, p. 42.
[6] Cf. *ibid.* Its functions became less political and more judicial.
[7] Cf. *ibid.*

within its precincts.   They preferred to suffer the loss of their estates and to emigrate to Poland.[1]

There, attempts on the part of the Polish nobility to establish serfdom, and attempts on the part of the Latin clergy to suppress Greek Orthodoxy, led to flights of peasants.   Meanwhile the growth of serfdom in the Moscow State was producing similar flights.   The two streams of fleeing peasants met and formed bands, armed for defensive and offensive purposes.   The dying out of the Kalita dynasty and the unsuccessful attempt on the part of the Godunovs to establish a new one led to the absence of a masterful hand.   Absolutism under these conditions was impossible, and anarchy supervened.

During the period of anarchy the question of choosing a new Tsar brought into relief the conditions under which the new Tsar must accept his high office.   To begin with, the *boyars* agreed that the new Tsar should be a foreigner, that he should uphold the Orthodox Church, that he should acknowledge the right of the *boyars* to counsel the Tsar, and that there should be held a general assembly of the people—the *Zemsky Sobor*.[2]   Vladislav, son of Sigismund of Poland, accepted these terms ; but the conduct of the Poles and the rising spirit of the Russians brought his brief reign to an end, and after prolonged intrigues Mikhail, the first Romanov, was elected by the *boyars*.[3]   That Mikhail, who was only sixteen years of age at his accession, accepted the throne with conditions, there seems to be no doubt, but what these conditions were is not definitely known.   It is clear, however, that they included concessions to the *boyars* by whom and by the Cossacks he was elected.   In the early years of the reign of Mikhail, the *Zemsky Sobor*, or popular assembly, was frequently summoned in order that money might be granted to the Tsar ; but later, when his father, Philaret Romanov, returned to Russia from Poland, his influence came to be felt, and, in the interests of his son, he seems to have prevented the *Sobor* from being summoned.[4]   For a time Russia was a theocracy, the Patriarch having power at least equal to that of the Tsar, and reigning with him.

[1] *Cf.* Kovalevsky, *op. cit.*, p. 47.
[2] *Ibid.*, p. 58.   This general popular assembly was not an indigenous Russian institution.   It seems to have been suggested by the existence of a similar institution in the Polish-Lithuanian kingdom (cf. *ibid.*).   On the *Zemsky Sobor*, see *supra*, vol. i. p. 42, &c.
[3] And, not unimportantly, the Cossacks.
[4] Kovalevsky, *op. cit.*, p. 61.

Although the Tsar Alexis, the son of Mikhail, does not seem to have entered into any *pacta conventa*, yet the *Zemsky Sobor* was convened to confirm the act of coronation, and later was called to codify the law, and to advise concerning the method of dealing with insurrectionary movements.[1]   In all these matters at this time its influence was recognized, but later it fell into decay ; and during the period of the consolidation of the Moscow State, the personal power of the Tsar increased, and the importance of the *Zemsky Sobor* diminished.

It is not surprising that in the processes of welding numerous races into one mass and of forcing the reconciliation of divergent national and economical interests, the highest importance should be attached to the principle of unity.   Cohesion was necessary to enable the Russian people to resist the pressure of the Tartars, the Poles, and the Swedes, and unity was necessary to place the nation beyond the danger of internal divisions after the inroad of the moment was overcome.   This notion of the necessity of unity, and of its corollary, unanimity, appears to be quite fundamental in Russian local and national life.   In the village as in the State, dissent must not exist.   Where opinions differ, the differences must be resolved.   People must not agree to differ ; they must not differ.   Thus in the local assemblies decisions must be unanimous.[2]   The " sentence " must be the " sentence " of the whole assembly.[3]   This conception of the cardinal importance of unanimity with its implications may be regarded as the principal feature which distinguishes Russian political ideas from those of Western Europe.

The principle of unity is not merely a political conception. It is based upon a theory of morals.   The late M. Pobyedonostsev, Procurator of the Holy Synod, puts this quite clearly :

" Les esprits forts, les érudits prétendent : ' l'État n'a rien à voir dans l'Église, ni l'Église dans l'État ' ; donc l'humanité doit évolver en deux sphères, de telle sorte que le corps aura sa place dans l'une et l'esprit dans l'autre, et entre ces deux sphères il y aura l'espace comme entre le ciel et la terre.   Cela est-il possible ?

---

[1] Kovalevsky, *op. cit.*, p. 68.
[2] In the Polish Diet, the principle of individual veto prevented the passing of any but unanimously accepted measures.
[3] For an exception see *supra*, vol. i. p. 144.

On ne peut séparer le corps de l'esprit ; le corps et l'esprit vivent d'une vie unique, inséparable. . . . Le principe moral est unique. Il ne peut être divisé de telle façon qu'il y ait une doctrine de morale privée et une autre de morale publique ; la première séculière, la seconde religieuse. . . . L'État ne peut se borner à representer les intérêts matériels de la société, car alors il se dépouillerait lui-même de sa force morale et détruirait son union spirituelle avec la nation. Ce n'est qu'à cette condition que se maintiendront dans le peuple le sentiment de la legalité, le respect de la loi et la confiance dans le pouvoir. . . . Le pouvoir politique est appelé à agir et à ordonner ; ses actes sont des manifestations d'une volonté unique : sans cela, aucun gouvernement n'est possible." [1]

Although it is conceivable that political unification of disparate elements should be accomplished and sustained by the general will, and not by an "unique will," the necessity of unification, in the absence of demonstrative manifestation of the general will, affords the appropriate soil for the growth of autocratic power. In one of its aspects the history of Russia is the history of the growth of autocracy under these conditions. The "inflexible will "[2] of the Tsar[3] is "the unique will." He is at once head of the State and of the Church. He is ordained of God to be the arbiter of the destinies of his people. While absolutism is not a peculiarly Russian phenomenon, and while its characteristics in Russia were gradually developed, not without imitation of the models of Byzantium and of Western Europe prior to the eighteenth century, the fundamental idea of it was not out of harmony with the principle of unity which was deeply rooted in the Russian mind as a social necessity of the first order. The difficulty which the Slavs and their allies experienced in making themselves masters

[1] Pobiedonostsev, *Questions religieuses, sociales et politiques* (Paris), pp. 10, 11, 17, and 37.
[2] This is the expression employed in the imperial ukases. It is used even in the manifesto of 17th October 1905, announcing the advent of liberty.
[3] According to Professor Kluchevsky, " Tsar " is an abbreviated South Slavonic and Russian form of " Cæsar " or *Tsĕsare*, by the ancient transcription *Tsesare*, the unaccented *e*'s being silent in both transcriptions. The elision of the silent letters and of the superfluous *s* gave " Tsar " as an abbreviation. See *Kluchevsky, op. cit.*, vol. ii. p. 152. The title of the sovereign used in internal official documents in the reign of Ivan III and sometimes in that of Ivan IV (the Terrible) is *Samoderjets*, which is the Slavonian translation of the title αὐτοκράτωρ used by the Byzantine Emperors. (*Cf.* Bury, J. B., *Later Roman Empire*, ii. p. 173.)

of the vast region which they were colonising thus led perhaps inevitably under the conditions of the time, internal and external, to absolutism.

Deficient as they were in knowledge of the social and political development of contemporary France and England, and of the impossibility of the permanent re-establishment of arbitrary power in the West, successive Russian Tsars, from Alexander I (1801–1825) onwards, and most conspicuously Nicholas I (1825–55), seem to have looked upon themselves as instruments of Heaven entrusted with the high task of stemming the revolutionary tide. They have conceived the idea that popular government would be fatal to Russia, and they have rightly foreseen that if it were granted to the rest of the world, its advent in Russia could not for long be delayed. While self-interest thus impelled them to observe and even to share in the affairs of countries other than their own, they no doubt honestly conceived that popular government would be as fatal to these countries as they supposed it would be to Russia. Consumed with a desire to play a great rôle in the history of humanity, they threw themselves in 1814, in 1849, and again in 1854, into the struggle against what they conceived to be the spirit of revolution—in 1814 against Napoleon I, in 1849 against Hungary, and in 1854 against Napoleon III.

So early as 1804 the Tsar Alexander I formulated a plan for a European Confederation, by means of which continental wars would be rendered impossible. To this confederation there might be submitted " the positive rights of nations," and by it there might be drawn up " a new code of the law of nations." Attempts to infringe this code " would risk bringing upon " the nations by whom these attempts might be made " the forces of the new union." [1]

Although this project was formed at a time when Alexander I was in one of his liberal phases, it is really conceived not only in an anti-revolutionary spirit, but even in an anti-liberal spirit. The nations were to be confederated under a code, and whoever attempted to infringe the provisions of the code was to suffer the

---

[1] See extract from despatch of 11th September 1804, by Alexander I. containing a plan for a European Confederation to be submitted by Novossilzev, the Russian Special Envoy to Great Britain. Quoted by W. A. Phillips in " The Congresses, 1815–1822," in *The Cambridge Modern History*, x. p. 3.

weight of the forces of the " new union." Clearly such a confederation might be used for the purpose of crushing a movement
like the French Revolution, and for the re-establishment of absolutism on a firmer basis than ever, as well as for the extinction
of small nationalities like Belgium and Switzerland.[1]

Stein no doubt accurately represents the attitude of mind of
Alexander I when, after the retreat from Moscow, the question
arose as to what next must be done. Defensive tactics had been
so far successful, and Napoleon had, so to say, committed *felo de
se*. But should such tactics continue ?

" A false and crafty policy or ignorance may perhaps counsel
a defensive war, destructive to the armies that carry it on and the
country which will be its arena, and allowing the enemy time to
avail himself of all the resources of the west and south of Europe.
. . . Such timorous and unsound notions are repugnant to the
Emperor Alexander's noble and magnanimous character ; he will
choose to be the benefactor and pacificator of Europe, as he has
been the saviour of his kingdom. . . . He will offer his alliance to
Austria and Prussia, and it will be accepted with gratitude ; he
will demand that England form an army . . . which may contribute to the execution of these plans, and in co-operation with
that Power he will set up a political organization in Germany which
may restore to the nation its independence and put it in a condition to withstand France and secure Europe against the attempts
of the violent and capricious nation which inhabits it." [2]

According to Stein also, the Emperor Alexander I " was set by
Providence in his happy and splendid position to be a benefactor
to the present generation." [3]   Stein's view of unity as the solvent
for contemporary German difficulties is substantially the same as
the Russian view. " The old rotten forms " associated with the
decaying medieval castles and the private jurisdictions of their
possessors must go down before the idea of unity, as these castles
must crumble before modern artillery. " My confession of faith is

---

[1] It is difficult to avoid the suspicion that any League of Peace might
have an outcome of this kind. Appreciation of this danger caused the smaller
states of the American Union to resist consolidation between 1776 and 1789 ;
and their influence sufficed to prevent union in the strict sense.

[2] Quoted in Seeley's *Life and Times of Stein* (Cambridge, 1878), iii.
p. 13.

[3] *Ibid.*

unity, and if that is not attainable, then some shift, some transition stage." [1] Throughout all this there is definitive association between unity and absolutism, between the fitting together into one whole of the national elements and highly centralized autocratic government.

The penetrative analysis of the character of Alexander I by Metternich [2] throws further light upon the mental states of an absolute monarch. While Katherine II was in her liberal phase, she entrusted the education of Alexander to the Swiss, La Harpe, [3] who, from Metternich's point of view, filled " the mind of his pupil with doctrines wrong in themselves and ridiculous in their application. . . . Convinced, no doubt, that the empire which his pupil would one day be called upon to govern was not sufficiently advanced in civilization to bear immediately the practice of these doctrines, he thought of preparing in the future autocrat a mighty lever to secure the upheaval of other countries which he considered more ripe for the purpose, and especially his own fatherland, Switzerland."

Metternich relates that in 1805 Alexander was liberal in the largest sense of the word, but in 1807 " a great change came over his mode of thinking " ; in 1812 he reverted to his former liberal views, which in 1814 reached their highest point. He was then thirty-seven years of age. In 1815 he became a religious mystic ; in 1817 he reacted from mysticism and became " a champion of monarchic and conservative principles " ; in 1818 he was already on his way back to mysticism. In 1823 he realized that not only in other countries, but even in Russia, revolutionary opinions were increasing, and that those who were beginning to suffer for them under his rule might fairly " reproach him with having been the cause of their error."

When, in 1849, Nicholas I sent two army corps (40,000 men) to help Austria to suppress the Hungarian revolution, he thought

[1] Quoted in Seeley's *Life and Times of Stein* (Cambridge, 1878), iii. p. 17.
[2] *Memoirs of Prince Metternich*, 1773–1815 (English translation, London, 1880), i. p. 314 *et seq.*
[3] For La Harpe's account of his pupil, see *Le Gouverneur d'un Prince*, F. C. de La Harpe et Alexandre I (Paris, 1902). See also for La Harpe's influence upon Alexander I, Semevsky, V. E., *Peasant Question in Russia in the Eighteenth and First Half of the Nineteenth Centuries* (St. Petersburg, 1888), i. p. 236.

that all the monarchs in Europe should recognize him as the bulwark of monarchical power. In his own country the crushing of the incipient revolutionary movement of the *Dekabristi* in the beginning of his reign, and the suppression of the Polish insurrection in 1830, had, so far as concerned Russia, stamped out the influences of the French Revolution as well as those of separatist national ambitions.

Although the causes of the Crimean War were very complex, yet one important factor in the situation which immediately preceded the war was the attitude of the Tsar Nicholas I towards Napoleon III. Not only did he look upon him as a *parvenu*, as belonging to the scum which the turmoil of the Revolution had thrown to the surface, but he looked upon him as representing the Revolution, and as the ostentatious advocate of oppressed nationalities.[1] Moreover, he must have been fully aware of the fact that already in the peasant villages the people were talking of a war which was to be waged by France against Russia for the purpose of emancipating the peasantry from bondage.[2] Tradition and policy combined to provoke the Tsar to inflexibility; and ample opportunity was given to Napoleon, Stratford de Redcliffe, and Palmerston to embroil England and France with Russia. The consequences of the war to Russia were manifold. The course of events was not unlike that of the Russo-Japanese War.[3] Military disasters followed one after another. There were no roads, and the means of transport were most inadequate. Ammunition was deficient. Exposures of the incompetence of the commanders and of the officers, and of the fraudulent conduct of the commissariat, infuriated the people against the Government. The military system and the Government were alike discredited.[4]

[1] On the reasons for the adoption of this rôle by Napoleon III, see Rose, J. H., *Development of European Nations* (London, 1905), p. 25. When a young man of twenty-two, Louis Napoleon was on his way to join the Polish insurgents in 1830, when he was met in Germany with the news of the suppression of the revolt.

[2] After the fall of Sevastopol a story became current that Napoleon III had stipulated that the liberation of the peasants must be a condition of peace. *Cf.* Simkhovitch, V. S., "The Russian Peasant and the Autocracy," in *Political Science Quarterly*, xxi. p. 569.

[3] Russian public men of all shades of opinion were almost unanimously in favour of the Crimean War, as they were in favour of the Japanese War. For the Russian point of view, see, *e.g.*, article by de Martens in *Vestnik Evropy*, 1897.

[4] *Cf. supra*, vol. i. p. 365.

The collapse of his lofty pretensions was deeply mortifying to the pride of the Tsar. The country was in disorder, but the Emancipation brought new hopes, and the autocracy entered upon another lease of power.

The Tsars Alexander II, Alexander III, and Nicholas II have also played a Quixotic part in tilting against windmills. All have been inspired by the desire to exercise and to bequeath unimpaired to their successors sole autocratic power within their own dominions, as well as by ambition to confer the benefits of autocracy upon other nations. There is reason to believe that some of them, in moments of religious exaltation, have regarded themselves as being in very direct relations with the Divine Power and as sharing in its attributes. The touch of fanaticism which this suggests accounts for the vacillation of the " inflexible will," for the general benevolence of intention, for frequent lapses into barbaric cruelty, for the lack of judgment with which successive Tsars have chosen their advisers, and for the ardour with which many of them, notably Alexander III, endeavoured to control every department of Government down to the smallest detail. The practice just mentioned was followed by Nicholas II; and this circumstance accounts for the confusion in which the administration was plunged in the revolutionary years of 1905–1906. When the Tsar held himself responsible for everything, there is little wonder that the people also held him responsible.

The effect of autocracy in detail upon the duration of life of the Tsars is significant. Omitting Paul I, who, after a reign of four years, was assassinated by a group of palace conspirators in 1801, the mean age at death of the four remaining Tsars who died during the nineteenth century was only fifty-four years. Alexander II was assassinated at the age of sixty-three; Alexander I and Nicholas I died, the first at forty-eight and the second at fifty-nine, for want of the will to live; Alexander III died at forty-nine, a nervous wreck, in close retirement. Yet all, especially the last, were physically strong men, well endowed with physical courage. The mean period of their reigns was $23\frac{1}{4}$ years. " The trade " [1] of autocracy is an exhausting and dangerous business, imposing a

---

[1] The phrase alleged to have been applied to his office by King Humbert of Italy after he was struck by his assassin.

severe strain upon the physical constitution and tending to the disturbance of mental equilibrium.

Autocracy upon a small scale may conceivably be successful in maintaining " good government," but the demands of a numerous nation of manifold racial origins, upon an autocrat who is at once priest, soldier, judge, official, and " first policeman," tend to become cumulative and to reach beyond the endurance of the human mind or body on their present plane. An ideal Tsar must not merely be divinely anointed—he must himself be indeed a god. When an autocrat attempts to govern an empire which has rapidly attained a population of 150,000,000, the inherent difficulties of the system develop into impossibilities, and the situation approaches an *impasse*.

The history of the movement for the emancipation of the peasantry from bondage right [1] shows how, autocratic as the Tsar was, the real foundation of the autocracy was the good-will of the landowning gentry, and that, if this good-will were forfeited, the stability of the system would be most seriously compromised. It was quite indispensable, therefore, for the autocracy to conciliate the gentry, and to provide for the carrying out of emancipation and other reforms without permitting any of the cost of these to fall upon them. Emancipation was retarded for years, and when it came it was deprived of its full value because no scheme could be devised which would liberate the peasants from the authority of the *pomyetschĕk*, and at the same time preserve that authority unimpaired. In the immediate interests of the gentry, and in the ultimate interests of the autocracy, Tsar after Tsar attempted this impossible task. The emancipation of the peasantry and the maintenance of the influence over them of the gentry appeared alike to be necessary for the safety of the autocratic state, and they were incompatible. In the early ages of serfdom, the Tsar appeared as impartial arbiter between the peasant and his lord ; but as the discussions upon emancipation proceeded, it became gradually patent that there was a fundamental identity of interest between the autocrat of the State and the owner of the serf. Government and serf-ownership were alike autocratic. As this identity of interest came to be recognized, the recognition was fatal to the peasant view of the functions of the Tsar as disinter-

[1] Cf. *supra*, vol. i. pp. 316 *et seq*.

ested arbiter ; but for a time the autocracy succeeded in rehabilitating itself in the eyes of the peasants by temporarily assuming the cost of emancipation. The peasants were ultimately to bear the whole burden, but the financial operations were facilitated and emancipation was hastened by the Government. The relations between the autocracy and the landed gentry which have been described account for the almost ferocious bitterness with which in successive reigns the autocracy has borne itself towards those of the gentry who have exhibited revolutionary sympathies.

Up till the recent revolutionary epoch popular recognition of the impossibility of the adequate performance of the traditional rôle of the Tsarship, as well as remnants of Cæsar-worship which lingered among the simple rural folk, combined to render the public attitude towards the Tsar one of large tolerance. " The Dear Father [1] does not know our situation, or he would change it," was the popular formula. One sign of the great change which passed over Russia during the first decade of the twentieth century is that this formula was recognized to be no longer applicable. The Tsar must know what everyone else knows. He had the power to effect radical changes in the condition of the peasantry; although he has retained this power, he has not exercised it, therefore he is responsible. Although from the peasant point of view Nicholas II was not worse than any, perhaps even better than most, of his predecessors, his failure only proved that hereditary autocracy was worn out.

Thus stage by stage the revolutionary state of mind develops. Private grievances and difficulties come to be intermingled with public grievances and difficulties. " Lawlessness " [2] on the part of the Government has its inevitable counterpart in " rightlessness " on the part of the people. Gradually class after class comes to be infected with the desire for drastic political change. In countries which enjoy the advantages, such as they are, of representative and " responsible " government, this desire is expressed and expended in the polling booths; in an autocracy it can only be expressed in sullen discontent, or expended in conspirative or open attacks upon the representatives of authority.

[1] "Dear Father" represents more exactly the Russian expression than the customary "Little Father."

[2] As in procedure by administrative order instead of by ordinary process of law.

To this factor—the desire for drastic political change—must be added the fatalistic habit of thought which is characteristic of the Russian mind ; once the necessity of change is realised, it must take place somehow immediately. The practical means of carrying out any change are not really considered, nor is the character of the change itself at all deeply regarded. The means might have to be violent ; who might know ? The character of it would have to be left to the people to determine ; who might know the result ? A " Constituent Assembly " might be convened, and this would reveal " the will of the people." Such was the state of mind of Russia in 1905.

The suppression of criticism and the destruction or exile of the bearers of critical intelligence were paid for heavily in the confused and haphazard projects which the Government and the bolder publicists now began to advance. All this fermentation, troublesome and painful as it must be, is nevertheless an evidence of growth. It means that the lethargic masses of the Russian people were shaking themselves into waking life. This was the real revolution— the rousing of the people from stagnation. For the moment their immediate material interests sank into the background ; and not until the necessity of caring for these brought the people back to practical exigencies did the result of the fermentation become a new organic part of the national life. People cannot live for any great length of time at white heat. Human nerves will not endure indefinitely such an experience. The acute stage of the revolution through which Russia passed in 1905 and 1906 left the autocracy and the people alike in a state of nervous exhaustion. Like the campaign in Manchuria, the conflict was not fought out to the bitter end. Neither combatant was completely defeated, but both had gone nearly as far as their strength at the time permitted. Although the advantage remained with the autocracy, the people gained much. When all is said, and the reaction notwithstanding, Russia stood upon a level substantially higher in point of political development than she did before the Russo-Japanese War and the incomplete revolution which followed.

In all great revolutions there is this widespread or universal " state of mind." Distinct from it, although acquiring their force from the prevalence of the revolutionary state of mind, are the various revolutionary propagandas. These are conducted by enthusiasts sometimes numerically insignificant, sometimes influenced largely by hysteria ; but frequently inspired by disinterested love of country and of humanity. With the uttermost self-abnegation, these enthusiasts throw themselves against authority, well knowing that they must perish, but believing that the blood of the " martyrs is the seed," not in their case of the Church, but of liberty. These enthusiasts and their propagandas of action or education, or both, are rather the result of the revolutionary state of mind than the cause of it ; reaction of one upon the other being of course constant.

The history of revolutionary movements must therefore be considered as having two sides—the history of the emergence and development of the revolutionary state of mind and the history of the movements considered as propagandas. These histories are so closely related, however, that they must for the most part be told together.

CHAPTER II

THE DISTURBANCES AMONG THE COSSACKS AND THE
PEASANTS AND THE RISING OF PUGACHEV (1773-1775).

THROUGHOUT the period of the Kalita dynasty the nomadic tribes
on the frontier of the Moscow State continued to harass the settlements on the edge of the steppe. This was especially true of the
region situated immediately to the south of Moscow—the region
of Ryazan. Here peaceful agriculture was impossible, and the region
could be occupied only by warlike people.[1] Ryazan thus drew
to itself a population different from that of Moscow—a population
peculiarly adapted to frontier conditions. From an early period
this population was composed of two elements—landless people,
who were accustomed to earn their own living upon the land of
others, and who were drawn into the region by offers of high wages,
and adventurous people who liked the free life of the steppe, who
liked to fight, and who preferred to live partly by means of the
military pay which they derived from the Government and partly
by means of plunder which they might derive from their defeated
enemies. These two elements were both known as *Kazaki* or
Cossacks.[2] While such elements of the population were to be found
from early times and in every part of the Moscow State, they make
their appearance as a compact localized group for the first time in
the middle of the fifteenth century and in the region of Ryazan.[3]
It is not surprising that on both sides of the indefinite frontier, people
of a similar character should be found, and thus there were Tartar
as well as Russian Cossacks. The latter were Mohammedans, and
were in the same relation to the Sultan as were the Russian Cossacks
to the Tsar. The Cossacks on both sides of the frontier appear to

---

[1] *Cf.* Soloviev, *History of Russia from the Earliest Times* (ed. St. Petersburg, *n.d., cir.* 1911), vol. v. p. 1684.
[2] In the Teurki group of languages *Kazak* means *bachelor*, and in its
derived Russian form it meant originally a man without a settled domicile.
[3] *Cf.* Soloviev, *loc. cit.*, and Kluchevsky, *op. cit.*, iii. p. 132 (English translation, iii. p. 107).

have been mercenary troops.   So long as they were paid and were
not interfered with they seem in general to have refrained from disturbance, although they sometimes engaged in raids or even in
formal warfare on their own account.   For example, the Cossacks
of the Don and those of the Yaēk, or Ural River, engaged,
in 1632, in a war with Persia on the Caspian Sea.[1]   Occasionally
they attacked and plundered the Russian cities in their neighbourhood, and then escaped into the steppe, where they were practically
immune from pursuit.[2]   The Cossacks sometimes allied themselves
with frontier tribes, as they did, for example, with the Kalmuks,
who were subsidized both by the Tsar and by the Khan of the
Crimea ;[3] and as they did with the Bashkirs.   So also in the wars
with Poland and Sweden, they constituted an uncertain element,
disposed to serve the power which offered them most conspicuous
advantages.

The Cossacks did not belong to one racial group ; on the contrary, they were drawn from many races, although those who settled
on the Dnieper were predominantly of Little Russian origin.   They
collected together near the Falls of Sula, and there fortified an
island, which came to be known as the *Syech*, and the community
which they formed as the *Zaporojtsi*, or Zaporojian.[4]   So also the
Cossacks of the Don and the Yaēk, or Ural River, formed communities and regarded these communities as independent of any
State.   The Cossack settlements which were near the places populated by Russians, were in general kept under restraint with comparative ease ; but those settlements which were far in the steppe
were occupied by practically autonomous communities over whom
the rule of the central State was very slender.[5]   Such Cossack
communities elected each its own *ataman* or headman, who conducted their communal affairs.   The *ataman* also acted as the
representative of the Cossacks in communications with the Moscow
authorities.[6]   Even the *ataman* was usually illiterate.   The Cos-

---

[1] Soloviev, ii. p. 1247.
[2] As in their attack upon Guriev in 1677.   See Soloviev, iii. p. 860.
[3] *Ibid.*, iii. p. 574.
[4] For an account of the Zaporojians, see Soloviev, ed. 1911, iii. p. 12 *et
seq*.   There is a vivid description of them in *With Fire and Sword*, by Senkie-
vich.
[5] Soloviev, *op. cit.*, i. p. 1684.
[6] The Moscow Government assumed to appoint the *ataman*, but such
appointment was recognized only when the Cossack communities were

sacks of the seventeenth and eighteenth centuries were, therefore, unacquainted with the Russian laws, and were, moreover, at the mercy of the army clerks who were sent to settle accounts with them. Their own *atamans* were sometimes dishonest and often negligent in their dealings alike with the Cossack communities and with the Government. Disputes and disorders occurred frequently from the attempts of officials to take advantage of the ignorance of the Cossacks.[1] Payments for military service were customarily made partly in money and partly in kind, or the Cossacks were granted rights (to fisheries, *e.g.*), and the value of these rights was counted as part of their payment, or the wages of the Cossacks were counted as part payment for the rights which had been granted. Sometimes through alleged embezzlement of funds by the *ataman*, sometimes through alteration in the amounts imposed by the Government or collected by its officials, disturbances in connection with settlements of balances took place in the seventeenth century.[2]

Although in proportion to the total peasant mass the Cossacks were not numerous, and although, as we have seen, all the Cossack communities were not free and autonomous, the withdrawal from among the peasants of the more energetic and courageous for the free life of the steppe resulted in diminution of will and power to resist oppression on the part of the peasantry as a class. The recruiting of the ranks of the Cossacks by these enterprising elements, therefore, at once localized such elements, increased the subserviency of the peasantry remaining under bondage, and contributed with the intensification of bondage right to promote the disarticulation of Russian society. We have seen that at frequent intervals in the history of the peasantry, flights occurred of peasants from the estates to which they belonged, the peasants sometimes fleeing in masses. On these occasions the peasants often went out into the steppe and took refuge among the Cossacks. On the complaints of the *pomyetschēkē*, the Government demanded of the Cossacks the return of the peasants because their evasion

within reach of the arm of the Government. Cossack *atamans* spoke with pride of having been elected by their fellows, even when they were at the same time appointed by the Tsar.

[1] For this reason Tatishev suggested, in 1737, that Cossack schools should be established. *Cf.* Soloviev, iv. p. 1546.

[2] *Cf.* Soloviev, ii. p. 1058 ; so also in the eighteenth century, see *infra.*

diminished the numbers on the tax rolls.   When the Government was strong enough to enforce its demands the peasants were returned to their owners; but when the central authority was weak— as it was, for instance, in the time of the Tsar Alexis, the father of Peter the Great—the Cossacks were able either to dissemble or to resist actively.   The first open revolt of the Cossacks on account of demands from Moscow for the return of fleeing peasants took place in 1670, under Stenka Razēn, *ataman* of the Don Cossacks. This revolt was suppressed, but the practice of flight still continued, and in the next reign the Cossacks and the refugees again engaged in armed rebellion in 1716 under Bulavin.   The Cossacks were again defeated, on this occasion by a comparatively insignificant force.   The policy of Peter, who was then engaged in his formidable industrial enterprises, in which he had the greatest difficulty in securing a sufficient number of working hands, was not compatible with the drawing off of productive powers to the non-productive steppe.   He forbade the Cossacks to build new towns and destroyed the refuges of the runaways.[1]

The power of Moscow, which had always been disputed by the Cossacks, was now vindicated for the time, and the Cossack communities became more compact and less influenced by accession from the peasantry.   The character of the Cossack comes now to be differentiated from that of the peasant.

The success of the free Cossack life inspired the Cossack with hope, while increase of burdens and intensification of bondage continued to oppress the peasant with gloom and despair.   The Cossacks had by their own valour and energy conquered for themselves a large element of independence, and they therefore looked with some contempt upon the peasantry who were humbly submitting to excessive burdens.   There is to be found the historical ground of the hostility which, save on rare occasions, the Cossacks have entertained against the peasantry, and of the confidence with which the Government has been able to rely upon the Cossacks in punitive expeditions and the like.   Yet there were and are many traits of peasant character which the Cossacks presented even in an exaggerated form.   For example, alike among the peasantry and among the Cossacks, every administrative change, and still more every change in the occupancy of the Imperial Throne, pro-

[1] See Soloviev, *op. cit.*, iii. pp. 291 and 1472.

duced a fermentation in their narrow worlds. Both alike formed exaggerated anticipations of the benefits to be derived from "the grace of the new Tsar," and when disappointment ensued, disturbances occurred. The accession of a new Tsar was thus usually the occasion for Cossack and peasant outbreaks.[1] If that which they expected did not happen immediately, they soon began to exhibit symptoms of disorder. For example, when they learned that Peter III had forbidden the purchase of peasants for the factories, the previously purchased peasants understood that this meant freedom for them, and forthwith began to act upon this belief.[2] So also when the peasants of the Church were transferred to the State, and when the nobility were released from compulsory service, the peasants thought that freedom for them must ensue.[3] When this result did not follow, they regarded themselves as being defrauded by the proprietors of the benefits which had been conferred upon them by the Tsar. In general they refused to believe that ukases were genuine unless the ukases gave them what they wanted. If an alleged ukase met their views, they customarily regarded it as genuine, in spite of evidence to the contrary. Peasants and Cossacks alike were thus peculiarly exposed to deception by false ukases [4] and by impostors. It may be that this and other peasant traits were the natural consequences of habitual oppression,[5] and that the peasant psychology predisposed peasant and Cossack alike to look always for some benefit from above—to hope always for some ukase of the Tsar which would by a stroke of the pen alter all the conditions of their life. The peasants were indeed always in an attitude of expectancy that a Messiah would arise among them and by a mere announcement prevent oppression and bestow upon them economical prosperity.

The grievances of the peasants, alike of the State and of the *pomyetschēkē*, in the first half of the eighteenth century have already been described. From the details which have been given it may be surmised that almost at any time the mood of the peasants, in spite of their humility, predisposed them to revolt against their

---

[1] Cf. Fērsov, N. N., "Peasant Agitation up till the Nineteenth Century," in *The Great Reform*, ii. p. 45.
[2] *Ibid.*   [3] *Ibid.*
[4] The circulation of false ukases is frequently mentioned above (see, *e.g.*, i. p. 240).
[5] As suggested by Fērsov, *op. cit.*, p. 46.

masters and against the officials with whom they came in contact. Leadership among them was, however, hard to find. They were dispersed over an immense area in comparatively small communities. They were habitually insubordinate to authority, and they were mutually suspicious of one another.

The situation in the reign of Katherine II had become acute. Enormous grants of land and of peasants to Court favourites, and the intensification of bondage right, especially through ascription to industrial enterprises, had brought about a " state of mind " among the peasants, chiefly among those of the Volga region, which rendered them ripe for revolt.

The Cossacks had simultaneously their own grievances. They disliked the new military system which had been introduced by Peter the Great, although it had been very gradually applied to them ; and they were frequently engaged in disputes with the local authorities about their payments to the Government.

The discontent among the Cossacks, which eventually developed into the formidable rebellion of 1773–1775, appears to have had its specific origin soon after 1752 among the Cossacks of the Ural River (in the earlier part of the eighteenth century called the Cossacks of the Yaëk). These Cossacks took from the Empress a lease of the fishings of the Yaëk River, and undertook the collection of the duties within that region upon wine. They were also granted a monopoly of the sale of salt fish. For these privileges the Cossacks were to pay to the Government a yearly sum of 10,450 rubles. An *ataman* called Borodin was appointed by the Military Collegium for the collection of this sum as well as for other duties in connection with the affairs of the Cossacks. His appointment was the first grievance. The Cossacks had been accustomed to elect their own *ataman*, and they naturally usually chose one of themselves. Borodin was an appointee of the Government and was, moreover, not a Cossack. He appears to have collected the sums due by the Cossacks, but the Cossacks alleged that for three years previous to 1767 he had not rendered any accounts of his intromissions. When some of the Cossacks reminded Borodin of the conditions of his appointment, and demanded the rendering of accounts, they were " punished with lashes as insolent and riotous people." [1]

[1] State Archive VI, Affair No. 505, cited by Dubrovin, N., *Pugachev and His Accomplices* (St. Petersburg, 1884), i. p. 2.

About 1760 a certain Loginov, described as a person of doubtful integrity, who had been an *ataman* of the town of Sakmarsk, applied to Borodin for employment as a tax-collector. Borodin refused to employ him, and thereafter Loginov appears to have devoted himself to the destruction of Borodin. Loginov went to St. Petersburg and secured an appointment in the administrative office of the Yaēk Cossacks. On his return Borodin refused to receive him, and Loginov then placed himself at the head of the party of Cossacks who had been opposing Borodin, advising the Cossacks to refrain from paying their duties to Borodin until accounts had been rendered showing the intromissions of the previous fifteen years, and accusing Borodin of levying duties unjustly and of embezzling the amounts illegally collected.[1] In 1762 the Military Collegium sent a Commission to Yaēk to inquire into the quarrel between Borodin and Loginov and into the consequent disturbances among the Cossacks. The Commissioner (Brookfeld) reported that undoubtedly Borodin had embezzled funds and had exacted money illegally from the Cossacks ; but that there was no one in the region who could be trusted to do otherwise.[2] The Military Collegium, however, ordered that if Borodin had really abused his office, he should be dismissed and a staff officer from Orenburg sent to take his place, with two aldermen elected by the Cossacks to advise him. The Senate did not, however, approve of this plan, on the ground that it might lead to further disturbances. Nothing was done. Brookfeld remained on the Yaēk ; Borodin continued nominally to act as *ataman*, and Loginov continued to collect the taxes. In February 1763 two Cossacks went to Moscow to lay the affair before the Military Collegium, and at the same time a complaint against Borodin was sent to the Empress by Mir-Ali-Khan on account of the Kirghiz.

The result of these complaints was the appointment of a new Commission of Inquiry into Cossack grievances with certain executive powers. Major-General Potapov was appointed head of the Commission, and was required to dismiss Borodin, to arrest Loginov for insubordination, and to appoint another *ataman* from Orenburg, and not from among the Cossacks. The Cossacks protested against the latter measure. They said that it involved infringement of their privileges. The Empress Katherine II,

---

[1] Dubrovin, *op. cit.*, i. p. 7.   [2] *Ibid.*, i. p. 9.

usually good-natured in such matters, wrote to Prince Trubetskoy to the effect that if it was customary for the Cossacks to elect an *ataman* from among themselves, they should be allowed to elect anybody they chose.[1] Potapov considered the carrying out of this order impracticable ; but he eventually agreed that the Cossacks should elect an *ataman* from among themselves. They chose a young nephew of Loginov. His election appeared to mean that the real power should be in the hands of the latter. On that ground Potapov objected to ratify the election and on leaving for St. Petersburg, appointed an officer of dragoons from Kazan as temporary *ataman*. The nephew of Loginov at once made friends with this officer, hoping to have his own election confirmed, and proceeded to act in a manner very similar to that in which Borodin had been acting, thus simultaneously opposing his uncle, the Cossack party, and the Borodin party.

Meanwhile a new ukase upon Cossack affairs was promulgated in December 1765. Under this ukase the anomalous status of the Cossacks was altered. Instead of being free to render military service or not, as formerly, the Cossacks were now obliged to serve by turn—every able-bodied Cossack being obliged to serve. The practice of election of their own officers was abolished. This adjustment of their affairs was not what the Cossacks expected. They were gratified by the dismissal of Borodin, but they were disturbed by the new military regulations, which they regarded as infringing upon their privileges. The Cossacks were further irritated by the orders of the Military Collegium, under which Loginov was banished to Tobolsk in Siberia, and the forty representatives who had been elected under the instructions of Potapov were to be beaten and exiled because they were unable to prove some of their accusations.[2]

In order to prevent disturbance on the part of the Cossacks in the execution of the instructions of the Military Collegium, dragoons were sent from Orenburg to the Yaёk town. The Cossacks continued to make complaints, and deputations were sent to St. Petersburg. One of the deputations succeeded in presenting a petition personally to the Empress, who seems to have taken a more serious view of the situation than did the Military

---

[1] Dubrovin, i. p. 14.
[2] State Archives VI, Affair No. 505, and Dubrovin, i. p. 16.

Collegium.[1] That department appears to have evaded the instructions of the Empress, for it ordered that in future, petitioners should not be permitted to leave the Cossack communities. Katherine, however, sent a confidential agent to the Yaëk with instructions to endeavour to put an end to the disturbances. This agent (Captain Chebyshov) found that it was impossible to settle the triangular dispute—the Cossack party, the party of Borodin, and the Military Collegium all representing different and irreconcilable interests. A new *ataman* was eventually elected and his election was confirmed; but the primary causes of the dispute still remained, aggravated as these were by the regulations of the ukase of 1765 abolishing the system of volunteering and establishing that of compulsory service.

In 1769 the Cossacks were still refusing to render service under the new regulations. Conscripts were taken by force, but they escaped from their captors, and the agitation against the ex-*ataman* Borodin gradually became an agitation against the Government. On the one hand the war with Turkey rendered it necessary to secure all possible troops, and on the other, the quarrels among and with the Cossacks rendered it impossible to secure troops from among them excepting on the customary terms. The Cossacks steadfastly refused to be enrolled as " regular " soldiers, and they regarded enrolment as a kind of punishment imposed by the Government for their exercise of what they considered the indefeasible right of petition.[2]

In 1770 also there appears a ground of objection to serve as regular soldiers other than that based upon the established practice of volunteering. This ground of objection was that the regular soldiers were obliged by the regulations to shave off their beards. The Cossacks, who were mostly *raskolnēkē*, or dissenters from the Orthodox Greek Church, entertained religious scruples about shaving. The new system thus not only interfered with previously established practice, but interfered with religious beliefs. The Military Collegium gave way upon this point, and offered to allow the Cossacks to retain their beards if they wished to do so. But the Cossacks still obstinately refused to submit. The local authorities then attempted to reduce them to submission by preventing

[1] Letter of Katherine II to Count Chernyshev, Moscow Archives of the General Staff, cxix, sec. 4. Affair No. 43; cited by Dubrovin, i. p. 21.
[2] Dubrovin, *op. cit.*, i. p. 36.

the Cossacks from engaging in their usual employment of fishing during the season.   This measure produced fresh complications, for by means of it the Cossacks were more impoverished and became more discontented than formerly.   The Cossacks sent messengers to Orenburg to complain to the Governor and to ask for passports to St. Petersburg in order that they might carry their new grievances to the Throne.   These messengers were arrested and imprisoned, but others were sent direct to St. Petersburg, where now (September 1770) there were eighty deputies from the Cossacks of the Yaëk. Katherine received the new petition, and ordered the Military Collegium to remedy nearly all the grievances which it detailed, to see that the Cossacks were paid the five years' arrears of money due to them if their statements on this head were found to be accurate, to liberate those who had been arrested, &c. An ukase in these terms was read to twenty-six of the petitioners at the Military Collegium, but they indignantly refused to be satisfied with the terms of it.   They demanded simply that they should be allowed to live and to render military service as formerly.   The Military Collegium then ordered all the Yaëk Cossacks who might be found in St. Petersburg to be arrested and conveyed under a convoy to their homes on the Yaëk River.   Many were arrested and despatched, but some could not be found.   Of those who were secured, only six reached the Yaëk; the others escaped in the course of the journey.[1]

With a pertinacity characteristic of Cossack and peasant alike, those who escaped succeeded in returning to St. Petersburg and in presenting another petition to the Empress, begging to be relieved of the obligation to serve in regiments of the regular army, and continuing to complain of the abuses to which the petitioners alleged they had been subjected by Borodin's allies—the so-called aldermen's party.   Again Katherine sent an emissary to the Yaëk and withdrew the regulation respecting enlistment in the regular army.[2]   For the moment the Cossacks were content, and the large group of petitioners returned to their homes.

---

[1] *Memorials of New Russian History*, part ii. p. 291 ; cited by Dubrovin, i. p. 44.

[2] The project had involved the formation of so-called foreign legions in the regular army.   It had never been proposed to make the Cossacks troops of the line.   The objectionable ukase had been issued in December 1765, the cancelling ukase was dated 7th December 1770.

Almost simultaneously with these disturbances among the Cossacks there was observable in 1771 a movement among the Kalmuk Mongols, among whom was then beginning the agitation which eventually led to the flight of the Kalmuks across Asia. This distraction caused the local military authorities to be more anxious than formerly to placate the Cossacks and to reconcile the two contending parties. They, therefore, conciliated one party by exacting a fine which had been imposed upon the aldermen, together with an accounting of their intromissions, and at the same time hesitated to carry out to the full extent the instructions of the ukase by dismissing the aldermen and rendering them incapable of being re-elected. The result of this compromise was that neither party was satisfied. The aldermen's party had been punished; but in the opinion of the other party, they remained in a position to commit fresh offences.

It appeared also that, as frequently occurred at that period even on grave occasions, the copy of the ukase of 7th December 1770 which had been given to the Cossack petitioners at St. Petersburg was an inaccurate copy. Instead of merely relieving the Cossacks from the obligation to serve in the regular army, and thus leaving them in the position in which they were before the ukase of 1765 was issued, the ukase of 1770, as they had it, appeared to relieve them of service of any kind. The Cossacks were not slow to attach this meaning to the ukase, so that when a demand was made upon them for a draft of 500 troops to pursue the Kalmuks, only the aldermen's party supplied troops, the " disobedient " Cossacks declaring that they were now by ukase exempted from military service. They objected even to volunteer unless they were permitted to elect all their own officers.[1]

Another large group of petitioners made their way to St. Petersburg, the journey occupying from Easter until June. When they arrived one of their number, Kĕrpĕchnikov, went to the Military Collegium and asked Count Chernyshev to hand their petition to the Empress. Chernyshev seems to have lost his temper and to have literally kicked the Cossack out of his presence. This act rankled in the mind of the Cossack, who at once drew up a petition of complaint against Chernyshev, and succeeded in having it placed

[1] Dubrovin, i. p. 49.

in the hands of the Empress.[1]   The petitioners disguised themselves
as coachmen and other working men, and distributed themselves
about the city in order to escape the arrest they knew must follow.
Most of them were, however, hunted down and confined in the
fortress of Peter and Paul.

The petition was both quaint and cunning.   It was written in
a spirit of servility to Katherine, and was cunningly contrived to
enable the Cossacks to profit by the intrigues of the Court.   Count
Chernyshev was denounced, but the Cossacks invited the protection of his rivals the Orlovs.   Kěrpěchnikov succeeded in escaping
from St. Petersburg, carrying with him a letter which he had procured from Orlov.   Meanwhile the attitude of the Cossack party
on the Yaěk had become more bellicose.   They refused to supply
troops for the pursuit of the Kalmuks, and a conspiracy was discovered which had as its objects the seizure of the guns and ammunition and an attack upon the *ataman*.   Under these circumstances
an officer, Major von Traubenberg, was sent from Orenburg to the
Yaěk.   He was familiar with Cossack affairs, but he was irritated
at the refusal of the Cossacks to supply men for his command, and

---

[1] The following extracts from the petition are given by way of illustration
of such documents :

"To God and you, most gracious Empress, the deputies are writing.
Your most devoted slaves are falling with bitter tears at your feet.   Mercy,
most gracious Empress, upon all those who live on the Yaěk, and who depend
upon your life, and who exist under your Imperial protection.   Have pity,
most gracious Empress, on us for the offences which we have survived, as is
known to your Imperial Highness personally through our petitions.   We,
unfortunates, and most devoted slaves, not only do not have satisfaction, but
we suffer most inhuman tortures from the *ataman*, Peter Tambovtsev, and
his aldermen, who are still appointed by the Military Collegium, and especially
by Count Chernyshev. . . . Most august, most gracious Monarch ! at your
sacred feet we fall, your most devoted slaves.   With tears we implore you
to deliver us, by your monarchical grace, from insupportable ruin.   Not only
are we decayed (economically), but we have become beggars.   By God, we
are brought to such conditions that we cannot continue any more your
Imperial service on account of our case having been continued for eleven
years, and of our having spent so long a time here (in St. Petersburg).   We
are short of funds for food and for other expenses, and we are deeply in debt.
Have pity, most gracious Empress, defend us from the attacks of the *ataman*
and all the aldermen, and the generals, staff, and over-officers. . . . Honour
us as we were honoured in the time of the father of the country, the Emperor
Peter the Great. . . . We want to be under His Excellency Count G. G.
Orlov, in order that our Yaěk troops may be saved from invasion, and this
mother's pity of yours we shall count not otherwise than as new life given
to us " (State Archives VII, D, No. 2331 ; cited by Dubrovin, i. pp. 51–2).

he proceeded at once to punitive measures. Those Cossacks who were most active in promoting resistance were ordered by him to be flogged, and he ordered the necessary number of men for the command to have their beards shaved off and to be sent on under convoy. The convoy was, however, inadequate, the 300 Cossacks who had been taken forcibly, turned upon the convoy and carried it back to the Yaēk.[1]

In January 1772 Kērpēchnikov returned from St. Petersburg, told the Cossacks of the failure of his mission, and urged them to send an ultimatum to the *ataman* to the effect that unless the over-due fines were paid and the offending aldermen dismissed within three days, the Cossacks would act by " armed uprising." [2] Kēr-pēchnikov was ordered to report himself to Traubenberg at the Military Chancellery. He refused, and a riot ensued, in which the " disobedient " Cossacks fought the " obedient," and prisoners were taken on both sides. Traubenberg then called a general meeting of all Cossacks to discuss the affair—a very hazardous proceeding under the circumstances. The " disobedient " Cossacks poured into the town of Yaēk until they numbered a thousand, while Traubenberg had only seventy men of the regular troops and fifty " obedient " Cossacks upon whom he might rely in case of disorder. Traubenberg despatched a messenger to Orenburg for assistance. Dragoons and infantry were sent at once, but they did not arrive in time to prevent the catastrophe which took place on 13th January. On that day a large crowd of " disobedient " Cossacks attended a service in the cathedral, and then carrying three *ikons*—one of them a thaumaturgical picture of Christ which was believed to weep when perils threatened the Cossacks—marched along the street towards the Military Chancellery. Fearing an attack, Trau-benberg ordered his regular soldiers to attack the crowd. The Cossacks then threw aside all disguise, rushed upon the Chancellery, turned the guns in it upon the defenders, killed many of them, including Traubenberg, and wounded severely the next in command, an officer named Durnovo. The latter was only saved from being killed through the efforts of Shegaev, a Cossack, who afterwards was one of the chief supporters of Pugachev. The *ataman* and

---

[1] Report of Durnovo, August 1772. *Military-Scientific Affairs*, No. 104, Division 15, cited by Dubrovin, i. p. 55.
[2] Dubrovin, i. p. 53.

some of the aldermen were killed. In blind fury the Cossacks looted the houses of the officials and destroyed the records. Many barbarities were committed—*e.g.* two of Traubenberg's fingers were cut off in order to secure the rings which he wore upon them.[1]

On the evening of the 13th the Cossacks dispersed to their homes, but marvellous to relate, a deputation of them went to Durnovo, who lay severely wounded and a prisoner, and asked him to permit them to elect a new *ataman* and new aldermen, as all were either dead or in prison. Durnovo naturally said, " Do as you please. I am not in a position to give orders." The Cossacks replied that they looked upon him as the military commander appointed by the Empress, that in acting as they had done they had carried out the will of the Empress as expressed in the ukases, and that they were prepared now to take his orders in respect to a new election. Fearing further disturbance, Durnovo consented, whereupon they required him to countermand the order for assistance which had been sent to Orenburg. This he was obliged to do.

On the morning of the 14th the victorious Cossacks held a meeting at which they decided that some of the prisoners they had captured on the previous day should be executed, that then the party quarrels should be forgotten, and that no one should go to St. Petersburg of his own volition. It was also decided to send deputies to St. Petersburg for the purpose of explaining the reason for the action of the Cossacks. The executions took place, and the deputies departed with a formidable array of documents, some of the signatures to which, as in the case of Durnovo, were procured through fear of consequences.

The authorities at St. Petersburg now determined to deal drastically with the situation, by abolishing the locally elective offices in the Cossack communities and by compelling the Cossacks to enter the regular army service. They did not realize, however, the extent of the military measures which might be necessary to enforce this answer to the Cossack question, and they proceeded to impose upon the military forces which they detailed, an impossible task. Had the Military Collegium decided to send a properly equipped force of 10,000 men into the disturbed district in the summer of 1772, several years of bloodshed might have been prevented, although,

<hr />

[1] Dubrovin, i, p. 70.

postor was Theodore Bogomolov, a bonded peasant of one of the Vorontsevs, who had fled from the estate to which he belonged. Bogomolov had been a boatman on the Volga, had been serving in some capacity among the Kalmuks, and for a time had been with the Cossacks of the Volga working as a farm labourer. In 1772 he volunteered for military service, describing himself as a Don Cossack. The fifth impostor was Emilian Pugachev, a Cossack of the Don.

The three earlier impostors need not detain us, the career of the fourth is significant, that of the fifth highly important. The significance of all of the impostors is that they emerged at psychological moments. Had Peter really survived, and had he conducted himself with any sagacity, the impostures suggest that he might have regained his throne as the head of a great popular movement. The character and the methods of both of the two later impostors were almost precisely identical. They were both illiterate, therefore they had at the very beginning of their careers of imposture to find literate persons to act as secretaries. They both founded their claims upon alleged Tsar's signs or marks upon the body, and they both possessed a certain power of attracting adherents notwithstanding the risk which was inevitably incurred. In both cases their immediate supporters were, with high probability in the case of Bogomolov, and with certainty in the case of Pugachev, rather accomplices than dupes. Many among the Cossacks realized the advantage of having a central figure round whom a tradition had gathered, or might gather, and against whom the governmental vengeance might turn in case of non-success, while the accomplices might escape on the ground that they had been deceived. On the other hand, in the improbable event of success, the impostor would be wholly at the mercy of his accomplices, who would be able to extort any concession from him they might desire.[1]

In 1772, soon after he went among the Cossacks of the Volga, Bogomolov, being " immeasurably drunk," declared himself as the Emperor Peter III.[2] The rumour that the expected Tsar had made his appearance spread rapidly among the Cossacks of the Volga, and many people visited Bogomolov for the purpose of ascertain-

[1] The temporary successes of pseudo-Demetrius I and II gave colour to this view.
[2] Dubrovin, i. p. 107.

ing whether or not he resembled the portraits of the Tsar Peter which they had seen. They seem to have agreed that the resemblance was at least doubtful, but that the lapse of years might account for a change. A definite adherent made his appearance in a soldier named Dolotin, who, either convinced of the validity of the claim of Bogomolov, or acutely discerning the importance of the rôle played by him at that juncture, attached himself as secretary and proceeded to circulate the rumour of the reappearance of the Tsar Peter.

In May 1772 the rumour had spread so widely that the Cossacks immediately surrounding Bogomolov prepared to take advantage of the situation. They arrested their officers, but one of these had the courage to ask an interview with the alleged Emperor. Immediately upon seeing him he struck him in the face, saying, "What kind of an Emperor is this ? Arrest him."

From the manner in which Bogomolov took the insult he stood revealed to the Cossacks, who put him in irons and, together with his secretary, despatched him to headquarters. The two prisoners were sentenced by the Military Collegium to be publicly whipped, and to be banished to Nerchinsk with hard labour for life. In addition Bogomolov was to have his nostrils slit and was to be otherwise marked. While Bogomolov was awaiting his sentence he was not idle. He did not contrive to escape, but he succeeded in setting afloat, through conversations with his guards, rumours about the reappearance of Peter III, and these rumours spread among the Cossacks of the Don as they had previously spread among the Cossacks of the Volga.

The Don Cossacks had experienced grievances somewhat similar to those of which the Yaëk troops complained. They had, however, a stronger *ataman* to deal with. This *ataman*, Daniel Efremov, persuaded Katherine II to appoint as his successor his own son in order to begin a hereditary atamanship. He also proposed to enlarge the powers of the *ataman* in such a way as to give him control alike of the civil and military affairs of the Don Cossacks. This would have made the Efremovs practical dictators of the community. The younger Efremov was, however, denounced to the Military Collegium by a Cossack, and accused of abuse of authority. The Military Collegium ordered him to St. Petersburg, ostensibly to consult about the military situation in the Don region.

Efremov understood the risk he ran in putting himself into the hands of the authorities, and refused to comply with the order. He then began a journey through the Cossack stations announcing that the Government was demanding more recruits from the Cossacks, and urging them to petition against the proposed recruiting, and as well to demand the return of recruits previously sent to Azov and Taganrog. This astute manœuvre brought the Cossacks round to the side of Efremov, who now proceeded to defy the Military Collegium. Major-General Cherepov, who was sent to demand the presence of Efremov at St. Petersburg, was roughly used by the Cossacks, and orders were then given by the Empress to arrest Efremov. The arrest was effected on 9th November 1772, and Efremov was conveyed to Rostov-on-Don and immediately afterwards to St. Petersburg. The alarm bell was rung in the Cossack towns, and the whole population became greatly agitated. Efremov was tried at St. Petersburg for accepting bribes and for embezzlement. He was found guilty and sentenced to be hanged. The sentence was afterwards commuted to banishment for life.

While these agitations were going on among the Cossacks of the Don, one of the discontented Cossacks, a Little Russian called Pevchy, decided to go to Tsaritsin, where Bogomolov was confined, to investigate for himself the rumours about the reappearance of Peter III. He had two interviews with the impostor, who showed certain marks upon his body which he alleged were Tsar's marks, or marks which were made upon the heirs to the throne. The exhibition of this alleged Tsar's cross convinced Pevchy, who undertook to endeavour to secure the adherence of a hundred Cossacks and to attempt the rescue of Bogomolov. Pevchy went a second time to Tsaritsin, carrying a small sum of money which had been subscribed by the Cossacks. He gave the money to Bogomolov and asked for a receipt. The impostor, who was quite illiterate, made the pretence that he had no writing materials. The influence which Bogomolov, in spite of his imprisonment, was exerting upon the Cossacks became known to the Empress, and she ordered[1] that immediate steps be taken to punish the impostor. Bogomolov was mutilated and whipped, and was then sent off secretly under convoy in August 1772 to Nerchinsk. He died on the way.

[1] In an autograph letter to Chernyshev.

Some of the accomplices of Bogomolov who had escaped were still being searched for in 1774, when the fifth impostor appeared upon the scene. This was a fugitive Cossack of the Don, Emilian Ivanovich Pugachev. According to his own statement, Pugachev was born in 1744.[1] Since Peter III was born in 1728, there was so great disparity in age that there seems little excuse for the Cossacks being deceived, simple-minded as they were. Certainly those immediately about the impostor were not. Yet it appears that he looked older than he was.[2] Pugachev was born on the Don, was married to a Cossack girl, and was enlisted in the army. He fought in Prussia in the Russian campaign during the Seven Years War. In one of the minor engagements he lost a horse belonging to his Colonel, and for this was "mercilessly beaten."[3] The Russian troops were withdrawn from Prussia on the accession of Peter III in January 1762, and six months afterwards, on the death of Peter, the Cossack troops were disbanded. In 1764 Pugachev was in service again in Poland, and afterwards on the frontier in the war with Turkey. During the latter campaign he was invalided. In February 1771 he appeared at Cherkask on the Don, and later at Taganrog. In the course of these visits Pugachev became acquainted with the grievances of the Cossacks, his long period of service abroad having prevented him from knowing of them earlier. Pugachev compromised himself in the first instance by aiding his sister and her husband to escape across the Don from the Cossack territory. They were arrested, but at that time he evaded capture, and then began the odyssey of Pugachev which led later to momentous consequences. Pugachev was arrested repeatedly, but he escaped as often. In the course of these earlier wanderings Pugachev was being driven on the steppe when the following conversation took place between him and his driver. This conversation and another which followed both throw light upon the manners and way of life of the steppe in the third quarter of the eighteenth century.

The travellers, Pugachev and his young driver,[4] had halted for

[1] Statement of Pugachev to Sheshkovsky, 4th November 1774. State Archives VI, Affair No. 512 ; cited by Dubrovin, i. p. 132.

[2] Peter was deeply pitted with smallpox, a fact which was probably unknown to the Cossacks.

[3] Dubrovin, i. p. 133, quoting State Archives VI, Affair No. 506.

[4] Alexis Koverin, step-son of Ivan Koverin, from whose statement the narrative is taken. The statement is dated 11th December 1774. State Archives VI, Affair No. 512 ; cited by Dubrovin, i. pp. 142 et seq.

supper. Pugachev remarked "insinuatingly" to his companion, who was a *raskolnēk* or dissenter:

"I want to live for God, and I do not know where to find God-fearing people."

"I know where to find a God-fearing man," said the driver. "He accepts people who want to live for God."

"Please take me to him. Who is that God-fearing man, and where does he live?"

"This man is a Cossack of Kabaria settlement. He lives on his own farm; and his name is Korovka."

On the next evening they arrived at the farm of Korovka. Pugachev remained concealed in the cart while the driver went to reconnoitre and to interview the farmer.

"Who are you?" asked Korovka.

"I am an emigrant from Poland, a *raskolnēk*, an inhabitant of Belgorodskaya *gub.*, of Volnysky *uezd* (district) of the Courts' (Court peasants) *raskolnēk* settlement Chernigovka on the river Koysukha, Alexey Ivanovich Koverin. I have brought here a man who wants to live for God alone."

"Where is that man?"

Pugachev then emerged from the cart.

"What is your rank?" asked Korovka.

"I am a Don Cossack, Emelian Ivanovich Pugachev. . . . I want to live for God. Let me live here in service, doing what good for God a man can do."

"I should be glad," said Korovka, "but it is quite impossible. I have kept such people, but they have often robbed me. Indeed, I am afraid they have almost ruined me. . . . Life is hard here for us Old Believers. I have suffered for beard and cross[1] in Belgorod; but God give good health to our gracious Empress. She gave her ukase, and I was relieved."

Korovka kept Pugachev for two days, sent his son with him to guide him, and gave him money, two horses, and a passport in Korovka's own name. Throughout his wanderings this extraordinary man found always charitable persons, dupes, or shrewd allies who protected and assisted him. In the course of these

---

[1] In being taxed for wearing a beard and for dissent by the tax laws of Peter the Great. The Old Believers attached extreme importance to symbolism. They approved only the eight-branched cross.

wanderings Pugachev heard the story of Bogomolov. He learned that Bogomolov had been sent secretly to Siberia, and that his fate was unknown. He learned also of the disturbances on the Yaëk. Much of this information was derived from a monk called Philaret, whom he found at a hermitage at the village of Malikovka (now the town of Volsk, near Saratov). This monk appears to have recognized in Pugachev some capacity for leadership, and to have suggested to him the idea of raising another insurrection among the Cossacks.[1] Pugachev adopted the suggestion, and seems to have added an idea of his own, namely, that he should induce the Cossacks to leave the Yaëk and to enlist in the service of the Sultan of Turkey. As he approached the Yaëk he learned of the flights of Cossacks from that region, and he was confirmed in the impression that by directing these flights he might become *ataman* of the transferred Yaëk Cossacks. Pugachev arrived at the town of Yaëk on 22nd November 1772.[2]

Two months earlier the Commission charged with the investigation of the occurrences at the Yaëk had reported and recommended that of the Cossacks found guilty of participation in the uprising, twelve should be quartered, forty-seven hanged, three decapitated, twenty beaten, and eight shaved and sent into the regular army. The property of those who had been found guilty, but who had been able to escape, was to be confiscated, and on recovery of their persons they were to be hanged. The children of those who were punished were to be sent into the regular army.[3] This formidable sentence was sent to St. Petersburg for confirmation, and those to whom it applied were kept in prison. Pugachev found the Cossacks in deep depression. Their leaders were awaiting death, and the fear of punishment hung over the community. He also heard renewed rumours about the appearance at Tsaritsin of the Emperor Peter in the person of Bogomolov. Pugachev was aware that that impostor had disappeared, and he seems then to have determined

---

[1] In more than one of the insurrections of peasants and Cossacks at this period, incitement by the clergy appears as a prominent incident. It is difficult to dissociate this fact from clerical antagonism to Katherine on account of the secularization of the Church lands in 1764, although the process was begun in 1762, under the nominal rule of Peter III. Cf. *supra*, i. p. 233, and [Tooke] *Life of Catherine II* (London, 1800), ii. p. 184.

[2] From the statements of Pugachev and others made in 1774. State Archives VI, Affairs Nos. 506 and 512. See Dubrovin, i. pp. 150–4.

[3] Archives of the General Staff, Moscow, Inventory No. 93, Roll 492, No. 517; cited by Dubrovin, i. p. 155.

to personate him, and thus to secure what benefit might be derived from Cossack sympathy with him. He therefore began cautiously to announce that he was himself the Emperor Peter, and that he had escaped death in Tsaritsin as well as in St. Petersburg. The fact that Pugachev had entertained the design of leading the Cossacks away from the Yaëk was betrayed to the authorities. He was arrested, and in January 1773 he was sent to Kazan. There he was detained in prison until the end of May, when he escaped. Advice of the escape of Pugachev was accidentally delayed, and was not in the hands of Prince Vyazemsky, to whom it was directed, until the beginning of August. At St. Petersburg it was at once taken seriously. It was reported at midnight to Count Chernyshev, vice-president of the Military Collegium, and on the following morning orders were despatched to take every possible measure to find Pugachev. It was too late ; Pugachev had already declared himself to be the Emperor Peter, had succeeded in surrounding himself with a considerable force of armed Cossacks of the Yaëk, had captured an outpost, and had nearly reached the Cossack town. Imitating Bogomolov, Pugachev had exhibited to his adherents certain marks upon his body which he said were Tsar's signs. He remained on the steppe receiving visitors and disseminating the idea that he was the Emperor and that he had come to redress the wrongs of the Cossacks.

The sentence upon the Cossacks which had been formulated by the investigating Commission was not approved by the Military Collegium. Instead, an order was sent to deport to Siberia a number of the Cossacks, and to impose a heavy fine upon the Cossack community as a whole,[1] the amount of individual assessment being left to the local authorities. Although the proposed punishment was greatly diminished, the Cossacks were still dissatisfied. Among the visitors of Pugachev were some of the leading spirits of the Cossack disturbances who had contrived to evade arrest. One of these, a Cossack named Karavayev, was interrogated by another Cossack called Chika, who afterwards took a very active share in the revolutionary campaign, and who obtained the title of " Count " from Pugachev.

" Tell me the truth, what kind of man is he whom we regard as an Emperor ? "

[1] The fine was 36,000 rubles. Dubrovin, i. p. 185.

" Even if he is not an Emperor, but only a Cossack of the Don, he shall intervene for us instead of an Emperor. It does not matter to us what he is."

" Very good; so let it be. This means that he is necessary for the Cossacks." [1]

Chika took an early opportunity of interrogating Pugachev.

" Tell me, little father, the essential truth. Are you a real Emperor ? "

" I am a real Emperor to you," said Pugachev.

Chika then said, " You may conceal it from men, but you shall not be able to conceal it from God. . . . I have sworn that I will tell no one. . . . It is not of much importance whether you are a Don Cossack or not, if we have accepted you as Emperor. So be it."

" If so, then, keep it secret. I am really a Don Cossack," said Pugachev. " I have told this to a few of the other Cossacks. But under the name of Peter I shall acquire power and shall have many people with me, and I shall capture Moscow, where there are no troops."

Chika at once imparted this confession of Pugachev to another Cossack, Myasnikov, who said :

" It does not concern us whether he is an Emperor or not. Out of earth we can make a prince. Even if he does not conquer the Moscow State, we shall make the Yaēk our own kingdom."

Pugachev was thus in a large measure a tool of the Cossacks. They required a man of his type to act as nominal leader and possible scapegoat, and they found in Pugachev the man they wanted.[2] Myasnikov afterwards confessed this fully. " When Pugachev came to us and told us that he had escaped from Kazan, that he had been wandering about the steppe, and that he needed shelter in order to escape the search which was being made for him, we had many conversations about him, and we recognized in him a certain shrewdness and talent. We, therefore, thought of protecting him and of making him master over us, and of re-establishing our suppressed habits and customs. . . . For this reason we have accepted him as our Emperor, so that we may re-establish our customs and destroy all the boyars who think themselves so much cleverer

---

[1] State Archives VI, Affair No. 506 ; cited by Dubrovin, i. p. 217.

[2] In this respect the history of Pugachev resembled the history of Father Gapon in 1905. Cf. *infra*, p. 455.

than other people. We hoped that our undertaking would be supported, and that our power would grow by the adhesion of the common people, who are oppressed and ruined to an extreme extent." [1]

By the 18th September 1773 Pugachev felt himself strong enough to use force to compel the Cossacks to resort to his standard. He caused a loyal Cossack to be hanged, and he circulated a manifesto to the effect that he would confer great benefits upon the Cossacks if they supported him, and that he would hang and torture them if they did not. When he appeared in force before an outpost, the Cossacks realized that they were on the horns of a dilemma. If they joined him they were certain to be punished by the Government in the future ; if they did not join him they were to be hanged immediately. A future punishment was less to be dreaded than a present one, therefore they decided to join Pugachev's forces. They marched out of their small fortified posts, accompanied by their priests, and prostrated themselves before Pugachev, offering him " bread and salt." This occurred, for example, on 21st September at one of the outposts. The commandant, deserted by the Cossacks, was hanged, and Pugachev went to the church, ordering that the name of the Empress should be excluded from the prayer and the name of Peter substituted. After the service the people, beginning with the priest, took an oath of fealty ; and Pugachev promised on his part to relieve the people from " oppression and poverty," saying that he would take the villages from the boyars, and give them, as well as money, to the peasants.[2] Such captures enabled Pugachev to recruit his forces, to acquire money, which he took from the administrative offices, and to obtain ammunition and guns. He had gun carriages made for the latter, and converted small fortress guns into field artillery. When resistance was made, Pugachev easily overpowered the small garrisons, hanged the commandant, and sometimes also his wife, as well as any active defenders, and then compelled the remainder of the garrison to join his standard.

Although Pugachev went within a few miles of the Yaēk town, he did not feel himself strong enough to attack it, but he proceeded

---

[1] State Archives VI, Affair No. 421, statement of 8th May 1774 ; cited by Dubrovin, i. p. 221.

[2] Dubrovin, ii. pp. 16 and 17.

on his way towards a more important place—the fortress of Orenburg—slaying and recruiting as he went.   The Cossacks everywhere not only joined his ranks, but information about his movements did not circulate, and the people and garrison of Orenburg were quite unaware of his rapid approach.   Even when news was received it was discredited.   Reynsdorp, the commandant, refused to accept verbal reports.   There were no others, for the excellent reason that those who should have given them had been hanged. Only on the 24th September, in consequence of a message from the Khan of the Kirghiz horde, which indicated Pugachev's movements, did Reynsdorp take the matter seriously.   He then despatched an officer named Bilov with a detachment of 400 men and six field guns, with orders to intercept and capture Pugachev.   In addition Reynsdorp ordered 500 Kalmuk Tartars to go to the reinforcement of this detachment.   On the 26th, Bilov arrived at an outpost 82 *versts* from Orenburg, where he received a message from the commandant of one of the outposts which Pugachev had attacked. The message was a pathetic appeal for assistance, the Cossack garrison having deserted and left the commandant to his fate.   By the time the message reached Bilov the commandant had been cut to pieces.   Such information as Bilov could obtain showed that Pugachev had now at his disposal a force of 3000, with an unknown number of guns.   He therefore retired upon the fortress of Tatisheva, which was situated upon a hill overlooking the confluence of the Ural River and one of its tributaries.   This was looked upon as an important place, military supplies were stored there, and the garrison consisted of 1000 men equipped with 13 guns.   The fortress was under the command of Colonel Elagin, a brave and capable officer.   On the 27th September Elagin sent out a party to reconnoitre.   The officer was killed and almost all the party taken prisoners.   A sortie of Orenburg Cossacks from the fortress was then ordered, with the object of frightening the rebel forces.   The Cossacks deserted in a body, and went over to Pugachev.   The fortress was then attacked by the rebels in force, set on fire, and captured, Elagin and Bilov both being killed.   The fall of Tatisheva not only gave Pugachev a quantity of plunder and some additional guns, but it produced a great moral effect upon the surrounding Cossack population, and moreover opened the way to Orenburg. Pugachev was joined by a large body of Kalmuks and by 500 Bashkirs, and was now within 28 *versts* from Orenburg, without any intervening fortress. The city was practically defenceless. The garrison of regular troops was small (only 1200 men), and it was scattered in different outposts; the Cossacks, who had been relied upon only for resistance to the Tartar hordes, were under strong suspicion. The people were panic-stricken; the excesses of Pugachev had become known, and had excited the utmost horror. The inhabitants proceeded desperately to repair the neglected defences.

Pugachev did not attack the city immediately. Had he done so he might have taken it. He proceeded by making himself master of the surrounding region and by isolating Orenburg. Reynsdorp, the Governor of Orenburg, suggests that Pugachev's object in going into the surrounding country was to announce to the peasants that he was going to emancipate them, and by this means inducing them to join him. He certainly destroyed many houses of *pomyetschēkē* and caused a general flight of serf-owners and their families.

The news that Pugachev was investing Orenburg reached St. Petersburg on the 19th October 1773, but in spite of the transparent gravity of the situation, action was difficult. Russia was engaged in the war with Turkey, and France and Sweden together were threatening Russia in the Baltic. A Cossack attack upon a remote outskirt like Orenburg appeared to be a minor affair. Besides, to send any considerable reinforcement of troops to the Volga was to disclose the interior troubles, and thus to compromise external relations; and to send any large number was difficult, because of the demands of the unsuccessful Turkish campaign and the need for defensive measures in the north. Thus, although Katherine seems to have grasped from the beginning the gravity of the Cossack movement, she found herself in a dilemma. Detached bodies of troops were thus sent to Kazan in such a manner as to avoid attracting attention.

Meanwhile Pugachev circulated through the whole region manifestoes ordering the liberation of peasants and promising religious freedom, abolition of bondage right, and the allotment of land to the liberated peasants. He invited all " enslaved persons " to join his ranks and to fight for their liberty. Emissaries were sent by him among the peasants at the State and " possessional " factories. Since the adoption of a policy of concentrating the military forces became necessary in consequence of the growth of Pugachev's army, the outlying posts were abandoned, and thus in the regions round about these posts the influence of the Government declined and the influence of Pugachev increased.[1] Cossacks of the Yaĕk belonging to Pugachev's army went about among the estates, collected the peasants, and told them that by the order of Pugachev they were liberated. To make this manifest, they burned the houses of the *pomyetschĕkĕ*. At the works where bonded peasants were engaged, they killed the managers, plundered the works, and carried off the peasants as recruits. Some of the commanders of outposts, being deserted by their troops, capitulated to Pugachev in preference to being hanged by him.[2]

As in all such historical cases, Pugachev's army was a very fluctuating quantity, but he succeeded in maintaining the investment of Orenburg, although he feared to attack the town. He destroyed the hay in the suburbs and prevented any supplies from being taken in, hoping to reduce the population to submission by famine.

In the beginning of November (1773) Pugachev learned of the advance of General Kar,[3] who had been sent by the Government to take command of the troops on the Volga and to endeavour to relieve Orenburg. Kar collected the scattered elements of an army and proceeded towards Orenburg, but he found himself in a hostile country. The whole of the Russian population was agitated and more or less disloyal, while the Kalmuks and Bashkirs were in open rebellion, marauding and disappearing on the steppe.[4] Advance was difficult, because provisions and forage could not readily be procured, and from the middle of October there had been a heavy fall of snow. Kar had under his command very few regular troops,[5] and the irregulars could not be relied upon. The country had never been surveyed, and the distances between points were not accurately known. In addition to the forces under Kar himself, there were moving upon Orenburg, or available to move upon it, about 4000 regular and irregular troops from Tobolsk, under the command of Dekalong, a smaller detachment under Chernyshev

---

[1] Dubrovin, ii. p. 81.   [2] *Ibid.*, p. 83.
[3] Properly Ker, a Scotch soldier of fortune in the Russian service.
[4] Dubrovin, ii. p. 98.
[5] Only 631. *Ibid.*, p. 99.

on the Volga, and another detachment under Korf, in one of the fortresses south of Kazan. Had all of these various forces been able to precipitate themselves at the same moment upon Pugachev, the rebellion would have been at an end. But the distances were great, means of communication in a hostile country difficult, and each commander was unaware of the whereabouts of the others.[1] Pugachev, whose information was much more ample, was thus able to meet the various detachments individually, and to defeat them in detail. Nor was Pugachev left to act alone. The emissaries whom he had sent to rouse the peasants on the estates and at the " possessional " and State works were highly successful. They were received with " joy " at the works at Avzyano-Petrovsk, for instance, where Prince Vyazemsky had found the ascribed peasants had been drawn to the works from immense distances, and had been for this and other reasons connected with the administration of the works in a state of discontent for years.[2] Pugachev's emissaries obtained at these and other works men, money, and materials of war. Forming a force they were able to attack Kar, to prevent reinforcements from reaching him, and even to induce the desertion of some of his troops.[3] In spite of the need of haste, which he felt necessary to accomplish his object, Kar was obliged to retire and to await reinforcements before continuing his advance.

Korf and Chernyshev, however, succeeded in reaching, one within 20 and the other within 40 *versts* of Orenburg, and they contrived to convey despatches to Reynsdorp, who ordered them to march towards the town at daybreak on the morning of the 13th November, on which morning he would make a sally. On the night of the 12th Chernyshev received news of the defeat and retirement of Kar, and also of a threatened attack by Pugachev upon himself. He was urged by the Cossacks, who gave him this information, to endeavour to reach Orenburg by a night march, and under cover of the night to try to evade Pugachev, through whose lines he must pass. Pugachev, by whom probably the plan was concocted, had prepared an ambush, and in the early morning, on emerging from a defile, the head of Chernyshev's column was attacked by Pugachev in force. The column was demoralized, the irregulars first deserted, and

[1] Dubrovin, ii. p. 100.   [2] Cf. *supra*, i. pp. 458–9.
[3] Economical (formerly Church) peasants deserted, for instance. Dubrovin, ii. p. 104.

then the garrison troops. Chernyshev was made prisoner and almost immediately afterwards was hanged, together with thirty-three officers and one officer's wife. Elated with this victory and occupied with the despatch of his unfortunate prisoners, Pugachev allowed Korf to slip past him and to enter Orenburg with 2500 men and 22 guns.[1] This accession of numbers was at once too many and too few. The fresh troops were too many to feed and too few to relieve the town. Reynsdorp ordered a sally the following day, but the force was defeated by Pugachev, who now had before Orenburg 10,000 men and 40 guns. This was not, however, all his force. In December 1773 he appears to have had altogether 15,000 men and 86 guns. The rebel army was, as might be expected, indifferently organized and badly armed. Following the Cossack practice, the officers were elected, the Cossacks of the Yaēk taking the leading part in the elections and allowing only those of whom they approved to be elected. Pugachev established a so-called military collegium, with whose proceedings it appears he did not interfere. Some were armed with pikes, some with pistols, some with the swords of captured officers, a very few with rifles.[2] They were all or nearly all well mounted.[3] The armed crowd was, however, only a small part of the total of Pugachev's adherents. There were about him a number, unknown even to himself,[4] of escaped *dvorovie lyudē*, agricultural peasants, State works peasants, ascribed peasants, Kirghizes, Bashkirs, and others. Of all of these the most zealous were the peasants ascribed to the works to whom Pugachev meant liberty from the intolerable conditions to which they had been subjected.[5]

The discipline of Pugachev in certain directions was very severe. One of his confederates, who ventured in his cups to say that he knew where the " emperor " came from, was hanged the following morning, although he had been personally intimate with Pugachev and a useful commander. From an early period denunciations and treachery were frequent in the camp of the impostor.

While the investment of Orenburg occupied the greater number

---

[1] Dubrovin, ii. p. 111.   [2] *Ibid.*, p. 135.
[3] Reynsdorp complained that they had all the good horses in the region.
[4] Pugachev's statement, 4th November 1774. State Archives VI, Affair No. 512 ; cited by Dubrovin, ii. p. 136.
[5] Report of the Orenburg Secret Commission, 21st May 1774. State Archives, Affair No. 508 (2) ; cited by Dubrovin, ii. p. 136. See also *supra*, i. pp. 434–521.

of the immediate adherents of the impostor, the unrest which his movement produced spread far and wide. In Kazan the situation was very serious. The disturbances of the previous years, the rigorous enforcement of the laws, and the arbitrary action of the authorities, both local and central, had filled the prisons. The local militia was composed of tribesmen of the native races of the Upper Volga—the Cheremissi, the Mordva,[1] and others—all more or less unreliable elements, and there were few regular troops. Migrations in mass of the gentry of Kazan to Moscow began early in the winter of 1773.[2]

General Kar, who had been driven back by the adherents of Pugachev, found himself in the beginning of winter without reliable infantry and without cavalry. He determined, suffering from fever as he was, to leave his command in winter quarters, and to go to St. Petersburg for the purpose of consulting with the authorities and endeavouring to induce them to send an adequate force to put down the rebellion. On his arrival at Moscow he was dismissed the service for leaving his command without orders.[3] He was replaced by General A. I. Bibikov,[4] who was given one regiment of cavalry and two of infantry, although the reinforcements which Kar had asked for had been refused. The infantry regiments were to be forwarded from Moscow to Kazan in post-carts in order to save time.

A manifesto written by Katherine was read to the Council at which Bibikov was present, on the eve of his departure. " My spirit," Katherine said, " shivers when I think of the times (150 years earlier) of Godunov (Boris) and Otrepiev (the pseudo-Demetrius I), in which Russia was plunged in civil war, when, because of the appearance of an impostor, the towns and villages were ruined by fire and sword, when the blood of Russians was shed by Russians, and when the unity of the State was destroyed by Russians themselves." [5]

---

[1] See *supra*, i. p. 580. Dubrovin, ii. p. 147.

[3] *The Eighteenth Century*, ed. Bertener, i. p. 102 ; cited by Dubrovin, ii. p. 162.

[4] Cf. *supra*, i. p. 465.

[5] *Moscow Society of History and Antiquities* (1860), ii. p. 72 ; cited by Dubrovin, ii. p. 168. Both Chernyshev and Orlov objected to the comparison between Pugachev and the pseudo-Demetrius, and the names of Godunov and Otrepiev were deleted ; but Katherine had a clearer idea of the significance of the rebellion than had any one about her.

Bibikov had previous experience, both as soldier and as diplomatist. Katherine gave him large powers, advised him to inform himself fully upon the whole situation, and then to act, attacking the insurgents with the " superiority which science, education, and courage always give against a mob which is moved only by stormy and fanatical religious or political inspiration." [1]

The Government, however, perversely forbore to bring common sense to bear upon the problem which confronted it. In the first manifesto which Bibikov was required to promulgate an appeal was made to the Greek Orthodox to defend Holy Russia, and pardon was offered to those who should leave Pugachev. Since the backbone of Pugachev's force was composed of Russians who were *raskolnēkē*, and of Tartars who were either Mohammedans or pagans, the appeal not merely failed of its purpose, it excited hostility, because it suggested the continuance of the intolerant measures which had been among the causes of the rebellion.

During the winter of 1773-1774 the influence of Pugachev extended still more widely. The flight of *pomyetschēkē* from their estates facilitated the growth of the movement among the peasants. They declared themselves free, and they attributed their freedom to the Tsar Peter III, who for them was really alive. The peasants had now no taxes to pay, for there was no one to collect them, and this again they attributed to the Tsar Peter. " Our time has come," said the common people ; " we shall get to the top, and we have nothing to fear." [2]

The officers sent on in advance by Bibikov found that throughout the Volga region the authority of the Government had simply disappeared. The pseudo-Peter III reigned in no real sense, but his influence was diffused everywhere. The nomad tribes, now unimpeded by the forces of the Government, which were shut up in Orenburg, Kazan, and a few other fortresses, passed their usual boundaries and pillaged indiscriminately, driving off the peasants' cattle and plundering their crops. But this fact, troublesome as it was, had no importance compared with the fact that the peasantry throughout the Volga region had been liberated, partly through

---

[1] *Collections of Imperial Historical Society*, xiii. p. 371 ; cited by Dubrovin, ii. p. 174.

[2] Report of an officer, Captain Mavrin, 27th May 1774 ; quoted by Dubrovin, ii. p. 181.

their having joined an uprising of the Cossacks and partly through the flight of their owners. This fact gave importance to the rebellion of Pugachev. His own share in it, as we have seen, was insignificant. Urged by the Cossacks, he acted as a standard round which they rallied; but the rising would have been a mere riot had it not affected the peasants. It became a peasant revolt of a character similar to those revolts which occurred in France almost, if not quite, simultaneously.[1] Bibikov recognized the signs at once. " This is a riot of poor against rich, *kholopi* against their masters." [2]

When Kar left his post south of Kazan he left General Freiman in command. Freiman had scarcely any cavalry, and he therefore spent an anxious winter, almost surrounded as he was by an extremely mobile enemy, not only well mounted, but taking with them, in order to increase the rapidity of movement, a supply of spare horses. The meagreness of the force of Freiman greatly increased his peril. The peasants at the works and on the estates remarked the delay in sending troops from the capitals. If, they said, the leader of the Cossacks before Orenburg is an impostor, why does the Government not send troops to put him down. That months have passed during which nothing has been done, shows that he is the real Emperor.[3] In some cases the officials and their

[1] The beginning of the peasant revolts, which were among the premonitory symptoms of the French Revolution, appears to have taken place immediately after the death of Louis XV in 1774. The harvest of that year was inferior, and this fact, together with the relaxation of authority which ensued on the death of the King and the exaggerated hopes which were entertained by the peasants of benefits to be conferred by his successor, led to riots in the winter of 1774–1775 at Dijon, Auxerre, Amiens, Lille, Pontoise, Passy, and St. Germain, at least. (*Cf.* Kropotkin, *La Grande Revolution*, 1789–1793, Paris, 1909, p. 31.) For the issue of false decrees in France (as in Russia) at this time, and for other revolutionary indications similar to those which appeared in Russia, see Rocquain, Felix, *The Revolutionary Spirit preceding the French Revolution* (English translation, London, 1891, pp. 126 *et seq.*). In the winter of 1788–1789, several months before the fall of the Bastille (14th July 1789), " spontaneous anarchy " broke out in the provinces. The peasants seized their liberty in the same way that the Russian peasants had done a few years before. They refused to pay taxes or to render " personal dues "; they refused to pay *octrois* on produce entering the towns; they announced explicitly that they " had declared a sort of war against landowners and property . . . and that they would pay nothing, neither taxes nor debts." Taine, *The French Revolution* (English translation, London 1878), vol. i. chap. i.
[2] Quoted by N. Fĕrsov in *The Participation of the Peasantry, &c., in the Great Reform* (Moscow, 1911), ii. p. 48.
[3] Dubrovin, ii. p. 195.

families, being without protection, left the works, and the peasants then elected their own chiefs, maintained order among themselves, and continued their occupations as usual, without troubling themselves about either Empress or impostor, excepting to send a few men to the " Cossack troops " in order to secure immunity for the remainder.[1]

During the winter, Chika, the Cossack, Pugachev's "Count Chernyshev," made himself master of Bashkiria and of the whole of the region on the east of the Kama River.   He appointed *atamans* and administered the district he had acquired.[2]

When Bibikov arrived at Kazan on 26th December 1773, he found the administration in a hopeless condition.   The Governor, von Brandt, was an aged man, who thought only of keeping Pugachev out of Kazan, and who had no grasp of the general situation. He was surrounded by officials whom Bibikov found not only useless, but obstructive.   In some of the neighbouring towns the officials had simply fled.   It was necessary to reorganize the whole military and civil government of the region, and for this purpose a new group of able and courageous officials was necessary.   Bibikov insisted upon such a group being sent, and a number of experienced officers joined him early in 1774.   At this moment the rebels broke into the *gubernie* of Kazan and crossed the Urals into Siberia.[3]   The investment of Chelyabinsk indeed imperilled communication between Siberia and European Russia.[4]

The Military Collegium, advised by Bibikov of the immense difficulty of a campaign against Pugachev, offered a reward of ten thousand rubles for his capture.   Although Bibikov recognized very well that Pugachev in himself was insignificant—" a scarecrow " he called him—he also recognized that " the general movement was important," [5] and that since circumstances had determined that the general movement had centred upon Pugachev, it was necessary that he should be secured as an early step in the " pacification " of the country.

There were contradictory incidents—on the one hand, the Cossacks of the Don, to whom Pugachev himself belonged, remained

---

[1] Dubrovin, ii. pp. 196–7.   [2] *Ibid*., pp. 197 *et seq*.
[3] *Ibid*., p. 228.   [4] *Ibid*.
[5] Letter dated 29th January 1774 in *Memoirs of Bibikov* (Moscow, 1865), Supplement, p. 76 ; quoted by Dubrovin, ii. p. 248.

generally loyal, while among the regular troops from other parts of Russia there was much discontent. They grumbled at the hardness of the service and the insufficiency of their allowances. It appeared also that the clergy of the towns were very generally in favour of the rebellion.[1] The monks in the monasteries were not.

In spite of the difficulty of campaigning in winter, when the snow rendered movement of troops extremely arduous and the movement of heavy guns almost impossible, Bibikov spent an active January. His subordinates, Prince Golētsin and his own relative, Colonel Bibikov, drove the rebels hither and thither, and brought a large region once more under the authority of the Government. The peasants began once more to pay their taxes and to bring in fodder for the use of the troops. Orenburg still held out, but Samara and the Yaēk town had been taken, although the garrison of the latter still held a portion of the fortifications to which they were confined, while the rebels held the town.

On 21st March 1774 Golētsin arrived before Tatisheva fortress, occupied by Pugachev with about 8000 men. Golētsin had at his disposal 6500.[2] After a stubborn engagement the fortress was taken, but not until after Pugachev and his chief supporters had fled. Between two and three thousand of Pugachev's following were killed in this engagement. It was believed in St. Petersburg, and widely announced, that this was the end of the rebellion; but this was by no means the case. Pugachev had still a large force, for the most part concentrated at Berda before Orenburg.

His confederate Chika, who had acquired control of Bashkiria, was investing Ufa, and in the spring of 1774 Mikhelson, one of Bibikov's active officers, was sent to take command of the troops in that region. He attacked Chika, and on 27th March completely defeated him, Chika himself escaping with a few Cossacks. In both of these engagements it appears that the rebel forces fought with determination, and that they were commanded with skill.

From the defeat at Tatisheva Pugachev fled to Berda, and there began immediately among the Cossacks intrigues towards his

---

[1] There were numerous cases in which they received Pugachev with open arms, either through fear or through sympathy with the revolt. Witness the case of the clergy of Samara. Dubrovin, i. p. 251.

[2] Archives of the General Staff, Moscow, 47, vii.; cited by Dubrovin, ii. p. 215.

capture by them and the surrender of him to the Government.[1] Having made of him all the use possible, the Cossacks were now preparing to make a scapegoat of him. Pugachev, who was not destitute of sagacity, discovered the plot, and in the early morning, with two thousand Cossacks of the Yaēk upon whom he thought he could rely, he evacuated Berda and left the rest of his army to its fate and Orenburg still nominally invested. On the afternoon of the same day (23rd March) Berda was occupied by troops from Orenburg, and the stores of the rebel forces were pillaged by the inhabitants, who, after a close investment of six months, had been reduced to starvation. Then began the hunt for Pugachev, who was as yet by no means at the end of his support, although his personal initiative seems to have been temporarily diminished. He was joined by about two thousand Bashkirs, and he was still prepared to offer resistance to the forces of Golētsin, by whom he was pursued. On 1st April Golētsin engaged Pugachev and defeated him, but Pugachev escaped with 500 men, leaving all of his principal accomplices and supporters in the hands of Golētsin, who made 2800 prisoners.[2] On the 15th the Government forces reached the Yaēk town, and the small force confined in a portion of the fortifications, who had eaten their last morsel of food two days before, was relieved.[3] It appeared now as though the Pugachev episode were closed, but it was not so. General Bibikov, who had with great energy and skill set himself to the task of putting down the rebellion, became ill in March and died on 9th April. When the news reached St. Petersburg, Sir Robert Gunning, the British Ambassador, wrote to Lord Suffolk, saying that it seemed " likely that his death would raise the spirit of the rebels." [4]

The prophecy was true ; the rebellion was rekindled, it became more formidable than ever, and six months elapsed before it was finally extinguished. This was not foreseen by the Government, which was moreover embarrassed by the war with Turkey and very unwilling to be distracted by interior affairs more than appeared at the time to be absolutely necessary. A successor to Bibikov was therefore not immediately appointed. It was hoped that the local authorities, aided by the officers on the staff of Bibikov, would be able to deal with the small bands of rioters to whom the con-

[1] Cf. Dubrovin, ii. p. 374.   [2] Ibid., p. 387.
[3] Ibid., ii. p. 394.   [4] Quoted by Dubrovin, ibid., p. 399.

tinuance of the insurrection was attributed.   Upon Prince Sh'cher-batov, who had been Bibikov's second in command, there devolved the duty of succeeding him at Kazan, while Reynsdorp was en-trusted with affairs at Orenburg.   At the latter place there was an enormous number of prisoners (4700) whose presence embarrassed the local authorities and perplexed the Government.

Whether these people were punished or were liberated, further disturbance might be excited.   They were sent in large numbers to Kazan for trial.   After Berda, Pugachev had disappeared, in spite of active pursuit, and three of his armies had been killed, captured, or dispersed.   He had already lost some 15,000 men.   There re-mained in the field numerous large groups, with whose organization Pugachev had little or nothing to do, and these kept the troops moving over large areas in guerilla warfare for months.   Pugachev himself reappeared in May in Bashkiria with a formidable force of Bashkirs.   He was attacked and defeated by Dekalong, losing 4000 men and 28 guns, together with more than 3000 people, includ-ing women and children, who had composed part of his camp. Again Pugachev disappeared, to reappear in the Ural Mountains, sweeping through small fortresses with an army of works peasants and of well-mounted Bashkirs, clothed in chain-armour and pro-tected otherwise by cuirasses made of tin, procured at the tin works in the mountains.[1]   There he was attacked by Mikhelson.   The Bashkirs defended themselves against regular troops with great stubbornness, and large numbers of them were killed.   When re-sistance was no longer possible, the survivors dispersed, carrying off Pugachev with them.   Pugachev again procured reinforcements, and ravaged the works in the Urals in the neighbourhood of the Mias River, upon which he established himself, and even delivered a counter-attack upon Mikhelson.

Up till May 1774 the disturbances had been confined to the outskirts—to the *gubernie* of Orenburg, Perm, Ufa, Samara, Saratov, and the borders of Kazan.   In that month St. Petersburg was alarmed by the news that disaffection had made its appearance in Voronej and other adjoining *gubernie* in Great Russia.   The peasants of these *gubernie* had learned that beyond the Volga the Tsar Peter III had liberated the peasants from the *pomyetschēkē*, and some peasants had been sent off as a deputation to him to ask him to

[1] Dubrovin, iii. p. 37.

liberate the peasants on the west of the Volga.[1]   Katherine now urged upon all the Governors to be careful not to exact unusual work from the peasants, and to avoid irritating them in any way.

Pugachev issued manifestoes, which he disseminated widely, promising freedom from bondage, reduction of poll-tax, and relief from compulsory military service.   " No more," he said, " will the nobility burden the peasantry with great wars." [2]

The effect of these manifestoes was enormous.   In spite of the repeated defeats inflicted upon Pugachev, the movement had spread far beyond Cossack spheres.   The Bashkirs and the Kalmuks were wholly up in arms, and the peasants from the State works and the Possessional factories were almost unanimously implicated in the rising.   Works and estates were pillaged everywhere, not merely by forces over which Pugachev had control, but by spontaneously formed groups in many regions.   The Cossack revolt had become a mass-rising of the peasants.   The sheep had turned in its rage.

Prince Sh'cherbatov being appealed to for protecting forces for individual works, replied that it was impossible to provide a guard for each establishment, and added, " the cruelty of the owners of the works towards their peasants arouses the hate of the peasants against their masters." [3]

Pugachev and his Bashkirs fought only when they were forced to fight.   They evaded the troops that were sent to surround them, and their great mobility enabled them to appear suddenly in unexpected places, to levy toll and to disappear.[4]   The rebels were individually much better acquainted with the country than were the Russian generals, and they were able to make their way through forests impenetrable to regular troops with their munitions of war.

Wherever he went Pugachev was able to raise local forces, and to invest and attack fortresses by means of the peasants of the immediate neighbourhood, as reinforcements of his nuclear troops of Cossacks of the Yaëk and Bashkirs, with other tribesmen.   This circumstance accounts for Pugachev's being able to change his

---

[1] Dubrovin, iii. p. 44.
[2] Archives of the General Staff, Moscow, 47, x., quoted by Dubrovin, ibid., p. 53.
[3] Ibid., iv., quoted by Dubrovin, iii. p. 53.
[4] The parallel between this condition and the later phases of the South African War is obvious.

field of operations in such a way as to draw into one region the Government forces, and then suddenly to appear in a distant region where the troops were inadequate to impede his movements. In this way Pugachev passed rapidly from Bashkiria to Orenburg, and from Orenburg to the Yaēk, and then northwards towards Kazan. Having seized the town of Osa, and burned it, no considerable place remained between Pugachev and Kazan, upon which towards the end of June he advanced with a force of about 7000.[1] The local authorities had refused to believe that the town was within the possible field of Pugachev's operations, the defences had been neglected, and the garrison had been allowed to fall to a low point. On the 12th July Pugachev, avoiding the principal defences, stormed and entered the town, and large numbers of the inhabitants threw themselves at his feet. The surviving defenders retired to the citadel, which they succeeded in holding, while the town was given up to fire and pillage. Out of 2873 houses, 2063 were burned or plundered.[2] Pugachev withdrew from the burning town to his camp where he had now 12,000 men.[3]

Mikhelson, who had been following up Pugachev by forced marches, reached Kazan on the day after the capture of the town, but in time to relieve the refugees in the fortress, a portion of which was now on fire. The rebels were immediately attacked by Mikhelson, although his forces were as one to ten; he was able to rout them, but unable at once to follow up his advantage. On the following day (14th July) there was another engagement in which the troops from the fortress participated. Pugachev's forces were dispersed in all directions, but no cavalry was available for pursuit, and thus Pugachev was enabled to collect his scattered forces, and even to add to them from the peasants in the neighbourhood, so that on 15th July he had 15,000 men within 20 *versts* of Kazan.[4] On that day, after an engagement of four hours, Mikhelson defeated Pugachev, who escaped with difficulty, losing 2000 killed and wounded, and 5000 prisoners, with all his artillery.

[1] Statement of Pugachev, 4th November 1774, State Archives VI, Affair No. 512, quoted by Dubrovin, iii. p. 77.

[2] Tscherbatov to Chernyshev, 1st August 1774, Archives of the General Staff, Moscow, 47, iv.

[3] MSS. Journal of Mikhelson, Collection of Count Uvarov, No. 559, cited by Dubrovin, iii. p. 98.

[4] Dubrovin, iii. p. 100,

The dispersal of the survivors of Pugachev's forces, which followed the defeat and pursuit, resulted in the spreading over the Kazanskaya and Nijigorodskaya *guberni* of detached parties of desperate people. They pillaged the estates, hanged the proprietors, and drew off the peasants as they had done elsewhere. These parties infested the roads and destroyed the means of communication.[1] The forests were set on fire, and there was no material wherewith the burned-out towns and villages might be rebuilt. " There was no bread, no hay, no fuel ; the population lived under the open sky ; where houses remained they were occupied by the military ; but the houses had neither roofs nor windows. The churches were filled with ruined people." [2] Not alone the parties resulting from the decomposition of Pugachev's forces, but the peasants everywhere rose against their *pomyetschĕkĕ*, and either put them to flight or hanged them. With characteristic reliance upon authority of some kind the peasants submitted themselves to Pugachev or his representatives wherever he went. They sent to Pugachev petitions asking him to settle disputes among the peasants about the distribution of grain and the like, which, owing to the flight or death of the proprietors, had fallen into the hands of the peasants.[3] Fears began to be entertained that the agitation might envelope Moscow, and that the wave of discontent might carry the impostor to the capital.

On 23rd July 1774 the news of Rumyantsev's victory over the Turks and of the consequent peace [4] came as a welcome relief to the horrible situation. It was now possible to turn the whole forces of the Empire against the interior rebellion. It was high time. Moscow, which had suffered severely from the plague of 1771, was in a state of disaffection, and the whole of the Volga region had been ravaged. Katherine entrusted Count Peter Panin, brother of the minister, with the task of subduing the rebellion. The real labour,

[1] " The damned owl frightened Kazan on the 12th July, and although his wings are damaged, it is evident that his bats are flying all over the outskirts, barring all the roads, so that during this month there have been neither couriers nor post from or to Kazan." Lubarsky to Bantysh-Kamensky, 24th July 1774, State Archives VI, Affair No. 527, cited by Dubrovin, iii. p. 104.

[2] Dubrovin, *ibid.*, p. 109. [3] *Ibid.*, iii. pp. 103–114.

[4] The Treaty (of Cainargi) was signed 10/21 July 1774. It was drawn up in Italian. A copy of the original is printed in De Marten's *Recueil des principaux Traites, &c.* (Göttingen, 1795), iv. pp. 606 *et seq.*

however, fell upon Mikhelson, who pursued Pugachev with tireless energy, and succeeded in cutting him off from the Moscow road. The most active of Pugachev's officers had been captured, and the excesses of his troops had induced a reaction. The back of the rebellion was already broken. One of his confederates, a certain Dolgopolov, made up his mind to betray him. He went to St. Petersburg, had an interview with Count Orlov, and afterwards with the Empress, and offered to deliver up Pugachev to the authorities on receipt of 20,000 rubles. The money was paid. Pugachev was delivered, brought to Moscow in an iron cage, tried in September 1774, and executed in January 1775.

The significance of the rebellion of Pugachev lay in the fact that it was a really revolutionary movement. When all the adventitious elements are allowed for, the incitement of the clergy in revenge for the secularization of the church lands,[1] the sordid grievances and petty party quarrels of the Cossacks, and the personality of Pugachev, there remains the substantial fact that the revolt was essentially the spontaneous outcome of the exercise of bondage right. This right had, as we have seen, been greatly intensified in the immediately preceding period. The policy of Peter the Great in forcing industry and in ascribing large numbers of peasants to the works of the State and to Possessional factories led to abuses so grave that only the abolition of the system and the freedom of the peasants could cure the evil.

The agricultural peasant was also being kept down by the incidents of bondage, and in his case also there was no outlet but economic freedom, and under the then existing régime in Russia there seemed to be no hope that this should be granted from above.

The growth of bondage had disintegrated Russian society. The sharpness of the division between the classes prevented homogeneous social progress, and embittered the classes against each other. One fraction thus rose against the other fraction in a civil war, in which the masters were on one side and the bonded peasants on the other. The partial success of the revolt was due to the numbers of disaffected peasantry as well as to the numbers of the

---

[1] Such incitement could not have been successful directly with the Cossacks, who were *raskolnĕkĕ*, nor with the peasants, who had been by no means unwilling to be transferred from the hands of the Church to the hands of the State. It could not be otherwise applied than through leaders, and even, perhaps, through impostors.

frontier tribes who joined the rebellion, and the partial failure of it was due to the absence of a town proletariat, which might have co-operated in the rebellion.[1] The forces of the revolt were also compromised by the absence of intellectual capacity on the part of the leaders, who were unable to grasp the situation, and who were led into excesses of mere destructiveness. At no period did they reveal any constructive powers.[2]

It may be held that the rebellion of Pugachev threw the whole question of reform back for perhaps fifty years. It frightened the mass of the people as well as the governing classes by " the red glare in the sky," the sign of a *jacquerie*. The French Revolution, which followed it closely, had a similar influence. Yet these popular uprisings proved that society might hover on the brink of reform too long, and that delay was perhaps more dangerous than precipitation.

[1] As was the case in the French Revolution, *e.g.* It was the Paris proletariat which made the Revolution possible, although it did not begin it and did not profit by it.

[2] On the times of Katherine II. generally see Soloviev, *History of Russia* (St. Petersburg), *v.d.*, vols. xxi.–xxix.

CHAPTER III

THE REVOLUTIONARY MOVEMENTS OF 1824-1825, 1830, AND 1848-1850

THE first modern revolutionary movement in Russia was that of the *Dekabristi* in 1824-1825. The movement had been in the making from about 1814.[1] The revolutionary ideas of that epoch were the outcome of the "impact"[2] of Western European liberalizing tendencies upon the minds of the younger nobles, and especially upon those of the younger officers, who had become acquainted with the currents of political thought in France and Germany.[3] Many young officers had studied in the latter country during the later Napoleonic days, while others had become infected with revolutionary impulses

[1] Perhaps even a few years earlier. Prince Kropotkin (*Ideals and Realities of Russian Literature*, p. 35) has observed that the character of Pierre in Tolstoy's *War and Peace* is that of the young men who afterwards became *Dekabristi*. Pierre's enthusiasm for the humanitarian movement received its impetus from Freemasonry in 1809. During and since the year 1905, much light has been thrown upon the Dekabrist movement by the publication of documents and memoirs. The most important material is to be found in *Popular Movements in Russia in the First Half of the Nineteenth Century*, vol. i., the *Dekabristi*, by V. E. Semevsky, V. Bogucharsky, and P. E. Sh'chegolyev (St. Petersburg, 1905). There have also been published *Letters and Confessions of the Dekabristi*, by A. R. Borozdin (St. Petersburg, 1906); *Memoirs of the Dekabristi* (Kiev, 1906); *The Secret Society of the Dekabristi* (Moscow, 1906); *The Ideals of the Dekabristi* (Kiev, 1906); all by M. V. Dovnar-Zapolsky; *The Dekabristi*, by A. Kotlyarevsky (St. Petersburg, 1907), *Russkaya Pravda*, by Paul Péstel (St. Petersburg, 1906), and *Political and Social Ideas of the Dekabristi*, by V. E. Semevsky (St. Petersburg, 1909). An excellent account of the Dekabrist movement is given in the *Cambridge Modern History*, vol. x., by Professor S. Askenazy. See also "The *Dekabristi* and the Peasant Question," by V. E. Semevsky, in *The Great Reforms*, vol. ii. p. 176 (Moscow, 1911).

[2] A phrase of William Godwin's in relation to the effect of the French Revolution.

[3] *Cf.* Pushkin, *Eugene Oneguine* (translation by Col. Spalding, London, 1881). For a lively account of the German influence upon the Russian youth in 1814-1815 and in 1848, see Vicomte E.-M. de Vogué, *Le Roman Russe* (Paris, 1892). N. E. Turgueniev, General Orlov, and Count Dmitriev-Mamonov, *e.g.*, studied at Göttingen under Stein. See Kleinschmidt, *Drei Jahrhunderte russischer Geschichte* (Berlin, 1898), p. 316. Stein was invited to Russia during the period immediately preceding the French invasion.

in France during the Russian occupation of a part of that country in 1814–15.[1]

The situation of the peasantry at that epoch, and the scanty numbers of the urban proletariat, rendered this movement inevitably aristocratic rather than popular. Yet it was inspired by humanitarian aims, among which were the abolition of serfdom,[2] the education of the people, political equality, and "constitutional guarantees" against the exercise of arbitrary power. A few of the adherents of the movement thought of a return to the federal system of city republics [3] as in pre-Variagian days.

Alarmed at the progress of liberalism in Western Europe, Alexander I abandoned his previously sympathetic attitude towards liberal ideas, and devoted himself in the later years of his reign to German mysticism and political reaction. Under the influence of Madame Krüdener and General Arakchéev, he set himself to combat the ideas he had derived from La Harpe, and formerly espoused. The effect of this attitude was that liberalism was driven "underground." Numerous secret societies were formed, e.g. "The Welfare Union" and "The Bund of Public Weal." The latter came to be divided into two factions, the Southern,[4] which fell under the influence of Péstel, and the Northern, which fell under that of Prince Obolensky.[5] In 1824 these societies [6] carried on an active revolutionary propaganda in the army. When Alexander I died, Constantine was proclaimed Tsar. His immediate abdication and the elevation of his younger brother, Nicholas, to the throne, was accompanied by the denunciation of the group of conspirators. On the 26th December, two days after Nicholas had announced by manifesto, his accession,[7] the Dekabristi, with some hundreds of men from the regiments of the Guard and some men from the fleet, appeared before the Winter Palace. For several hours the fortunes of the new Tsar hung in the balance, but towards evening a salvo of

---

[1] Prince Kropotkin in *Ideals and Realities of Russian Literature* (London, 1905), p. 34.

[2] On the influence of surviving *Dekabristi* on the emancipation movement, see *supra*, vol. i. p. 388.

[3] Prince Kropotkin, *op. cit.*, p. 35.

[4] Cf. *supra*, vol. i. p. 360.   [5] Cf. *supra*. vol. i. p. 388.

[6] There was also founded at the same time a patriotic society in Poland.

[7] For an account of the reasons for the abdication of Constantine and the accession of Nicholas, see Skrine, F. H., *The Expansion of Russia*, 1815–1900, pp. 74 *et seq.* ; see also Kleinschmidt, *op. cit.*

artillery scattered the insurgents, and the *Dekabrist* movement was at an end.

The leaders were arrested, and in June 1826 their trial took place. On 25th July, five were hanged, and afterwards eighty-five were exiled to Siberia, where the survivors remained until 1856. Although the *Dekabrist* movement was in effect confined to the aristocratic circle, it comprised many of the most intellectual and patriotic figures of their time, and their " sudden disappearance was disastrous." For thirty years Russia remained under the vigorous rule of Nicholas, and " every spark of free thought was stifled as soon as it appeared." [1]

The importance of the *Dekabristi* lies in their having effected the first organized revolutionary movement against the autocracy.

The stagnation which characterized the revolutionary movement after the collapse of the *Dekabrist* conspiracy was broken only by sporadic attempts to organize secret societies more or less on the *Dekabrist* model ; but since the *Dekabrist* time no similar movement has affected the army to the same extent, until the recent instances of military revolt. Among the sporadic movements referred to there was that promoted by the Kērēl-Methodian Society [2] (1846–1847), a small Slavophil movement, in which Kostomarov, the Russian historian and the first Pan-Slavist, was implicated. In 1830 there occurred the insurrection in Poland which, together with the revolution in Paris of the same year, influenced the Russian youth to a considerable extent. Still the field affected by the revolutionary tendencies was comparatively small. The peasant question had been the subject of continuous discussion, but the peasants, although they were discontented, were nevertheless practically untouched by these tendencies. The urban proletariat was as yet too slender in numbers and too fluctuating owing to the habit of returning periodically to the villages practised by the artisans who were also peasants, for that class to be materially influenced. The revolutionary impulses affected exclusively the youth of the aristocracy, those of the merchant class, and to a small extent the sons of the clergy. These impulses were thus predominantly of a political rather than of a social-economic char-

---

[1] Prince Kropotkin, *op. cit.*, p. 35.
[2] For an account of this society, see Semevsky, V., " Kērēl-Methodian Society, 1846–1847," in *Russkoë Bogatstvo*, 1911.

acter; the inevitable association of these had not at that time become fully apparent. In the early forties, however, there was observable among the Russian youth a new intellectual movement which expressed itself in a revived interest in the French Encyclopedists, in the Physiocrats, and in the Socialist writers—Saint-Simon, Fourier, Leroux, and Proudhon, for example. This interest seems to have arisen in various ways. Herzen,[1] for instance, one of the youths of the time, made his first acquaintance with the French writers in his father's library.

The absence of a free press and of open public discussion of all fundamental questions led to the formation of small groups or clubs, which came to be known as "circles," in which the intellectual movements of the time had their origin.[2] Such "circles" came to be identified with their leaders or those around whom the "circles" grew, and sometimes the influence of these leaders was very great, even although they may "never have written anything."[3] Among the young men who came under the influence of the "circle" movement was M. A. Butashevich-Petrashevsky,[4] who became the

---

[1] Alexander Herzen (1812–1870), an illegitimate son of a Russian Senator and a German governess, was educated in the old "Equerries (or nobility) Quarter" of Moscow. Exiled to the Urals in 1834 for six years, then to Novgorod in 1842 for five years, he left Russia in 1847, and till the close of his life lived abroad. He collaborated with Proudhon in the newspaper *L'Ami du Peuple.* He suffered expulsion from France, and finally settled in London in 1857, started *The Polar Star,* and later *The Bell.* Died in Switzerland in 1870. *Cf.* Kropotkin, *Ideals and Realities of Russian Literature* (London, 1905), pp. 270–5.

[2] See also *supra,* vol. i. p. 354. There were numerous similar "circles" in Paris at various epochs, notably between 1860 and 1870.

[3] Kropotkin, *op. cit.,* p. 266.

[4] M. A. Butashevich-Petrashevsky (1822–?) was educated at the Alexander Lyceum. At the age of fourteen, he had already attracted attention as a lad of a "liberal shape of mind." He went to the University, where he took his diploma in the Faculty of Law in 1841. At this time he was already a republican, an advocate of international peace, and of complete toleration in religion. When he left the University he "gave himself up with zeal to the study of Fourier." He formed his "circle" in 1845, and immediately afterwards began the publication of his *Pocket Dictionary of Russian Words,* which was, in effect, a medium for the expression of his views. In 1849 the members of the "circle" were arrested, and several of them were condemned to death. See Semevsky, V. E., *Peasant Question in Russia in the Eighteenth and the First Half of the Nineteenth Century* (St. Petersburg, 1888), vol. ii. p. 370. *Cf.* also *Peasant Law and Peasant Reform in Operation in the Works of M. E. Saltikov,* by V. E. Semevsky (Rostov on Don, 1905).

centre of a large group, among whom was the celebrated writer Dostoievsky.[1]

The rôle of the Slavophils in the discussion of the peasant question has already been noticed.[2] The Slavophil groups were numerous and influential up till the period of emancipation of the serfs in 1861. While some of the Slavophils were merely reactionary Chauvinists, the school as a whole may be said to have rendered the greatest services to Russian historical and juridical studies. The enthusiasm for Russian culture led to more serious study of its early phases, and this led to the disappearance of the illusions about the early history of Russia which had been prevalent.

Slavophil historians like Byelyaev, for example, investigated for the first time the growth of serfdom and the growth of the autocratic power of the Moscow princes ; and the Slavophil jurists discriminated sharply between the imperial law and the customary laws of the people.[3]

Even after emancipation the characteristics of Slavophilism appear in the *Narodnēkē* movement,[4] and also as a stimulating influence in the collection of *Zemstvo* statistics. The social revolutionary party of the present [5] is not untinctured with Slavophil ideas, as also are the Socialist *Narodnēkē*.[6] In the 'forties (of the nineteenth century) the propagation of Slavophil ideas led to the counter-propaganda of the *Zapadnēkē*,[7] or advocates of the thesis that Russia is likely to follow the same course of development as the countries of Western Europe. This clash of theories appears in the polemical literature of the two parties.

---

[1] F. M. Dostoievsky (1821–1881) was educated as a military engineer. He went to St. Petersburg in 1845, and soon acquired reputation as a writer by his novel *Poor People*. In 1849 he was arrested, together with other members of the Petrashevsky circle, tried *in camera*, and sentenced to death. He was reprieved on the scaffold at the moment fixed for his execution, but he never quite recovered from the shock of this horrible experience. He was exiled to Siberia, where he remained for ten years. He was pardoned in 1859. He then returned to Russia in broken health, but survived to write his best-known work, *Crime and Punishment*, and probably his best, *Memoirs from a Dead-House*. Cf. Kropotkin, *op. cit.*, p. 165, and De Vogüé, *Le Roman Russe* (Paris, 1892), pp. 203 *et seq.*

[2] See Book II, chap. xv. [3] Cf. Kropotkin, *op. cit.*, p. 269.

[4] Represented by " V. V." (Vasili Vorontsev) and Nikolai-On (N. Danielson), *e.g.* Cf. *infra.*

[5] Represented by Victor Chernov, *e.g.* Gershuni and Gotz, both now dead, were also important figures. Cf. *infra.*

[6] *e.g.* H. F. Annensky and A. V. Pachekhanov.   [7] " Westerners."

These movements, sporadic and general alike, were the results of a widespread fermentation, produced partly by the rapidity of the changes in the structure of Russian society and partly by stimulus from without. This fermentation had been, as we have seen, in progress throughout the nineteenth century. The net result of it was the " revolt of the individual." [1] In Russia, the family, the community, and the State had counted for everything, the individual for nothing. Patriarchalism had retained its force in the family ; a strong sense of communal interest, together with the long-continued " mutual guarantee," had subordinated the individual to the communal group ; and the service system had predestined the upper classes to the service of the State—all had combined to make life subject to rigorous regulation. Under these conditions individual initiative was tabooed, because it made inevitably for political and social disintegration. The revolt of the individual meant a revolt against established order in every field. It meant the revolt of the youth against his father, and against the collective interests of his family. It meant the revolt of the daughter against her mother, and against the conventions which prevented her from exercising her own will. It meant the revolt of the youth of both sexes against the restraints of village discipline in the rural districts, and against the social restraints in the towns. It meant also revolt against the Church, which sanctioned and emphasized these restraints, and against the State, which on occasion lent its strong arm to enforce them. The revolt of the individual will against external coercion meant inevitably revolution in all the fields of restraint. The most potent influence in producing this reaction of the individual will against external restraint was probably the mere increase in numbers, together with the rapidity of that increase. The family became too large for patriarchalism ; the community became too large for the effective exercise of the communal spirit ; the State became too large for the effective centralized control which the whole system implied. Yet the concentrated forces of conservatism, aided as they were by the mere inertia of the mass, were strong enough to isolate the scattered and unorganized groups of individual protestants. The prospect of the disintegration of the society to which they were accustomed, and the possibility of reactions whose ulti-

[1] Kropotkin, *op. cit.*, p. 296.

mate tendencies could not be foreseen, frightened even people of relatively progressive impulses, and thus the incipient insurrection against established order was met with a certain vindictiveness even by those whose general attitude of mind was benevolent. But while the individuals who thrust themselves forward with determined expression of their own individuality might be dealt with in detail, banished to Siberia in detachments, immured in fortresses, or even executed, the disintegration which these proceedings were designed to prevent was going on. The family was breaking up through the operation of intricate forces, some of which have been described above ; the community was breaking up from similar causes ; and the State administration was rapidly becoming unworkable. The revolutionary spirit was an outcome of these conditions, and the growth of it went on in spite of suppression— indeed, suppression made it more and more active.[1]

The absence in Russia of the modes of expression of intellectual movements customary in Western Europe, due to the hostility of the autocracy and the ecclesiastical authorities against everything whatsoever that in their opinion tended to disturb the established order, seriously affected the character of the discussions which ensued. Immensely able as many of the best men of the literary circles of St. Petersburg and Moscow in the years 1840–1860 undoubtedly were, such men, for example, as Bakúnin, Byelinsky, Herzen, Turgénev, politician, literary critic, publicist, and novelist, all exhibit in their writings a certain fretful impatience and rhetorical exaggeration, very natural and very interesting as historical evidence, but detracting somewhat from the permanent artistic value of their respective works.[2] These characteristics arose out of the conditions of the time. The autocracy was either blind to the progress of West European society, and to the inevitable effect of this progress upon the Russian youth, or it greatly overestimated the power of effective antagonism to its authority which the renascent

[1] A most vivid account of the psychology of the Russian youth between 1848 and 1870 is given by Prince Kropotkin in his *Memoirs* (chap. xii.): " During the years 1860–1865 in nearly every wealthy family a bitter struggle was going on between the fathers, who wanted to maintain the old traditions, and the sons and daughters, who defended their right to dispose of their lives according to their own ideals " (*op. cit.*, p. 301).   So also Turgénev in his *Fathers and Sons*, and Goncharóv in his *Oblomov*.

[2] Cf. *infra* on the rôle of the *Intelligentsia* in the revolution, *infra*, pp. 585 *et seq.*

youth could possibly exercise. From the point of view of the remarkable group whose names have just been mentioned, the autocracy was merely stupid, and their impatience was simply the impatience of intellectual men with an impossibly unintellectual Government.[1]

[1] Cf. *supra*, vol. i. p. 352. The relations of these groups to the peasant question is described *supra*, vol. i. Book II.

CHAPTER IV

THE REVOLUTIONARY MOVEMENTS, 1860–1874

THE declaration of the Emancipation of the Serfs, which was issued on 5th March 1861, although it was not to go into force until 1863, was received with unbounded enthusiasm. The peasants appeared generally to be making honest attempts to understand the bulky document which described how the abolition of bondage right was to be accomplished. The nobility and the merchants also on the whole looked forward to a revivified national life. The period was coincident with the beginning of extensive railway construction, for which a plentiful supply of labour was necessary. Wages advanced for reasons explained in a previous chapter. Land rose sharply in value. There was a general air of optimism and good-will. Yet some of the older nobility did not share these feelings. They seemed even to be anxious to prevent the full accomplishment of the design of emancipation. Nor were all of the peasants more content. Ere long in the rural districts they began to be agitated. " After all," they thought, " we are being cheated." Disturbances took place in many *guberni* on the eastern frontier of European Russia. These sporadic attacks upon unpopular landowners may or may not have been excited sometimes by reactionaries who desired to demonstrate that the prophecies of the conservatives had been fulfilled, that the murders of landowners which they had predicted would occur the day after emancipation had taken place. This " provocation " may have occurred in some cases ; but of the numerous peasant riots,[1] the majority were undoubtedly spontaneous. The peasants had their own crude anticipation of what emancipation must mean. If the interpretations of the landowners or of the local authorities differed from those of the peasants the difference must arise from intentional or unintentional error. In either case the peasants could not suffer themselves to

---

[1] Stepniak speaks of one hundred such riots.

be deprived of what they considered to be their rights.   They therefore proceeded to take what they held to be their own.   Those who resisted were attacked, and their property was sometimes destroyed.[1]

The Government drafted considerable bodies of troops into the rural districts, and although repressive measures were frequently severe and sporadic disturbances continued for several years, the danger of a general peasant rebellion was avoided, partly by repression and partly by concession.

The Russian youth, successive generations of whom had been excited about the conditions of the peasantry throughout the first half of the nineteenth century, became very ardent about it as the discussions upon emancipation went on.   The fluctuations of hope and fear in the " higher spheres " have already been recounted.[2] Similar oscillations between optimism and despair were observable among the students of the universities at least as early as 1860, and the feelings which were inspired ripened in the University of Moscow into a social movement in which, in 1861, two professors—Granovsky and Kudryavtsev—took part.[3]   This movement led many students into the rural districts round Moscow to speak to the peasants about the coming liberties.

In 1861 there appeared the beginnings of a similar social movement in the Universities of St. Petersburg and Kazan ; and circles were formed of a character similar to those of an earlier time.[4]   At this moment foreign influences do not seem to have played an important rôle, save in a very general sense.   It is possible that some suggestions came from the " non-political " propaganda of Schulze-Delitsch for co-operative and mutual credit associations, which had been going on actively in Germany for ten years ; but the main current of ideas arose out of the currents of Russian life.   Slavophilism was active, and new economic problems arising from the liberation of the peasants confronted everyone.

It was in many ways a great misfortune for Russia that at this critical moment many of her ablest, most candid, and most experienced public men were in exile.   This fact at once embittered the

---

[1] Similar incidents occurred in 1905 and 1906.   See *infra*, p. 301 *et seq.*

[2] Lênda, V. N., " Moscow Students in 1861 and their Relation to Peasant Emancipation (Reminiscences) " in *The Great Reforms* (Moscow, 1911), vol. v. p. 269.

[3] *Ibid.*   [4] Cf. *supra*, vol. i. p. 354, and vol. ii. p. 66.

attitude of such men and deprived the country of the advantage of their presence either as effective critics or as constructive statesmen.[1] Moreover, it was impossible for them to appreciate fully in detail the conditions of the problems which the recent liberation of the peasantry presented.

The circumstance of expatriation notwithstanding, exiles like Herzen were not urging in the early sixties an immediate revolution, or even an agrarian uprising. They knew too well the absence of preparation for such an adventure. Vague and diversified as the movement among the *intelligentsia* was in 1861, it grew in 1862 into a revolutionary movement which came to be known as *Zemlya e Volya* (Land and Liberty) ; and for the first time for many years there was a more or less definitely organized revolutionary party.

On 26th May 1862 there broke out in St. Petersburg a fire which seemed at one moment likely to destroy the Ministry of the Interior and the Bank of Russia. Means of extinguishing fire were at that time practically non-existent in St. Petersburg. There was no wind, otherwise half the city might have been destroyed.[2] Accusations [3] were not wanting that the fire had been caused by Poles and by Russian revolutionaries, but the origin of it was never discovered. Other fires of a similarly mysterious character took place in other cities, and an uneasy feeling began to manifest itself. Meanwhile the Poles were preparing for a revolt. They secured the sympathy of Bakúnin and of the *Zemlya e Volya* group.[4] Herzen implored them to delay, and told the Poles bluntly that the number of revolutionaries in Russia was too insignificant to render material assistance. The Polish revolt broke out on 21st January 1863, and the small group of Russian revolutionaries was dragged into it. But the

---

[1] One of the most distinguished of these voluntary exiles told the writer that while no doubt he had saved his life by leaving Russia, it would probably have been more advantageous to his country if he had not done so. A public man, he thought, should not expatriate himself.

> " It is my country. Danger in its bounds
> Weighs more than foreign safety."
> DISRAELI'S *Count Alarcos.*

Or there may be recalled the speech of Theodora to Justinian—" Yonder is the sea, and there are the ships. Yet reflect whether, when once you have escaped to a place of security, you will not prefer death to safety."

[2] A most lively account of this fire is given by Prince Kropotkin, *Memoirs*, &c., p. 157.

[3] *e.g.* by Katkov, *ibid.*, p. 162.

[4] See Mélyukov, P., *Russia and its Crisis* (Chicago, 1905), p. 390.

Polish uprising was a national and racial rather than a social movement, and the sympathy of the Russian liberal elements was soon
sacrificed. A peasant insurrection was planned to take place on
the Volga simultaneously with the Polish revolt ; but this incipient
rebellion was easily put down, and the Polish peasants were separated from the revolt of their landowners by extreme concessions
on the part of the Russian Government and by confiscatory
measures at the landowners' expense. The Polish revolt had assumed the form of a guerilla campaign, but whenever the sympathy
of the peasants was secured by Russia the revolt came rapidly to
an end.[1]

After the Polish insurrection there were two years of extreme
reaction, during which the ameliorating influences of the emancipation were largely neutralized, and the revolutionary forces, defeated for the time, were driven " underground " to prepare for
fresh assaults upon the autocracy. In 1864 the remnants of
Zemlya e Volya, now divided into the two usual factions—
the party of permeation, and the party of immediate action—
prepared for further activity. The attempt of Karakózov, on
16th April 1866, to assassinate the Tsar was apparently the outcome of the latter faction.[2] This attempt was followed by the
sternest measures. Mikhail Muravióv, who had been entrusted
with the suppression of the Polish revolt, was now endowed with
exceptional powers to deal with what was regarded as an extensive
conspiracy. Although it does not appear that anyone but Karakózov was actually implicated, wholesale arrests were made, and
everyone whose tendencies were in the least radical either was
arrested or was compelled to remain silent.[3]

Again reaction with suppression, voluntary or compulsory, of
all oppositional forces, whether revolutionary or otherwise, intervened for nearly three years ; and, as before, once again ardent
and reckless spirits made their appearance to continue the attack
against the Government. In 1869 a secret revolutionary group

---

[1] At the conclusion of the revolt, Poland was treated with remorseless
severity. A hundred and twenty-eight Poles were hanged, and 18,672 were
sent to Siberia, where a large number of them again revolted on account of
the treatment to which they were subjected there.

[2] It is alleged that Karakózov acted on his individual initiative, and
against the wishes of his friends. Mélyukov, *op. cit.*, p. 394.

[3] The result has been described by Turguéniev in his *Fathers and Sons*.
See also Kropotkin, *Memoirs*, p. 256.

of no special significance was formed among the students at various higher institutions of learning in St. Petersburg and Moscow.[1] The leader of this group was Necháiev. " He resorted to the ways of the old conspirators, without recoiling even before deceit when he wanted his associates to follow his lead. Such methods could have no success in Russia, and very soon his society broke down " [2] Necháiev dragged down with him a large number of Russian youths. One of them, Ivanov, who opposed the measures of Necháiev,[3] was murdered at his instigation. Necháiev fled, but was arrested in Switzerland and extradited as an ordinary accused. The remaining members of the " circle " were arrested for complicity in the murder, tried, found guilty, and sent to Siberia.

Meanwhile a new party of permeation opposed to the reckless violence of Necháiev was organized, and was known as " The circle of Tchaikovsky." [4] To begin with this was simply a " circle for self-education." Its importance lay rather in the character of the men and women whom it attracted than in its definite programme. From its ranks there came in 1874 the chief figures, and from the " circle " came one of the chief impulses of the *V Narod* movement, which altered for a time the whole course of Russian revolutionary history, and in a large measure altered the character of Russian society.[5] In 1872 the " circle " was distributing books authorized by the censor but of a liberal tendency. It was quite eclectic in its selection—*e.g.* Russian historical works, and, on the social question, the works of Lassalle and of Marx. Some of the members of the " circle " aspired to enter the provincial Zemstvos (or local government councils) which had been organized in 1864, and to this end studied seriously the rural economical conditions.[6] These hopes were doomed to disappointment, but they indicated an entirely new phase of social activity. In

---

[1] Mēlyukóv, *op. cit.*, p. 394.   [2] Kropotkin, *op. cit.*, p. 305.

[3] The programme of Necháiev is given by Mēlyukóv, *op. cit.*, pp. 395, 396.

[4] Nicholas Tchaikovsky (*b. circa* 1840). Educated as a chemist. Arrested twice during the period of the activity of his " circle," but discharged, sufficient evidence to justify his punishment not being forthcoming. Went to America in the seventies, and later to London, where he went into business and resided until after the outbreak of the revolutionary movement in 1905. He was arrested in St. Petersburg, but was released on bail. Afterwards he was tried and discharged.

[5] For an account of the *V Narod* movement, see *infra*, chap. vi.

[6] An excellent account of the activities of the circle of Tchaikovsky is given by Prince Kropotkin in his *Memoirs*, pp. 304–42.

1872 it would appear that the youths who were engaged in this movement were opposed altogether to terroristic enterprises,[1] and were convinced that, while a constitution should be aimed at for Russia, much preparatory work would have to be done among all classes if the experiment of a constitution could be expected to be successful. The utmost which they attempted to do was to contribute to the creation of a situation in which a " Parliament " might be and would be summoned.[2] The Tchaikovsky "circle" came in 1873–1874 to be merged in the general *V Narod* movement ; some of its members exiled themselves voluntarily, many of them were arrested.

[1] Prince Kropotkin narrates a remarkable story of an occasion when the " circle " not only tried to dissuade by argument a young man from the southern provinces who went to St. Petersburg with the intention of assassinating Alexander II, but intimated that they would keep a watch over him and prevent him by force from carrying out his purpose. *Memoirs*, p. 316.

[2] Cf. *ibid.*, p. 315.

CHAPTER V

THE INFLUENCE OF WESTERN EUROPEAN SOCIALISM UPON THE RUSSIAN MOVEMENT

THE Russian oppositional groups having been influenced both positively and negatively by contemporary thought and by contemporary events in Western Europe, it is necessary to notice those movements by which Russian parties have been most conspicuously affected. Each of the Russian groups took from Western Europe what suited its purpose, and attached importance to foreign progress and to foreign speculation in proportion as their elements harmonized with its own point of view. The nationalist aims of some of the West European political movements were regarded sympathetically by the Slavophils, while the internationalist propagandas were approved and to some extent even adopted by the *Zapadnēkē* and their successors. The Russia of Peter the Great and that of Katherine II had both gone to fantastic extremes in attempting to adopt by crude and wholesale methods some of the elements of West European culture. These efforts were not conspicuously successful, yet each succeeding age produced new enthusiasts.

The influence of the French Revolution and of the events of the first quarter of the nineteenth century upon the state of mind which produced the *Dekabrist* movement has already been noticed. That influence, together with the influences of the revolution in Paris in 1830 and of the general revolutionary movement of 1848, affected profoundly the successors of the *Dekabristi*. The French Revolution did not merely involve the destruction of the contemporary social system—it involved also efforts towards a new order.[1] It seemed to the system-mongers to be necessary to reconstruct society upon a fresh basis, alike in the spheres of politics, economics, and morals, as if society were a mechanism whose parts had been

[1] *Cf.* Harrison, Frederic, *The Meaning of History* (London, 1906), p. 180 *et seq.*

worn out by ages of use, and had been in some measure broken in pieces by the Revolution.   It seemed also as if the next task were to clear away the debris of the past and to construct an entirely new social order.   The difficulty which the system-mongers encountered did not lie in the invention of a new social order so much as in contriving means to get rid of what remained of the old.   The reason for this appears to lie in the fact that while there are in the social structure certain mechanical elements, as there are in all organic and inorganic bodies, the organic character of the social structure, and even of these mechanical elements, was somewhat generally overlooked.   So also was the essentially organic character of the changes which society had been undergoing.   These changes had already resulted in a new society, in which there had been abundantly disclosed, that revolution notwithstanding, human nature had not undergone material alteration.

Towards the end of the eighteenth and in the beginning of the nineteenth century, great emphasis had been laid upon the influence of surroundings upon the formation of character, yet by 1840, surroundings had been subjected to important changes, but the character of the people had changed slightly and slowly.

The state of international relations in the last years of the eighteenth century and throughout the first half of the nineteenth suggested, in the contemporary mood, a new order of those relations in which reason rather than passion should be the dominant influence.   Thus from 1791, when the Concert of Europe had its rise,[1] international diplomacy was directed towards the concerted action of the European powers against revolutionary impulses. The diplomatists had indeed acutely discerned in the humanitarian enthusiasm of the post-revolutionary period a means of arresting the furore for political change.   Whether or not the social order was really in peril the statesmen of the time proceeded to " make common cause for the purpose of preserving ' public peace, the tranquillity of states, the inviolability of possessions, and the faith of treaties.' "[2]   In 1804 the Tsar Alexander I proposed a scheme for an European Confederation,[3] and Napoleon I conceived the idea of a Central Assembly or European Congress on the model of the American Congress, to which all the European States were to send representatives.[1]

These high policies, visionary as they were, cannot be said to have had any effect upon the working masses. Had any effect been produced, there must have arisen in their minds a reaction against policies which, were they realized, must render the task of the working class in its struggle for political influence incomparably more arduous than it otherwise would be. A federal authority endowed with the collective power of half a dozen great states could deal with a revolution in any one of them with irresistible effect. Nor could the bourgeoisie of liberal tendencies see in this form of internationalism other than hostility to the growth of the political influence of the middle class. The urban middle class of all countries is, indeed, inevitably of particularist rather than of internationalist tendencies. It is even sometimes obsessed with municipal as opposed to national points of view. The middle class is thus always the advocate of local self-government and the opponent of centralized authority. The years immediately before and immediately after the year 1830 appear to exhibit the high-water mark of the influence of the urban middle class. It is not surprising that during this period the characteristic political phenomenon was by no means the development of internationalism. It was rather the intensification of nationalism under middle-class domination as a reaction against the imperialism of Napoleon I and Alexander I alike.

At the close of the first thirty years of the nineteenth century there came the unsuccessful struggle for the independence of Poland and the successful struggles for the independence of Greece and of Belgium. Meanwhile there came the rise of Prussia, beginning with national, although it proceeded with imperial ambitions which led incidentally to a United Italy. The struggles for independence in Greece and Italy, though predominantly bourgeois rather than agrarian or proletarian struggles, were regarded sympathetically by the working class especially of England, probably chiefly because the first struggle was against a Mohammedan and the second against a Catholic power.

The years of peace which followed the collapse of Napoleon I were characterized by unprecedented development of industrial

[1] Phillips, *op. cit.*, p. 1.

activity. The great inventions of the eighteenth century were perfected and the systems of manufacture and transport were transformed. The movement of population upon the industrial centres, which had always existed, was greatly accelerated, and the population of the towns outgrew the municipal machinery and the locally developed powers of administration. The national debts and the disorganized national finances, which were the inheritance of prolonged war, led to excessive taxation, and diversion of capital and labour from agriculture into industry led to enhanced prices of the necessaries of life. The disintegration of the family and the rupture of social relations which accompanied these movements, with the consequent destruction of the elements of social cohesion present in the older society, contributed to the general revolt against authority and precedent which now became apparent in all directions. Abrupt changes in the social order are at once caused by and are provocative of individuality. " The wisdom of our ancestors " was the subject of common jest in the fields of philosophy,[1] economics,[2] natural science,[3] art,[4] and religion,[5] as well as in those of politics. Destructive criticism in many fields induced discredit of the State and of its rôle as representative of the general will. But criticism does not always yield negative results ; by the middle of the nineteenth century reaction had begun, and so far as the State was concerned a new ideal State began to emerge from the critical discussions. The outcome of *laisser-faire* and aggressive individualism, unrestrained as it was at least for a time by tradition, was an apparent contradiction between vastly increased

[1] Feuerbach (Neo-Hegelian) published his first book in 1830 ; Bentham's " subversive " influence was dominant at this time, alike in philosophy, law, and economics.

[2] Comte's attack upon the " orthodox " political economy may be said to begin with the publication of his *Cours de Philosophie positive* in 1839.

[3] Laplace lived till 1827, and Lamarck till 1829.

[4] On " the revolution of the arts " about 1830, see W. E. Henley, *Memorial Catalogue of French and Dutch Loan Collection* (Edinburgh, 1888). The inspiration proceeded largely from England. Constable exhibited in the Louvre in 1824, and profoundly affected the French painters of the immediately succeeding time. Delacroix exhibited his *Massacres de Scio* in 1829. In the drama, Victor Hugo announced the literary revolution in his *Hernani*, produced in 1830 ; and in criticism Sainte-Beuve had already written *Joseph Delorme* and *Consolations*. Scottish and English romanticism was in full vigour.

[5] The critical attack upon the foundations of the Christian religion may be said to have been formally inaugurated by the publication of Strauss's *Leben Jesu* in 1835.

powers of production and apparently contemporaneous diminution of well-being among the masses of the people. This contradiction led many thoughtful and conscientious, if too optimistic, persons to formulate numerous schemes to "remedy the distress of nations," and to undertake numerous inquiries into the "condition of the people" question.[1] In the more far-reaching of these schemes the international aspects of social problems assumed a large place. Among the first, if not the first, to promote the idea that a reorganization of society should be regarded as an international affair was Robert Owen, who developed the idea in 1817.[2] Owen, who was himself of authoritative temperament, appears to have thought that an absolute government was on the whole most likely to act with the rapidity which the case seemed to demand.[3] He proposed to form an " Association of all classes of all nations," [4] but Owen seemed to have in his mind the idea that a working class regenerated by his " rational religion " would dominate the whole. The international character of his society was more formal than real ; the only importance of the society lies in the fact that it foreshadowed the international association, not of all classes, but explicitly of the working class which was to follow thirty years later.

The association which gave rise to the Chartist movement had international filiations and sympathies.[5] It issued, e.g., manifestoes to the working classes of Europe, and especially to the French and

[1] The effect of some of these upon contemporary Russian *intelligentsia* is discussed *infra*, Book VII, chap. xiv.

[2] At meetings held in London in August and September 1817, and afterwards before the German Diet at Frankfort on the Main, and through Lord Castlereagh at the Conference of Aix-la-Chapelle in 1818. See Owen, *The New Existence of Man upon the Earth* (London, 1854), pp. 3 and 4 and p. xxxv., and *The Millennial Gazette*, No. 4, 15th May 1856 and 1st August 1857.

[3] Cf. *The New Existence of Man upon the Earth*, part ii., p. 5, and [Thompson, Wm.] *Labour Rewarded* . . . (London, 1827), p. 99. It should be observed that while Owen exhibited a preference for action through the State, he gave the primary impulse towards the foundation of the English co-operative system, which is based wholly upon voluntary action, and is not in any way indebted to State support or recognition. On the other hand, the writings of his contemporary, Thompson, strongly impregnated as they are with voluntary mutualism, and antagonistic as they are to State control or State action, seem to have given, if not the initial impulse to the State collectivism of Marx, at all events to have contributed to it important suggestions.

[4] *The Constitution and Laws of the Univ. Com. Soc. of Rational Religionists* (London, 1839), p. 20.

[5] " The Working Men's Association for Benefiting politically, socially and morally the Useful Classes."

to the Polish people.[1] These manifestoes urge the united action of the working class of all nations. " Fellow-producers of wealth, seeing our oppressors are . . . united, why should not we, too, have our bond of brotherhood and holy alliance ? "[2] The Chartist movement, had it been fully understood by contemporary Russians, would have been regarded as characterized by politicalism ; because although some of the Chartists had ulterior economic aims, these did not occupy a place in their programme.[3]

During the period which elapsed between the French Revolution of 1830 and that of 1848, there were practically numberless schemes for the reformation of society in a national or an international sense and for the regeneration of humanity. A new literature and a new vocabulary sprang into existence. " In 1830, Socialism was nothing ; to-day, Socialism is everything," Considerant wrote in 1848 ; and he continued, " A new order is about to be created. All creation is preceded by a chaos. Socialism has been, has to be, and is still but a chaos. . . . The problem of Socialism contains two historical formulæ. The emancipation of the slave produced the serf. The emancipation of the serf produced the bourgeois and the proletarian. . . . There remains the social and, following, the political emancipation of the wage-earner, the proletarian."[4]

This was in effect the text of numerous pamphlets and manifestoes issued during the period from 1830 till 1848. In the forties of the nineteenth century Paris teemed with social speculators. Saint-Simon[5] had died in 1825, and Fourier[6] died in 1837 ; but during the forties, Proudhon,[7] Buchez,[8] Cabet,[9] Leroux,[10] Dupin,[11] Considerant,[12] and Louis Blanc,[13] were all alive and at the full height

[1] Issued in 1838. In the manifesto to the working classes there is a lively summary of the democratic movement in Europe.
[2] *Address to the Working Classes of Europe* (London, 1838), p. 7.
[3] The Chartists refused to be diverted from their political propaganda by the contemporary movements of Owenism, communism, and free trade. Cf. *The Chartist Circular* (Glasgow, 19th October 1839), and letter from Mac-Donnell, the Chartist, to Cabet, in *Procès du Communisme à Toulouse* (Paris, 1843), p. 29.
[4] Considerant, V., *Le Socialisme devant le mieux monde ou le vivant devant les morts* (Paris, 1849), pp. 18–19.
[5] Saint-Simon (1760–1825), *Œuvres* (1832). See also Fournel, *Bibliographie Saint-Simonienne* (Paris, 1833).
[6] Fourier (1772–1837), *Théorie des Quatre Mouvements* (1808).
[7] Proudhon (1809–1865).   [8] Buchez (1796–1865).
[9] Cabet (1788–1856), *Voyage en Icarie* (1840).   [10] Leroux (1798–1871).
[11] Dupin (1784–1873).   [12] Considerant (1808–1893).
[13] Louis Blanc (1811–1882).

of their activity, each with his social specific. No doubt Socialism was a chaos, but the chaos was in a state of fermentation. The activity of the continental governments, and their determination to put down what they considered as subversive movements prevented any but small, isolated, and ephemeral associations of working men from being established, in spite of assistance from sympathizers among the " intellectuals." Up till 1848, when revolutionary movements occurred in Paris, Berlin, and Vienna, no open revolutionary association was possible, but there were many secret societies, especially in France, Belgium, and Switzerland. In 1843 Karl Marx[1] went for the first time to Paris. He was then twenty-five years of age, almost fresh from the University of Bonn, where he had become impregnated with the philosophy of Hegel, and had become inclined towards the school of Neo-Hegelians, then led by Feuerbach. Marx plunged into the contemporary discussions of the Paris group, whose names have been mentioned, and he seems to have adopted their vocabulary and to have absorbed some of their ideas. A group of German workmen in Paris had formed themselves into a Communist League in 1836 ; in 1839 a number of these workmen were expelled from Paris, and in the following year they founded a similar society in London.[2] Marx was expelled from Paris in 1844, and after three years of migration was to be found in London, where he attended a congress of the Communist League, founded by the German workmen in Paris eleven years before. Marx made himself conspicuous at this congress, and with his friend Engels undertook to draw up a manifesto. This manifesto (the celebrated *Kommunistische Manifest*) was written in German in January 1848, the manuscript being sent to the printer a few weeks before the French Revolution of 24th February.[3] A French translation appeared in Paris shortly before the insurrection of June 1848. Danish and Polish editions were published about the same time.

The Communist manifesto is a controversial pamphlet in which

---

[1] Karl Marx (1818–1883). See Stammhammer, *Bibliographie des Socialismus und Communismus*, 3 vols. (Jena, 1909). For career of Marx, see Meyer, R., *Der Emancipationskampf des vierten Standes* (Berlin, 1892), i. pp. 114 *et seq.* For an admirable criticism of the philosophical basis of Marx's opinions, see Bonar, J., *Philosophy and Political Economy* . . . (London, 1893). See also Simkhovich, *Marxism* versus *Socialism* (New York, 1913).

[2] Rae, John, *Contemporary Socialism* (London, 1884), p. 135.

[3] Preface by F. Engels to the *Manifesto of the Communist Party.* . . . Authorized English translation (London, 1886), p. 1.

Marx attacks almost all previous writers upon the subject. He develops in it what is usually described as a materialistic view of history—in other words, he lays emphasis upon the economical causes of political and social changes. The claim of originality which Engels afterwards advanced on the part of Marx and himself, cannot be regarded as tenable. Irrespective of earlier examples, Montesquieu had laid great stress upon the influence of climate and of the nature of the soil upon the laws of " civil slavery," upon the laws of " political servitude," and upon laws in general. This is undoubtedly, in modern phrase, the economic interpretation or the materialist view of history.[1]

What Marx really did was to emphasize the influence, perhaps even to the point of exaggeration, of the economical struggle of the social classes upon the political struggle of the same classes. The force of his conclusions thus varies with the intensity of the economical struggle and with the character of the contemporary political struggle.

The issue of the manifesto caused a schism in the League, and a second manifesto, also by Marx, caused another schism, in which Liebknecht, afterwards well known as a Social Democratic member of the German Reichstag, left Marx.[2]

The revolution of 24th February 1848 at Paris was followed by the " massacres of Rouen " in April, and by the " inexpiable hecatomb of June " in Paris in the same year, and these, with the results of the various revolutionary movements throughout Europe during that period, left the working class discomfited and disorganized.[3] It had compromised its immediate interests by its political filiations, and it had been attacked in detail and defeated. The associations of French working men,[4] which had been formed with internationalist aims, were dispersed after the *coup d'état* on 2nd December 1851,

---

[1] *Cf.* Montesquieu, *De l'Esprit des Lois*, liv. xiii–xxiii. Two writers of communist tendency, Mably and Dupin, annotated Montesquieu, and both added notes to these very books. Marx's indebtedness to Mably and Dupin and their group otherwise cannot be questioned.

[2] *Cf.* Lavollée, *Les Classes ouvrières en Europe* (Paris, 1884), i. p. 244.

[3] Emigration from Europe to the United States was greatly stimulated in 1847 by the economical and political conditions combined. *Cf.* statistics in Bromwell, W. J., *History of Immigration to the United States . . .* (New York, 1856), pp. 175 *et seq.*

[4] *Cf.* Malon, B., *L'Internationale, son Histoire et ses Principes* (Lyons, 1872), p. 7.

and the international labour movement, such as it was, was thrown into the background for ten years. During this period the conditions were preparing for the further uprising of the internationalist idea. The processes of social disintegration, whose beginnings have already been noticed, had now gone far. The development of the American wheatfields had thrown cheap food into the English and continental markets, and domestic agriculture had everywhere receded, while the industrial centres had grown rapidly. The proletariat, whose numbers were relatively small when the existence of the class began to attract attention in the beginning of the nineteenth century, now assumed formidable proportions. Factory Acts notwithstanding, and notwithstanding the considerable development of trade unions, the temper of the working class fluctuated closely with the state of trade. A single bad harvest was sufficient to produce an outbreak of discontent. There was as yet no national system of education and no broadening of the franchise even in England. The trade union movement was in effect under a ban. On the Continent working-class meetings and movements were prevented by the police and by the expulsion of influential advocates of working-class interests. The inevitable consequence of the banishment of propagandists from their own country and the suppression of their propaganda within its limits, is the spreading of their propaganda in other countries. Extreme nationalism on the part of governments leads to internationalism on the part of their opponents. Enthusiasts cast off by different countries have a common oppositional ground ; they tend to unite in formal or in informal alliances against all national governments. So, too, the exclusion of certain classes of people from sharing in the government of a country, or from representation in its assemblies, tends to create in the minds of these classes hostility towards their own Government, and therefore sympathy with those classes which in other countries are similarly excluded. This sympathetic hostility to all governments induces a certain cosmopolitan attitude of mind,[1] which, although not identical with, may nevertheless prepare the way for internationalism.

Where this cosmopolitan attitude has no deeper foundation than mere exclusion from representation it may disappear whenever

[1] Cf. Hutton, Richard Holt, in *Essays on Reform* (by various writers) (London, 1867), p. 33.

the representation is granted.   In so far as it exists, from whatever cause, it tends to make for a fresh classification of humanity.   The national boundaries become less important, and the vertical cleavage of society which the nation involves assumes a sinister aspect to the mass of the people, and seems to account for the economical and political disadvantages under which the people labour.   The existence of a horizontal cleavage becomes apparent in which the proletariat of all countries form one mass at the base of society, while superimposed upon it are the other classes in whose hands appear to rest the instruments of economical and political power.   The result of the fermentation of such ideas in the minds of the working class is the development of " class consciousness," a kind of patriotism of class in which the feelings of kinship and of common interest, which constitute patriotism proper, are transferred, not to all humanity, but to the working class in all countries.   Although in a vague and uncertain way, excited partly by experience and partly by propaganda, this feeling of " class consciousness " seems at certain epochs gradually to gain ground and then to be mitigated by returning racial animosities, which throw back the working class into reassociation with people of their own kin, even though they may belong to the classes whom they regard as exploitative. Such recurring waves of national feeling which exhibit themselves in the familiar episodes of chauvinism and jingoism illustrate the important fact that history cannot be interpreted exclusively in terms of economical conditions in the narrow sense.

The initial impulse towards a recrudescence of the international working men's movement upon a more important scale than before was to come from an unexpected source.   During the International Exhibition which was held in London in 1862, Napoleon III had permitted the election of some French workmen to visit London as delegates.[1]   A meeting was held at the Freemasons' Tavern on 5th August 1862, and an address was presented to the French delegates by representatives of the English working men.   This address urged that an organized union should be effected of working men in all countries in order that their interests might be protected,

[1] The idea seems to have originated with some manufacturers and certain newspapers, e.g. Le Temps and L'Opinion Nationale (de Laveleye, E., Socialism of To-day (London, n. d.), p. 149).   Napoleon III is alleged to have desired to patronize the International at a later date.   See a curious note by Kropotkin, Memoirs, p. 485.

because these interests were everywhere identical. To this address the French workmen replied that the working class in all countries must go hand in hand by means of a "holy alliance" to obtain their freedom.[1] In the address a suggestion was made that committees of working men should be formed in order to provide a "medium for the interchange of ideas on international trade";[2] but the trade unions held aloof, and the international union remained a mere phrase.[3]

The Polish revolt began on 21st January 1863, and on the 22nd July of the same year a meeting was held in St. Paul's Hall, London, to express sympathy with the Poles. To this meeting five French delegates were sent by French workmen.[4] In the address of George Odger to the "French brethren," suggesting a "Universal Labour Congress," Rudolf Meyer finds the "germ" of the "International."[5] The outcome of this suggestion was a meeting in St. Martin's Hall on 28th September 1864. The French delegates were again prominent, and there were also present Major Wolff, private secretary of Mazzini, who represented Italian working men, and Marx and Eccarius, who represented Germany. Altogether five foreign nations were represented. Professor Beesly presided.[6] The address of the Paris working men, whose spokesman was Tolain, after referring briefly to the situation in Poland, went on to lament the absence of solidarity among working men and the commanding position which capital had acquired under the influence of the development of mechanical industry and free trade, and to urge the union of workers in a class struggle.[7] After the discussion of this address, the meeting resolved to appoint a provisional committee, which was empowered to draw up a constitution of an International Working Men's Association, and to arrange for an international congress to be held in Brussels in 1865. This provisional committee

[1] Meyer, R., *Der Emancipationskampf*, i. p. 119.
[2] De Laveleye, *op. cit.*, p. 150.
[3] Meyer, R., *loc. cit.*
[4] Palmerston had refused to agree to the proposal of an European Congress upon the affairs of Poland. How far this meeting was engineered from Paris as a protest against the action of the British Government it is not necessary here to inquire. (*Cf.* Meyer, *op. cit.*, p. 120.)
[5] Meyer, *op. cit.*, p. 120.
[6] Professor Beesly was at that time advocating internationalism with special ardour. His point of view is put with great clearness in his "England and the Sea," contributed to *International Policy: Essays on the Foreign Relations of England* (London, 1866), pp. 153 *et seq.*   [7] Meyer, *op. cit.*, p. 121.

consisted of twenty-seven English representatives and eight foreigners, among whom were Wolff and Marx.

Almost immediately there occurred a dispute between Mazzini and Marx. Mazzini had composed an inaugural address and a constitution. In the address he developed his political programme, deprecated the class struggle, and proposed a highly centralized organization for the International. With the exception of the last point, the policy of Mazzini did not meet with the approval of Marx, who prepared a rival address and constitution. Mazzini thereupon withdrew from the association.[1] Marx probably realized that to draw the International at the outset of its existence into an individual national movement, in which the primary object of its existence, viz. to convert the national struggle into a class war, would be submerged, must be fatal to the association. Mazzini, for his part, undoubtedly desired to utilize the International, for so much as it availed, as an instrument in the campaign for Italian unity. The two views were irreconcilable.

By the middle of 1865 the " International " consisted of a group in London, one in Brussels, one in Geneva, and one in Paris. There were a few adherents in Rouen, Caen, Lyons, Neuville-sur-Saone, and Marseilles, " and that was all." [2] It had been intended that a congress should be held in Brussels in September 1865, but the Belgian Government took fright, and, bringing into force an old law against foreigners, prevented the congress from being held there. This action served, however, to advertise the " International," and adhesions began to pour in.[3] Sections were formed in Germany

---

[1] Mazzini's views upon the Socialism and Communism of Saint-Simon and Fourier as he understood them are expressed at considerable length in his *Thoughts upon Democracy* (1847). See English translation in *Joseph Mazzini : A Memoir*, by [Madame] E. A. V[enturi] (London, 1875). Although Mazzini had not kept himself *en rapport* with the development of the social question in France and England, M. de Laveleye is far from just in attributing to him inability to see anything " outside of Carbonarism " (*Contemporary Socialism* (London, n. d.), p. 151). Bakúnin, while opposed to Mazzini, is much fairer to him. *Cf.* Bakúnin, *La Théologie politique de Mazzini et l'Internationale* (Neuchâtel, 1871). At that period Marx had not grappled with the agrarian question, nor, indeed, did he ever do so fully ; and Mazzini must have realized that an exclusive appeal to the urban proletariat of Italy (not numerous at that period) would involve the sacrifice at once of the support and of the interests of the revolutionary middle class and of the peasantry.

[2] Malon, B., *L'Internationale, son Histoire et ses Principes* (Lyons, 1872), p. 19.

[3] *Ibid.*

and in the south of Italy, and when the first congress was actually held in Geneva on 3rd September 1866, the number of adherents was estimated at 70,000.[1] Marx's address had become a manifesto of the General Council at London, and now his project of a constitution was adopted by the congress at Geneva. This constitution remained without modification until 1873.

Marx's address, though briefer and more moderate in tone than the Communist manifesto of 1848, was not inconsistent with that document. It refers to the identity of wage and slave labour, and calls upon the working men to take into their own hands the determination of international policy, and to watch the proceedings of the diplomatists, thwarting them in case of need. It declares that such a struggle is a part of the struggle for the emancipation of the working class, and concludes with the watchword, " Proletarians of all countries, unite." [2] These were the words which concluded the Communist manifesto of 1848. There can be no doubt that in Marx's mind at least the Communist League had come to life again.[3]

The constitution formulated by Marx—and adopted by the congress—employs substantially the same expressions as the earlier manifesto. " The emancipation of the working class must be achieved by the working class itself. . . . The struggle for the emancipation of the working class is not a struggle for class privileges and monopoly, but for equal rights and duties and for the abolition of all class domination." It goes on to say that the final purpose of all political action is the economical emancipation of the working class. This emancipation is not a local, nor a national, but is a social problem which affects all countries. It further declares that there are no duties without rights and no rights without duties. The by-laws of the association provide for a yearly congress and for the election of a general council, which shall act as " international agent between the different national and local groups." [4] The principal topics of discussion at the Geneva congress (3rd to 10th September 1866) were the eight-hours working day, child labour, the trade union movement (which was reproached

---

[1] Malon, L'Internationale, son Histoire et ses Principes (Lyons, 1872), p. 9.
[2] Meyer, R., Der Emancipationskampf, i. p. 123.
[3] Cf. Rae, J., Contemporary Socialism (London, 1884), p. 144.
[4] The text is given in full by Meyer, op. cit., pp. 124-6.

for too close adhesion to the wages question), and direct taxation (which was favoured). On the question of the admission of members who did not belong to the working class, the French delegates declared themselves against the admission of mere *parleurs*—advocates and journalists. The German and English delegates, who themselves chiefly belonged to such classes, objected to their exclusion. Had the French proposition been carried, the International might have been a purely working class organization, but it would have had to expel at the outset Marx and the others who had at least rendered important aid in bringing it into existence, and who had stamped upon it its special character.

Depression of trade in 1866, with strikes in France, Belgium, and Italy, brought accessions by the thousand.[1] When the congress met at Lausanne in 1867, there were over 300,000 nominal adherents.[2] Whether or not these adherents were fully convinced internationalists is not so much a matter of moment as the facts that, under the circumstances of the time, the International had its doors wide open, that all comers were admitted, and that large groups were added *en masse*. It is true that many of the adherents were likely to desert the cause, and that eventually differences of opinion on cardinal points must develop ; yet the numbers in gross were unquestionably becoming formidable, and the leaders of the movement, as well as the European Governments, began to exaggerate the importance of the following of the Association. The French Government in particular became alarmed, and endeavoured, but without success, to secure the co-operation of the British Government in suppressing the Association.[3]

During a strike of bronze workers in Paris in 1864, and during strikes in England in 1867, the International intervened successfully.[4] Annual congresses were held. The congress of Lausanne in 1867 is important because of the events to which it gave rise. Marx was not present, and the resolutions bear the marks of his absence.

The principal resolution was to the following effect : Social emancipation is inseparable from political emancipation, and the establishment of political freedom is a first and an absolute necessity ; to this end it is decided to form an alliance with the

---

[1] Malon, B., *L'Internationale, son Histoire et ses Principes* (Lyons, 1872), p. 19.
[2] *Ibid.*, p. 20,   [3] Meyer, *op. cit.*, p. 128.   [4] *Ibid.*, p. 129.

intelligent bourgeoisie, and to send delegates to the Peace and Liberty Congress at Geneva, for the purpose of carrying this into effect.[1] Had Marx been present, Rudolf Meyer says, this nonsense would never have been carried. In other resolutions the Lausanne congress decided to aim at the acquisition by the State of the means of transportation and at the breaking down of the monopoly of the great industrial companies.

The third congress was held in Brussels from 5th to 11th September 1868. At this congress the communistic ideas accomplished a complete victory.[2] It was decided that as all mines and railways belong to society as represented by the State, they should be exploited by it, and not by capitalistic associations. Land, canals, highways, and telegraphs should be similarly possessed and exploited by the State. Mechanical industries were, however, to be organized through co-operative societies and systems of credit and rewards for inventions by working men. The congress approved of properly organized strikes, but pointed out that the strike cannot in itself be regarded as the means of securing freedom for the worker. It also announced its adherence to the principle that the worker had the right to the whole produce of his labour. The congress called upon the working men of both countries to strike against a war between Germany and France. " As a farce following the congress of the International at Brussels, came the Liberty Congress at Berne." [3] To this congress of " La Ligue internationale de la Paix et de la Liberté," [4] which was held at Berne, 22nd to 26th September 1868, the International sent representatives, who, however, were expected not to speak, but to vote. The resolutions adopted at the Berne congress were to the following effect : That standing armies are an obstacle to peace and to liberty, that they therefore should be abolished, and that they should be replaced by a system in which every citizen, as an inseparable part of popular education, should be trained in the use

---

[1] Meyer, *op. cit.*, p. 131.   [2] *Ibid.*, p. 132.   [3] *Ibid.*, p. 136.
[4] This league was founded at Geneva in 1867, when it held its first congress, which was presided over by Garibaldi. The second congress (at Berne) was presided over by Gustav Vogt, one of the founders, and the third (at Lausanne in 1869) by Victor Hugo. The fundamental principle of the League was declared to be the subordination of politics to morals. See *Ligue internationale de la Paix et de la Liberté : Résolutions votées par les vingt-un premiers Congrès. Recueil Officiel* (Geneva, 1888).

of arms for the purpose of defending his country; and that the congress could not commit itself definitively upon the social question further than to say that it regards the freedom of the individual as a necessary corner-stone of all social reform. The congress also declared itself as in favour of a federative republican system, as opposed to Cæsarism, and as in favour of the autonomy of Poland.[1]

From our present point of view the most interesting incident of this congress, which Rudolf Meyer not quite fairly regards as farcical, was the appearance there of a remarkable man whose influence upon the Russian youth of that time was very great, although his writings and utterances had been fragmentary and although a great part of his life had been spent in prison and in exile. Bakúnin[2] had attended the first congress of the " Ligue," which had been held in Geneva in 1867, and he had been made a member of the permanent committee which met during the succeeding winter. In the end of October 1867 Bakúnin proposed to the committee to adopt a programme—" socialist, anti-authorita-

---

[1] *Ligue internationale de la Paix et de la Liberté : Résolutions*, &c., pp. 18–27.

[2] Mikhail Bakúnin (1814–1876) was born of a noble family at Torjok, Tverskaya *gub*. His first publication of importance was an introduction to a translation of some papers by Hegel, which appeared in the *Moskovsky Nablyudatel* in 1836 (Nettlau, M., *Bibliographie de l'Anarchie* (Paris, 1897), p. 42). In 1838 he entered the army, and in 1840 he left it, going to Germany and refusing to return to his military duties. During the succeeding decade he threw himself into revolutionary movements in Austria and in Germany. In 1848 he took part in the disturbances at Prague, and in 1849 those at Dresden. In the latter city he was arrested and sentenced to death. His sentence was commuted to imprisonment. After two years in a German prison he was handed over to the Austrian Government, which demanded his extradition on account of his complicity in the Prague uprising. In 1851 he was again sentenced to death, and his sentence was again commuted. He spent some time in an Austrian prison chained by a foot to a cannon ball. On the demand of the Russian Government he was sent to Russia, where he was confined in the fortress of Schlusselburg until 1855, when he was sent to Irkutsk. There he found his distant relative, Count Muraviev-Amursky (cf. *infra*, p. 219), Governor-General of Eastern Siberia. Bakúnin spent some time in the society of Muraviev, discussing quaint projects for the future of Siberia, one of which involved the separation of the country from the Russian Empire and the federation of the United States of Siberia to the United States of North America. (*Cf.* Kropotkin, *Memoirs*, &c., p. 169). In 1861 Bakúnin escaped from Siberia and returned to Europe *via* Japan. During the remainder of his life he lived chiefly at Locarno, asthmatic and dropsical, but actively engaged in socialistic controversy and in revolutionary agitation in Italy. He died at Berne in 1876. See also *infra*, p. 99.

tarian, and anti-religious." [1] For the congress of 1868 he prepared an address (afterwards published under the title, *Fédéralisme, Socialisme et Anti-théologisme*),[2] in which he developed those views upon anarchism which eventually led to the disruption of the International, and which at the same time exerted a profound influence upon the youth of Russia.

Bakúnin was undoubtedly a disturbing element in the League of Peace and Liberty. His address, able fragment of a summary of social and political development as it was, the peculiarities of the author's point of view being taken into account, was also an ironical criticism of the membership of the League. " Here we have," he said, " *Sabreurs* and priests—why not also *gens d'armes?* " The League was, in fact, composed of well-meaning sentimentalists and of persons who found association with it the most convenient means of making themselves internationally conspicuous. Bakúnin endeavoured by means of a resolution to capture the League for the Socialist propaganda. This resolution was defeated by eighty votes to thirty, and he thereupon seceded from the League and established a new organization which, though it was short-lived, was nevertheless not wanting in significance. He called this association " L'Alliance internationale de la Democratie socialiste." Its programme left little to be desired by the most thoroughgoing nihilism. " The Alliance declares itself for atheism. It desires the abolition of all cults, the replacement of faith by science, and of divine by human justice, and the abolition of marriage as a political, religious, juridical, and civil institution. It desires also definitive and complete abolition of classes, and political, economic, and social equality of individuals and of sexes, ' involving equal profit of production and equal means of education in all branches of knowledge, industry, and art.' " [3]

The International now became a field in which four different but related struggles were waged with great animosity, until eventually the International was wrecked by them. These struggles were : *first*, the struggle between the statists and the anti-statists, or

---

[1] Introduction by " N." to Bakúnin, *Œuvres* (Paris, 1895), p. xxiv.

[2] *Œuvres*, pp. 1–205.

[3] Meyer, *op. cit.*, p. 136. The groundwork of the programme is to be found in *Fédéralisme, Socialisme et Anti-théologisme*, mentioned above. Bakúnin seems to have developed his theory of anarchism in Siberia. His first writings which exhibit this tendency appear to have been composed in 1863. (*Cf.* Nettlau, *op. cit.*, p. 43.)

between the Social Democrats, who aimed at a powerful democratic republic, and the anarchists, who objected to the exercise of authority, whether this authority were in the hands of a despot or of a democracy ; *second*, the struggle as regards method between those who desired to proceed by legal and constitutional steps towards the capture of the representative chambers and the control of the mechanism of government, and those who conceived that the only effective path of reform was through " riot "—the former being in general statists and the latter anti-statists ; *third*, the struggle between those who advocated the individual autonomy of the national groups which composed the International, and those who advocated control by a strong central executive ; and *fourth*, the struggle between the revolutionary socio-political aims and the aims of the trade unions properly so called, involving merely the control of wages and of the conditions of employment, and not involving any drastic political or social changes.

Bakûnin, almost from the beginning of his relations with the International, was hostile to Marx, partly because of the fundamental divergence of their views in the first three struggles which have been described, and partly because of radical difference of temperament. Not only Bakûnin, however, but many others, among them notably the French group, found Marx domineering. The plain fact was that Marx exhibited the faults of his qualities. He was, moreover, generally consistent with his central point of view,[1] a circumstance which brought him into conflict with those whose opinions upon social progress were even more fluid than his own.

Meanwhile the general economic movement had been bringing the industrial problem through new phases. The Civil War in America reacted upon England and Western Europe through the diminution of demand for general merchandise and the cessation of the supply of cotton. Unemployment and distress followed, but during the years of war and of trade depression money was plentiful and cheap, and a furore of company promotion made its appearance. This furore had its appropriate conclusion in the collapse and panic of 1866, intensified as these were by the economic

---

[1] How far this central point of view was *Socialist* in any incontrovertible sense is open to question.   *Cf*. the acute criticism of Marx by V. Simkhovich, in *Marxism* versus *Socialism* (New York, 1913).

disturbance caused by the Prussian campaign against Austria. Sadowa (3rd July 1866) brought peace, but five years elapsed before trade resumed its previous channels, the period of depression being prolonged by the Franco-Prussian War. Immediately after the close of that war trade recovered rapidly, and the following years, 1871–1874, were years of unusual industrial prosperity. During the period of inferior activity, deepening into depression, or between 1861 and 1871, wages were low and profits were insignificant. All the conditions existed for the emergence of industrial disputes. These disputes, resulting as they did in numerous strikes in every part of Europe, provided for the time " rich material for agitation " ; but when conditions changed and when wages advanced, as they did by leaps and bounds between 1871 and 1874, the agitation, deprived of its material stimulus, became less influential. These conditions reflected themselves in the congresses of the International. In 1868 the French Government had suppressed the French branch of the International, though some of the individual members still retained their connection with the central organization. In 1869 a congress was held at Basle (6th to 9th September). The influence of the trade union principle is evident in the resolutions of this congress. Current events determined this. Strikes had been going on throughout the winter in the cotton trade, among coal miners, &c. These strikes had been entered upon by local organizations of the industries in question. The value of these strikes and of the local organizations to the International in a propagandist sense was obvious. It became therefore politic to encourage the formation of individual groups, proposing only to support their proceedings by the united force of the International. In this way the International assumed a practical character which had not previously been very manifest.[1]

Although the International had been to a large extent dominated by Germans, it had not succeeded in establishing itself in Germany. This was due to the fact that the German Socialist

---

[1] At the congress held in Brussels in 1868 the number of working men represented is stated at 1,000,000, and at the congress at Basle, at 2,000,000 (Malon, *op. cit.*, p. 20). These figures and others issued at the time of various congresses are open to suspicion ; yet the number of nominal adherents was considerable. The number of effective leaders was small, but they were formidable, because of their activity and because, like stormy petrels, they appeared wherever the political atmosphere was tempestuous.

elements had been organized under the leadership of Lassalle.[1] After the death of Lassalle, in 1864, the "Universal German Workers' Association," [2] which he had formed, was presided over successively by Becker, Tölcke, and Schweitzer. On 1st July 1867 the North German Bund was created, and shortly afterwards the elections to the North German Reichstag were open to universal male suffrage.[3] Schweitzer, Bebel, and other leading Socialists were elected. The original "Universal Association" was suppressed by the police at Leipzig on 16th September 1868.[4] Although another similar association was immediately founded by Schweitzer in Berlin,[5] the leadership of German Socialism was destined to fall into other hands.

Liebknecht and Bebel, at the general meeting of the new association held at Barmen on 28th March 1869, brought an impeachment against Schweitzer. Their attack was unsuccessful,[6] but Schweitzer's authority was seriously impaired. Schweitzer was, moreover, shortly afterwards arrested and imprisoned.

Meanwhile Liebknecht and Bebel were endeavouring to enlist the sympathies of the Saxon and South German working men for the International. From 1866 they had been availing themselves of every opportunity, and by 1868 they had won over a majority of the German working men's associations. The struggle between the group upon whom the mantle of Lassalle had fallen and the group led by Marx through Liebknecht and Bebel came to a head at the Eisenach congress, held 7th to 9th August 1869. The combatants formed a curious group. According to Franz Mehring, on one side were Schweitzer, a "hireling" of Bismarck, and Tölcke, an "uneasy criminal"; while on the other side were Liebknecht, an easy-going ally of the middle class, and Bebel, a stipendiary of

---

[1] Ferdinand Lassalle (1825–1864). For a sketch of his career, see Dawson, W. H., *German Socialism and Lassalle* (London, 1891); for Lassalle's point of view, see his *Working Man's Programme* (English translation, London, n. d.).

[2] *Allgemeiner Deutscher Arbeiterverein.*

[3] *Cf.* Election Law of 31st May 1869, which embodied the previous law.

[4] For an account of the proceedings which led to its suppression, see Mehring, F., *Geschichte der Deutschen Sozialdemokratie*, 4th edition (Stuttgart, 1909), iii. pp. 314–29.

[5] 10th October 1868. Mehring, *op. cit.*, iii. p. 341.

[6] Forty-two delegates, representing 7400 members, voted confidence in Schweitzer, and fourteen delegates refrained from voting, out of a total of fifty-seven delegates. Mehring, *op. cit.*, iii. pp. 352–53.

the ex-King of Hanover.[1] The German labour movement had fallen into strange hands. Schweitzer was still in prison; but Tölcke appeared at Eisenach at the head of 100 delegates with mandates from 102,000 workers. On the other side there were 262 delegates with mandates from 140,000 workers. The struggle began with mutual recriminations and accusations of " mandate swindles." [2] It is possible that both sides were equally offenders. The Eisenach congress marked the close of the influence of Lassalle; but another " strife of factions " took place immediately afterwards at the Basle congress of the International.[3] The result of these struggles was an undoubted victory for Marxism. The International had passed through its early eclectic phase and had become more and more a Marxist organization. The congress at Basle represents, however, the high-water mark of the influence of the International. From that moment it began to decline. The reasons for this are complex ; but the more important may be thus summarized. The Franco-Prussian war, which was looked upon as a war of defence by the German working men's associations, was not so regarded in France. The budding alliance between the German working men and their fellows in other countries through the International was thus nipped almost in the beginning. The growth of a new and very powerful State, uniting the North German political units, brought in many ways a new factor into the field of international relations. Although the full effect of the readjustment did not become obvious until much later, the decay of international proletarian feeling may be traced from that moment, as well as the growth of nationalist and even rival nationalist aims among the working men. It is therefore not surprising that contemporaneously with the victory of the Marxists' dialectics and tactics, there should have been a real defeat of Internationalism. This became evident in the year 1870. The congress was to have been held in Paris, but the outbreak of war rendered the holding of it there impossible, and it was not held at all. When in the spring of 1871 the rising of the Commune of Paris occurred, Marx endeavoured to organize its operations in detail from London,[4] a

[1] Mehring, op. cit., iii. p. 364.   [2] Ibid., p. 366.
[3] The Eisenach congress was held from 7th to 9th August, and the Basle congress from 5th to 12th September 1869.
[4] Yet the rising of the Commune had little in common with Marxism. Marx's attempt to control it was one of the inconsistencies of his career.

proceeding which was not merely futile, but was also quite destructive of the influence of the International both with the French
socialists and with the English trade unions.[1]   No congress was
held in 1871; but in September 1872 a congress was held at the
Hague, where the struggle of factions was resumed.

The controversies at the Hague may be divided into two related
groups—those relating to Marx's personal dictatorship and to his
control of the General Council, whose policy he had been directing
since the Basle congress of 1869 ; and those upon questions of
principle—the most important of these being the controversy
between the advocates of political and those of non-political
Socialism.   The first controversies issued in an attempt to abolish
the General Council.   This was only defeated by a strategic manœuvre of Marx, who proposed that it be removed from Europe
to America.   The second controversy was the more important.
The leader of those who were opposed to political action of a constitutional character by the International was Bakúnin, who now
came forward as the chief antagonist of Marx.   There was nothing
new in non-political propaganda—the trade union movement in
England had been predominantly non-political in its agitation,
the co-operative movement and the friendly society movement
had both been wholly non-political—the two last, at least, entirely
peaceful and non-revolutionary movements.   But Bakúnin did not
advocate measures of that kind.   He urged strongly that the con-
ventional political methods were understood and practised with
greater skill and success by the bourgeoisie than by the proletariat,
and that, therefore, the proletariat must always in that field either
be cheated or defeated by the bourgeoisie.   Bakúnin also urged that
the bourgeoisie must succeed better than the proletariat in all
contests of speech-making or of writing.   Propaganda carried on
by these means must thus in the end be recognized as useless.
Therefore, the only effective propaganda is the " Propaganda of
the Deed."   Moreover, he looked upon political action on the part
of the proletariat as contributing in so far as it might be successful
to the increase of the power of the State and, therefore, to the
diminution of individual liberty.

[1] Marx thus fell between two stools.   In his more recent polemics he had
scouted the idea of revolutionary as opposed to evolutionary processes.   He
plunged ineffectively and gratuitously into the one and offended those whom
he had induced to believe in the other.

The moderate elements of the International had been offended by Marx's patronage of the Commune, and deprived of their aid Marx had no sufficient majority to obtain a clear victory over Bakúnin. He nevertheless defended himself against the attack of Bakúnin with great skill ;[1] but the International was doomed. One more congress was held in Geneva in 1873. Then the International passed to New York, where it expired in 1876. In its later years neither Marx nor Engels took any interest in its proceedings.

The International played in its day a considerable rôle. It frightened every Government in Europe rather by what it appeared to be able to do than by what it actually did. This dread was after all created rather by what Marx opposed than by what he initiated.

It is now necessary to notice the effect of these Western European incidents and controversies upon contemporary Russian youth.

The interpretation given by one of them of the disputes of the International in 1873 may serve as illustration.

" The West European International Association of Working Men, or as it was called at that time, ' The International,' had fallen into two camps—Social Democratic and anarchistic. The Social Democrats proposed that they should take possession of the Reichstag gradually by means of legal agitation and elections, in order, in the more or less remote future, to transform the German bourgeois-constitutional Empire into a Socialist State. The anarchists proposed completely to destroy the State as an authoritative establishment. They denied that the influence of authority is beneficial, no matter in whose hands the authority might be placed, and affirmed that real equality could be brought into existence only by free agreement between people, and not at all by means of State decrees and State reforms. The first appeared to be statists and the second anti-statists. When these two adverse propositions were placed before the Russian youth, they expressed themselves by a great majority for anarchy. I do not undertake here to point out the causes of this phenomenon. May be it was caused by the facts that we Russians have become tired of State intervention, and that in the State we see an enemy to progress

[1] Mehring, *op. cit.*, iv. pp. 53 and 54.

rather than an aid to it ; and also that we have no Reichstag, and nowhere to send our deputies. However it was, almost all expressed themselves in favour of anarchist theories." [1]

The distinction is put with more precision by Prince Kropotkin.

" The conflict between the Marxists and the Bakúnists was not a personal affair. It was the necessary conflict between the principles of federalism and those of centralization, the free commune and the State's paternal rule, the free action of the masses of the people and the betterment of existing capitalist conditions through legislation—a conflict between the Latin spirit and the German *Geist*, which, after the defeat of France on the battlefield, claimed supremacy in science, politics, philosophy, and in Socialism too, representing its own conception of Socialism as ' scientific,' while all other interpretations it described as ' utopian.' " [2]

The controversy was not a new one. It had been waged with bitterness in the eighteenth century. Centralization had been one of the causes of the French Revolution, and federalism had been the leading principle of the constitution of the United States. The political history of Russia had been a history of progressive centralization ; but in the solitary respect in which the superiority of the system was universally admitted, viz. in the consolidation of a great military power, the system had ignominiously broken down.[3] The Crimean War had shown that incompetent centralization was quite fatal. It was thus not surprising that to the Russian mind of that period federalism should offer more promise of political and material progress ; nor is it surprising that the characteristic enthusiasm and directness of Russian speculative thought should carry it to extremes.

The principal avenue of federalist and anarchist influences through which they reached the Russian youth at that time was Zurich, where some three hundred Russians were living either as

---

[1] Debogoriy-Mokrievich, *Reminiscences* (St Petersburg, 1906), p. 81.

[2] Prince Kropotkin, *Memoirs*, p. 386. At this period Marx had no influence in North Germany, where the Lassallists held the field, and but little influence in South Germany. He had also but little influence in Russia at that time.

[3] *Cf.* the discussion upon Federalism *versus* Centralization in De Tocqueville, *Democracy in America* (ed. New York, 1838), p. 152, chap. ix. ; in J. S. Mill's *Representative Government*, and in Freeman's *History of Federal Governments*. See also the disputes about centralization among the Russian Social Democratic groups, *infra*, chap. ix.

students or as political exiles. Although all were favourable to anarchist rather than to Social Democratic opinions, they were by no means agreed upon one form of federalism.

There were, indeed, two sharply divided schools. One was the school of Bakúnin, who lived at Locarno; and the other was the school of Lavrov,[1] who resided in Zurich.

The distinction between these two groups was a customary distinction in such cases. Both approved of revolutionary means to achieve the social revolution; but the Lavrists believed in the policy of permeation—the gradual spreading of revolutionary ideas among the people, while the Bakúnists believed in " riot " as an instrument of progress, because dissatisfaction with the existing order was already prevalent, and a riot always afforded an opportunity of transference into a popular uprising or a revolution. Even if the riot were suppressed, rioting would, nevertheless, be a school in which the people might be educated in the desired direction and in which the people might be revolutionized—that is, made capable of creating the revolution.[2]

The various ideas of the International, irreconcilable as they proved, were fructifying in the minds of the Russian youth, discontented as they were with the political condition of their own country and with the oppression under which they believed the working men of all countries were suffering. Questions of principle were hotly discussed among the Russian youth at Zurich generally, as is the Russian manner, in loud voices on the streets, in restaurants, or in their rooms.[3]

The idea, which had been from the beginning more or less widely

[1] Piotr Lavrovich Lavrov (1823–1901), colonel of artillery and Professor of Mathematics. Arrested and sent to the Ural Mountains, from which he escaped. In 1874 he went to London, where he published a newspaper, *Forward*. " He belonged to the Social Democratic wing of the Socialist movement; but he was too widely learned and too much of a philosopher to join the German Social Democrats in their ideals of a centralized communist State, or in their narrow interpretation of history" (Prince Kropotkin, *Ideals and Realities in Russian Literature* (London, 1905), p. 277). Lavrov published an unfinished *History of Modern Thought*, in four or five vols., from an evolutionary point of view. His chief influence upon the Russian youth was exercised in 1870–1873 through his *Historical Letters*, published under the pseudonym of "Mirtov" (Kropotkin, *loc. cit.*). For a sketch of the life of Lavrov, see *L'Humanité Nouvelle* (Paris, 1900), xxxvii. pp. 35–49.
[2] *Cf.* Debogoriy-Mokrievich, *op. cit.*, pp. 95, 96.
[3] Debogoriy-Mokrievich, *op. cit.*, p. 80.

accepted in the International, and which had been also in accordance with the general attitude both of Lavrov and of Bakúnin, to the effect that the working class must work out its own political and social salvation, came to be widely entertained by the Russian youth in Zurich and elsewhere. Their acceptance of this notion did not, however, soothe them into inaction ; on the contrary, it presented itself to them as an imperative impulse towards themselves becoming working men. To join the working class thus became an object of ambition. The only means by which the people could be understood and aided was to become one of them.[1] Beside this idea, the strife of factions in the International and the splitting up of its ranks into rival sects, occupying themselves with economical and political dogmatics, assumed a small place.

In Russia this idea sent in the early seventies large numbers of educated persons into the country to live the life and to share the burdens of the peasants. At the same time and under the same influences, Russian students and others living abroad went to work as artisans, and even as railway navvies on the lines then being constructed in Switzerland. Having qualified in such ways, they then became members of one of the local branches of the International. This movement towards the people came to be known as *V Narod*.[2] There remains merely to be indicated, as arising out of the activities of Bakúnin, the formation of the " Federation of the Jura"[3] and the propaganda of anarchist opinions among working men, especially in the Latin countries, by Bakúnin and his adherents, Varlin in France, Cæsar de Paepe in Belgium, Cafiero in Italy, and others.

[1] Bakúnin had himself attempted this in Lyons in 1871. Cf. *ibid.*, p. 85.
[2] For an account of the *V Narod* movement, see next chapter.
[3] *Cf.* the letters of Bakúnin to the Jura Internationals, *Œuvres* (Paris, 1895), pp. 207 *et seq.*, and Kropotkin, *Memoirs*, pp. 387 *et seq.*

CHAPTER VI

THE *V NAROD* MOVEMENT

THE movement which impelled the educated youth of Russia to go among the people and to *be* of the people arose partly out of the general state of feeling which the International had done much to engender in Western Europe, and which had had an echo in the minds of the Russian youth. Yet the movement was nevertheless characteristically Russian. It had no counterpart elsewhere. It was the logical outcome of a state of mind which had gradually been subject to intensification, especially since emancipation. The disasters of the Crimean War had aroused everyone to the fact that the Russian people occupied two quite separate and distant worlds. There could be no national cohesion so long as this phenomenon presented itself. Emancipation had formally restored the peasant to human dignity in a juridical sense, but some organic change was necessary in order that he might be able to avail himself of his newly acquired opportunities. The " knot " of bondage had left an impression upon him. He hardly yet felt his limbs released from its pressure. The formality of emancipation was not enough. Society could not become homogeneous unless one-half knew how the other half lived, and as it was they did not do so. If it was difficult for a gentleman to see the world through the eyes of a peasant, it was still more difficult for a peasant to see the world through the eyes of a gentleman. Education had been in effect a monopoly of the superior class, and so long as it remained so the freedom ensured by emancipation was a mere juridical fact, destitute of social value. How was all this to be altered ?

This problem struck the Russian aristocratic youth like a blow in the face, and produced in them varying emotions. Some of them, trained as they were in the physical and mental sciences, experienced a revolt against the apparent selfishness of pursuing these studies while the mass of the people were not only deprived of the luxury of doing so,[1] but were hardly able to keep body and soul together. Some of these proceeded to apply their training, such as it was, to the solving of this momentous question. But science afforded no cut-and-dried solution. Ages of discussion notwithstanding, patent and obvious facts of human life were still unexplained. To some this proved the futility of study. All questions could not be solved even by the most arduous labour. Therefore it were best to act, and not to waste time in researches. Others insisted that intellectual labour simply removed the student farther from the people. The peasant was not intelligent, thus it was useless to hope to become like him by cultivating the intelligence. This attitude led to the adoption of mere formulæ. " Do you consent to go at once to the people ? " " Yes." " Then you are ours ! " What the convert was to do when he went to the people was a detail unworthy of attention. Peasants and working men alike were idealized, and when by actual contact was some real understanding achieved, the disillusionment was frequently too great for the raw enthusiast. Many working men were themselves demoralized by the flattery of the ardent *intelligentsia*. " Working men are heroes, and the gentlemen are useless ! " Such phrases and " such an attitude of mind were a logical consequence of our outlook," Debogoriy-Mokrievich says in his frank and interesting *Reminiscences*.[2] In the winter of 1873–1874 the members of various groups and circles remained in the cities, working at carpentry and the like, living with and as working men. Their work was inefficient and unreal ; sometimes even from mere restlessness, sometimes from desire to see as many phases as possible, they moved about from place to place, and learned little in any of them. In the spring of 1874 there was a great migration to the villages. Enthusiastic youths bought sheepskin coats, manufactured passports, and prepared for assuming the life of peasants. Again they wandered about ; the novelty of the impressions kept them interested for a time, but it soon became apparent that nothing could come of these wanderings. Then arose an enthusiasm for entering

---

[1] " What right had I to these highest joys " (original researches upon the influence of the polar-ice cap) " when all around me was nothing but misery and struggle for a mouldy bit of bread." Prince Kropotkin, *Memoirs*, p. 240.

[2] Debogoriy-Mokrievich, *op. cit.*, p. 117.

into the life of the people in an organic way. One enthusiast became a teacher, another a male nurse, another a craftsman, and so on. More might be hoped for from this, but no effect could be expected from the process in any short time.

When the *V Narod* movement began, it was supposed that the peasants were eager for some drastic settlement of the land question, and that they would listen to any revolutionary solution of it. Soon it became apparent that the peasants were waiting for some miracle to happen, and that the idea of their doing anything to facilitate this miracle was quite out of the question. All changes must come from above. Even when the peasants realized that they were the victims of some specific act of injustice, either at the hands of the authorities or at those of the landowners, they simply murmured : " It seems that from our birth it was so designed."[1] " If, on one hand, poverty and perpetual oppression may bring a man to acts of desperation, on the other they may bring him to idiotcy."[2] " The peasants were moreover afraid to leave the known present for the unknown future. . . . They were accustomed to obey and never to protest, and the purpose seemed to them too remote."[3]

Ardent and picturesque as in the best the *V Narod* movement was, the flippant student was speedily discouraged, and even serious observers and workers found that they made little progress. The plain fact was that the peasants were not ready even for so mild a revolutionary movement as the *V Narod* offered. There is little evidence to show that the movement contained any peril for the Government. Had it been left alone, it would almost inevitably have died a natural death, both in the towns and in the country. But the Government fell into a state of panic. It felt that the *V Narod* movement must be suppressed. Suppressed it was. Wholesale arrests were made. Those who went into the people were hunted down. " The hunt spread all over Russia. They grasped right and left, innocent and guilty alike, sparing nobody, and halting for nothing."[4] This state of matters demoralized the police and the authorities. Careers were made by those who engaged in these battues. Fear settled down upon everyone.

---

[1] E. Breshkovsky, quoted by Debogoriy-Mokrievich, *op. cit.*, p. 180.
[2] *Ibid.*   [3] *Ibid.*, p. 181.
[4] Debogoriy-Mokrievich, *op. cit.*, p. 182.

Even those who disapproved of these proceedings were compelled to keep silence.[1]

" The *V Narod* movement was a failure. Yet," says Debogoriy-Mokrievich, " we succeeded in producing that about which we did not care at all—the sympathy of the thinking layers of Russian society." [2] The Government prosecutions intensified this sympathy, and little by little there began to grow the struggle between the Russian *intelligentsia* and the autocracy." [3] Thus failure as it was so far as immediate results were concerned, the *V Narod* movement undoubtedly contributed, in spite of the hostility of the Government, and largely because of it, towards bringing more closely together the different elements of Russian society, and towards a better understanding of the real nature of the problems presented by the lives of peasants but recently brought out of bondage.

According to the secret report of Count Pahlen, written in 1875,[4] the greater part of European Russia was covered, towards the end of the year 1874, by a network of revolutionary groups. Thirty-seven out of fifty-one *guberni* were affected. The number of persons described as belonging to these groups was 770, of whom 158 were women. At the date of the report 265 were in prison, 452 were allowed to be at large, and 53 were undiscovered. Among the groups were persons of all ages and of all social positions.[5] This report became the foundation of the prosecution of the 193, which marked the close of the peaceful agitation of the *V Narod* movement.[6]

It seems to be quite clear that for a considerable time after the *V Narod* movement began there was in it nothing of a conspirative character. If there was, it was sporadic and trifling. The movement was too open and too eclectic for it to assume a general character of a conspirative order. Its very eclecticism rendered it open, no doubt, to entrance by conspirators, but in the nature of the case,

---

[1] Debogoriy-Mokrievich, *op. cit.*, p. 183.   [2] *Ibid.*   [3] *Ibid.*, p. 184.
[4] Published in *Deutsche Rundschau*, vol. xxvii. (Berlin, 1881), p. 351 *et seq.*
[5] *Op. cit.*, p. 358.
[6] Stepniak says that the total number of imprisonments in connection with the trial was 1400, of whom 700 were shortly set free. The remainder were kept in prison for periods of from one to four years. Of the 193, 73 either became insane or committed suicide, or both, during the four years over which the trials extended. Yet only 40 of the total number were eventually found guilty. *Russia under the Tsars*, chap. xiv,

adherents of this type must have been few in number. When the suppression began, and when " going to the people " involved risk of prosecution, the more timid elements tended to drop out and the bolder elements to remain ; and thus, although the two movements were distinct, even peaceful adherents of *V Narod*, proscribed and hunted, gradually formulated for themselves ideas hostile to the State, and some of them became active revolutionaries. Their mode of life was inimical to any settled ideas. They moved about continually, now in Russia, now in Switzerland, smuggling broadsheets and pamphlets printed on thin so-called " conspirative " paper, sometimes succeeding in circulating these and sometimes falling into the hands of the police. In the latter event they were consigned to solitary confinement in some fortress. Deprived of books and of communication with their fellows even before trial, when they came before their judges, already generally prejudiced against them, they frequently exhibited the effects of the nervous strain to which they had been subjected.[1] Many of them became insane, some committed suicide, or deliberately assailed their guards, hoping that a shot would put an end to their sufferings.

Meanwhile the Government was passing through its most corrupt phase. It seemed to have fallen altogether into the hands of a formidable combination of peculators—Shouvalov, Potapov, Trépov —" while all the active men of the reform period had been brushed aside."[2] The State lands and the Treasury were plundered remorselessly. Through an isolated revolutionary act the scandalous situation was disclosed. Trépov, who was chief of the St. Petersburg police, had ordered a political prisoner[3] to be flogged in prison. Aroused by this act, Vera Zasúlich shot at Trépov.[4] Although he afterwards recovered, Trépov believed himself to be mortally wounded, and made his will. This document revealed the possession of a considerable and previously unsuspected fortune, and gave rise to an investigation before the Senate sitting as a court of justice. Trépov

[1] Witness the case of Mushkin, whose speech in court is given by Debogoriy-Mokrievich, *op. cit.*, pp. 188–90. The speech is described by Stepniak as having had an extraordinary effect throughout the country. *Russia under the Tsars*, chap. xviii.

[2] Kropotkin, *Memoirs*, p. 242.

[3] The student Bogolyubov, who had been arrested for participation in the demonstration before the Kazan Cathedral in St. Petersburg.

[4] 23rd January 1878.

was found guilty of peculation and dismissed. His assailant was tried, and acquitted. The deed of Vera Zasúlich created a profound impression throughout the *V Narod* groups.

Up till the period of the wholesale arrests, the activities of those who went into the *V Narod* movement seem to have consisted in the circulation of books and pamphlets, and in propaganda of a more or less socialistic character among peasants and working men. In neither case could it be said that the revolutionary effects were important. When, however, these activities were arrested, some of those who had been engaged in them formed groups for propaganda of another kind. Various as were the types of socialism represented in the *V Narod* movement, their adherents agreed in general in the doctrine that changes in the administration of government could not alone bring about the regeneration of society. They looked with scorn upon contemporary liberalism, and indeed upon political action of all kinds. But they found by experience that whether or not political measures could promote a social revolution, they could do much to retard one. In spite of their doctrines they felt themselves drawn into the position that the political situation must be altered, otherwise the social situation would remain as it was. Numerous groups formed themselves upon this new platform. Among these there was, in the year 1877, a small group at Kiev composed of some half a dozen students and others.[1] According to Debogoriy-Mokrievich, it would appear that on the initiative of Valerian Osinsky,[2] two or three members of this group decided upon an attempt to kill Kotlyarevsky, who, as public prosecutor, had investigated the Chigirin case.[3]

The attempt was a failure,[4] but the group decided that it was

---

[1] A lively account is given of this group by Debogoriy-Mokrievich, *op. cit.*, pp. 326 *et seq.*

[2] For sketches of Osinsky, see Stepniak, *Underground Russia*, and *Narodnaya Volya*, No. 2, 1st October 1879 (reprinted in *Literature of the Social-Revolutionary Party*, Narodnoë Volë (Paris, 1905), pp. 101–16). See also *infra*, p. 120.

[3] The Chigirin case arose out of an accusation that the peasants of Chigirin were robbed by the *Narodnëkë*. The charges were that the peasants had been called upon to subscribe 5 kopeks each monthly, and that one-half of this sum only was devoted to the purposes of the movement ; the other half being appropriated by the *Narodnëkë* personally. (*Cf.* Osinsky's speech before the court in *Literature*, &c., p. 113.)

[4] It was made on 23rd February 1878, a month after the attack upon Trépov by Vera Zasúlich. (*Cf.* Debogoriy-Mokrievich, *op. cit.*, p. 329. See also *infra*, pp. 120–122.)

expedient to make a public declaration of the reasons for the attempt. This they did by means of printed placards which were posted at night in the streets of Kiev. In order to give this declaration a formidable air, the placards were stamped " The Executive Committee." Debogoriy-Mokrievich says that this was the origin of the Executive Committee which afterwards entered upon the Terror that ended with the assassination of Alexander II.[1] " Of whom this Executive Committee consisted (in 1878) it would be difficult to say, because it did not possess any definite organization. Everybody acted according to his own opinions. Osinsky, Ivichevich, and some others apparently looked upon the affair very seriously. So also did my brother, who saw in it an attempt at a struggle of a political character. ' Up till now,' he said to me, ' you have been discussing about *V Narod ;* there has been in all this very little of revolutionism. You have been throwing the beans upon the kissel.[2] As soon as the affair has reached your own interests, you see the result. They are shooting there at Trépov, here at Kotlyarevsky. There is no use in shutting one's eyes. These are facts of political struggle. . . . Just think of how many peasants have been flogged by *ispravnēkē*[3] and governors ; nobody shoots them for that ; but Trépov tried once to flog an *intelligent* revolutionary, and he was punished. Thus, my brother, neither socialism nor *V Narod* is concerned in this thing.' "[4]

This was undoubtedly a sound diagnosis. However natural and inevitable the transition from *Narodnechestvo* or the *V Narod* movement to the revolutionary *Narodnaya Volya*, the spirit of the two movements was not the same. The old *Narodnechestvo* looked upon political freedom as an advantage for the upper classes of society, because it would give them a definite political status and would greatly strengthen their position ; but this result would be disadvantageous for the mass of the people, because the more powerful are the enemies of the masses, the worse for the masses themselves.[5] The revolutionary *Narodovoltsi*, on the other hand, while they began by demanding political freedom in the form of constitutional guarantees, went on later to urge that, since a con-

---

[1] There was, however, no precise continuity. For an account of the origin of the Executive Committee as eventually organized, see *infra*, p. 125.
[2] That is, wasting time.   [3] District chiefs of police.
[4] Debogoriy-Mokrievich, *op. cit.*, pp. 333-4.
[5] *Ibid.*, p. 599. This was the view of Bakúnin.

stitutional régime might be utilized by the bourgeoisie for their own advantage, political freedom must be employed for the purpose of securing a fundamental change in the whole social structure.[1] Debogoriy-Mokrievich points out quite soundly that, if the *Narodovoltsi* had confined themselves to the single aim of securing a constitution, they would have gained allies among the Liberal elements. Apart from the characteristic reluctance of all Russian parties to ally themselves with one another, the *Narodovoltsi* were embarrassed by two ideas of doubtful validity : first, the possibility of transforming directly, without an intermediate phase of parliamentary constitutionalism, a "semi-Asiatic"[2] and highly heterogeneous Empire into a socialist state, corresponding more or less closely to their utopist ideas of what such a state ought to be ; and second, the possibility of overthrowing a Government whose weakness, as events showed almost immediately, was greatly exaggerated by them.

While the *Narodovoltsi* laid stress upon political freedom, and the *V Narod* propagandists did not, they were in a strict sense both engaged in political movements. Stepniak,[3] who was a member of both groups, recognizes this fully. "This movement" (the early *V Narod*) "was in reality directed against our political system, for only a new free State could successfully take up and solve the agrarian question."[4] Stepniak goes on to say that the reason for the failure of the *V Narod* movement was that "the young generation could not formulate its real desires, and the educated class could not understand the young generation. The

[1] Debogoriy-Mokrievich, *op. cit.*, p. 570.   [2] *Ibid.*

[3] Sergius Stepniak (1852–1894) (real name Serghei Kravchinsky) was a lieutenant of artillery when he threw himself, in 1873, into the *V Narod* movement. In Count Pahlen's secret report (cited above) he is described as one of the four or five principal figures in the propaganda among St. Petersburg working men. He also carried on a propaganda among the peasants. Under the influence of the repressions, Stepniak became an active member of the *Narodovoltsi*, being at the time about twenty-six years of age. On 4th August 1878, he shot and killed in broad daylight in St. Petersburg, General Mezentsev, chief of the Third Section. He escaped from Russia and spent some years in Italy, where he wrote his *Underground Russia*, originally in Italian (afterwards in Russian and in English). He reached England about 1882, and resided there until his death by accident at a railway crossing near London in 1894. Stepniak possessed a singularly attractive personality. His writings, especially his *Career of a Nihilist* (London, 1889) (written originally in English), exhibit very high artistic powers which, however, were even more observable in his conversation.

[4] *Nihilism as It is* (London, n.d.), p. 16.

young extremists were left to depend upon their own powers, and this fact condemned the movement beforehand to complete and fruitless destruction." [1]

Yet some of the *V Narod* groups refused to be drawn into *Narodnaya Volya*. By temperament or conviction they were indisposed to engage in the Terror which now began to make its appearance. Those who adopted this attitude may be said to have fallen into two camps—one the old *Narodnechestvo*, the other the so-called *Chorno Peredyeltsi*.[2] The latter group devoted itself especially to the agrarian question, which it proposed to settle by a drastic redistribution of the land, retaining in general the old *V Narod* ideas. The *Chorno Peredyeltsi* seem to have consisted for the most part of students who were " preparing themselves " for revolutionary activity among the people. But " preparation " did not always go very far. In the older *V Narod* movement, those who were " preparing themselves " were also making perpetual attempts in practice.[3] They were really learning in the school of life. From the point of view of the adherents of the old agitation, the *Chorno Peredyeltsi* were engaged in endless " preparation," and in endless discussions and drafting of programmes.

The definite division of the *Narodnēchestvo* into *Narodovoltsi* and *Chorno Peredyeltsi* took place at a meeting of revolutionary parties held at Lipetsk, 17th to 21st June 1879,[4] when the party of action emerged as a new party, and the party of permeation, represented by the *Chorno Peredyeltsi*, remained, adhering so far as programme was concerned to the original ideal of the *V Narod* movement. From this time onwards there was a struggle between the two revolutionary wings for influence upon the Russian youth. Both published newspapers. The party of action issued the *Narodnaya Volya*, and the other the *Chorno Peredyel*.[5]

---

[1] *Nihilism as It is* (London, n.d.), p. 16.
[2] Literally " Black repartition "—the black referring to the soil.
[3] Debogoriy-Mokrievich, *op. cit.*, p. 574.
[4] This meeting was continued at Voronej. Cf. *infra*.
[5] The first number of *Narodnaya Volya* is dated 1st October 1879. It was suppressed in January 1880. This issue was succeeded by *Listok Narodnoĕ Volĕ*, the first number of which is dated 1st June 1880. At the fifth number of that issue the title was changed to *Narodnaya Volya*. It continued to be published at intervals under this title until October 1885. The *Chorno Peredyel* was suspended in March 1880.

The history of the *Narodnaya Volya*, which gave rise to the social-revolutionary party, is recounted later ; that of the *Chorno Peredyeltsi* may be briefly concluded. Although during the period of its existence it represented incipient social democracy, and while many of its members became social democrats, the activity of the group was practically destroyed in the reaction after 1881. Some of its members went abroad, and carried on from Switzerland and elsewhere a desultory propaganda. In the famine year of 1891 there was a revival of the spirit of the *Chorniy Peredyel* in the *Narodnoye Pravo*, or Folks' Right Party. Many enthusiasts went to the people, as others had done eighteen years before. The movement was sternly put down by the Government in 1893.

The close of the year 1876 and the whole course of the year 1877 formed an important period in Russian revolutionary history, because the repressions of the Government in connection with the *V Narod* movement at least contributed to the separation of the groups engaged in that agitation into two camps, one of which grew into a formidable force. Apart, however, from this incident, there were other signs of a new phase of revolutionary activity. The first revolutionary demonstration of this epoch took place in the Nevsky Prospekt, St. Petersburg, in front of the Kazan Cathedral, on 6th December 1876. This demonstration was organized by the group known as *Zemlya e Volya* [1] (Land and Freedom). Although this group was not a distinctively working men's society, the demonstration was attended by some working men. The bulk of the persons who attended the demonstration were, however, *intelligentsia*. The first revolutionary society of working men organized during this epoch was the North Russian Working Men's Union. [2] This union had a combined economical and political platform. Its principal demands were " the limitation of working hours," " the prohibition of the labour of children," " the institution of co-operative associations," [3] the establishment of " land credit banks with free credit for working men's

---

[1] See *supra*, p. 73.
[2] *Cf.* Svyatlovsky, V. V., *The Labour Movement in Russia* (St. Petersburg, 1907), p. 386. See also Stepniak, *The Russian Storm Cloud*, chap. ii.
[3] The prominence of " co-operation " was due to the desire of the union to put an end to the system of " truck."

associations."[1]   According to the constitution of the union, only working men might become members.[2]

[1] This meant free State credit, or loans without interest to working men's associations.

[2] In this respect the union resembled the typical trade union in England. In Canada and in the United States the line is not customarily so sharply drawn.   Small masters and even Government officials occasionally find their way into labour councils.   At the head of the North Russian Working Men's Union stood Victor Obnorsky and Stepàn Khaltùrin (cf. *infra*, p. 127).   The principal success of the union was among the St. Petersburg working men. The first issue of their newspaper, *The Dawn of the Worker*, was confiscated, and the printing office seized in February 1880.   The views of the union were similar to those of Lassalle, and were probably derived from him. The Union was attacked by the *Narodovolsti*.   Its reply to the attack is to be found in *Zemlya è Volya*, Nos. 3 and 5.   On the activities of the Union, see also Stepniak, *The Russian Storm Cloud*, ch. ii.

CHAPTER VII

NARODNAYA VOLYA

THE transition from *V Narod*, or "Into the people," movement to
Narodnaya Volya, or "The People's Will," has been described in
the immediately preceding chapter. We have now to examine
the significance of the rôle of the new group in Russian revolutionary history. Authentic data concerning terrorist parties are
invariably difficult to procure. Conspirators do not usually en-
cumber themselves with unnecessary *pièces de conviction*. Even
the evidence brought before the courts during the more important
trials throws somewhat meagre light upon the psychology of
terrorist groups, and the actual share of individuals in the operations of these groups is, for obvious reasons, in general elaborately
concealed. Significant indications of the " state of mind " of the
members of revolutionary parties are, however, to be obtained to
a certain extent from the revolutionary newspapers, issued in
spite of police surveillance and frequent suppression, and from the
occasional manifestoes, broadsheets, and pamphlets printed abroad
or in " underground " printing offices, as well as from memoirs
published subsequently to the termination of the particular phases
of the movement to which they refer.

The documentary material relating to the *Narodnaya Volya* is
not voluminous. From its beginning the *Narodnaya Volya* was
harassed by the police. Such documents as were issued by it were
issued in small numbers, and it does not appear that any complete
collection of them exists, save possibly in the archives of the Department of Police in St. Petersburg.[1]

An article entitled " Delenda est Carthago," in the first issue
of the *Narodnaya Volya*,[2] the party organ, reveals fairly the point

---

[1] A collection of these documents, admittedly incomplete, has been published in Paris by the Social Revolutionary Central Committee, entitled,
Literature of the Social-Revolutionary Party Narodnoë Volé, 1905.

[2] No. 1, 1st October 1879, reprinted in volume above quoted.

of view of the *Narodovoltsi*, or adherents of the party. According to this article, the political theory upon which the Russian Government is based involves the idea that the people exist for the Government, as opposed to the idea that the Government exists for the people. " The Russian State is thus unlike an European State. . . . It is not a commission of delegates of a ruling class, as in Europe, but it is an independent, self-existent organization, a hierarchical, disciplined association which holds the people in economical and political slavery. Even if there were no exploiting class, the State would remain as private owner of half of the territory of Russia. One-half of the peasants are merely lessees of the lands of the State." Yet this formidable association can only maintain its unique position by constant repression, by prosecutions and by executions and exiles. " The northern provinces and Siberia are full of exiles " who have incurred the displeasure of the Government. The Government, self-existent as it is, lives apart from the people ; it leans not upon them, but upon the rude force which it commands through the discipline and passive obedience of those in its own ranks and through the political ignorance of the masses. These masses, like all masses, " are inert and cowardly. They desire peace first of all, and they cease to prefer existing evil to an unknown and risky future, only when the pressure of the Government reaches a certain point." Thus all oppositional parties must watch for the moment when this point arrives. Social thought develops beneath the surface ; under Government repression, indeed, a spirit of criticism is fertilized by this very repression. But this spirit of criticism is timid and negative, and the social thought of the general mass is limited and " without comprehension of the chief necessities of the time." There is thus opportunity for the oppositional party which boldly announces " I know the way out (of this apparent *impasse*) and where to go." " If such a party is able to seize the real needs of the time it must be a power, because the social problems may be solved under its guidance. A party which pretends to point the way to the future must, however, base its principles upon a real and severe relation to actual life. The most rosy ideal is useless, and even dangerous, if it cannot be projected into actuality." A propaganda of idealism may be injurious if its proposed methods of action are impracticable, and if they are opposed to those methods of action by means of which alone the first barriers in the path of the people may be removed. A party of action must therefore set before it concrete, directly useful tasks, and choose those means that are at the particular moment most effective. In its prosecution of the *Narodněkě* (or the adherents of the *V Narod* movement) " the Government has declared war upon us. Whether we wish it or not, the Government prosecutes us. Certainly it is open to us to refrain from defending ourselves, but nobody ever gained anything by adopting that course. Our direct policy must be to approach and to throw down the obstacle that prevents us from acting, and that every day takes from us our best workers, that surrounds us with a network of espionage, and attacks us by denunciations. In the struggle with this obstacle we are spending 90 per cent. of our force. We do not deny that it is possible to carry on a propaganda among the people, or that riotous activity might not arise among them, but under existing conditions activities of these kinds are too difficult.

" The power of the Government need not frighten us. It is an iron giant with feet of clay." It is true that it may in time die a natural death, but " for our party it is very important that the new order of things should correspond to the interests of the people and of the party itself. It would be a great mistake to allow the new order of things to be without the management and influence of the people, or, while liberating the other classes and opening up the possibility of activities to other parties, to permit the new order to leave the mass of the people and also the Socialist party in the conditions under which they now exist. Even if the revolution were accomplished, the party might condemn itself for centuries to hard (and merely) preparatory work. The present moment is a moment of great importance. Persecution, prosecution, imprisonment are nothing compared with the results of the present moment to the people, if the Socialist party is able to comprehend the situation and to control it. . . . We are sure that the time is coming when the Socialist party shall stand against the Governmental system, not spasmodically, but systematically and steadily, and, destroying the oppressive Governmental mechanism, shall assure to the people . . . the possibility of free development of its thoughts, ideals, and forms of social life." [1]

[1] *Literature*, &c., pp. 3–11.

In the second issue of the same organ, the necessity of political activity is similarly urged. " First of all it is necessary to liberate the people from the yoke of the Government. For this reason our activity must be of a *political* character. . . . It is to be understood, however, that in calling upon the people to engage in a struggle with the Government, we do not object to a social and economical revolution—we only say that in our circumstances, the political and social revolution are inextricably coupled, and that one without the other is impossible. For the politico-social revolution we are only pointing out a new path—a path indeed not wholly new, but merely ill-recognized by our party." The article goes on to urge that a Constituent Assembly, after the model of the *Assemblée constituante,* should be convened.[1] In this Constituent Assembly nine-tenths of the members must represent the peasantry. Thus the outcome of the Assembly must be "a complete revolution of all economical and State relations."

An article in the same issue deals with the question, " On which Side is Morality ? " It accuses the officials of corruption, and refers to conspicuous cases—those of Trépov and Prince Volkonsky, for example.[2] " Profiting by the impossibility of defending ourselves, we are set before the eyes of society as bloodthirsty, merciless monsters ; on the contrary, we give to spiritual, and especially to moral questions, a new meaning." When the political prosecutions and the system of espionage are considered, " do not be surprised that there are a few murders, but that there are so few." . . . " Russian revolutionaries are not adepts in terror ; they are humane and not given to bloodshed."

The principles and methods of the *Narodnaya Volya* party are, however, most fully disclosed in the " Programme of the Executive Committee," first published in 1879.[3] According to this document, the Executive Committee are " socialists and *narodněkě.*" [4] " We are convinced," they say, " that only by means of socialist prin-

[1] This became one of the watchwords of the revolutionary year 1905. See *infra*, p. 489.
[2] The Trépov case has already been noticed. Volkonsky was accused of robbing the Griaze-Tsaritsinsky Railway of 600,000 rubles.
[3] *Narodnaya Volya*, No. 3, 1st January 1880, reprinted in *Literature*, &c., cited, p. 162.
[4] *Narodněkě* may be rendered " populists," but their position should not be confounded with that of the almost contemporary " populists " of the United States.

ciples can humanity incorporate in its life, freedom, equality, and brotherhood, in order to secure common well-being and a full and large development of the individual, and therefore to secure progress. We are convinced that only ' the will of the people' (*narodnaya volya*) can sanction social forms, that the development of the people is sound only when it is independent and free, when every idea which is incorporated in its life is so through the conscience and will of the people. The well-being of the people and the will of the people—these are our most sacred and most indissolubly binding principles." This is by way of introduction, the chief points of the programme follow :

1. The people are in a state of complete economical and political servitude. " The working man labours merely to feed and keep the parasitical classes. He is deprived of the rights of a citizen." Not only does Russian life exist apart from his will, but he has no right to express this will. Pressed upon from all sides, the people become physically degenerate and dull, and are crushed into poverty and slavery in all senses.

2. Chained in rows (like galley slaves), oppressed by layers of exploiters, who are brought into existence and defended by the Government. The State is the greatest capitalistic force in the country. It is the only political oppressor of the people. There is a complete absence of sanction by the people of this oppressive power, which forcibly introduces and maintains political and economical principles and forms which have nothing in common with the wishes and ideals of the people.

3. Notwithstanding these conditions, there are still alive among the people old traditional ideas—of the right of the people to the land, of communal and district self-government, of the beginnings of federal organization, freedom of conscience and speech. These ideas would be developed and would give a wholly new direction to the history of Russia, if only the people could live as they wished.

4. Therefore the nearest task is to remove from the people the crushing weight of the existing system, and to make a political revolution with the object of giving the power into the hands of the people. The results of this revolution would be—(*a*) that the development of the people would go on independently, in accordance with its will, and (*b*) that pure socialist principles (common to the

Narodnaya Volya party and to the people) would be recognized and supported.

5. The will of the people would be quite well expressed in a Constituent Assembly, elected freely by universal suffrage, with " instructions " from the electors. A Constituent Assembly is, however, far from an ideal institution for the expression of the will of the people, but it is the only practicable form of such an institution at present.

6. " We therefore aim at the removal of power from the existing Government and the transference of it to a Constituent Assembly. This Assembly would have as its task to survey all our State and social institutions, and to rebuild them according to the instructions received from the electors.

7. " While we submit to the will of the people, we consider it our duty, as a party, to place our programme before it. We shall make it our propaganda before the revolution, we shall recommend it throughout the period of agitation, we shall defend it before the Constituent Assembly."

8. The specific points of the programme are : (*a*) A gradual popular representation, with full powers (to be enjoyed, it is to be presumed by the representative assembly) over all affairs of State ; (*b*) a large measure of local autonomy, secured by the independence of the *mir* and the economical independence of the people ; (*c*) " the land must belong to the people " ;[1] (*d*) the transference to the workmen of all mills and factories ; (*e*) complete freedom of conscience, speech, press, meeting, associations, and election ; (*f*) universal suffrage, without any class or property limitation ; (*g*) the replacement of the standing army by a territorial militia.

9. The means of realizing this programme are as follows : (*a*) Propaganda with the general objects of familiarizing all classes of the population with the idea of a democratic political revolution as a means towards social reform, and of popularizing the programme of the party, and with the special aims of protesting continually against the existing order, and of demanding the convocation of a Constituent Assembly : the forms of protest being meetings, demonstrations, petitions, addresses, and refusal to pay taxes, &c. ; (*b*) destructive and terroristic activity, consisting in the exter-

---

[1] Like some other points in the programme, this is vague. The phrase might mean State, provincial, communal, or individual ownership.

mination of the most prejudicial persons in the Government, in defending the party against espionage, in punishing those who engage in the most important acts of violence on behalf of the Government : the objects of these activities is to destroy the influence of governmental power, and to give continuous evidence of the possibility of struggling against it, and by this means to raise a revolutionary spirit among the people ; (c) the organization of secret societies and the binding of them about one centre ; (d) to acquire influential connections and position in the administration, in society, and among the people ; (e) it is necessary for the party (of *Narodnaya Volya*) to take the initiative in the revolution,[1] and not to wait until the people do it without the party.

In the separate issue of the programme as a manifesto there were added the following points :

" 1. Towards the Government, as an enemy, the end justifies the means ; we regard as permissible every means leading towards the end.

" 2. All oppositional elements, even although not associated with us, will find in us help and defence.

" 3. Individuals and social groups which are exterior to our struggle are regarded as neutral ; their persons and property will be respected.

" 4. Individuals and social groups consciously and actively helping the Government in our struggle with it, are regarded as committing a breach of neutrality, and therefore as enemies." [2]

These documents disclose sufficiently the point of view of the *Narodnaya Volya ;* there remains to be noticed the personalities of those who composed its inner circle, and the more important of the terroristic attempts in which they engaged.

The first " Executive Committee " seems to have been indefinitely self-appointed within the ranks of the *Narodněkě*, or adherents of the *V Narod* movement.[3] The leading spirit in this committee was Valerian Osinsky, whose first attempt at political crime is graphically described by Debogoriy-Mokrievich. " At night, on the 23rd February 1878, I was aroused by a slight tapping at my window. I found that the tapping was by Valerian, and

---

[1] Here there apparently followed a specific plan which was not published.
[2] Third edition of the Programme, 15th August 1881.
[3] See *supra*, p. 1022.

I hastened to open the door. He was accompanied by two comrades. The night was damp and cold, and I immediately returned to bed. Osinsky approached me, and, looking over his *pince-nez*, the glasses of which were damp, whispered, ' Kotlyarevsky is killed.' ' When ? ' I asked, feeling as if tar were being poured upon me, ' Just now. We are directly from there.' I pulled down the curtain at the window, so that the light could not be seen from the street, and began to inquire how it was done. Osinsky told me that they had overtaken Kotlyarevsky near his own house, and that they had fired upon him. After the first shot he fell, with an awful cry. They had fired one or two more shots, and had then run away. Ivichevich (one of the comrades of Osinsky) had proposed to make sure by stabbing Kotlyarevsky, but the others dissuaded him, because it was dangerous to remain. ' All the same, the affair is completed,' Osinsky said. I sat up in bed in silence, trying to digest the fact, and I confess that I could not digest it. A shiver ran down my spine, and a burdensome and awfully unpleasant feeling gradually took possession of me. ' Are you going to spend the night here ? ' I inquired. ' Necessarily ; where else could we go ? A terrible hunt is going on all over the streets.' ' Then let us go to bed. The light must be put out.' Beds were made on the floor, and the three lay down. I put out the lamp, and the room became dark. For a certain time I lay in silence, then I asked Osinsky by what streets they had escaped. When he had replied, I said, ' Very well, let us sleep.' ' But we cannot sleep.' My nerves were agitated ; my hands and feet became cold. I listened intently in the calmness of the night, but everything was still. After a time there came suddenly from a distance a continuous noise. ' They are beating the alarm.' Whenever the idea entered into my mind, I felt a new wave of unpleasant feeling, never before experienced by me, and involuntarily I rose slightly in order to bear it. It is difficult to define of what sort was this feeling. There was fear—fear not merely of responsibility and of punishment, but, so to say, of the very fact, as well as a feeling of satisfaction with this fact. I realized that for Osinsky this was his own immediate affair, but for me it was strange. ' Valerian ! do you hear ? ' I whispered. ' Yes ! ' as if the drumbeats had revived him. We fell into silence. ' Which of you is snoring so noisily ? ' I asked. ' It is Ivan ' (Ivichevich), answered

Osinsky. 'They are both sleeping.' I also began to slumber, but I heard Osinsky turning on the floor and coughing quietly. Next day it came out that Kotlyarevsky was not only not killed, but was not even wounded. His thick fur coat had saved him." [1]

Although this passage from real life ends in the spirit of comedy, it is most stimulating to the imagination and pregnant with suggestion of the psychology of the *Narodovoltsi*.

The change of attitude which had been in progress among the *Narodnēkē* in South Russia during 1878 had its counterpart among the *Narodnēkē* of St. Petersburg. On 4th August in that year General Mezentsev, chief of the Third Section, was killed by Sergey

[1] Debogoriy-Mokrievich, *op. cit.*, pp. 329–31. Valerian Osinsky (1853–1879) was the son of a landowner near Taganrog. His father, who had been an engineer in the service of the Government, was a man of liberal tendencies, who, becoming dejected and embittered, partly through defects in his own character, and partly through the unfavourable social conditions in which he felt himself involved, gave way to drink, and ill-treated his family. Young Osinsky, otherwise unhappy in his home life, enjoyed the advantage of a good library, although his education was miscellaneous rather than systematic. At an early age he was influenced by the writings of Dobrolubov, Pisarev, and Turgenev, and of other writers of the sixties. After studying at the Institute of Ways of Communication in St. Petersburg, he entered into the service of the Landvarovo-Romensky Railway, which was then under construction. The period was a bad one. Corruption on the part of officials and contractors was rampant, and the exploitation of the labourers, usual in such cases, was none the less that traditions of bondage relations still remained, and that there was a great surplus of labour (*cf.* p. 362). The conditions of the labourers affected Osinsky profoundly. At that moment the hopes of social reform were concentrated upon the *Zemstvos*, and Osinsky returned to St. Petersburg determined to study social science in order that he might be able to take some share in *Zemstvo* administration. After three years of such studies he became a clerk in the Rostov *Zemstvo* bureau. Here also he was disappointed. He found the *Zemstvo* controlled by people who did not desire any change in the existing system. Reflecting that this inertia was reproduced in the higher spheres of State administration, his mind was prepared for the admission of extreme views. While he was under the influence of disappointed enthusiasm he became acquainted with the ideas of Lavrov (*cf.* p. 101 *ff.*), and joined a "circle" devoted to his views. But even here he was disappointed. The propaganda of Lavrov was too mild and too slow. In 1875, at the age of twenty-two, he joined the *V Narod* party, and in 1877, and 1878 gradually drifted to the extreme wing of that party, becoming eventually one of the *Narodovoltsi*. He exercised a considerable influence over his contemporaries in that group, and came to be known as "the empirical creator of terrorism." He was arrested in May 1879, and accused of forming a secret society, having for its object the overthrowal of the State. When asked to what class and profession he belonged, Osinsky boldly announced himself as a social revolutionary. He was found guilty by the military court before which he was brought, and was hanged on 15th May 1879. See *Narodnaya Volya*, No. 2 ; *Literature*, &c., p. 101–16.

Kravchinsky,[1] who immediately drove off in a carriage and escaped. One of the consequences of this act was the promulgation of an ukase which transferred cases of political murder and attempts at murder from the ordinary criminal courts to courts martial. Further assassinations and attempted assassinations of high personages followed at intervals throughout 1879. On 9th February 1879 Prince Dmitri N. Kropotkin, Governor-General of Kharkov, was assassinated by Goldenberg. On 12th March the successor of General Mezentsev, General Drenteln, was killed by Mirsky. On 2nd April Soloviev fired five shots at the Tsar Alexander II without wounding him. The Government now took fresh measures. The whole country was divided into six general governorships, and systematic attempts were made everywhere to hunt down the revolutionaries; but these strenuous measures seemed to serve only to increase their numbers and their boldness. From 17th June to 21st June 1879 what was called a congress was held at Lipetsk.[2] To this meeting there came leading members of the *Zemlya ē Volya* party, as well as *Narodnēkē* of many shades of opinion. It was decided to meet shortly at Voronej with a worked-out plan of action.[3]

The outcome of the Lipetsk-Voronej meeting was the election of a terrorist committee composed of Tikhomirov,[4] Frolenko, and Alexander Mikhaelov.[5] But the chief advocate of terrorism at

---

[1] Better known as Sergius Stepniak. Cf. *supra*, p. 110.   [2] See *supra*, p. 111.

[3] A. Tun, *History of the Revolutionary Movement in Russia* (Paris, 1904), p. 198.

[4] Tikhomirov, who took at this time so leading a part in the terrorist camp, afterwards recanted, became an official, and afterwards became editor of the *Moscow Gazette*.

[5] Alexander Mikhaelov was born in 1855 or 1856 at Putivl, in Kurskaya *gub*. His father was a land surveyor. Like many others who became conspicuous in the revolutionary movement, he began his career as an agitator while he was a schoolboy. He organized a " self-education " circle and a secret library in the Gymnasium of Putivl, and there also led a revolt against his teachers, and engaged actively in spreading popular pamphlets among the people. These activities interfered so much with his studies that he was obliged to leave the classical course at the Gymnasium and to enter a *Real Schule* in another town. In 1875 he entered the Technological Institute at St. Petersburg, and immediately began to organize " self-education " groups in that institution. In a short time he had succeeded in forming a students' society, with branches in various universities. Again his activities resulted in neglect of his studies, and in a few months he was rusticated. He spent the winter of 1875-1876 in an " Odyssey " over all Russia. In the first instance he went to Kiev, where he made the acquaintance of the revolutionary groups then concentrated there. Among them he found propagandists, rioters (*buntari*), and Jacobins, the groups in which the

the Voronej meeting was Andrey Jelyàbov,[1] who startled the older and more moderate *Narodnēkē* by his advocacy of what appeared to them to be purely political terrorism. Jelyàbov's appearance, indeed, almost resulted in the fruitless dissolution of the meeting. In the end a compromise was effected. The programme remained

revolutionary party was at that time divided. But the division of the oppositional forces disappointed him. He saw in it the impossibility of creating a great All-Russian movement. In Kiev there were only generals and officers ; there were no rank and file wherewith to form an effective force. In the summer of 1876 he returned to St. Petersburg and frequented the " communes " (*obtschina*) or meetings of students. He also became acquainted with the then newly founded society of the " Troglodites," which afterwards became the *Zemlya ē Volya* (Land and Liberty). In the spring of 1877 he joined the stream of *Narodnēkē*, and went "into the people." Mikhaelov, with Olga Natanson and other members of the central group, went to Saratov. Mikhaelov established himself at the house of a dissenting sectarian (*raskolnik*), and undertook the study of the Scriptures and of the dogmas of the sect for the purpose of becoming a sectarian teacher. At that time and for long after many revolutionaries entertained the idea that sectarianism offered a favourable field for revolutionary propaganda, because the sectarians were traditionally opposed to Orthodoxy, and therefore to the Government. (Stepniak went so far as to think, as he told the writer, that the revolution might be brought about through the growth of religious dissent.) This anticipation was, however, not realised. Saratov became the scene of a police battue, and Mikhaelov went to St. Petersburg, where he became the leading spirit in the *Zemlya ē Volya* (Tun, *op. cit.*, pp. 145–7). In April and May 1878, in discussions upon party organisation, Mikhaelov urged a complete change involving high centralisation and submission of the local groups to the central committee. On 15th September 1878 nearly all the members of the *Zemlya ē Volya* were arrested. Of fifty or sixty members, only five or six remained at liberty. But among these was Mikhaelov. With characteristic energy he set himself to rehabilitate the party. " He collected money, fabricated passports, and established connections," so that the *Zemlya ē Volya* not only did not fall to pieces but continued (its underground printing office having been saved) to issue its organ regularly. Mikhaelov himself was everywhere. He lived like " a Red Indian on the war-path " (Tun, *op. cit.*, p. 254). He thought of everything and for everybody. He knew every one of the spies, and spied upon them. " Russians are not, as a rule, good conspirators ; Sophie Perovskaya and Mikhaelov were rare exceptions " (Stepniak, *Underground Russia* (London Russian edition, 1893), p. 166). Eventually Mikhaelov was captured by the police. He was one of the twenty-two who were prosecuted on 9th February 1882, and with nine others he was sentenced to death. His sentence was, however, commuted. In his speech before the court he admitted that he was a member of a revolutionary organization. " The struggle," he said, " has made us personal enemies of His Majesty the Emperor " (*Literature of Soc.-Rev. Party, N.-V.*, p. 589).

[1] Andrey Jelyàbov (1850–1881) was born in the Crimea. His parents were *dvorovie lyudē* (domestic serfs). Among his first impressions were the flogging of his uncle and the dishonouring of his aunt. His grandfather, a *raskolnik* (dissenting sectarian) taught him the Old Slavonic or ecclesiastical alphabet and obliged him to commit the Psalter to memory. The *pomyet-schēk* (landowner) to whom his family belonged was attracted by the boy,

unchanged; but it was agreed that the activity of the struggle against the Government should be increased, and that in the event of the infliction of capital punishment for propaganda, " the tyrant should be punished also." [1]

The Executive Committee, which was composed of terrorists

and taught him the modern Russian or civil alphabet, and afterwards sent him to school, where he distinguished himself alike for his industry and for his bad conduct. He entered the University in 1868, and soon became a leader in a demonstration against a professor. For this he was expelled. He was permitted to return ; but again, for a similar offence, he had to submit to expulsion. After he left the University, he became an adherent of Necháiev (cf. *supra*, p. 75). In 1872–1873 he came to be associated with the less aggressive " circle " of Tchaikovsky (*cf.* pp. 75–76). Under the influence of the *V Narod* movement, he went " into the people " and sold cucumbers in the market. But work of this kind was unsuited to his passionate and eager disposition. Rapid and even dangerous movement was necessary for him. He was always ready for an exploit which involved unusual risk. Between 1873 and 1877, however, he lived for the most part in his native village, married, and worked as a peasant, but nevertheless engaged in propaganda. He was a man of powerful physique ; and notwithstanding his education, fragmentary as it was, he exhibited in his character many peasant traits. When the prosecution of the 193 took place in 1877 (*cf.* p. 106) he was among the accused. After undergoing imprisonment for seven months in St. Petersburg, he was released. This experience made him more bitterly hostile towards the Government than he had been formerly. Up till this period, save for his brief connection with the conspiracy of Necháiev, he had allied himself with the more moderate groups of the revolutionary party. Now he threw himself into the active wing. He had made himself conspicuous at the meetings at Lipetsk and at Voronej. In the autumn of 1879 he laid the mine at Aleksandrovsk, which on 19th November 1879 was intended to destroy the train by which Alexander II was travelling. The attempt was a failure, and Jelyàbov went immediately to St. Petersburg, where he was placed by the committee, in charge of the preparation of dynamite. He organized the plan for the assassination of Alexander II ; but was arrested on 27th February 1881, two days before the assassination took place. He is reported to have heard in the cell in which he was confined the explosions on the Katherine Canal, which told of the carrying out of his design. Jelyàbov was executed, along with those who had actually accomplished the deed. Jelyàbov seems in some fashion to have modelled himself upon Taras Bulba, the Cossack leader immortalized by Gogol. He hated the principle of despotism—the uncontrolled power of one person—and he entertained the belief that in liberating the peasants the Tsar had merely the intention to increase the power of the Government, and to increase its income by means of the exploitation of the peasants, while at the same time the rising power of the nobles was curtailed. Muraviev the public prosecutor at Jelyàbov's trial characterized him as " a typical conspirator in his gesticulations, mimicry, movements, speeches, and theatrical effects. That he has cleverness, talents, and acuteness cannot be denied." Stepniak makes Jelyàbov, under the name of Andrey Kojukhov, the hero of his remarkable novel, *The Career of a Nihilist* (London, 1889). For Jelyàbov's career, see A. Tun, *History of the Revolutionary Movement in Russia* [Paris ?], 1904 ; and Debogoriy-Mokrievich, *op. cit.*

[1] A. Tun, *op. cit.*, p. 199.

drawn from various groups, was organized in three sections, according to the degree of confidence.[1] Jelyàbov, for example, was of the inner circle. The members of this circle selected their agents and devised the methods of attack.[2] The committee entered upon its terroristic programme at once. During the summer elaborate preparations for the destruction of the imperial train which was to convey the Tsar from the Crimea to St. Petersburg were made. Three mines were laid—one at Aleksandrovsk, a second at Moscow, and a third at Odessa, in case the Tsar made a detour by that city. The chief mine was at Aleksandrovsk, where it was intended to throw the imperial train into a ravine. In October 1879 Jelyàbov purchased a piece of land adjoining the railway at Aleksandrovsk, ostensibly for a leather factory. From this land two mines were driven beneath the railway line.[3] The train passed on the 19th November, but owing to some defect in the mechanism the anticipated explosion did not take place.

At the same time two revolutionists, Hartmann[4] and Sophie Perovskaya,[5] took a house in the neighbourhood of Moscow and pretended to carry on trade. The house was otherwise occupied

---

[1] This was the account given by Goldenberg, who assassinated Prince D. N. Kropotkin ; his statement was objected to by Mikhaelov. *Cf.* Tun, *op. cit.*, p. 208.

[2] Their secrets were well guarded. None of the attempts upon Alexander II were betrayed to the police. *Cf.* Tun, *op. cit.*, p. 208.

[3] Tun, *op. cit.*, p. 210.

[4] Hartmann was the son of a German colonist at Archangel. He became a village clerk near Saratov. Because of his knowledge of chemistry he was enlisted in the Moscow affair. He escaped to the United States, and afterwards went to England, where he was employed as an electrical engineer.

[5] Sophie Perovskaya (1854–1881) belonged to the higher aristocracy. Her grandfather, Leo Perovsky, was Minister of Interior (cf. *supra*, vol. i. p. 369.) ; her father was the Governor of Pskov ; her uncle won some of the Central Asiatic provinces for the Tsar. The family of Perovsky was the younger branch of that of Razumovsky, which owed its origin to a morganatic union of the Empress Elizabeth. Sophie Perovskaya, like many other Russian revolutionaries, suffered in her early years from parental neglect and tyranny. She was not taught to read until she was eight years of age, and her education was assumed to be finished when she was fourteen. She began, however, to read serious books on her own account, and when the family removed to St. Petersburg from the Crimea, where they had been residing, she went to the Gymnasium, where she became acquainted with several girls who afterwards entered the ranks of the revolution. Her father objected to such friendships, and at the age of sixteen she left her home, and soon afterwards joined the Tchaikovsky circle, going " to the people " in the *V Narod* movement. She prepared herself to become a village teacher, and went from village to village in Tverskaya *gub.* and elsewhere, sometimes suffering great privations. In November 1873 she was arrested, but was liberated on a bail of 5000 rubles.

by a number of men who made the excavation. On the 19th November the mine was exploded at a signal from Sophie Perovskaya; but the train that was blown up was not the imperial train, which passed safely to St. Petersburg. The perpetrators of both of the attempts escaped.

Undismayed by these failures, the terrorists organized more definitely than formerly the *Narodnaya Volya* party, and proceeded to the execution of a still more elaborate and bold design, the preliminary stages of which had previously been in progress in case the attempts on the railway line should fail. This design consisted in the blowing up of the imperial family in their own palace. Its accomplishment was entrusted to Stepàn Khaltùrin.[1] Khaltùrin had organized the North Russian Labour Union,[2] and had published a newspaper as its organ. His printing-office was visited by the police, and his work appeared to be destroyed. He seems then to have conceived the idea of putting an end to the life of the Tsar. Khaltùrin's trade was that of a varnisher, and he was a workman of unusual skill. He therefore readily obtained employment in the Winter Palace. In October 1879, during the absence of the imperial family at their palace of Livadia in the

She then decided to be a nurse. After having taken a course in nursing at Simferopol she associated herself once more with the *V Narod* groups. She was one of the 193, but was released, and was sent into " administrative exile " in Olonetskaya *gub.* She escaped from her station, and returned to St. Petersburg in 1878. There she joined *Zemlya e Volya.* At Voronej she agreed with both parties, urged the continuance of agitation among the people, and at the same time urged the assassination of the Tsar, arguing that the latter occurrence would pass unnoticed unless the agitation among the people were continued. Yet she did not join either the *Chorno Peredyeltsi* or the terrorists, although she helped both. Her share in the explosion near Moscow (19th November 1879) is described in the text. After this event she returned to St. Petersburg and offered to join the *Chorno Peredyeltsi* if they would consent to organize a large movement among the people. They declined, and she said, " Then I have only to join the *Narodnaya Volya!* " On 1st March 1881, she gave the signal for the assassination of Alexander II. She was not arrested at the time, and up till the moment of her arrest on 10th March she probably might have escaped abroad. But she did not seek to do so, either from fatalism or from love of Jelyàbov, who had already been arrested before the attempt took place. Sophie Perovskaya was hanged on 3rd April 1881.

[1] Stepàn Khaltùrin, one of the organizers of the North Russian Working Men's Union, was himself a working man. Patient, obedient, and resourceful, he seems to have carried out the plan of Jelyàbov. An unknown revolutionist was hanged in Odessa on 22nd March 1882. He was afterwards discovered to be Khaltùrin (*Literature of the Soc.-Rev. Party, N.-V.*, p. 610).

[2] Cf. *supra*, p. 113.

Crimea, Khaltùrin had opportunities of examining the imperial apartments. He discovered that the private dining-room was above the carpenters' workshop, although separated from it by one floor, the intervening room being occupied by the guard. Kvyatkovsky, one of the members of the Executive Committee, who maintained communications with Khaltùrin, was arrested. A plan of the Winter Palace, with the dining-room marked with a cross, was found in his possession. This circumstance led to searches in the basement of the palace. A gendarme was posted in the carpenters' workshop, and the guards were warned to be careful. These precautions delayed, but did not prevent Khaltùrin's proceedings. The dynamite had to be brought into the palace in very small quantities. Khaltùrin stored it under his pillow.[1] Meanwhile he continued with his varnishing work, with so great satisfaction to the authorities of the palace that he received a present of a hundred rubles. Otherwise he was not idle. He came to be on very friendly terms with the guard, and the gendarme on duty in the carpenters' workshop even wanted him to marry his daughter. Khaltùrin is said to have felt that in any case many lives would have to be sacrificed, and therefore he wanted to have at his disposal as much dynamite as possible, in order to make sure of the death of the chief victim. Jelyàbov is said to have insisted upon haste, and, moreover, the risk of discovery became greater every day. The guard was stronger and more careful. The dynamite cartridges were put in the corner of the main wall of the palace beneath the dining-room on 5th February 1880, and shortly after the hour of dinner the fuse was fired. The explosion committed tremendous havoc — ten people were killed and fifty-three were injured; but the Tsar escaped. He had been late for dinner, having waited for the arrival of a high personage. Khaltùrin also escaped into the palace yard before the explosion took place.[2]

Meanwhile, the Government had been endeavouring to cope with the forces of the revolution by the employment of spies, and by frequent wholesale arrests of persons who were betrayed or who were suspected of having revolutionary literature in their posses-

---

[1] Khaltùrin is reported to have suffered from headaches in consequence of evaporation from the nitro-glycerine cartridges.
[2] Tun, *op. cit.*, pp. 212–4.

sion. On the other hand, they were endeavouring to counteract the influence of the *V Narod* movement amongst the peasantry by contradicting the rumours of a redistribution of the land, which had obtained currency among the peasants. The circular[1] of Makov, the Minister of the Interior, was issued with this intention. Referring to the rumours, the Minister says that, on the instructions of his Imperial Majesty, he has to announce that " neither now, nor at any future time, will any additional amount of land be added to peasant lots. Under our laws upon the right of ownership, such an injustice as the taking of land from its lawful owner and transferring it to another cannot be permitted. The peasants themselves own the land given to them under the Act of 19th February 1861. Such being the case, according to law, they are peacefully profiting by their lots, and they have the right to obtain more land from other owners on terms voluntarily agreed upon with them. By this means the laws leave everyone his own, and do not permit the appropriation of the things of others. Thus the peace of the State is secured. The false rumours about the repartition of the land, and about the distribution of supplementary lots for the benefit of the peasants, are disseminated in the villages by evil-intentioned persons whose interest lies in the agitation of the people and in the disturbance of the social peace. Unfortunately these rumours are frequently believed by simple-minded people who propagate them, not suspecting their falsity and not thinking of the misfortunes into which they might themselves fall, dragging others with them. In accordance with the will of the Emperor, I therefore warn the inhabitants of villages against these insidiously inspired rumours, and I impose upon all village, volost, and police officials the duty to observe vigilantly the appearance of evil-minded newsmongers, and to explain and prevent from spreading these injurious devices."

The wisdom of the issue of such a circular is, from any point of view, extremely doubtful. It increased rather than allayed the unrest among the peasants, whose demands for more land were becoming urgent, and it gave into the hands of the *Narodněkě* fresh material for agitation.

The explosion at the Winter Palace led immediately to a change in general policy on the part of the Government. In the weeks

[1] Dated 16th July 1879.

immediately following the 9th February 1880, Count Lóris Mélikóv [1] was appointed to a practical dictatorship, and Count Pahlen and Count Dmitri Tolstoy were dismissed. It seemed to be necessary to provide a lightning conductor to draw from the Tsar the revolutionary electrical discharge. In spite of their repeated failures to accomplish what they aimed at, the revolutionists had contributed to bring about a decided change in the political situation. In the " higher spheres " people began to talk about a National Assembly. In spite of the formal maintenance of the self-existent autocracy, efforts were made to rally important elements of society to the support of the throne. Counsel was sought of the leading people in St. Petersburg, interviews were given to journalists, and above all, rumours were set afloat of the approaching dissolution of the celebrated Third Section—the political police.[2] Lóris Mélikóv had the general reputation of being a Liberal, and those who believed in the desirability of a National Assembly began to build their hopes upon him. During the period of revolutionary quiescence after the Winter Palace explosion, there were no attempts upon the life of the Tsar. Mélikóv's dictatorship in effect ceased, and he became simply Minister of the Interior. Mélikóv had prepared a constitutional scheme, but the Tsar vacillated and hesitated. He proposed to leave it to his successor, in order that a constitution might be his gift to the Russian people. In February 1881 an attempt was made upon the life of Mélikóv,[3] and at the same time Mélikóv intimated to the Tsar that preparations were being made by the Executive Committee for another attempt upon his life. Alexander then decided that an Assembly should be convoked, which should comprise delegates from the provinces. He is said to have called it *Assemblée des Notables*, under the influence of the idea which seems to have possessed him, that his fate would be the same as that of Louis XVI.[4] The scheme was prepared, and after some hesitation and " a final warning " from Lóris Mélikóv, the Tsar on the morning of Sunday, 1st March 1881, ordered it to be placed before the Council of State. Mélikóv endeavoured to persuade the Tsar not to go into the streets of St.

---

[1] Lóris Mélikóv was of Armenian extraction. He had been chief of Tverskaya Oblast and Governor of Kharkovskaya *gub*. Although his administration in these posts had not been without severity, he was generally supposed to be of liberal tendencies.

[2] Cf. *infra*, p. 573.

[3] By Molodetsky, who was hanged for the attempt on 22nd February 1881.

[4] Kropotkin, *Memoirs*, p. 431.

Petersburg on that day, his agents having warned him of the probability of an attempt upon his life ;[1] but the Tsar desired to visit his cousin, the Grand Duchess Catherine (daughter of Elena Pavlovna, the advocate of emancipation).[2] He went, and on his way back to the palace he met his fate. A bomb thrown under his iron-clad carriage injured it, and killed several of his Circassian escort. The Tsar, who possessed the traditional courage of the Romanovs, alighted from the carriage, in spite of the protests of the coachman, and approached the wounded Circassians. He even spoke to Rysakov, the youth who had thrown the bomb. He passed another of the conspirators, Grēnevetsky, who threw another bomb. So close was the Tsar to his assassin that the bomb killed both. According to Prince Kropotkin, the guards whose duty it was to attend the Tsar, and who had survived the first explosion, had disappeared before the second bomb was thrown. The Tsar was raised from the snow by cadets from the School of Pages, was placed by them in a sleigh, covered with the cloak and cap of one of them, and conveyed to the Palace.[3] He died in the afternoon. Had the Tsar escaped the bombs which killed him and his escort, it is known that there were others in the hands of several revolutionaries who were near the spot where he fell. Moreover, Little Sadovaya and the bridge over the canal were both mined. Jelyàbov had laid his plans with skill and the Executive Committee had accomplished its design.

After the assassination of Alexander II the numerically insignificant forces of the *Narodnaya Volya* were depleted by arrests, followed by imprisonments and executions. Those who were immediately executed on account of their participation in the conspiracy for the assassination of the Tsar were : Jelyàbov,[4] Sophie Perovskaya,[5] Kēbalchēch,[6] Timothy Mikhaelov, and Nikolai Rysa-

---

[1] Jelyàbov, the organizer of the attempt, had been arrested on the previous Friday (cf. *supra*, p. 125 *n.*).

[2] Kropotkin, *loc. cit.* See also *supra*, vol. i. 377 *n.* &c.

[3] Prince Kropotkin relates that one of the terrorists (Emeliánov), who even had a bomb under his arm, went to the assistance of the wounded Tsar and aided the cadets in placing him in the sleigh (*loc. cit.*, p. 432).

[4] See *supra*, p. 124.   [5] See *supra*, p. 126.

[6] Nikolaï Kēbalchēch (*c.* 1850–1881) was a Little Russian. In the early seventies he was a student in a military medical high school. He organized there " circles " of self-education among the students, as well as lectures on political economy, &c. In 1875 a girl friend, hearing of a domiciliary visit of the police, asked Kēbalchēch to take charge of some books which had been sent to her from abroad. Kēbalchēch took them ; a few days afterwards he

kov.[1] Grĕnevetsky, who threw the bomb which killed the Tsar, was also killed by the explosion. Nikolai Sablĕn committed suicide upon being arrested. The two most active survivors of the Executive Committee, and of its immediate outer circle, seem to have been Bogdanòvich [2] and Khaltùrin, who began at once to organize plans for the escape of members of the party who were in prison, and in administrative exile in Siberia. The partial success of these plans enabled them to recruit their ranks to some extent. But these ranks were again thinned through the activities of Sudeikin, the astute chief of the Third Section. Sudeikin adopted the plan of visiting the accused members of the *Narodnaya Volya* in prison, and of endeavouring to convert them into spies upon their former comrades. He succeeded in this design in the case of a revolutionary called Degaiëv, by whose means a large number of members of the *Narodnaya Volya* and their sympathizers were arrested.[3] Yet simultaneously with these occurrences there was proceeding a considerable increase of revolutionary organization in the army. Degaiëv and another spy, Zlatopolsky, turned their attention to this, Degaiëv having been himself formerly an officer. The result of his operations at Kronstadt and elsewhere was the arrest of about two hundred officers.[4] The members of the Executive Committee who

received himself a domiciliary visit, and he was put in prison. After having been in prison for three years, he was tried and sentenced to *two months'* imprisonment. The prison affected his health seriously; but it also transformed him into a revolutionary. When he emerged in 1878, he began to study explosives. The use of dynamite as a revolutionary agent seems to have been suggested by him. He studied the literature of the subject in French, German, and English, and although he was not regarded as a good conspirator so far as practice was concerned, his theoretical knowledge and his facility in rapid calculation, *e.g.* of the quantities of explosive necessary for a given operation, and of the least expensive and most convenient method of arriving at a given result, were of the greatest service to the Executive Committee. His time was wholly spent in the laboratory making experiments and fabricating the cartridges for terroristic attempts. For some time before his arrest he had been devising a flying-machine, which was to be operated with a powerful motor actuated by a high explosive. He was arrested on 17th March 1881, and on 3rd April was executed. (See *Russian Revolutionaries* (issued by the Socialist-Revolutionary Party), ii., Nikolaï Ivanovich Kĕbalchĕch (Paris ?), 1903.

[1] Rysakov was a boy of nineteen years.

[2] Bogdanòvich had controlled the mine under Little Sadovaya Street in St. Petersburg on 1st March 1881.

[3] As a result of the activity of Sudeikin upwards of seventy were arrested in the summer and autumn of 1881. In 1882 further arrests followed (Tun, *op. cit.*, p. 310).

[4] Tun, *op. cit.*, p. 317.

had escaped arrest up till the end of 1882 were now all abroad, excepting Vera Figner, who remained at her post. She was arrested at Kharkov on 10th February 1883. These wholesale arrests put an end to the activities of the Executive Committee in Russia ; but they also suggested to those who were abroad the presence of a traitor in their ranks. Spies had occasionally made their way into revolutionary circles ; but the traitorous defection of a trusted member of the party was previously probably altogether unknown. Eventually the principal traitor was found to be Degaiëv, who thought it expedient to leave Russia. He went to Geneva, where he was discovered.[1] Fearful that his life would be endangered he offered to return to St. Petersburg and to assassinate Sudeikin. The assassination was committed by him, or with his connivance, in his house in St. Petersburg, on 16th December 1883.[2] The arrests resulting from the operations of Degaiëv are understood not to have affected exclusively those who were engaged in conspiracy, or even in propaganda. He is alleged to have organized " self-education " circles of youths, and then to have betrayed them to the police.[3] These events, together with the effect of the assassination of the Tsar upon the minds of the groups from which the revolutionary elements were recruited, the general influence of governmental activity and of the political reaction, and the beginnings of active industrial development combined to put an end altogether to the operations of the Executive Committee. Yet in January 1884 the emigrants of the *Narodnaya Volya* group assembled in Paris to devise means of reorganization. The result of this meeting was the election of a new committee, of which the principal member was Lopatin, " an old revolutionary, well known and very popular." [4] Lopatin returned to Russia and organized a number of groups, principally of students in Moscow, Kiev, and more importantly in Rostov-on-Don. Slenderly as the *Narodnaya Volya* had been supported either by the working men of the towns or by the peasants, the support given to the new organization was still more slender.

---

[1] Tun says by Tikhomirov, who was then in the ranks of the *Narodnaya Volya* (cf. *supra*, p. 123).

[2] The Socialist-Revolutionary party afterwards considered that the acceptance of Degaiëv's offer was unwise from a revolutionary point of view.

[3] For later instances of this so-called " provocation," see *infra*, 188 and 572.

[4] Tun, *op. cit.*, p. 334. Lopatin was tried in 1887 for complicity in the murder of Sudeikin. He was sent to Schlüsselburg, and was released in 1906.

Lopatin was, moreover, arrested in the Nevsky Prospekt, St. Petersburg, on 7th October 1884. Upon him was found a list of sympathizers. He attempted, unsuccessfully, to destroy this list by swallowing it. About five hundred persons were afterwards arrested. The revolutionary forces were thus once more defeated and disorganized. Yet the revolutionary movement of this period was not yet over. Ivanov, Orgich, Bogoraz, and others attempted to organize a fresh group. They held a meeting at Ekaterinoslav in September 1885. Throughout the autumn preparations went on for another onslaught upon the Government. Dynamite bombs were manufactured, and new relations were established with sympathizers in the army. In 1886 Orgich was arrested at Taganrog, and his printing-office was seized ; the organization was conducted for a short time by Bogoraz, but nothing was accomplished. With these futile efforts the *Narodnaya Volya* came finally to an end. A small group of independent terrorists, representing themselves as a fraction of the *Narodnaya Volya*, were arrested in St. Petersburg on 1st March 1887, with bombs in their possession. They were executed on 8th May 1887, and with them died the last expiring embers of the revolutionary movement which began in 1879.

CHAPTER VIII

THE REACTION

THE dictatorship of Count Lóris Mélikóv failed of its apparent object. The struggle against the Tsar in person had continued, and after repeated attempts he had eventually fallen. Alexander III was at first apparently inclined to adopt the project of a constitution prepared by Lóris Mélikóv, but he speedily came under the influence of his former tutor, Pobyedonóstsev,[1] then Ober-Procurator of the Holy Synod. Pobyedonóstsev was an able man and a jurist of high reputation, but his belief in autocracy was as profound as his scepticism of all forms of democracy. To him the movement of Western Europe was towards decay and not towards progress. His ideal of government was Asiatic rather than European. Under such influence the way was open for the victory of reaction, and this victory came speedily. A certain exhaustion of spirit which supervened among the Liberal elements after the assassination of the Tsar, and a widespread fear lest organized government should be rendered impossible by continued assassination, must be regarded as accounting for the weakness of the resistance to a reactionary policy.[2] Moreover, there appeared a general disposition to give the new Tsar his opportunity, a phenomenon which, under similar circumstances, is almost invariable in Russian history. Yet the ceremonial of the coronation was postponed until two years

[1] Constantine Petrovich Pobyedonóstsev (1827–1907), author of *Course of Civil Law*, 3 vols. (St. Petersburg, 1868–1875), and *Reflections of a Russian Statesman* (translated, London, 1898).

[2] Yet those who had been looking forward to some form of constitution were reluctant to resign the struggle. According to a pamphlet published in London (mentioned by Prince Kropotkin in his *Memoirs*, p. 435) and purporting to contain the posthumously available papers of Lóris Mélikóv, General Skobelov (famous for his assault on the redoubts at Plevna on 11th September 1877) proposed to Mélikóv and to Ignatiëv to arrest Alexander III, and to compel him to sign a constitutional manifesto. Ignatiëv is said to have denounced the scheme, and thus to have secured his appointment as minister. (Kropotkin, *op. cit.*, p. 436.)

after the accession of Alexander III, for the administration was nervous and apprehensive of hostility. In course of time the revolutionary party, formidable in the intelligent and self-regardless utilization of its numerically insignificant forces, was destroyed or dispersed, and the wave of reaction gradually overwhelmed the national life.

The revolutionary movement had been recruited largely from the universities and professional institutions, medical and technical colleges, and the like. The government of these institutions had been retained in the hands of the Minister of Education, but prior to the period of reaction the teaching bodies enjoyed a considerable amount of autonomy. In 1884 the universities were completely subordinated,[1] even in academic affairs, to the Minister. The control of examinations was removed from the professors and transferred to commissions appointed by the Government. Students were forbidden to pass from one academic course to another without permission from the Government nominees. These also were required to advise the students not to be carried away by crude doctrines, and not to permit themselves to be distracted by studies other than those to which they were assigned. The wearing of uniform was insisted upon strictly. For the purpose of excluding Jews, the State stipendium, or scholarship stipend, was to be paid only to Christians. Professors of liberal or independent tendencies were either dismissed, like Maxime Kovalevsky,[2] or their positions were rendered so uncomfortable that they resigned, like Stasyulevich. In the gymnasia the pupils were forbidden to read any " civil books " (*i.e.* non-theological books) without the consent of the authorities. In the theological seminaries the pupils were forbidden to leave their houses after five o'clock in the evening. The possession of an unauthorized book or the suspicion of politically unorthodox opinions, if discovered, resulted in imprisonment, and sometimes in bodily punishment. Many gymnasium pupils committed suicide. The public elementary schools were not suppressed, but efforts were made to replace them by schools under

---

[1] By the statute of Delyánov, Minister of Education, 13th August 1884. The project of the statute had been prepared by Count Dmitri Tolstoy. The majority of the Council of State was opposed to the measure, but it was nevertheless passed into law. Brockhaus and Ephron, *Russia* (St. Petersburg, 1900), p. 390.

[2] Editor of *Vestnik Evropy*.

the control of the clergy, in which education was practically confined to theology and vocal music. Wherever there was a clerical school, a " civil " school could not be established without the consent of the bishop.

In the law courts the principle of the irremovability of judges was abrogated. Judges who did not meet the wishes of the administration were moved from one place to another or dismissed. The jury system was modified, and the practice of changing the venue, when it was unlikely that a conviction could be secured, was extended. Local officials, eager to propitiate the Government and to secure promotion, utilized these measures to their own advantage.

It is true that even democratic countries are not without experience of many of these measures, that most governments have interfered with the course of justice, that the venue has been changed in political causes, that criticism of governmental action has frequently resulted in condign punishment; but in the case of Russia a self-existent autocracy lay behind the measures, and they were adopted avowedly rather for the maintenance of that autocracy than for the benefit of the people. Moreover, proceedings which are in democratic countries after all only occasional, and, when they occur, are openly criticized and generally condemned, became in Russia normal incidents. Behind the acts of repression there lay the desire to determine the direction of the development of the national life and to exclude influences which might come from the progress of Western Europe. " In Russia the Government fears the current of fresh air which comes eastwards, and would like to close all the windows." [1]

The destructive effect of the reaction upon the incipient organization of the artisans in towns into groups analogous to trade unions has already been noticed.[2] The policy of the Government undoubtedly rendered the exploitation of the working class easier, and therefore more frequent. Between 1880 and 1885 the depression of trade which had been affecting industrial Europe since 1876 had not been without influence in Russia, now being gradually drawn into the industrial and commercial network. Prices fell

---

[1] *Narodnaya Volya*, Nos. 11-12, October 1885; *Literature*, &c., p. 756.
[2] See *supra*, pp. 106 and 127, and Svyatlovsky, *The Trade Union Movement in Russia* (St. Petersburg, 1908), pp. 11-12.

sharply, and, high protection notwithstanding, profits disappeared and wages remained low or diminished.   Large numbers of work-men were thrown out of employment.   The conditions of labour revealed the survival of pre-Emancipation oppression—they were, indeed, frequently destructive of human dignity—while the con-ditions of life were often debasing.   Prohibited from combination by the Government,[1] the workmen were at the mercy of their employers.   Inevitably the workmen were disposed to throw the blame of every evil upon the Government.   The employers on their side were disposed to censure the Government whenever it failed, as it frequently did, to make immediate military dispositions to protect their property.   The centralization of authority had its counterpart in local weakness.

The peasants urgently demanded more land, but the circular of Makov[2] brusquely refused any governmental assistance in procuring it.   The congestion of the population in Central and Southern Russia, and the scantiness of the population in the vast cultivable area of Siberia, suggested a generous system of coloniza-tion ; but there were at that time inadequate means of communi-cation, and the different departments of the Government could not agree upon a colonizing policy.   At the same moment free grants of land were offered in Siberia, and emigration from certain *guberni* was prohibited.[3]   Peasants were even refused permission to leave their villages.[4]   Notwithstanding these conditions, flights of peasants became frequent.   Many wandered they knew not whither.   Great masses of peasants, with their wives and children, suffering from lack of food and clothing, wandered over the regions of Rostov, Saratov, Samara, and Ekaterinburg.   Some found their way to America.   In the Caucasus some peasants squatted upon free lands and built houses upon them.   Their houses were destroyed and the peasants were ruined.

On the non-Russian elements in the Russian Empire the Govern-ment re-enforced its disciplinary measures.   In the Baltic Pro-

[1] The situation was similar to that which existed in England in the first twenty years of the nineteenth century.

[2] See *supra*, p. 129.

[3] In Voronej the Governor forbade emigration altogether.   Peasants were forbidden, without special permission, to go to the Caucasus, where there were free lands.

[4] Two circulars were issued, on 22nd April and 7th May 1882, forbidding emigration without special permission.

vinces the Russian language replaced German in the law courts and in the schools. In Poland restrictions were imposed upon the acquisition of land by Poles. The Bank of Poland was closed, and branches of the State Bank of Russia were established in place of them. The Russification of Finland began.[1]

In brief, the Government was doing its utmost " to turn the nation into human dust."[2] Had the nation submitted tamely to this process, it would, as Professor Kluchevsky said of the Russia of an earlier period, have been lacking in the elements of human dignity.[3] The demoralization of the Government had its counterpart in the demoralization of the people.

Freedom is not invariably wisely used, for the mere absence of restriction permits growth in all directions. On the other hand, restriction in one direction induces, and sometimes forces, growth in other directions. The insistent thwarting of movement in Russia reproduced for many the conditions of a prison, involving abnormal mental phenomena. Mania of all kinds resulted from the widespread psychological disturbance. Suicide became epidemic. There were many outbursts of religious fanaticism.[4] New sects made their appearance.[5] A false Tsar, a characteristic of many movements of political unrest in Russia, was not wanting. This man appeared in Bogoduchovsky, attired in uniform and accompanied by an " aide-de-camp." Under his influence the peasants stopped payment of their taxes. Disorders in the villages were frequent, and in the towns riots occurred through conflicts of people of different races. There were outbreaks of brigandage in the Caucasus, and pillage was committed in many places. Murders became more numerous. Industrial strikes in factories produced many disturbances and much loss of life. In the industrial cities of Poland there was much unemployment and much unrest. In Russia proper there were strikes of weavers at Ivanovo-Voznesensk, of railwaymen at Sevastopol, and of dock labourers at Ribinsk. Jewish pogroms occurred in Rovno (Volynskaya *gub.*), where the

---

[1] On the Finnish question, see *infra*, p. 246.
[2] Svyatlovsky, *op. cit.*, p. 11.   [3] Cf. *supra*, vol. i. p. 79.
[4] There was a revival among the Stundists in Bogoduchovsky district, and an " Old Mohammedan " movement led by a preacher called Vaisov, in Kazan.
[5] A new sect calling itself " Golubchēkē " (good fellows), of a character similar to that of the Molokani appeared in Atkarsk (Saratovskaya *gub.*).

houses of Jews were destroyed ; one Jew was killed and two were wounded. In Kovno (Kovenskaya *gub.*) a fight took place between Germans and Russians over some village quarrel ; ten were killed and twenty wounded. In the district of Bogorodsky the peasants of two villages quarrelled and fought. The peasants fought with the authorities at Kuban, and also at Novo-Slavkin (Saratovskaya *gub.*), where they fought the police who came with a veterinary surgeon to kill plague-infested cattle. There were many such disturbances in different villages. In Belebeyevsky district (Ufimskaya *gub.*) the Tartar peasants disapproved of the insurance of their cattle by the village clerk and *starosta* (alderman), and beat them both. Property was damaged everywhere. In 1885, 192,000 complaints were made of damage to forests, a number about one-fourth more than that of the previous year. Such was the situation in 1885,[1] about one year after the reaction had begun in earnest.

In the same year the Government sought for support in the most powerful class of the population, in a manifesto to the nobility on 21st April 1885. While the peasants had been making demands upon the Government, the nobility had been having dreams of their own. They were willing to support the central authority of the Government, but they desired to have for themselves the leading part in local affairs. They desired also exclusive right to occupy the higher offices in the service of the State, and the right of acceptance or rejection of new-comers into their ranks. The Government yielded to a certain extent. Plebeian officials were in some cases discharged from public offices and replaced by noblemen. To propitiate the mercantile class, the Government gave subsidies to industrial enterprises and increased the already protective tariff. Not for the first time in Russian history did the higher classes secure advantage for themselves from political disturbance by selling their support at a high price to an enfeebled and unstable Government.

While these measures placated the superior orders, the working men in the towns and the peasants in the villages were becoming quiescent from other causes. The fever of political and social unrest has, like other fevers, its periods of high and its periods of low

---

[1] Several of these details are drawn from *Narodnaya Volya*, Nos. 11 and 12 (October 1885). The " legal " newspapers of the time were prevented by the pencil of the censor from full disclosure of the state of the country.

temperature, as well as an exhausting influence upon the frame. Moreover, the revival of trade which occurred in Western Europe from about 1886 reacted upon Russia. Industrial employment increased and wages advanced, while fairly good harvests improved the condition of the peasants.

In the decade of the nineties conditions were otherwise. The crop deficiency of 1891 produced famine throughout a great part of Russia ; and there were again serious deficiencies in the crops of 1897, 1898, and 1899.[1] But starving peasants do not revolt, and these economically critical periods passed over, the Government having taken exceptional means to meet the emergencies.

Such incidents, trade *malaise*, and trade prosperity, famine, and relief did not affect the idealists, who saw in them only temporary material advantages or disadvantages unaccompanied by any of those radical changes which they regarded as indispensable for permanent well-being. But among the general mass of the Russian intelligent public there was a real reaction, not merely against revolutionary violence, but also against serious political thought. The problems which presented themselves were too intricate and too exhausting. The nation needed a mental rest. The general mass of the peasantry and the working men in the towns became supine sometimes through increased prosperity, sometimes through increased misery. Under these conditions the task of the Government was easy. The revolutionary forces were destroyed or dispersed, and what was even more to the purpose, widespread sympathy with them had disappeared. Only in a new epoch could new forces arise.

[1] See *Collection of Answers to Questions issued by the Imperial Free Economical Society on the Crop Deficiency of the Year* 1891, edited by Ya. O. Kalinsky (St. Petersburg, 1893) ; *Issue of Provision* (Issue of Governmental Assistance from Grain Reserves) *in* 1897–1898 ; *Discussion in the Free Economical Society* (St. Petersburg, 1898), and *infra*, p. 289.

CHAPTER IX

THE SOCIAL DEMOCRATIC MOVEMENT IN RUSSIA

THE Government had scattered its enemies ; but danger lay in this fact. Following upon the destruction of the *Narodnaya Volya,* the *Chorno Peredyeltsi* had gone abroad, principally to Switzerland, where Zurich, Geneva, and some of the smaller towns had been " cities of refuge " for Russian propagandists during intervals of reaction. Among the refugees, in 1883, there were Plekhanov, Akselrod, Deitch, Ignatov, and Vera Zasulich, all of whom had been *Chorno Peredyeltsi,* including the last-mentioned, who had passed over from *Narodnaya Volya.* This group seems at first to have devoted itself to the examination of the question why their movement had failed of its purpose. They appeared to have arrived at the conclusion that their methods had been too naïve, and that it was necessary for them to call in the aid of science. They seemed to feel that while the social gulf between the revolutionary *intelligentsia* and the peasantry might be crossed, the intellectual gulf remained, and it appeared to the disappointed *Narodnĕkĕ* that the will of the people—that is, of the peasantry—was an inadequate guide; that, indeed, the peasants were seeking guidance from the *Narodnĕkĕ* themselves. Relatively educated as the propagandists were, they felt a need for more knowledge of the laws of human progress to enable them to deal with the situation, if not to the advantage of the peasants, at least to their own satisfaction. They were thus thrown back upon the studies with which many of them had begun. They now became acquainted with the socialist movement as it had been developing in Western Europe, and they began to be sceptical of the soundness of the " Utopist " views of " the old Russian revolutionaries," when " political tendencies began to develop amongst them." [1] " Being convinced that our ideas were wrong or out of date, we shall see what place in the political struggle is reserved for

[1] Plekhanov, *Socialism and the Political Struggle* (Geneva, 1905), p. 7.

the science to which even bourgeois opponents do not refuse the name of ' scientific socialism.' Afterwards we have to make what modifications in our conclusions may be necessary, because of the peculiarity of our contemporary conditions in Russia ; and the political struggle of the working class in Russia will be more clearly understood when it is considered in relation to general problems." [1] That a few revolutionaries, even if they could obtain possession of the Government, would be quite powerless to liberate the people in any real sense, and that the people alone could liberate itself, and that by consciously discarding the old order, became clear to the group.[2]

In 1883 this group of refugees in Switzerland formed the first definite social democratic organization in the Russian movement. It was called *Osvobojdenie Truda*, the Emancipation of Labour. The programme of the new party was issued in 1885. The views expressed in this document are the familiar Marxist views of that period. " The Russian social democrats " (the small group in question) " like the social democrats of other countries are seeking complete liberation from the yoke of capital." . . . " The present development of international commerce has made it inevitable that the revolution can be forced only by the participation in it of the society of the whole civilized world. The solidarity of the interests of the producers of all countries is recognized and declared by the International Brotherhood of Working Men. Since the liberation of the working men must be the act of the working men themselves, and since the interests of labour are in general diametrically opposed to the interests of the exploiters, and since, therefore, the upper classes must always try to prevent the reorganization of the social relations, the inevitable condition precedent to this reorganization must be the *taking possession by the working classes of the political power in any given country*. Only the rule for a time of the working class can paralyze the forces of the counter-revolution, and put an end to the existence of classes and to the struggle between them." The programme goes on to point out that the practical problems which are encountered by the democracies must vary with the varying phases of economical development. A country, for example,

---

[1] Plekhanov, *Socialism and the Political Struggle* (Geneva, 1905), p. 7.
[2] Lyadov, *The History of the Russian Social Democratic Labour Party* (St. Petersburg, 1906), vol. i. p. 35.

which possesses fully developed capitalistic production and distribution presents problems different from those presented by a country " where the labouring masses find themselves under the double yoke of capitalism and of an expiring patriarchal economy." Russia is in the latter position. Since the abolition of bondage right there has been a great growth of capitalistic enterprise. " The old system of natural economy is giving place to commercial production, and a large interior market has thus been opened up for the products of industry conducted upon a large scale." The chief support of the autocracy lies in the political indifference and mental backwardness of the peasantry. As a consequence of that condition there is weakness and timidity among the educated classes who find the present political system inimical to their own material and moral interests. When they raise their voices in favour of the people, they find the people indifferent. Thus there arises instability of political opinions and complete disillusionment among the Russian *intelligentsia*. The situation would be quite hopeless were it not that the economical development of Russia creates at the present time " fresh opportunities for the defenders of the interests of the labouring classes." The means of political struggle are the spreading of socialistic ideas among the working men, and the aim of it is a democratic constitution.[1]

This project of a programme was written chiefly by Plekhanov, and, as he afterwards observed, it was rather a leading article than a programme. The " project " is not free from a strain of Utopism. It is optimistic in respect to the " conscious " action of the working class in a socialist direction, and in respect to their eventually adopting, of their own volition, methods of governmental administration founded upon socialist doctrines, which methods must result in an ideal commonwealth. Yet the " project " brings sharply into the field of Russian discussion the questions of the inevitability of the process and the inevitability of the share in it of the working class. From this point of view there was an important deduction— viz. that the process, being an organic one, was most effectually facilitated by organic means, and that, while revolutionary violence might hasten, such violence might retard the process. This deduction was fully accepted, and Plekhanov and his group ceased to have any

[1] " The Project of a Programme of the Russian Social Democrats, 1885," *Soc. Dem. Calendar* (Geneva, 1902); quoted by Lyadov, *op. cit.*, vol. i. pp. 35–8.

direct connection with the revolutionary movement in Russia. The principal converts to the doctrines of the new group were among the Russian students who were attending the universities in Switzerland.[1] Through them it exercised a considerable influence upon the direction of the Russian movement afterwards. One of its members, Deitch, who probably alone among the group possessed organizing ability, was arrested.

Subsequently Plekhanov gave a more definite indication of the programme which he considered his party should adopt. " We think," he says, in his first pamphlet on social democracy, " that the sole non-fantastic aim of the Russian Socialists must now be the conquest of free political institutions on the one hand, and, on the other, the working out of the elements for the formation of a *future* Russian social democratic party. . . . The working men . . . will join our revolutionary *intelligentsia* in its struggle with absolutism, and then, gaining political freedom, they will organize themselves into a labour socialist party."[2] Akselrod supported this view, but considered that there was a possibility of organizing a socialist labour party even before the fall of absolutism, and during the process of struggle.[3]

Arising out of the interest in social democratic ideas popularized among the Russian *intelligentsia* by the Plekhanov group in Switzerland, and derived from direct study of Marxist literature, there appeared in St. Petersburg, in 1885, a social democratic group formed by Blagoev (a Bulgarian), Kharitonov, and others.[4] This group issued two numbers of a newspaper, *Rabochnaya Gazeta* (Workmen's Gazette). They were then arrested. Their ideas seem to be a mixture of Marxist socialism and Lavrism.[5] The aim of the group was to separate the working class and to form it into an independent political party, the final object of which was to be the reorganization of society upon a socialist basis—viz. the

---

[1] Lyadov. *op. cit.*, vol. i. p. 45.

[2] Plekhanov, *Socialism and the Political Struggle*, in collection, *On Two Fronts* (Geneva, 1905), p. 75 ; cited by Lyadov, *op. cit.*, vol. ii. p. 39. The pamphlet was originally issued in 1894.

[3] Lyadov, *loc. cit.*

[4] Egorov, A., " The Germination of Political Parties and their Activity," in *Social Movements in Russia in the Beginning of the Twentieth Century* (St. Petersburg, 1909), vol. i. p. 375. Lyadov (*op. cit.*, pp. 46–49) says that this group was formed quite independently of the Plekhanov group, and that it did not have any connection with it until some time after its formation.

[5] Lyadov, *op. cit.*, p. 46.

collective use of the means of production.   In order to achieve that object the working man's party must struggle for a constitution ; but a constitution would be a dream unless there was a working man's party with aims independent of those of the bourgeoisie. Plekhanov contributed an article to the second number, in which he called the social democratic party an " exclusively working men's party." . . . "Our revolutionary *intelligentsia* must go *with the working men*, and the peasantry *must follow them*." This blunt statement of the determinism of undiluted Marxist doctrine probably represents fairly the view of the few Russian Marxists of that time.   From such a point of view there are two courses— either to await inactively the operation of the implied social law, or to study intimately the actual working of the social forces in order to be in a position to estimate their direction and rate of movement, and to utilize this knowledge in practical action.   In the middle of the eighties the first part of this latter course was adopted, not exclusively by people of tendencies in opposition to the Government, but also by many who found a new field of scientific research in which they might work without ulterior social or political aims.   The result of this state of mind was a greatly renewed interest in problems of local government, and in economic questions leading, *e.g.*, to the collection of exact data upon the movements of commodities in the interior market, upon wages, cost of living, and the like.[1]   A great mass of official and non-official studies were undertaken, and reports of great value were issued upon the economical state of the nation.   In such studies the Imperial Free Economical Society of St. Petersburg was especially active.[2]   With renewed interest in life, Russian students returned from foreign universities and plunged into economical inquiries.   They also plunged headlong into recondite studies for which in many cases no doubt their preliminary preparation was inadequate—into history, sociology, ethnography, and philosophy.[3]   Some of them developed a varied if not very

---

[1] For activities in the latter direction, see, *e.g.*, Lyatschenko, *Outlines of Agrarian Evolution in Russia*, vol. i. p. 285–6.

[2] *Cf*. Beketov, A. N., *Historical Sketch of Twenty-Five Years' Activity of the Imperial Free Economical Society*, 1865–1890 (St. Petersburg, 1890); and *Zemstvo Year Book*, 1885–1886, edited by L. V. Khodsky (St. Petersburg, 1890).

[3] Lyadov, *op. cit.*, vol. i. p. 56.

deep erudition. The older *intelligentsia*, and even many of the revolutionary youth, looked askance at this rapid absorption and application of knowledge. To the former, educational methods seemed to have been turned upside down ; to the latter, the doctrines of Marx and his social democratic followers seemed abruptly contradictory to all that they had learned from Lavrov, Mikhailovsky, and the moderate collectivists.

The strength of the Marxist movement was thus devoted up till 1890 to self-education and inquiry. Foreign writings upon socialist questions were devoured with avidity—Marx, Engels, Kautsky, Liebknecht, Bebel, Lafargue, and Guesde.[1] There was an insatiable appetite for all knowledge that might bear upon the social question.[2] Meanwhile there was an almost entire absence of political agitation. Politicians and " economists " alike were peacefully engaged in the equipment of their intellectual arsenal.

With the famine of 1891 there came a psychological moment. Not merely did this occurrence provide material for agitation, but it brought the idealists, and even a large number of moderate liberals, to a new point of view. Famines were ascribed to a number of causes. Incompetence and impoverishment of landowners, incompetence and impoverishment of peasants, absence of agricultural organization, absence of insurance against the consequences of fluctuation of seasons, absence of communications by which the deficiency of one region might be instantly compensated from elsewhere, and the like. That all these deficiencies could be prevented by competence and capital seemed obvious ; that such competence and capital were more likely to be applied, and applied continuously, by a democratic State, which should have full ownership and control of all production and all of means of communication and distribution, was suggested in effect by the famine itself. The social democratic gospel from that moment became " a fashionable doctrine," and Marxist collectivism became so popular that recruits appeared for it from all social ranks.

The small group of emigrants, led by Plekhanov, attempted to take advantage of the situation produced by the famine and of the general state of mind, by formulating a policy based upon the

---

[1] Lyadov, *op. cit.*, p. 56.

[2] There was a similar outbreak of enthusiasm for such studies among the working men of St. Petersburg in 1905. Cf. *infra*, p. 457.

famine. They sought to unite with the liberal and the democratic oppositional elements in carrying on a propaganda against the Government. Although this movement had no definite political aim it had a certain effect among the radical youth.[1] Simultaneously in those *Zemstvo* Assemblies in which there were active liberal elements, there was developed a considerable amount of opposition to the Government. This opposition was maintained for about four years, when it subsided.

The social democratic agrarian programme, indefinite as it was, was swept into the background in the years immediately succeeding 1891 by the revival of industry and by the diversion of the energies of the social democratic groups into the industrial field, which indeed was more appropriate to their activities. The incipient attempts to form trade unions which the working men were making at that time were aided by the social democrats, who then found at once a platform for their propaganda and an opportunity for practical action. These proceedings had, however, a certain disintegrating effect, for, in order that they might not excite the attention of the Government, the social democrats were most careful to avoid not merely centralization, but even association of the various groups and various unions.[2] They also studiously kept themselves apart alike from the " active " groups of social revolutionary tendencies and from the social democratic groups abroad. By these means they concentrated their activities upon the local organization of social democratic groups among working men, and they frequently promoted strikes.[3] This policy was very effective in forming organizations analogous to the " trade clubs " or " trade societies," of the pre- " trade union " days in England ; [4] but it led to the absence of common ideas and of common action, and it neutralized the force of the social democratic movement when it was summoned by the course of events at a later period. It is true that in 1896 there was formed in St. Petersburg the *Union for the Liberation of the Working Classes*, to which the Government appeared at the time to attach importance, and in Moscow the *Working Men's*

---

[1] Egorov, A., *op. cit.*, p. 375. [2] *Ibid.*
[3] *e.g.* at Vilna, in 1893–1894, among Jewish tradesmen ; in 1894 in Moscow, in 1895 and 1896 in St. Petersburg, and in 1897 at Ekaterinoslav. *Cf.* Egorov, *op. cit.*, p. 376.
[4] That is, before 1830. *Cf.* Webb, S. and B., *History of Trade Unionism* (London, 1894), pp. 99–103.

Union, afterwards the *Union for Struggle*. Similar unions were formed at Nijni-Novgorod, Vilna, Minsk, and Kharkov. But these unions were composed almost exclusively of social democrats from the *intelligentsia*. They were rarely entered by even the most advanced working men.[1] These unions, however, distributed both legal and illegal literature,[2] and kept their members informed of the state of affairs. They also maintained, principally through students, and thus only periodically, connections with the local organizations. But they had no power over the working men's societies and no very intimate association with them. The need for union among the latter soon made itself felt. The local unions began to develop an incipient federation by appointing influential working men " who played the rôle of connectors," and who contributed to common action. The local unions also began to form interior " circles " of young working men, who occupied themselves with the study of socialism under the leadership of propagandists.[3] At the same time there were organized " treasuries," which were supported by contributions from the organized working men. The funds of these " treasuries " were used for assistance during strikes, for forming libraries (of legal and illegal literature), and for helping " victims of police repression." [4]

The important fact about the working-class movement from 1892–1896 was that for the first time it was really spontaneous. It was aided, no doubt, by the social democratic elements of the *intelligentsia*, but it was not originated by them. They found in the working men's organizations a favourable field for their propaganda, but they did not initiate and could not direct the movement. While, however, the working-class movement of this period was a genuine working-class movement, it was by no means either originated in, nor did it materially affect, the general mass of working men. It was initiated by a comparatively small number of " advanced " working men, some of whom had been previously more or less connected with revolutionary circles, and some of whom had in the

---

[1] Egorov, *loc. cit.*
[2] " Legal " literature comprised those publications which had passed the censor. Illegal literature was published abroad and smuggled into Russia or was printed in " underground " printing offices.
[3] Egorov, *loc. cit.*
[4] These " treasuries " were formed, *e.g.* at Vilna, Minsk (in 1895), and Moscow (1895–1896).

capitals acquired a knowledge of the Marxist ideas. Many of the smaller trade societies were formed, however, originally on purely economical grounds, and only after their existence had become known were they entered by propagandist elements, either from the working class or from the *intelligentsia*.

The activities of the social democrats among the working men in helping them to organize into trade societies, and in aiding them to form " treasuries," gave a practical direction to social democratic energies, and drew into their ranks enthusiasts who were willing to undertake practical functions. Experience in organic contact with working men gave them also a certain knowledge of actual conditions, and also, no doubt, a better knowledge of the limitations of the working man's mind and character. But all this implied neglect of development on the side of theory. The Marxian dogmatics were accepted as final truth, and although some of the social democrats realized that Russia presented many problems with which Marx had not dealt at all, they were unable at that moment to formulate the modifications upon the *Credo* of Marxism which Russian conditions rendered necessary. They were thus driven to accept the Marxian position pure and simple, and so far as their practical tactics were concerned, rather to follow the working men than to lead them. To a certain extent they tended to imitate the German social democrats, and when the Erfurt programme was promulgated in 1892, the Russian groups generally accepted it. At the same time they appear to have considered, and to have deliberately rejected, the English trade-union policy on the ground that it was destitute of ulterior socio-political aims.[1]

It is difficult to estimate the numerical importance of the various societies among working men that were at this time more or less directly influenced by social democratic tactics and ideas. There were, however, probably a few thousand working-men members of these societies, and there were besides a few hundred social democrats of the *intelligentsia* who assisted in forming or in directing the local working-class groups. There were, in addition to these, the societies formed on purely economical grounds, and not as yet affected by propagandist ideas.

About 1894 the Government turned its attention to the movement. They began to arrest those of the *intelligentsia* who had

[1] Lyadov, *op. cit.*, p. 70.

taken part in the organization of working-men's societies. Large numbers of students were arrested ; but so great was the enthusiasm that their places were quickly filled, so that the ranks of the social democrats, far from being depleted, became more numerous. The Government also " banished " to their villages the working-men members of the organizations ; but in so doing it contributed to the dissemination of the opinions which it desired to suppress, for the banished working men carried the social democratic propaganda into every part of the country, especially into the villages, and at the same time carried in their hearts a bitter feeling against the Government. Under the influence of these events, the social democratic *intelligentsia* began to see in the working-class movement a " lever " which might be employed by them to force the Government into political reforms.[1] Disappointed with the results of previous attempts to agitate among the peasants, they now looked forward with hope to the organization of the working men as a means of forcing concessions from the Government.

In the end of April 1895 the Moscow social democratic organization determined to make a census of the working men who had definitively enlisted under their banner, by holding on 1st May a meeting which would have the character of a demonstration, invisible, however, to the authorities. Secret Labour Day meetings had been held in 1891 at St. Petersburg and in 1892 at Vilna ; but no other demonstrations, secret or otherwise, had been made. The Moscow meeting, which was held in the country near Moscow, was attended by about 250 working men and 5 *intelligentsia*. At this meeting it was decided to create immediately " a widespread organization," to be called " The Moscow Working Men's Union," and to be not merely a working-man's union, but to be also inclusive of sympathetic *intelligentsia*.[2]

The social democratic *intelligentsia*, small in number as they were, gained experience in these movements, and they contributed to regularize strikes when they occurred, and to replace the elemental forms of struggle—indiscriminate riot and the like—by more peaceful and dignified demonstrations.

Meanwhile Russian industry was developing with immense rapidity. The peasants were leaving the villages and streaming into the industrial centres ; the small towns even were deserted for

[1] Egorov, *op. cit.*, p. 378.   [2] Lyadov, *op. cit.*, pp. 115–16.

these. Among the economic results of this movement of population were the disturbance of the interior markets, the fall of prices in the villages which were in the neighbourhood of the depopulated small towns,[1] and the increase of the industrial cities. The characteristic of the time was the growth of huge industrial enterprises. It seemed as if Russia were going to leap at once from an agricultural economy to an economy of great industry. Moreover, these industrial enterprises were of a magnitude to which there is no parallel save in the recent great combinations in the United States. The exploitation of the natural resources of Russia attracted capital from Western Europe, and the high protective tariff enabled promoters to offer highly remunerative returns.[2]

Some influential persons in the " higher spheres " [3] began to see in these movements a serious danger to the autocracy. Others saw in them a period of prosperity in which revolutionary impulses might subside.[4] The general drift of orthodox Marxism, on its purely economical side and apart from its democratic elements, was not out of consonance with the industrial policy of the Government. The Government was not only by far the greatest landowner in Russia, it was by far the greatest capitalist and the greatest employer of labour. Its railways, its mines, its factories of many different kinds, were in every part of the country. An economical policy which urged the extension of governmental enterprise over all fields was thus of itself not obnoxious to the Government. The obnoxious feature of the social democratic propaganda was its democratic character, the insistence that the existing Government should be dismounted and a democratic Government put in its place. There thus arose in the minds of the authorities a sharp distinction between Marxism as an economical theory and social democracy as a political propaganda. Moreover, the labour movement, which had been in progress from 1892, could not escape the notice of the " legal " press. The character of the movement was discussed in the leading newspapers, and the influence of Marxist

---

[1] This process was very manifest in the Upper Dnieper region, where numbers of people from the small towns migrated into the industrial towns of Poland. Cf. *infra*, p. 374.

[2] Cf. *infra*, p. 372.

[3] M. von Plehvĕ, for example, who is reported to have said that M. Wittĕ, through his policy of high protection, was creating revolutionists.

[4] Like M. Wittĕ, *e.g.*

economics could not fail to be noticed. The antagonism of the Marxist doctrines to those of the *Narodovoltsi* was brought out sharply. Thus, when Peter Struvë published in 1894 his *Critical Essays*,[1] the book passed the censor, and "legal" Marxism was a fact. The writings of Marx were also admitted to circulation, so that from that date onwards they were exposed for sale in the windows of the ordinary booksellers.[2] There also arose a group of "legal" Marxists, comprising persons who adhered to the Marxist economic theories without taking part in social demo-cratic organizations.[3] "Legal Marxism" did not, however, be-come of importance immediately. Its evolution was conditioned by the gradual acceptance of the doctrines of Marx as consonant with the negative aspects of philosophical materialism, which represented then, as it does now, the predominant point of view in philosophy of Russian men of science.[4] The growth of "legal" Marxism and the open discussion of the Marxist dialectics to which it gave rise led to an attitude towards collectivism not as a doctrine concerning merely a struggle of classes ending inevitably with the victory of the proletariat, but towards it as belonging to the theory of social evolution in general. Not all of those who were fairly entitled to be called "legal Marxists" remained within the fold of orthodox Marxism ; many of them either joined the social democratic groups, or became advocates of constitutional and social reform.[5]

The defence of the Marxist position was not, however, left to the "legal Marxists" properly so called. Plekhanov made a direct appeal to the *intelligentsia* in his book, *Towards the Development of the Monistic View of History*, published in 1895.[6] According to this lively polemic, the *Narodnēkē* were Utopists similar to the

---

[1] Struvē, P., *Critical Essays* (St. Petersburg, 1894).

[2] Although when Marx's writings were found on domiciliary visits, they continued to be regarded as confirmatory evidence of undue interest in political questions.

[3] Among these there was, *e.g.* the well-known Professor of Political Economy, M. Tugan-Baranovsky. There were also many of the junior members of the teaching staffs of nearly all the universities.

[4] *Cf.* Egorov, *op. cit.*, p. 379.

[5] Some of them identified themselves at a later period with the consti-tutional democrats, and some of them became merely observant critics of all parties.

[6] Published under the pseudonym of "N. Beltov," republished St. Peters-burg, 1905.

Utopists of Western Europe. They had nothing in common with revolution. They were not liberals, or conservatives, or monarchists, or republicans, but, consecrated to their own *idées fixés*, they were ready to follow any of them in so far as by doing so they might hope to realize their own " practical " plans. Plekhanov similarly attacked the Russian " subjectivists." He accused them of failing to understand Marx's materialistic theory of history, when they reproach the Marxists for the passive observance of the social forces to which they consider the theory logically leads them. " The degree of development of the productive forces," says Plekhanov, " defines the measure of power over nature. The dialectical method " (the method of Marx) " not only strives, as its enemies recognize, to convince people that it is absurd to make an uprising against economical necessity, but for the first time it shows how to deal with it. Once we *understand* the *iron law*, it devolves upon us to throw off its yoke and to make *necessity* an obedient slave to *reason*. ' I am a worm,' says the idealist. ' I *am* a worm,' says the materialist dialectician, ' so long as I am ignorant. I am a god when I know. *Tantum possumus, quantum scimus.* ' " [1]

One of the consequences of " legal Marxism " was the publication of several newspapers [2] in which " legal Marxism " was propagated, although the contributors to these were frequently members of the revolutionary social democratic ranks. The association of these discordant elements in the production of party newspapers contributed in the first instance to an absence of definite theoretical basis, as the result of compromise on questions of principle, and led afterwards to divisions in the ranks of the social democrats. From the Marxist point of view, the association of these groups led also to the transformation of the labour movement into a liberal " tail." [3]

Up till the year 1895, partly because of the comparatively slender growth of great industries in Russia, and more largely because of the hostility of the Government to labour combinations,

---

[1] " Beltov " (Plekhanov), *op. cit.*, p. 232; quoted by Lyadov, *op. cit.*, vol. i. p. 151.

[2] The first of these was *Deenas Lapa*, published at Riga in Lettish. Then followed the *Samara Gazette*, *Novoe Slovo* (New Word), *Nachalo*, and *Jizn* (Life). *Cf.* Lyadov, *op. cit.*, vol. i. p. 154.

[3] Cf. *e.g.* Lenin, *What to do*, p. 10 ; cited by Lyadov, *op. cit.*, vol. i. p. 155.

there had been few strikes. In that year they began to increase, in 1896 there were many more, and in 1897 the number of strikes and the numbers of men involved were the highest during that period.[1] The causes of these strikes were exclusively economical. The era of the political strike had not yet begun. In 1895 about 75 per cent. of the men who were on strike struck for higher wages, 3 per cent. for reduction in the number of hours of labour, and 22 per cent. for improvement in the conditions of labour. In 1896 the proportions were quite different ; only about 36 per cent. struck for advance in wages, while about 60 per cent. struck for reduction in the number of hours of labour. In 1897 the numbers striking for each of the two principal causes was almost equal, the number striking for improved conditions being 5 per cent.[2]

The growth of great industries now brought a new factor into the situation. Large fortunes were made by merchants and by financiers who had embarked in various enterprises. The factories, employing many thousands of hands, had sometimes in their immediate vicinity the new and costly houses of their owners. For the first time in Russian history since the absorption of the free towns into the Moscow State there arose definitely a bourgeoisie, exercising, autocracy notwithstanding, a certain political influence. This bourgeoisie was small in number, but it was important because the conditions of Russian finance had brought it into relations with the network of the international money market. If, for example, the Russian Government was unwilling to serve certain ends of the great manufacturers, pressure which was difficult to resist might be brought to bear from Belgium, France, Germany,

[1] The official statistics are :

		1895.	1896.	1897.
Number of establishments involved . . .		68	118	145
,, workmen involved		31,195	29,527	59,870
,, days lost		156,843	189,213	321,349
,, ,, where workmen gained .		59,332	8,143	128,988
,, ,, where employers gained .		15,417	173,087	132,662
,, ,, where there was a compromise		82,094	7,659	59,594
,, ,, where result is unknown .		...	324	105

Ministry of Trade and Industry: Statistical Reports of Labour Strikes in Factories and Foundries, 1895–1904, V. E. Varzar (St. Petersburg, 1905), p. 72, and App., p. 3.

[2] *Cf.* Varzar, *op. cit.*, p. 55.

or England. Moreover, many of the very large industries had been established by foreigners, who remained subjects of their respective countries,[1] and who on occasion called upon, as they were entitled to do, for the diplomatic services of their respective ambassadors. From the point of view of the social democrats, the landowning nobility were effete and powerless. Their political influence had been quite unable to prevent the development of the protective tariff, and was now a " negligible quantity," and their liberal elements, which had shown themselves in the Zemstvos, had easily been rendered useless. The new bourgeoisie, rising into power through the great industry, though small in number, was the really formidable supporter of the Government and the formidable enemy of the working class. This was, of course, in complete accordance with the Marxist hypothesis, and to the social democrats the rise of the bourgeoisie in the nick of time to justify the prescience of Marx was no accident, but was an inevitable necessity.[2] The only real antagonist of the allied forces of the bureaucratic autocracy and the great factory-owning bourgeoisie was the proletariat. The peasantry, in spite of the years of hard toil among them of the Narodnik groups, were politically valueless. The intelligentsia, in view of the current reaction in the opinion of the working class against the previous idealization of their political virtues by the Narodovoltsi and the subjectivists, were described by Struvë as " in sociological relations ' une quantité négligeable.' "[3]

From this point of view it became evident that the working class, in its struggle against the employing class, must endeavour to secure its victories by means of changes in the legislation and administration of the State. It must thus be brought soon into collision with " the whole State mechanism."[4] Thus the working

[1] Conspicuous instances of this are the woollen mills of the Thorntons on the Neva and the engineering works of the Maxwells at St. Petersburg, belonging to and managed by Englishmen, and of the silk factory of Girot at Moscow, belonging to and managed by Frenchmen. The Nobels (English and French capital) have large interests in Southern Russia.

[2] Struvë, P. B., Critical Essays (St. Petersburg, 1894), quoted by Egorov, op. cit., p. 380.

[3] It is to be observed that historical conditions in Russia have made for the sharper division of the classes than in any other country. Moreover, there is there no such diffusion of industrial and commercial capital as there is in Western Europe. Russian enterprises are indeed, as pointed out above, largely financed from abroad.   [4] Egorov, op. cit., p. 380.

class, even if it conquered an eight-hour day by means of an economical strike, must insist further upon a legal eight-hour day; or,
if it conquered a recognition by the employers of the right of combination, it must further have that right secured by law, and so
forth. Such appears to have been the psychology of the social
democratic movement in and among the working class in the period
succeeding 1894. This came to be known as the period of " economism."[1]

These views necessarily isolated the working-class social democrats from all other social groups. The movement came to be regarded as a " pure working-class movement " by its advocates, and
as merely " opportunist " by its critics. The latter, indeed, regarded
it as opposed in principle to the ultimate aims of the older social
democratic groups, as, for instance, that of Plekhanov, and as
struggling for no aims other than those which might with pressure
be realized without displacing the existing form of government, and
without altering the fundamental character of the administration
of law.[2] The development of " economism " had indeed led the
social democratic working men's movement unconsciously, but substantially, to the point of view of English trade unionism, as interpreted by Brentano. Indeed the critics of " economism " applied
also to it the name " Brentanism."[3] Their views, however, corresponded more closely and directly with those of Bernstein, whose
polemics against Kautsky are well known.[4]

It seems advisable now to glance at the fluctuations of opinion

[1] Egorov, *op. cit.*, p. 380.
[2] *Cf.* Egorov, *op. cit.*, p. 381. Some social democrats afterwards recognized in the " economist " movement of this period a direct playing into
the hand of the great bourgeoisie through concentration of attention upon
merely trade-union methods. *Cf.* Lyadov, *op. cit.*, p. 158.
[3] Professor Lujo Brentano published in 1872 the second volume of his
Die Arbeitergilden der Gegenwart, in which he endeavoured " to demonstrate
the possibility of a solution of the labour question under the social and
political order of the present." (Preface to his *Das Arbeitsverhältniss Gemäss
dem heutigen Recht* (Leipzig, 1877).) He had further developed the same
theme in " Meine Polemik mit Karl Marx: Zugleich ein Betrag zur Frage des
Fortschrittes der Arbeiterclasse und seiner Ursachen " (in *Deutschen Wochen-
blatt*, 6th November 1890). See also Bernstein, Edouard, *Brentano über
die Socialdemokratie und das Lohngesetz* (1890–1891), republished in his
Zur Geschichte und Theorie des Socialismus (Berlin, 1901), pp. 32–6.
[4] Book V, chap. xi. Bernstein indeed was very popular at this time.
Three editions of a collection of his writings were published in Russia. He was
one of the writers recommended by Zubátov to be read by those whom he
wished to convert from social democracy. (Cf. *infra*, p. 189 *n.*)

within the groups whose principle was characterized as "econo-mism." The "Unions for Struggle" were composed for the most part of working men, whose principal objects were to improve the conditions of their own labour and incidentally of the labour of other working men, alike as regards the physical conditions, the number of working hours, and the remuneration. Only a relatively small number of them could be described as being consciously engaged in a struggle between the working class and the owners of capital allied with the Government. On the "peripheries"[1] of these circles there were such working men, and in the centre there were groups of *intelligents* who guided the organization. These latter groups maintained, to begin with, their association with the immediately preceding socio-political elements from whom they had, indeed, inherited or acquired their starting-point. Such groups appear to have regarded "economism" as a temporary phase—as, indeed, an evil which should have to be abandoned. But in the periphery of the circle, occupied by working men of the character described, and by *intelligents* of similar character, there was a ten-dency towards the increase of the influence of "economism." In those unions where the *intelligent* guides at the centre were new-comers, the working men at all stages of "socialist education" were inclined to insist upon managing the unions themselves.[2] As the unions grew in dimensions, the working men in them greatly outnumbered the *intelligents*, and thus the control of the unions by the latter came to have more and more an undemocratic aspect, and "democratism" became a new watchword in this interior struggle. In St. Petersburg and in Kiev, *e.g.* there emerged a party within the unions which proposed a unification of the unions, and the formation of a political party, on the basis, however, of a programme which was confined within the limits of "economism." This pro-posal was not received with favour either by the working men on the "periphery" or by those who were "socially educated," and were therefore well within the circle. They saw in the project a means of strengthening the central control and of diminishing the democratic character of the structure of the unions. They saw in it also the increase of the influence of the "ideologists" over that of the "practitioners." They urged that a working men's party can grow only organically from the inside, and that the formation

---

[1] A phrase of Egorov's, *op. cit.*, p. 381.   [2] According to Lyadov.

of a social democratic political party would be a mistake. They also anticipated the moment when the local organizations, losing their " hierarchical character and *intelligentsia* influence shall become (really) working men's organizations, which would embrace all of the struggling portion of the proletariat." They denounced any other way of forming a party as being " conspirative," and as savouring of *Narodnaya Volya*.[1]

In spite of the adverse interior conditions of the social democratic groups, they appeared to be making progress in so far as concerned the arousal of the working men from political ignorance and apathy. It is difficult to assess the proportions of the purely spontaneous labour movement apart from the social democratic and " active " revolutionary propaganda. It is possible that it was very considerable. The dispersal of working men, occasioned by the Government's policy of banishing by administrative order,[2] was undoubtedly influential in spreading discontent as well as in spreading the social democratic ideas with which at least some of them had become inoculated.

Towards the end of the year 1896 it became quite apparent that an incipient mass movement was in progress. Where it would end, no one could tell. The liberal elements in Russian society were conscious of an altered state of affairs, but they seemed to be unable to grasp the situation. The feeling that the working men and the peasants were too ignorant to be trusted with political power completely possessed them, and their prevailing mood throughout the nineties was one of pessimism. This attitude on the part of the liberals was undoubtedly favourable to the reactionaries, and the policy of arrest, imprisonment, banishment, and exile went on. So long as social democratic *intelligents* only were imprisoned, the tendency was for them to be idealized by the working men; now that social democratic working men were arrested, they came to be idealized by the *intelligents*. It was only a step farther for them to idealize the whole working class. The Russian youth following in this direction found so great a spontaneous revival among the working men, that they refused to give the social democratic *intelligents* the whole credit of the movement.[3] They thus discounted the

---

[1] Egorov, *loc. cit.*
[2] The prisons could not have held the workmen banished by the local governmental authorities.
[3] Lyadov, *op. cit.*, vol. ii. p. 21.

effect of propaganda, and came to attach great importance to organization. This attitude was to a certain extent confirmed by the demands of the strike period, when practical organizing ability was called for on all hands. The result of this " state of mind " was the formation of groups of the younger men rivalling the groups of the older propagandists of various shades of opinion. The *Molodykh* (youths) group, and other groups of the same kind, were formed in St. Petersburg, and in one case a number of " Technologists " left their union and formed a group of their own. The *Molodykh* group developed interior differences and divided into two factions.

These divisions and subdivisions gave rise to a situation in which it was said that wherever two Russian social democrats meet together, there will be three social democratic parties ; [1] and that in the mouths of self-styled social democrats " nonsense was elevated into a principle." [2] In Russia socialism was still a " chaos." [3]

One way out of this chaos seemed to be to convene a congress. The Moscow group had proposed in 1894 to convene a congress in order to fix the " political physiognomy " of the party ; but the arrest of nearly all of its members prevented this project from being carried out.

Projects of unification of the unions were repeatedly made, but they were always met by the same objections, advanced by the same groups, who came to be known as the " Men of the Nineties." The reaction against the formation of what they considered " immature parties out of innumerous and unstable circles," culminated in 1897.

Two different currents combined to bring about a partial change of view among the social democrats : the growth of industry, accompanied as it was by strikes in the winter of 1896–1897 ; and the popularization of " orthodox " Marxism through the legal press. The strike situation brought the need of union into the first place, and the percolation of Marxist opinions prepared the way for a political programme. Notwithstanding the traditional opposition to such a project, and in consequence of these currents, the central groups of the " Unions for Struggle " in St. Petersburg and in Kiev, and the central committee of the Jewish " Bund," convened a con-

[1] Akimov, *Outline of the Development of Social Democracy in Russia* (St. Petersburg, 1906), p. 46 ; cited by Lyadov, *op. cit.*, vol. ii. p. 24.
[2] Lyadov, *op. cit.*, vol. ii. p. 25. [3] *Cf.* the phrase of V. Considerant.

gress at Minsk for February 1898. The congress was held in March ; there met, besides the groups mentioned, the representatives of the " Unions for Struggle " of Moscow and Ekaterinoslav. The meeting was held in strict secrecy; even the working men of the "periphery" knew nothing about it. The occasion was, however, important, for there was then formed a " Russian Social Democratic Working Men's Party." The congress appeared to be divided into three groups, representing three streams of tendency, which had manifested themselves in the isolated and disparate organizations.[1] There were some adherents of the " Group for the Emancipation of Labour," who adopted the platform of Plekhanov, which has already been described. The second group represented local organization and " economism," the idea of the " immediate improvement of the condition of every working man." The third group represented the idea of limited centralization, involving the preservation of the secret or conspirative character of the " general staff " or central organization, but by gradually enlarging its structure to bring it into more direct contact with the locally organized groups, otherwise the " army." According to this group, the organized mass should not have any control of the " party." The mass should be " disciplined by continuous agitation," strikes should be steadily " developed," and it should take part in " propaganda circles " and in managing the strike funds. The principal exponent of the ideas of the last-mentioned group was Lenin, who had issued a pamphlet advocating them immediately before the congress was held.[2] The congress practically adopted the position of Lenin. The drift of the manifesto is interesting because it exhibits the mental content of the groups that were at that time endeavouring to change the current of Russian life. The manifesto begins by drawing a comparison between the French revolution of 1848 and the future Russian revolution. From the customary Marxist point of view, this revolution marked the beginning of the proletarian struggle in Western Europe. The reference to the revolution of 1848 in pre-

---

[1] According to Lyadov, no account of the proceedings at this congress has been preserved. All that remains are the programme of the initiators and the manifesto of the congress. The manifesto was printed in *The Workman's Gazette* (*Lëstka Rabotnëka*), No. 8, June 1898, pp. 3–8. It is quoted *in extenso* by Lyadov, *op. cit.*, ii. pp. 67–72.

[2] Lyadov, *op. cit.*, ii. p. 64.

ference to the revolution of 1789 is significant, because the authors of the manifesto seemed to think that in Russia a social revolution would be either contemporaneous with, or precedent to, a political revolution. But either social democrats of the congress did not agree with the Marxist position, or were careless in their historical allusion, for they went on to say, that it is necessary for the Russian proletariat to struggle first for " political freedom," because this is as needful for them " as pure air is for healthy respiration." Profiting by the lessons derived from Western European experience, the Russian proletariat will achieve this conquest alone without waiting for help from the bourgeoisie. While the accomplishment of the socialist revolution must be " the great historical mission of the proletariat, the first step must be the political revolution." So far as the congress was concerned, here was the end of " economism." There could be no question of limiting the aims of the social democratic labour movement to the immediate economic needs. The congress also pronounced in favour of centralization. " All the organizations must act according to one plan, and must obey the directors." At the same time, the Jewish " Bund," which was already a centralized organization within the social democratic movement, was given full separate autonomy.[1] The congress also decided that the *Working Men's Gazette* should be the organ of the central committee. It is significant that the manifesto contains no reference to the agrarian question. The document appears to have been drawn up by P. B. Struvë, who, however, seems to have expressed, not his personal opinions, but those eventually agreed upon by the congress.

The document was not well received. The unions refused to circulate it, and the " periphery " elements resented the action of the *intelligent* centres in summoning a meeting without their knowledge and without representation from them. The unions on the frontier held a congress in the autumn of 1898, and rejected a motion of sympathizers with the " Group for the Emancipation

[1] The reasons for this are stated in an article in the organ of the *Bund*, published immediately after the congress. These reasons were: the peculiar situation of the Jews in Russia, the policy of the Government towards them, the fact that the Jews have a separate language, and the like. (Quoted by Lyadov, vol. ii. p. 74.) The Jewish " Bund," or " The Pan-Jewish Working men's Union of Russia and Poland," was composed of Jewish Lithuanian and Polish social democrats.

of Labour" to the effect that the principle of the manifesto should be accepted.[1]

It appeared that the hostility to the policy of centralization was not merely justifiable from a democratic point of view, but that, in the condition of Russian affairs at that time, to centralize organization was to make the task of suppression by the Government easier. No sooner were the details of the organization of the central committee and of its relations to the local committees settled, than the members of all of these, together with the editors of their newspaper, were arrested, and the newspaper office was seized by the police. There had been a spy at the centre, and all were arrested who were in any way engaged in the organization. " Economism " was justified after all, in spite of its neglect of the distant aims of the " politicians." Yet in some of the groups there remained the conviction that the new organization, which must arise upon the ruins of the old, must be centralized. The destruction of the centres by the measures of the Government, together with the interior disputes between " economism " and " politicalism," resulted in the pulverization of the unions into small detached groups of varying tendencies. There remained a so-called " committee " of the party, but this committee was composed chiefly of representatives of the " periphery " elements ; it was destitute of political aims, and it did not engage in political action. In the autumn of 1898 there was not a single strong social democratic organization of " political " tendencies.[2] The labour movement as a social democratic movement existed, but only as independent and dissociated fragments. Trusting, as the local groups did, in the " experience and erudition " of the emigrants in the " Group for the Emancipation of Labour " headed by Ple-khanov, they naturally looked for guidance and for a supply of pamphlet literature suitable for propaganda purposes, but neither of these was forthcoming. There was a lack of comprehension of the real needs of the hour on the part of the emigrants, and Ple-

[1] Egorov quotes a document of this time called the *Credo*, which denounced the idea of the formation of a social democratic political party on the ground that such a party would be an imitation of Western European examples, and urges the social democrats to unite with the liberal opposition in its struggle against the Government. He says that this document was " very influential " among the unions of the frontier. Egorov, *op. cit.*, p. 383, and cf. *infra*, p. 166.

[2] Egorov, *op. cit.*, p. 384.

khanov's learned polemics were not suited either to the understand-
ings or to the stage of " social education " of the working men, and
still less to those of the peasants.[1] The emigrants spoke constantly
of " the future labour movement," but the labour movement was
in being, and they did not realize the fact. But among the emigrants movements were in progress corresponding to those in the
interior of the social democratic circles in Russia. A crisis was
precipitated by some of them, who separated themselves from
the " Group for the Emancipation of Labour " and formed a new
group, which they called the " Union of Russian Social Democrats
Abroad." The members of this group were, for the most part, young
emigrant students who had had connections with the social democratic organizations in Russia. In one of the publications of this
group [2] Akselrod [3] wrote " a mild criticism " of the course of Russian
social democracy, and suggested that the scope of its immediate
aims might well be enlarged. During the winter of 1897–1898 the
relations between the " Union " and the " Group for the Emancipation of Labour " became very strained over the question of " economism," and the " Group " abandoned its publications, while soon
afterwards the " Union " was split into two fractions. The larger
fraction was led by the editors of the newspaper *Working Men's
Activities*, who adopted an eclectic attitude towards " economism "
and " political activity " alike. The smaller fraction united
with the members of the " Group for the Emancipation of
Labour," and formed the " Revolutionists' Organization of Social
Democrats." [4]

The critical paper of Akselrod, referred to above,[5] spoke of the
fundamental solidarity of interests of all classes of society in so
far as these were progressive, and of the identity of interest of
the democratic *intelligentsia* and the democratic working men.

---

[1] *Cf.* Lyadov, *op. cit.*, vol. i. p. 161.
[2] The series of publications comprised, *About Agitation ; Towards the
Question of the Fundamental Problems and Tactics of the Russian Social Democrats ; Historical Conditions and the Relations of the Liberal and Social Democracy ; A Letter to the Editors of " Workmen's Activities."* *Cf.* Egorov, *op.
cit.*, p. 381.
[3] Formerly one of the *Chorno Peredyeltsi*, then one of Plekhanov's group.
Cf. *supra*, p. 111.
[4] Egorov, *op. cit.*, p. 382.
[5] "On the Question of the Contemporary Problems and Tactics of the
Russian Socialists." *Rabotnik*, No. 56 (1899).

Akselrod's critics pointed out that in this view Akselrod looked upon the labour party not as a class party, but as a democratic bourgeois party, acting upon and among working men, and that his view did not differ materially from " the pale liberalism " of the bourgeoisie. They insisted that the " general national problem " did not coincide with, and that it was indeed hostile to, the problem of the class interests of the proletariat.[1] It is clear that these critics decidedly undervalued the " social point of view." They appear to have thought that disinterested movement was quite impossible, and that, since the point of the social democratic agitation among the proletariat was to provoke what they called class consciousness, that therefore any movement among the bourgeoisie or any fraction of it must be a class-conscious movement also. As one of them puts it : " Akselrod did not believe in the class character of the demands of the landowners and the lawyers, because he thought they were able to stand upon the revolutionary point of view of the proletariat owing to their common hatred of capitalism." [2]

Akselrod was, however, probably more Marxian than his critics, for Marx always insisted that the class war was a temporary though necessary phase, and that the end of it would be the abolition of classes and the merging of society into one social group. Akselrod was, therefore, not antagonistic to Marxist principles when he advocated the utilization of the democratic *intelligentsia*, so far as this *intelligentsia* would go.[3]

According to Lyadov,[4] one of these critics, the great misfortune of the social democratic party in the late nineties was the fact that it absorbed " too great a dose of the bourgeois *intelligentsia*—so much of it that the latter did not even desire to organize into separate bourgeois revolutionary circles or fractions." He considered that the social democracy of the bourgeois *intelligentsia*, including among them the " legal Marxists," had not left one stone upon another of the fabric of scientific socialism, to the great joy of the survivors

---

[1] As stated by Lyadov, *op. cit.*, vol. ii. pp. 96–8.
[2] Lyadov, ii. p. 98.
[3] The question had been fought out in the *International*. Had it been decided in accordance with the views of the social democrats, who were opposed to Akselrod, Marx himself would have been excluded from the Association he was instrumental in bringing into existence.
[4] See Lyadov, *op. cit.*, ii. p. 115.

among the old *Narodnik* elements, and to the neutralization of the efforts of the other revolutionary oppositional organizations. The *intelligentsia* had cultivated an innocuous socialism, and had been at pains to direct the movement into the channels of trade unionism. The two documents in which the views of the *intelligentsia* and the supposititious views[1] of the proletariat are most sharply contrasted are the *Credo* and the *Protest*.[2] The former, which bears the marks of the views of Akselrod, although its authorship appears to be unknown, states its general point of view in these terms : " The Marxism which is negative, the primitive, intolerant Marxism (which employs in a too schematical way its division of societies into classes) must give way to democratic Marxism, and the position of the party in contemporary society will thereby be greatly changed. The party will find its *narrow corporative* and mostly sectarian aims changed into a tendency to reform contemporary society in the democratic direction adapted to the contemporary state of affairs, with the aim of more successfully and completely defending the rights (which vary) of the labouring classes." [3] The *Credo* originated in St. Petersburg. The *Protest*, which was compiled by seventeen social democratic exiles in Switzerland, warned the party of what it considered the danger which menaced it, in the attempt to divert it from the path it had chosen—viz. the formation of an independent political labour party, inseparable from the class struggle of the proletariat, with the primary object of conquering political freedom.[4]

In his criticism of the *Credo* and of the policy of " economism," Lyadov argues that " economism " was really a political movement, and that the effect of inducing the working men to adhere closely to economical demands must be to leave politics in the hands either of the bureaucratic autocracy or of the bourgeois *intelligentsia*.[5] He also pointed out that the latter groups had

---

[1] By supposititious is meant that the views in question were expressed rather for than by the proletariat. The controversy was really between *intelligents*.

[2] Both were published in *Vade mecum for the Editors of Workmen's Affairs* (Geneva, 1900).

[3] Quoted by Lyadov, *op. cit.*, ii. p. 116.

[4] *Ibid.*, p. 121.

[5] *Cf.* the idea of Zubátov, *infra*, p. 188.

drifted away from their revolutionary sympathies of the seventies and the eighties, and, together with the " agrarians," or advocates of agrarian reform, had organized a merely liberal opposition, attaching significance to the possibility of the success of the Zemstvos in a struggle against the autocracy.

There were thus two main currents tending towards the cessation of revolutionary activity — one in the bourgeois *intelligentsia* and the other in the working class. The former had arrived at its position by means of a destructive criticism of the doctrines of Marx, and through the sense of the absence of preparation on the part of the town artisans for the assumption of a rôle so important as the "dictatorship of the proletariat." The latter had found in combination and in strikes a cure for their immediate ills, and although they identified the interests of their employers with the interests of the Government, they found continuous organizatior and continuous pressure towards gaining material advantage more advantageous than spasmodic outbreaks of violence which appeared to result only in suppression by the Government.[1] The percentage of strikes after which the workmen gained was high in 1895 ; it was low in 1896 ; it rose again in 1897.[2] The strike movement on any considerable scale was quite new in 1895, and these were looked upon as satisfactory results. But these gains, and the attitude of the working men in so far as it was dependent upon continuous gains, came to an abrupt ending when, in consequence of the inferior harvests of 1897 and 1898, and in consequence of depression of trade abroad, employment on any terms became more difficult to procure. The stream of people from the villages to the industrial centres continued, and the supply of labour being in excess of the demand for it, and that demand being steadily subsiding, strikes became in 1899 at once more numerous and more unsuccessful so far as the working men were concerned. Judged by its practical results, "economism" had been pronounced a wise and materially profitable policy ; now, judged

[1] The appointment of factory inspectors, and the enforcement of factory legislation, though not regarded entirely with favour by the working class, had a certain influence in producing the state of mind described in the text. For factory legislation, see *supra*, p. 407 *et seq.*

[2] See table following.

by its results, it appeared to be doomed to be a thing of the past.[1]

Up till the year 1895 arrests among the social democratic ranks had been chiefly of *intelligentsia ;* from that time onwards larger numbers of working men were arrested, although the practice of

[1] Table I, showing the numbers of strikes in Russia and of workmen involved in respect to the causes of the strikes.

	1895.	1896.	1897.	1898.	1899.	1900.	1901.	1902.	1903.	1904.
I. For advance of wages	53 / 23,376	75 / 8,890	71 / 27,503	152 / 16,430	132 / 40,490	66 / 15,203	95 / 8,654	68 / 16,394	309 / 41,671	50 / 9,840
II. For reduction of time	6 / 1,021	27 / 19,063	66 / 28,818	35 / 17,633	36 / 9,825	40 / 9,300	53 / 15,933	24 / 7,126	95 / 16,706	4 / 3,943
III. For improvement of labour conditions	11 / 6,938	11 / 1,235	6 / 3,042	22 / 7,527	10 / 4,051	9 / 707	11 / 7,111	21 / 8,009	20 / 9,433	12 / 10,619
IV. Other causes	...	5 / 239	2 / 517	6 / 1,560	11 / 3,123	10 / 4,179	5 / 520	11 / 5,042	126 / 19,022	2 / 501

Table II, showing numbers of strikes in Russia and of workmen involved in which the workmen and the employers gained respectively and in which compromises were effected during the years 1895-1904.

	Workmen Gained.	Employers Gained.	Compromised.	Result Indecisive.
1895	37 / 59,332	12 / 15,417	19 / 82,094	...
1896	26 / 8,143	77 / 173,087	8 / 7,659	7 / 324
1897	44 / 128,988	84 / 132,662	15 / 56,594	2 / 105
1898	49 / 30,732	52 / 39,012	113 / 89,010	1 / 144
1899	31 / 47,030	131 / 171,125	27 / 46,701	...
1900	31 / 13,576	56 / 57,214	36 / 44,435	2 / 4,300
1901	67 / 37,365	64 / 59,109	33 / 13,719	...
1902	37 / 35,949	68 / 81,866	16 / 10,000	1 / 385
1903	147 / 78,893	226 / 248,765	109 / 76,498	68 / 40,763
1904	28 / 7,448	32 / 170,504	8 / 7,460	...
Totals	478 / 447,456	802 / 1,148,761	384 / 437,170	81 / 46,021

From Varzar, V. E., *op. cit.,* pp. 55 and 72.

banishment still continued. In many of the industrial and commercial centres—in Warsaw, Lodz, Moscow, St. Petersburg, Nijni-Novgorod, &c.—the most active working men belonging to the social democratic groups were arrested.[1] Partly spontaneously, and partly through the propaganda of the social democratic *intelligentsia*, the mass movement had really begun. The arrests of so large numbers of working men were convincing proofs that this was the case, or, at all events, that the Government believed, or affected to believe, that it was.

"The appearance" in the prisons and "in the streets of the political mujik soon destroyed the ice which separated the few revolutionaries from the mass of the people, and created a series of cords which bound the revolutionaries to the mass."[2] The strikes not only brought together the working men and the revolutionary elements, but they inflicted a severe blow upon the traditions of factory employment which had come down from pre-Emancipation days. The obvious success of "economism" in producing this effect had an important influence upon the "state of mind" of the working men. They began to see in the strike a cure for everything, and to feel that, after all, a complete political change was not so necessary as appeared at first sight. But the continuance of this attitude was dependent upon the continuance of successful strikes, and external influences contributed to render such continuance impossible.

Up till 1898 Western European capital, increasing rapidly in volume, sought employment in all countries where the rate of interest was relatively higher than in England and in France. The United States, Canada, Germany, and Russia all benefited by this condition. Immense sums flowed from the Western European money market to all of these countries. The South African War broke out in 1899, the supply of gold from the Transvaal suddenly ceased, the money market in Western Europe became stringent, and the supply of capital for Russian enterprises was checked at its source. Inferior crops in Russia in 1897, 1898, and 1899 intensi-

---

[1] Between 1894 and 1896, according to Lyadov, there were 726 political cases, and 3531 persons were brought to trial. This number does not include those who were dealt with by "police-administrative order," and who were banished to the northern provinces or to Siberia. See Lyadov, *op. cit.*, i. p. 125.

[2] *Ibid.*, ii. p. 5.

fied the situation, and industry became stagnant. Wages fell, especially in the south of Russia. In the great ports of Odessa and Nikolayev starving labourers wrecked the shops. Disorder spread all over the south. There were few strikes, but there was much unemployment. The labourers who had left their villages for the high wages current during the preceding period readily returned to the villages. They felt the instability of employment which depends upon foreign commerce and large industry. In the north, too, there were hordes of unemployed. In Riga there were strikes against reduction of wages, and the city was given over to riot. Police and troops were used to quell the disturbances; crowds were beaten with the *nagaïka*.[1] The mob was desperate. Always on the edge of subsistence, deprivation for a day meant starvation. There was no organization of any effective kind for dealing with such a situation. The working men and the advocates of " economism " blamed the employers. The critics in general of the Government found in the autocracy the explanation of the *impasse*. The social democrats denounced the autocracy and the employers alike, and urged that the only exit was by means of a social revolution and a socialist State, under which industry would be organized in such a way as to obviate commercial and industrial crises, or at least to mitigate their effects. On the other hand, the employers complained that the Government gave them inadequate protection, in spite of a promise that their property would be protected. The Government was indeed between two fires. If it refrained from protecting the factories, it practically abdicated its functions; if it protected them, it excited the forces of the revolution, already sufficiently perturbed. The Government was thus inevitably brought into the position of an enemy of the working class. " The struggle of the labouring class with the capitalists," says one of the social democratic newspapers of that time, " has brought into the field a new enemy, the Government of the Tsar, and we must fight with it for our political rights." [2]

The commercial and industrial crisis which began in 1899 afforded ' rich material for agitation," and in spite of the watchfulness of the

[1] " The Labour Riots in Riga," in *Working Men's Affairs* (Geneva, August 1899), p. 65; quoted by Lyadov, ii. p. 158.
[2] *Forwards* (Kiev), No. 4, January 1899; quoted by Lyadov, ii. p. 164.

police and the hostility of the Government, fresh social democratic organizations sprang up everywhere, and the previously existing fragments of older organizations, frequently harried by the police, were revivified. The political propaganda became active; "illegal literature" from the Russian presses abroad once more came into Russia in great quantities. The "Group for the Liberation of Labour," under the leadership of Plekhanov and Akselrod, was again active, after having been relegated to the background during the period of "economism." New journals made their appearance.[1]

These events gave a fresh impetus to controversy. The forces of the opposition were once more distracted by disputes upon the familiar topics. Bernsteinism and all that it implied were again subjected to attack.

Meanwhile, the spontaneous movement of labour, regardless of the *contestations stériles* of the social democratic scholastics, was spreading widely—its branches ran along the Siberian Railway so far as Krasnoyarsk and penetrated the Caucasus to Tiflis.

Among the students there were also spontaneous movements, leading to strikes, in which the students demanded "guarantee of personality." The Government replied by issuing "temporary regulations" about the enlistment of students in the army.[2] Revolutionary impulses began to make their appearance, and the students denounced in resolutions the action of the "Asiatic Government," demanding "freer forms of life." At Kharkov the medical students joined the social democrats, and attempted to make a demonstration. The demonstration was a failure, many of the students who took part in it being arrested. In the evening of the same day (19th February 1900) the working men of Kharkov made a demonstration in favour of the students, singing the "Marseillaise" and other revolutionary songs.[3] The crowd was charged by Cossacks, and at midnight was dispersed with difficulty, the demonstration having lasted for five hours. At St. Petersburg a similar demonstration of students on the same day—the anniversary of peasant emancipation—failed, but in Moscow a meeting of students was held, only to be surrounded and captured by the police.

---

[1] e.g. *Iskra*.
[2] One hundred and eighty-three students were enlisted as a consequence of these disturbances.
[3] Lyadov, *op. cit.*, ii. p. 223.

Crowds of working men came, however, to the rescue, and succeeded in liberating about half of the students who had been arrested. Disturbances continued to take place in the neighbourhood of the University for several days. Arrests of working men and of students continued. On Sunday, 25th February, the day upon which Count Leo N. Tolstoy was excommunicated, crowds surged along the principal streets of Moscow in spite of the efforts of the Cossacks and the police. In Lubianka the crowd recognized Tolstoy, who was walking in the street. He received an ovation, and with difficulty escaped from the pressure of his admirers. The crowds were not dispersed until three o'clock the following morning.

On 4th March a demonstration, accompanied by charges of troops and bloodshed, took place at the Kazan Cathedral, St. Petersburg.

Demonstrations now became frequent in the capitals and elsewhere. The working men seem to have thrown timidity, and even prudence, aside. On 11th March there was a demonstration on a small scale at Kazan ; on 19th September about 400 persons made a demonstration in St. Petersburg, nearly all being arrested ; on 7th November a demonstration to protest against the exile of Maxim Gorki took place at Nijni Novgorod. On the following day a similar demonstration for a like reason was made at Moscow to greet Gorki who was passing through the city. On 18th November a meeting to be held in memory of Dobrolubov [1] was prohibited, and a demonstration in protest was held. On 2nd December there was a demonstration at Kharkov, in which students and working men took part. On 15th and 16th December students and working men made a demonstration, revolutionary songs were sung, and shouts were heard, " Away with the autocracy ! " " *Vive* political freedom ! " " *Vive* social democracy ! " The crowds were attacked by soldiers and police.

In 1902 another series of demonstrations began at Kiev on 2nd February, and continued at Ekaterinoslav, Rostov-on-Don, and Odessa. On 9th February, at the University of Moscow, a number of students made a demonstration within the walls of the University, and barricaded themselves in one of the buildings. In the night the barricades were carried by the police, the students who were behind them were arrested and sent to Eastern Siberia.

In March, April, and May numerous arrests were made, yet the

[1] 1836-1861. One of the allies of Chernishevesky in *The Contemporary*.

enthusiasm for demonstration continued, to die down somewhat in the summer, and then later, in the beginning of 1903, to come up with renewed force.

The value of the policy of demonstration could not be denied. The practice of meeting in great numbers thrust the conspirative groups into the background. Yet the social democrats lost heavily, partly by wholesale arrests during these large open meetings, and partly through the eclectic phase in which the social democratic groups had come to be involved. The idealists among the social democrats saw in demonstration a further means of " unifying " the interests of the numerous groups of *intelligentsia*, and later they began to see in demonstration an entirely new means of propaganda. As the meetings grew larger it became more difficult for the police to disperse them. While people on the outskirts of the crowds might be arrested, it was practically impossible to arrest social democratic orators surrounded by thousands of people in a dense mass. The result of these conditions was that in 1902 and 1903 the social democratic movement in the towns became, in a propagandist sense, a formidable force, especially in the south of Russia.[1]

So great was the success of the social democrats among the working men in the towns, so eager did the audiences appear in listening to social democratic speakers, that the latter came to the conclusion that they were the centre of a mass movement which was destined soon to sweep over the whole of Russia. At the same time they proceeded to denounce the rival revolutionary elements. They accused the social revolutionaries of serving the interests of the liberal bourgeoisie.

---

[1] For the share of the social democrats in the strike movement in South Russia in 1903, see *infra*, p. 442 *et seq*.

CHAPTER X

THE SOCIAL REVOLUTIONARY MOVEMENT

WE have seen how, during the reaction which succeeded the assassination of Alexander II on 1st March 1881, the revolutionary groups were hunted down, and how the *Narodnaya Volya* was finally suppressed in 1887. The depression of trade of the early nineties produced much discontent among the city proletariat, and the famine of 1891 reduced large numbers of the peasantry to starvation. People who are really starving do not revolt, though there may be sympathetic revolts by those who are not starving. It was not until the revival of trade had been in progress for some years—not, indeed, until 1897 and 1899—that, under the influence of the strike movement of these years, there came about a new revolutionary agitation. This movement may be regarded as having two not very intimately associated sides. On the one hand there was the spontaneous labour movement, expressing itself in strikes, and becoming of revolutionary tendencies at intervals, but even then only in a vague way ; and, on the other hand, there was the propagandist revolutionary movement, those who took part in it being for the most part *intelligentsia* drawn from different classes, who sought to take advantage of the state of mind of the working men and to utilize the strikes for revolutionary purposes. On both sides the new movement, if such it may be called, sprang up spontaneously and therefore lacked organization. The alertness of the police, indeed, made organization almost impossible. Yet there was in the movement a fresh feature. This was the extent to which it was an agitation among the masses of the working men spontaneously arising among themselves, similar in this respect to the mass movements among the peasantry in the eighteenth century. Like these movements, the agitation of the late nineties was, to begin with, of a purely economical character. In so far as the strikes were successful the movement remained purely

economical ; only in the unsuccessful strikes did it exhibit a tendency towards political aims.   This tendency was reinforced by
the propagandist elements ; but the hands of the more purely
revolutionary fractions of these were tied, partly by the watchfulness of the police, and partly by their own want of sympathy for
the " economism " of other fractions and for the " strikism " of the
working men.   On the one hand the workmen demanded leadership, and " not merely empty scholasticism " ; [1] on the other hand,
the revolutionists despised the narrow aims of the workmen, and
felt aggrieved because the latter capitulated when their economical
demands were met.   The social democrats of the nineties were
undoubtedly nearer to the working men and to their point of view
than were the social revolutionaries.   The latter were more purely
idealistic, and were therefore impatient with social democrat and
workman alike.   This attitude of mind produced during the
nineties a pessimistic mood so profound that there was among
the revolutionaries an epidemic of suicides.[2]   From the point of
view of the social democrats, the strike movement of the nineties
was the sign of the existence of class consciousness in the city
proletariat ; from the point of view of the social revolutionists, it
was merely the first awakening of the working men to the fact
of the immaturity of the development of this class consciousness.
The social revolutionists laboured to explain to the working men
that striking could not be an end in itself—that the serious problem
with which they had to grapple was, what next ?   This propaganda led many of the working men to the belief that the revolutionists were opposed to the labour movement, and such an attitude
inevitably increased the difficulties of the revolutionary propaganda among the city proletariat.

Towards the close of 1899 the industrial crisis caused reduction
in the demand for labour, while contemporaneously the agricultural
crisis drove peasants into the towns to seek for employment in a
market already overstocked.   Wages fell sharply, and the working
men were powerless to prevent this consequence of the economic
conditions through strikes or any other means.   Confidence in the

---

[1] *Towards the Question of Programme and Tactics.*   Collection of articles
from *Revolutionary Russia* (Paris ? 1903), p. 5.

[2] Among the better-known revolutionaries who died in this way at this
time, were A. L. Safonov, A. T. Oryekhov, and N. V. Efêmov.   *Ibid.*, p. 4.

utility of strikes speedily declined, and the working men, having no other weapon in their arsenal, turned helplessly to the *intelligentsia* for leadership. At this moment, the beginning of the year 1900, the students' movement for a " guarantee of personality," which has been alluded to in the previous chapter, broke out in open demonstrations. The workmen took their cue from the students, joined the demonstrations of the students, and organized demonstrations of their own. This gave them a new form of struggle.[1] Demonstration, in spite of the risk involved through conflict with the police, became a habit. Both sexes and all ages took part in it.[2] " The furore for strikes was readily changed into a furore for demonstration." [3] For what were they demonstrating ? It cannot be said that the crowds of workmen and workwomen, most of them youths, had any clear or uniform idea of what they wanted.

These chaotic demonstrations forced the revolutionists into a dilemma. They knew the futility of them perfectly well. They knew that unarmed demonstrationists would never frighten the Government into any positive action. They knew also that the demonstrations played into the hands of the reactionaries by frightening those who regard public order as a primary necessity. Yet if they refrained from throwing in their lot with the demonstrationists they sacrificed their revolutionary reputation. They were not ready for a serious struggle with the Government, and yet they had to engage in one. " Taking into consideration the fact that the Government of the Tsar always tries to show that revolutionists are agitators who thrust the people forward before the bullet and the rod, and then take themselves to flight, we have to remember that, in case of bloodshed at demonstrations which we have brought about, we must be in the foremost ranks, and we must show the example of self-sacrifice." [4] The socialist revolutionary groups were thus compelled by the force of circumstances to do what they could to assist the working class in its economical struggle, while at the same time they recognized that

---

[1] *Towards the Question of Programme and Tactics,* &c., p. 14.
[2] Young Russian workpeople who became addicted to the habit of demonstration and who afterwards emigrated to America, found conditions there intolerably dull and uninteresting because there were no demonstrations.
[3] *Towards the Question of Programme and Tactics,* &c., p. 15.
[4] *Ibid.,* p. 19.

the economical struggle was only an incident in the political conflict which they were themselves attempting to wage.

In 1899 the authorities discovered the existence of a revolutionary propaganda among the peasants of Saratov, Tambov, and other places. This propaganda was conducted by means of the circulation of " illegal literature " by small isolated revolutionary groups. In order to carry on the propaganda more effectively, larger groups were formed—*e.g.* the " Brotherhood for the Defence of the Rights of the People," and in 1900 the " Agrarian Socialist League."

" In the end of the 'nineties " groups of this kind united themselves under the general name of socialist revolutionaries, and out of this union there grew the Socialist Revolutionary Party,[1] which issued its first manifesto in 1900. It was not, however, until the end of 1901 that *all* the socialist revolutionary organizations associated themselves with the party.[2] From the date of the Congress of Socialist Revolutionaries in 1898 the propaganda among the peasants was looked upon as of great importance, and one of the first publications of the party in 1900, before the final union, was a pamphlet, specially designed for the use of peasants, entitled " *19th February*," the date of Emancipation in 1861. In 1902 the Peasants' Union issued an appeal to all socialist revolutionaries which was published in *Revolutionary Russia*, the organ of the united party.[3] This document is important because it shows how in 1902, before the outbreak of the Russo-Japanese War, the revolutionary state of mind was already a factor with which the Government had to reckon. After reciting a portion of the history of previous revolutionary movements, and especially that of *Zemlya ē Volya*, and narrating some of the incidents of the reaction, the manifesto goes on to say : " The terrible time has passed when, after a great struggle, the expenditure of our forces exceeded the income. Now when the powerful resources of the working masses are opened to us, no police terror can frighten us ; we can only

---

[1] There had been previously in existence the " Union of Socialist Revolutionaries " which sent representatives to the Socialist Congress held in London in 1896; but they were excluded from the Congress, leaving the Social Democratic Party group as the sole representatives of Russia, the old *Narodovoltsi* group, which had been accepted, having withdrawn by way of protest against the exclusion of the socialist revolutionaries. *Revolutionary Russia*, No. 8 (1902), p. 25.　　[2] *Ibid.*, p. 26.

[3] The first number of *Revolutionary Russia* appeared in 1900.

become stronger every year. We, the founders of the ' Peasant Union of the Party of Socialist Revolutionaries,' as a result of a critical examination of our programme in consequence of the emergence of new conditions, have arrived at the conclusion that these conditions permit and demand the enlargement of our activities and the guidance by us of the labouring masses, and hence of the peasantry, and the introduction into our programme of all the means of struggle, beginning with peaceful propaganda, until armed terroristical attacks upon the autocracy are included. . . . The labouring masses are swallowing tens of thousands of proclamations, revolutionary pamphlets, papers, &c. . . . The dogma of Russian social democracy of the end of the 'eighties and the middle of the 'nineties, to the effect that no revolutionary force can exist outside of the city proletariat, was wholly based upon belief in the remoteness of open political struggle and in the inevitability, as a preparation for this, of some decades of proletarianization of the peasantry. But is it wise to set ablaze a revolutionary fire among hundreds of thousands, or even millions, of proletarians, when tens of millions of peasantry may come like ice-cold water and extinguish the fire ? In order to do so it is not even necessary for the peasantry to act against the proletariat, it is sufficient if they only remain neutral." From this condition the manifesto draws the conclusion that propaganda among the peasants is desirable. It also considers it possible, because not only are the peasants dissatisfied with their economical position, but they are advancing steadily in cultural development. Formerly the peasant wandered little ; now " ten million peasants " are tramping all over Russia and are coming in contact with " wealth and poverty, education and ignorance." For these reasons the manifesto rejects the " superstition which depicts the peasantry as a dark, hopeless, inert, and reactionary force. . . . That the patience of the peasant masses is almost exhausted, that the mass may rise up at the first acute moment in its chronic suffering—this, after the movement of the peasants in Little Russia, is unnecessary to show . . . and we shall ourselves set fire to this combustible material with the torch of the struggle for liberty, and this flame shall join the other. In the streets of the towns and in the fire of the terror the rotten structure of the autocracy shall be destroyed. . . . Our final aim is the accomplishment of the socialist ideal in its fullness; but we do not think that, woven out of brotherhood and freedom, the socialist order can be born immediately from the soil of our contemporary enslaved Russia. We are convinced that the different elements of our ideal shall be accomplished partially and in various forms, because some of them are logically and historically necessary phases. Therefore the problem of our work is not in preparing for a fantastic giant jump at once to the final aim, but in a deliberate and measured advance through the phases of changes and revolutions as they occur in history. . . . For the peasantry in the *first* place we put the socialization of the land— that is, the passing of the land into social property, and the raising up of those who cultivate it ; *second*, the development among the peasantry of different forms of social union, economical co-operation, for the dual aim of the liberation of the peasants from the power of money capital and for the preparation of the forthcoming collective agricultural production. . . . In printed and verbal addresses to the peasants we must emphasize especially the political element, and must employ the economical mainly as an argument in agitation. . . . We have to show the impossibility of serious improvement in the economical conditions of the peasants until free universal suffrage shall place their fate in their own hands. We have to repeat to the peasant that, when everything shall depend upon his will, he shall be given land. We have to call the peasant by Land to Freedom, and lead him through Freedom to Land." [1]

The forces by means of which the " revolutionization of the peasant " was to be carried out were to be drawn largely from prison and from the exiles in Siberia. " Escapes are becoming more and more frequent." [2] Efforts were to be made by the revolutionary propagandists to influence the peasants in all *mir* affairs, to try to secure the election of their own men to elective offices, to endeavour to induce the peasants to unite in mutual cultural-educational and other useful associations. Finally, the authors of the manifesto fully acknowledge that, besides these peaceful although illegal measures, they recognize from the beginning the possibility of the secret revolutionary peasants' organization passing at some time into an armed struggle.[3]

---

[1] *Revolutionary Russia*, No. 8, April 1902.
[2] *Ibid.*   [3] *Ibid.*

In February 1903 the socialist revolutionary party addressed a manifesto to the Russian youth in the universities and in other higher educational institutions, calling upon the students not to neglect their studies, but to consecrate these to social ends ; and concluding " When the youth went to demonstrations in 1901, there was no thought of resistance. Now the possibility and necessity of armed demonstration is in the air. Peaceful demonstrations have revealed the necessity of open struggle and have uplifted the fighting mood of the masses." [1]

The activities of isolated socialist revolutionaries did not disturb the social democratic organizations, but when they united themselves and formed a party, the social democrats found that their own propaganda was imperilled. In 1903 in the second issue of the *Red Banner*, the then new organ of the " Union of Russian Social Democrats," there appeared what the social revolutionists interpreted as a declaration of war. " The chief political sin " of the latter, from the social democratic point of view, "was that they desired to unite the mass of labouring *intelligentsia* into one party with the proletariat, and that they desired to unite into one party all the labouring peasantry with the proletariat. Such a party would be wider than a social democratic party, but would be so unstable that its building up would be an impossibility. Thus, instead of a socialist programme, the socialist revolutionaries present only a ' socialist mist,' which merely obscures the class-consciousness of the proletariat."

The socialist revolutionists answered by accusing the social democrats of lack of political perspicacity. The social democrats, they said, certainly sought the aid of the *intelligentsia* in their struggle with the autocracy ; and they realized that so soon as political oppression should disappear, there might suddenly be disclosed a situation in which only a small part of the *intelligentsia* would unite their fortune with the tempestuous fate of the working man's life, while the remainder " would go over into the service of the bourgeoisie." What they did not realize was that some portion of the proletariat would pursue the same course. The socialist revolutionaries pointed out that such had been the case in England, where the working men were satisfied with the purely economical

---

[1] *Revolutionary Russia*, February 1903.

movement. Even in Germany, social democracy had not yet succeeded in uniting all the proletariat.

It is not surprising, they say, that when political freedom is gained and when an economical struggle becomes legal, the working men should abandon socialism. It is thus necessary to develop among working men the *socialistic conscience*. " To us," the socialist revolutionists say, " all labouring interests summed up and coordinated in the highest ideals of socialism are equally precious. We have ideals ; but we have no idols. The proletariat is not an idol to us ; and we shall not worship it by erecting an altar for sacrifices, in which we would offer up the interests of other labouring and exploited classes. If union with social democracy can only be purchased at the price of our convictions, we do not want it and must struggle against it." The socialist revolutionary author continues. The social democrats find in Russia two revolutionary classes—the proletariat and the peasantry ; but they do not recognize an identity of interest. According to them only the proletarians are the grave-diggers of bourgeois society, the peasants are impostors. Both can obtain satisfaction, from the socialist revolutionary point of view, only by the abolition of private property. The aims of the socialist revolutionary party then are—free popular rule, nationalization of the land, and nationalization of all great industries. This programme, they think, " will unite working men and peasants under one fighting banner." [1]

The socialist revolutionary party found itself almost at the outset of its existence confronted with a problem. Propaganda among the peasants and among the working men was necessary to bring them out of the narrow economic views and interests in which they were involved ; but propaganda not only took time, it involved continual conflict with the authorities. The propagandists were beaten, imprisoned, sent into the army, sometimes into the penal battalions, or exiled to the extreme north of European Russia or the far eastern regions of Siberia. How were they to be protected ? Measures might be organised for their escape, and such measures were taken ; but when they returned to active revolutionary service as " illegal men " they were again liable to arrest and imprisonment. Revolutionary movements of the past had been slowly and surely pounded

[1] *Revolutionary Russia*, January 1903, and *Towards the Question*, &c., pp. 56–71.

to pieces in this way. The socialist revolutionists believed strongly in their ideals, and these ideals appeared to them to be saturated with a moral force and a disinterestedness which distinguished them not only from those of governmental and bourgeois society, but even from those of the social democrats. They were fully aware that the mass of Russian society was excited almost to the pitch necessary for a vigorous open movement against the autocracy, and, in point of fact, subsequent events showed that in this they made a correct diagnosis. The continuance of their propaganda was essential, the means of protecting it remained to be considered. The propaganda was a fundamental condition precedent to open revolt, therefore it could be protected only by conspirative actions. By this mental process the socialist revolutionists seem to have been led into terrorism. While the preparation of individual acts was carefully guarded no attempt was made to conceal the fact of the terror. Notwithstanding the collapse of previous terroristic movements, like that of the *Narodnaya Volya*, for example, they found consolation in the fact that these movements were conducted by very small numbers of persons against a strong Government and in the teeth of a public opinion acquiescent to, if not even sympathetic with, governmental authority. Yet, to a certain extent, even these insignificant forces had succeeded in altering the course of events. Now, the case was different. The growth of the proletariat in numbers, its concentration in the cities, the famines and the discontent among the peasantry, the industrial and agricultural crises, together with the apparent inability of the Government to grapple with these questions, and the consequent diminution of its prestige, combined to prepare the soil for propaganda as it had never been prepared before. Therefore it appeared that terroristic blows delivered with skill might at the right moment change the current of things and re-enforce the propaganda. So much for diagnosis of the state of mind of the revolutionaries, we shall see how far their utterances at this period (1902–1904) support this view.

An article in *Revolutionary Russia* for June 1902 puts the case for terrorism on the formation of the new party.

" We should be the first," says this article, " to protest against one-sided isolated terrorism. We do not by any means want to exchange the mass struggle for the courageous blows of our advance-guard, but rather to aid and reinforce the mass struggle. Terroristic acts must be organized. They have to be supported by the party, which must regulate their direction and must undertake the moral responsibility for them. But although in a *tactical* sense there is a necessary co-ordination between the terrorist struggle and other forms of revolutionary activity, in a *technical* sense the separation of the terrorist struggle from the other functions of the party is not less necessary. There must be a severe unity of principle and a not less severe division of organization. In accordance with the decision of the party there exists apart from it a special fighting organization,' which has taken upon itself the functions of an isolated disorganizational terroristic activity on the foundation of hard conspiracy and division of labour. The revolutionization of the masses, that is our fundamental affair as a socialist revolutionary party. Terror is one of the temporary and transitory technical means which we adopt, not for itself, but as a very heavy duty which we have to perform, and which we have derived from conditions of Russian life thrice as heavy as the duty itself." [1]

From the point of view of the socialist revolutionists the conflict with the Government had become a civil war, in which the campaign on one side was conducted by the Government, possessing all the instruments with which a modern Government can be equipped for the maintenance of order, and supported by the active assistance of great numbers of people and by the inertia of the masses, and, on the other side, a small but active irregular force of self-regardless men who were prepared to take their lives in their hands and to attack the enemy. In such a campaign every hope is a forlorn hope. The combatants are sustained alone by the idea that their end must be gained eventually, and that the sacrifices, though inevitable, are not futile. The socialist revolutionaries pointed out, not without justice, that peaceful demonstrations involved sacrifices. The demonstrators were arrested, imprisoned or exiled, in many cases prematurely aged or killed by their experiences. Terror has its sacrifices, but so also have peace and acquiescence. Moreover, they said, an armed struggle is necessary, but an armed demonstration cannot be created of a sudden ; it must be prepared. Terror can be created by individual action.

[1] *Towards the Question,* &c., pp. 71–84.

These extracts and summaries from the literature of the socialist revolutionists during the course of the propaganda before the outbreak of the Russo-Japanese War show that there was in existence a more or less widespread revolutionary spirit, and that those who were imbued with it were of similar temperament to the adherents of *Zemlya ē Volya* and of the *Narodnaya Volya*, and that, therefore, a similar result might be anticipated. Soon after the formation of the Fighting Organization of the Socialist Revolutionary Party, they seem to have pronounced sentence of death upon Sipiaghin, the Minister of the Interior, and upon the aged Pobyedonostsev, the Over-Procurator of the Holy Synod.[1] A youth of twenty-one years, named Balmashev, was selected as the slayer of Sipiaghin. This young man was the son of a revolutionist of the seventies, and he had during his childhood been with his father in banishment in a remote part of Arkhangelskaya *gub.* In 1891 he was sent to the gymnasium at Saratov, where he at once organized reading circles for the purpose of reading the revolutionary journals and the works of Dobrolubov, Pesarev, Chernyshevsky, Lavrov, and others. In 1899 he entered the University of Kazan, and subsequently went to Kiev. Here he also engaged in organization and connected himself with the *Obrazovanie* group. In January 1901 Balmashev was arrested within the buildings of the university, the total number of arrests of students at that time being 183. Along with many others he was sent into the army. In September 1901, however, we find him again in Kiev University busily engaged in organization, and shortly afterwards in Saratov, and a member of the Fighting Organization of the Socialist Revolutionaries. In February 1902 he disappeared from Saratov. On 2nd April in St. Petersburg he shot and killed Sipiaghin. On 3rd May he was hanged. The Minister of Interior, with a view to extracting from him information about the organization to which he belonged, had encouraged him to make an appeal for mercy, but Balmashev is reported to have said to him : " You seem to find it harder to kill me, than it is for me to die. All I ask of you is that the rope should be strong enough, for you are not very competent

---

[1] Some light upon these proceedings was afterwards shed by the publication of details in the Azef and Lopukhin cases. It is highly probable that from the very beginning of the socialist revolutionary party there were spies in their camp. Cf. *infra*, p. 577.

even as hangmen." [1] There were many such—human bullets fired at the heads of the Government.

From the tone of the articles in the socialist revolutionary press of this period it is evident that, although there was a certain animus against the social democrats, and although between them and the social revolutionists there was much difference in methods of action, especially in the pre-revolutionary days, there was little difference in point of ultimate aim. Both desired the overthrowal of the autocracy, and both desired a social revolution. Both also desired the nationalization of the land and the nationalization of all the means of production. The social democrats were in general Marxists *pur sang*, and the socialist revolutionists took from Marx what suited their purpose. In 1903, for example, they drew attention to Marx's suggestion, advanced rather casually, that the revolutionary movement in Russia should have as its aim one or other of the following—either (1) to compel the Tsar to convene a Constituent Assembly, or (2) to frighten the Tsar and his entourage by creating deep disturbances which would compel the convocation of a Constituent Assembly.[2] The socialist revolutionists thought that Marx looked upon Russia as developing rapidly into a capitalist industrial State, and that the Constituent Assembly must *inevitably* lead not to a mere liberal constitution, but to a radical social change. Whether the original suggestion came from this source or not does not appear, but, as we shall see later, in 1905 the phrase " Constituent Assembly " was in every one's mouth. The phrase was being shouted in the streets by people whose pronunciation of the words showed that they had not the slightest idea of their meaning. So diversified a group as the socialist revolutionaries cannot be regarded as representing any formal dogma. Many of them threw themselves into the movement from motives of revenge for imprisonment or exile on the ground that they were found guilty of possessing some book of which a policeman did not approve, or for standing on the outskirts of some unlicensed meeting. Others threw themselves into it because they were convinced that at all hazards one revolutionary dogma or another ought to be

[1] *Zasvobodu* (" For Liberty ") [Album of revolutionary portraits with biographies].   Nagasaki, Japan [n.d.], fo. 16.

[2] Letter of Hermann Lopatin on his conversations with Marx and Engels, published in 1893 ; cited by *Revolutionary Russia*, No. 20, 15th March 1903, p. 4.

propagated, others because of their deep sympathy with people whom they looked upon as oppressed by employers or by Government, or by both. There were many men and many minds. In general, however, while the social democrats were anxious that, when the new order came, it should bear their stamp, the socialist revolutionists seemed to be more anxious to destroy the old order than prematurely to determine the direction of the new.

In the light of later disclosures of political and police intrigues, and of the alleged manipulation of the social revolutionary forces by unscrupulous officials to gain private ends, it is as yet quite impossible to discriminate between those terroristic acts which were the outcome of spontaneous action on the part of the militant division of the socialist revolutionary party and those which were suggested to them by *provocators*. The only persons who are in a position to tell the truth about these mysterious transactions are persons whose actions have rendered their evidence valueless. It is, however, certain that during the terroristic periods which immediately preceded and immediately succeeded the war with Japan there were many acts for which the militant social revolutionists were exclusively responsible. Notices of the following kind are not infrequent in the pages of *Revolutionary Russia* :

" On 13th March 1903 the Governor of Ufa, N. M. Bogdanovich, ordered the troops at Zlatoust to fire upon a group of striking workmen. The crowd ran away, but the troops continued to fire. Twenty-eight people were killed, and about 200 were wounded. Among the killed and wounded were many women and children. . . . On 6th May, by the order of the Fighting Organization of the Party of Socialist Revolutionaries, two of its members shot and killed N. M. Bogdanovich, Governor of Ufa." [1]

" On Thursday, 15th July 1904, about 9.50 A.M., at the Ismaïlovsky Prospect in St. Petersburg, there was killed by means of a bomb the Minister of Interior, Plehvë." [2]

" On 28th June 1905 the Chief of the city of Moscow, Count P. Shuvalov, was killed by a member of the Fighting Drujina of the Moscow Committee of the Party of Socialist Revolutionaries." [3]

When the general strike occurred in South Russia in 1903 [4]

---

[1] *Revolutionary Russia*, 15th May 1903, No. 24, p. 1.
[2] *Ibid.*, supplement to No. 56.
[3] *Ibid.*, 1st July 1905, No. 70, p. 1.   [4] See *infra*, p. 443.

the socialist revolutionaries hastened to give it their approval. " The ' general strike,' " they said, " is one of the best forms of struggle, and therefore we include it in our programme, not instead of other methods, but together with them." [1]

Many of the local branches of the socialist revolutionaries had their fighting contingent, sometimes well armed, who attended demonstrations and carried out conspirative acts. In the capitals these contingents played an important rôle in the open outbreaks which occurred throughout 1905. In that year the terror became submerged in the general movement.

The rôle of the social revolutionaries in the acute stage of the revolutionary period is described in the following book.

[1] *Revolutionary Russia*, 5th August 1903, No. 29, p. 1.

CHAPTER XI

"POLICE SOCIALISM" AND THE LABOUR
MOVEMENT—"ZUBÁTOVSHINA"

The course of the political as well as of the labour movement was
seriously influenced, from 1900 till 1905, by attempts on the part of
the political police to control the labour movement in detail. The
design was elaborated by a police officer in Moscow called Zubátov,[1]

[1] Sergey Vasilyevich Zubátov was born in Moscow (?) about 1864. In
1880 he entered the Fifth Moscow Gymnasium. The young Zubátov is
described as an "ugly and old-fashioned" boy (Osvobojdenie, vol. i., 1902–
1903 (No. 26), p. 393). Within a year he had so far conquered the first
unfavourable impression that he succeeded in forming a group of fellow-
pupils and in organizing a debating society. Zubátov seems to have been
especially attractive to the youths in the school because he was the only
member of his group who had relations with the representatives of the revolutionary party, then the Narodnaya Volya. Zubátov appears to have been
already a traitor (Osvobojdenie, loc. cit.). The meetings of the society of
schoolboys organized by Zubátov were held at a circulating library where,
among others, prohibited books were to be obtained. In 1882–1883 Zubátov
left the Gymnasium and formed "a more active" revolutionary circle.
About the same time he married the proprietress of the circulating library,
which was thenceforward carried on under his name. In 1883 the circle
was entered by another spy, who actively "revolutionized" all the young
company, so that after a few months the members of it were arrested (Osvobojdenie, loc. cit.), and one of them shortly afterwards died in banishment.
Although Zubátov was owner of the premises in which the meetings were
held, and although he was the organizer of the group, he was not arrested.
It was known that he was called to the Department of Political Police, and from
that time he was regarded with suspicion. For about three years he appears to
have been quiescent ; but in 1886 he proposed to some former fellow-pupils
of the Gymnasium to form a "self-education circle" among the students
of the Petrovsky Academy (a Forestry-Agricultural High School). After the
organization of this circle Zubátov proposed to form a united library for
all such circles in Moscow and for working men. The object of Zubátov in
interesting himself in the Petrovsky students soon became apparent. That
Academy had always been noted for its revolutionary tendencies, and when
the Moscow branch of the Narodnaya Volya party was arrested, during the
general debâcle of the party which followed the assassination of Alexander II,
some of the students of the Academy had attempted to keep together the
wreck of the Moscow branch. They took over the printing office of the
organization and its cash and entered into relations with the provincial
members. They had thus lists of sympathizers with the Narodnaya Volya;
and these lists might be made of value in skilful hands. At first the revolutionary group at the Academy would have nothing to do with Zubátov;

and for that reason the episode has come to be known as the " Zubátovshina." The idea, though probably original, was not

but he managed ultimately to obtain admittance to it.   Shortly afterwards, when one of the provincial members of the former *Narodnaya Volya* came to Moscow, he was arrested on his return, and Zubátov once more fell under suspicion.   Meanwhile Zubátov was busily occupied in forming " self-education circles " among young men and girls attending pedagogical courses and among gymnasium girls and boys, and especially among the pupils of the Moscow Technical School.   In 1887 Zubátov's circulating library was a regular storing place for revolutionary literature, which was distributed from it in bundles.   On 17th May 1887, Zubátov's blow fell upon the Petrovsky Academy, and numerous arrests were made.   The first certainty of the rôle of Zubátov as " provocative agent " and spy was obtained by his former comrades in prison, when, previously unknown to one another, they compared notes.   All were found to be united by the personality of Zubátov.   (*Osvobojdenie*, loc. cit.)   Most of those who were arrested were raw youths, who learned to their astonishment that they were accused of complicity in a gigantic conspiracy (*ibid.*).   Many were banished to Siberia.   Zubátov was rewarded for this exploit by his appointment as Deputy Chief of the Moscow Political Police.   It is alleged that by means of an intrigue he shortly after procured the dismissal of his chief and his own appointment as his successor. (*Osvobojdenie*, loc. cit.)   In this position he continued to carry out his policy of keeping in touch, now through others, with the revolutionary groups, and to recruit his army of spies by corrupting members of these groups.   Under his influence many political prisoners in the Moscow gaols were given quite unprecedented privileges.   " They were allowed to go out of the prisons, and to go to the theatres " and other places of amusement (F. Dan, *History of the Labour Movement and Social Democracy in Russia*, 2nd ed. (St. Petersburg, 1905), p. 41).   Zubátov had long conversations with these selected prisoners (Dan), " mostly after midnight " (according to a correspondent), arguing with them upon the subjects of the revolutionary propaganda, professing his ardent devotion to the cause of labour, and assuring them that " the struggle for political freedom in the existing state of affairs is only an idea of the bourgeois *intelligentsia*, and that it could only injure the interests of the working men."   (Dan, *loc. cit.*)   He told them that the Government was now " willing to give to the working men freedom to form themselves into unions and to strike, and was also willing to assist them in their struggle against their employers.   What stops the Government " (in this benevolent design) " ' is the political agitation on the part of the social democrats.' Further, Zubátov pointed out that in Western Europe, Marxism had reached a ' crisis,' and that this had confirmed him in his views.   At the same time he recommended them to read the works of Bernstein and Sombart, as well as those of the Russian ' Revisionists.' "   (Dan, *op. cit.*, p. 42.)   I am informed by a correspondent that for some time prior to this period, Zubátov had been accumulating a library of forbidden books upon the social question. At all events he had informed himself upon the controversies in which the leading Marxists had become involved.   The movement described in the text began in 1900 and ended in 1904.   In the course of it Zabátov was promoted.

After the Odessa disorders (described below), which were the direct outcome of his proceedings, and were regarded by M. von Plehvé as proving fully the dangers of his manœuvres, Zubátov was dismissed, and was banished to Arkhangelskaya *gub.*, while his subordinate agents were arrested and some of them were sent to Siberia.

novel. In one form or another attempts have been made to control the labour movement by administrative means even in democratic countries. Those who were responsible for the policy in Russia seemed to realize that the labour movement could not be suppressed by administrative severity, and to imagine that it was possible to control and direct it into channels chosen by themselves.

The object of controlling the labour movement was to separate the economical from the political aspect, by concentrating the attention of the working men upon the improvement of the conditions of their labour, and thus to withdraw them from the influences of political agitation and revolutionary propaganda.[1] By this means the attack by the working men upon the Government might be foiled by converting it into an attack upon employers.

It thus appears to have occurred to Zubátov, then chief of the Political Department of the Moscow police, that it might be possible to draw off the working men from the revolutionary propaganda by inducing and encouraging them to engage in a purely economical struggle with their employers.

It cannot be denied that the idea was a bold and ingenious one, nor that the time was ripe for such a suggestion. The immediate and considerable success of the movement of Zubátov cannot be otherwise accounted for. The revolutionary propagandists had all along insisted that the autocracy was the chief obstacle to any improvement of their condition, and that nothing could be hoped for until the autocracy was overwhelmed. But the process was evidently a long one, and meanwhile the workers were suffering. The offer of immediate relief was too seductive to reject.

So far as it is possible, from the available evidence, to fathom the personal motives of Zubátov, it appears that his design was to make a career by a *grand coup* which should earn for himself the gratitude of " the highest authority." The course of events induces the inevitable suspicion that he intended to produce a premature rising which might easily be crushed, and the futility of a labour revolutionary movement be thus fully demonstrated ; but there is no certain evidence of this. The views of Zubátov were not without a certain breadth, and his manner of carrying them

[1] See Svyatlovsky, V. V., *Professional* (Trade Union) *Movement in Russia* (St. Petersburg, 1907), p. 53, and F. Dan, *op. cit.*, p. 6.

into effect did not lack boldness. Realizing that the organization of workmen into societies, secret or open, was an inevitable concomitant of factory industry on a large scale,[1] he determined to recommend, not only that such organizations should not, as hitherto, be impeded or prevented, but, on the contrary, that they should be permitted and encouraged. He intended, however, that the organizations should be completely under the control of the police. The organizations were to have exclusively economical aims, and by diverting into this channel the enthusiasm of the working men, he hoped to keep them out of the revolutionary movement, which would be dealt with otherwise. If the revolutionary parties could be isolated from the working men, and if they could thus be deprived of their chief numerical support, they might be more easily crushed.

The state of mind of the working men at this time is described as having been " very ominous."[2] The most intelligent groups were showing an extraordinary interest in political questions; even those working men who were opposed to interference in politics were discussing political affairs. They began to discuss such questions as " Is an income tax necessary ? " " How should universal education be instituted ? " &c.

Zubátov's idea was, on the one hand, to keep the revolutionary ranks and the ranks of the working men distinct, and, on the other hand, to prevent spontaneous political discussion among the working men by inducing them to discuss economical questions only.

In order to earn the confidence of the working men, Zubátov proposed that under certain circumstances, strikes for higher wages should not merely be permitted by the police, but should be facilitated, and even suggested, by them. Of course, the fact of the direction of the whole movement by the police, as well as the real springs and final purposes of the movement, were to be kept a profound secret. The organization of labour was to be effected by

---

[1] He was not alone in this view. M. von Plehvë had consistently opposed M. Witte's policy of industrial and commercial expansion, on the ground that it must lead to the growth of an urban proletariat, and therefore to revolution.

[2] The social democratic organ *Iskra*, No. 89, 24th February 1905, p. 3. (Reprinted St. Petersburg, 1906, in *Iskra za dva goda* (*Iskra for two years*), vol. i. p. 293.)

means of carefully selected agents, who were not to be known to have any connection with the political police department. Although many persons were in the secret, it was well kept, and sympathy with the movement was enlisted in quarters both honest and influential.[1]

Zubátov appears at an early stage to have secured for the execution of his plan the sanction of the Grand Duke Sergey,[2] then General Governor of the Moskovskaya *gub.*, and General Trepov,[3] then chief of the Moscow police.

Both Zubátov and his Moscow superiors appear to have undertaken the experiment of " playing with fire " with a light heart.[4]

Zubátov's first step was to effect, in 1901, the organization in Moscow of "The Society of Mutual Assistance of Workers in the Mechanical Industries," and also of " The Council of Workers in the Mechanical Industries." [5] The organization of these societies was accomplished with great ingenuity.

In the spring of 1901 some working men, directly or indirectly inspired by Zubátov, called upon Professor Ozerov,[6] of the University of Moscow, and invited him to assist in the formation of working men's societies. Professor Ozerov consented, and together with

---

[1] As in the case of Professor Ozerov, cf. *infra.*

[2] During the " reign " of the Grand Duke Sergey, Moscow was practically a "State within the State." The Grand Duke, who was the fourth son of Alexander II and uncle of Nicholas II, was assassinated in Moscow on 4th February 1905.

[3] General Trepov, then Chief of Police in Moscow, was the son of the General Trepov who was shot by Vera Zassúlich. General Trepov *fils* was a thoroughly honest but not very able officer, who evidently did not see to the end of Zubátov's designs.

[4] Subsequent events showed that M. von Plehvë disapproved of Zubátov's plan from the beginning. Probably the influence of the Grand Duke Sergey sufficed to prevent his interference with it until a late stage ; but when M. von Plehvë did interfere, he used the failure of the plan in Moscow and its still more disastrous outcome at Odessa to discredit M. Wittë. Zubátov was thus a mere pawn in the political game.

[5] Svyatlovsky, *op. cit.*, p. 53.

[6] Professor I. Kh. Ozerov was at that time incumbent of the chair of Finance Law in the University of Moscow. Since then he has been appointed to the chair in the same subject in the University of St. Petersburg. He is a productive writer, his principal works being upon financial policy and taxation. One of these is *Podohodnie Nalog v Anglie* (Income Tax in England) [chiefly in relation to the struggle of classes], Moscow, 1898. He has also written upon co-operation. His "*Politika po rabochemu voprosu v Rossie*" (Policy on the Labour Question in Russia), Moscow, 1906, is the principal available authority for the early phases of the Zubátov movement, in which Professor Ozerov played a conspicuous though unconscious part.

Mr. V. J. Den, Privat-docent in the University of Moscow, drew up a form of constitution. This constitution was modelled upon that of the Society of Craftsmen of Kharkov. After some formal objections by General Trepov, to whom the constitution had inevitably to be submitted, the document was forwarded with his endorsation to the Minister of the Interior (M. von Plehvë).

Meanwhile Professor Ozerov and Mr. Den were occupied in discussions with the working men upon the whole question of labour organization, explaining to them the methods of friendly societies in England, about co-operative societies, labour exchanges, workmen's dwellings, duration of the working day, factory legislation, collective contracts, arbitration courts, workmen's clubs, hygiene, &c. &c.[1] These meetings were held in the auditorium of the Historical Museum. They were attended by large numbers, although a fee of 20 kopeks (5d.) per month was charged, and none were admitted who had not paid their fees. By the autumn of 1901 the meetings were multiplied in different working men's districts, and the determination of the programmes of these meetings, together with the arrangements for the discussions, led to the formation of a so-called " Board of Working Men in the Mechanical Trades of Moscow." The first indefinite indications of the agency of Zubátov appear in the " Instructions " of this board to the branches or " regional meetings." These instructions were understood to be prepared by the working men themselves, but Professor Ozerov remarks, that " in them was seen the hand of someone else."[2] Who that " someone else " was does not appear to have been suspected at the time by the academic allies of the working men. When, after some delay, the " constitution " prepared by Professor Ozerov came back from St. Petersburg,[3] there was no doubt about the intimacy of the control of the society intended to be carried on by the police.

Professor's Ozerov's draft had provided for the submission of a yearly report to the chief of police ; but this was not regarded as sufficient. Clause after clause required submission to the chief of police on practically every point.

" The new constitution bound the organization hand and foot.

---

[1] Ozerov, I. Kh., *Policy on the Labour Question in Russia* (Moscow, 1906), pp. 195-254.
[2] *Ibid.*, p. 206.   [3] It was granted on 14th February 1902.

It was not permitted to make a step without the approval of the local authorities. ' The seal of the police spirit was stamped upon this constitution in dense colours,' " writes Professor Ozerov.[1]

It is evident that M. von Plehvë had little confidence in the administrative supervision of Zubátov and his agents in the unions, and that he determined to secure so far as possible a definite admission of the supervision of the police in the constitution of the society. It is improbable that this overt control was any part of the plan of Zubátov. Indeed, it may be held to have led to the disclosure which ere long deprived him of the unconscious participation in his designs of those who made his organization possible.

While the " constitution " was still under the consideration of the St. Petersburg authorities, the " Board of Workers engaged in the Mechanical Industries" was extending its influence. It was the first open and legal organization of the working class in Russia. Its meetings were permitted by the police. The close supervision was effected by means of spies, and was invisible. The possibility which this organization afforded of discussing the conditions of labour, under legalized circumstances, drew into its ranks the working men of Moscow in the trades which it concerned, practically *en masse*. Zubátov's organization had succeeded in attracting numbers beyond his most sanguine hopes. So far there was neither revolution nor politics in the discussions. They were concerned, to all appearance, exclusively with the conditions of employment. Soon the meetings resulted in demands being made upon the Factories and Mill Administration for the Moscow district. These demands are summarized by Mr. Grigoryevsky from the unpublished reports of the Moscow factory inspectors.[2] The demands were made by mechanics and weavers.

1. Demands for improved conditions of labour generally, by means of changes in the terms of contracts, considerable increase in wages, and at the same time reduction in working hours.

2. Demands for payment for several previous years (sometimes for the whole of the period of the working men's employment in the factory), for unemployment through no fault of the

---

[1] Svyatlovsky, *op. cit.*, p. 60, and Ozerov, *op. cit.*, p. 226.
[2] Quoted by Svyatlovsky, *op. cit.*, p. 60, from Grigoryevsky, *Police Socialism in Russia*, pp. 14 and 15.

working men, for loss of time while waiting for materials,
payment for giving out finished goods, and for carrying them
to warehouses, &c.

3. Demands for payment (*a*) for idleness through no fault of the
workers, to the amount of average piecework wages (payment was
usually made for idleness from this cause by day wages, which are
considerably lower than the usual piecework rate in the same employment) ; (*b*) for remuneration for repairing or putting in working
order mills or looms, for joining threads in weaving, for spooling,
for cleaning materials, for sweeping passages between spinning
mules, for loss of time owing to defects in the warp. [These details
were understood to be provided for in the wages scales, yet in the
general review of the position, they became the subject of special
demands] ; (*c*) for overtime work for all past years, for payment
for carrying ' mules ' from one place to another, for washing floors
in the workmen's rooms (in the barracks of the factory), and for
cleaning oil lamps.

4. Demands for changes in the following conditions of work :
(*a*) The institution of a more exact manner of receiving goods
(recording and crediting piecework payments due to workers), the
workers being very distrustful (of the methods customarily employed) ; (*b*) the institution of a rule whereby the spool boys
should be provided by the employers, and not by the weavers
themselves ; (*c*) the abolition of charges made to the working
men for lodging, use of dining-rooms, and for water, firewood, &c.,
in the common kitchens.

There were in addition numerous other complaints and demands, some of them of a trivial, and some of even an obviously
unfair, character from any point of view.[1] The demand for payment on account of retrospective claims is characteristic. These
demands were made through the factory inspectors for the Moscow
district in the first four months of 1902. How far Zubátov was
actually responsible for the demands does not appear ; but these
afford sufficient evidence, confirmed by the nature of others not
detailed, that the workmen who were at the head of the movement
(many of whom, like Afanasyev, the chairman of the board, were
undoubtedly agents of Zubátov) were a thoroughly inferior class of

---

[1] The working men " were anxious ' to scalp ' " the employer ; to take
from him " as much money as possible." See Grigoryevsky, *op. cit.*, p. 15.

men, whose presence in the labour movement could under any circumstances only compromise and discredit it.

In the spring of 1902 the first steps in presenting and enforcing these demands took effect. The most important attack was made upon a factory established by French capital and under French management—the factory of Goujon—one of the best-managed factories in Moscow. Two men, one representing himself as president and the other as secretary of the " Moscow Union of Workers," presented themselves to the factory manager and asked to be allowed to meet the workers in the factory. Their request was refused on the ground that the right of visiting workers *tête-à-tête* belonged exclusively to the factory inspector. The visitors disappeared, to return almost immediately with a requisition from the president of the Moscow Council on Factory Affairs, to the effect that the men be admitted for a *tête-à-tête* conference with the workers. The meeting took place, and on the evening of the same day the workers intimated to the manager that they were ordered not to return to work on the following day, on the ground that the firm owed them 40,000 rubles for retrospective claims.[1] The factory stopped work next morning. The Political Police Department, for some strange reason, showed its hand for the first time in these proceedings. The police intimated to M. Goujon that he must either grant the demands of his workers or submit to be banished from Moscow.[2]

It appears that at the same moment the working men at the head of the movement threatened those who were reluctant to join in it that if they did not concur in presenting the demands they would be " *transplanted from Moscow* "[3]—an evident indication that they had, or thought they had, the power of the police behind them. The upshot of the affair was very natural. M. Goujon appealed to the French Ambassador, who at once interviewed M. von Plehvë, and the result was an imperative order to the Moscow authorities to put an end to the strike.[4]

---

[1] See *Russkoë Dyelo* (Russian Affairs) (1905), No. 3, p. 9, and Svyatlovsky, *op. cit.*, p. 62.

[2] Svyatlovsky, *loc. cit.*

[3] Report of the manager of Smirnovoy's factory, published in *Torgovo-Promishlennaya Gazeta* (1906), No. 36 ; quoted by Svyatlovsky, *op. cit.*, p. 63.

[4] Svyatlovsky, *op. cit.*, p. 62. This appears to have been done in spite of the support of the strike by General Trepov.

The circumstance that Zubátov or his agents selected a well-managed factory established by foreign capital for their operations is significant. It exhibits the hollowness of the movement, if even it does not suggest sinister aims. There were undoubtedly in the Moscow district factories in which abuses were rampant, and in reference to which even a Zubátov strike might have done some good, but in this particular case the answer was easy and effective. The attack, notwithstanding its ostentatious support by the police, failed, and in its failure suggested to the working people the impossibility of labour organization. The motives are obscure, and the evidence, copious though it is, is lacking in some links, so that conclusions upon the affair must be taken as provisional.

While the Goujon strike was in progress the movement developed rapidly. The spirit, so long repressed, of the ventilation of grievances, real and imaginary, was in the air, and infected the working masses in Moscow practically as a whole. " Enormous and unprecedented quantities of collective announcements of grievances "[1] came into the offices of the factory inspectors. These inspectors report that complaints came, in January and February 1902, almost " exclusively " from the factories in the city of Moscow, while in March about one-third of the complaints come from out-lying districts, thus showing the rapid spreading of the movement initiated in Moscow. The *Digest of Factory Inspectors' Reports*,[2] issued by the Ministry of Finance, contains the following details: In the district of Kharkov the total number of complaints diminished in 1902 to about one-half of the number of 1901. They also diminished in Kiev and in Warsaw. In St. Petersburg the number increased by approximately one-third, while in Moscow district the complaints increased three times, and in 1902 composed more than half of the total number of complaints from workers against the managers of industrial factories in all districts.[3] Still more striking is the circumstance that, while in other districts the percentage of well-grounded complaints to the total number either increased or remained without change, the percentage of well-

[1] Unpublished reports of the factory inspectors, quoted by Professor Ozerov from papers in the Ministry of Finance ; cited by Svyatlovsky, *op. cit.*, p. 63.
[2] Quoted by Svyatlovsky at length, *op. cit.*, pp. 64 *et seq.*
[3] The figures were for Moscow in 1901, 16,815 complaints ; in 1902, 52,051. Total number from all districts, 97,843. Svyatlovsky, *op. cit.*, p. 64.

grounded complaints in Moscow greatly diminished. The number of well-grounded complaints varied in 1902 between 68 per cent. in Kharkov and 78.4 per cent. in Kiev, while in Moscow district the percentage in 1902 was 40.2. In 1901, before the manœuvres of Zubátov, the percentage of well-founded complaints was 71.5. In Moscow government (the city of Moscow) the number shrank from 72 per cent. in 1901 to 37.5 per cent. in 1902.[1] While thus there was a very considerable increase in complaints for which on inquiry insufficient foundation was found, it is very significant that the number of serious, well-founded complaints increased very materially. The number of complaints in the Moscow district of bad treatment and of beating of workers in factories in 1901 was 161. In 1902 " this number increased more than ten times, and reached 2146." In the government of Moscow alone there were 2098 complaints. The district factory inspector also points out that, whereas the well-founded complaints of bad treatment and of beating did not exceed 56 per cent. in 1901, the percentage of well-founded cases of such treatment in 1902 was 95. The conclusions of the factory inspector are as follows :

1. All these unfavourable appearances (referring to the increase in the number of all complaints, together with the increase in the percentage of ill-founded complaints) coincide with some movement among the workers during the year. That movement appeared most considerably in Moscow, and it evidently accounts for the advancing of many demands which had not previously been made, and which were not always well founded.

2. The workers, influenced by the above-mentioned movement, began to consider more closely the behaviour of managers and owners of factories, &c., and began to make complaints of actions which they had formerly disregarded.[2]

In June 1902 Zubátov convened a meeting of Moscow manufacturers in order to give to them some explanations of his policy. This meeting was held in Testov's Hotel on 26th June. To them Zubátov formally announced his " programme " in sixteen clauses.

---

[1] Of the total number of 52,051 complaints in the Moscow district, there were found well grounded only 20,914 ; for Moskovskaya *gub.* there were 48,074 complaints, of which 18,029 were well grounded. *Digest for* 1902, pp. 58–61.
[2] Condensed from *Digest of Factory Inspectors' Reports* (1902), p. xviii. ; cited by Svyatlovsky, *op. cit.*, pp. 64–6.

These clauses were committed to writing by some of the manufacturers and confidentially communicated to St. Petersburg " spheres."[1] By way of introduction, Zubátov is alleged to have addressed the manufacturers in some abrupt and uncomplimentary phrases. According to the report, he told them that their exploitation of their workpeople had made them universally detested in Moscow, not merely among the workers, but among the whole population. He told them that the people generally regarded them as *moshennēkē*, which can only be translated as " fakirs." He reminded them of the outbreaks, with attacks upon private property, which had taken place during the spring of that year in two districts of Poltavskaya *gub.*, and in certain districts in the government of Kharkov.[2] In order to prevent the spread of this spirit of disorder, Zubátov said that it was imperative that " the rights of workers should be widened," and that " not by legislation, but by means of administrative action."

The principal points in Zubátov's " programme " were as follows :

" 1. At present the law confides the safeguarding of the legal rights of employers and employees to the factory inspectorship ; but this institution, in the opinion of the Political Police Department, has proved to be powerless to discharge this function, having forfeited the confidence of the workers owing to its partiality to the employers. Therefore the Political Police Department, from considerations of State importance, has not only decided to take upon itself that part of factory inspectorship duties which comprises the mutual relations of employers and employed, but even is almost inclined to put an end to the institution as an anachronism. . . .

" 2. The widening of the rights of factory workers (in spite of the statute law) shall consist in uniting the workers of each factory into separate groups, each having its committee, voluntarily elected by workers of both sexes from among themselves. These committees must point out changes desirable for workers, in the scale of wages, distribution of working time, and general changes in the rules of internal order. The employer must communicate in future

---

[1] Svyatlovsky, *op. cit.*, p. 54. This " programme " was published in *Russkoë Dyelo* (Russian Affairs) in 1905, Nos. 3–5.

[2] These disturbances occurred in the last months of the " reign " of Sipiaghin and the first months of that of von Plehvë. Châteaux had been robbed and granaries looted by the peasants.

not immediately with his workers, but through the committee. The committees of separate factories of a given district are in communication with each other with a view to uniformity of action, the general supervision of the committees being centralized in the Political Police Department. For the purposes of this supervision the department appoints special agents from among the experienced and promising workers who are wise by long experience in the art of ruling the masses of the people.

" 3. In order to form this institution, mutually useful as it must be for employees and employers alike, the Political Police Department, in order that the coming occurrences should not take it unaware, took care not only to seek workers promising and experienced in strikes, even from among those who had been in administrative banishment, but also of establishing a school[1] for training the future actors, under the management of people experienced in this branch. All these teachers receive decent remuneration.

" 4. The sums required for the support of this institution are afforded by the 'Society of Mutual Assistance of the Workers in Mechanical Industries,' the constitution of which was granted on 14th February 1902. In this society there are taking part as members thousands of workers of both sexes, and even those under age. Besides contributions from these, there are the subscriptions from high exalted personages, educated classes, clergy, and different persons, but as yet no merchants or manufacturers.

" 5. By the means described the Political Police Department succeeded in a short time in inspiring the most sincere confidence of the working men, because they became convinced that every humbled and insulted person finds in the Political Police Department paternal attention, advice, support, and assistance by word and deed ; so that even the Museum of Labour, established by the Imperial Technical Society, began to lose ground." [2]

After he had succeeded in establishing the society of workers in the mechanical trades, Zubátov set himself to organize the weavers, especially in the cotton factories, of which there are a very large number in the Moscow district. On 21st December 1902 there began the enrolment of members in a " Union of

[1] Zubátov actually used the word " stud."
[2] These points are slightly condensed from Svyatlovsky, *op. cit.*, pp. 54–6.

Weavers." On 19th January 1903 there were 800 members. The president of the union was an agent of the Political Police called Krasivsky. This union numbered among its honorary members the Metropolitan, Vladimir, the Right Rev. Parfeni, the chief of police, Trepov, the editor of the *Moscow Viedomosti*, N. J. Prokhorov (the largest manufacturer in Moscow) and others. The workers in towns other than Moscow began to become aware of the growth of trade unionism in that city, and imitative unions sprang up in many places. For example, the factory inspectors reported that in 1902, in the government of Vladimir, " the success achieved by the Moscow working men is known to the locksmiths of Kovrov, is hotly discussed by them, and is evidently agitating them." In Perm, Ryazanskaya *gub.*, and other places the working men were becoming greatly excited. Meanwhile in Moscow fresh organizations were brought rapidly into existence ; button-makers, candy-makers, perfume-makers, cigar-makers, &c., were organized. The activity of the pupils of Zubátov manifested itself, however, most conspicuously, apart from Moscow, in St. Petersburg, Odessa, and Minsk.

In the autumn of 1902, the first steps towards open organization of working men took place in St. Petersburg. The application to form a society similar to the Moscow societies was presented to the Chief of Police of St. Petersburg (V. J. Frēsh). This functionary not only gave the applicants an attentive hearing, but the application to hold a meeting of working men was granted by the Director of the Imperial Police Department (Lopukhin).[1] This meeting, the first meeting of working men officially permitted in St. Petersburg, was held on Sunday, 17th November 1902. On 21st November the representatives of the working men were received by M. von Plehvë.[2] These representatives (agents of Zubátov) thanked M. von Plehvë for giving them permission to hold the meeting. Yet this attempt bore no fruit. The St. Petersburg working men seem to have been more wary than their comrades in Moscow, for they looked upon the movement with undisguised hostility.[3] The attempt also created some alarm among the publicists, who were more or less in

---

[1] *Svyet* (St. Petersburg). Quoted by Svyatlovsky, *op. cit.*, pp. 68 and 69. For Lopukhin, see *infra*, pp. 572 *et seq.*
[2] Svyatlovsky, *op. cit.*, p. 69.
[3] Dan, F., *History of the Labour Movement and Social Democracy in Russia*, pp. 42 and 43.

the confidence of the Tsar, although it is doubtful if at this time they fully understood its real origin. For example, Prince Metschersky wrote in his newspaper, *Grajdanin*,[1] " It must be remembered that in this labour question, there is fire, and with fire one must not joke, because of the risk of burning. If they (the organizers) are not sincere, and speak for effect only, nothing except harm can come of these public honours to factory workers. Why is there such honour to Moscow working men ? may be asked by other workers."

More important in the history of the Zubátov movement are the proceedings at Minsk and at Odessa. Zubátov's special agents at Minsk appear to have been two women ; but the movement there was carried on under the open patronage of an officer of gensdarmes, Vasilyev. Under his auspices there was formed " The Jewish Independent Labour Party." The policy of the party was set forth as a purely economical one, strictly legal modes of action were advocated, and profession was made of loyalty towards the Government. Here also Zubátov's agents met with opposition, especially from the " Universal Jewish Labour Union in Russia and Poland," a spontaneous organization of Jewish working men. This society devoted itself to exposure of the alleged independent party. The want of success in St. Petersburg and in Minsk led Zubátov to concentrate his attention upon the cities of Southern Russia. In the beginning of 1903 an agent of Zubátov, known as " Dr." Shaëvich, engaged in the organization of labour unions.

[1] Prince Metschersky, grandson of Karamsin the historian, is a characteristic figure in Russian society. Oriental not merely in his habits, but also in his ideas, which " are those of the Dahomey of fifty years ago or the Bokhara of to-day, modified in two important points." According to him, every governor of a province, every village *starosta*, should share the irresponsible power of the autocrat, and when dealing with the peasantry need observe no law. " Questions of the Zemstvo have no more to do with law courts," he writes, " than questions of family life. If a father may chastise his son severely without invoking the help of the courts, the authorities— local, provincial, and central—should be invested with a similar power to imprison, flog, and otherwise overawe and punish the people." (Art. " The Tsar " in the *Quarterly Review*, No. 399, July 1904.) Prince Metschersky edited and published *Grajdanin*, a newspaper which he maintained for the dissemination of his ideas. The title was recently changed to *Diary of a Conservative*. Not infrequently he spoke out against the Government in a manner for which only his birth and high position enabled him to secure immunity. Together with the late M. Pobyedonostsev, he was of the inner circle of the confidants of the Tsar. Both represented the autocracy in its most extreme and uncompromising form. (Cf. *Quarterly Review*, art. cited.)

The factory-owners were ordered by the police to employ only workers belonging to the union, the conditions of employment were dictated, and wages were fixed also by the police. Workmen who refused to belong to the union were expelled from the factories, and were even beaten in the streets, under the eyes and with the acquiescence of the police. " The acting chief of police at Odessa received delegates from unions and strikers, entered into negotiations with them, and sympathized with the unions." [1]

The movement at Odessa seems at an early stage to have passed wholly beyond the control of Zubátov as well as of the local police.[2] The general strike of July 1903 was put down with much bloodshed, for which it is impossible to hold Zubátov as otherwise than guilty.

The Odessa affair was the undoing of Zubátov. Events there led to inquiry into the whole system of police organization of labour on the part of the St. Petersburg authorities. Shaëvich and Zubátov were banished to the North of Russia, and this phase of police patronage of the labour movement was brought to an abrupt conclusion. Meanwhile among the working men strong suspicion of Zubátov and his agents had been developing into active hostility. The official fall of Zubátov had been in a large measure discounted so far as the working men of St. Petersburg, Moscow, and Minsk were concerned.

These details of the manœuvres of Zubátov are not without serious significance. They show that, notwithstanding the doubtful origin of the police " unions," and notwithstanding the doubtful character of many of their chief promoters, they did have an important influence upon the beginnings of Russian labour organization. Universal long hours, low wages, and unfavourable conditions of labour, rendered the whole industrial fabric insecure.

Socialist revolutionary propaganda, or any propaganda which offered a prospect of relief, found a favourable soil for the dissemination of its ideas. Zubátov was indisputably right on that point ; and, honest or otherwise, he saw farther than his superiors. His " unions " came at a psychological moment. His mistake lay in

---

[1] Report cited by Professor Ozerov, *op. cit.*, pp. 238-9.
[2] The history of the Zubátov movement in Odessa is told at length in *Iskra*. See also *infra*.

supposing that it was possible to control the forces which his "unions" concentrated. Zubátov thus "builded better than he knew"; for his "unions," the first "open" trade unions in Russia, taught the working men how to organize, and gave them a taste for power.

Profiting by the example of the Zubátov unions, other organizations made their appearance, to the great perplexity of the authorities. M. von Plehvë in particular felt that the furore for labour organization had already gone so far that it was impossible to stop it. He got rid of Zubátov; but it was not easy to get rid of the Frankenstein's monster which Zubátov appeared to have been instrumental in creating.[1]

The policy of controlling the labour movement, and of separating it from the revolutionary movement, with the design of turning it to account in the interests of the autocracy, came, in all the three cases of which account has been given, to a disastrous end. There is nothing novel in an attempt on the part of the Crown, of adherents acting in the assumed interest of the Crown, or of an oligarchy, to enlist the sympathies of one class against another, and thus, by producing internecine dissension, to divide the forces of the nation.[2]

Nor was there any novelty in the idea that the police system might be utilised for the purpose of carrying out the design in detail.[3] The gravamen of the charge against Zubátov is that he deliberately incited the working men to make unprecedented demands upon their employers, to strike when these demands were not granted, and to create by this means a condition of social unrest

[1] M. von Plehvë did not give evidence in this affair of insight into the conditions with which he had to deal. The event proved that Zubátov's dangerous activity should have been arrested at its beginning. Even if it be admitted that the relations between MM. von Plehvë and Wittë demanded a complete exposure of the results of M. Witte's industrial policy, the national risk of exposing them in this way was clearly too great from any point of view.

[2] Historical examples abound; instances are to be found in the sales of grain at nominal prices in Rome (see Mommsen, iii. chap. xii.; iv. chap. iii.); in the legislation of Basil I (Finlay, *Hist. of the Byzantine Empire*, bk. ii. chap. i.); and in Russian history in the reigns of Ivan IV and Paul I.

[3] It is alleged by social democrats that the police had been similarly employed in "assisting" in the organization of the labour movement by Napoleon III and Bismarck. The view of the *intelligentsia* is expressed sharply by Moskvitch in art. "Die Polizei" in *Russen über Russland* (J. Melnik ed., Frankfurt-am-Main, 1905), p. 439.

which would divert attention from the shortcomings of the Government to the shortcomings of private employers. At the same time, by preoccupying the working men with the wages question to the exclusion of interest in political propaganda, Zubátov contributed to the antagonism between the working men and the *intelligentsia*, and deprived the latter of numerical support to their propaganda. Moreover, Zubátov proposed to deal with the whole matter " administratively "—that is, that there was to be no question of legislation, but that orders were to be given (as they were given in the Goujon case), which proceeded from the authorities, and the full credit for which was to go to them. The employers were indeed to be despoiled, and the spoils handed over to the workmen. Thus the socialist revolutionaries were outbid by promises of immediate realization of excessive largesse extorted from the employers.

When it was eventually exposed, the method of Zubátov incurred the disapprobation not only of the employing class, but also of the reactionary party, which felt itself discredited by the dishonesty of the proceedings, as well as compromised by the danger of international complications, and of the working men, who felt themselves deceived by Zubátov and his agents. Everywhere the working people hastened to dissociate themselves from the wreck of the societies founded by Zubátov or under his influence.

While the Zubátovshina was submerged under a wave of general disapprobation, it must be held to be significant in so far as it taught the working men how to combine, and gave them experience of what open combination without continual fear of police suppression meant for them. The discussions of social questions, especially at Moscow and St. Petersburg, were unquestionably of educational value, although the social democratic writers [1] are inclined to depreciate them. Altogether, with other incidents of the time, the Zubátov series of movements must be held to have rendered an important though unintentional service in the initial stages of the revolution. The panic into which the authorities in Odessa, in Moscow, and in St. Petersburg were thrown showed that they had arrived at complete mistrust of police methods, and the chapter of police socialism, so far as it relates to labour combination, was,

[1] F. Dan, *e.g. op. cit.*

at all events for the time, wholly closed.[1] Police socialism, however, assumed a new and much more dangerous aspect in the hands of others than Zubátov—viz. in those of Rajkovsky, Lopukhin, and most of all of Azef, the account of whose proceedings will be given in a subsequent chapter.[2]

[1] The movement of Father Gapon is described *infra*. Some writers ascribe this movement to the influence of Zubátov. The validity of this ascription is discussed also *infra*.

[2] See *infra*, pp. 572–584.

CHAPTER XII

JEWISH POGROMS

JEWS are permitted to reside only in the so-called *Cherta Osedlosti*, or line of settlement—that is, in the following *guberni* : Bessarabskaya, Vilēnskaya, Vitebskaya, Volinskaya, Grodnēnskaya, Ekaterinoslavskaya, Kievskaya (excepting the city of Kiev), Kovēnskaya, Minskaya, Mohilevskaya, Podolskaya, Poltavskaya, Tavricheskaya (the cities of Sevastopol and Yalta excepted), Khersonskaya (the city of Nikolayev excepted), Chernigovskaya, and in the tsardom of Poland. In Poland Jews may live anywhere, but in the other localities mentioned their " right of residence " is limited to urban places, and it is also limited to an area within a zone of 50 *versts* round the boundaries. According to an ukase of 1882, certificates of sale of estates and mortgages upon estates may not be drawn in favour of Jews, nor may they enter into rent contracts for estates outside the limits of cities and towns, nor may they act as proxies for the management or sale of property. These restrictions, however, do not apply to certain classes of Jews. They do not apply to Karaïm or non-Talmudical Jews, nor do they apply to Jews who have received a university or equivalent education, nor to dentists, pharmacists, merchants of the first and second gilds, nor to direct descendants of persons who rendered military service in the time of Nicholas I.[1]

Jew-baiting is not new in Russia. The following is an account of a characteristic scene. A group of idlers who have lounged out of bars, tea-rooms, dens of various kinds, stand at a street corner. A Jew passes. The group of idlers jeer at him. If he answers the jeers, the idlers attack him. Other Jews come to his assistance. These are attacked. Then stones are thrown into the neighbouring houses. The rioters enter the houses and drag out the people. Gradually the disorder spreads from one district to another. Shouts

[1] Cf. *Osvobojdenie* (Stuttgart), i. No. 22, 8th May 1903, p. 378.

of "*Bey jēdov !*" (Beat the Jews !) are heard in the streets. Sometimes the Jews form into groups and defend themselves ; then the police, and even the troops, come into action, and the Jews find themselves attacked by those whose duty it is to protect them. Frequently the Jews offer money to escape worse consequences at the hands of the rioters. Jewish women offer themselves to escape death.

In the early seventies of the nineteenth century, and again in the early eighties, such *pogroms* or riots occurred. The principal scene of these riots was Kishenev, the capital of Bessarabia. The fundamental cause of the *pogroms* was described by the Russian review *Vestnik Evropy* in 1883 [1] as the legislation of Russia, in which the Jew is regarded as " a stranger, a pariah," and therefore beyond the protection of the law. Yet there is probably some foundation for the assertion of *Osvobojdenie*,[2] that the anti-Semitic feeling had died down in Russia after the *pogrom* at Odessa in 1873. It was aroused once more in 1881, when M. von Plehvë became Director of the Department of Police during the reaction which followed the assassination of Alexander II. " All this year there were continual anti-Jewish *pogroms*, in which even the official communications could not always conceal the fact of the actual participation of the local authorities." [3] In 1882 and later years *pogroms* were sporadic ; but they had practically disappeared for some years when, in 1903, once more the control of the police passed into the hands of M. von Plehvë, when immediately *pogroms* began again to occur. They began at Kishenev. Since 1897 the press of Kishenev had been suppressed, with the exception of two newspapers, *Bessarabits* and *Znamya* (Banner), both edited by a certain Krushevan. The close relation between these newspapers and the local administration is undoubted. In March 1903 *Bessarabits* published an account of an alleged ritual murder by Jews at Dubossari, a small town in the province of which Kishenev is the capital. This account was false, and on its exposure M. von Plehvë issued a circular on 22nd March prohibiting further newspaper reference to the subject. Whether under the auspices of M. von Plehvë or of Krushevan does not appear, but soon after the Jewish Passover, some

[1] *Vestnik Evropy* (1883), part ix. p. 354.
[2] Edited by P. Struvë, vol. i. No. 22, 8th May 1903.
[3] *Osvobojdenie* (Stuttgart), vol. i No. 22, 8th May 1903. p. 379.

persons made their appearance in Kishenev as agitators in favour of a Jewish *pogrom*. The Jews became alarmed, and sent a deputation to the governor to request protection. The governor promised to take measures for their safety. This he failed to do, and the destruction of Jewish houses began, while the police stood by indifferently, or even attacked those Jews who attempted to defend themselves. According to *Osvobojdenie* the people who took part in the *pogroms* were, in the first instance, peasants from the neighbouring country districts, who had had no previous relation with the Jews of Kishenev. Later the local inhabitants, who found the Jews keen competitors in their business, joined the anti-Semitic movement, and engaged in *pogroms*. The Kishenev *pogrom* took place on 6th and 7th April. About a fortnight previously (on 25th March) von Plehvë, then Minister of Interior, had sent a despatch to General von Raben, Governor of Kishenev. This despatch, which was published at the time by *The Times*, was as follows :

" I have been informed that in the locality entrusted to you there are in preparation vast disorders against Jews who are exploiting the local population. Because of the generally unquiet state of mind of the people of the city, a state of mind which is seeking for an outlet, and also because of the undesirability of exciting anti-governmental feelings among the population not yet touched by the propaganda, and of applying too severe measures, your Excellency will not fail to stop immediately by persuasion, not using armed force, the disorders which are about to begin." [1]

This despatch was naturally interpreted at the time as a callous instruction to leave the Jews to the mercy of the rioters in the interests of the Government, which von Plehvë seemed to think would be served by the diversion of popular fury from an anti-governmental to an anti-Semitic direction. *Znamya* and *Bessarabits*, Krushevan's newspapers, offer another explanation. The Jews of Kishenev were, he said, " the redeeming sacrifice for the revolutionary propaganda of their fellow-Jews." [2] That the Jewish *pogroms* were intended as a counter-revolutionary stroke appears also from the circumstance that the dates fixed for revolutionary demonstrations were also the dates fixed beforehand for the Jewish *pog-*

---

[1] *Osvobojdenie*, ibid.
[2] Quoted by *Osvobojdenie*, No. 22, p. 380.

roms.[1] The policy, if such it may be called, was to some extent successful. The revolutionary groups, realizing the connection between their proceedings and the *pogroms* against the Jews, cancelled many of these demonstrations,[2] and thus it may be said that throughout the south of Russia, the revolutionary movement was thrown back for about two years. In May 1903 a deputation of three influential Jews went from Odessa to St. Petersburg to remonstrate with von Plehvë and to endeavour to see the Tsar. The case for the Jews was skilfully put by Königshatz, a Jewish lawyer. Von Plehvë answered that he was considering measures for the improvement of the condition of the Jews ; " but," he said (according to the report of the deputation, drawing himself up to his full height and assuming a menacing tone), " tell this to the Jewish youth, your sons and daughters—tell all your *intelligentsia.* Let them not think that Russia is an old and rotting organism ; the new developing Russia will win, and will put down the revolutionary movement. Much is said about the cowardice of Jews. This is not true. The Jews are the boldest of people. In Western Russia about 90 per cent. of the revolutionists are Jews, and in Russia as a whole, about 40 per cent.[3] I will not conceal from you that the revolutionary movement in Russia is disturbing us. From time to time when, here and there, demonstrations are arranged, we come even to confusion ; but we shall control this. I wish to let you understand that unless you detain your youth from the revolutionary movement, we will make your situation so intolerable that you will have to go away from Russia to the last man." [4]

This was undoubtedly the true explanation of the *pogroms ;* and M. von Plehvë must have known that in putting it in set terms, he was pronouncing his own sentence of death.

---

[1] *Osvobojdenie,* ibid.   [2] *Ibid.*
[3] This was probably correct at the time when von Plehvë spoke. It would not, of course, have been true in 1905 and 1906.
[4] From *Latest Information* (the organ of the Jewish Bund), No. 132 ; quoted in *Osvobojdenie,* No. 1 (25), July 1903.

CHAPTER XIII

RUSSIA IN THE FAR EAST

THE eastward expansion of Russia and her conflict with Japan have been important incidents in her economic, as well as in her political history ; but the progress of the one and the causes of the other have extended over so long a period of time, and in the earlier stages these were so far removed from the main currents of Russian economic life, that it has appeared to be necessary to treat them separately in this place.

The Russians reached the Ural Mountains early in the fifteenth century,[1] and settlements were established upon the western slopes by enterprising adventurers, who engaged in the fur trade and in salt-boiling. Amongst these early adventurers was the founder of the celebrated family of Strogonov.[2]

Towards the end of the sixteenth century the hostile tribes beyond the low range of hills which constitute the Ural Mountains, on the frontiers of which are now the *guberni* of Perm and Ufa, distressed the fur traders by frequent attacks upon their settlements. These attacks led the Strogonovs to petition the *voyevoda* of the district to authorize them to raise a force for the purpose of repelling the tribesmen. Permission was given, and a force under the command of a Cossack *ataman* was sent across the mountains.

---

[1] The relations of Russia with the Far East began, however, much earlier. Russia had been repeatedly overrun, and in the thirteenth century had been subjugated by Asiatic hordes. (For ethnical affinities between some of the races of Russia and the Northern Mongols, see Vol. I. Appendix No. II.) The great Asiatic empire of Genghis Khan and of Oktai extended from the Pacific Ocean to the western shores of the Black Sea. The Mongolo-Tartar conquerors were masters of the plains of Asia and of Russia. They were stayed only by the mountaineers of Moravia and Bohemia. There are Chinese traditions of Russian guards being taken to Peking in the thirteenth century. (*Cf.* Parker, E. H., *China, Her History, Diplomacy, and Commerce* (London, 1901), p. 96.)

[2] *The Industries of Russia*, vol. v. *Siberia and the Great Siberian Railway*, edited by J. M. Crawford (St. Petersburg (in English), 1893), p. 3.

The Cossack *ataman* was Yermak Timofeyevich, whose energetic conduct of the expedition won Siberia for the Tsar.

Ivan IV (the Terrible), whose policy was one of consolidation of conquests rather than of extension of territory, disapproved of the aggressive character which the ostensibly merely punitive expedition had assumed in the hands of Yermak, and ordered its recall. It was too late. The Siberian tribes were unacquainted with gunpowder, and they fell before the bullets of Yermak's insignificant army. Yermak was drowned in 1584, but the conquest and settlement of the vast Siberian region went on rapidly. In 1587 Tobolsk was founded, in 1604 Tomsk, in 1619 Yeniseisk, and in 1632 Yakutsk. A party of Cossacks was sent in 1636 from Tomsk to the Aldan River, in order to reduce a band of Tunguses to subjection. The Aldan has its rise on the northern slopes of the Stanovoi Mountains, on the southern slopes of which rise many of the tributaries of the Amur. Rumours of the existence of a mighty stream to the south reached the Cossacks, who, however, at that time made no attempt to visit it, but pushed eastwards to the Sea of Okhotsk, on whose shores they arrived in 1639. In this year the rumours about the Amur region were confirmed, and in 1643 an expedition was despatched from Yakutsk for the purpose of exploring it. The party was injudiciously led, and its leaders succeeded in converting friendly peoples with whom they came in contact into formidable enemies. The Russians were driven back famished and decimated. Nevertheless, they had reached the junction of the Sungari with the Amur, and had acquired much knowledge of the resources and defences of the region. In 1649 another expedition was fitted out at the expense of Khabarov, a wealthy Cossack. With seventy Cossacks, Khabarov reached the Amur, and found at the mouth of the Urka, a Daurian prince, Lavkai, who interrogated him about his object in visiting the country. Khabarov professed trade, but Lavkai suggested conquest.

The expedition was mainly for reconnaissance, and Khabarov returned to Yakutsk. In the following year, 1650, he commanded a second and stronger expeditionary force for the region of the Amur. Khabarov's company was, after all, of no great strength, considering the magnitude of the task he was about to undertake ; but men were scarce in Eastern Siberia, and his total force consisted of twenty-one Cossacks and one hundred and seventeen volunteers.

On the advance of the Russians into the Amur region, most of the inhabitants fled ; those who resisted were cut to pieces without quarter. Arrows [1] were useless against bullets. The Daurian princes and their people retired everywhere before the Russians ; occasionally some of them were surprised and killed or captured. The Manchu Emperor at Peking, Shun-chih, claimed suzerainty over the Daurians and collected tribute from them, but the few Manchu horsemen who were in the region, and whose duty it was to protect the tributaries of their master, fled before the Russians and left the Daurians to their fate. The policy of the Russians and the tactics of the Daurians, who deserted their villages, carrying off their food supplies, together rendered the continued occupation of the region by Khabarov's company impossible. Khabarov built a fort, and sent out foraging expeditions ; but he was repeatedly attacked by the Ducheri and the Achani, Khabarov having moved his quarters into the country of the latter. He was also attacked by Manchus, who were then armed with matchlocks and artillery. Khabarov repulsed these attacks at the expense of a considerable number of his force ; but he was obliged to reascend the Amur. As Khabarov was returning to Yakutsk, he met in the pass of the Bureya Mountains a party nearly as large as his own original company, which had been sent to reinforce him. Khabarov therefore retraced his steps ; but he was speedily embarrassed by a mutiny among his men and the desertion of more than a third of them.

These expeditions were unquestionably conducted with cruelty unusual even in such adventures. Khabarov admitted that he tortured and burnt his hostages.[2] The memory of his atrocities remained among the natives of the Amur until our own day, and doubtless still remains.[3] The number of the natives slaughtered by him does not appear, but the loss of natives and Manchus together, killed in frequent attacks, is put at 1600 men. Khabarov's own losses are stated at 233 by death or desertion.[4]

The irregular and non-productive exploits of Khabarov led the Moscow Government to decide to send out an army of 3000 men for the occupation of the Amur region. Khabarov himself had suggested

[1] There is a very interesting collection of bows and arrows in the Royal Palace of the Manchus at Mukden. The bows are of great size ; their use must have involved the exercise of a high degree of muscular strength.
[2] Ravenstein, E. G., *The Russians on the Amur* (London, 1861), p. 19.
[3] *Ibid.*   [4] *Ibid.*, p. 25.

double that number, on the ground that the number of Manchus which would have to be reckoned with was about 40,000. The most exaggerated reports of the riches of the Amur were circulated by Khabarov's returning Cossacks. The result of these reports was a stream of adventurers. " Lawless bands " of such people passed through Eastern Siberia, plundering the villages as they went. The expeditionary force which was to have been sent from Moscow to the Amur was sent only to Siberia, where its presence was more necessary. The Chinese were aroused, numerous Manchu troops were sent into the region, the small Russian forces, now under Stepanov, who had succeeded Khabarov, were inadequately supplied with ammunition, and thus, in spite of considerable gallantry exhibited in the face of overwhelming numbers of Manchus, the main force of the Russians was killed or captured. The Lower Amur was completely evacuated by 1660. Although the Russians had consolidated themselves upon the Shilka, an important tributary of the Upper Amur, had occupied Trans-Baïkalia and had founded Nerchinsk, they allowed several years to pass before any renewed attempts were made to occupy the Lower Amur.

The adventurous spirit of the Russians in Eastern Siberia led to the occupation, in 1665, of Albazin, on the Amur, by a bandit of Siberia, named Nikita Chernigovsky.[1] Chernigovsky was, as his name implied, of Little Russian extraction. He had been exiled to Siberia, where he became the leader of a predatory band. The *voyevoda* of Ilimsk having fallen at his hands, Chernigovsky, with about eighty of his followers, fled to Albazin, where they found one of the old forts of Lavkai, the Daurian prince. Here the bandits established themselves. Recruits came to them in groups, contributed by the lawless bands of Eastern Siberia. In 1671 the command of this little settlement was placed in the hands of an official sent from Nerchinsk. In 1672 the group of settlers assumed a new character. Formerly they had lived chiefly upon the exploitation, by forced tribute and otherwise, of the native population. This they had been able to carry on in spite of protests to Moscow from Peking. Now peasants began to go into the country, to cultivate the soil, and to deal with the natural resources. Many villages began to be built in a wide region, the centre of which naturally was Albazin, which thenceforward came to be a position of importance.

[1] Crawford, *op. cit.*, p. 7.

The Russians were now after a manner established on the Amur, within territory over which the Chinese had exercised a somewhat ineffective sovereignty, collecting tribute from tribal groups whom they did not attack so long as the tribute was paid, but whom they did little to protect except from one another. As the event proved, the Chinese were unable to protect them against the Russians. Towards the east the river Bureya flows into the Amur at Skobeltsin, about 700 miles above the mouth, and the river Amgun, which, although its sources are on the slopes of the Bureya Mountains at no great distance from those of the Bureya, flows into the Amur near the mouth.

The valleys of these rivers were occupied by tribal groups which admitted no allegiance and paid no tribute either to the Chinese or to the Russians. In spite of interior difficulties at Albazin, by 1682 several posts had been established by the Russians in widely separated parts of the region embraced by the great bend of the Amur and watered by its northern tributaries.

It is necessary now to turn to the region upon which the Russians had encroached. The valley of the Amur had formed the heart of successive Tungusian empires,[1] whose boundaries from the beginning of the tenth until the beginning of the twelfth century had extended from the Great Wall of China northwards to the Altai Mountains, and westwards so far as Kashgar, in what is now Chinese Turkestan. Even China fell under the control of the Tungusian Emperors, for a Tungusic dynasty ruled North China from Peking (960–1260), during approximately the same period as the Sung dynasties ruled South China from Nanking, Hangchow, and other capitals (915–1232),[2] the latter power paying tribute to the former during a great part of the period. Among the Tungusic peoples, the group which has made more impression than any other upon history has been the Manchu. These people, whose cradle was probably either the plains through which the Sungari River flows, or the Shan Alin range to the south of these, appear to have invited Koreans and Chinese into their country, and to have cultivated the arts and sciences at an early period. In the tenth century they were conquered by the Kitans, another Tungusic people, who were masters

[1] The origin of the name Tungus is obscure. See discussion upon it by A. H. Keane, *Man, Past and Present* (Cambridge, 1900), p. 287.
[2] The reign of the Sung dynasties embraces the great literary and artistic period of China.

of the region between the Liao-tung peninsula [1] and the Amur, as well as all that is now Mongolia. These were the people who gave China her Tungusic Emperors, and who through Marco Polo gave the name by which China is known in Russia (Kitai), and also gave the name Cathay. During the period of Mongol domination in China from 1260 till 1368, Manchuria seems to have been the battle-ground of constant wars between the Mongol Emperors and the Tunguses, now represented chiefly by the *Chin* or Golden dynasty. The population was decimated and the towns destroyed. The Mongol power was overthrown by a revolution in 1368, and the Ming dynasty came to the throne. Manchuria was divided into three provinces in the fourteenth century ; and in the early part of the fifteenth these provinces were made tributary to China.

In one of these, the province of Tsyan-chzu, there lived about the middle of the fourteenth century a certain Aishin-goro, who was recognized as a descendant of the Golden dynasty, several villages acknowledging his sovereignty. A reputed descendant of this man, three hundred years later—in the end of the sixteenth century—succeeded in enlarging the boundaries of Manchu influence. This heir to the Golden Throne was Nurkhatzi.[2] The gradual growth of his power enabled him to establish himself at Mukden, which became his capital. He threw off the yoke of the Chinese and declared himself Emperor. The Chinese troops sent against him were defeated. Nurkhatzi died in 1626; but his successor, on being invited to Peking as recognized vassal of the Chinese Emperor, in order to aid in the suppression of a rebellion, not only put down that rebellion, but himself seized the throne of China (1644) as the first Emperor of the dynasty which fell in 1911. Nurkhatzi's successor died in the year of his triumph, and the throne fell to a child of six years. During the minority of the young Emperor, and for many years afterwards, the position of the dynasty was by no means secure.

Although the Manchus from the beginning had disputed the Russian advance, and had prevented the invaders from establishing

---

[1] The Liao-tung peninsula was from early ages an independent kingdom, until about the beginning of the Christian era. Under the Han dynasty, the region was annexed to China. Then followed successively the suzerainty of China, independence, conquest by Korea, Chinese rule, Tungusian control. With the seizure of power in China by the Manchus, it passed once more into the hands of China.

[2] Or Nurhachu.

themselves on the Sungari, the ancient cradle of the Manchus, they had not been able altogether to expel the Russians from the Amur region.

In 1683 the Manchu Emperor K'anghi determined to adopt vigorous measures to recover the rich alluvial soils of the Amur basin, some portion of which had fallen into the hands of Russia. A considerable force was sent to Aigun in the summer of 1683, and many of the smaller Russian settlements were captured or dispersed. In the following year Albazin was besieged and was forced to surrender. The Russians were permitted to withdraw. They retreated to Nerchinsk, meeting on their way too tardy reinforcements. The Chinese forces, having driven out the Russians, withdrew up the Sungari River. Within a few days after the withdrawal of the Chinese, Albazin was reoccupied by the Russians. They immediately proceeded to improve the defences. In the following year the Chinese returned in force, and invested Albazin. They tried to carry the place by assault, but failed. Although they had reduced the garrison to small numbers and to great extremities, they voluntarily raised the siege after an investment of five months ; and left the region altogether in the following year (1687).

The reason for this action, inexplicable to the besieged, was a diplomatic one. An emissary had been despatched from Moscow to Peking, where he had arrived in 1686. The negotiations thus initiated by Russia led, in the first instance, to the raising of the siege of Albazin, and, secondly, to an agreement that representatives of Russia and China should meet at Selenginsk to arrange about the delimitation of the frontier between the two countries.

Plenipotentiaries were despatched by each power, one from Peking and one from Moscow, suitably escorted. Strangely enough, both embassies were attacked by Mongols as they approached their meeting place ; the Russians beat off their assailants, but the Chinese were compelled to retire. A fresh arrangement was necessary, and after some delay the plenipotentiaries met at Nerchinsk, the Chinese appearing in considerable force, greatly outnumbering the Russians. After many difficulties and at least one moment when hostilities seemed likely to break out immediately, the Russians being surrounded by hostile Chinese, the draft of a treaty, afterwards known as the Treaty of Nerchinsk, was signed, 29th August 1689. The Stanovoi Mountains and the Argun River were accepted as the boundaries, the Russians having the north and the Chinese the south banks of the latter river. The Russian fortress of Albazin was to be demolished, and hunting was prohibited on either side to the " nationals " of the other; commerce and intercourse were, however, permitted. The terms of the treaty were to be graven upon stones in Tataric (Manchu) Chinese, Russian, and Latin, and these stones were to be erected on the frontier. The treaty was a complete victory for the Chinese; not only were they left with the rich basin of the Amur, but they retained also the valuable hunting grounds on the southern slopes of the Stanovoi Mountains, as well as the basins of the numerous tributaries of the Amur which had their sources in them.

During the eighteenth century the colonization of Siberia proceeded after a fashion, the aboriginal tribes were driven away from the settlements, stockaded posts and fortresses being built at intervals for purposes of protection. Meanwhile, exploration of Siberia was carried out by several scientific expeditions. Under Peter the Great, and on his initiative, an expedition was despatched in 1725 to find whether there existed a passage into the Arctic Ocean from the Pacific between America and Asia.[1] This expedition was commanded by Vitus Berend, a Danish sailor in the Russian service. The successful issue of this voyage led to a series of expeditions, which resulted in the gradual discovery and occupation by the Russians of the region which came to be known as Alaska. During the same period the Aleutian Islands were discovered and occupied. These expeditions were performed between 1739 and 1769.[2]

During the eighteenth century the Chinese seat of government of the Amur was Tsitsikar, at which town and at Aigun there was a military governor. Both of these, together with the Governor of Kirin, were under the authority of the Governor-General of Manchuria at Mukden. The males of the Manchu population were practically all under arms. In addition to the Manchus there were nomadic tribes, who were for the most part hunters. The former paid taxes and the latter tribute. The tribute exacted (in sables and in grain) was heavy, and the tribesmen were thus not reluctant to pass under the rule of Russia. Up till 1820 a policy of rigid

---

[1] The existence of such a passage had already been demonstrated by Simeon Dejnyev in 1648; but Peter seems to have been unaware of the fact. Cf. *Siberia and the Great Siberian Railway*, edited Crawford, pp. 526–810.
[2] *Ibid.*, p. 11.

exclusion was carried out by China, and immigration into Manchuria was prevented even in the case of Chinese. In that year, however, the policy was changed and the Chinese flocked into the country.

Throughout the eighteenth century the Chinese were frequently requested by Russia to permit the free navigation of the Amur, but they persistently refused. Meanwhile Russian settlements had been formed on the Pacific coast, and the supplies for these had to be transported by land at considerable cost.[1] The Russian Government was, however, reluctant to employ coercive measures at so great distance from any military base. The region was comparatively little known and little valued. The event which ultimately changed altogether the attitude of Russia towards the Pacific and towards the Amur was the appointment of Count Nikolas N. Muraviev as Governor of Eastern Siberia in 1847. This officer became an enthusiastic advocate of Russian advance in Eastern Asia, and although his ardent appeals fell into dull ears at St. Petersburg, he persevered until the force of circumstances came to his aid. His first step was to send in 1848 a small party of four Cossacks with an officer down the Amur.[2] The party was never heard of again. The next step was the despatch, through Muraviev's initiative, of a surveying vessel from the Baltic to the Pacific with instructions to explore the coasts of the Sea of Okhotsk and the mouth of the Amur. In 1850 this vessel entered the mouth of the river, and in 1851 two towns were established upon the banks. Although the Russians had been shut off by China from the upper waters of the Amur, they had now succeeded in establishing themselves some distance above its mouth.[3]

The decisive event which precipitated action on the part of Muraviev was the outbreak of the Crimean War. In 1854 there were three Russian frigates on the Pacific coast. Whether or not there was real risk of these vessels running short of supplies owing

[1] In 1816 the price of flour in Kamchatka was 8½d. per lb. Ravenstein, *op. cit.*, p. 114. The cost of transport by pack-horses at that time was, however, only about 1d. per cwt. per mile.

[2] This was not the first attempt to navigate the river. The first vessel to appear upon the waters of the Amur was the *Constantine*, which, under the command of Gavrilov, entered the estuary of the river on 5th May 1846 (Crawford, p. 230).

[3] On the history of the Amur, see Temonov, *Sketch of the Principal Watercourses of the Amur Region* (St. Petersburg, 1897), and *Reports of the Imperial Russian Geographical Society*, and those of *The Imperial Academy of Science*. See also Bussye, *Literature of the Amur Region* (St. Petersburg, 1882), and bibliography by Ravenstein, *op. cit.*

to the difficulty of getting them by sea or by land by the usual pack-horse route in time, the possibility of this contingency was sufficient, in Muraviev's mind, to justify him in adopting an unusual course. He determined to send the supplies down the Amur from Shilkinsk on the Shilka, and to take command of the expedition himself. He applied to the Chinese Governor of Kiakhta and to the Viceroy at Urga for permission to navigate the Amur, but these functionaries declined to grant permission without consulting their Government at Peking. Muraviev left Shilkinsk on 27th May 1854, without permission. He had one small steamer and about fifty barges, besides numerous rafts. He took with him about a thousand troops and several guns. He reached Marünsk, on the Lower Amur, without mishap on 27th June. Muraviev found that the Chinese garrisons of the posts on the Amur were miserably armed, and were quite unable to do more than make a formal protest against his passage.

Meanwhile war had been declared, and a small allied squadron was making its way from Callao to the Sea of Okhotsk. The only armed vessels belonging to Russia in these seas at that time were one frigate and a hulk, a store ship, and two transports. Their total armament was 130 guns. The allied squadron consisted of two English frigates, a steamer, and a brig, and of one French frigate and a corvette, with altogether 190 guns and about 2000 men.

The Russian ships concentrated at Petropavlovsk. While the allied squadron was about to attack, the English Admiral committed suicide. The French Admiral succeeded to the command, but being unable to exercise sufficient authority over the officers of the squadron, he was obliged to permit a premature and ill-managed assault, which was repulsed. Five days after the arrival of the squadron, it sailed away without having accomplished the object of the expedition. In the spring of 1855 the Russians abandoned Petropavlovsk, the Russian vessels slipping unobserved in a fog, past the allied fleet, which had returned reinforced with instructions to take the port. The Allies landed, found the town deserted, destroyed the batteries, and then departed. Some engagements of no moment took place later ; but the Pacific naval operations had no more influence upon the course of the campaign than had the similarly fruitless expedition to the White Sea.[1] Quite otherwise

[1] When a few shots were fired at the Solovietsky Monastery by the fleet under Admiral Erasmus Ommaney.

was the influence of the attack upon the Amur with regard to the development of the region and the extension of Russian authority over it.

The experiment of unlicensed navigation carried out successfully by Muraviev led to the diversion of the traffic between Eastern Siberia and the Pacific from the land route to the Amur. The Russo-American Company [1] also used the river for the transportation of colonists and goods destined for Alaska. Muraviev's policy of expansion now received a definite impulse. In order to protect the trade which had grown up on the Amur, in 1857, it was necessary to occupy certain posts on the river in force. Muraviev went to St. Petersburg and obtained the means and the men to carry out this design. When, however, he arrived with his forces at Nerchinsk, the situation on the Amur had changed.

The Chinese had observed, no doubt with misgiving, the use made of the Amur by the Russians, but they were evidently unwilling to provoke hostilities. An attempt had been made in Southern China in 1840 to put an end to foreign trade.[2] This attempt had brought on the war of 1840–1842, and had resulted not only in the compulsory opening of Canton, Shanghai, Ningpo, Foochow, and Amoy to foreign commerce, but also in the loss to China of the island of Hong-Kong. In 1856 the anti-foreign feeling in China again became acute and resulted in the war of 1858–1859, in which Great Britain and France took part. The Allies at first were repulsed by the Taku Forts, but later they marched upon Peking, destroying the Summer Palace [3] to the north of the city, and demanded the opening of Tientsin, Chefoo, Swatow, Hankow, Kiu-Kiang, and Chinkiang. These incidents revealed to the Chinese more demonstratively than before the material force which might be brought into play by European powers.

Thus when Muraviev arrived on the Amur in May 1858, he found the local Chinese authorities much more complaisant than he had expected. He was indeed able to achieve without any display of force the Treaty of Aigun (28th May 1858), by which the north bank

---

[1] Founded in 1799 and liquidated in 1867 in consequence of the sale of Alaska to the United States. *Siberia and the Great Siberian Railway*, p. 12.

[2] Not only to the trade in opium. *Cf.* Parker, E. H., *China, Her History, Diplomacy, and Commerce* (London, 1901), p. 92.

[3] The ruins of this palace still lie north of the outer walls of Peking. At a distance of a few miles farther north is situated the modern Summer Palace with its lake and beautiful park.

of the Amur was ceded so far as the Ussuri River, as well as both banks of the Ussuri. The Sungari, the Ussuri, and the Amur were to be open to Russian trade. Count Putiatin, who had been sent by the Russian Government to Peking, concluded almost at the same date (13th June) the Treaty of Tientsin, by which certain ports were opened to Russian trade and Russia was permitted to maintain an embassy at Peking.[1] During the negotiations the Chinese Government is alleged to have invited the Russians to assist it in repelling the attacks of England and France, but the Russian envoy turned a deaf ear to the solicitation.

During the summer of 1858 Muraviev was not idle. He founded Blagovesh'chensk, near the Chinese fortress of Aigun, Khabarovsk at the mouth of the Ussuri, and Sofyevsk on the Lower Amur.

The Russian Government had, in an ukase of 31st October 1857, assumed possession of the Amur region, and for administrative purposes had constituted it, together with the coast of the Sea of Okhotsk and Kamchatka, the "Maritime Province of Eastern Siberia." On 31st December 1858 another ukase was issued referring to the "reacquisition" of the Amur region, and recognizing it as the "Province of the Amur," separating it from the Maritime Province. Settlement upon the Amur was carried out too speedily to be effectual. Cossacks and their families, to the number of 20,000, were established there prior to 1859; but the Cossacks are not good farmers, and their agricultural settlements cannot be held to have been successful. The Amur Company, incorporated 23rd January 1858, was founded for the purpose of the commercial exploitation of the region. This company also projected a telegraph line from Moscow to the Amur.

The Government gave facilities in money and otherwise to political exiles, sailors, and others who were willing to establish themselves in colonies. In the beginning of 1859, 10,000 colonists passed through Irkutsk from European Russia and Western Siberia on their way to the Amur.

In the summer of 1859 China, having for the moment relieved herself of the pressure of the Allies, repented of the generosity of

---

[1] A so-called "clerical mission" at Peking had been established in 1692. This mission had served the purpose to a certain extent of a diplomatic mission, although it had been at least partly maintained by the Chinese Government. [Cf. Art. 10, Treaty of Tientsin (Russian Chinese).]

the terms of the Treaty of Aigun, forbade the ascent of the Sungari by a group of Russians, and even interfered with Russian navigation on the Amur. At an opportune moment, however, the Allies marched upon Peking ; and this diversion enabled the Russians to avoid the use of force in insisting upon the observation of the terms of their treaty.

Meanwhile the Russian Government engaged to a small extent in colonizing experiments. Forty-seven German families were taken from California, and a hundred Mennonites from South Russia.

In November 1860 Russia concluded a new treaty with China. This treaty gave Russia the whole coast of Manchuria to the Korean frontier, and provided for trade free of all duties and restrictions between Russia and China on the land frontiers. The new territory thus acquired enabled Russia to found her great eastern seaport— Vladivostok—(" Dominion of the East "). Writing immediately afterwards, Ravenstein predicted that when the Chinese Empire fell to pieces, Russia would possess herself of the whole of Manchuria, including the Liao-tung peninsula.[1]

The efforts of Russia to colonize the basin of the Amur were not very successful ; while, meantime, immigrants from China poured not only into Manchuria south of the Amur, but even into the region ceded to Russia on the north bank. Koreans also crossed the frontier into Maritime Manchuria and formed colonies there. The reason for the non-success of Russia in the colonization of the region she had acquired, undoubtedly lay in the circumstance that until after emancipation had been fully carried into effect, and until the system of " mutual guarantee " for the payment of taxes was abolished, it was quite impossible to promote any considerable voluntary emigration movement from European Russia, either to Siberia or to Manchuria. Further reason may be found in the facts that owing to serfdom the peasants were destitute of the funds which were necessary to undertake so great a land journey as was involved in traversing Siberia, then without railways, and that Siberia itself was most scantily populated, although great areas were nearly as fertile as the soils of the Amur basin. Those peasants who did make their way in the predatory bands, whose existence has already been mentioned, did not form sufficiently stable communities to occupy outposts of the Empire. Even in Siberia the

[1] Ravenstein, *The Russians on the Amur*, p. 154.

pioneers were " vagabonds and nomad adventurers, so that the Government had to make great efforts to bind them to the land." [1] It was also apparent that the climate of the north bank of the Amur was severe in winter, and that settlers were inclined to go south-wards,[2] impelled by a desire for a milder climate. This southerly tendency meant, however, ultimate conflict with the Chinese authorities.

The Amur was too distant from European Russia to benefit by the presence of those peasants who, fleeing from their proprietors in Russia, populated the *gub.* of Tobolsk,[3] and even made their way farther east. It must also be realized that, simultaneously with the attempt to settle the Amur region, Russia was engaged in the colonization of the Zaïlüsh slopes on the frontier of Central Asia, as well as in the occupation of Turkestan. In this region also Russia and China came into contact.

After the suppression of the Tai-ping rebellion a Mohammedan revolt took place in China ; and Russia occupied the province of Ili, in the extreme west of the Chinese Empire, to the south of Lake Balkash. This occupation continued up till 1881, when China negotiated a treaty with Russia, providing for the evacuation of Ili, and for the security of Russian merchants on the land routes. One of the most important of these passes from Hankow by the river Han, through Ili to Kashgar and Russia.[4]

The effective colonization of Siberia really began only after Emancipation in 1861 ; and then began also a serious effort to attract colonists to the Amur. The obligatory settlement of Cossacks promising at best a restricted colonization, it was necessary to offer inducements to peasants to migrate thither from the con-gested regions in European Russia. The Government did not grant free land, but it offered 100 *dessyatin* per family in free use for twenty years, with right of purchase or of renting at the end of that period. If immediate purchase was desired, the land was sold at three rubles per *dessyatin*. The settlers were also exempted from

---

[1] *Siberia and the Great Siberian Railway,* cit., p. 3.
[2] Kropotkin, Prince, *Memoirs* (Boston, 1899), p. 269.
[3] *Siberia and the Great Siberian Railway,* p. 9.
[4] This route was discovered about the beginning of the Christian era by Han Wu Ti. It is the shortest existing route between China and the Western world. " Sooner or later it must be the line of China's chief trunk railway to the west." Parker, E. H., *China, Her History, Diplomacy, and Commerce,* p. 149.

imperial taxation for twenty years, from military service for ten years, and from rural taxes for three years.

Even when Emancipation had been effected, however, there remained the great obstacles of distance and of the inadequacy of the means of communication across the immense Siberian region, which intervened between European Russia and the Amur.

It thus became indispensably necessary, if the acquisition of the territory was to bear any fruit for Russia, that cheap and rapid means of communication should be established between European Russia and the head waters of the Amur. In other words, the construction of the Siberian Railway became from 1860 an imperious necessity.

This necessity was clearly foreseen by Muraviev. Several projects were advanced for partial or complete railway communication. The earliest of these projects was brought forward in 1850, when the Russians had only just established themselves upon the Lower Amur. From time to time projects were brought before the authorities at St. Petersburg, but they met with small encouragement, partly because the railway system of European Russia was as yet very imperfectly developed ; while the Crimean War, the advances of Russia in Central Asia, and the Russo-Turkish War, successively preoccupied the Government. The finances were not in a flourishing condition, and the administration of public works was costly and corrupt. Even after the financial feasibility of the construction of a line came to be admitted, the question of the route to be followed occasioned prolonged controversy. In the seventies of the nineteenth century three routes were proposed, and each of them had many adherents—the northern route, the middle, and the southern.[1]

The discussion of these routes concerned itself not so much with the line through Siberia, as with the point in the Ural Mountains which should be connected with the Russian European lines, and divergent interests at once manifested themselves. The Eastern Siberian interests began to clamour for local lines ; e.g. a petition was sent in 1875 from Vladivostok to provide a line from that port to Lake Khanko.[2] Meanwhile the construction of the European network brought the Russian railways to the Ural Mountains in 1880,[3] when the great bridge across the Volga was completed. The ques-

---

[1] *Siberia and the Great Siberian Railway*, p. 240.
[2] *Ibid.*, p. 241.   [3] *Ibid.*

tion of a Siberian line now assumed a new phase. The construction of the Obi-Yenesei canal, together with a project for the removal of the rapids in the river Angara, had offered an alternative combined rail and water route from the Urals to the Amur. A special commission was appointed in the end of 1890 for the purpose of determining what was to be done. The principal consideration of the Commission seems to have been the economical development of Siberia, rather than the political and strategic consequences of the construction of a trans-Asiatic line. Although the increasing military importance of Japan had been very manifest from about 1886, yet this does not seem to have had any material influence upon the Russian plans prior to 1890 or 1891. In the former year Russian attention was drawn to the surveys which were being made by an English railway engineer, Mr. Kinder, in the employment of the Chinese Government. These surveys were performed at the instance of Li Hung Chang, who was then in a powerful position at Peking. His instructions to Mr. Kinder were to the following effect : to survey a line from Shanhaikwan, a Chinese military camp at the point where the Great Wall reaches the Gulf of Chihli, in a north-easterly direction by Mukden and Kirin towards the Russo-Chinese frontier.[1] A survey was also to be made of a branch line to New-chwang, then the principal port from which Manchurian produce was shipped.

The visit to Japan and to Maritime Manchuria of the Tsar Nicholas II, then Tsarevich, accompanied as he was by Prince Ukhtomsky, one of the most enthusiastic of Imperialists, further excited activity in the " higher spheres " at St. Petersburg, and the construction of the Trans-Siberian Railway was decided upon on 21st February 1891. Construction was commenced immediately at both ends, surveys being pushed forward from Chelyabinsk and from Vladivostok simultaneously.[2]

[1] These surveys were intended to be performed secretly ; but before the surveying party started upon its mission, its object, as is usually the case in China, leaked out. "The Chinese move certainly had the effect of forcing Russia's hand to the extent of compelling her to hasten the execution of her plans." Kent, P. H., *Railway Enterprise in China : An Account of its Origin and Development* (London, 1908), p. 41.

[2] Actual construction was begun at Vladivostok on 19/31 May 1891, and at Cheliabinsk on 17/29 July 1892. See *Administration de la Construction des Chemins de Fer de l'Empire* (Russe) (Paris, 1900), p. 15. The construction was begun under M. Hubbenet, Minister of Ways of Communication, and was continued under MM. Witte, Krivoshéïne, and Prince Khilkov.

The line as projected in 1891 extended from Cheliabinsk, on the eastern slope of the Urals, by Omsk, Krasnoyarsk, Irkutsk, Chita, Stretinsk, and Albazin, on the north bank of the Amur, to Khabarovsk and Vladivostok. It was, so far as the Amur and Ussuri sections were concerned, entirely within the territory ceded by China to Russia in the Treaty of Aigun in 1858. The project of a railway from Irkutsk through Northern Mongolia and Northern Manchuria south of the Amur, to Vladivostok, had been proposed and rejected.[1] The Vladivostok-Khabarovsk section, commenced in 1891, was finished in 1902. The sections between Chelyabinsk, and Irkutsk, commenced in 1892, were finished in 1900 ; the section between the eastern shore of Lake Baïkal and Khabarovsk, commenced in 1895, was finished in 1904. The short section round the southern shore of Lake Baïkal was finished during the war in 1905. The length of the Siberian line proper from Chelyabinsk to Vladivostok was 6484 kilometres.[2] The total distance from St Petersburg to Vladivostok was 9431 kilometres. The cost of the Siberian line proper was about 400,000,000 rubles.

The desire on the part of Russia to extend her markets arose naturally, for Russia has comparatively little sea-going commerce ;[3] and her exports to European countries consist chiefly of grain and raw materials. But from the remotest time her caravan trade with China had been very considerable, and thus traffic from the opening of the line was assured in silks, tea, and furs, by way of imports, while the development of Manchuria as a grain-producing country might be calculated upon to produce a demand for manufactured cotton and other commodities.[4]

It is well now to pause and to reflect upon the evidence which the above historical recital affords of " land hunger," and of deep and far-reaching designs on the part of Russia. How far is it true that the Government up to the moment of embarkation upon

[1] See map in *Siberia and the Great Siberian Railway*.

[2] It is now considerably reduced by improvements, chiefly in Central Siberia.

[3] From 1872, however, Russia had developed a sea-going trade with China. At the present time large steamers run from Hankow, on the Yiangtse Kiang, to Odessa and to Kronstadt. Parker, E. H., *China, Her History, Diplomacy, and Commerce* (London, 1901), p. 155.

[4] Of late years the principal exports from Manchuria have been beans and wild silk cocoons. The seaports of Newchwang, Dalny, and Vladivostok are practically built upon the bean trade.

Siberian railway enterprise in 1891 was consciously striving to possess itself of the whole of Manchuria and of Korea, of checking the growth of Japan, and of exercising a dominant influence over China ? It must be recognized that while Muraviev saw in the fifties the value of the region of the Amur, and while he realized that it formed an important route between Trans-Baïkalia and the Pacific, he was able with great difficulty to induce the " higher spheres " in St. Petersburg to share his views.[1] They were naïvely ignorant of the region which had inspired in him so much enthusiasm. The opening of Japan to foreign intercourse had not taken place until eleven years after Muraviev arrived in Trans-Baïkalia. He could not see the portentous potential strength of Japan, nor could he foresee the intricate political relations that would result from her emergence as a great power in the Pacific. It must be allowed that up till 1891, there is no proof of aggressiveness on the part of the Russian Government in the Far East.[2] The evidence goes to show that the Government was reluctantly forced into acquiescence in the earlier projects for a Siberian line, partly through the advocacy of enthusiasts and interested merchants, and partly by circumstances chiefly connected with the economical development of Siberia. Indeed, so far as the motives which inspired the scheme of a Siberian railway were concerned, these may be regarded as primarily economical and as only secondarily strategical.[3] But when the construction of the line through to the Pacific coast was actually undertaken in 1891, there can be no doubt that the strategical advantage began to loom up in large proportions.

We have now to consider the effect of the construction of the line upon the political relations of Russia, Japan, and China.

[1] See the very interesting account of the attitude of St. Petersburg officials towards Manchuria at this period, in Prince Kropotkin's *Memoirs*, p. 196. Prince Kropotkin was aide-de-camp to Korsakov, the Governor-General of Eastern Siberia, successor of Muraviev.

[2] Earlier than this period there was undoubtedly in Russia a party, more or less influential, which had designs upon India. In the time of the Tsar Paul I, this party induced that eccentric monarch to make preparations for an invasion of India through her northern frontier, and inheritors of this policy have not been lacking. Their influence contributed to the advance of Russia in Central Asia, and this advance, so long as it continued, preoccupied Russia and prevented similar adventures in the Far East.

[3] This is shown by the circumstance that the early projects did not involve a through railway line, but merely separate lines linking up the waterways. Even in 1901 the lines were discontinuous and the steamer service on the Amur was defective.

Up till 1891 the preoccupation of Russia in the Balkans and in Central Asia, together with the jealousies of the Powers and the uncertainty of the defensive strength of China, combined to prevent the advance of Russia south of the Amur and west of the Ussuri. The colonization of Maritime Manchuria had proceeded slowly. Few Russian settlers had migrated there ; the chief immigrants had been Koreans, for whom the Russians had established schools. In the Amur province, on the north bank of the river, the Chinese had settled in considerable and the Russians in lesser numbers. Affairs were in this posture when the construction of the Siberian Railway was begun in 1891. For some years before that date the Japanese Government had undoubtedly viewed with apprehension the inevitability of the Russian advance southward so soon as convenient opportunity should arise.

The geographical situation involved the masking of the Russian advance by China and her quasi-dependency Korea, and at the same time involved the practical immunity of Russia from effective attack at the mouth of the Amur or on the coast of Maritime Manchuria. A naval defeat might have been inflicted upon Russia by Japan, and might readily have been inflicted at any period subsequent to 1886 ; but a naval victory would have been fruitless without a land campaign. For a land campaign of the necessary magnitude, Japan was not ready in 1891 nor for several years after that date. Wisdom, therefore, dictated to Japan, Fabian tactics. It was wise to wait until Russia by her own acts should extend her operations, as she must do, ever farther and farther from her military base and ever nearer the military base of Japan. If Japan were able to prepare herself to strike hard when the moment to strike should arrive, Russia would be compelled to retire probably for a generation.

The preparation was a long and formidable task. If it failed, not only would the whole of Manchuria and Korea fall into the hands of Russia, but Japan might become a mere province of the Empire.[1]

An essential part of the preparation for the driving back of Russia was the control by Japan of Korea and the neutralization of China. No power understood China better than Japan. It was

---

[1] The opinion is prevalent in well-informed circles in Russia that prior to the war of 1904–1905, this idea was actually in the minds of the " higher spheres."

perfectly evident to the latter power that China could not resist the advance of Russia, and that, so far as she was concerned, the existence of Manchuria and Korea as buffer States between Russia and Japan was a negligible quantity.

It was also evident that so soon as the opportune moment arrived, Japan must bring about a quarrel with China, and, if possible, occupy a portion of Southern Manchuria as well as Korea, in order to enable her to offer effective resistance to Russia when that power made her southward advance. The Korean question was sufficiently apposite to afford an excuse for the adoption of the military measures necessary to eliminate China from the field, and to prevent a futile attempt on her part to avoid the occupation of South Manchuria by Russia. The Sino-Japanese War of 1895 resulted in the complete victory of Japan. China was compelled to surrender, and the weakness of her military position was laid bare to all the world. Japanese ambition was satisfied with the outcome of the war, for she was now entitled to interfere in Manchurian and Korean affairs; but she had disclosed her hand, and in doing so had stimulated Russian diplomacy to the exercise of the greatest ingenuity in order to deprive her of the substantial fruits of her victory. It was inevitable that Russia should rely upon diplomatic action, for military measures were not at that time practicable. The Siberian Railway was not completed, and it would have been impossible for her to throw into Manchuria a force sufficient to effect the seizure of the Liao-tung peninsula from Japan. She therefore used the Yellow Peril argument with such effect that Germany and France joined her in insisting upon the withdrawal of Japan from Port Arthur and from Korea. Japan had to accept the inevitable, and to withdraw, for she could not have withstood a naval attack upon her shores by three allied powers.[1] She had, however, gained something; she had exhibited the helplessness of China, and although in doing so she had encouraged Russia to encroach upon Manchuria, she had justified her title to interfere

---

[1] The Russian fleet, together with two German cruisers, lay off Chefoo, opposite Port Arthur, on 8th May 1895, when the ratifications of the treaty were being exchanged. The French Admiral de la Bonninière de Beaumont did not join in this demonstration although France was acting with the other two powers and in the event of the refusal of Japan to agree to the compromise urged by the three powers, the French ships might have been brought into action. *Cf.*, however, Pierre Leroy-Beaulieu, *The Awakening of the East* (New York, 1900), pp. 250–252.

whenever that encroachment had proceeded to what she might consider a dangerous extent.

To suppose that Japan foresaw precisely the events which followed the restoration of the Liao-tung peninsula to China would be to imply an incredible prescience ; yet there can be no doubt that the astute Japanese statesmen saw somewhat of the future, and there can equally be no doubt that the surrender appeared to them to be temporary. The principles of *jiu-jitsu* have penetrated so deeply into the Japanese mind that it is permissible to believe that, consciously or unconsciously, these principles were applied to the titanic struggle between the two powers.[1] It thus appeared that while Russia was able to effect an agreement with China which gave her not only permission to build a railway across the north-eastern corner of Mongolia and the northern part of Manchuria, but also a lease of the Liao-tung peninsula, she had gained without a campaign an important strategic advantage. Yet, to the Japanese mind, the very advance which this advantage implied brought Russia within striking distance when the appropriate moment arrived.

The history of the series of agreements by means of which Russia obtained a footing in Southern Manchuria has not yet been fully disclosed. Russian diplomacy was exceedingly active at Peking in 1890 and 1891, and it was directed towards delaying the construction by China of the Manchurian railways projected by Li Hung Chang, in order that concessions for railways in this region should be granted to Russia. What the relations between Li Hung Chang and Russia were at this time may perhaps never be known.[2] He may or may not have intended from the beginning to concede these lines to Russia for a consideration.

The war between Japan and China came to an end on 17th April 1895, when the Treaty of Shimonoseki was concluded. Li Hung Chang was the plenipotentiary of China in the negotiations which preceded the conclusion of the treaty. His conduct during the

---

[1] The first maxim of the Japanese *Jiu-jitsu* is, " Do not resist an opponent, but gain the victory by pliancy." In other words, yield precisely at the right moment, so that the opponent exhausts himself. The weight and the impetus of an opponent will, under given circumstances, even cause him to break his own arm. For an interesting technical account of *Jiu-jitsu*, see "The Legacy of the Samurai," by R. Tait -Mackenzie, M.D., in *American Physical Education Review*, December 1906.

[2] Li Hung Chang's papers and those of his English secretary are supposed to have disappeared. They may have been destroyed.

negotiations, when viewed in the light of subsequent events, requires explanation, which has not yet been fully forthcoming. He seemed to be indifferent about the cession of the Liao-tung peninsula and Korea, and devoted his energies to an attempt to save Formosa from falling into the hands of Japan.[1] Had he succeeded in this attempt, Japan would have had to be content with a pecuniary indemnity alone, and would not have gained any territory as the result of the campaign.

Upon the supposition that Li Hung Chang knew of the project by which Russia hoped to thwart Japan, his conduct is intelligible.[2] The proceedings of Russia after the conclusion of the Treaty of Shimonoseki have already been alluded to. After the war was over, the continuation of the railway beyond Shanhaikwan was not proceeded with by the Chinese. Again it is alleged the hand of Russia is discoverable, although the delay may have been due to the fluctuation of exclusively Chinese political influences in Peking.

One year after these events Li Hung Chang was sent as Plenipotentiary Extraordinary to be present at the coronation of the Tsar in Moscow.[3] During his visit to Russia there were rumours of the confirmation by him of a secret convention which had been entered into between China and Russia in 1895,[4] the so-called Cassini Convention. Official denials were at once published ; but subsequent occurrences justified the belief that an agreement of some kind had been arrived at, which enabled Russia to take her next important step. This step was the establishment of the Russo-Chinese Bank, which was destined to play a great rôle in the immediately succeeding events. The bank was founded by imperial ukase on 10th December 1895, after the Cassini Convention, and a few months before the alleged confirmation of that convention by Li Hung Chang. The capital stock of the Russo-Chinese Bank was opened

[1] Cf. Kent, op. cit., p. 43.

[2] It has been hinted (by Mr. Michie) that Russia had intimated to Li Hung Chang before the treaty negotiations began that, should he be obliged to cede territory on the mainland, Russia would bring pressure to bear upon Japan to have such a provision annulled. Cf. Kent, op. cit., p. 43, and Weale, Manchu and Muscovite, p. 129. It may also be mentioned here that diplomatic gossip of the time attributed the speedy fall of Port Arthur to a pecuniary arrangement between Li and certain Japanese. If any credence can be given to this story, the conduct of Li appears in a still more unfavourable light.

[3] The coronation took place on 14th May (O.S.) 1896.

[4] The terms of this alleged document were published by Mr. R. W. Little in the North China Daily News, and were copied in the newspapers of the time. Cf. Kent, op. cit., p. 47.

to public subscription, and was largely subscribed for in Paris, Brussels, and in Amsterdam.[1] Li Hung Chang arrived in China, via Vancouver, in August 1896, and on the 29th of that month an " agreement " was concluded " between the Chinese Government and the Russo-Chinese Bank for the construction and management of the Chinese Eastern Railway." [2] This agreement, together with a supplementary document, entitled " Statutes of the Chinese Eastern Railway Company," provided for the formation of the company by the Russo-Chinese Bank, and for the construction by it of a railway of the Russian gauge (5 feet) from the western border of the province of Hei-Lun-Tsian to the eastern border of the province of Kirin, and for the connection of this railway with the imperial Russian railways by the Trans-Baïkalian and the Southern Ussuri lines. The Chinese Eastern Railway was to be under Chinese direction ; but in the event of disagreement between the Chinese railway authorities and those of the Russian railways, the Russian Minister of Finance was to decide the points in dispute. Imports and exports by this railway were to be subject to preferential customs duties to the extent of a diminution of one-third. The railway company was to have its own police ; but the Chinese Government undertook to protect the line against extraneous attacks. The ordinary shares of the company were not to be guaranteed, but the bonds were to be guaranteed by the Russian Government.[3]

This agreement enabled Russia to dispense with the originally projected line along the north bank of the Amur to connect Nerchinsk with Khabarovsk, and also prepared the way for further extensions southwards. The construction of the line through Northern Manchuria was quite indispensable for Russia if any material advantage was to be gained by the possession of Maritime Manchuria, apart altogether from any adventures in Southern Manchuria or in China or Korea. The building of the extension of the Trans-Siberian line as originally planned, along the northern bank of the Amur, was recognized at an early stage as very difficult from an engineering point of view.[4] The river Amur presented

---

[1] Weale, *op. cit.*, p. 126.

[2] This agreement was signed on 8th September 1896. A translation from the Chinese text is given by Kent, *op. cit.*, p. 211.

[3] In addition, the line was redeemable by purchase in thirty-six years, and was to revert to China without payment in eighty years.

[4] It is now (1913), however, in course of construction.

grave difficulties in bridging. The variation in its waters between the wet and the dry seasons was so great that bridges of unheard-of length would have had to be constructed, with piers of unusual depth, in order to reach secure foundation in the river bed. The cost of such a line was at the time in effect prohibitive.

The construction of the Chinese Eastern Railway was begun in 1897. Meanwhile diplomacy appears to have been active in preparing for the southern extension of the line towards the Gulf of Chihli in order to secure a port which should be free from the disadvantage which attached to Vladivostok of being annually icebound for several months. Events again facilitated and hastened Russian movements. Germany had compelled the Chinese Government to give a lease of the region round Kiaochau Bay for ninety-nine years, by way of compensation for the murder of two German missionaries in the province of Shantung. It has been suggested that China was under promise to grant Russia a concession in the Kiaochau region, and that Russia embraced the opportunity of the grant to Germany to insist upon a lease of the Liao-tung peninsula, including the harbour and fortress of Port Arthur, for twenty-five years, and upon the right to construct a railway to connect Port Arthur with the Chinese Eastern Railway. The lease of the Liao-tung peninsula was granted on 27th March 1898, including the right to build a railway connecting Port Arthur with Kharbin, and another connecting Talien-wan (later Dalny [1]) with Newchwang. There was, however, the proviso that the railway concession was " never to be used as a pretext for encroachment on Chinese territory, nor to be allowed to interfere with Chinese authority or interests." [2] The gauge of this railway was to conform to the Russian standard, viz. 5 feet.

The extension of the Chinese railways beyond the Great Wall at Shanhaikwan now began to engage the attention both of Russia and of Great Britain. During the discussions which ensued, Russia openly declared her intention of preventing " the provinces of China bordering upon the Russian frontier from coming under the influence of any nation except Russia." [3] The discussions arose out of the proposed loan to the Chinese Government for the con-

---

[1] Now called Dairen by the Japanese.

[2] Clause 8 of the agreement quoted by Kent, *op. cit.*, p. 49. The branch to Newchwang was completed in 1899.

[3] M. Pavlov, quoted by Sir Claude Macdonald in despatch to Lord Salisbury, 19th October 1897. Parliamentary Paper, *China, No.* 1 (1898), p. 5.

struction of the line by the Hong-Kong and Shanghai Bank. A compromise was eventually arrived at, Great Britain receiving, so far as Russia was concerned, a free hand in the Yangtse Valley, the Hong-Kong and Shanghai Bank agreeing to advance the capital required on the security of the Peking-Shanhaikwan section with a charge upon the revenues of the extension. There thus remained no mortgage to a foreign Power of the line, which extended from Shanhaikwan to Newchwang and Mukden.[1] This arrangement between Great Britain and Russia gave the former the right to construct railways in the Yangtse Valley, so far as Russia was concerned, and gave Russia the right to construct railways beyond the Great Wall at Shanhaikwan so far as Great Britain was concerned.[2]

In 1900 the Boxer disturbances threw the whole of North China into chaos ; and Russia immediately occupied Manchuria, ostensibly to secure the maintenance of order. After the Legations had been relieved by the international expeditionary force, the Powers proceeded to negotiate with China upon the terms under which they they would evacuate Peking. These terms included, of course, the settlement of the amount and periods of payment of the indemnity exacted for the cost of the expedition. Until a general treaty was concluded between China and the co-operating Powers, it was obvious that it would be at least inappropriate for any individual Power to seek to negotiate a separate treaty with China. The obligations of China to the Powers jointly might be prevented from being implemented if China were beforehand to transfer any material portion of her liquifiable resources to an individual Power.

On 3rd January 1901 *The Times* published the draft of an agreement into which China was alleged to have entered with Russia, respecting Manchuria. The existence of such an agreement was denied by Count Lamsdorf, the Russian Foreign Minister, to both the British and the Japanese Ambassadors at St. Petersburg,[3] and

---

[1] See Kent, *op. cit.*, pp. 51–5 ; and Identic Note, 28th April 1899, quoted by Kent, *op. cit.*, p. 220.

[2] The arrangement was not a favourable one for Great Britain, for the Yangtse Valley had already been tapped at Hankow by the concession granted in August 1898 to a Franco-Belgian Syndicate for the construction of a railway from that port to Peking and no *quid pro quo* was really obtained. On the other hand, Russia was permitted to expand her influence in Manchuria. *Cf.* Kent, *op. cit.*, p. 56.

[3] See Despatches Nos. 30, 31, &c., *China, No. 6* (1901), *Further Correspondence respecting the Disturbances in China* (Cd. 675) (London, 1901).

China was warned by both Great Britain and Japan that no separate agreements should be made with any individual Power.[1]   In spite of Count Lamsdorf's disclaimer, it appeared that an agreement respecting Manchuria was being urged upon China by Russia.[2]

The Chinese Ministers furnished a copy of this proposed agreement to the Powers, and requested their advice. This meant, of course, that should the Powers advise China to refuse to accept the agreement, they should be prepared to guarantee China against the consequences of such refusal. The explanation of Count Lamsdorf was to the effect that the proposed agreement was of a limited and temporary character, and that it did not affect the permanent interests of China. The Powers did not in effect accept this disclaimer. China delayed the conclusion of the agreement until after the time stipulated for its conclusion had elapsed, and the project came to nothing.[3] The negotiations were clearly intended by Russia to be regarded as " most secret," [4] but, as might have been readily foreseen, the Chinese Government attempted to make the most out of international rivalries and to break up the concert of the Powers by promptly revealing the terms of the draft.

The clumsy diplomacy of Russia at this time contributed materially to her isolation. The ardour of the Franco-Russian *entente* had cooled steadily since 1898 ; [5] and all the Powers, including Germany, who had supported Russia in protesting against the Japanese occupation of the Liao-tung peninsula and Korea, were unanimous in opposing the transparent attempt on the part of Russia to secure exclusive advantages for herself out of the confusion of Chinese affairs. In 1858 Russia had successfully played a diplomatic game of this kind ; but then her diplomacy was in more skilful hands, and Great Britain and France, who had made the

---

[1] A similar view was taken later by the United States and the German Governments. (*Cf.* Despatches Nos. 153 and 156, *China*, &c.)

[2] The text of this agreement is given in No. 158, *ibid.*

[3] Its withdrawal was announced by Russia in a despatch on 5th April 1901 (No. 237, *ibid.*).

[4] Even after the existence of the draft treaty was demonstrated by the disclosure of its terms by the Chinese Government, Count Lamsdorf continued to express himself ambiguously and to refuse to supply the Powers with an authentic copy of the proposed treaty, while at the same time he affected to throw doubts upon the genuineness of the Chinese copy. (Cf. *ibid.*)

[5] The Dreyfus affair diminished the confidence of Russia in France, and the Fashoda affair (1898), during which France appealed to Russia for assistance in case of need, and received a refusal, diminished the confidence of France in Russia. See note at end of this chapter.

gratuitous success of Russia possible, had just defeated Russia in a long and costly campaign, and did not desire a renewal of hostilities. Moreover, the region in which Russia gained her advantage was at that time very remote from the spheres of interest of either Power. In 1901, however, the case was different. The Powers were engaged in the humanitarian task of relieving their embassies from investment during a period of barbaric anarchy, and none of them had been more profuse than Russia had been in announcements of the purity of motive which had dictated the operations.[1] Each Power was on the *qui vive* in case an advantage should be gained by any other, and alliances might easily be made against any Power which attempted to act selfishly.

The incidents connected with the projected treaty and those connected with the seizure by Russia of railway lands and material at Tientsin and Newchwang,[2] convinced the Powers that Russia was determined to gain important advantages for herself. In these proceedings and in the ambidexterous conduct of them Russia was preparing the way for an inevitable combination against her. This combination came in the Anglo-Japanese Treaty, negotiated in 1902 by Lord Lansdowne, and in the simultaneous isolation of Russia from France and Germany.

The fatuous diplomacy of Russia was accompanied by hurried exploitation on the part of Russian speculators of the valuable timber region of the Yalu River,[3] by encroachments upon Korea, by enormous expenditures at Dalny, which the Russians destined for a great commercial port,[4] and by extraordinary neglect of the military measures necessary to maintain the security of the hostages she had given to fortune in so extended and advanced outposts.

In these adventures and in the neglect of military precautions, Russia was simply playing the game of Japan and hastening the moment when, with greatly diminished prestige, she should have

[1] See, *e.g.*, Despatches Nos. 149, 238, and 239, in *China, No.* 3 (1900) (Cd. 257) (London, 1900).
[2] For correspondence in connection with the Tientsin and Newchwang disputes, see *China, No.* 7 (1901), *Correspondence respecting the Imperial Railway of North China* (Cd. 770) (London, 1901).
[3] An account of the relation of the Russian Timber Company with the political situation in 1903 is given in *Osvobojdenie, No.* 75 (Stuttgart, 19th August 1905).
[4] To Count Witte is attributed the expenditure, unauthorized probably, upon Dalny and the determination to make it instead of Port Arthur the terminus of the Siberian line. *Cf.* Kuropatkin, *Military and Political Memoirs*.

to submit to be driven back towards the Amur. Whatever the unrevealed ambitions of Russia may have been, and however she may have been convinced of the legitimacy of her efforts to force Russian civilization upon the Far East, perhaps even to the extent of playing the same rôle in North China and Japan which England had played in India, the mode of approach was hopelessly ineffectual. The morale of the Russian civil official class was not equal, save in rare cases, to any such task, nor was the morale of the superior officers of the army by any means equal to the momentous demands which such an enterprise would have made upon them.[1]

Incompetent guidance in St. Petersburg, incompetent and even dishonest conduct by her agents in the Far East, led Russia along the road to ruin. The occupation of Manchuria, which had been effected in order to re-establish order during the Boxer outbreak in 1900, was still maintained in 1904, notwithstanding repeated promises to evacuate the region. There is abundant evidence of divided counsels at St. Petersburg. Now one party and now another secured ascendency, and sometimes the Tsar appears to have acted upon his own initiative.[2]

The incidents of the war need not be recounted here. It is necessary, however, to consider the position in which Russia stood in the Far East at the conclusion of the war with Japan. The Chinese Eastern Railway, which extends from Manchuria, a station on the Russo-Chinese frontier between Trans-Baïkalia and Manchuria and the border of Primorskaya *oblast* and Vladivostok, is now wholly in her hands, together with the region through which it runs. The Chinese Government possesses, under the agreement of 1896, the right of purchase of the line thirty-six years after the commencement of traffic. This period expires about the year 1937. It is impossible to determine whether or not China will be in a position at that distant period of time to exercise the option of purchase.

[1] A view of the Russian occupation of Manchuria, somewhat distorted by prejudice, is to be found in *Manchu and Muscovite*, by B. L. Putnam Weale (London, 1907), *passim*.

[2] The division of parties was not constant. At one moment M. von Plehvë, who was in general opposed to commercial and industrial development, had the ear of the Tsar, and had as an ally Bezobrazov, the promoter and speculator, who manipulated the Russian Trading Company, the exploiters of the timber limits on the Yalu River ; at another moment the influence of M. Witte was dominant, and this influence was exerted towards the commercial enterprises of Russia in the Liao-tung peninsula and the foundation of the port of Dalny.

It is, however, more than likely that Russia will plead conquest, and will retain the line.[1] Russia may be held therefore to have gained permanently a large portion of North Manchuria to which previously she had no real claim. The post-bellum agreement between Russia and Japan suggests that Japan and Russia have made up their minds to divide Manchuria between them, and to get rid at the first convenient opportunity of the presence of Chinese Government officials in the country. Meanwhile, of course, as regards Southern Manchuria, Japan has possession of the railway line and the stations alone, together with the Liao-tung peninsula, the remainder of the lease of which to Russia has been taken by her as war spoil. This lease, which was originally drawn for twenty-five years from 27th March 1898, expires on 26th March 1923, although in terms of the original agreement it may be renewed. The unknown quantity in both cases is China. If China develops during the next few years a formidable military strength, which is quite within the bounds of possibility, the lease may not be renewed by her, and thus Russia and Japan alike may be driven out of South Manchuria.

It should be observed that grave difficulties present themselves in cases where Powers attempt to hold permanently regions which are occupied entirely by alien peoples belonging to vigorous neighbouring nations ; and that if Russia is unable to populate Northern Manchuria with a population predominantly or largely Russian, and if Japan is unable to populate the Liao-tung peninsula with a population predominantly or largely Japanese, neither of these Powers can expect to hold the respective regions permanently. The Russian migration into Northern Manchuria is at present inconsiderable, while as regards Japan, she has been up till the present time unable to induce her people to settle in the Liao-tung peninsula in any considerable numbers. Manchurian winters seem to be too severe for Japanese, and Manchurian wages are too low to induce migration.[2] Under these circumstances, the principal determining point in the future of Manchuria is the result of the military and political development of China.

[1] The original agreement provided that the shareholders should be exclusively Russian or Chinese. As no Chinese are understood to have invested in the stock, it may be presumed to be wholly in Russian hands.

[2] Cf. "The Emigration Question in Japan," in The Round Table, London, vol. i. (1911), p. 263.

It is now necessary to consider the effect of these events in the Far East upon the military and diplomatic position of Russia in Europe. During the war and during the revolutionary period which followed, Russia was reduced to impotency. She found herself isolated. The Franco-Russian *entente* had become cold ; and two events occurred almost immediately which could not have occurred had not Russian prestige been seriously weakened. These were the separation of Norway and Sweden and the annexation of Bosnia and Herzegovina by Austria. The desire of Russia to secure a port in the North Sea by the continuation of the Finnish railway line from Uleåborg via Torneå across Sweden to Hammerfest, or some other port on the North Sea, had scarcely been concealed. Alone Sweden could not dare to hope to resist the pressure of Russia, the continuation of the union with Norway was therefore indispensable for her. The preoccupation of Russia in Manchuria and the diminished prestige of an unsuccessful campaign, offered the opportunity of which Norway availed herself. Almost at the same moment Austria seized the opportunity for which she had long lain in wait, to appropriate the two Balkan provinces, without fear of the strenuous protest which would otherwise have come from Russia.

Up till 1910, there had been no obvious recrudescence of Russian activity in Western Europe; although such recrudescence might at any time occur in the troubled waters of Balkan politics. That Russia preferred to permit the Balkan peoples to exhaust one another instead of interfering prematurely in their disputes is a tenable hypothesis; but there may have been another reason. The Far East still contained immense possibilities for Russia, and it was indispensable to prepare for eventualities there. That ever since the close of the Russo-Japanese war the position of China has been precarious had obviously been the view of Russia. In accordance with this view, she concentrated troops upon her new Manchurian frontier.[1] Russia, moreover, established a new military base at Krasnoyarsk, in Siberia, at which place she con-

---

[1] During the winter of 1910, on the outbreak of plague at Kharbin, Russia is reported to have taken advantage of the situation to mass troops upon the Chinese frontier ostensibly for the purpose of preventing Chinese from crossing it. Under these circumstances encroachments upon the indefinite boundaries between Russian and Chinese territories are more than probable.

centrated immense military stores. China was in no position to resist encroachments should they be made. When the war of 1914–18 was over, one of the reactions of the struggle was a rapprochement between Russia and China.

Thus, so far from having been thrown back upon Europe, as it were, Russia may one day attempt to recover some of her lost ground in the East, if a suitable opportunity should arise for its recovery. In addition to the corner of Mongolia which is traversed by the Chinese Eastern Railway, now an integral portion of the Siberian line, the vast region of Mongolia lies along the southern frontier of the Russian Empire from Transcaspia to the Khingan Mountains, upon the crest of which the Great Wall still constitutes a formidable barrier. Even in February 1910 when the treaty of 1881 between China and Russia expired, Russia embraced the opportunity to reopen the Far Eastern question. This treaty was concluded for the purpose of putting an end to the Russian occupation of the province of Ili, and of facilitating the trade in brick tea, which was conveyed from Hankow, on the Yangtse-kiang, to Ili and Kashgar for Russia. The importance of this great land route has already been noticed. It is not without reason that Russia laid her hand upon Ili.[1] Secluded as it is in the heart of Asia, no Power could dispute the possession of it with Russia; and lying across, as it does, the route for caravan tea from China, as well as offering facilities for tapping the trade of the Upper Yangste Valley by means of the river Han, it possesses enormous economic importance. Extension of the Transcaspian railways of Russia to Ili would being Russia by another route to the back door of China—a route from which she could with difficulty be driven by any conceivable combination of Powers. In the event of a second Trans-Asiatic line being constructed by this route, as it might be, the guarantees respecting the Yangtse Valley, which Great Britain secured from Russia, would be worthless, and a most serious situation might readily arise between the two countries. Moreover, checked as she has been in Manchuria by Japan, the seizure of the whole of Mongolia looms up as a possibility. Indeed Mongolia became in

[1] On the events in the province of Ili in 1912, see Major Pereira's Report of Journey from Kashgar to Lanchou Fu in *China*, No. 3 (1913), Parliamentary Paper, August 1913, London [Cd. 7054], pp. 47–52.

effect a protectorate of Russia under the Russo-Mongolian Agreement and Protocol, 21st October–3rd November 1912.[1]

The relations between Russia and China cannot be understood without taking into account the fact that, in spite of encroachments upon China by Russia, the two countries, excepting for the affair in Ili during the Mohammedan disturbances, have not actually been in a state of conflict since the siege of Albazin in 1687. No European Power has quite the same sympathetic relations with China as has Russia. While European powers in general were not permitted to send diplomatic representatives to Peking until 1858, Russia had maintained a semi-official embassy there from 1692.[2] The Russian representative has always been *persona grata* at the Court of China, and has thus been able to enjoy a confidence denied to others.[3]

The attitude of Russia towards Asiatic peoples and the rule by her of subject races in Asia, are less humane, conscientious, and educative than the attitude of England and the rule by her of Asiatic subject races; but the Russians who exercise the administrative functions in the East are naturally more affable than the English. Both, no doubt, have the faults of their qualities; but the Russians are habitually more indifferent than the English, and when hostile, much more hostile to moral and religious propagandas which disturb the settled course of Asiatic life and affect profoundly the social structure.[4] In brief, from origin, temperament, and personal

---

[1] See *China, No. 1* (1913): *Despatches . . . transmitting the Russo-Mongolian Agreement . . .* Parliamentary Paper, February 1913, London [Cd. 6604]. For a rather passionate account of the economical interests of Russia in Mongolia, see Ular, Alexandre, *Un Empire Russo-Chinois*. English version, London, 1904. See also for an account of later phases of the Mongolian question, *With the Russians in Mongolia*, by H. G. C. Perry-Ayscough and Captain R. B. Otter-Barry (London, 1914). The relations of Soviet Russia to the Far East are fully discussed in Dennis, A. L. P., *The Foreign Policies of Soviet Russia*, New York [1924], pp. 269–338.

[2] Ravenstein, *The Russians on the Amur*, p. 71. Cf. *Supra*, p. 222.

[3] It should be observed, however, that the abuses of Russian officials in Manchuria and the cruelties perpetrated by them during the occupation (cf. *e.g.* Veretschagēn, V. V., *Memoirs*), sometimes under the influence of panic, as at Blagoveschensk by the late General Grodekhov, for example, seriously compromised the relations between Russians and Chinese. During the Russo-Japanese War the Chinese assisted the Japanese actively. They were by no means strictly neutral.

[4] For example, notwithstanding its domestic policy of anti-clericalism, France encourages missionary enterprise, as also do Great Britain and Germany. Russia, on the other hand, is spared the friction which is due to an intricate

liabits, and through intimate contact with Asiatics from the dawn of history, the Russian is nearer to the Asiatic point of view than is the Englishman, whose origin, if Asiatic, is so only in a sense inconceivably remote, whose temperament is more active and less reflective, whose habits are more fastidious, and whose desire for personal comfort is more insistent than those of the Russian or the Asiatic. The English have, moreover, come into contact with the Asiatic, in any serious sense, only in very modern times.[1]

series of reactions arising out of missionary attempts to change the current of Asiatic life. This is due to the fact that the Greek Orthodox Church does not proselytize.

[1] *Cf.* the suggestive treatment of this subject by Mr. Townsend Meredith in *Asia and Europe* (London, 1901), *passim.*

NOTE (1924).—I have left the expression " The Franco-Russian *entente* had melted away " (p. 240) as it was written in 1914. At that moment, although the documents confirming the *entente* were in force, the spirit of the *entente* had distinctly declined during the immediately preceding years. The decline was due to the military weakness of Russia as disclosed in the Russo-Japanese War and was made manifest in the apparent indifference of France in 1908, when Austria annexed Bosnia and Herzegovina. The spirit of the *entente* revived with the increasing truculence of Germany.

The anticipation that the next crisis in which Russia might become involved would arise in " the troubled waters of Balkan politics " (also p. 240) turned out to be well founded.

CHAPTER XIV

NATIONAL PARTICULARISM WITHIN THE RUSSIAN EMPIRE

THE ethnical and linguistic distribution of the population, which has been described,[1] indicates to some extent the lines of national cleavage, but it does not do so fully.

The principal nationalities which came to be incorporated in the Russian Empire are the following:

The " Russians," or people of Moscow, whose Grand Princes (*Velikye Kniazia*) gradually encroached upon the surrounding nations and absorbed them. While the " Russian " national feeling cannot be regarded as particularist, there is a very definite distinction, in the mind of the Russian, between the " Russian " and the " non-Russian " elements. The reactionary Russian party advocated the complete absorption and assimilation of the non-Russian peoples; the Liberal parties in general objected to the Russification even of the smaller nationalities. The latter parties advocated the " self-definition " of the constituent nationalities of the Empire. They said, for example, that each nationality should have the right to decide what language should be taught in the local schools and should be used in the churches and in the courts of law. This implied a certain exclusive Russian national feeling,[2] and a willingness on the part of the Liberals to permit a similar feeling to other than the Russian constituents of the Empire.

Between no two of the main races in the above catalogue are the relations very cordial.[3]

The Little Russians.—The most numerous of the non-Great

---

[1] See *supra*, vol. i., App. II.

[2] The disfranchisement of several non-Russian elements under the Electoral Law of 1905 is one of the evidences of this exclusive nationalism.

[3] Strategic use of racial antagonism was made in the military administration.

Russian groups is the Little Russian. The aim of the patriotic Little Russian movement was an independent Ukraine. It had its chief adherents among the *intelligentsia*; yet the *intelligents* were for the most part members of the Constitutional Democratic Party, and were thus brought into friendly relations with Russian Liberalism.[1]

The Poles.—The historical struggle between Russia and Poland was undoubtedly promoted and sustained by deep racial antagonisms. The Russians alleged that the Poles were cruel and vindictive, and that in early times their captives taken in war were tortured. The Poles in more recent times had experience of the remorseless severity of the Russian Government. The difference in religion, the Poles being Roman Catholics, counts for much, and the different personal habits of the two peoples count for even more in their mutual attitude. The Polish artisan dresses smartly, and he is conspicuous for his polite manners. He is frequently well educated and even cultivated. The Russian workman dresses himself as a rule in a slovenly fashion. His peasant traits exhibit themselves in his manners, and he is rarely educated.

Notwithstanding the partition of Poland among Russia, Austria, and Prussia, a strong Polish national feeling remained; and this feeling lent much force to the revolutionary movement within the Tsardom of Poland. The Polish Socialist Party, *e.g.*, advocated autonomy, although it did not advocate separation from Russia. It desired the admission of Poland as an equal partner in a federation of Russian States. On the other hand, the Polish Patriotic Party undoubtedly desired separation, and the re-establishment of a Polish kingdom, dreaming even of the acquisition of at least a portion of Prussian Poland.[2] The adherents of the autocracy in Russia, and even some Russian Liberals, pointed out with much

---

[1] While a Ukrainian Republic was established independence has not been achieved, for the Ukraine remains under the control of Moscow.

[2] The Polish population in the United States in 1900 was 668,536, including only persons born in Poland or born in the United States, both parents being Polish. [See *Reports of Twelfth Census* (Washington, 1901), i. p. 810.] This large group, of which about one-third was concentrated in Chicago, New York, and Milwaukee, was not without its patriotic dream. They entertained the fantastic idea of a Kingdom of Poland in America (*Krulevstvo Polskov Ameritze*). Extensive agricultural colonies of Poles have settled in a region officially called "New Poland," in the State of Parana in Brazil. [See B. J. de Siemiradzki, " *La Nouvelle Pologne,*" *État de Parana (Brésil)* (Brussels, 1899).]

force that complete autonomy would be simply a step towards separation, and that separation must lead to an attack on an independent Poland by Germany, in order to crush similar ambitions on the part of her own Polish population. Austria, whose interests are similar, would also have to be reckoned with.[1]

The Finlanders.—The most successful of all the groups in preserving their national institutions and privileges, were the Finlanders. In spite of attempts at Russianization, they retained a large measure of constitutional liberty.

While Finland adhered strongly to the principle of autonomy, there was until the collapse of Germany and the fall of the Romanov Dynasty no manifestation of any desire for separation, nor even for the abolition of autocracy excepting so far as concerned Finland.[2]

The dislike of Russian and Finn is mutual. The general level of culture in Finland is unquestionably higher than it is in Russia; but the Russians look upon the Finns as narrow-minded and selfish. The Finlanders, on the other hand, look upon all Russians as merely stupid peasants. They thus never sympathized either with the liberal movements in Russia or with the imperialism of the autocracy. From the Russian point of view, all that they desired was to be let alone and enjoy selfishly the benefits, such as they were, of belonging to a great empire, without paying for them in men or money, and without being subjected to any imperial control. This was the Russian view of the case, and thus at most moments when either people was struggling against the autocracy, no effective moral or material support came from the other.[3]

The general doubt and suspicion entertained in respect to the " non-Russian elements " in the population appears in the manifestos of the Tsar, especially after the dissolution of the Second Duma, when their influence was diminished seriously by depriving some of them of the franchise.

[1] The outcome of the war of 1914–18 reunited Poland, cancelling the partitions and establishing an autonomous Polish State.
[2] The Finnish constitutional question gave rise to a special literature.
[3] For example, during the Finnish constitutional struggle of 1899, the Finns obtained practically no assistance from Russians, even from those beyond the reach of autocratic reprisals.

The hereditary autocracy has been swept aside, yet the racial difficulties and racial prejudices remain.

The Letts.—Since about 1895 a literary revival of the Lettish language has led to the development of a strong nationalist movement in Livland. Where formerly German alone was spoken, the people now speak Lettish.

The Georgians.—The Georgian kingdom became Russian in the time of Paul I. Among the masses of the Georgian population in the Caucasus there is a very strong national feeling. Especially from about 1900 there has been a considerable intellectual movement, having its centre in Tiflis, but extending to the small towns. This movement appears in scientific and literary periodicals in the Georgian language.[1] The Georgian nobility entered the Russian service and made itself conspicuous by its loyalty.[2]

Remnants of other small nationalities which have been absorbed and Russianized are not of sufficient magnitude to produce national feeling properly so called. Some of them (the Crimean Tartars, *e.g.*) have a feeling of nationality as against other peoples, but they have exhibited no positive nationalist feeling as against the Russian Empire.

The immense variety of languages in Russia gives rise to grave practical difficulties. Desire for uniformity and for complete Russification of the minor nationalities led to the compulsory teaching of Russian in the schools and to the prevention of the teaching of the native languages. The result was that in those regions where the national feeling was strong, "not to learn" became a patriotic duty. Thus in Livland the people lapsed into indifference to all education. Only after the relaxation of the regulations on the language question was there any revival of intellectual life.[3] The inconvenience of the state of mind induced by the Russifying regulations made itself very manifest in the army. Large numbers of conscripts do not speak Russian, and they had to be taught

[1] The monthly journal, *Moambe* (Newsletter), (in Georgian), published in Tiflis, was an outcome of this intellectual movement.

[2] A Georgian Republic was established on the breaking up of the imperial system; but the government remained under the control of the Moscow Soviet.

[3] This renaissance of intellectual energy expressed itself, in the Baltic provinces especially, in many unexpected directions. For example, the chess players of these provinces became famous for the originality of their end-game compositions.

in the regimental schools. The teaching in these schools was not efficient, and as a rule the young conscript learned little more than the words of command and other purely military terms, even when he was drafted into a regiment where there were few of his special compatriots.

In spite of the attempts on the part of the Imperial Russian Government ever since the conquest or annexation of the regions occupied by the nationalities which have been mentioned, to Russianize the respective peoples, and perhaps because of these attempts, the national spirit remained more or less intense. In each important case—Poland, Finland, Georgia—there was at the root of the national spirit, and constantly stimulating it, a romantic tradition and history, and a flexible and living language. These national possessions have contributed greatly to the intellectual life of the different peoples, and have conduced, especially in recent years, to extraordinary outbursts of literary activity. The romantic episodes of Polish history have, for example, been rewritten by popular novelists, and Finnish and Georgian writers are even enriching their respective languages with new forms of expression conceived in the traditional spirit. While these incidents vitalized the intellectual life of the people, they also undoubtedly tended to separatism, and contributed greatly to the complexities of the political situation in successive epochs. It will be recognized that among the incidental effects of the various nationalist movements, there has been the practical disappearance of Pan-Slavism. If Pan-Slavism united the Slavonic elements, it would set in still greater relief than is now the case the non-Slavonic elements, and thus, so far from uniting the various factions in Russia, would tend to emphasize their differences. Excepting among the masses, and there only to an insignificant extent, and among the extreme obscurantists, the Pan-Slavic movement before the end of the twentieth century had ceased to have any force. Nevertheless, the Slavic races are dominant in the Russian group of peoples and the sympathy of these with the Southern Slavs living beyond the boundaries of Russia is inevitable.

BOOK V

THE AGRARIAN QUESTION AND ITS
REVOLUTIONARY PHASES

INTRODUCTION

THE special feature of the revolutionary movement of 1905-1907, which distinguished it from all other Russian movements of the same order, was the association of the peasant masses, for at least a short time, with the urban artisan. During the epoch of agrarian disturbances in the eighteenth century there was no urban artisan class, or none sufficiently numerous to aid in any material way the revolting peasants. The seats of the central government thus remained secure, although not without anxiety, while the peasants and the Cossacks attacked the outskirts and the frontier fortresses and small towns. At the time of the *Dekabristi* there was again a want of cohesion in the oppositional forces. The *Dekabrist* movement was conducted by intellectuals, who, while advocating liberation of the serfs, were not in contact in any real sense with the peasantry, and who, therefore, were not in a position to obtain their aid, even if they had desired to do so. The growth of an urban proletariat altered the relation of the constituent elements of society. It came as a class between the peasantry and the *intelligentsia*, and, touching both, brought them in a sense together. That which the *V Narod* movement failed to accomplish was in a large measure realized by the working men who oscillated between the village and the industrial town. When they became inoculated with social democratic or social revolutionary ideas they disseminated these either by means of their customary migrations or through banishment to their native places.

The interior changes in the structure of society, the decomposition of the family, and the increasing individualism of the members of the disintegrated family groups, accompanied as these were by disturbance of the incidence of taxation, must also be regarded as important revolutionary agents.

The *pomyetschēk* of the twentieth century was not so harsh as his forefathers of the eighteenth century, but was perhaps even more anxious to obtain, through high rents and low wages, as large a return from his estate as possible. Emancipation notwithstanding, the interests of the peasant were with difficulty reconcilable with those of the landowner, and, allotment notwithstanding, the peasant found it hard to obtain sufficient land for his needs under the existing conditions of agriculture. The social classes remained sharply differentiated, and the proprietors of land retained by far the larger share of local authority. The slenderness of agricultural capital and of agricultural credit placed the peasant landowner at a great disadvantage, and the large landowner often found it difficult to obtain sufficiently competent working hands. The skilful peasants were in some regions reluctant to become mere wage-earners, excepting where it was impossible to obtain land for cultivation on their own account.

It is clear that the peasants were impatient with the slowly moving processes of law, and that they did not have the West European conception of constitutional government and regularized administration. Having made up their minds that there must be popular government, and regarding themselves as " the people," they saw no use in waiting for debates and discussions, but proceeded immediately to act upon their belief. The land must belong to the peasants, therefore the land should at once be taken from the proprietors and given to the peasants. Although the manners of the age were not quite so violent as they were in the age of Pugachev, the process of *l'action directe* was not dissimilar from the process adopted by the peasants in 1773–1775.

CHAPTER I

PEASANT CHARACTER AND PEASANT CLASSES

THE dweller in cities and the " habitant," or rural person, appear to one another more or less mutually shrouded in mystery. The contents of their minds are different, and they look at life from different angles. When a man leaves the country and goes to the town, he never completely shakes off his rusticity ; but he never completely retains it. When a man leaves the city and goes to the country, he never completely shakes off, nor does he ever completely retain, his urbanity. Thus full mutual understanding between the townsman and the countryman is exceedingly rare. To the peasant the townsman is a person of dissolute habits and dishonest character ; while the idea is prevalent among townsmen that the peasantry of all countries is stationary and stupid. Inarticulate as the peasant appears to the civilian, it is not surprising that this opinion should be common ; but it cannot be accepted without qualification. The peasant's vocabulary is limited so far as polite, or urban, language is concerned, but he has an ample vocabulary of his own, appropriate to his own purposes. So also with the contents of his mind. These are limited enough from the point of view of the urban person, but they are ample in directions wholly unknown to dwellers in towns. Life is made easy for people who live in large groups ; they organize existence for each other, and they combine to employ people to organize life for them. The peasant organizes life for himself or as a member of a relatively small group. He is, therefore, brought more immediately into the presence of the facts of raw nature, and the energy of his mind is occupied with those to an extent from which the townsman is relieved by the organized life to which he is accustomed. In the absence of this organized life the townsman is helpless ; but the peasant is Jack of all trades, and incipient professor of all the arts and sciences.[1] In his crude, primitive, and empirical way he knows some things thoroughly well, and he is full of confidence and resource when the town dweller is confused, helpless, and ignorant. His methods, often based upon centuries of tradition, are shorter and more direct than the complicated and longer methods of organized production, and these methods are not necessarily employed without intelligent understanding. When he is credited with the possession of mysterious powers by his neighbours, as in finding water, for instance, inquiry will generally show—although the water-finder will not always admit the fact—that he simply applies his intelligence to the problem. The peasant is sometimes even skilled in rude but effective surgery, and some of their women make unrivalled nurses. Far from being stationary, peasant life, to an intimate view, is extremely fluctuating. Peasants frequently discuss matters concerning the most fundamental conditions of their economic life, and sometimes arrive at decisions which have the effect of tearing this life up, as it were, by the roots. They oscillate between the extremes of individualism and communalism, and often carry suddenly into effect the most drastic changes. The limits of these fluctuations and the substance of them vary in different races, and at different times in the same race; but everywhere, and at all times, within the hard shell of the economic system in which the peasants find themselves encased by external pressure, this animated life goes on like the movement of microscopic creatures in a drop of water. Occasionally the shell itself is ruptured by

[1] The writer lived for a short time with a group of Russian peasants who had just migrated to a new neighbourhood. They took with them practically nothing but some flour, some leather, some iron bars, and their tools for carpentry and blacksmithing. Immediately upon their arrival on the site they had chosen, they searched for clay, found it, made bricks, sun-dried them, and built two sets of ovens. In one set the women made the bread for the group, in the other the men burned wood for charcoal. Within two days after their arrival they had six blacksmiths' forges going by means of the charcoal, and bellows which they made out of the leather. Within other two days they had made several dozen spades and a wagon, whose wheels were rimmed with iron forged by them on the spot. During the same time they had made shoes for their horses. During the four days some of them had been engaged in building houses, and within a few more days these were completed. Yet not one of these peasants could either read or write. They could nevertheless discuss with great gravity and intelligence their reasons for adopting an immovable instead of a movable whiffle tree on their wagon, for making their spades with long instead of short handles, and for their preference for the light Russian plough in stony ground to the heavy plough of the manufacturer.

interior changes, and these changes become more obvious to the observer. Inert or slow in its movements as the peasant mind appears to be when confronted with problems to which it is unaccustomed, its instant and decisive grasp of other problems disproves the common charge of mental inactivity. In this real activity, limited as its range may be, lies the immense reserve power which enables the peasant blood to reinforce the blood of the classes deteriorated and rendered infertile through inbreeding and relatively high living. The reinvigoration of the governing class by draughts of peasant blood has not only prevented the former from dying out, but it has enabled it to lead a vigorous life in all countries where this reinvigoration has taken place. The normal peasantry, physically strong, with good teeth, good digestion, appetite unjaded by excess, and good heredity, constitutes, as it were, the well of life from which life intellectually superior is ultimately drawn.[1]

In the historical sketch given in a preceding book it has been shown that the course of Russian history resulted in the separation of the governing classes from the peasantry—that is to say, that the supply of invigorating influences for the upper classes was stopped at its source. The classes suffered from lack of reinforcement, and the peasant mass suffered not merely from the lack of sympathy which such a condition involved, but suffered also from the accumulation of untrained and unused powers. The major part of peasant energy thus ran to mere fecundity. Nature revenged herself upon the whole system by producing enormous numbers separated from, yet indissolubly united in their fate with, an exclusive and for many generations increasingly inept governing class. The dislocation of national life caused by bondage, and perpetuated by the class prejudice which outlived bondage, has apparently been chiefly responsible for bringing the national life to the pass at which it had arrived before the fall of the autocracy in 1917.

The Russian peasant is not customarily suspicious about the ordinary affairs of life. He is, however, extremely suspicious about all " papers " or documents to which he is asked to put

---

[1] It may be observed, however, that the psychological and moral consequences of migration of peasants are sometimes very unfavourable to the development of improved types. The peasant who migrates not infrequently loses his primitive culture without acquiring any other, or without acquiring it for some generations. The history of all colonization affords ample evidence of this fact.

his signature,[1] and he is similarly suspicious about all contracts or arrangements concerning land. It is probable that the origin of the first suspicion is to be found in the " Kabala" days, and in the tradition of documentary binding of the peasant in land or personal bondage; and of the second to the tradition of the frauds which were perpetrated in the carrying out of emancipation under the ukase of 1803, and later under that of 19th February 1861.

The following description of peasant life applies to the period immediately before the war of 1914–18.

It is impossible to refer accurately to Russian peasants as a whole. Their characteristics and habits of life vary widely in different parts of the country, nor can the migratory habits of large numbers of the peasants be left out of account. For example, the peasants of Northern Russia, since the abolition of the mutual guarantee and since the removal of restrictions upon their mobility, have been migrating southwards. Moreover, during the earlier years of the twentieth century they exhibited a preference for employing themselves as labourers upon large estates rather than for cultivating land of their own. The responsibilities were less, and the return to their labour was more certain, and sometimes much greater because their labour was better organized and more productive. Some of the northern peasants—*e.g.* those of Yaroslavskaya *gub.*—were very enterprising. The men left their villages, and even the district towns, to go to St. Petersburg, where they became street vendors or artisans, or they went in the season of grain shipment to the Volga, and worked as labourers in operations connected with the grain trade. Thus in many of the towns and villages in this *guberni* the men all went; only the women, children, and old men remained.[2]

Some regions acquired special celebrity for the supply of labourers in certain occupations. For example, the Zubtsovsky district, in Tverskaya *gub.*, supplied shepherds, and the Pokrovsky district of

[1] The rationale of this is, with high probability, the primitive idea that in placing his name or his mark upon a paper which is given into the hands of another, a part of the writer himself is transferred, and that through the possession of this part, the owner of the paper may exercise power over the personality of the writer. So also in the case of signatures with blood marks which were affixed by the Daimios of Japan to the oath of fealty to the Shogun.

[2] Examples of deserted towns in this *gub.* are Mishkin (2238 inhabitants) and Uglich (9500 inhabitants).

Vladimirskaya *gub.* supplied carpenters, bricklayers, and painters for all Russia.

The manufacturing centres drew their permanent recruits chiefly from Middle Russia. The harvest season, extending from the beginning of June, when the hay harvest may be said to begin, until August, when other crops are reaped, drew an immense migratory population southwards from Northern and Middle Russia. The annual migration involved about a million and a half of peasants. To some regions they went only for the hay harvest, returning to their villages to reap their own crops. In the less fertile and less skilfully cultivated regions in the north the yield of crops, usually about two and a half to three times the quantity of seed sown,[1] did not afford sufficient subsistence for the cultivators, and it was therefore necessary for the peasants to supplement their income by going for a period to the more fertile regions, where labour during harvest was relatively highly paid. The migration was not well organized. Owing to the absence of employment bureaux or similar agencies,[2] the farmers in one region in the south during harvest-time found it impossible to procure a sufficient number of labourers, although they offer as much as ten rubles a day, while a few miles away thousands of labourers were starving because they can find no employment.[3]

The habits of the peasantry vary very much in different parts of Russia and among different races. In the north, drunkenness was perhaps more common than in the central and southern regions. A statement is current among officials in the north that the State peasants in five of the northern *guberni* " drank up " the forests since Emancipation.[4] But, indeed, drunkenness everywhere was spasmodic rather than continuous. On festival days, of which there are a great number, it was not unusual for peasants to drink to excess, but only well-to-do peasants could afford to do so frequently. In the regions where beer was made, and where it was cheap, as in the *guberni* of Kharkov, the consumption was very great. During the harvest-time peasants were expected to work on Sundays, but

---

[1] In very good years the yield reached 4½ times only.

[2] Up till 1901 the Zemstvos organized employment bureaux; but they were discontinued because they were supposed to be utilized for purposes of propaganda.

[3] The principal centres to which these annual migrants went were Rostov-on-Don, Novi Cherkask, and Simferopol.

[4] In the far north, among the Ziranes, for example, drunken orgies seem to be not infrequent. Cf. *Russkoë Bogatstvo*, No. 8, August 1905, p. 29.

they did not usually receive wages for this work. They were customarily satisfied with a collation of bread and cucumbers, washed down with a few glasses of *vodka*. Drunkenness on such occasions was very unusual.

The wants of a Russian peasant are, as a rule, very simple. The prison allowance for the food of prisoners of inferior rank was six kopeks per day, the ration being bread, bouillon, small pieces of meat, small quantities of barley, and vegetables. Peasant prisoners are reported to find this ration quite satisfactory; it is probably more than they customarily enjoy. If even they have bread enough they consider themselves fortunate. In the villages the peasants subsist largely on *murtsofka*—water in which bread and salt are put. This fare is supplemented with berries, vegetables, and mushrooms in the summer. The indispensable " luxuries " of the peasant are a watch, a pair of long boots, a red shirt, music from a German accordion—his own or someone else's—and a dance on Sundays. If, in addition to these, he has a drink now and again on Sunday or on a holiday, he is usually happy and contented.[1]

Different regions in Russia present different economic conditions, and therefore various social habits, and thus a general picture is not likely to be universally faithful. Moreover, each village includes in its population various classes of peasants.

These classes may be summarized as follows:

1. The well-to-do peasants, who form the backbone of the community. These have usually a sufficient amount of land, and some of the members of the family have earnings other than agricultural earnings. They are what is known as " firm " peasants. They go to church regularly, and they can be relied upon by the *Zemskiy Nachalnik* to support him in the *volost*. They are not usually addicted to revolutionary tendencies. They are popularly known as *kulaki* or " fists." [2]

2. There are the " middle " peasants, not so well off as the first, possessing little land and cultivating, for the most part, land for which they pay rent in labour upon the estate of the landlord, but whose agricultural labour and whose extra-agricultural earnings together yield a fair living. This class feels the need of land, and some

---

[1] The temperamental contentment of the Russian peasant has, of course, permitted the exploitation to which for ages he has been subjected.

[2] There are such peasants in all countries. In Scotland the term *pechler* corresponds closely to the Russian *kulak*. For description of the class in Scotland see Tait's *Edinburgh Magazine*, Edinburgh (1832), i. 65.

of the members of it could find the necessary resources to cultivate more than they can, under present conditions, obtain at reasonable rents. They have cattle, and could obtain implements to work the land.

3. Beneath these two classes there is the village proletariat. Landless, or almost landless, almost destitute of agricultural capital of any kind, feeling at once the " need of land " and the impossibility of purchasing or of renting it. This is the class for whom schemes of purchase through the Peasant Bank have practically no interest, and for whom any scheme, revolutionary or otherwise, which will give land without the necessity of burdensome redemption payments, offers invincible attractions. The agricultural skill of this class is small, and the members of it are in chronic need. When a bad season occurs they suffer more than others, because their land is not in good condition, and their produce is proportionately much smaller than that of their neighbours. These peasants, working for themselves on minute holdings, or working for low agricultural wages, comprise a very large fraction of the 97,000,000 of Russian peasants, and their difficulties constitute the crux of the agrarian problem.

Primitive Customs.—Primitive customs abound in all parts of Russia. The following examples may suffice. Land is usually measured by the peasants with a pole. Although this pole is not divided into fractions by any marks, the peasants are accustomed to estimate the fractions very exactly. The strips of land are so long that even an inch in width means a large number of square yards.

Tally sticks are still kept by shepherds and herdsmen. On these sticks they cut the number of sheep, calves, horses, &c., under their charge. This stick is handed to the *starosta*, who places it before the *mir* once a year. On the record provided by these tallies, the *Zemstvo* statistician bases his calculations, and upon them also the payments to the landowners for pasturage and the payments to the herdsmen are based. These tallies receive different names in different regions. For example, in Vladimirskaya *gub.*, the tally is called a *dokùment*; while in Kharkovskaya *gub.* it is called a *gramota*.

Modes of observance of great holidays vary in different regions. The following account of the observance of Christmas was obtained from a peasant of Vitebskaya *gub.*[1] Early in the morning of the day before Christmas the head of the family goes into the town and

---

[1] He was a peasant of the village Barshuksky, Strunskaya *volost*, near the town of Polovtsi. The conversation took place in 1909.

buys fish and *vodka*. The supper of Christmas Eve is called *kolada*.[1]
At this supper all of the fish which has been purchased in the morning must be consumed, no matter what the quantity may be. At
midnight, between Christmas Eve and Christmas Day, the women
begin to prepare the Christmas dinner, one of the great events of
the year in the peasant household. This feast is called *razgovenye*."[2]
The traditional menu is composed of sausages, made from liver and
from beef, and boiled pork.[3] Before dinner a candle is lighted beneath the *ikon*, which finds a place in every Russian dwelling, and
even in every place of business. The whole family kneel, pray, and
prostrate themselves several times. The head of the family occupies
a conspicuous place at the table, and the other members sit around
him. The dinner begins with a service of peppered *vodka*. Usually
all, beginning with the head of the family and ending with the
youngest member, drink in succession from the same glass or silver
cup. Then they eat without ceremony, and to such an extent that the
youths often drop off to sleep towards the afternoon. After dinner
the head of the family goes to church.[4] Sometimes during the
service non-canonical incidents occur. The *mujìki* prostrate themselves, and their long locks rest on the pavement. Drunken comrades, with their boots well tarred for the holiday, accidentally or by
intention step upon the hair of the prostrate *mujìki*, who reproach
them with remarks little appropriate to the occasion and the edifice.
In the evening the youths go to the *egrēshya*,[5] or play-house, usually
the house of the *starosta* or village elder, or of some other important
villager. This play-house is the primitive village club. In those
families where the peasants are too poor to buy *vodka*, they sometimes buy cabinetmaker's varnish. Out of this, by a method of
his own, the peasant makes an evil-smelling liquid which he con-
sumes instead of *vodka*.[6]

---

[1] In the district in question. In general, the word *kolada* is applied to the
carols sung on Christmas Eve. The ordinary Great Russian word for supper
is *ujèn*.

[2] The same word is used in Byelozerskoë district, and no doubt elsewhere.

[3] About 1 *pùd* (36.11 lbs. avoir.) per ten persons.

[4] In Byelozerskoë, the head of the family goes to church before dinner.

[5] From *ēgrat*, to play. In Byelozerskoë district the play-house is called
beseda in the Korellian villages, and *posedka* in the villages inhabited by Great
Russians.

[6] Well-to-do peasants drink *vodka* made from corn, less well-to-do drink
that made from potatoes.

Disregard of Private Property among the Peasantry.—Everyone who has spent any time in rural Russia must have noticed the enormous iron bars and the huge padlocks which fastened even inner rooms in country houses, and perhaps may have experienced petty thefts. One condition was necessary to prevent the other. The explanation of the prevalence of petty thieving seems to lie in the survival of ideas originating in bondage. Under bondage the peasant had no legal right to any property. It was therefore difficult for him to conceive of any such right on the part of anyone else.[1] The *pomyetschēk* assumed himself to have the right of possession, but the peasant never fully admitted this right. Moreover, the community of occupancy of land and the community of use of agricultural instruments—although not invariable or universal—bred in the peasant a certain indifference to property considered as an individual possession. Appropriation by a neighbour of the goods of another peasant was looked upon as a venial offence, if, indeed, it were an offence; but appropriation by a stranger of the cattle or goods of a village or of a villager was in a different category. Horse-stealing is, for example, a common crime in Russia, and it is punished by the villagers with frightful severity.[1]

It is not always easy to know how much importance to attach to general statements made by peasants about the prevalence or otherwise of theft in their districts. Yet peasant evidence is of value on such a point, because the authorities as a rule know only those cases which have been brought to their notice or which have been made the subject of public inquiry. The peasants, on the other hand, know probably all the cases, although their accounts of the circumstances may not always be impartial. For example, " orthodox " peasants will narrate lurid stories of the crimes of their neighbours who are *raskolnēkē*, or dissenters, while Jews will be equally vociferous about the offences of adherents of all faiths except their own. The following details upon the conditions in this respect in Vitebskaya *gub.* were obtained for the

---

[1] *Cf.* Peter Struve in *The Slavonic Review*, London (1922), vol. i. p. 33.

[2] The writer has before him a statement contained in a letter from a peasant to his brother, of revolting details of torture applied to a horse thief in a village of Strunskaya *volost* in the spring of the year 1909. The participants in this fiendish outrage were prosecuted, and the headman of the village was punished. The case came up in the court at Vitebsk.

writer by a very astute observer, himself a peasant, in whose good faith he has every reason to have the fullest confidence. It appears that theft is highly prevalent in the *guberni*. The Jews steal by cheating in money and in weight. Orthodox (*i.e.* Greek Orthodox) peasants steal timber only, but *raskolnēkē* steal anything. This latter remark applies especially to the sect of " Old Believers." The sectarians, " Old Believers," are in this particular *guberni* traditionally thieves until they reach the age of thirty years. They steal anything, from home-woven cloth to horses. The peasants hobble their horses with heavy iron chains, but these are cut, and the horses are driven away. This practice prevails to such an extent that the peasants are unable to keep good horses, even when they are sufficiently well off to do so. Up till the age of thirty the " Old Believer " (*starovyer*) is known as *mirskoy*, or " of the world "—a worldly man ; afterwards he becomes a *rabskoy*, or " of service "—*i.e.* a servant of God. The peasants say that he devotes himself to the service of God when he has been beaten so soundly by those whom he has robbed that he can serve Mammon no more. The *rabskoy* will not eat with a *mirskoy*, any more than he would do so with an " Orthodox." The peasant view is that an " Old Believer," while forbidden to smoke or drink, is nevertheless allowed to steal. If a *mirskoy* steals the last horse of a peasant, his priest orders him to fast and to prostrate himself ; but if he steals from abundance, he is not obliged to undergo penance. The " Old Believers," according to the peasants, steal wives, and if they become tired of them they turn them away. On predatory expeditions the " Old Believers " go armed with a crowbar for breaking open lockfast places, and with knives for defence. They usually go in pairs, one watching while the other abstracts the horse they have determined to steal. When they make a raid upon the granary of a *pomyetschēk* they go in a large group, with carts and horses to carry off the plunder. The " Old Believers " are conspicuous for their loyalty to one another. If one of them falls into the hands of the police, the utmost torture will not suffice to draw from him the names of his accomplices. While he is in durance his fellows support his family. When an " Orthodox " peasant takes an oath in a court of justice, he usually regards the oath as a matter of great importance, and in general tells the truth ; but an " Old Believer " is indifferent about an oath when testimony is to be borne against a member of his own sect.   Orthodox peasants, when they are robbed by " Old Believers," are very severe upon them when they succeed in capturing the offenders.   The thieves are beaten unmercifully, and are sometimes killed by the peasants.

The reasons advanced by the "Orthodox" peasants for the inclination to steal exhibited by the " Old Believers " are these. The sectarians were, during bondage times, generally free peasants. They had therefore no allotments ; and since their religion forbids them to work for or to eat with pagans, among whom they regard all who are not of their communion, they were obliged to steal in order to support themselves.   As a rule, in Vitebskaya *gub.* at the present time the " Old Believers " are wealthier than the Orthodox peasants in whose neighbourhood they live.

These notes upon the customs of the sectarians in Vitebskaya *gub.* are of value chiefly because of the light they throw upon the opinions about the sectarians entertained by the Orthodox peasants. Whether the evil reputation of the sectarians is well deserved or not, the fact that the peasants in general think that it is accounts for the difficulty of uniting the peasants in any common action for the benefit of the peasantry as a whole.

CHAPTER II

SURVIVALS OF PRIMITIVE FAMILY CUSTOMS AND OF POPULAR
CONCEPTIONS REGARDING THE TENURE OF LAND

THE UNDIVIDED OR JOINT FAMILY

THE survival of the undivided family in Russia long after this in
stitution had ceased to have any living force in Western Europe[1]
has been a potent factor in determining the character of social and
economic life. The German observer, von Haxthausen,[2] described
very fully the undivided family as he found it in Russia about the
year 1840. Although the number of such families has greatly
diminished since that time, his description is still true so far as
regards the main features of the institution, the minor features
varying with the character of the head of the household. The
characteristic family of this kind appears to have consisted of
from ten to twenty, and occasionally even of fifty or more persons,[3]
engaging in common labour. Among the members of the family
are " the grandfather [4] and grandmother, the father and mother,

---

[1] The undivided or joint family is prevalent throughout Asia, and is
still to be found in Eastern Europe, elsewhere than in Russia. See, for
example, notes on the joint family among the Croats in Hungary, by Professor A. Herrmann in *The Millennium of Hungary and its People*, ed. by
J. de Jékelfalussy (Buda Pest, 1897), p. 407. It has been highly prevalent
in Turkey, where separations, which had been discouraged by the Government, have been taking place since the revolution in 1908 ; and in Japan
where separations have also been taking place since the revolution in 1869.
[2] *Études sur la Situation intérieure, la Vie nationale, et les Institutions rurales
de la Russie* (Hanovre, 1847–1848), vol. i. pp. 115 *et seq.* A more recent
description is given by M. Kovalevsky in *Modern Customs and Ancient Laws
of Russia* (London, 1890), pp. 15 and 47 *et seq.* See also Maine, *Ancient Law*
(London, 1874) (5th ed.), pp. 133, 260, and 266, and Hearn, *The Aryan Household, Its Structure and Development* (London, 1891), pp. 188 and 230.
[3] I have been informed by a trustworthy correspondent that in the village
of Stepankova (Moskovskaya *gub.*) there was an undivided family which consisted in 1886–1887 of seventy-five persons. The family possessions included
thirty-seven horses and sixty cows. The family was considered to be very well
off. Large undivided families are now rare.
[4] Even also sometimes a great-grandfather.

264

sons and daughters, grandsons and granddaughters, brothers and sisters, nephews and nieces, with such other persons as may be united to them by ties of marriage, as daughters-in-law in right of their husbands, and sons-in-law in right of their wives." [1] Close relationship is, however, not invariable.[2] " The house elder is *primus inter pares.*" He is chief of the family council, and representative of his household before the authorities. He appears in court to answer complaints against the members of his own household, and to make complaints against those of others. He is regarded as responsible for the payment of taxes due by the members of the family, collectively or individually. Yet he has no right to dispose of the family property without the consent of all its adult members. The house elder arranges the daily labour of the members of the family. If there is a surplus of labour for the agricultural purposes of the group, which often occurs when the family is large and when for any reason there is difficulty in obtaining land, members of the family may be sent, or may be permitted to go, abroad to earn money, their surplus earnings being required to be remitted to the house elder for the benefit of the household, while the dependents of the absentees are meanwhile nourished at the common charge. This, at all events, is the law of the household. The law is not improbably frequently evaded by concealment of individual resources.

The system of land occupation and cultivation under the undivided family may be regarded as semi-communal. Although the family group is strictly communal, there is a certain recognition of individual interests. Thus, although the land remains undivided so long as the family holds together, each member of the household has his recognized share. Nor are the shares equal. Brothers have equal shares, but others have lesser fractions of the common heritage. Any partner in the property of the family group may sell his land to a relative or to a stranger, but the purchaser is expected to conform

---

[1] Kovalevsky, *op. cit.*, pp. 53 and 54.
[2] Haxthausen, *op. cit.*, i. p. 90. Although Haxthausen quotes a specific case, there is no reason to believe that " adoption " of strangers into the family was customary. Orphans were, however, confided to peasant families by the great orphanages at St. Petersburg and Moscow, and payment was made for them by the orphanages, usually two rubles per month, until the age of sixteen years. These orphans might marry into the peasant families ; but they do not appear to have been legally adopted by them, the process of adoption being expensive and troublesome.

to the family regulations. The meadows are undivided, but they are annually apportioned for mowing, and for the purposes of each individual family in the larger family group. Pasture and forest are also common property, although they may not belong to one undivided family. They may belong in common to a larger group of several undivided families, or even to undivided families together with families which had been " separated " from their own family kin.

The prevalence and the persistence of the undivided family has affected profoundly the character of the peasant. To the regulations of the undivided family may be attributed to a large extent the customary submissiveness of the Russian peasant to authority. Even adult men are under the system obliged to be submissive to their elders. The prevalence during recent years of separations has undoubtedly contributed to the new spirit of resistance to authority which animated the peasant youth especially in the revolutionary year of 1905, and, in general, separations have effected a considerable change in the attitude of the peasant towards regulative authority of any kind.

" That the character of the Russian *mujik* has been modified by the system of the great family is proved by the fact that wherever a division of the common property has taken place, wherever the peasant has been reduced by his own will to depend entirely upon his personal industry for his success in life, he has become the pushing, unscrupulous man whom the American novelist has rendered familiar to us." [1]

The causes of the survival of the undivided family in spite of individualistic tendencies which naturally emerge within the family itself, and the causes of the breaking up of the family, have been partly spontaneous and partly administrative.

Spontaneous Disintegration of the Undivided Family.—The undivided family implied the exercise of authority by the elders, and conduced to a considerable degree of ease on their part. The *paterfamilias* oppressed his sons, acting, indeed, as a driving foreman of the working force of the family, while the *materfamilias* equally oppressed her daughters-in-law.[2] The reasons given by the peasantry for separation are these :

---

[1] Kovalevsky, *op. cit.*, p. 61.
[2] Peasant lads generally marry at about eighteen or nineteen years of age. At twenty-one they go to military service. Their wives remain members

" Non-division causes the able and laborious to work for the idle and incapable. It is unjust to force an unmarried person to divide his savings with a relative enjoying the pleasures of married life and a numerous progeny, who, on account of their youth, are not yet able to earn anything by the work of their hands. They also affirm that as the dwelling-place is too small to accommodate a large family, they are forced to divide in order to live with decency." [1] The strongest motive, however, making for " separations " has been the excessive labour of the subordinate members of the undivided family. Family quarrels arising out of this excessive labour frequently rendered separation inevitable, and when separation occurred from this cause, the filial relations were altered, and this circumstance contributed importantly to the revolutionary state of mind of the younger and more vigorous peasants. Thus the younger inhabitants of the villages, suffering at once from exactions by their family elders, by the community, and by the Government, suffering from interferences with their personal freedom and mobility practised by all of these external forces, and suffering also from want of land and of agricultural capital, took the lead in the revolutionary movements, feeling that some extraordinary demonstration was necessary to improve their condition. In many cases they dragged their elders after them into these movements. In the acts of revolt against administrative authority there thus often lay concealed acts of revolt against the authority of their parents and elders. The breaking up of the undivided family thus plays an important rôle in the revolutionary movement by preparing the minds of the younger people in the peasant communities.

But the tendency towards separations has been at intervals checked by the spontaneous action of the communities themselves. The elders found that separation was being used by the younger people to enable them to escape the payment of their share of the redemption

of the paternal households during the four years of the military service rendered by their husbands. This practice leads to undesirable results. The young husbands are corrupted in the army, and the young wives (contemptuously called by the peasants *soldatki*) are too frequently corrupted at home. On the return of the young soldiers, family quarrels take place, and for this reason, and because of the hard toil of the peasant life, to which during his military service he has been unaccustomed, the reservist often leaves his family and goes into the city, where he becomes a policeman or a janitor. His wife is frequently left permanently behind.

[1] Kovalevsky, *op. cit.*, p. 66.

tax. They thus attempted to check the tendency by refusing to permit separations even of a temporary character. This attitude of the communities led those who desired separation to undertake to continue to pay their share of the tax after separation. On this understanding conditional separations took place.[1]

Administrative Discouragements of Separations.—It is obvious that the administration was under the necessity either of discouraging separations, because they compromised the collection of taxes, or of altering the system of taxation, and of abolishing the system of mutual responsibility for the punctual payment of taxes. Prior to the emancipation of the serfs in 1861, separations were discouraged by the landowners, because the management of the serfs by their owners was greatly facilitated by the circumstance that the number of heads of households was small, while their authority over the members of their households was great. After Emancipation, when the redemption tax came to be imposed, the head of the family became responsible for the whole of the tax due by his household. The collection of the tax was simpler than it would have been had the tax-collector been obliged to deal with each member individually. Thus when the question of tax responsibility was fixed upon the head of the household the difficulty of breaking up the family by separations was greatly increased.

Yet separations continued, permitted and unpermitted, the latter sometimes greatly predominating over the former. Where the head of an undivided family was a man of strong character, separations were unusual. When, however, the contrary was the case, there was a tendency to disputes which led ultimately to separations. These were frequently postponed, however, until the death of the head of the household, or until the return of some member of the family from military service. The effects of the separations upon the prosperity of the peasants involved in them were very serious. The separated groups took with them their shares of the farm implements and the cattle, and the family land was frequently subject also to division ; but the separated groups had rarely sufficient means to establish themselves independently with any likelihood of success. The need for land, which had manifested itself even in the undivided family, became more insistent as separa-

---

[1] It is said that sometimes permission to separate was obtained from the *volost* courts by treating the people of the village to *vodka*.

tions took place, and the prosperity of the peasants affected was diminished. Many were for this reason, as well as on account of the attractions in the form of opportunities of labour and for amusements, driven or drawn into the industrial towns. The economic consequences of these separations having become obvious, a committee was appointed by Alexander III to make inquiry into the matter. The local functionaries reported that in spite of the prohibition of separations by the authorities, and in spite of reluctance on the part of the communities to permit them, separations were going on in great numbers. Peasants who separated from joint families were put in gaol. They served their terms, returned to their villages, and separated again. Only five per cent. of all separations in villages are said to have been permitted separations.

Divisions were, indeed, going on, in spite of administrative and communal discouragement, to such an extent that the Government became increasingly embarrassed in the collection of the redemption tax, the *mutual guarantee* notwithstanding. The redemption tax fell heavily into arrear. The embarrassment of the Government led to the law of April 1889, and later to that of 10th April 1894, both having for their object the limitation of the number of permitted family separations. As a result of these laws, about 5 per cent. only of the applications for separation were granted by the local authorities.

Vacillation of the Government on the Separation Question.— While M. Yermolov was Minister of State Domains and Agriculture, he proposed in 1889 to check separations by abolishing the duties on artificial manure and agricultural implements, in order that the larger peasant family groups might cultivate their land to more advantage by devoting their family capital to improvements. M. Witté, however, opposed this measure on the ground that it was inconsistent with the protective policy then advocated by him, and brought to a high point in 1891. In this attitude M. Witté was quite consistent with his general policy of promoting Russian industrial development. From his point of view separations were to be desired rather than prevented. The organic family group, occupying itself as it did in ineffective agriculture, were better broken up, in order that its constituent elements might enter into fresh artificial combinations under the auspices of capitalistic industry.

From the commercial and industrial point of view the breaking up of the undivided family was to be desired ; from the communal, agricultural, and Slavophil points of view it was to be deprecated. To the communalists the new order meant new slavery, to the industrialists it meant escape from the practical slavery of the younger generations which the communal system involved.

Impetus to Separations given by the Abolition of the Redemption Tax.—The attitude of the Government, of the local authorities, and of the community changed only when the redemption tax was abolished. The abolition gave a great impetus to separations through the removal of the obligation of mutual guarantee. The increase of individualism, or, at all events, the increase in the manifestation of it, the altered parental relations consequent upon separation, and the increased self-assertiveness of the young resulted, at least temporarily, in the diminution of social solidarity, as well as in increased migration from the village to the town. The disintegration of the undivided family has thus been a structural change, involving an alteration in the character of the peasant, in which some of the finer peasant qualities may not improbably be lost during the transition from an old to a new family order.

Peasant Views about the Tenure of Land.—Associated with the conceptions naturally arising out of the conditions of the undivided household are the views about the land common to the peasantry in different parts of Russia. These views are illustrated in the writings of several of the Russian novelists — *e.g.* in Turgenev's sketch *Moumou*, in Tolstoy's *Russian Proprietor*, in Uspensky's *Ivan Afanasiev*, and in Zlatovratsky's *Oustoy* (The Solid Base).[1] A vivid description of the attitude of the *mujik* towards the land is given by Stepniak in his *Russian Peasantry*. Stepniak quotes the translation in John Stuart Mill's *Political Economy* [2] of a passage from Michelet's *People*,[3] in which he describes with warmth the passion of a French peasant for his land, for the purpose of contrasting it with Uspensky's sketch in his *Ivan Afanasiev* of a Russian peasant, " a genuine husbandman, indissolubly bound to the soil both in mind and heart. The land was in his conception his real

---

[1] Quoted by Kovalevsky, *op. cit.*, p. 62.
[2] Mill, J. S., *Political Economy*, p. 172 *n.*
[3] Michelet's *People*, pt. i. chap. i.

foster-mother and benefactress, the source of all his joys and sorrows, and the object of his daily prayers and thanksgivings to God. . . . He and his land are almost living parts of the same whole. Nevertheless Ivan Afanasiev does not feel in the least like a bondsman chained to the soil ; on the contrary, the union between the man and the object of his cares has nothing compulsory in it. It is free and pure because it springs spontaneously from the unmixed and evident good the land is bestowing on the man. Quite independently of any selfish incentive, the man begins to feel convinced that for this good received he must repay his land, his benefactress, with care and labour.'[1] Stepniak points out that, unlike the French peasant, the Russian *mujik* has in his " longing after land more of the love of a labourer for a certain kind of work which is congenial to him, than of a concrete attachment of an owner to a thing possessed."[2]

The attitude of the Russian peasant to the land is quaintly put in a petition to the Canadian Government by Peter Veregin, the leader of the Dukhobortsi in Canada.

"The earth is God's creation, created for the benefit of the human race, and for all that live on it. The earth is our common mother, who feeds us, protects us, rejoices us, and warms us with love from the moment of our birth until we go to take our eternal rest in her maternal bosom."[3]

From this point of view land is a gift of God to the cultivator, to use, but not to appropriate. This was undoubtedly the ancient Russian view. " The word *property*, as applied to land, hardly existed in ancient Russia. No equivalent to this neologism is to be found in old archives, charters, or patents. On the other hand, we meet at every step with rights acquired by use and occupation. The land is recognized as being the natural possession of the husbandman, the fisher, or the hunter—of him ' who sits upon it.' "[4] " In the living language of peasants of modern times there is no

---

[1] Uspensky, *Ivan Afanasiev*, quoted in Stepniak, *Russian Peasantry* (ed. New York, 1888) pp. 148 *et seq.*
[2] Stepniak, *op. cit.*, p. 148.
[3] *Petition to the Minister of the Interior and all People of Canada from the Christian Community of the Universal Brotherhood of the Doukhobors in Canada*, 7th March 1907.
[4] Prince Vasilchikov, *Land Tenure and Rural Economy* (St. Petersburg, 1881), quoted by Stepniak, *op. cit.*, p. 6.

term which expresses the idea of property over the land in the usual sense of the word." [1]

This conception, not by any means entertained by the peasants in Russia exclusively, of the use of land as the function of the peasant, while the appropriation of it in any form of ownership is regarded as inadmissible, is probably a survival of the idea of land occupancy which naturally arises in the minds of pastoral people. Among such people land belongs to no one ; it is, so to say, free as air, but its use is enjoyed by those who traverse it. From this point of view rent is an anomaly. Yet the quarrels of pastoral tribes about their routes upon the steppes show that even they had definite ideas of a tribal interest in the land traversed by them periodically. Although this conception frequently reappears in peasants' discussions about land,[2] the practical difficulties of distinguishing between rights of permanent occupancy and rights of ownership become very great, especially when population is increasing and the available area of land is naturally or artificially limited. These difficulties appear even in the " undivided family," whose definite regulations about ownership of land within the family have been noticed above.

PEASANT CONCEPTIONS OF EQUALITY AND UNANIMITY

A firm sense of equality within the class pervades Russian peasant opinion. This sense of equality tends to prevent the rise of aggressive individuals, although it is not always effectual in doing so. With it is very definitely associated the practice, universal in peasant assemblies, of requiring unanimity in decisions. In the beginning of discussions there is always a majority and a minority, but as the discussion proceeds one party convinces the other or induces or compels the other into acquiescence. This practice involves often very noisy proceedings. The orators try to shout one another down, although the most influential are not always the most vociferous. The practice of securing unanimity also involves sometimes very long meetings, one party relying upon its physical endurance to wear the other out. Eventually the opposition melts away or

---

[1] Stepniak, loc. cit.
[2] An account of some of the discussions is given in the next chapter. The peasant views about land are further discussed in chapter x., infra.

abandons its position, and the measure, whatever it is, is passed.[1] Frequently, however, hard feelings remain, to accumulate in course of time into more or less formidable hostility. Thus beneath apparent harmony in a village community there often lurks real discord, and then unanimity being regarded as essential, there is nothing to be done but for the malcontents to leave the community or to be expelled from it. Unanimity is inconsistent with agreement to differ. The rule of the majority, with the proviso that the rights of minorities will be respected, seems less likely to result in tyranny than a system of compulsory unanimity. The extent to which the *mir* has availed itself of its powers to flog and to exile its members shows that "unanimity" is not unaccompanied by tyranny. Yet in certain phases of social development the universality of the practice of unanimity seems to suggest advantages in securing the safety and the continuity of the political and social structure. The nonconformist and the heretic are enemies to the family hearth, and they must be got rid of. The practice of the autocracy in stamping out what it considers as subversive tendencies, and in exiling or destroying all who presume to criticize the administration, may be related, along with the peasant conception of compulsory unanimity, to primitive social conceptions, naturally arising under conditions when social solidarity is the first essential.[2]

It may be regarded as doubtful that the tradition of unanimity would have prevented the disintegration of the family had it not been reinforced by the powerful agency of the mutual guarantee. The friction produced by the mutual guarantee was, nevertheless, an important factor in producing family disintegration, the tendency to unanimity notwithstanding.

REDISTRIBUTION OF PEASANT LANDS IN PRACTICE

The practice of redistribution of peasant lands varies widely in different parts of Russia. In the following sketch two typical districts are taken by way of example : (1) A district in the forest region in the north, where the soil is poor ; and (2) a district in the rich Black Soil region.

[1] For a very lively account of such an assembly among the Ziranes in the Arkhangelskaya *gub.*, see Shukin, P., " With the Ziranes," in *Russkoë Bogatstvo*, No. 8, August 1905, pp. 17 *et seq.*
[2] See also *supra*, pp. 10 *et seq.*

1. *The District of Byelozersk.*—This district is in Novgorodskaya *gub.* The land is too poor for wheat cultivation ; the chief crops are rye and oats. The three-field system of rotation is generally adopted—rye, oats, and fallow. The redistribution of the land takes place at no fixed period ; but whenever a number of people become dissatisfied with the quality of the land allotted to them, or with the quantity of it in relation to the number of revision souls in their families, such people complain to the *skhod*, or village as-sembly, and if they succeed in convincing the *skhod* that the time for redistribution has arrived, a sentence of the *skhod* is passed, and redistribution takes place. The *skhod* is not bound to divide the land in accordance with the number of revision souls ; but it usually does so, because this is the traditional basis of division. The system of redistribution does not, however, apply to all the land in the possession of the community. Meadow land which has been cleared by a peasant is allowed to remain in his possession, and is not subject to redivision ; nor is the peasant who has brought it into cultivation liable for taxes in respect to it. Meadow land, however, on the banks of the rivers, which overflow and which deposit mud upon the meadows, and thus enrich them, is subject to distribution like the field lands.

Until about 1904 garden land was also exempt, but now garden as well as " field " land, or land under oats and rye, is subject to division on complaint to the *skhod*. If a widow, whose husband had cultivated land and paid taxes for one revision soul, is able to work the land, either by her own labour or by that of her family, and if she can pay the taxes to the amount due by one revision soul, she is not disturbed in possession ; but if she is unable to pay the taxes, the land will be taken from her by the *skhod*, and will be handed over by it to someone who undertakes to pay taxes in respect to one revision soul more than the number to which he had been himself entitled. If a peasant who is entitled to land in respect to two revision souls finds the corresponding taxes burdensome, he may transfer, if the *skhod* permit, one-half of his privileges and obligations, retaining the right to the amount of land due to one revision soul and undertaking to pay the taxes in respect to one soul. In this way the equilibrium of the distribution is preserved among the able-bodied members of the village community.

As the village grows and the number of *ēzbas* increases, a peasant often builds his *ēzba* on the land allotted to another. Complaint is made to the *skhod*, and the peasant upon whose land the *ēzba* of another has been built receives compensation in land elsewhere. It is, however, now usual for a peasant to get permission from the *skhod* before he builds his dwelling. Formerly the land upon which the *ēzba* was built was not taken into account in allotting the lands, but now it is taken into account.

2. *Saratovskaya Gub.*—In the Black Soil region, where the land is relatively valuable, the land is, as a rule, redistributed every four, or at farthest every six, years. The distribution is effected in terms not of revision souls, but of male souls in the family. There are no forests, and thus the whole of the land tends to become field land and subject to redivision. The allotments are relatively small— 4–5 dessiatines per revision soul. As the land deteriorates in quality from continuous cropping it becomes more sensitive to climatic changes, and thus two important influences make for diminished crops. Although, in consequence of the scarcity of land other than the field land, there is little pasture, the peasants have some cattle ; but the manure from these is not put upon the land to fertilize it, but is made into fuel, because there is no timber. The manure is put into piles, dried by its own combustion, and then trampled into powder by the treading of horses. The powdered material is mixed with water, pressed into briquettes, and so used as fuel. Some of the peasants who have knowledge of what is done elsewhere object to the system of distribution, on the ground that it does not conduce to high cultivation ; but this effect may be due to other causes, and perhaps chiefly to the absence of agricultural knowledge as well as to the absence of agricultural capital.[1]

[1] These details have been obtained from peasants in the districts in question.

CHAPTER III

THE *POMYETSCHĒK* OF 1914

THE *pomyetschĕk*, or estate proprietor, of the period before the War of 1914–1917, belonged to one or other of several classes. The peculiarities of each class will necessarily be described in various ways by people who have had different opportunities for observation and who have varied prepossessions. On the great estates, the administration of which is in the hands of German managers, skilled in the technique of agriculture and in the management of labourers, the great proprietors seldom live. In the winter they are to be found in St. Petersburg, as members of the Council of State or of the Duma, or merely as members of the fashionable society of the capital, in Moscow in society there, at their villas at Yalta, Alupka, or Gurzùf, in the Crimea—on the Riviera or in Italy—cultivated, intelligent, and benevolent, or ignorant, dull, and cynical, according to their temperament. In rare cases proprietors of large estates reside almost altogether upon them, taking an active share in their management, and, on the whole, working them not only to their own advantage but to the advantage of the peasantry upon them. Another class of large proprietors rent their lands to Jews, who pay a stipulated amount to the proprietors, and then sub-let the land to peasants, exacting from these in most cases as much as is possible. Such proprietors come little in contact with the peasants even when they live in their country houses. They frequently travel abroad for sport or pleasure, and if they are members of one or other of the important bodies by means of which the central government is carried on, they spend a portion of each year at St. Petersburg. Members of the first or second classes above mentioned are usually members of the local administration of the district or *gubernie* in which their estates are situated— the government of the *gubernie* or the Zemstvo Assembly. The third class may be regarded as much more numerous than either the first or the second. This class embraces the proprietors of estates of from three thousand to five thousand dessiatines—considerable, but not large, estates. Many such proprietors are also public officials—spending the larger part of the year either in one or other of the capitals, or in the capital of the *gubernie*. Some of them are judges, some are members of the central or local governments, some are military men. The estates of members of this class are sometimes managed very efficiently, even although the proprietors may not spend more than a few months in each year upon them. The proprietors are in many cases not merely well-educated men, but they are also skilled in estate management. They have attended forestry or agricultural schools, and have kept in touch with improved methods of agriculture in their own or in other countries. Other members of the same class, who are not officials, have similarly acquired a knowledge of the business of estate management, live continuously upon their estates, and maintain production upon them at a high level.

In all the above groups, with the exception of some of those whose estates have been let to Jews, the estates are as a rule well managed, the roads are in good order, the buildings properly maintained, the forests not depleted,[1] and the industry of the peasants is well organized in such a way as to provide continuous employment.

A fourth group may be regarded as comprising those proprietors of estates of the same magnitude as the last who from ignorance, indolence, or otherwise, allow their estates to be incompetently managed, the roads and buildings to fall into disrepair, and the fields, forests, and orchards, to be neglected. On such estates the peasants are sometimes subjected to severe exactions, while no efforts, or merely spasmodic efforts, are made to enable them to live prosperously. The consequences of this state of matters are easily discernible in the aspect of the villages. The peasants' houses fall into cureless ruin.[2] The negligence of the *pomyetschēk* is reflected in the negligence of the peasants. Even where the fields of the *pomyetschēk* are well cultivated, the contiguous fields of the peasants

[1] There are stringent forest regulations ; but in some parts of Russia these are habitually neglected.

[2] The writer has seen on such estates in 1899 peasants' houses fairly well built of brick, erected under the influence of spasmodic energy. In 1910 these same houses were found by him to be rapidly tumbling to pieces under the influence of a careless proprietor and hopeless and indifferent peasants.

are not always so ; but where the fields of the *pomyetschēk* are neglected, the peasants' fields are invariably neglected also.

A fifth group might be discerned, in which there might be included the proprietors of estates of less than 3000 dessiatines, in which there would also appear a similar subdivision into intelligent and conscientious proprietors who conceived their duty in a high sense, and those who were indolent, dissolute, and careless—both disseminating their qualities round about them among the peasantry.[1]

In his very interesting *Notes of a Governor : Kishēniev*, Prince S. D. Urusov gives an estimate of the changes which have been occurring in the inner life of the *pomyetschēk* class during the past thirty years.

" I have known well," he says, " the customs, character, traditions, and peculiarities of the gentry of the Great Russian provinces, particularly the provinces of the Moscow region. . . . In the eighties and nineties of the nineteenth century there might be found not seldom large estates with traces of former greatness, with parks, centuries old, with artificial lakes and peach orchards, with valuable furniture, rare bronzes, family portraits, and libraries in large rooms in old but still quite habitable houses. It was, however, even then to be noticed that the former life of the nobility on such estates was declining, that old houses and old luxuries could not in the majority of cases be maintained on the former plane ; yet the spirit of the old nobility still survived, and the sight of all this antiquity might inspire a certain amount of æsthetic satisfaction. . . ." Besides these, there were at that time, " households more closely adapted to the contemporary conditions—households without agricultural experts or managers, but being managed by the owner himself, who lived upon his estate, and who had as assistants a *starosta* (or peasant foreman) or a clerk. In the majority of such estates there was no luxury.[2] A few days of hunting in the autumn, three homebred horses, and some pet colt, upon whom there were placed exaggerated and in most cases false hopes—these comprised the luxuries of the *pomyetschēk*, who received from his estate modest but

---

[1] Many of the smaller gentry are scarcely, if at all, superior in respect to education to the peasantry. The writer has met with cases in which educated peasants were applied to by indifferently-educated *pomyetschēkē* to conduct for them official correspondence which they were unable to conduct for themselves.

[2] There was, however, a certain rude comfort and general evidence of well-being.

genuine profits in those rubles which, according to the Russian proverb, ' are thin but long.'   Quick enrichment from the management of such estates could not be expected.   Yet notwithstanding complaints of bad yields, of dearness of labour, of dishonesty of neighbouring peasants, the possessors of small estates were living modestly, but with satisfaction, and although sometimes they adorned the pages of bank publications, they nevertheless were becoming rich owing to the slow but continuous advance in the price of land.   Of such steady landowning gentry I knew many, especially in the non-Black Soil region, and I should say that they constituted a phenomenon—in general favourable.   Their relations with peasants, in spite of occasional disagreements, were in most cases not uncordial. Exploitation of peasants on their part was rare ; on the contrary, there was in their relations with working peasants a certain kind of union, which was developed by continuous mutual activity. . . . Simplicity of life, absence of class exclusiveness and class pride in the sense of ostentation, a laborious rural life, understanding of popular wants, and considerate relations with the neighbouring peasantry characterized the average *pomyetschēk* with whom I was acquainted in Kalujskaya *gub*.

" Quite another picture was presented in Bessarabia.   There on the estates of rich *pomyetschēkē* great luxury might be met with ; but in them there was none of that old magnificence which in Great Russia had come from the time of Katherine II and Alexander I. The houses of the Bessarabian gentry are sometimes lighted with electricity, but there are not to be found the oil lamps of the style of the First Empire, or the bronze candelabra and lustres by which in Central Russia the houses of the old gentry are distinguished.[1]   The book-presses of the Bessarabian gentry are full of the latest romances; but there are no French encyclopædists of the eighteenth century, bound in leather with gold letters.   Nor could there be seen in their houses the old furniture made by home-bred carpenters.   In them everything is made according to the prevailing fashion—everything is new and everything is often changed.   Perhaps there is much more of convenience in these houses than there is with us, but they are, after all, only splendidly furnished rooms—they are not old Russian gentry nests.   Moreover, among the Bessarabian gentry there was not noticeable that love for the estate which with us is indepen-

[1] These are also to be found in such houses in St. Petersburg.

dent of the beauty and profitableness of it. We look upon our estates as upon inanimate persons, and love them for themselves, and not for what they bring to us." [1]

In Bessarabia, owing to the advance in the price of wheat and rye during recent years, the accessibility of two important seaports—Odessa and Nikolaiev—greatly increased facilities in these ports, differential railway rates, which favoured exportation, the income from the possession of land greatly increased, and the prices of land advanced rapidly. " Estates which were obtained in the seventies for 25 to 35 rubles per dessiatine were transferred in my time into fifth hands for 250 to 350 rubles per dessiatine." [2] At the first-mentioned period enrichment of the soil by manure was unusual. The increasing value of land, coupled with the fact that the landowning gentry were frequently very indifferent farmers, led to the sale of the land to others who were better able to exploit them. Thus the estates of the landholding families speedily melted away.

Even when the estates fell into the hands of competent owners, these were not always succeeded by competent heirs, and thus the process of enrichment and impoverishment contributed to frequent changes of ownership and to the disappearance of successive landowning families.[3]

---

[1] Prince S. D. Urusov, *Notes of a Governor : Kishēniev* (Berlin, 1907), pp. 128–32.

[2] Urusov, *op. cit.*, p. 133.

[3] Fondness for the pleasures of the table is a usual trait among landed proprietors almost throughout Russia. The following is the daily routine even in households which pride themselves upon their simplicity : 8 o'clock light breakfast—tea, bread, and honey, *e.g.* ; 11 o'clock, breakfast *à la four-chette*—a formidable meal ; 1 o'clock, lunch of similar character ; 4–5 o'clock, tea and bread, &c. ; 7 o'clock, dinner of numerous courses ; 9 o'clock, supper ; 11 o'clock, a snack before retiral. Prince Urusov gives an amusing picture of the *ménage* of a Bessarabian *pomyetschĕk* whose hospitality he had accepted upon the distinct understanding that simple fare must alone be provided. " At three o'clock in the afternoon we sat down to dinner. The table was filled with bottles and *zakuska* (*hors d'œuvres*) of various kinds. Having moderated our hunger, we continued our dinner at leisure. We were served with four courses of nutritious food without soup. Having sat at the table for an hour and a half, I waited impatiently for an opportunity to take a walk ; but I found that what we had despatched had been merely the Bessarabian *zakuska*, and that the Bessarabian dinner had not yet begun. Two soups were then served, followed by seven different enormous heavy dishes. By way of tacit protest I refrained from touching the dishes served in this unexpected continuation of the dinner. I regarded the conduct of my host as an attempt upon my health. We rose from the table about seven o'clock, having sat for four hours." Urusov, *op. cit.*, p. 136.

Apart from his function of landowner, the typical *pomyetschĕk* is expected to bear his share in local administration.   If he is a great landowner he will probably be marshal of the nobility of his *guberniya*, or he may serve as a district marshal, or as an honorary judge for a district, or he may be a member or the president of the Zemstvo Assembly.   Sometimes these offices are filled conscientiously and efficiently.   During the period prior to 1905 the Zemstvo Assemblies were composed very largely of men of liberal tendencies.   They promoted on the one hand educational enterprises, and on the other sought to improve agriculture by employing the services of *agronoms*, whose function it was to advise about the improvement of agriculture.   Frequently their relations with the central Government were those of not unfriendly critics.   They enjoyed and availed themselves of a considerable freedom of speech.   But the agrarian movements of 1905 excited much anxiety among them.   They began to see in the agrarian movement a force that might make for their impoverishment or even their ruin.   Thus there came about the so-called " Righting of the Zemstvos," or their turning from an attitude of benevolent, though sometimes, perhaps, supercilious, interest in the peasantry, to one of extreme devotion to the Throne.

In Bessarabia up till this moment the Zemstvos, led by enthusiasts among the nobility, had embarked in many enterprises which were designed to educate or in some way to serve the peasantry.   These enterprises sometimes consisted in the erection in the casual Bessarabian way of handsome buildings for various purposes—houses for pensioners, museums, asylums, and the like.   Sometimes the funds for the erection of these came from the central Government, and sometimes they came from the Zemstvo taxes.   In spite of the good intentions with which these enterprises were conceived, they were constructed on a scale of magnificence which heavily taxed the Zemstvos to maintain.   Thus, although many of them were works of utility, the Zemstvos were unable sometimes even to utilize them, because of the continuous expense involved in their use.[1]

[1] An instance of this is given by Prince Urusov, *op. cit.*, p. 141.

CHAPTER IV

AGRICULTURE AFTER EMANCIPATION

BETWEEN the period of Emancipation and 1887, the arable land of Russia increased 25 per cent. This increase was not, however, extended all over Russia ; in the Black Soil regions the arable land increased 50 per cent., while in the non-Black Soil it decreased 10 per cent. The area of arable land in forty-six *guberni* of European Russia (excluding from the fifty *guberni* Penzinskaya, Astrakhanskaya, Liflandskaya, and Donskoye *oblast*) was estimated in 1887 at 107.3 millions of dessiatines, or 28.2 per cent. of the total area. In the Black Soil zone the proportion of arable land was 55.2 per cent., and in the non-Black Soil regions 12.7 per cent. The proportion is highest in Khersonskaya *gub.*, where it is 77.6 per cent., and lowest in Arkhangelskaya *gub.*, where it is 0.1 per cent. Of the total of arable land 62.5 millions of dessiatines, or 58.3 per cent., was under crop ; 23.5 millions of dessiatines, or 21.9 per cent., under annual fallow ; 6.6 millions of dessiatines, or 6.1 per cent., under grass, and 14.7 millions of dessiatines under fallow for several years. This last is known as *zalesh*, or resting land.[1] Peasant lands at that time (in 1887) were being ploughed more than lands in the hands of landowners. In peasant lands 61 per cent. was under seed, while in landowners' lands only 53 per cent.

Between 1861 and 1887 the proportion of land under winter and spring grains respectively altered considerably, the land under spring grains increasing. Spring wheat, *e.g.* increased by 39.5 per cent. in area, while winter wheat increased by only 7.5 per cent.

---

[1] Such land is common in intermediate " economies," not in large economies or in peasant holdings.

In 1900, in the fifty *guberni* of European Russia, the area under crop was 71,276,925 dessiatines, distributed as follows :

	Dessiatines.
Rye	24,350,271
Spring wheat	11,360,819
Winter wheat	2,730,564
Oats	13,853,117
Barley	6,513,848
Other crops	...
	71,276,925

Rye is the chief crop everywhere in Russia, except in the New Russian and Middle Volga (steppe) regions, where wheat predominates. Maize is cultivated to the extent of 32.4 per cent. of the total arable area in Bessarabskaya *gub.* ; oats to the extent of 20 per cent. in the Middle Volga region and in the Black Soil zone, and barley 55 per cent. in Arkhangelskaya *gub.*[1] " Everywhere and for all plants the crops on landowners' lands yield more than on peasant lands." [2] The yields are highest in the Ad-Baltic region ; they are lowest in the New Russian district and in Minskaya, Astrakhanskaya, Samarskaya, and Orenburgskaya *gub.*

The yields from Russian agriculture fluctuate very greatly, yet over any long period of time there does not appear any tendency either to the increase or the diminution of the yields. Landowners' crops and peasants' crops fluctuate alike.

The average of fifty *guberni* shows that the lands in peasants' hands produce 68.1 per cent. of the total yield, or more than two-thirds. The statistics of yield show that the increase is due, not to increase of crops, but to the increase of arable area.

The cultivation of the sugar beet has spread over almost one-half of the *guberni* of European Russia. In the twenty-three *guberni* in which sugar beet is cultivated, there were in 1902–1903, 278 factories. In ten years, 1892–1902, the number of factories increased 19 per cent. and the area of plantations 73 per cent. The fields in cultivation increased 97 per cent. Poland gives the highest yield and the best beet ; the eastern region gives the lowest yield. Tobacco is culti-

---

[1] Chermak, L., in *Brockhaus*, Supplementary Volume, p. xliii.
[2] *Ibid.*

vated in thirty *guberni* of European Russia. The principal seat of the cultivation is in Chernigovskaya and Poltavskaya *gub.* ; but it is also cultivated in the Caucasus, Trans-Caucasus, and in Poland.[1] Tea is grown in Batùmskoë district ; cotton is grown in Middle Asia.

Fertilizers are being increasingly used throughout European Russia, natural manure being chiefly employed. Peasants are as a rule applying less manure than private owners, a natural consequence of the deficiency of cattle among the peasants. In the Black Soil zone the quantities of manure used by peasants and by land-owners respectively are 2000 and 2800 *pùds* per dessiatine. The use of artificial fertilizers is increasing yearly ; the imports of slag from Thomas furnaces and superphosphates have increased largely, while the production in Russia has also increased, some of the product being utilized in Russia, and a large quantity being exported. The total quantity of artificial fertilizers consumed in 1901 is stated as 6,800,000 *pùds*.

Agricultural implements of modern character are being increasingly used. In 1900 there were 162 factories for manufacturing such implements, producing yearly 12,000,000 rubles worth. In addition there were imported in 1904 agricultural implements of the value of 18,903,000 rubles. Between 1896 and 1905 the weight of agricultural implements imported increased by 360 per cent.

Cattle Raising.—In fifty *gubernie* of European Russia there were in 1900, 113,775,000 head of all cattle, of which 18.4 per cent. belonged to landowners and 81.6 per cent. to peasants. The proportions of different animals were as follow : In each 1000 head of all cattle in peasants' herds there were 173 horses, 289 head of horned cattle, 436 sheep, 100 swine, and 2 head of others. Landowners had proportionately fewer horses, more sheep, and more swine. In the Black Soil zone there are more sheep and fewer horned cattle, and in the non-Black Soil vice versa.

The increase of ploughing has driven the sheep to the cheaper lands of Northern Caucasus and the south-east, so that in European Russia the number of sheep has contracted from 14 to 9 million head. The deficiency in cattle experienced by the peasantry is shown in a general way in the following table :

[1] The total quantity of tobacco produced in 1903 was 6,169,000 *pùds*, 38 per cent. being of the finer qualities. Chermak, *loc. cit.*

HEAD OF CATTLE PER 1000.

	Dessiatines.		Souls of both Sexes.	Working Males.	House-yards.
	Land suitable for Cattle.	Arable Land.			
1870 . .	664	1144	1456	6344	9329
1880 . .	655	1130	1238	5416	8345
1890 . .	631	1062	1135	4948	7294
1900 . .	602	887	1026	4426	6474

This table illustrates vividly the progressive decline of peasant well-being, the number of all cattle per peasant houseyard having declined within thirty years about 30 per cent. During the same period the number of working horses per 1000 dessiatines declined from 163 to 126 per head, or 23 per cent. ; per 1000 working males from 904 to 629, or 30.5 per cent. ; and per 1000 houseyards from 1329 to 920, or 30.5 per cent. Thus, in 1870, on the average every houseyard had at least one horse, now not nearly all houseyards have even one horse. In forty-three *gubernie* of European Russia, according to the military horse census of 1899–1901, there were of each 100 peasant houseyards 29.6 without horses, 32.2 with one horse, 21.4 with two horses, and 17.8 with three horses or more.

While European Russia has been impoverished in cattle, there has been a great development of cattle raising in Western Siberia. The immense prairie regions in the region of Omsk sustain enormous herds. Statistics of these are wanting ; but the exportation of butter from Siberia has already reached great dimensions, and the Siberian railway enables beef to be sent into the markets of European Russia in considerable quantities. Much remains to be done, however, in improving the breed of the cattle.

Systems of Agriculture.—Great changes have been effected during recent years in the systems of agriculture in vogue in Russia. Up till ten or fifteen years ago exhaustion of the soil by continuous cropping may be said to have been the rule. Where the soil was enriched, this was effected by burning timber upon it, a wasteful method,[1] which has come to be impracticable in all but the extreme northern parts of Russia, because timber has become scarce and dear.

Since about 1900 Russia has come to be divided into three regions: the timber region of the north, the central region, where the " resting land " system is adopted—a system involving leaving land in fallow for several years in succession, and the regions of the east and south, where the three field system is adopted. The latter system is, of course, the most advanced in an agricultural sense, whether the land left in fallow is treated with fertilizers or not. The second system is the inevitable outcome of continuous cropping ; the land requires years to recover its productive powers.[2]   In the Moscow district there appears to be a tendency to pass from the three field system to a many field system.   An extensive rotation of crops is of course possible only within a reasonable distance of an extensive market in which there is a varied demand.   The organization of the market in products, even other than the great staples, has facilitated this change.   On the peasant lands there is inevitably a tendency to produce exclusively those crops which are required for peasant consumption, viz. principally rye, wheat, oats, potatoes, and vegetables.   The area of peasant land per household is too small for the production of any considerable surplus for sale. The peasant agricultural economy is thus in general more varied, because it is more self-contained than the agricultural economy of the landowner, who cultivates his land by the aid of peasant labour, and who sells almost all the product.   In Central and Southern Russia and in the Ad-Baltic, Polish, and north-eastern regions, the proprietors engage chiefly in the production of grain and potatoes for the manufacture of alcohol in their own distilleries, for sale to the Government, which possesses a monopoly for the sale of vodka.[3]   Very few of the landowners devote themselves to cattle raising.   The scarcity of peasant cattle is noticed elsewhere.

[1] The writer saw this method in practice in the north of Finland in 1899. It is probably still employed there, but it is understood to be now unusual in European Russia.

[2] In the Black Soil regions continuous cropping has in the course of eighty years in some cases reduced the yield to an insignificant amount.   This " mining " of the land is the usual practice in the United States and Canada. Unless it ceases impoverishment of the farmers there must ensue.

[3] In 1903 the number of such estates to which distilleries were attached throughout Russia was 1952.

The Zemstvos have played an important part in the spreading of agricultural knowledge among the peasants, and also among the smaller landowners, who stood as much in need of instruction as did the peasants. Among the most active of the Zemstvos in this connection those of Moscow and Kharkov take a high place. Altogether the Zemstvos of European Russia, between 1895 and 1904, increased their expenditure on this account from about 1,000,000 rubles to nearly 4,000,000 rubles. The Zemstvos found that in Russia, as elsewhere, the agricultural schools led their scholars away from peasant life. In order to counteract this tendency some of the Zemstvos devoted themselves to the organization of special courses of instruction in dairying and of lectures at country fairs upon agricultural questions. They have established more numerous experimental stations and agricultural museums, and have organized more frequently agricultural exhibitions. They have also employed in large numbers *agronoms*, or agricultural experts, whose services are placed at the disposal of peasants, and by these numerous local agricultural associations [1] have been established. The Zemstvos have assisted the peasants in certain localities in the struggle against quicksands, in drying up swamps, in irrigation,[2] and in the establishment of shops for the sale of agricultural implements, artificial manure, and pure seeds, as well as workshops for the repair of agricultural implements. In addition to these activities the Zemstvos have done much to improve cattle breeding by establishing breeding points and studs. They have also contributed to the encouragement and improvement of flax culture, grape growing, the cultivation of hops, &c. The Zemstvos have organized the granting of small loans to peasants to enable them to adopt improved means of production, and to enable them to buy land.[3]

Most of the Zemstvo statisticians have embraced their calling from idealistic motives. Many of them are *intelligents* who have left the universities voluntarily or compulsorily on account of their liberal views. Occasionally university professors work as Zemstvo statisticians, because the exercise of their functions brings them into direct contact with the conditions of the peasantry. Among the statisticians are to be found many *privat-docenten* of the universities.

[1] There were 956 of these associations in Russia in 1906.
[2] The Government has also engaged in extensive irrigation works in Turkestan, *e.g.*, and has expended large sums in combating insect pests.
[3] Chermak, *loc. cit.*

The Zemstvo statisticians and the Zemstvo agronoms are not usually regarded with favour by the officials of the Central Government, nevertheless their statistics are universally regarded as reliable, and they are accepted for administrative purposes. The taxation of land is based upon the valuations made in the Zemstvo offices, and these valuations are founded upon the statistics furnished by the Zemstvo statisticians.

In addition to private mortgages upon land, which in Russia are not registered in any public office, the following enormous indebtedness had accumulated upon land up till 1st July 1905 :[1]

Mortgages upon land in the hands of the—	Million Rubles.
1. Nobility Bank	716.0
2. Nobility Bank Special Department . . .	47.6
3. Peasants' Bank	405.1
4. Other Banks	959.4
Total . . .	2128.1

[1] Groman, *Agrarian Question and Agrarian Projects* (Moscow, 1906), p. 39.

CHAPTER V

GRAIN DEFICIENCY AND THE MARKETING OF CROPS[1]

THE peasant produces primarily for his own needs. His land allotment, unless it is supplemented by land purchased or rented by him, excepting in the case of rich peasants, is insufficient to produce grain beyond these needs. Yet after harvest each year the peasant sells grain, even although he may reserve an inadequate quantity to maintain his family until the next harvest, and even although he may reserve no seed. Why does he do this ? The answer is that in the autumn he requires money to pay his quit-rent and his taxes and to meet the principal or the interest of his other obligations. Ere long he has to go into the market to buy back his own or other grain, sometimes from the very persons to whom he has sold it. But the price of grain in August and September, when the granaries are full, is at its minimum ; in January or February, when exports have drawn off a large part of the crop and when consumption has diminished the supplies, the price is usually higher, in the spring the price approaches its maximum. Thus the peasant sells in a cheap market and buys in a dear one. All this is so common that the practice is the subject of quaintly humorous jests among the peasants. After his manner, when the *mujik* loads his grain to take it to market, he addresses it :

" Don't thou be sorry, Mother Rye ! that thy path is city-wards. In spring I will overpay ; but I will take thee back."

" Don't be sorry, Oats ! that I brought you into Moscow. Afterwards I will pay three times more ; but I will take you home again." [2]

This practice involves a very expensive form of credit. The peasant really pawns his grain in the autumn and redeems it in the spring or earlier at a considerable cost for the loan.

According to investigations conducted in 1895, the quantity of

[1] The conditions described in this chapter were those of the period before the Revolution of October 1917.

[2] " Towards the Theory of the Class Struggle," in *Revolutsionnaya Rossiya*, No. 34, 15th October 1903, p. 7.

breadstuffs, which barely sufficed to meet the needs of peasants, was found to be 19 *pùds* per soul, while the quantity required to meet these needs fully was 26.5 *pùds* per soul.[1]   Only in cases where the production in any group amounted to 26.5 *pùds* per soul could there be, properly speaking, any excess of grain for sale.

In forty-six *gubernie* of European Russia the following is the result of investigations conducted upon the basis of the normal quantities as indicated above:

	Thousand Souls.	Percentage of Total.
Peasants experiencing inadequate production for necessary consumption	33,533	52.0
Peasants just secured — that is with an exact balance of production and consumption . .	20,428	31.8
Peasants having an excess of production over quantities required for consumption	10,176	15.9

All of these figures are open to criticism, and the net conclusion of subsequent inquiries of the same character is that they are too favourable, that in brief the numbers of peasants who do not produce grain enough for their subsistence is considerably more than 52 per cent.   They must make up the deficiency by working upon land other than their own—an indication either that they have too little land, or that their methods of production do not utilize fully what they have—or the deficiency must remain with its inevitable concomitants, reduced standard of living and accumulating debt.   The reduced standard of living expresses itself partly in the purchase of foodstuffs of inferior nutrition—potatoes, oats, and barley, *e.g.* in the domestic manufacture of inferior *kvass* or *turia*, an indigestible mechanical mixture of water, flaxseed, and flour,[2] and partly in mere abstinence.

The Zemstvo statistics disclose these conditions very clearly. The Central Black Soil region possesses the richest agricultural land in Russia, and yet these statistics show that even there the defici-

[1] Mares: "The Production and Consumption of Breadstuffs in Peasant Economy," in *The Influence of Yield and Breadstuff Prices on some sides of Russian Economic Life*, edited by Chuprov and Posnikov (St. Petersburg, 1895), i. p. 35.

[2] Cf. *Statistical Description of Kalujskaya Gub.* (Kaluga, 1898), i. pp. 666 *et seq.*

ency of grain is considerable in very many districts. In Orlovsky district, for example, the deficiency of grain, or the difference between the quantity normally requisite for peasant consumption and the quantity available, is stated at 326,000 *pùds* of rye. " Of the total number of peasant households, 84.6 per cent. have a deficit, and only 15.4 per cent. have a real excess." [1] Local investigations show that sales of foodstuffs by the peasants are " nearly always " followed by subsequent purchases. The difference between the autumn and the spring prices amounts to 24.6 kopeks per *pùd* of rye, and 39.4 kopeks per *pùd* of oats. Moreover, the prices in the villages and small towns are usually higher than they are in the cities. In other districts of the same *guberni*, the same conditions obtain. In Bolkhovsky district, for example, in some villages all peasants have to buy breadstuffs every year. Some are reduced to the purchase of food by the middle of November, 20 per cent. are able to refrain from buying until Christmas, only a few are able to postpone buying until the middle of February. In the neighbouring *guberni* of Tula, in the district of Tula, there is a deficiency of grain even in the most fertile part of the district. In seven *volosts* of this district only 38.7 per cent. of all households have enough breadstuff for their annual consumption, 24.3 per cent. have enough for from two to six months only, while 7.9 households rent their allotments to others and thus require to supply themselves by purchase exclusively. In Ryazanskaya *gub.*, from which large quantities of grain are exported, the shortage of grain was 950,000 *chetverti* each year. In poor years some peasants begin to buy immediately after harvest, and by February three-fourths of the peasants are buying. In Mikhaelovsky district of this *guberni*, the peasants in years of deficient crops, *e.g.* in 1897, began to buy in August, 16.1 per cent. of their households being under the necessity of doing so. By December more than one half were buying. Cattle were sold by 23 per cent. in order to secure money wherewith to buy food. These peasants were obliged during that year to sell 35.3 per cent. of their cattle. In that year also, after the cattle, the buildings began to be used up.[2] It became necessary to deroof the houses in order to

---

[1] *Book of Statistical Information about Orlovskaya Gub.*, viii. (Orel, 1895). Quoted by Lyatschenko, P. J., *Outlines of Agrarian Evolution in Russia* (St. Petersburg, 1908), i. p. 389.

[2] Lyatschenko, *op. cit.*, p. 391.

give the straw to the remaining cattle, while some were wholly utilized either for food for cattle or for fuel. The cattle were, of course, purchased by well-to-do peasants ; but there remained the impoverished families, who were in effect ruined.

In Samarskaya *gub.*, a rich region, in 1899, although the crops were above the average and much above the crops of the immediately preceding years, the Zemstvo office reported a shortage of foodstuffs *before* the beginning of field work in 62.3 per cent. of all peasant statements. In some districts this percentage was very much higher, in Nikolayevsk for instance it was 86 per cent., and in Boozuluk 94 per cent. Immediately *after* the harvest, 25 per cent. of the peasant statements of the whole *guberni* showed that the peasants concerned had recourse to loans for consumption, 32 per cent. had to buy grain, and about 28 per cent. had to "work out." In years of average crop in this *guberni* 38.6 per cent. of all houseyards have an excess of breadstuffs, and the remaining 61.4 per cent. are compelled to sell and to buy again, or to buy inferior foodstuffs.

In Ostrogorjsky district of Voronejskaya *gub.*, according to the Zemstvo statistics of 1886, 58.1 per cent. of peasant households could not subsist upon their own grain production. The incidence of this shortage was as follows : [1]

	Per Cent. of Household.
Landless peasants	63.00
Households having 1–5 dessiatines	64.20
Households having 5–15 dessiatines . . .	61.30
Households having 15–25 dessiatines . . .	48.30
Households having over 25 dessiatines . . .	36.60

The statistics of Ufimskaya *gub.* show the same results in another way. If the whole of the yield of grain on landowners' estates is sent to market, and if the peasants have an excess of grain, calculating the net excess of all peasants, the result for the whole *guberni* would be as follows :

	Million pùds.
Landowners' grain	4
Surplus of peasant grain above normal requirements for consumption	2.5
	6.5

[1] *Statistical Information for Voronejskaya Gub.*, iii. (Voronej, 1886).

But the balance of grain exported from the *guberni* is 14.2 million *pùds*, so that there is left a deficiency which presses wholly upon the peasants of 7.7 million *pùds*.[1]

In many *gubernie* the grain is purchased from the peasants by small dealers, who do not export it out of the district in which it is bought ; they simply store it, well knowing that the peasants will return and will require to pay an enhanced price for it. In Slobodskoy district of Viatskaya *gub.*, for example, the difference between the price in autumn and the price in spring represents interest at the rate of 38 per cent. for rye, and of 62 per cent. for oats.[2] Similar rates of interest might be calculated for other *guberni*.

Even in Khersonskaya *gub.*, which is one of the richest grain-producing regions in Russia, peasants having less than 11 dessiatines of land per household experience a deficiency of rye for consumption, while those who have less than 6 dessiatines have a deficit of wheat and millet as well.

In Moskovskaya *gub.* the total requirement, at the very small figure of 16 *pùds* per soul, is 20,324,000 *pùds*. The ordinary yield is about 7,555,000 *pùds*, so that there is a normal deficit of bread-stuffs in the *guberni* of 12,769,000 *pùds*, or 10 *pùds* per soul. That is to say, that the population can be fed by means of breadstuffs of local production for only four months and a half in the year. Not-withstanding this general deficiency, rye is sold in autumn in order to provide cash for quit-rent payments at from 50–60 kopeks per *pùd*, and is bought in spring at 90 kopeks.[3]

These are the conditions in the best agricultural regions of European Russia. Into the forest regions of the north, where grain is produced in small quantity, imports of grain must take place.

Statistical material regarding the internal trade of all countries is obtainable with difficulty, and in no case can it be held to be complete. The means of communication are varied and of some of them no records are kept. Moreover there is much urban and village interchange which is too elusive to record, yet which is, nevertheless, in the aggregate probably in general greater in magnitude in respect to quantity and value than the export and import trade of the country.

[1] Lyatschenko, *op. cit.*, p. 392–4.
[2] *Ibid.*, p. 395.
[3] *Ibid.*, p. 397.

The change from a self-contained to a money economy, in spite of the increase in individual liberty which such a change usually implies, may result in the increasing dependence of those whose productive powers and whose capacity for bargaining are alike inferior. On the other hand, such a change may redound greatly to the advantage of those who possess either high productive or high bargaining powers, and still more of those who possess both. Thus in the village there speedily arise the two classes whose characteristic features have already been described—the poor peasants, who gravitate into a landless class, and the rich peasants, *kulaki* or fists, who gradually accumulate both land and capital.

Under a self-contained system, such as obtained prior to the emancipation of the serfs, production in the villages was varied, and for this reason relatively inefficient when compared with high specialization in each of the varied activities. The weaver and the fruit-grower, who specializes in his particular business, must in general produce more than the non-specialist can produce in either of the occupations in question. The life of the specialist may be more monotonous than the life of the general producer, but it is within its limits more productive in a physical sense. Where there is a sufficiency of free and suitable land, and where the generally producing peasant is industrious, given good atmospheric conditions, the peasant will in general be able to subsist himself and even perhaps to accumulate a reserve in various products. Money economy introduces numerous factors of which the following are the most important :

1. Exchange of products on terms determined partly by relative powers of bargain making and partly by conditions beyond the control of the parties to the bargain.

2. Competition of buyers and sellers respectively within the local market, and competition of external buyers and sellers.

3. The necessity of selling in order to buy.

4. The specialization of production, which is induced by the need of producing, not what is required to be consumed by the producer, but what can be sold.

5. The acquisition by land of value which it did not formerly possess, because it was neither bought nor sold. This value is acquired by land because of the relative suitability of it for productive purposes.

The reactions of those factors upon the character and the habits of the peasants who fall under the influence of money economy result in the changes in the structure of peasant society which bring into relief the agrarian problem. The social outcome of the process is the gradual dissolution of the self-sufficing rural community, its dispersal among towns and concentration in them, and the growth there of industries. These industries afford the means of producing a mass of industrial goods available for exchange for the means of life which are produced by the remaining rural population. This process as a whole involves the creation of reserves, which are above all necessary in towns where, notwithstanding increasing facilities of communication, supplies of certain commodities are not immediately available, the scenes of their production being more or less distant. Only in highly developed urban societies are the supplies which are daily and hourly required for consumption delivered so constantly that large reserves become no longer necessary. But this continuous supply requires organization and means of communication. These can only be created by means of capital, and thus urban and rural communities alike come to be more and more dependent upon capital and upon those who control its movements. The urban communities require urgently goods for consumption, and the rural communities which devote themselves to the specialized production of products for town consumption become themselves dependent upon the towns for those commodities which they need, but cannot produce because their productive powers are otherwise employed.

The principal fact, then, which demands study in connection with peasant economy is the movement of the staples of urban consumption from the village to the town.

The fundamental material for the study of the economical condition of an agricultural country lies in the statistics of the reserves, if any, carried over from one year to another, and of the yields of successive years. Unfortunately, the first element is not readily ascertainable with exactitude for Russia.[1] Comparison of yields of

[1] For the United States and for Canada reserves are customarily estimated by adding together the quantities of grain in the elevators and " in farmers' hands " on 31st August. The former is susceptible of exact statement; the latter can be merely an estimate. Such statistics, however, leave out of account grain in the hands of millers and in transport, as well as all flour,

early dates is difficult owing to the questionable reliability of the earlier data ; but since 1883 statistics of yields are available.[1]

Two principal causes induce the movement of grain from the hands of the producer. These are the price which is to be obtained for it, and the need for selling it at any price which may be obtained. The scale of prices in different centres determines the direction of the movement. It is obvious that this direction is determined, not by the peasant when he sells the grain, because he cannot be supposed to be familiar with the markets external to his locality, but by the middleman who buys his grain, and who, keeping himself acquainted with the conditions of the grain trade, disposes of it in the market which yields him the greatest net advantage. Even the large landowners sell their grain through such middlemen.

During the past ten or twelve years great facilities have been afforded by the Government and otherwise for the movement of grain. Stores and " elevators " have been provided, and differential railway rates have been instituted between interior producing centres and the great shipping ports of Odessa and Nikolayev.

These differential rates are lower from the producing centres to the ports than they are from these centres to the interior consuming centres, so that it is more profitable to export grain than to send it to the cities for domestic consumption. The object of this policy on the part of the Government railways when it was initiated was to excite the exportation of grain in order to induce imports. Imports were, however, checked by a highly protective tariff. This condition was expected to result in the influx of gold, the special object of this desired influx being the rehabilitation of the paper ruble, which had become depreciated through over-issue. The policy has been successfully carried out ; an enormous hoard of gold has been accumulated ; the paper ruble has been completely rehabilitated ; industrial enterprise has been fostered ; the cities have grown rapidly ; and the reactions of all of these conditions have involved the growth of a discontented city proletariat on the one hand, and of an impoverished peasantry on the other.

---

[1] An excellent account of the development of agricultural statistical methods is given by P. J. Lyatschenko in his *Outlines of Agrarian Evolution in Russia* (St. Petersburg, 1908), vol. i. pp. 278 *et seq.*

CHAPTER VI

THE PEASANTS' UNION[1]

SIDE by side with the propaganda carried on in the villages by the social democrats and by the social revolutionary parties, there grew up in the villages a special peasant movement in the early summer of 1905. This movement appears to have arisen out of antagonism to an attempt on the part of ardent adherents of the bureaucracy to secure from the peasants' assemblies formal approval of the war, and of the projects of agrarian legislation known as the Plehve-Stishinsky reforms.

The leader in this attempt was Samarin, marshal of the Moscow nobility, who had distinguished himself also as leader of " The Union of the Russian People." [1] Samarin endeavoured, by careful manipulation, through the *Zemskiye Nachalnëkë* and the police, to obtain the passing of " sentences " of a patriotic character by the Zemstvos in the Bogorodsky district of Moscow Government. These " sentences " contained a declaration of the acceptance by the peasants of the principle of " unlimited supremacy of the landowners and authorities over the Russian peasantry." [2] By careful selection of obedient peasants it was possible in many cases to get such resolutions passed, but the attempt aroused antagonism among those who were already more or less infected with revolutionary ideas. Some of those who lived in villages in the Bogorodsky district, associated with peasants living in the cities and with *intelligentsia* living in villages and in the cities alike, seem to have made up their minds to convoke a " congress " of peasants and their immediate sympathizers, for the purpose of counteracting the influence of Samarin and his concocted " sentences." This " congress," which took place

---

[1] " Krestyanski Soyooz," or " Black Hundred," *cf.* p. 499, *infra.*
[2] V. Groman, ed. *Materials on the Peasant Question.* Report of Sessions of the Assembly of Delegates of the All-Russian Peasant Union, 6–10th November 1905 (Moscow, 1905), p. 3.

in Moscow in May 1905, contented itself with passing resolutions in effect simply negativing Samarin's " sentences."   At the same time it was decided to form an " All-Russian Peasant Union." [1]   The formation of a bureau of organization was assisted by the " Agronoms' and Statisticians' Union," which had in March pronounced itself in favour of the " transference of the land to the hands of the people."   The result of this co-operation between the peasants and *intelligentsia* was the convocation of a " congress " or assembly, which was held in Moscow on 31st July and 1st August 1905.   The membership of this assembly consisted of one hundred peasant representatives from twenty-two *guberni*,[2] and of twenty-five *intelligentsia*.

From the report of the proceedings at the first assembly it may be gathered that in the villages the universal topic was "Land."   This ancient topic had, however, through force of circumstances, acquired for the peasant a new meaning.   Although there was no unanimity in the speeches or resolutions, the majority of the peasant representatives seem to have given their adhesion to the " sentence " of the peasants of the village of Ekaterinovka (in the Donyetsky district,[3] in the Black Soil zone in South Russia).   In addition to the political demands, this " sentence " formulates the following agrarian programme.   " To abolish all private property in land, and to transfer all private, fiscal, *udelnya*, monastery, and Church lands to the disposal of all the people.   The use of the land is to be enjoyed only by those who by their families or by partnership, but without hired labour, cultivate the land, and to the extent only of such powers of cultivation." [4]

Some thought that the abolition of private property in land should be accomplished by means of redemption, others thought that redemption would be unjust, as already the landowners had received enough.   Some argued that the redemption money should

[1] Groman, *op. cit.*, p. 4.   It will be recognized that this Union had nothing to do with the " Peasants' Alliance " mentioned, *e.g.* by Professor Milyukov in *Russia and its Crisis* (Chicago, 1905), p. 510.

[2] Vladimir, Vologda, Voronej, Vyatka, Kazan, Kostroma, Kursk, Moscow, Nijni Novgorod, Orel, Poltava, Ryazan, Saratov, Smolensk, Tula, Kharkov, Kherson, Chernigov, Yaroslav, Black Sea, and Don *oblast*. See Groman, *op. cit.*, p. 4.

[3] District of the Don troops (mostly Cossacks).

[4] Unsigned article summarizing the agrarian question in 1905 in *Russkiya Viedomosti*, 1st January 1906.

be paid by the State, not by peasants. Very rarely did anyone propose to postpone the question until a constitutional and representative assembly should be established. One representative said that it was " quite clear that land would not be given without redemption. It will be necessary to pay for it in blood. If this is the case, would it not be better to agree to redemption in order to avoid the shedding of peasants' blood ? " One pointed out the indirect social effects of confiscation in the annihilation of the credit of the landowners and loss to their creditors. This, he said, would create much hostility to the union. A social democratic representative, who was present at this assembly, insisted that redemption should not be discussed. Eventually the assembly passed a resolution to the following effect :

" That the land must be considered the common property of all the people, that private property must be abolished, that the monastery, Church, *udelnya*, cabinet, and Tsar's lands must be taken without compensation, and that the lands of private owners must be taken partly with and partly without compensation; that the detailed conditions of the mobilization of private lands must be defined by the coming Constitutional Convention or Constituent Assembly." [1]

By November 1905 the new peasants' movement had spread practically over all the *guberni* of European Russia ; and from the 6th to the 10th of that month another meeting of the peasants' representatives took place in Moscow. The reports of the proceedings at the meeting in August [2] and those of the meeting in November [3] are of the greatest importance, because a comparison of them confirms the conclusion already stated, viz. that the peasants were really more extreme than the revolutionary parties, and that the latter had been obliged to amend their programmes in accordance with the views of the peasants. As an integral element in the peasants' programme, there was the contribution of " banished " peasant working men already familiar, through their residence in the towns,

[1] Unsigned article summarizing the agrarian question in 1905 in *Russkiya Viedomosti*, 1st January 1906.
[2] The " Protokolls " of the first assembly were published under the title, *The Constituent Assembly of the All-Russian Peasants' Union*, issued by the Chief Committee of the Union (Moscow, 1905). The Protokoll of the " Assembly " of 6-10th November 1905, together with the party programme, are given in full in Groman's *Materials*, cited above. He gives also a good analysis of both Protokolls.
[3] Groman, *op. cit.*, p. 33.

with the revolutionary propaganda which had been going on there. Yet the net influence of the propaganda upon the peasant was inconsiderable. His fundamental views about land were the same as before. If he used new words, caught from the propaganda, he said always the same thing. " The land is ours—give it to us, and let us cultivate it."

The peasant probably did not see through the tactical manœuvre of the social democrats. Their evident purpose was to utilize the peasant for the revolution, which to their mind was chiefly for the benefit of the urban artisan. The peasant must benefit, too, in the long run ; but, meanwhile, as a revolution in Russia was impossible without the aid of the peasant, it was necessary to utilize him, and to utilize him it was necessary to compromise on points of economic doctrine. The social revolutionary party was not quite in the same position, but they also undoubtedly felt that there was a danger in the possible separation of the interests of the city proletariat and those of the peasantry.

The second note, dominant at least in the addresses of the representative peasants who attended the assembly, was *volya* or " will " —the will of the people. This word represented for them the whole question of their local autonomy and of what they conceived to be their rights, including as an important element the " right " to land.

In the first assembly there were complaints of the *Zemiskiye Nachalnēkē*. " Those gentlemen stop all endeavours of the peasants towards education for instance." They " stack " the " sentences." [1] Some complained also of the village priests. A peasant from Orel said that the landowners' lands came up close to the houses in the villages, so that it was impossible to prevent cattle from trespassing, and that fines for trespass were imposed daily.[2]

The first assembly decided, with only one dissentient voice, that *the land should be considered as the common property of the whole nation*.[3] The first assembly also declared itself as in favour of the popular election of judges.[4]

In the first assembly there is no definite tendency towards advocacy of a change in the form of government, although there is

---

[1] A peasant delegate from Vologda. " Stack the sentences " is a vulgarism for arranging the resolutions as if cheating at cards.

[2] Groman, *op. cit.*, p. 8. One ruble for a horse, 50 kopeks for a cow, and 35 kopeks for a sheep.

[3] Groman, *loc. cit.*

[4] *Ibid.*, p. 9.

observable a vague idea of a possible " supremacy of the nation " [1] to replace the supremacy of the Tsar. This idea makes its appearance vaguely and doubtfully in the speeches alone, not in the resolutions.[2] The peasant attitude upon the question of the autocracy may be gathered from the few quaint words of a peasant from Kursk in the first assembly :

" The Tsar ought not to be touched. He is still breathing as something great to the peasants. This in its turn will be over." [3]

This literally translated cryptic utterance almost needs interpretation. The Tsar, it means, must not be attacked in the proclamations and party manifestoes. He still exists as the " Dear Father " of his people ; but, after all, in this benevolent rôle, he only just exists—breathes, and no more. In a short while all will be over. This may be taken as significant of the peasant mind at the date of the first assembly in July and August 1905.

The peasants may thus be described, as they were at this date, as being hopeful, calm, and moderate. They were anxious to get more land and to obtain relief from abuses of various kinds ; but they did not obviously connect the land scarcity and the abuses with the autocracy. They seemed to think that the autocracy was, in any event, at the point of death from natural causes, and that therefore it was a matter which would be waste of energy to trouble about. The *Zemski Nachalnēk* was a much more closely pressing autocrat than the Tsar.[4] It was necessary to protest against him. The village priest was troublesome, and his services were expensive. He also must be put in his place. The land scarcity question must be dealt with, and private property in land somehow abolished.[5]

When the second assembly met on 6th November 1905 there was immediately observable a somewhat different tone. At the November meeting the effect of the revolutionary propaganda in the villages

---

[1] Groman, *op. cit.*, p. 9. [2] *Ibid.* [3] *Ibid.*

[4] The peasants were not alone in their belief that the *Zemski Nachalnēk* was a petty autocrat. This was the view of the position taken, for example, by so renowned an exponent of autocracy as Prince Meshtchersky. See *Quarterly Review*, article, " The Tsar," July 1904.

[5] This phase of opinion makes its appearance in all countries contemporaneously with the emergence of definite schemes of expropriation. See, for instance, the scheme of "a progressive agrarian law" developed by W. Ogilvie in *The Right of Property in Land* (London, 1782) (republished London, 1891), in which he completely ignores the difficulties of the transition. Schemes of expropriation appeared about the same time, *e.g.* Thomas Spence's *Lecture at Newcastle-on-Tyne* (1775), reprinted London, 1882.

becomes evident in the resolution calling upon the Peasants' Union not merely to lead in the agrarian question, but to agree with the urban proletariat, " with factory and mill workers, with railway and other unions and organizations formed to defend the interests of the toiling classes." The meeting also resolved to adopt as principles of immediate action, " Not to buy lands from owners at all. Not to rent lands. Not to enter upon land contracts of any kind with owners. In case the demands of the people are not complied with, the Peasants' Union will have recourse to a general strike." [1]

The peasants seemed to consider that the solution of the agrarian question was to be imposed upon the new State Duma, but they regarded the Duma as bound to solve it in accordance with the mandate of the Peasants' Union. It was, therefore, necessary that they should formulate their demands unmistakably in order that the Duma might know what was necessary to be done.

In the event of the prosecution of the Peasants' Union, the meeting resolved to refuse to pay taxes, to refuse to supply recruits and reservists for the army, to demand the payment of all deposits from the State Savings Banks (the only Savings Banks), and to close all the State liquor shops—by destroying them. [2]

Thus, in spite of the possibility of agrarian reform of a more or less important character being proposed by the Duma, the agitation went on even more vigorously than formerly, the seizures of land by peasants and peasant riots continued, and at the close of the year fears came to be felt that a new Pugachevshina,[3] or peasant revolt, was imminent.

The Government threw a sop to Cerberus by remitting the instalment payment on account of the redemption, first by reduction to one-half for 1906, and then by abolition from 1907.[4] Had the Government made this concession earlier rather than incur great risk by delay until it was vociferously demanded by the revolutionary parties, a much better impression would have been created, and much bloodshed might have been saved.

It is now necessary to turn to detailed reports from the villages in order to ascertain the actual course of events as well as the motives and phases of opinion which affected the masses of the peasantry during the autumn of 1905 and the spring of 1906.

[1] *Russkiya Viedomosti*, 1st January 1906.   [2] *Ibid.*
[3] Pugachev. See *supra*.   [4] By the ukase of 3rd November 1905.

CHAPTER VII

INQUIRIES INTO THE CONDITION OF THE PEASANTRY IN 1905

In the year 1906 the Imperial Free Economical Society of St. Petersburg instituted an extensive inquiry into the condition of the peasantry and into the facts of the discontent and disturbances among them which manifested themselves in 1905. These inquiries were conducted by means of a series of questions submitted to persons in different districts in forty-eight *gubernie* of European Russia. Altogether 1400 answers were received. These answers inevitably vary very much in value ; but sometimes they amount to an exhaustive account of the subject so far as the districts in question are concerned. Before attempting to draw any general conclusions from the voluminous evidence which is presented in the *Transactions* of the Society, it seems well to give examples of some of the details which this evidence contains.[1]

The group of reports from the *gubernie* of Novgorod and Pskov has been analyzed and reported upon by M. Rikachov. He remarks that the best of all the reports is the detailed description of the agrarian movement in Byelozyersky district, Ncvgorodskaya *gub.*, by S. S. Kholopov, until recently chief of the *Zemstvo* Board of Byelozyersky.[2]

The report was written in October 1907 ; it refers especially to the agrarian movement in 1905–1906. The movement began in November 1905. It affected almost the whole district ; but it was especially strong in the Markovskaya, Megrinskaya, and Churinovskaya *volosts*. The people of Markovskaya *volost* had an old standing grievance against a timber firm in respect to a piece of land which they held had been a " gifted allotment," and which had not been cut off from the estate of the *pomyetschĕk* from whom the timber firm had

---

[1] *Transactions of the Imperial Free Economical Society*, Nos. 3–5, May-June 1908 (St. Petersburg, 1908).

[2] Independent inquiries about Mr. Kholopov show that although he is a man of liberal tendencies, his report is singularly free from bias.

bought their property. It does not appear that this dispute was brought into court ; but between 1890 and 1900 [1] the peasants retaliated upon the firm by cutting timber upon the disputed land, regarding it as common property. The firm appealed to the Government, and several peasants were arrested by " administrative order " and sent to Siberia for settlement. The cutting of timber was stopped ; but the peasants continued to regard themselves as unjustly treated.[2]

In the same way, prior to the recent disturbances, a dispute arose between the peasants of the villages of Sorky and Malakhova and the owners of the estate upon which these villages were situated, the Messrs. B. " From old time " the peasants had " possessed," in addition to their allotments, a " waste," extending to about 1200 dessiatines, although they had no documents to show that they were entitled to possession. In the nineties the manager of Messrs. B. claimed possession of this land and began to prevent the peasants from using it. He acted resolutely, ordering the hay which had been cut upon the land by the peasants to be destroyed.[3] This action seemed likely to lead to violence when the District Circuit Court decided, on the ground of long possession, that the " waste " belonged to the peasants. An appeal was taken to a higher court, and it was there decided in favour of Messrs. B. While the affair was in dispute, the peasants cut timber upon the land. The police seized the timber and took it back. Then the peasants were accused of offering armed resistance to the police, and some were sentenced to imprisonment. Ultimately Messrs. B. sold the disputed land to the peasants through the Peasants' Bank. In other places in the same district there were similar disputes about land, fisheries, and the like. They usually ended, as in one of the cases above mentioned, in some compromise, the subjects in dispute being sold to the peasants through the Peasants' Bank. In one of the above cases and in many others, painful memories remained of imprisoned and expatriated peasants. The peasants had often no documentary evidence to present in support of their claims. They

[1] The writer is informed by a resident of this *volost* at the time that the dispute came to a head in 1895.

[2] A new survey was ordered in 1907, and the firm offered to surrender part of the land in its possession. Kholopov, *Transactions*, No. 3, p. 266.

[3] The writer is informed by a peasant that this manager was a German-Russian, " very strict and unsociable with his peasant neighbours."

founded these upon tradition, long possession, or established usage ; and " they were firmly satisfied that they were claiming justly." [1] The general movement of 1905 began in the Byelozyersky district quite independently, no similar movement being observable in the surrounding districts. But Mr. Kholopov says that it is possible that the newspaper accounts of the agrarian movement in South Russia " gave a push to it." [2]

The movement began in November 1905 by the cutting of timber upon the lands of private owners and upon those of the State. Secret stealing of timber had been previously practised, but now the illegal cutting was open, whole villages participating in it. In Markovo the greater part of the land of the *volost* belongs to two proprietors—one the timber firm above mentioned, and the other a timber dealer ; and the cutting was performed chiefly on their lands. " The previously existing acute relations with the firm and the belief of the people in their right to the use of the estate, made the peasants very resolute." The peasants cut openly and to a great extent. The local administration tried ineffectually to put a stop by persuasion to this wholesale cutting, and the Governor of the *gubernie* went down to the place, but the peasants treated him discourteously, and told him that they intended to go on with their cutting.

The *Zemstvo* Board attempted to influence the peasants by a proclamation in which the poverty of the peasants was admitted, together with the need for additional allotments of land. It was pointed out that representative government was approaching, and that no long time could elapse before the position of the peasants must be improved. Therefore violence and its inevitable result, punishment, were alike unnecessary. The proclamation pointed out that application had been made for military force, that that application had been granted, and that violence would be punished, while at the same time it would be represented that the people were not ripe for freedom. The proclamation also said that all political parties, with the exception of the " Black Hundred," [3] united in deprecating violence. But the peasants were not moved by these pacific representations, and the proclamation was torn up in the villages. The outcome of the timber-cutting of Markovo was

---

[1] Kholopov, report cited, p. 266.
[2] *Ibid.*, p. 267. [3] *Cf.* p. 499, *infra.*

the death of the local chief of police after a severe beating,[1] the arrival of troops, arrests, banishments, and the seizure of the illegally cut timber.

In Megrinskaya *volost* the movement had other features. The whole of the land of this *volost* was formerly State or Treasury land. There were no *pomyetschĕkē* in the *volost*, and the peasants were all formerly State peasants. At the Emancipation the peasants received allotments, otherwise all the land belongs to the State. Under the Emancipation arrangements the peasants of this *volost*, like nearly all the peasant population elsewhere, received in allotment less land than they had used under the bondage system. A considerable part of their former possessions was "cut off" and remained in the hands of the Treasury. Seven of the nineteen villages of which the *volost* is composed are situated on the shores of Byeloye Lake, and the peasants of these villages are fishermen as well as farmers. The remaining twelve villages are inland, and for the peasants of these, agriculture is the principal means of livelihood. The movement arose in the farming villages. The land formerly cultivated by the peasants prior to Emancipation, which had been "cut off," had been allowed to go out of cultivation, and had been afforested. Upon it during the forty years since Emancipation there had grown up a quantity of building timber (large pine), and the State began to sell this timber to dealers. "The peasants of Goroditschsky Parish could not accustom themselves to the idea that the land upon which this timber was growing was not their own possession"; [2] and therefore, when the dealers who had bought the standing timber from the Treasury began to cut it, the peasants protested. The work was stopped, but the Treasury did not abandon the land. In November 1905 the peasants resolved to enforce what they considered their rights upon these forest sections, and by "general consent of the villages" began openly to cut down the trees. The Treasury manager tried to persuade them to stop cutting, but without success. A high police functionary (*Stanovoy prestav*, chief over several *volosts*) was arrested by the peasants and kept in durance for two days. The peasants proposed to sell

[1] He was really an employé of the timber firm.
[2] Kholopov, report cited, p. 268.

the timber to dealers.[1] The results were the same as in Markovskaya *volost*. Troops were brought, and numerous arrests were made. In this case, however, " administrative order " was not employed. The accused were brought before the ordinary court nearly two years after the offences were committed. Of sixty-six accused, eleven were found not guilty, and the remaining fifty-five were sent to prison or to " penal battalions " in the army. Among those who were found not guilty was a local teacher who had been regarded by the authorities as the leader of the movement. He had been in prison for more than a year and a half.

In Churinovskaya *volost*, however, affairs took a happier turn. The chief of the *Zemstvo* Board persuaded the peasants to agree to stop arbitrary cutting, provided he obtained permission for them to cut what they required for repairing their houses. He did so, and the arbitrary cutting was stopped.

But elsewhere arbitrary cutting of timber took place all over the district. No assessment of the damage can be accurately made. Landowners even can estimate the damage to their estates only approximately. Mr. Kholopov says that it is equally impossible to state precisely what was the dominant motive in the minds of the peasants at the time. The movement appears to him to have been " spontaneous and original." It was not regulated by any plan worked out beforehand or by any external influences, but there appeared to be an underlying current of knowledge about the approach of freedom and about the reorganization of the State. With this knowledge in their minds the peasants rushed instinctively to get what they wanted. Moreover, the bulk of the timber lands in the Byelozyersky district was the property of wealthy companies, which were being further enriched by the exploitation of these estates. It is significant to notice that, excepting in the single instance of the Churinovskaya *volost*, where, after all, the proceedings were easily stopped, the smaller estates belonging to individual owners were not touched. The peasants recognized

---

[1] This may have been actually carried out in this case, but in the Markovskaya case, I am informed that the peasants immediately proceeded to build *ēzbas* with the cut timber, showing that they probably really needed it. Only *kulaki*, or " fists," are said to have been able, by means of hired assistance, to cut more timber than they really needed. An ordinary peasant family of four persons with two horses could not cut and drive, under the conditions at the time, more than the family could use.

that the *pomyetschēkē* on these small estates lived in a modest way, and even had difficulty in making their income meet their necessary expenditure. The peasants refrained from touching the estates of such owners as they knew to be poor, but they attacked the estates of the rich owners, and even those of owners not very rich, and they attacked also the estates of some of those owners with whom they had been on good terms. Some of those whose property was attacked had been looked upon by the peasants as their defenders, and some of them had been elected by means of peasant votes to represent the peasant interests in the State Duma.

Mr. Kholopov says also that the " cutters " of timber saw in the movement not merely a means of satisfying the immediate needs of their households, but a means of enriching themselves as well. This was apparent from the circumstances that " cuttings " on State and other lands were performed by villages which had their own uncut forests, and that timber in excess of the peasant requirements was exposed for sale. Finally, the movement died out last in the district round a town where timber might readily be sold.

The attitude of the proprietors towards these occurrences varied. *Pomyetschēkē* generally tried to persuade the peasants to desist from " arbitrary cutting," while the large timber firms applied to the Government for protection against depredations upon their property.

In addition to the arbitrary cutting of trees in this district, the movement also expressed itself in the discontinuance of payment of taxes by the peasants. This tax-boycott was applied not merely to State taxes, but also to the *Zemstvo* and *Mir* or local taxes. Subsequent fiscal arrangements had determined that the local offices receive all taxes, and that, after its full quota had been retained by the local administration, the balance only was payable to the State Treasury. In the district in question, out of each 100 rubles payable in taxes, the local administration should receive about 16½ rubles, and the State about 83½. Since the total collections in the district in 1905 amounted to only 37 per cent., the amount left for the State was about 25 per cent. of the assessed total of the State taxes.[1] The tax-boycott was an entirely new

[1] In 1905 in the Byelozyersky district the total assessed taxes amounted to 35,000 rubles. Of this only 37 per cent. was paid. In 1906 50 per cent.

feature in the agrarian movement. The peasant communities in the district had been, prior to 1905, most punctual taxpayers. Mr. Kholopov says that the boycott could not be ascribed wholly to the desire to embarrass the Government. It was due, he says, partly to the low yield of grain in the district and to the high prices of grain,[1] and partly to the inactivity of the administration. At the beginning of the movement the Government " lost its head and avoided all occasion of activity against the peasants." The fact seems to be that they were afraid of a general peasant uprising, and were naturally anxious to avoid any friction that might provoke such a movement. Its attention was, moreover, concentrated upon the rooting out of *kramòla* (sedition). In 1907, however, the Government began to set to itself the task of collecting taxes. This it accomplished by expeditionary forces which marched upon the villages.

It has already been noticed that the timber trade is the important industry of the Byelozyersky district. Large numbers of the peasants are employed in felling the timber and in " driving " the logs on the rivers. The logs are committed to the streams in the forests and allowed to float to the sawmills in the lower reaches. " Driving " consists in disengaging the logs when they become jammed or when they become lodged on the banks. In the spring of 1906, when the " drives " were in progress, the peasants whose villages were situated upon the driving rivers made artificial obstacles and stopped the " drives," at the same time demanding that they should all be employed by the timber merchants at increased rates of wages. Sometimes they demanded, also, compensation for the passing of timber on the rivers flowing through their land, on the ground that their meadows were damaged by logs lodging upon them during floods. These demands, according to the

was paid. (Kholopov, report cited, p. 269.) I am informed that in this district in 1909 many peasants were still refraining from paying their taxes, even although the State redemption tax had been abolished. The reason alleged for this boycott is that the taxes are not considered by the peasants to fall equably upon themselves and the landowners. When the peasant defaults in payment of his taxes, his movable goods are distrained; when the landowner defaults, he is allowed to remain in debt to the Zemstvo. The fiscal reasons for this are obvious, but the practice constitutes a grievance.

[1] Although some grain is produced in the district, there is not at any time sufficient for the normal consumption of the population. Grain is therefore imported into the district from other producing areas.

timber merchants, were excessive. The stoppage of the "drives" occasioned loss, and where, as sometimes occurred, the "booms" which impounded the timber were damaged and the workmen who were attending to the drive driven away, the situation became even dangerous. In addition, "arbitrary driving" of timber by the peasants themselves was resorted to. The timber was "driven" to the next village, which in turn presented similar demands, and so on. These proceedings took place upon almost all the "driving" rivers of the district. Sometimes the timber merchants and the peasants arrived at an agreement, but more frequently the military were called into the district.

Besides these unusual interferences with the ordinary routine, there were numerous strikes for higher wages, the strikers sometimes demanding that peasants of villages other than their own be not permitted to work. Such strikes were, however, usually brought to an end by mutual concessions.

All these occurrences were regarded so seriously by the timber merchants that they seem to have contemplated discontinuing their operations until the state of the peasant mind changed. This would have been a serious matter for the district, as timber "driving" and the labour connected with it form the sole occupation of the peasants in winter.

Another detail from Mr. Kholopov's report has certain significant features. This is the case of the so-called *tyaglo promishlennēk* movement. The Byelozyersky Circle Canal, which passes round Byeloye Lake, gives employment to about 1500 men and 3000 horses in drawing barges. These people are known as *tyaglo promishlennēkē*. Each spring, before the opening of navigation, at a definite date there begins registration of all who are willing to engage in this industry. The persons so registered form a society or corporation. There is no limit to the number of persons who may register, but the number of horses which each registered person may employ is limited. Formerly the number of horses was five, now it is three. The corporation thus organized elects an alderman or *starosta*. This *starosta* manages all the affairs of the corporation. He receives payment from the shipowners for services rendered by its members, hands over to the serving members the stipulated amount, arranges the rotation of work of the members, notifies them when their turn of work comes, and manages the capital of the corporation. The price for the work is fixed by the Department of Ways and Communications at St. Petersburg together with the Ribinsk Exchange Committee. The established rate is 7½ rubles for each horse for the course of 63 versts or return. In normal years more than 3000 ships pass through the canal. Each ship requires an average of four horses, so that the total summer earnings of the corporation amount to upwards of 100,000 rubles.[1]

In 1905 the Department of Ways and Communications, acting in concert with the Ribinsk Exchange Committee, decided to replace the horse-driven barges gradually by barges propelled or towed by steam. The *tyaglo promìshlennĕkĕ* were disturbed at the prospect of losing their profitable employment, and at the passing of the business into the hands of " rich steamship owners." They held numerous meetings, and uttered threats against the shipowners and against the Department of Ways and Communications. It seemed likely that attacks would be made upon any steamships that might make their appearance on the canal. The President of the Zemstvo intervened in order to prevent this ; but, notwithstanding, steam tugs which entered the canal were bombarded from the banks by stones and by rifle-shots. This led to their withdrawal and to a modification of the scheme of the Government Department, which, however, did not abandon the idea of introducing steam power. In 1906 the experiment was repeated, the steam tugs being placed under guard of *gens d'armes*. But the attacks continued, some of the *gens d'armes* being beaten. In 1907 a peasant who had thrown a stone at a steamboat was killed and several men were arrested. The struggle died out from natural causes. Owing to the falling off of trade by the canal, the use of steamboats was abandoned and the customary method of hauling by horse-power continued.

The above incidents seem to be characterized by spontaneity. There is no evidence that they were in any way connected with movements elsewhere, or that the disputes were fomented by outside influence or by propaganda. Had they not been contemporaneous with similar and different movements elsewhere, they would have been regarded as isolated phenomena. Yet they reveal, if not a change, at all events a development which had been

---

[1] About 66 rubles per man per year.

going on among the peasantry. There is evident in all of the cases a certain spirited resistance to those in authority, and a widespread determination on the part of the peasants to take their own measures for the purpose of securing their own interests.

We now pass to some cases in which the general movement which was going on all over Russia seems to have influenced the peasants of the Byelozyersky district.

Churinovskaya *volost*, occupied entirely by former State peasants, surrounds the town of Byelozyersk. The peasants of this *volost*, being habitually in contact with the townspeople, are reported to be more developed intellectually than those in the more rural districts. The peasant youths frequently continue their education beyond that afforded by the elementary schools, and pass into the towns as clerks, &c., "entering into intellectual employments." By this means they came to take a lively interest in the political struggle, and found their sympathies engaged by the " programmes " of one or other of the parties of the " Left." The domiciliary searches, arrests, banishment of peasants for attending political meetings, the " underground " literature which was being widely disseminated, all had an effect upon their minds. Their connection with their peasant families, maintained through close proximity to them, in spite of their urban employment, enabled them to influence the immediately surrounding peasantry. Mr. Kholopov conjectures, without being certain upon the point, that these conditions led to the germination among the peasants of Churinovskaya *volost* of the idea that they should organize themselves, and should join the Peasants' Union. At all events they did organize themselves, and a committee was formed of members of the union, which " determined to adopt the tactics of one of the parties of the ' Left.' " Although Mr. Kholopov does not say so, the party whose tactics they adopted was clearly the social revolutionary party.

Thus in the hay-harvest time of 1906 the peasant renters of meadows belonging to " merchantress " B and to peasant C,[1] offered a lower price for hay than had previously been customary, with the threat that, if this lower price were not accepted, the meadows would be mown, and nothing would be paid. The owners refused the price offered, and the meadows were mown ; but the

---

[1] This peasant was a *kulak*, or " fist."

hay was taken away from the peasants by troops. This " experiment in expropriation " was not repeated in this district. Some cases of arson were reported, but they were not traced to the members of the Peasant Union ; they were attributed to " separate disquiet elements."

In other *volosts* there were numerous cases of arson and attempted arson, and buildings of private owners and reserves of grain and hay were damaged or destroyed. Mr. Kholopov declines to accept the responsibility of an estimate of the losses occasioned by these occurrences, or to decide whether in particular cases the fires were due to intention or to carelessness ; but there were certain quite indisputable cases of firing with a purpose.

Opinions vary very widely upon the most prevalent motives for these acts. Some peasants explain that they were acts of personal resentment ; others that they were intended to terrorize the owners in order that they might surrender their possessions ; others that the disorderly acts were intended to proclaim to the Government the dissatisfaction of the peasants with their existing organization, this method of protest being employed because they conceived that they had no other ; still others that the acts were a form of revenge for the " Black Hundred " [1] *pogroms* and for the tendency of that group to assist the Government in a reactionary policy involving administrative repressions. The *first* alleged motive, viz. personal resentment, has been illustrated ; the *second*, the desire to terrorize the landowners, appears, according to Mr. Kholopov, a real motive only in the arson cases in Churinovskaya *volost*, although there does not appear to have existed any real object in such acts. He thinks that they were inspired by " ideals " —that is to say, by the state of mind into which the people were brought by the propaganda which was going on in the provinces. The estates upon which the arsons were committed are, with one exception, too small, and have upon them too small a number of peasant households for any important oppressive exploitation to have taken place. As regards the other forms of the movement in the district, rumours of a rent-boycott, or no-rent movement, were not confirmed. There was no " outside element " in the district, so that whatever was done seems to have been due either to original ideas arising in the minds of the peasants themselves, or to ideas derived

[1] *Cf.* p. 499, *infra.*

from the propaganda communicated to them through literature or through members of peasant families who had in some way come in contact with the general movement. From the details it is apparent that in some cases there was a preliminary agreement among the peasants to carry out the disorderly acts. The only case, however, in which such a preliminary agreement was the subject of a formal sentence was the case of Goroditschsky Parish, in Megrinskaya *volost*.[1]

The administrative authorities seemed to entertain the idea that the movement was originated by local teachers and Zemstvo officials, and a number of these were arrested and banished by " administrative process." As they were not brought before a court, they had no opportunity of defending themselves, save in the Megrinsk case, which has already been referred to. In that case the accused teacher was found not guilty. Mr. Kholopov, however, says that it cannot be denied that the teachers and Zemstvo officials, who form the class of village *intelligentsia*, did make the people aware of the general movement for political reform, and also of the principal points in the party struggle which was in progress. Immediately after the issue of the manifesto of the Tsar of 17th October 1905,[2] meetings were organized in the district by the *intelligentsia*. At these meetings newspapers and party programmes were read and discussed. The meetings were held openly in the schools, and were attended by all classes of the village communities. Mr. Kholopov says that he attended several of these meetings, and that he formed the impression that the character of the people who attended them formed the best guarantee against any call to violence being made, that they served to draw the different classes more closely together, that the controversies showed how much preliminary discussion was necessary upon the extremely intricate social and economic questions which were involved, and that for this reason these meetings formed an important means of political education.

But soon after the issue of the Manifesto of Liberties the meetings were forbidden, and the organizers of them were arrested and placed in prison. This did not put an end to discussion; it was merely driven underground. Secret meetings were held in the forests,

[1] This case was investigated in court, where the fact in question came out.
[2] Cf. *infra*, p. 493.

and secret plots were hatched. The action of the administration had deprived the movement of the moderating influence of the *intelligentsia*, whose members did not take part in these proceedings.

Arrests by "administrative order" were followed by reprisals on the part of the peasantry. Policemen were attacked, and some were killed.

These details from Mr. Kholopov's report may be supplemented by some additional information derived by the writer from village *intelligentsia* in the district in question.

The influence of teachers was probably greater in Markovskaya *volost* than anywhere else within the Novgorodskaya *gub*. This circumstance arose from the liberal character of the Zemstvo administration, during the preceding twelve years, under Mr. Kholopov himself. He had appointed "quick" young teachers, drawn from the ranks of the local peasantry, and many new schools had been opened. These young teachers, belonging to local peasant families, were very close to the peasants in their interests, and their education gave them considerable influence in their communities. This influence was exercised in many ways, but among them was the part which the teachers took in the *skhod*, or assembly of the *mir*. The clerk of the *mir*, although capable of drawing up the "sentences" or decrees of the *skhod* when they related to simple routine business, was frequently unable to draw up the more extended and formal "sentences" which now began to be passed by the *skhod* in relation to the interests of the community. The teacher was thus often called in to perform the functions of legal draughtsman for the "sentences" of the *skhod*. This gave the teacher a peculiar influence, and there is no doubt that the new spirit, which might be called self-assertiveness or class consciousness, exhibiting itself among the peasantry during recent years was due largely to the influence of the teachers.[1]

Up till 1905 the *pomyetschēkē* of the district, with few exceptions, were liberal in their tendencies. They were responsible for the election of Mr. Kholopov as President of the Zemstvo Board, and they supported him in his educational activities. In that year, however, they realized that the education of the peasants

---

[1] On the occasion of the visit of the Governor of Novgorodskaya *gub.*, Count Medem, above referred to, he was met by a band of village youths carrying red flags and singing revolutionary songs, led by the teacher.

was leading them to assertions of equality, and that the privileges of the upper classes were becoming serious matters of discussion in peasant "spheres." They realized, also, that their material interests were likely to suffer if the peasants continued to agitate about a redivision of the land and a readjustment of their relations to the landowners. Private interest clearly conflicted with their political principles, and the latter gave way. The landowners of the district thus reversed their policy, and, being masters of the Zemstvo, owing to the small share of influence which the peasants exercised, they were able to sweep away the liberal members of the local administration, and to elect others whose opinions were in conformity with those which they had just formed. Among the landowners, also, there were some whose social and political ambitions were served by supporting the central authority at a critical juncture. Private economical interests and their ambitions thus together induced them to throw the weight of their influence on the side of the reaction. They "killed two hares with one shot," pleasing the Government and acquiring influence in the Zemstvo.[1]

Another reason for the collapse of the peasant movement in the Byelozyersky district is to be found in the growth among the peasants of a class which has frequently made its appearance in such movements. This is the class of peasant "informers," or, in Russian terms, "provocators." These peasants, desiring to ingratiate themselves with the authorities, denounce their peasant acquaintances, or even invent conspiracies for the purpose of entrapping unwary enthusiasts.[2]

The general outcome of this situation was a complete change in local administration, and especially in educational policy. The "quick" young teachers,[3] themselves trained in the Zemstvo schools, were dismissed, and their places were taken by young men and women educated in the schools and seminaries of the

[1] The Russian analogue of the proverb, "killing two birds with one stone."

[2] A highly intelligent peasant of revolutionary tendencies, speaking of this matter, went so far as to suggest to me that treachery and despotism are both deeply engrained in the Russian people. He thought that they were inherited from Tartar times. Disagreements among the peasants about the division of the loot of the estates appeared in some districts.

[3] From the revolutionary point of view, there were two types of teachers, the "quick" and the dead.

Holy Synod, and therefore well indoctrinated in the Greek Catholic faith and in extreme loyalty. The whole current of life in the district had thus undergone a series of changes. Up till 1905 the landowners were liberal and generally philanthropic, encouraging the education of the peasants and sharing in plans for their welfare. From 1905 they threw themselves into the arms of the reaction, and turned the whole of the Zemstvo activities into other channels than formerly.

The description of the movement in Byelozyersky district given above may be held to apply generally to all the northern *guberni* of European Russia, saving those in the extreme north, where conditions are exceptional.

We now turn to similar inquiries into the causes and course of the movement in the central agricultural region. As a type of these we may take the analysis of the answers by correspondents of the Imperial Free Economical Society as composed by Mr. S. N. Prokopovich.[1] His report deals especially with Tambovskaya *gub*. From this *guberni* there were twenty-two answers, seventeen of which dealt with the agrarian movement.

The movement seems to have begun by arbitrary pasturing of cattle by peasants in the fields of landowners in Ivanovskaya *volost*. In the last days of October more serious manifestations occurred in Uvarovskaya and afterwards in Potgorinskaya *volosts*. These manifestations are reported to have occurred under the influence of the movement in Balashovsky district of Saratovskaya *gub*. They consisted in pillage of estates owned by *pomyetschëkë* and by merchants, in driving away grain and cattle, and in setting fire to the buildings with piles of hay and straw. Prior to these attacks upon the courtyards of the estate-owners, there had been numerous cases of burning of fodder and of arbitrary mowings and pasturings. In November the pillaging developed itself in Kirsanov Bogoroditsk, and in Tambov. In the last-mentioned district, in the end of October, the peasants began by cutting the timber at night. These acts had the character of ordinary theft, but in a few days the peasants began to cut in the daytime *en masse*. Within a week they had cut several dessiatines of timber. In the end of the month they burned the house of the constable in the village Arjenka,

---

[1] *Transactions*, No. 3, 1908, pp. 47–89 *et seq.* Mr. Prokopovich is a well-known writer, of Narodnik tendencies, upon social and agrarian subjects.

and in the night of the 31st October to 1st November the pillage of owners' " economies " became general in many *volosts*. On the eve of this night of pillage some of the peasants went to one of the *pomyetschēkē*, and " in the name of the students," [1] advised him to go away. About eleven o'clock they arrived with horses and carts, and, after firing several shots by way of demonstration, they took with them whatever they found—rye, oats, peas, &c. For light to aid them in their depredations they burned piles of straw. At first they took only grain, but when their passions were roused they took things for which they had no possible use—*e.g.* household furniture. [2]

In November, throughout the *gubernie*, arbitrary cutting of grain and hay, arbitrary pasturing, and driving away of cut grain and hay, &c., continued.

In January 1906 timber-cutting and arbitrary pasturing began in Shavskaya *volost*, and spread into other *volosts* in the same district.

These depredations were committed upon the estates of private owners. In the State forests arbitrary cutting began on the 17th November, and lasted until the 30th November, in the same districts. Peasants who were suffering from the bad yield really needed timber for heating purposes, but they did not confine themselves to such cutting. They arbitrarily cut building timber.

In the end of May and the beginning of June 1906 a movement began in Kozlovsky district, towards the north, and gradually spread southwards. The peasants demanded advance of wages and reduced rents. In the autumn of 1906 there were further arbitrary pasturings and mowings. In the spring of 1907, on the plea of lack of pasture, these arbitrary proceedings were repeated.

Some details of the proceedings in Kozlovsky district, derived chiefly from the *Kozlovskaya Jēzn*, [3] will give a more exact idea of the course of events than any general description.

On 30th May 1906 there was a representative meeting of peasants

---

[1] Peasants of revolutionary tendencies were at this time fond of regarding themselves as allied with the " students " or village *intelligentsia*. They simply used the expression as offering some authority for their acts.

[2] There is not, as a rule, any furniture in a peasant's *ēzba*. Fixed benches and a table constitute the sole fittings.

[3] Quoted from *Kozlovskaya Jēzn* in *Transactions*, No. 3, p. 73.

from all parts of the Kozlovsky district.[1]   There were seventy representatives of the *volosts*.   This meeting decided that in future the peasants themselves must regulate the rate of wages.   In order to do this, it was first necessary to arrive at a new wage scale, and, having done so, to enforce this scale by means of peaceful combination and strikes.[2]   The scales of wages were to be settled by the villages.   Immediately after this decision of the representative meeting, the villages began to draw up the new scales.   For example, in the large village of Kругloë, in Epanchinskaya *volost*, the peasants established the following scale :

	Rubles.
For harvesting rye, per dessiatine	15
For harvesting oats, per dessiatine	10 [3]
For ploughing fallow land, per dessiatine . . .	8
Daily wage for a man	2
Daily wage for a woman	$1\frac{1}{2}$
Monthly payment for a man	15
Monthly payment for a woman	8 [4]

A delegate was elected by the village to arrange about bringing this new scale into force.   Followed by peasants, he made a round of visits to the estate-owners.   He inquired about the number of persons employed, and about the wages they were receiving.   He then announced the new scale.   If the estate-owner agreed to it, he was required to sign a document to that effect ; if he did not agree, the peasants employed by him were carried off by the party. The demands of different villages varied very much, both in amount and in character.   Thus, *e.g.*, in the large village Ekaterinino, in Ekaterininskaya *volost*, the village assembly decided that wages should be 3 rubles for a man and $1\frac{1}{2}$ rubles for a woman per day ; monthly wages were not to be less than 30 rubles ; for harvesting rye, 20 rubles, and for oats, 15 rubles ; while the rent of land must not exceed 10 rubles per dessiatine.   These demands were formally entered in a village " sentence " or decree, and stamped with the stamp of the *starosta* or village alderman.   In

---

[1] This representative meeting is significant ; in none of the northern *guberni* of European Russia did the peasants have district meetings.

[2] Their expression was *mirna stachka e zabastovka*.   In the peasants language strikes are always referred to as *stachka e zabastovka*, literally *stachka* = agreement, and *zabastovka* = strike.   *Mirna* means peaceful.

[3] This means about two rubles per day per man.

[4] These latter payments are " with board."

order to prevent secret agreements between the estate-owner and individual peasants, the village assembly elected a delegate, whose duty was to receive all payments from the estate-owner and hand them over to the persons entitled to them. In the large village Novo Aleksandrovka, in Bogolubskaya *volost*, the peasants in a village assembly decided that the hours of labour should be from six o'clock in the morning till six o'clock at night, with three hours and a half for meals, leaving a working day of eight and a half hours. The labour of children was to be regulated by the peasants. If work beyond their strength was given to children to perform, this work was to be given to adults, and appropriate wages paid for it. Monthly wages were to be 25 rubles per month, excepting in winter, when the wages were to be 15 rubles. Food was to consist of fresh products; meat was to be given, 1 lb. per man per day, with porridge and potatoes as much as was necessary. Payment for work was to be made weekly, on Sundays.[1] Any peasant who accepted wages at less than the fixed scale was to be brought before the court—that is, before the village assembly sitting as a court.

The regulations passed by the peasants of the village of Aleksandrovka, Izosimovskaya *volost*, are interesting, because they illustrate the methods of agriculture presently practised in South Russia. The daily wages for a *mujik*, or peasant man, were fixed at 1 to 2 rubles, according to the season; and for a *baba*, or woman, at 50 kopeks to 1 ruble. A horse was to be paid for at the same rate as a man. Ploughing one dessiatine by small plough (*plujok*) was fixed at 10 rubles; and by *sokha*, or Russian plough, 6 rubles, for ploughing once. A team of horses with harrow was to be paid for at the rate of 5 rubles per dessiatine, and seeding 5 rubles per dessiatine. Gathering grain, mowing and binding rye, and putting into stooks, 12 rubles; oats, 10 rubles. Driving sheaves, 40 kopeks per kopina (10 sheaves). Ploughing of rye-field, 8 rubles per dessiatine; and by *sokha*, 4½ rubles.

All land, whether previously in fallow or not, is ploughed at least twice.[2] Fallow is ploughed in June, and is then ploughed again before seeding. The second ploughing does not cost so much as the first. This village also passed the following regulation:

---

[1] Peasants in this region work habitually on Sundays as on week-days.
[2] In another village the rate given is, for ploughing fallow land, three times.

Renting of fallow land, and land for winter rye or spring oats or barley, was to be for one seeding. After harvesting once, the renter has no right upon this land unless he rents it for the following year, the rent to be 10 rubles per dessiatine. Those who are employed by landowners at 20 rubles per month are obliged to pay 3 rubles per year for the needs of the community as a local tax. No work must be performed on holidays, under a penalty of 2 rubles.[1]

In Arkhangelskoë village, Ilovi-Dmetrievskaya *volost*, the village assembly demanded that the manager, clerks, and other servants of the landowner, should treat the working peasants with civility ; and, on the other hand, the peasants bound themselves to refrain from aggressive acts against the landowner. " We peasants accept an obligation to look after peace and order. No one of us must take anything from the economy of the *pomyetschĕk*, or spoil it. Those who break this decree of the *skhod* will be held responsible by the community." In one case, that of Vachovskoë, 10 kopeks were deducted from the daily pay of each man for the payment of the delegates who were to see that the decree of the *skhod* was enforced. In the decree of the peasants of Tuchevskaya *volost* it is provided that peasants from other villages may be employed by a landowner, but the wages due to them must be handed to the home village delegates, and by them paid to the incomers. A clause is also added to the effect that the peasants " mutually guarantee " the carrying out of the decree. The delegates must provide that all peasants work in turn.

In the large village of Volchok it had been customary for peasants to be paid in grain part of their wages for harvesting. The new scale provided that for harvesting one-third of the grain should be retained by the owner, and two-thirds should be given to the peasants.[2]

Numerous strikes followed upon the adoption by the peasants of these new scales. Sometimes the working peasants were simply taken from work by the delegates of the village, elected for the purpose. Sometimes the whole of the village population—in one reported case to the number of 700—took part in " taking off " the working peasants.[3] In some estates, where the general body

---

[1] In another village the fine for breach of rules is 5 rubles.
[2] This was probably a simple reversal of the previous arrangement.
[3] In Moshkova Suren. *Transactions*, No. 3, p. 76.

of peasants were " taken off," some were left to look after the cattle.[1]

We have now to consider what were the aims of the peasants in this district in advancing these demands. Opinions of different reporters vary. The most penetrative analysis of the motives is given by the correspondent of the *Kozlovskaya Jēzn*.[2] According to him, it would be incorrect to explain the demands by the mere desire to earn more wages from the landowner for work, and to pay less rent to him. The correspondent thinks that the demands form an entirely new phase of the agrarian movement. This was, in brief, an attempt to drive the landowner from the land. The peasants were well aware that the landowners could not pay the wages demanded by them, and that the cultivation of the land in the hands of landowners, under the new scales, must be unprofitable. But to leave the land uncultivated or the grain unharvested " cannot be allowed." The peasants are said to have believed that the Government would " punish " the landowners by taking the land from them unless they cultivate it.[3] They thought that only " a little firmness would be necessary and the end would be reached " ; the landowners were in a position from which they could not escape. Another report, from Khmeliovskaya *volost*, confirms this explanation of the aims of the peasants. " Peasants consider that it is obligatory for the landowner to harvest the crops," and that cultivation is a condition upon which they hold their land. They demand, therefore, that the new scale of wages and rents should be accepted, or that the whole of the yield of grain should be given up to the peasants.[4]

The correspondent of the *Kozlovskaya Jēzn* thinks that the peasants realized that nothing was to be gained by mere pillage and violence. Such acts could only draw upon themselves " the horrors of pacification "—that is, similar violence on the part of the authorities. They therefore resolved upon peaceful means to obtain what they wanted—viz. complete possession of the land. To this end they organized watching of the fields and orchards of the landowners, and even prosecuted children for stealing apples.

---

[1] In the large village of Pokrovsk. *Ibid.*   [2] No. 37.
[3] This seems to be a quaint survival in the peasant mind of the old form of tenure by service and of the right of resumption by the Government. Cf. *supra*.
[4] *Transactions*, No. 3, p. 76.

During the whole period of the strike movement in Kozlovo there is said to have been only one case of violence. In discussing the strikes with the chief of the district police, the peasants of Aleksandrovskaya *volost* told him :

"We have a right to work for that price which we ourselves consider convenient and profitable. The landowners were within their right in demanding 26 rubles per dessiatine for their land. This was a high rent, but they were not arrested on that account."

In the large village of Pokrovskoë the peasants reasoned in this way :

"We paid 20 rubles for a sajen of rotten straw, and 25 to 30 rubles of rent per dessiatine. It was dear. We wept, but paid. Now let them pay."

A correspondent from Spassky district attributes the rise of the movement to the influence of revolutionary newspapers and booklets. Another, from Tambovsky district, ascribes the rise of the movement to " anarchist agitators " ; another to the influence of the Tsar's manifesto of 17th October 1905 ; another to the *pogroms* against the Jews. The property of the Jews having been pillaged without the punishment of the pillagers, the peasants are alleged to have thought that they also might be permitted without punishment to pillage the property of the landowners. Peasants who had actually taken part in the *pogroms* against the Jews, returning from the towns to the villages, told their neighbours how the soldiers and the police looked on at the pillaging and did nothing.

Almost everywhere in the Tambovskaya *gub.* all classes of the village population participated. There were, however, some anomalous incidents. In Klunefskaya *volost*, Kozlovsky district, the poor peasants were at the head of the strike movement.[1] In Kaminskaya *volost* of Tambovsky district the landless peasants took little part in the movement, because they had no horses to enable them to carry off plunder from the pillage. In Usmansky district the movement was headed by rich peasants. In Kunievskaya *volost*, in Tambovsky district, the rich peasants were " unfriendly " to the strike. Generally in Tambovsky and Borislog-

[1] The pacific character of the strike movement in the Kozlovsky district has already been noticed.

lebsky districts the rich peasants took an active share in the pillage. In Kozlovsky and Lebedyansky districts peasants who had bought land through the Peasants' Bank or otherwise were unsympathetic to the movement. The activity of peasants who had been working in towns, and who had returned to their villages, is mentioned only in two communications out of seventeen. The activity of soldiers who had returned from Manchuria is mentioned in three communications out of the same number. The youthfulness of the leaders is remarked by three correspondents. Women generally took an active part, especially old women who themselves had experienced the burden of bondage.[1]

In Tambovsky district the larger landowners among the peasantry, peasants owning 100 dessiatines or thereabouts, took measures to protect themselves against the mobs. The smaller landowners divided their households into two ; the older people defended the family property, and the younger participated in the pillage.

After the acute stage of the movement had passed, disagreements began to break out among the peasantry of Tambovsky district. The distribution of the spoil was the first occasion of difficulty. Some had employed one horse, and some six. The result was inequality of distribution. A second occasion was afforded when the authorities made their appearance with police and military force to inquire into and to suppress the disorder. Some of the peasants began to seek favour with the authorities by denouncing others. These disagreements led to arsons, performed by peasants upon peasants' properties. In the large village of Ivanovka the manager of the estate promised to give the peasants 400 dessiatines of land. Under the influence of this liberality, and after entertainment with *vodka*, the peasants of this village raided other villages, beating the peasants in them. The district of Kozlovo in general again offers distinct phenomena. After the strike movement there no disagreements are reported. If there were any, they are alleged to have been due to fear of the authorities after the suppression of the movement. In Melevskaya *volost* of this district, however, there were disagreements. Those who had compelled working peasants to go on strike were driven away

[1] The *Khlisti* or *Lyudi Bojii* (People of God), sectarian flagellants, took no part in the disturbances, their tenets being very severe upon theft.

by those whom they had formerly obliged to leave work.[1] The landowners in this *volost* met the demands of the strikers to some extent. The wages in the *volost* had formerly been 50 kopeks and 30 kopeks a day for men and women respectively. They were now raised to 1 ruble 25 kopeks and 65 kopeks respectively, with board.

A general review of the evidence of all the districts in this *guberni* shows that ten correspondents attribute the movement to the insufficiency of arable land and meadows as fundamental cause. Five correspondents regard the bad yield of the immediately preceding years as an important cause. In regard to the first-mentioned cause, the correspondent from Kozlovsky district points out that the former State peasants of Lipetsk district, which adjoins that of Kozlovo, having comparatively large land allotments, took no part in the movement, although they endeavoured to make use of the disorders in the neighbouring region to their own advantage.

Two correspondents only deny, in respect to their regions, that the peasants do not suffer from insufficiency of land. In Morshansky district, *e.g.*, the peasants are reported as not wanting land because they do not rent it at the comparatively low rent of 7 to 14 rubles per dessiatine.[2] In Tambovsky district a landowner reports that the former State peasants, with large allotments—" 7 dessiatines per revision soul of first-class Black Soil land "—were most prominent in the violent attacks upon estates. Ten of the correspondents allude to personal and class hostility against the landowners. In Kirsanov, *e.g.*, the landowner incurred hostility because he refused to rent some land to peasants of the district, and rented it to " rich peasants of a far-distant village." He was also alleged to be in the habit of prosecuting the peasants about trifling matters, and of driving cattle off his pastures, even when the fields were covered with snow. In Tambovsky district the arbitrary cutting of timber is ascribed to revenge against an owner who " exploited the village mercilessly." This owner laid claim to the best part of the village, including the market-place, from which he derived 30,000 rubles annually. The

---

[1] Such disagreements were very common throughout European Russia.
[2] This may have been due to the circumstance that the peasants refused on grounds of policy to rent at any price.

peasants thought that he had no right to this land, and they had carried on protracted litigation about it without result.

In Spassky district the movement was directed against shop-keepers, who were alleged to be dealing dishonestly with the peasants, " and who were competing with them in renting land."

In Volchkovskaya and Tuchevskaya *volosts* the movement was general against all landowners ; but in Spassk, Morshansk, and in Kozlovo the movement was not general. In Morshansk, according to one correspondent, the peasants believe that the possessions of their former *pomyetschēkē*—that is, their former owners in bondage times—could not legally be sold to any but the peasants who had been in bondage or their descendants. They thought, also, that the land could not legally be rented to other than peasants. Two of the correspondents of Tambovsky and Borisoglebsky districts say that the movement was directed against large estates of more than 500 dessiatines to begin with, and later against estates of smaller dimensions.

In Kozlovsky district the *starosta*, or village alderman, was dismissed because he refused to sign the decree about the new scale of wages. The peasants elected a new *starosta*, and required him to affix the *starosta's* stamp upon the decree.

In Uvarovskaya *volost*, Borisoglebsky district, grain in the railway station was pillaged. In the same district the telephone station was pillaged, the reasons being a quarrel with the officials and a superstitious feeling about the instruments, which were looked upon as the invention of the devil. In Lebedyansky district the movement was partly agrarian and partly industrial. The peasants demanded that the wages of workers on the railway should be increased. At one of the railway stations there was a strike of " loaders," and at another one of workers who were repairing the permanent way. So also in Izosimovskaya *volost*, the village " decree " regulated not only agricultural labourers' wages, but also wages in " various kinds of industrial enterprises." In Kozlov the peasants tried to get domestic servants to join the strike.

Nor were the formal demands confined to wages and rents. The peasants of the large village of Mashkova Suren drew up a new scale for the performance of ceremonies by the priest. They proposed to pay 3 rubles instead of 8 rubles for a marriage ; for a funeral, 1 ruble instead of 3 rubles ; for baptizing or burying an infant, 12 kopeks instead of 50 kopeks ; for thanksgiving and for taking *ikons* out of church, 20 kopeks instead of 1 ruble.[1]

The action of the authorities in the districts above mentioned consisted in sending Cossacks and police, who were ordered to whip the offending peasants with *nagaïki*. Sometimes, upon entering a village, the Cossacks " beat the first people they met " ; sometimes the people were obliged to prostrate themselves and to apologize. In Poltavskaya *volost* the *Zemski Nachalnēk* arrived with an escort of dragoons, and ordered the peasants to take back hay which they had removed from an estate. A public meeting of the peasants was called, and those who refused to obey the order were beaten. In Pavlodar nineteen peasants were killed. In Kirsanovsky district the peasants were brought before the district court, and twenty-six men were sentenced to eight months in a penal battalion. In Lebedyansky district the landowners organized themselves for the defence of their property. In Kozlovsky district the landowners demanded that martial law should be adopted.

In relation to this demand the Agricultural Society of Kozlovo issued, on the 18th June 1906, a " sentence " to the following effect. The peasant movement in the Kozlovsky district is concerned chiefly with demands that wages should be advanced to a point which " does not correspond to the standard of cultivation of our agriculture at present." The movement had as a basis " chronic want of land and political lawlessness." According to the opinion of the peasants themselves, the intention of the movement is to force, by means of the difficulties created by the strike, the landowners to use all their efforts for the solution of the land question. Only general State reform on the basis of the reply of the State Duma to the Tsar will change fundamentally the conditions of the life of the people, and will really pacify the peasant masses. No private means are of any use, excepting tact, reason, and quietness in each separate case. To answer the movement partly by repressive measures or by martial law would be " excessively dangerous, and might result in transforming the movement, peaceful until the present time, into " a cruel play of passion and bloodshed." Only the State Duma and the Ministry can pacify the country and " create a ground for transition to new

[1] *Transactions*, No. 3, p. 80.

forms of life."[1] There were thus among the landowners in this district two currents—one in the direction of repression, and the other in that of profound agrarian reform."

The official view of the authorities in the same district may be gathered from the report of the Governor of Tambovskaya *gub.* to the Minister of the Interior, dated 5th June 1906.

This report narrates that the movement in Kozlovsky district spread from the neighbouring *volosts* of Ryazanskaya *gub.* The movement was characterized by demands for fabulous increases of wages, and by strikes. In order to re-establish order, 250 Cossacks were drawn into the district. In the towns all is quiet. The police guard is almost useless, and reinforcements of Cossacks, at least to the extent of an additional force of 200 to 300, are urgently required. Agitators are being " mercilessly prosecuted " under the law about strikes of 15th April 1906.

Among the " agitators " arrested and prosecuted during these proceedings were elected village aldermen (*starostas*), delegates elected to look after the payment of wages, and village teachers. Altogether 600 persons were arrested. These were kept in prison for periods ranging from two weeks to three months. In some cases the arrests were resisted. For example, all the peasants in Sergievskaya *volost*, and some of those in Pavlovskaya *volost*, left their ploughing, and, to the number of 2000, demanded the release of the arrested peasants. This body was attacked by 150 soldiers and dispersed. Some of the peasants carried *ikons*. Some threw these away, but others used them to protect themselves against the blows administered by the troops. In other villages the *nabat*, or alarm bell, was sounded, the peasants collected together, and sometimes the prisoners were forcibly released by them. In some villages where a *skhod* or public meeting had been called, it was dispersed by dragoons or by Cossacks.[2] In the village of Lebedyanka four peasants were killed by a volley fired by dragoons. The village was saved from " extermination " by the priest, who prayed for them on his knees.

As an immediate consequence of these proceedings, landowners

[1] *Transactions*, No. 3, p. 82.
[2] For examples, see *ibid.*, p. 84.

began to sell their lands, and there was at once a fall in the value of land and in rents [1]

The answers to questions about the changes in the disposition of peasants and about their attitude towards the landowners and towards the Government are somewhat indefinite. In one district alone, viz. Morshansky district, a correspondent gives some indications. He says that in the occasional meetings of the peasants they began to discuss questions more broadly than they did before ; but that they found the difficult question of their relation to the land still unsolvable. Still they seemed to think that in some way or other their demands might be satisfied and that they might get the land for nothing. In Tambovsky district the peasants seemed to think that they might buy the land through the Peasants' Bank, on the instalment principle, and that they then need not pay the instalments. Others spoke of taking as much as they could out of the land for a few years, and of then letting the Peasants' Bank have it. Still others were opposed to the purchase of land through the Peasants' Bank, and were hostile to any project initiated by the Government.

As regards the relation of the peasants to one another, the disagreements before mentioned were very prevalent, and out of these or otherwise there grew up in Kozlovsky district an aversion to " separations." The peasant communities refused " separation," and when the *Zemski Nachalnēk* intervened and forced them, under the Separation Act of M. Stolypin, to agree to it, they gave

[1] The following table shows the depreciation :

PRICES OF LAND PER DESSIATINE.

	Before the Movement.	After the Movement.
Spassk	200 rubles.	150-170 rubles.
Tambov	180-210 ,,	175 ,,
Borisoglyebsk	240-300 ,,	160-220 ,,
Lebedyan	200 ,,	150 ,,

RENTS PER DESSIATINE.

Kozlovo: Winter seeding .	.	25-30 rubles.	15 rubles.
Spring seeding .	.	20-25 ,,	...
Usman : Winter seeding .	.	25 ,,	23 rubles.
Spring seeding .	.	20 ,,	18 ,,

WAGES.

Spassk : Labourers . .	.	50 rubles per year with board.	70-90 rubles.
Domestics (women)	.	24 rubles	36-60 ,,
Morshansk : Ploughing a dessiatine	1½-2 ,,		2½-4 ,,
Harvesting a dessiatine	3½-4 ,,		5½-6¼ ,,

(See *Transactions*, &c., No. 3, p. 84.)

the separated peasants the poorest land and land farthest from the villages. In Usmansky district " separation " was looked upon as impossible.

We now pass to a typical portion of the Black Soil Region —Saratovskaya *gub.* The agrarian movement of recent times makes its first appearance in this *guberni.* Every year, from 1901 onwards, in one district or in another, there have been signs of the movement. In 1901–1902, Kamushynsky district was chiefly affected ; in 1902–1903, Balashovsky district ; in 1903– 1904, Serdobsky district. In the spring of 1905 the movement began " to brew " throughout the *guberni,* and in the second half of October, after the manifesto of the 17th October, the first serious wave swept over the villages ; the second wave passed in the summer of 1906. The chief features of the first wave were the pillage and burning of the estates of landowners, and of the second, these and the driving away of hay and grain, non-payment of rent, strikes, expropriations of land and arbitrary division of it among the peasants, fixation of arbitrary rents, cutting of timber, and arbitrary pasturing. The proceedings were similar in all the districts of the *gubernie.* Before the actual movement began, there was much talk among the peasants about " the equalization of land," " revolution," and " struggle for the right."

When the pillage began and there appeared " the redness in the sky," the sign of the burning of landowners' property, " unknown persons," made their appearance in the villages and took the leadership of the movement upon themselves. Before an attack began the peasants sometimes went to the landowner and demanded " keys, money, and arms " ; sometimes they demanded the books of the estate, in order that the records of their indebtedness might be destroyed. In other cases no warning was given.

One purpose alone animated the peasants—" to smoke out " the landowners, to force them to leave their estates, so that the peasants might obtain the land for nothing or for a low price. " If we pillage the landowners they will the sooner give up their land. Land is the gift of God. It must belong to the labouring people." [1]

---

[1] In one case, viz. the estate of Prince G. in Kamushensky district, the peasants demanded that rents should be reduced from 18 rubles to 3 rubles per dessiatine, and that wages for mowing should be raised from 1.75 rubles to 4 rubles per dessiatine.

All classes of the peasantry joined in the pillage—poor, middle-class, rich, and even very rich peasants. Each took his turn and carried off as much as he could. In all villages, however, the poor peasants gave direction to the movement. In some they forced the rich peasants to join in the pillage under threats of turning upon them ; in others they prevented the rich from engaging in the pillage on the ground that they would be inclined to take too much for themselves. " There were cases in which the rich peasants who were on a pillaging expedition found, on their return, that their own property had been pillaged by poorer peasants." Some rich peasants neither joined in the movement nor allowed themselves to be pillaged ; they collected their families and friends and defended their property against the pillagers. In general, the rich peasants, whether they took part in the movement by compulsion or not, were opposed to it. They spoke contemptuously of the *agrarnēkē*, in whose ranks were the idle and the poverty-stricken.

The village youth was everywhere in the front of the movement. The older men at the beginning tried to impede the movement—" to keep their sons from sin " ; but later they were drawn into the current. They saw enviously their neighbours enriching themselves, and they could not withstand the temptation. In some cases the old men succeeded in stopping the movement. The women in general were sympathetic, and occasionally were even more active in pillage than their husbands.

Soldiers returning from Manchuria found, in frequent cases, that their households had been impoverished by external economic causes or by bad management during their absence. They had nothing to eat, and no fuel to heat their houses with ; they found that their families were getting no regular assistance or no assistance at all. Such men threw themselves into the pillaging movement and increased the general excitement. " For what," they said, " did we shed our blood, when we have no land ? "

There were two types of strikes in Saratovskaya *gub.*—one had the same object as pillage, viz. the starving out of the landowners ; the other type was directed merely towards an improvement of the condition of the peasant and of his relations to the landowner, without seeking for the extermination of the latter. In strikes of the first type, the demands upon the landowners were clearly confiscatory. Such strikes were sometimes followed by demands that rent should be reduced.

In Serdobsky district, a strike of the second type occurred. The object of this strike was the improvement of the system of *izpolnya* renting. Under this system the peasant was allowed to cultivate for his own support and advantage one dessiatine of land on condition of his cultivating one and one-third dessiatine and driving three loads to the railway station for the landowner. The peasants demanded that they should receive one dessiatine of land for the cultivation of another dessiatine—that is, that they should in effect receive one-half of the produce. In addition to this, they demanded that money rents should be diminished and wages increased.

The movement assumed a third form in Kamushensky district, where the owners rented their land on varying conditions, determined by the method of payment of rents. Thus some tenants paid rent in advance, the rent of the land for the succeeding crop being paid in the autumn, some paid only after the harvest was reaped. The best land was thus taken by the peasants who had sufficient capital to pay the rent in advance, and the poor land was left for the poor people. Rents in the district were, moreover, advancing. The peasants, under the influence of the movement, divided the land arbitrarily and fixed a general arbitrary rent in order " to equalize the rented sections in respect to quality."

A special character was given to the struggle on the Treasury estates in the same district. The peasants organized periodical illegal pasturings and ploughing ; and they threatened the large renters to set fire to their buildings unless they gave up the payment of rent to the Treasury.

The agrarian movement in Saratovsky and Petrovsky districts, for example, was followed by the dismissal of former village authorities and the substitution of others favourable to the movement ; by reduction of the salaries of village functionaries, these salaries being settled by the village assembly ; and by expropriation of the glebe lands and reduction of the payments for the services of the clergy. The last-mentioned incidents took place especially where the local clergy were known to have sympathetic relations with the landowners. The shops kept by the Government for the sale of liquor under the *vodka* monopoly were pillaged and closed, and the stores of merchants who were accused of engrossing grain in the Balashovsky district were pillaged. These merchants who sometimes rented lands belonging to them for cultivation by peasants were accused of " squeezing the peasants, on the one hand, by high rents, and, on the other, by cheating them " in measuring the grain in which these rents were paid.

In the latter district the property of the employees of the landowners was not touched by the pillagers. " Take it away," the peasants said, " so that it may not be pillaged along with the property of the landowners." [1]

Throughout the Saratovskaya *guberni*, the correspondents state that the poor peasants and those with the smallest allotments were the most active in the movement. Throughout the *gubernie* also the correspondents unanimously regard the insufficiency of land and the poverty of the peasants as the chief causes of the movement. They think that if the disturbances had not broken out at that time they were inevitable sooner or later. " The peasants became wearied of living in poverty and of experiencing unsatisfied " need of land." " Not the agitators caused the movement, but the poverty of the peasants." " Even the so-called full allotment of the landowners was not adequate." " The peasants who had only the gifted allotments were subject to ever-lasting hunger." " There is no forest, not a single twig ; there are no meadows and no cultivated land, not a sajen." " The peasants have for a long time nourished hatred against the land-owners who were indifferent (to their sufferings) and always well fed " (while they went hungry). " The peasants are sitting upon small pieces of land while the lands and forests of the estate-owners surround them."

These are some of the statements of the correspondents from various districts in the *gubernie*. This normal state of poverty experienced by the peasants became more acute than usual during the two years immediately preceding 1905 owing to the inferior yields of grain.

The average area of land occupied by a peasant non-renter who had a gifted allotment in this *guberni* is stated at $1\frac{1}{2}$ dessia-tines, the average of a peasant renter upon the estates of private

---

[1] *Transactions*, &c., No. 3, p. 148.

owners, 4 dessiatines, and the average holding of a peasant on the State lands was 7 dessiatines.

Even 8 dessiatines per holding, which was the average of Kamushēnsky district, did not prevent the peasants from joining in the movement.

Throughout the *guberni* the movement was directed against all landowners—the gentry, the merchants, rich peasants and large renters of *pomyetschēk* and Treasury lands. The *pomyetschēk* or private landowner's peasants began to look upon the land as their own, while the peasants upon the Treasury lands desired that the lands should simply be transferred to them. Peasants who had formerly been subject to personal bondage were eager to get, and to divide amongst themselves, the lands of the *barin*[1] to whom they had formerly been bondaged.

While all forms of landownership were attacked, even State ownership, the movement assumed specially acute forms wherever there had been unusually high rents or where the conditions of labour had been exploitative.

In Petrovsky and Kamushēnsky districts, the rents had been rising during recent years on private and State lands alike. The system of *izpolya* or metayer tenancy had been gradually changed for money-renting. The employment of day labourers had been taking the place both of *izpolnya* and of *otrabotok* or rented land, the rent of which was paid in work. The meadows ceased to be given for *otrabotok*—the landowners demanded cash for them. Wood for fuel had formerly been given as payment for clearing the forests, now it was charged for in money.[2]

As a rule the military force sent by the Government to " pacify " the peasants was not sent until after the movement had spent itself. The effect of this proceeding upon the peasantry was not salutary. They became frightened, and began to betray one another to the authorities. Sometimes, however, they offered resistance *en masse*. In Kamushēnsky district, *e.g.*, forty-five peasants were wounded in a bayonet charge by the troops, six were wounded by bullets, and one old man and three women were killed.

---

[1] *Barin* is a corruption of *Boyarin*, the nom. sing. of the Russian word corresponding to the English " Boyard," nobleman.
[2] This was especially the case in Petrovsky and Kamushēnsky districts.

Immediately after the movement rents fell sharply, in some districts to the extent of 25 per cent., in others to the extent of 50 per cent. So far as the details in the answers permit of definite statement, the following illustrates the fact of the fall of rent:[1]

District.	Rent before Movement. Per dessiatine.		Rent after Movement. Per dessiatine.	
	Rubles	Kopeks	Rubles	Kopeks
Balashov	20	0	12	80
Petrovsk	14	40	10	70
Saratov	19	0	9	50
Kamushēn	10	0	5	50
Volsk	20	0	6	0

It should be noticed, however, that the correspondents do not refer the fall of rents to the movement, but to the inferior yields of the two years immediately preceding 1905. In some places the fall was only temporary, and rents began again to rise in 1907. Thus in Verhozimskaya *volost* of Petrovsky district, rents fell from 15 rubles in 1905 to 6 rubles in 1906, and rose to 12 rubles in 1907.[2] So also the conditions of *izpolnya* renting which had been improved in 1906 became less favourable to the peasant in 1907.[3]

[1] *Transactions*, &c., No. 3, p. 149.
[2] *Ibid.*
[3] This is stated especially with regard to such tenancies in Serdobsky district.

CHAPTER VIII

CONCLUSIONS FROM THE FOREGOING EVIDENCE RE-GARDING THE CONDITION OF THE PEASANTRY IN 1905

THE three regions selected for detailed examination have been the region of Novgorod and Pskov, that of Tambov, and that of Saratov. The first is a forest region, in which grain cultivation has a subordinate place; the other two are in the Black Soil Region, the most fertile part of Russia, and that in which the cultivation of grain is carried on to an immense extent. The prevalence in the two latter regions of grain cultivation on a large scale by means of wage-earning peasantry upon estates belonging to landowners has already been noticed. The movement seems to have been, in point of time, earlier in Saratov than elsewhere, but in all the districts of all the *gubernie* it is very evident that the " state of mind " of the peasants which resulted in the disturbances was practically universal; the impulse to overt action, however it came, found its appropriate soil ready everywhere. The characteristic of the movement seems to have been the new spirit of resistance to authority which emerged almost suddenly, the grounds of dissatisfaction being of old standing. A general review of the evidence suggests that everywhere the peasants were animated by the same general idea—viz. that the land must be obtained somehow. They seemed to think that they must secure possession of the land, and that they were being unjustly deprived of this possession by the existing owners, whether these were private owners, or whether, as State lands, the lands were in the hands of the Treasury. In either case, they thought that the lands should be transferred to them, in order that they might cultivate them. They were told—as, for example, by the proclamation of the Zemstvo of Byelozyersky district—that the Duma would speedily settle the land question in a way satisfactory to them; but they were impatient. They knew nothing of constitutional procedure. It was enough that they knew what they wanted. The only solution of the land question which they could recognize as effectual was to give the land to them, or to give at least as much of it as they could cultivate. Endless time might be consumed in debating about the terms of transference. These terms could be discussed afterwards. The important thing was to get the land at once into their hands. *L'action directe* was the simplest and speediest method. If they had force enough to take the land, the transference might be accomplished in that way; if they had not force enough to take the land, they had enough at least to make occupation of the land by anyone but themselves exceedingly uncomfortable and even dangerous. Landowner and State alike might be compelled to surrender the land to the peasants by making ownership of it by anyone else impracticable. So far as the peasants were concerned, there is no evidence of wider political ideas. The supreme question for them was the question of the land. Their demands were concentrated upon possession of land, without payment, if possible, but in any case, possession. The demand that rents be reduced must be construed in the sense that the reduction insisted upon was in many cases so great as to amount to complete confiscation of the land. The peasants knew very well that the rents offered by them were not economical rents in the strict sense.

While it is no doubt true, as alleged by the correspondents of the Imperial Free Economical Society, that the peasants in many cases deliberately made demands which could not be met by the landowners out of the resources which their lands afforded, it is also true that the peasants were quite familiar with ineconomical agriculture and landholding. In many districts the peasants, in order to enable themselves to live and pay their rents and taxes, were obliged to engage in industry—hunting, fishing, lumbering—and to obtain subventions from the absent members of their families. They thus saw no inconsistency in making demands upon the landowners which necessitated similar expedients on their part. If the landowner had or could obtain sources of income external to landowning pure and simple, good and well; if not, he might be forced to surrender the land to those who had. The peasants' own holdings were inadequate for their support, and they saw no reason why the landowners' holdings should support them through the labour of the peasants. The landowner might have a salary as a public functionary, or profit as a man of business. In any case, the peasant considered that it was no affair of his how the landowner might live, deprived of rent or ruined by high wages of labour. The peasant even had other sources of income, so, no doubt, had the landowner.

The peasantry in general seem to have thought that for ages they had been exploited by the landowners, and that now the turn of the wheel of fortune had brought them uppermost. Their hour had come. The new Duma was to be a peasants' Duma, therefore it must give the peasants what they wanted. What they wanted was land, therefore land must be given to them.

While in some cases the influence of the propaganda of the socialist revolutionary party is apparent, it must be realized that almost everywhere the movement in its essential features was spontaneous. Indeed, the peasants were " more advanced " than the revolutionists. Although they did not work out the implications of their movement, it meant in effect that the land was to be given to them, and that they were to be allowed to cultivate it without State taxes. They might collect taxes from themselves, but the funds produced by these taxes were to be expended locally. Under these conditions, of course, the State as such must disappear, and the nation must dissolve into loosely-connected groups of independent and autonomous communities. Without realizing the course of the development of their ideas, the peasants had arrived substantially at the position of Bakùnin.

It is very clear that the drift of opinion in the towns among the artisans, and in the capitals, even among the professional classes, was not at all in this direction. These were at least not unfavourable to nationalization of the land, but for that very reason they were not prepared for the disappearance of the State. They were inclined towards State organization of industry, and for that reason they desired the State to be powerful. The divergence of opinion and of interest between the peasants and the artisans, and the simultaneous forcing of the social and the political revolutions, together with the absence of constructive ideas at the critical juncture, seem to account for the abortive character of the revolution.

Behind this fundamental antagonism of the peasant and the

artisan there lay also the increasing antagonism between the rich and the poor peasant, between the peasant who had both land and agricultural capital and the peasant who had neither. In presence of these irreconcilable antagonisms, and in the absence of social solidarity which was their inevitable outcome, the autocracy, enfeebled as it was from inherent defects, was able after a struggle to control the situation, and for the time at least to stem the revolution. This cannot, however, be made fully evident until the contemporary industrial situation has been studied.

CHAPTER IX

THE LAW OF 9TH NOVEMBER 1906

THE law upon which all subsequent projects of land reform in Russia must be based is contained in the ukase of 9th November 1906. This law effected a fundamental change in the relation between the peasant and the land. Old Russian habits of thought about landownership had attached to the idea of land possession a collective character. The rights of the community in the land were more or less definitively recognized, both before and after the emancipation of the serfs. The proprietor of the land could not do with it precisely what he liked. It was, in early times, when held as a *votchina*, his own heritable property, and in later times the distinction between *votchinal* ownership and other forms being obscured or obliterated, it became also heritable whether it was in *votchinal* ownership, properly speaking, or not. But the later history of landownership is especially characterized by restrictions upon the mobility or free transference of land. Land could not be sold to persons not authorized to possess land, and in this category were large classes of the community ; land might not be sold without the peasants who cultivated and lived upon it, &c. The community, as represented by the State, imposed these regulations, and thus confirmed its claim to an interest in the land. Moreover, the taxes upon land being assessed in accordance with the number of peasants living upon it, it was the interest of the community to see that none of its members evaded his just obligations by leaving the community, which was responsible for the payment of his quota of the taxes. In order to make the " mutual guarantee " effective, it was necessary for the community, as represented in the *volost*, to regulate the distribution of the land, and to see that each peasant took enough land to enable him to support his family and to contribute his quota of the taxes. In short, the community appeared everywhere ; legislation was directed either towards securing the interest of the State or community as central authority, or of the *volost* or *mir* or community as local authority. The interest of the individual peasant family was secured by the presence of its head in the *volost* assemblies, and by his right to appear in the *volost* court. But the right of the individual peasant was not explicitly recognized, excepting that, with the permission of his family and of the *volost*, he could " separate," and in " separation " could receive a specific share of the land of the family. But, as has been shown above, the practice of " separation " was very fluctuating.[1] The cancellation of the balance of the redemption tax which remained put an end to the " mutual guarantee," and the peasant family was face to face with the tax-collector, and was so far free from the interference in its affairs by the *volost* which the " mutual guarantee " implied. But the community land and the community interest in it remained. There was practically no land in individual family heritable tenure.

The ukase of 9th November 1906 changed all that. Under it every householder, independently altogether of the will of the community, was endowed with the right to fix in property, personal to himself and heritable, that portion of land which belonged to his family at the last distribution. This right involved the further rights to sell the land, and to distribute it among his descendants at his own discretion, although his powers in this connection were much modified by local customs as well as by general civil law. In order to prevent the accumulation of large blocks of land in few hands, the ukase provided that no single purchaser might purchase more than 25 dessiatines from any individual seller. The ukase of 9th November 1906 may thus be held to have in reality introduced into Russian law the conception of individual ownership of property, and thus to have brought in this respect Russian law into conformity with the law of Western Europe upon the subject.[2]

---

[1] Cf. *supra*, pp. 266 *et seq*. " Separations " of late years have been very numerous where the peasants have forsaken the country for the town ; and " separations " from the family, but not from the village, have been frequent, so also have " separations " on account of distant migration ; but cases of " separation " where the peasant has carved out of the land of the community a lot for himself, has built a house upon it, and has elected to live an independent life, have been rare.

[2] *Cf*. A. Berezovsky (Member of Third Duma, President of the Executive Board of his Zemstvo and of the Land Reform Committee of his district), in *Russ*, 31st January and 13th February 1908 (O.S.), art. on " Land, Peasants, and New Laws."

While this ukase introduced in reality into Russian law the conception of individual private property in land, this conception had been previously introduced in form into the Emancipation Acts.[1]

The community was permitted, under these Acts, to allot to individual peasant members in private property their share of the lands purchased by the community ; it was also permitted to compound for such allotment by a money payment. The agreement was to be mutual ; but it is clear that, since the land belonged to the community, that body had the right to dispose of it or not, as it might think fit, under the terms of the Act. The legal definition of communal property as distinguished from other property held by members of the community has been put thus by the Senate in one of the decisions of the Civil Department :

" The substantial distinction between the property of the community and general property is that the proprietor of the former is the community as juridical person, apart from the members of the community ; and the proprietors of the latter are the separate persons, and not the community." [2]

The new ukase enables the individual householder to take the land allotted to him at the last distribution, and to hold it as his own or to sell it. He receives, in short, without compensation to the community, a title to that which formerly belonged to the community. Thus, whereas previous legislation had been on the whole favourable to the maintenance of landholding in community as a characteristic Russian institution, the new ukase was apparently designed, along with the encouragement of " separation," to break up not only the community, but the family. The full effect of this ukase remains to be seen. It is, however, clear that it endows the heads of peasant families with considerable powers, which they did not enjoy under previous laws, while, at the same time, it not only removes the control of the community and abrogates whatever rights it may be presumed to have had in the land, but it cancels a previously existing right of the children of the head of the family to a share in the family land.[3] The land

[1] The series of Acts by means of which Emancipation was effected were called " General Peasants' Acts " or " General Acts upon Peasant Affairs." The section in question is the 12th. Quoted by Berezovsky, *loc. cit.*
[2] *Ibid.*   [3] Cf. *ibid.*

ceases to be the possession of the family as a part of, and under the control of, the community, and becomes the possession of the head of the family alone. He may alienate it practically at will, the rights of others in the property being simply cancelled by the imperial ukase.

There is thus created with one hand a peasant proprietary, and with the other a peasant proletariat. It must be realized that the land had been allotted to the peasant household at the last distribution, as a rule, in proportion to the number of revision souls in the household. Thus those souls who were counted as belonging to the household at the last revision, were in exactly the same position as those who were born after the revision, and were, therefore, not counted. It is true that extreme subdivision of peasant holdings may, by these means, be avoided ; but it is also true that peasant heads of households who wish to do so may sell their lands to speculators. Unaccustomed to the possession of ready money and unacquainted with the means of turning it to advantage the peasant is unlikely to benefit by this arrangement. He and his family come to be separated from their customary means of livelihood, and they necessarily swell the ranks of the proletariat either in the villages or in the cities. The following case illustrates the working of the law :

In Simbirskaya *gub.*, Ardatovsky district, between 11th September and 25th December 1907, ten sales of peasant land, transferred into private property under the Act, were effected ; the land being sold *very cheaply*. This region is in the Black Soil Zone, and may, therefore, be regarded as a favourable case. In the district mentioned, and at that time the price paid for landowners' land by the Peasant Bank was 120–130 rubles. The price paid in the ten cases quoted was less than half as much, being from 35–60 rubles per dessiatine.[1]

But the ukase of 9th November 1906 does not stand alone. It must be taken in connection with other land reforming schemes of the Government. These schemes involve partly the utilization of previously existing agencies, for example, the Peasant Bank, and partly the formation of new administrative mechanism. The administrations of the State (Kazna) and that of Imperial Family (Udelni) lands are required to sell to land-seeking peasants, and

[1] Berezovsky, *loc. cit.*

these may also purchase lands of private owners through the Peasant Bank. In addition, the Government has brought before the Third Duma a plan for the regulation of the relations of peasant proprietors with the landowners of adjoining estates. The disposition of the landowners to inflict petty fines and other annoyances upon peasants owning land in their neighbourhood has been a fruitful source of friction, and accumulated grievances of this kind have often produced grave peasant riots. Measures are also to be taken to transfer peasants from congested districts to less populated places. For the purpose of elaborating these practical plans and applying them in detail appropriately to different districts the Government announced, on 4th May 1906, on the eve of the calling of the First Duma, the formation of local Land Reform Committees to assist the operations of the Peasant Bank, and otherwise to facilitate the carrying out of the projects of the Government.

These measures promised well, but, unfortunately, from the beginning the composition of these committees was such as to invite distrust. The *personnels* of the committees varied in different districts, but the principle upon which the *ex officio* membership of the committees was fixed threw the weight of the influence of the committees upon the side of the landowners and of the bureaucracy. This proceeding was in accordance with all precedents in Governmental action in agrarian reform. It was indeed another added to the long list of attempts, which have been recorded above, to benefit the peasants without diminishing the influence or the property of the landowners—in other words, to make the peasants pay out of their empty pockets for that which had in the nature of things either to be withheld from them or to be given to them at the expense of the State or the landowners, or both. The "indispensable members" of the Land Reform Committees were to be the inspector of taxes, the district member of the local government court, the *Zemski Nachalnēk*, together with the district marshal of nobility, the president of the Zemstvo Executive Board, three representatives of the Zemstvo Assembly,[1] and three peasant

---

[1] When the ukase establishing the Land Reform Committees was promulgated, the Zemstvo Assemblies were generally of liberal tendency ; but after the dissolution of the First Duma, when agrarian disorders occurred, the so-called " righting " of the Zemstvos took place, and their influence was then directed rather towards the neutralization of reforms than the promotion of them.

representatives. The large landowning and the official influence
thus predominated in the committees, and from the beginning they
did not inspire confidence. Moreover, the committees were not
left free to exercise their own judgment. They were constantly
being instructed by ministerial circulars.

The Land Reform Committees began their operations by
arranging for the purchase of the land of private owners by the
Peasant Bank. They added largely to the land fund of the bank,
sometimes at relatively high prices. Valuation of land is a special
business with which the members of the committees were rarely
acquainted. They employed no expert advice, they were themselves owners of land, and their inevitable inclinations were to
maintain rather than to reduce prices ; the cost, moreover, did
not come out of their own pockets. The consequences may be
imagined. Estates which had long been in the market for sale,
and which, owing to non-fertility of soil, neglect, or otherwise,
were practically unsaleable under ordinary condition, now suddenly
acquired a value, and found a facile purchaser.[1]

When the phase of purchase had lasted for some time, there
came the desirability of distributing the land among the peasants—
the end, indeed, of the whole scheme. But after the exertions of
purchase the Land Reform Committees fell asleep, and, in spite
of the efforts on the part of the central Government to stimulate
their activity through the local officials who were members of
them, and in spite of the fact that the Government sent out special
functionaries to insist upon the committees proceeding with their
work, they could not be galvanized into further activity. In so
far as they did exercise any influence upon the peasant situation,
they seem to have rather intensified existing evils than to have
removed them. One of the difficulties of the system of frequent
redistribution of land had been the cutting up of arable fields into
long strips—a form of field which is not convenient for intensive
cultivation. In any new distribution it was important to avoid
this so far as possible, yet the committees sometimes distributed

---

[1] A. Berezovsky, who was himself President of a Land Committee under
Kutler's scheme (Kutler was Minister of Finance for a few months), and also
of one of the new Land Reform Committees, narrates a case in which an
estate which was offered for sale to the first-mentioned committee, and rejected
on the ground that it was unsuitable for conversion from timber-bearing into
arable land, and was therefore not suitable for peasant occupation, was sold
at a high price to the Land Reform Committee. *Russ*, 1st February 1908.

the land in such a way as to intensify this inconvenience, not only by selling the land in long and very narrow strips,[1] but by making, as had to be done in the nature of the case, this division of the land permanent. Inconvenient as the practice was under the former system of community ownership, it might be altered ; but under the new system of private ownership alteration was practically impossible.

The failure of the Land Reform Committees to accomplish what was expected and required of them was extremely embarrassing to the Government, but censure for the failure cannot be withheld from the Government itself, which determined the composition of the committees in such a way that in the absence of an unusual amount of self-abnegation and of an unusual obliviousness of the narrower interests of their class, it would have been difficult for the members of the committees to perform their functions in such a way as to inspire confidence.

The net results of the activity of the Land Reform Committees appear to have been the accumulation in the hands of the Peasant Bank of an unrealisable fund in land at high prices, and the increase of prices of land generally owing to considerable areas being taken off the land market. All this was done in teeth of the clamour on the part of the peasants for more land and of the miserable condition of vast numbers of them because of land insufficiency. When the Land Reform Committees did sell land, they seem to have sold it to well-to-do peasants, while those who really were in need of land, chiefly the peasants whose only holdings were the " gifted allotments," were obliged to go without. In those cases where such peasants did purchase relatively highly-priced lands through the Peasant Bank, they became debtors to the State to an amount which, under the most favourable circumstances conceivable, they would never be able to extinguish. Under these conditions the State must suffer pecuniary loss and the peasant must suffer from hopeless insolvency.

[1] Berezovsky mentions a case in which a Land Reform Committee in Simbirskaya *gub.* sold strips to peasants 3500 ft. long by from 105–140 ft. wide. *Russ*, 1st February 1908.

CHAPTER X

THE AGRARIAN SITUATION SINCE 1906

THE minds of the peasants during the years 1905 and 1906 came, through many channels, to be filled with high hopes. The agrarian question was to be settled at last. Some practical steps had indeed been made in this direction. State lands had been thrown open to the peasants. The "State land reservation" amounted already to 40–50 millions of dessiatines.[1] It appeared that everyone was to have his "need of land" satisfied. The enthusiasts began to see glowing agricultural prospects. Destitution among the peasantry was to give way to plenty. The peasants were even to devote themselves to improvement in farming. "The work of raising the standard of agricultural technique began to boil," writes one, for example.[2] Anticipation of a drastic land policy which was to be adopted by the new State Duma in obedience to the demands of the peasants led to the development of agricultural co-operation. Even the farm labourer looked forward to the possibility of becoming a small holder, or at least a partner in a holding; while the small holders hoped to increase their holdings. For a time these anticipations gave a great stimulus to village life, and the "stagnation" of the village which the chronic "need of land" had engendered began to disappear.

But the dissolution of the Second Duma and the new electoral law which followed changed all that. The peasants awoke to find that they had been dreaming, and to realize that the Government had no intention, and perhaps no power, to give them what they wanted.

Prior to the election of the First State Duma, the Government seemed to think that the most effective method of limiting the extent of political change was to give a proportionately large repre-

[1] That is between 110 and 138 millions of acres.
[2] A. A. Chuprov, art. "The Reforms from Above and the Movement from Below in Agrarian Questions," in *Russkiya Viedomosti*, 1st January 1908.

sentation to the peasantry. It was supposed that the danger of too rapid change lay in the influence of the urban proletariat, and that the balance of political power ought to be so adjusted that the conservative instincts of the peasantry should be utilized in such a way as to counteract the radical and socialist tendencies of the city working men. To the apparent amazement of the Government and of the staunch supporters of the autocracy, the First Duma turned out to be strongly desirous of dealing with the land question in a way which meant the practical extinction of the large landowners as a class. The ulterior economical and social effects of this were set forth in lurid colours by the Oktabristi, who saw in the destruction of that class a danger to the national interests.[1]

From their point of view, the absorption of the large estates by the peasants had been going on quite fast enough, although from the peasant point of view it had been going on so slowly as to be an ineffectual solution of the problem of land scarcity. The influence of the large proprietors was sufficient to determine the character of the measures prepared by the Government in the interval between the dissolution of the Second Duma and the convocation of the Third.

These measures were formulated by the Premier, M. Stolypin, aided by M. Gourko, Deputy Minister of the Interior,[2] and Prince Vassilchikov.[3] The measures in question are characterized by two fundamental negative principles—(1) that " compulsory expropriation of land is not permissible," which is explicitly set forth, and (2) that the community system is to be steadily discouraged, which is implied in the detailed proposals. With these principles in view, the measures provide for the purchase by the State through the Peasants' Bank of those estates only which are voluntarily offered for sale and for the purchase of land by peasants for individual occupancy. Critics of the measures point out the following objections :

1. Land is most urgently needed in those localities where land

---

[1] The point of view of the large landowners is stated, for example, by Sir Donald Mackenzie Wallace, *Russia* (London, 1905), ii. p. 227.

[2] Afterwards dismissed from his office on account of the occurrence of irregularities in his department.

[3] Regarded by the peasants as an active organizer of the " Black Hundred " in Moscow in 1905.

is dear and rents are high. The lands which the proprietors are willing to transfer to the State are not necessarily situated in the localities where the " need of land " is the greatest. If the land voluntarily offered is situated in scantily populated localities, the Government will find itself under the necessity of engaging in migration and colonization schemes, more or less expensive and troublesome.[1]

2. Where lands voluntarily offered for sale to the Government are situated in localities in which there is a local demand for land, relatively high prices will have to be paid for it. Thus the tendency will be for the land to be purchased either by well-to-do peasants only or by speculators who will hold the land for further advances. The real " need of land " on the part of small-holding peasants will, for this reason, go unsatisfied.[2]

3. The small holder and the village proletariat would thus run the risk of being exploited by the class of " farmers " which would, under these circumstances, be created. The results of this exploitation, coupled with their disappointment at the failure of the " reforms " to affect their situation favourably, would be further discontent. This discontent would manifest itself chiefly against the " farmers " or well-to-do peasants, rather than, as now, against the great landed proprietors. From the point of view of administrative strategy, this might be counted as the outcome of an ingenious device, but the social and economic advantage of it is not apparent.[3]

4. The measures are objected to in general on the ground of their inadequacy. " The land reformers (in the Government) forget that they have before them, not an unpopulated desert, but a densely-populated country, with peasantry in convulsions and in the noose of land scarcity.[4]

" The present practice of land-reforming measures is creating with one hand the prosperity of a selected few, while, on the other hand, it bereaves the majority of the peasants needing land of

---

[1] Cf. A. A. Chuprov in Russkiya Viedomosti, 1st January 1908.
[2] Ibid.
[3] This point of view has been put by a correspondent, who even considers that this result is intended by the framers of the legislation. The device is said to be due to the inventive genius of MM. Shisinski and Sturmer. " They put in this way a wall between the landowners and the peasants, upon which the peasants expend themselves."
[4] A. A. Chuprov. Art. cited.

any hope, and devotes them to previously unknown privations.
. . . The present agrarian policy is not constructive, but destructive." [1]

It should be noticed, however, that, from the administrative
point of view, the agricultural districts, or many of them, may be
regarded as over-populated under the present conditions of agricultural technique, and that it is necessary, on the one hand, to
promote the improvement of this technique by encouraging the
cultivation of relatively large farms, occupied by farmers with a
sufficiency of farming capital, and, on the other hand, to promote
the growth of industry by driving into the towns labourers who,
if left to themselves, would remain in the rural districts. [2] The
conception of the inevitable transformation of Russia from an
almost purely agricultural to an extensively industrial country
naturally affects the view of the administration. From this stand-
point the Government may be held to be engaged in promoting
an industrial revolution, while at the same time it is energetically
resisting a political one.

The reactions of a disturbed system are not, however, to be
neglected. If the extension of the farms and the discouragement
of small holdings by restricting them to an inadequate area of
land are fully carried out, the inevitable result must be that the
village proletariat will to a certain extent be driven into the towns,
to increase the numbers of the urban proletariat. The very means
that are alleged to have been employed largely for the purpose of
strengthening the conservative forces, by increasing the number and
improving the condition of the well-to-do farmers, may thus react
in such a way as greatly to increase the urban proletariat, and thus
make for the net increase, rather than the diminution, of the forces
of revolution. It is not a little remarkable that, under the assumed
necessity of modern economic development, the Russian Government should be taking measures to diminish the rural population
by driving a certain proportion of it into the towns, at the very
moment when, in Great Britain, for example, efforts are being made,
by means of legislative encouragement of small holdings, to retain
the rural population upon the land. Russia has been a country

---

[1] A. J. Chuprov (Professor of Political Economy in the University of
Moscow), in art., " Struggle over the Need of Land, and Colonization," in
Russkiya Viedomosti, 1st January 1908.

[2] *Cf.* Sir Donald Mackenzie Wallace, *Russia*, ii. p. 221.

of small holdings, although not of the *petite culture* in the sense of intensive cultivation, and the working of the system has resulted in an increase of the population, so great and so rapid that either agriculture must be greatly and quickly improved, the population must be spread out over a greater area, or it must be forced into the industrial centres in sufficient numbers to relieve the pressure upon the rural districts.

The following details of wages, &c., in certain districts in 1907–1908 may be compared with similar statistics applicable to the period prior to 1905. It must be realized that by 1907 the agrarian disturbances had spent themselves. In Volinskaya *gub.* a daily worker (mower) received 35 to 40 kopeks per day without board. A yearly worker received 25 rubles with board, and with pasture for one cow. He was also allowed to keep a pig and some hens. Rent was from 5 to 7 rubles a year per dessiatine for sandy land, for " Black Soil " 10 to 15 rubles. The *izpolnya* system (metayer tenancy) is common in the district.[1]

In Grodnēnskaya *gub.* mowers' wages were 50 kopeks without board in 1907–1908 ; work from sunrise to sunset, one hour for dinner, and half an hour for lunch. The wages mentioned are those paid by a landowner. If the *mujik* is mowing for a peasant, he gets 45 kopeks and board. At the harvest-time a woman earns from 25 to 30 kopeks without board ; digging potatoes, 15 kopeks. Able-bodied youths from fifteen to twenty years of age get 20 to 30 rubles per year with board, lodging, dress, and boots.[2] A man engaged by the year received 50 to 60 rubles, with board and lodging. The board is the same as that chronicled for Mohilevskaya *gub.* in 1901. A woman engaged by the year received, in 1907–1908, 18 to 25 rubles, with board and lodging. The landowners do not employ daily workers in the winter, but the rich peasants sometimes employ daily workers in the winter for threshing, paying them 20 to 25 kop. per day, with board. They work from sunrise to sunset. Single workers employed by the year sleep in bunks in an *ēzba* belonging

---

[1] The author is indebted to correspondents in the various districts mentioned for the details.

[2] The boots in this district are made of the inner bark of the lime. (In the northern *gubernie* birch bark boots are used.) Such boots are called *lapti*. The feet are covered with linen wrapping, coiled about the foot and leg very neatly (puttee fashion). This wrapping is vulgarly known as *onuchi* or *portyanki*, or little trousers. The use of bark for boots is one of the results of the scarcity of cattle, there thus being few hides.

to the landowner, and are supplied with 2 to 3 lb. of usually badly-baked rye bread per day, barley groats, buckwheat, and pork fat for making soup, the quantities being approximately the same as those given above for Mohilevskaya *gub.* They are also supplied with soup made from beets and sour cabbage. Labourers with families live separately from the single workers, and have their own kitchen, to which the food is supplied by the landowner; they are allowed pasture for one cow, and may keep a pig and a couple of hens. Boys of twelve to fifteen years of age generally look after the pigs and sheep of the landowner, and receive as wages 7 rubles per year. The wife of a labourer, who feeds the pigs, geese, hens, &c., of the landowner receives 10 rubles per year. The treatment of workers is rough, but they are not beaten.[1] In Grodnēnskaya *gub.* the landowners in most cases prefer to rent their estates to Jews, and these subrent the land to the peasants.[2] The usual conditions are that one-third of the produce is given by the peasant to the Jew as rent. When the land is good, the peasants pay one-half of the produce. The landowners in the *gubernie* are nearly all Poles. Good board and lodging in the villages costs 5 rubles per month. The board consists of cabbage, rye bread, potatoes, fat, and a little milk. Beef is given occasionally. Boots are of bark, and all dress is of home manufacture. In the towns of the same *gubernie* the board and lodging of working men costs 10 to 12 rubles per month.[3]

The normal allotment in this district is 3 to 4 dessiatines.[4] The land is good as a rule. It is cultivated by the peasant on the three-field system. The landowners who farm their own land employ the six or eight-field system.

In the northern *guberni,* where the peasants engage in forest labour, hunting, &c., the land is poor, but they have usually at least one steer besides some sheep to kill each year in a peasant household, and hides are thus available for making boots.

These details show quite vividly that up till the present time, commercial econony cannot be said to have displaced natural economy in the rural districts so far as the peasants are concerned.

---

[1] Information from a peasant of this district.
[2] This is true also of some parts of Chernigovskaya *gub.*
[3] Information from a working man.
[4] These details are from a correspondent in the sub-town of Kartusherioze, in the *volost* of that name in Prujansky district, Grodnēnskaya *gub.*

The peasant weaves his own cloth and, as we have seen, makes his own boots from the bark of the trees grown on or near his own land. The soil gives him every article of his consumption, excepting, perhaps, salt. In the towns, to some extent in the larger villages, and in the landowners' families, commercial economy has made great inroads since Emancipation set free the *dvorovie* or household serfs. Yet natural economy is still predominant among the great mass of the Russian population.

The following are the results of an investigation into peasants' budgets in Ordatovsky district, Simbirskaya *gub.*, made by Mr. A. Berezovsky, President of the Land Reform Committee of that district.[1] The figures apply to an average peasant family consisting of three adult souls.[2] It is assumed that this family purchases three-quarters of a dessiatine per male soul.[3] This is the quantity of land which such a family would absolutely require for its subsistence in that district.

Value of Peasants' Buildings—	Rubles.
Ezba, with doorway, roofed with straw . . .	150
Shed (for cattle, implements, &c.)	50
Barn (for grain, &c.)	30
Stable (for horses)	20
Well	15
Hay loft and dairy (hay above ; below, milk and vegetables, &c.)	10
	——275

Value of Live Stock—	
2 horses	100
1 cow	35
5 sheep	20
2 pigs	15
	——170

Value of Implements—	
2 carts with wheels	15
2 ploughs, wood	5
2 yokes	12
2 sleighs	5
Sundries	8
	—— 45
	490

---

[1] See *Russ*, 6th February 1908.
[2] That is to say, three men with three wives and children.
[3] About 7 acres per family.

The average annual outlay in money of such a group is :

	Rubles.	Kopecks.
Heating, 98 cub. ft. firewood	20	0
Lighting, 4 *pùds* kerosene oil @ $2 per *pùd* .	8	0
Clothing, including shoes [1] (three men) . .	90	0
Furniture	10	0
Repairs	10	0
Taxes	6	70
Vodka on Church holidays	10	0
Church rites	5	0
	159	70

The allowance for clothing is for the three men only, the women are expected to provide their own clothing, earning the means to purchase the materials by spinning flax in the house or by day work elsewhere. The children's clothes are made from the cast-off clothing of their elders.

The average annual consumption of such a group is :

	Pùds.
Rye flour, 20 *pùds* per adult (children being fed also out of the total)	120
Millet meal, ⅛ Russian ℔ per day	18
Cattle food : Flour	100
Oats	50
	288

Annual outlay for clothing for one man :

	Rubles.	Kopecks.
Two shirts	3	0
Three pairs trousers	2	50
Thirty-six pairs bast shoes	3	60
One leg wrapper (thick)	1	0
Two pair wrappers (thin)	0	60
Cap and fur cap (lasting 2 years) per year . . .	1	0
Kaftan	5	0
Short overcoat (lasting 3 years) per year . . .	5	0
Summer overcoat (lasting 4 years) per year . . .	2	0
Warm overcoat (lasting 3 years) per year . . .	2	50
Warm boots (lasting 2 years) per year . . .	1	50
Leather boots (lasting 2 years) per year . . .	2	50
	30	20

The income of the family group is on the average :

	Rubles.
One man may be spared to work externally. His earnings will be	60
The whole family may be employed during harvest-time externally. They will harvest 2 dessiatines of rye for 5 rubles per dessiatine	10
And 3 dessiatines oats for 3 rubles per dessiatine	9
The horses will earn	20
One calf sold	10
Three lambs sold	10
Fifteen sucking pigs	15
	134

Out of the nine and three-quarters dessiatines of land, three-quarter dessiatines are used for buildings, &c. ; of the remaining, six dessiatines are, under the three-field system, annually available for cropping ; three are cropped with oats, and three with rye. The average yield of rye in the district in question is 50 *pùds* per dessiatine, and of oats 33.5 *pùds* per dessiatine. If the family obtains 50 *pùds* per dessiatine of seeded land, the total is 300 *pùds* of grain.

The grain is thus little more than sufficient to provide for the subsistence of the family and its animals ; there is practically no surplus for sale. The money expenses of the family are 159.70 rubles ; while the money income is only 134 rubles. There is thus an average annual deficit of 25.70 rubles. This deficit may be met by economies in some of the items of expenditure. There remains, however, to be considered the means of meeting the interest upon the cost of the land, apart from the amortization of the amount. Land in the district in question costs on the average 125 rubles per dessiatine. The Peasant Bank requires the purchaser to pay 4½ per cent. per annum upon the purchase price, which in the given case would be 1218 rubles. The interest upon this sum is 48.78 rubles per year. In addition, the Zemstvo taxes (of 6 rubles 60 kopeks per dessiatine) with inevitable fines for delay, would bring the average annual payments under the head of interest and taxes to 60 rubles per year. This is an additional deficit, and this deficit must be met somehow, otherwise the peasant family sinks into hopeless insolvency, and eventually loses the land by means of which they live. In order to raise the additional 60 rubles per year, the peasant family would require to add 50 per cent. to the yield of their crops—that is, they would require to increase the yield from 50 *pùds* per dessiatine to 75 *pùds*. Since the maximum yield in the best and most intensively cultivated lands in the district is only 59 *pùds* per dessiatine, this increase is unattainable.

It is, therefore, plain that even if the peasant has sufficient agricultural capital to erect his house, to provide himself with the necessary implements and the necessary stock, he cannot make his budget balance saving by severe economy, even without taking into account interest upon his own capital which he has invested in his house, or interest upon the cost of the land or taxes. In the worse case of a peasant who has no agricultural capital to start with, there does not appear to be any prospect of his ever acquiring any, because instead of a surplus he has always to encounter a deficit. In both cases the problem is an insoluble one on any terms as yet offered through the Peasant Bank or the Land Reform Committees. The quantity of land is too small, the price is too high, and the interest is too high also. It is small wonder that the peasants should refuse to purchase on these terms, and that they should demand that land—plenty of land—should be given to them.

From the foregoing the following provisional conclusion may be arrived at. The revolutionary "state of mind" among the peasantry seems to have arisen not merely because of the political disabilities to which they were subject, nor merely from the economical pressure caused by high rents and low wages, nor merely from famine and its results, nor merely from the propaganda of enthusiasts, but from all of these together. It must be allowed that, especially during the years immediately preceding the Russo-Japanese War, the position of the peasantry, though bad, had distinctly improved. People who are in the depths of despair through sheer want may be very discontented, but they rarely revolt. The prosperity of the *kulaki*, or well-to-do peasants, is one of the significant features of the period. The growth of this class was facilitated by the Peasants' Bank and its presence as an important fraction of the village population is noticed in all the reports from the districts of which details have been given. It would appear that while the village proletariat had not been similarly prosperous, while they had been undergoing exploitation at the hands of landowners and rich peasants alike, they had nevertheless succeeded owing to the economical conditions of the years from about 1900 till 1905,[1] in forcing their wages somewhat upwards. The spectacle of greater relative prosperity of the exploiting classes, contrasted with their own relatively deficient prosperity, seems to have inspired them with the desire to diminish the hardships of their own lot by a vigorous stroke. The occasion for this vigorous stroke came with the confusion of the war and the preoccupation of the Government, together with the relaxation of local authority which these incidents involved.

The policy of strikes which the peasants adopted in 1905 was successful up to a certain point. They lost some of the advantages which they gained during the disturbances, but they did not lose all of them. Their wages remained somewhat higher than they were before the agrarian movement began, and their rents were somewhat lower. The principal gain which they have secured lies, however, in the fact that authorities and landowners alike were thoroughly frightened. Punitive expeditions and military and police suppression of the movement notwithstanding, the peasants have exhibited an astonishing latent power, and the Government at least must have realized that the days of peasant revolts are by no means over. The landowners, too, must have realized that they had no longer to deal with a spiritless peasantry, who might suffer themselves to be exploited without protest. Whatever view may be held regarding the nature of the demands made by the peasants, and of the motives which lay behind these demands, it must be allowed that their character showed that the peasants were thoroughly aroused, and that they might at any moment, at some conjunction of events similar to that which occurred in 1905 and 1906, spring again at the landowners with arms in their hands. It is obvious that under these conditions contracts for land and for wages must be at least slightly more favourable to the peasants than they were formerly, and that thus the sacrifices made in the agrarian movement were not wholly fruitless.

[1] The harvests of these five years were all good.

BOOK VI

INDUSTRIAL DEVELOPMENT UNDER CAPITALISM

INTRODUCTION

WE have seen that there were large industrial establishments in Russia prior to Emancipation in 1861. These establishments belonged in some cases to the State, in other cases to great nobles and smaller gentry, and in others to merchants or even to prosperous peasants. Under pre-emancipation conditions peasants not infrequently left their villages by permission of their owners, and worked in the towns, paying *obròk* to their owners. In addition to such workers, who offered themselves for hire, there were freed peasants and proletarian or impecunious gentry, and other free or quasi-free people. There was thus the nucleus of a free hirable class of artisans, although the existence of such a class was not yet recognized.

But development in any serious sense of industrial enterprise was not compatible with bondage. Capitalistic enterprise could not grow, at least until the concurrent growth of a free and mobile class of artisans. This class begins to appear in considerable numbers only after Emancipation. Even then, however, there were limitations of the supply. The mobility of the peasant was still imperfect, for the system of *mutual guarantee* prevented the peasants from leaving their villages without permission of the *volost* court, and this permission was not always granted. When it was granted, the condition was attached that the payments of taxes and other customary payments by the absentees were to be maintained. One class of peasant was, however, at once set free for industrial employment. This was the class of *dvorovie lyudĕ*, or domestic serfs, who were not allotted any land and for whom there was no provision, restrictive or otherwise, under the Emancipation Act. Unless they desired to remain as domestic servants, and unless their former owners desired them to remain, they were practically obliged to resort to the towns for employment. They were not accustomed to field labour, and employment otherwise in the country was not to be obtained. They had as a rule no capital for the cultivation of rented land, nor had they any allotments even had they desired to become cultivators. Many of them were skilled artisans, and these thus provided immediately upon their emancipation a large landless class ready for industrial employment. In addition to these, there were members of peasant land-holding families who were open to employment owing to the inadequacy of the allotments and owing to the diminution of the area of land available for cultivation by the peasants without the payment of rent, when compared with the area formerly cultivated by them as serfs. Such peasants were, however, obliged by the system of *mutual guarantee* to send to their families the balance of their earnings in the same manner as in such cases the balance had formerly to be sent to the serf-owner. The result of this practice was that the rent of agricultural land was frequently paid out of these industrial earnings, so that non-economical agriculture came to be extensively practised from the moment of Emancipation. High rents were exacted, and paid not out of the earnings of cultivation proper, but largely out of industrial earnings by absentee members of peasant families. At the same time the *mutual guarantee* inspired the communities with a certain reluctance to allow their members to leave. Permission was not always granted, and even when it was granted for a limited period, it was not always renewed. From time to time migration from the rural districts to the towns was further impeded by the action of the Government, which attempted to prevent the breaking up of joint-families and to prevent the too liberal granting of passports to peasants. The maintenance of connection with his village by the urban artisan has thus been a very definite factor in his life. He was half a townsman and half a countryman. Until very recently it has been the practice for the peasant artisan to work for a few months in an industrial centre and then to return to his village, where he assisted the other members of his family in cultivation—in ploughing or in harvesting—returning to his employment in the town when these operations were over. As a rule, he left his wife and family in the village, and lived in the town in a factory barracks or in a workmen's lodging-house.

These practices have within the past four or five years been greatly modified for reasons which have been alluded to above, in connection with the agrarian question. So long as they endured they practically prevented the growth of an urban proletariat, and this circumstance has had a very important effect upon the industrial and political situation.

The close connection between the country villages and the industrial centres has, moreover, had an influence upon the dissemination of revolutionary ideas. These ideas have in particular been disseminated by " banished " workmen, who have carried from the towns to their villages, though indefinitely and crudely, the propaganda of the Social Democratic and Social Revolutionary Parties, with which they had become acquainted in their workshops.

Apart from the question of the supply of labour, the general economical conditions in Russia prior to the Emancipation were not favourable to the growth of industry on any extensive scale. The economic life of the country was highly self-contained. Each estate, and sometimes each village, was a little world practically complete within itself. Even the noble landowners, who spent a portion of the year in the capitals, transported to their town houses from their estates almost the whole of the produce necessary for their support and for the support of their numerous retinue of servants.[1] With the exception of iron, tea, cotton, and a few other staple commodities not at that time produced in Russia in sufficient quantities to satisfy the existing demand, only articles of luxury were imported, or even transferred from place to place. The great commerce which had been characteristic of early Russia, and which had been the basis of its economical and political strength, had disappeared. The " immobilization " of labour had as inevitable concomitant the " immobilization " of goods. There were, moreover, almost no railways. There was no banking system, and as yet there was but a trifling circulation of money in the country. Yet there are those who look back upon the age of

---

[1] *Cf.* the lively sketch in Prince Kropotkin's *Memoirs of a Revolutionist* (Boston, 1899), p. 28. While undoubtedly the conditions stated in the text applied fully (and to a large extent still apply) to the peasantry, the wealthier nobility did not always realize the ambition of having everything made by their own servants. The serf-domestic-artisan was often ill-trained and inefficient. " I must own," says Prince Kropotkin (*op. cit.*, p. 29), " that few of them became masters in their respective arts. The tailors and shoemakers were found only skilful enough to make clothes or shoes for the servants, and when a really good pastry was required for a dinner party, it was ordered at Tremblé's (the fashionable pastry-cook), while our own confectioner was beating his drum in the band."

bondage as an age of relative abundance—an age in which there was no freedom, but in which there was in general plenty to eat. All the conditions which have been described had to be greatly modified before extensive industry was possible. The changes began immediately after Emancipation. The creation of Land Redemption Banks and the negotiation of foreign loans provided a financial basis ; railways were built rapidly in European Russia, and numbers of foreign capitalists—principally English, German, Belgian, and French—established factories for the manufacture of cottons, woollens, &c., in the late sixties and in the seventies. Some of the ancient towns developed into industrial centres. The regions specially affected by the industrial movement at this time were the Moskovskaya *gub.*, St. Petersburg and its neighbourhood, the Baltic Provinces, and parts of Poland.

The growth of the railway system in the seventies and the protective tariff, which reached its fullest development in 1891, stimulated industry enormously. From this time onward the urban proletariat, which, owing to the various causes indicated above, had previously no considerable existence in Russia, began to become numerous and influential. Movement from the villages ceased to be impeded by the Government, and artisans began to crowd into the towns. The excess of labour at once rendered labour cheap, and rendered the employers indifferent to the comfort of the labourers. The beginning of the process of industrial development on an extensive scale was not accompanied by the ameliorative legislation which, initiated in England, had been carried far in Germany and France—in all countries, in fact, in which the concentration of workmen in industrial towns had been taking place. Ere long the rigorous exploitation of labour brought the grievances of the workmen under the notice of the Government. Long hours, inadequate wages, and still more importantly, the knowledge that workmen in other countries were reputed to be better off than those in Russia, led to demands upon the Government to intervene. In countries where a measure of *laisser faire* existed, the natural and obvious method of labour association was productive, to a certain extent, of improved conditions. Even in such countries the power of the State was invoked in restricting the hours of labour, in regulating the system of " truck," and in providing for the protection of the working men against exposed machinery and in inevitably dangerous occupations. But in Russia such steps were taken slowly, and they were regarded by the workmen as inadequate, while labour association was practically prohibited.

Side by side with private enterprises, there were established Government factories for the manufacture of cloth, paper, tinned provisions, &c., together with metal refineries, foundries, porcelain works, &c. &c. These activities of the Government were supplemented by the factories belonging to the Udeli,[1] in which large numbers of men were employed.

The circumstances that many of the private enterprises were brought into existence by the high protective duties, and that these enterprises were encouraged by the Government, as well as the circumstance that the Government in its own factories, and in those of the Udeli, pursued methods similar to those of the private firms, made it inevitable that the responsibility for the situation should rest upon the shoulders of the Government. The labour question thus from the middle of the seventies assumed a definite political aspect.

In Russia, labour combination, in the West European sense, was probihited. " Protection " appeared to exist solely for the manufacturer, whose enterprises received governmental assistance and encouragement. The Government not only facilitated the development of industries by high tariffs, but through the State Bank it financed industrial enterprises, and through the State domain it gave land, mining, and timber concessions to persons who were willing to undertake the task of industrial organization. Many of these persons were foreigners, or the agents of foreigners, who were specially protected by the Russian Government.[2] In brief, the hand of the Government was everywhere.

The effect of this situation was to direct against the Government a large part of the irritation engendered in the minds of the working men against their employers. If, for example, a foreman in a factory lost his temper and beat a workman, the latter might com-

[1] The imperial appanage.
[2] In case of strikes in factories owned by foreign firms or organized by means of foreign capital, representations through the ambassadors at St. Petersburg of the countries concerned were usually met by prompt action on the part of the authorities, in the interests of Russian credit abroad. *Cf.* the case of Goujon of Moscow, *supra*, p. 196.

plain to the Government factory inspector, but if the latter did not take the workman's view of the case, he came to be looked upon as a partner in the offence committed by the foreman.　The *chinovnēkē*, or official class, came to bear the burden of the faults of its members, and the whole governmental system came to be called in question.　Meanwhile the Government neglected to apply the ameliorating legislation which had been applied under similar conditions of protection and encouragement of industry by Germany, and the factory system, inspection notwithstanding, continued to be conducted in what the workmen now recognized fully to be an archaic manner.

The comparatively small number of working men in the cities, which before Emancipation were rather political and trading than manufacturing centres, accounts for the late appearance of labour organizations, excepting some of a rudimentary character. An account is given in the following pages of the growth of the trade union idea and of its rapid development during the revolutionary periods.　An account is also given of the attempts on the part of the Government to control the movement, and of the influence upon labour organization of the revolutionary propagandas.

While the development of industry on the large scale in Russia has lagged behind that of Western Europe in point of time, the late development, in the technical and commercial senses, has been accompanied by a late development in a social sense.　The exploitation of the working men and women has been more severe than for many years it has been in any Western European country. The practice of " search," [1] universal in Russia, the practice of beating workmen, and other similar practices, are incidents in a system of oppression which survived the Emancipation, but which recent events have done much to mitigate.　Low wages and unfavourable conditions of work have, as will be seen, played a conspicuous part in producing the " state of mind " which made the Revolution.

While the factory system has been developing in Russia with great rapidity, partly under the influence of a high protective tariff, there has been a spontaneous and very widespread development

[1] Searching the workers on leaving the factory for concealed tools or other small articles which they might have purloined.

of the so-called *kustarny* or household industry in villages. In some *gubernie*, notably in Moskovskaya *gub.*, the Zemstvos have encouraged the *kustars* or household artisans by organizing for them the direct supply of raw materials and by facilitating the formation of *artels*, or co-operative groups. It seems that in some industries, small iron ware, cardboard, leather, woodwork, &c., not only do the *kustari* compete with the large manufacturers, but they have in some cases succeeded in directing the trade wholly into their own hands.[1]

The foregoing and the following analysis of the situation bring these points into relief :

1. The changes in social structure due to increase in population, the pressure of the " need for land," and the abolition of the *mutual guarantee*.

2. The forced development of industry through the protective tariff.

3. The rapid growth of a proletariat class in the towns, with consequent inferior wages and conditions of labour.

4. The fixation by peasant and artisan alike of responsibility upon the Government for the evils they experienced.

5. The passing of the labour movement from a purely economical movement into a political rebellion, the nature of the demands being largely of an economical character.

[1] The centre of *kustarny* activity in the Moscow region is at Sergei Passad, about forty miles from Moscow, where is situated the great monastic fortress of Troitsky.

CHAPTER 1

THE FACTORY SYSTEM SINCE EMANCIPATION

THE fall of bondage right on the Emancipation of the peasants in February 1861 immediately and profoundly affected factory industry. It is true that the system of forced labour in the factories had fallen into decay, and that free workmen were employed to the extent probably of more than two-thirds of the working force of the days immediately before Emancipation, but nevertheless industry received a great shock through the sudden desertion of the factories by great numbers of labourers who had been forced to work in them.

The *votchinal* and possessional factory managements had been fully responsible for the peasants ascribed to the factories. They were obliged to maintain them whether there was work to do or not ; but if there was work to do, the peasants were obliged to do it. If they objected they might be—and, as we have seen, often were—compelled by force to fulfil their obligations. The system, apart from its moral and social aspects, was ineconomical, and was gradually undergoing liquidation from interior causes. Probably there still remained in the ranks of the bonded factory workmen, the less vigorous and intelligent, those who were otherwise having largely succeeded, by one means or another, in joining the ranks of hired labour, even although they still remained nominally subject to bondage right. Yet, especially on the outskirts, there were large establishments in which forced labour was chiefly or altogether employed. There thus remained, for example, in the Ural Mountains large numbers of peasants by whose bonded labour mining, iron-smelting, and other mechanical industries were carried on in large establishments. In the Bogoslovsky district of Permskaya *gub.* about three thousand previously bonded adult male peasants, or three-fourths of the total male working force of the district, left the works to which they had been ascribed. These men, representing a population of from 12,000 to 15,000, sold or even gave away their houses and left the region. From the Berezovsky works there went away 800 of the best workmen, and from the Mēassky gold mines there went 2000 families.[1] Thus from the outlying to the central regions of Russia there began a considerable migration. Isolated works in the mountains and in Eastern European Russia were suddenly deprived of a part or of the whole of their working force. The wages of labour rose rapidly—indeed, they multiplied at once two or three times—and yet labourers could not be obtained in scantily populated regions and in the heart of dense forests. Industries had been built up in these remote places by means of forced labour, and when force was withdrawn labour stopped. The general result of this state of matters was a diminution of production.

The industry which suffered most from the Emancipation was the iron industry. Above all it had retained forced labour, and it had not been adapting itself to the employment of free hired labour to the same extent as had most of the other industries. Textile industries suffered much less, because the power factory was not yet fully developed, and compulsory labour in factories, for the reasons explained in previous chapters, had fallen into decay. " The transformed technique of production required a free working man, and the factories which retained compulsory labour could not compete with the new capitalistic factories." [2] The new capitalist factories were concentrated chiefly in the Moscow district and in the Baltic provinces—at Narva, largely, for example— while the old *votchinal* and possessional factories had been distributed in many *guberni* of Central Russia. The former had been increasing both in size and in numbers, although the great increase of them occurred in the subsequent two decades, while the latter had been diminishing. Thus, in Kalujskaya *gub.* there had been fifteen factories, eleven of which were on the estates of nobles and belonged to them. In 1861 there were no nobles' factories, and there were only a few belonging to merchants. In Simbirskaya *gub.* there were, up till 1860, thirty cloth factories, only two of which belonged to merchants, the remainder being *votchinal*, with a few possessional factories. Ten years after Emancipation, only eight of the twenty-eight factories remained in the hands of nobles,

[1] Tugan-Baranovsky, p. 308.   [2] *Ibid.*, p. 310.

ten factories were closed, ten were rented to and two were acquired by merchants.[1] In the end of the eighteenth century and the beginning of the nineteenth century the seat of the woollen manufacture in factories was Voronej. Voronej was a factory city and all its suburbs were dotted with factories;[2] in 1856 only three were left, and in 1865 not one. Since the time of Peter the Great there had been at Kazan a great possessional woollen factory. In 1830 this factory employed 1000 men; in the forties it began to decline, in the fifties it employed only 450, and in the sixties only 260 men. This decline was not due to the introduction of machinery, for the production declined proportionately.[3] So also the woollen factories of *pomyetschĕkĕ* in Orel and in Smolensk disappeared, and those in Penza, Tambov, Ryazan, Samara, Poltava, Kharkov, and Podolsk diminished considerably.[4] Instead of them there appeared new factories belonging to the merchants.

The cotton industry had established itself chiefly at Moscow; but in the sixties, immediately after Emancipation, it had to encounter the crisis produced in the cotton trade by the American Civil War.[5] The manufacture of cotton was not, however, carried on at this time to any material extent in possessional factories. It had been, as we have seen, from a comparatively early period a capitalistic industry, whether it was carried on within the factory or outside of it. In the manufacture of silk, hired labour had been almost exclusively employed since the disastrous experiment at Akhtuba.[6]

It is always hard to differentiate the effects of different economic causes acting simultaneously and giving rise to complicated reactions. For this reason it is not safe to assume too readily that the most obvious is the most important cause. In addition to the causes of disturbance interior to Russian industry, some of which have been suggested in preceding chapters, there were two important causes external to Russia, one of which occurred before and the other after the Emancipation. These were the general commercial crisis of 1857 and the cotton famine due to the Civil War in America. The latter has already been alluded to. Begin-

---

[1] Tugan-Baranovsky, p. 310.
[2] *Ibid.*
[3] *Ibid.*, p. 311.
[4] *Ibid.*
[5] Garelin, J., *Ivanovo-Voznesensk*, ii. pp. 25, 27, contains interesting data for the cotton crisis of the sixties; cited by Tugan-Baranovsky, p. 312.
[6] See *supra*, vol. i. pp. 484–88.

ning in the United States in August 1857,[1] the commercial crisis affected England in November of the same year.[2] Russia was not affected so immediately as England was, but within a year Russia was in the throes of a commercial crisis not to be dissociated from the restriction of credit due to the crisis of the preceding year. Russian banks and joint-stock companies, industrial and commercial houses, suspended payment in large numbers. The immediate result of this financial crash was the diminution of production with consequent stagnation in industry.[3] The effects upon Russian factory industry of the cotton famine, and of the subsequent crisis of 1866, originating in England, had hardly disappeared when Russian commerce was again struck by an external blow. This blow came from the Austro-German crisis of 1873. This crisis began with a panic on the Vienna Bourse early in May of that year.[4] The effects of the crisis did not make their appearance until August, when there is held the great annual fair of Nijni-Novgorod. Three large merchants and a great number of small merchants became bankrupt there in the end of August. Immediately afterwards a crisis manifested itself at Odessa. Many merchants failed, and " money disappeared completely."[5]

There were, however, influences interior to Russia making also in the direction of financial and industrial disturbance. One of many concurrent causes of the European crisis of 1873 was the heavy drafts upon European credit caused by the building of railways in the United States ; and this cause produced reactions in the United States from the financial disturbances on the European bourses. Simultaneously with the railway movement in the United States there went on, especially between 1868 and 1871, a vigorous construction of railways in Russia. Upwards of a milliard of rubles was spent in about four years. The transformation of so large a capital into so highly permanent and inconvertible a form could not be so rapidly accomplished without disturbance, especially

[1] It may be held to have arisen out of inflation of credit due to the rapid opening up of the middle west and the hopes to which that gave rise, hopes which were too extravagant for immediate fulfilment.

[2] The Bank Act was suspended on 12th November 1857.

[3] Tugan-Baranovsky, p. 327.

[4] The panic began in the last days of April and reached its height on 10th May.

[5] Wirth, Max, *History of Commercial Crises*, 1877, p. 475 ; cited by Tugan-Baranovsky, p. 328.

in a country like Russia, where there is little fluid financial capital, and where the commercial and industrial capital is widely diffused, and is therefore not readily susceptible of concentration for purposes of credit. During the four years of railway construction there was a temporary inflation due to the pouring into the country of masses of Belgian and French capital. In 1870–1871 it was inevitable that the French source of supply should dry up during the war, and for some time afterwards. Railway construction was resumed in 1873 and 1874, but the sudden stoppage in 1870 affected seriously in the following year the demand for goods.[1]

The recovery of the Russian factory industry and of Russian commerce from the effects of these interior and exterior cataclysms was extraordinarily rapid. After the Russo-Turkish War was concluded, an epoch of prosperity began. Profits became enormous. Joint-stock companies, according to their annual reports published from 1878 onwards until 1880, were earning up to 70 per cent. upon their capital.[2] These enormous profits led to great increase in production. Cotton manufacture was especially stimulated. In 1879 upwards of 1,000,000 spindles were installed, thus raising the previously-existing 3,500,000 spindles to 4,500,000.[3] This sudden expansion was due, Bezobrazov[4] thinks, to the issues of Government bank-notes for the purpose of financing the expenditure upon the Turkish War. Speculative activity was directed at this period almost wholly to the promotion of new joint-stock enterprises. The speculation had thus " a bourse character " to a greater extent than had any previous speculative period. By the beginning of the eighties of the nineteenth century Russia had been well drawn into the network of international trade and finance, so that the depression of trade which began in England in 1877–1878, and continued until 1886—the " long depression," as it came to be called—affected Russia seriously, as also did the various crises of that period, wherever they originated. Paris and New York both experienced financial crises in 1882 ; and in Russia in 1884 there came the railway *debâcle*. The stimulus

---

[1] Tugan-Baranovsky, p. 329.
[2] Bezobrazov, V., *The Economy of the People of Russia*, i. p. 277 ; cited by Tugan-Baranovsky, p. 330.
[3] *Ibid.*, p. 330.   [4] Bezobrazov, *ibid.* ; cited, *ibid.*

of war funds having come to an end, the period from 1882–1886 was marked everywhere by the shortening of production and by commercial stagnation.[1] The meagre fairs at Nijni-Novgorod between 1882 and 1887 afforded visible evidence of general depression in Russia.[2]

The effect of these movements upon Russian industry was also visible in St. Petersburg, which had already, in the winter of 1880–1881, a heavy unemployment roll. The great factory of Bird discharged about 3000 workmen, retaining only 1000 ; at the Alexandrovo works 350 only were left out of 800 ; at the St. Samson works 450 out of from 1200 to 1500.

Industrial depression affected Moscow so early as the spring of 1880. There the *kustarni* industry suffered even more than the factory. Throughout the winter of 1880–1881 there was much unemployment in Ivanovo. At the same time two thousand workmen were thrown out of employment by discharge from the works of Khludov, in the district of Dukhovtschina. In Klēntsi Posàd (*faubourg*), in Chernigovskaya *gub.*, the number of workmen was diminished by 40 per cent., and the wages were reduced by from 30 to 40 per cent. for those who remained. In Poland, during the summer of 1882, there were 20,000 unemployed in Warsaw alone.[3]

The long industrial depression thus began in Russia about a year and a half later than it began in England, and the revival took place about one year later than the revival of trade in England. There was a slight check in Russia in 1890, but in 1895–1896 Russia shared to the full in the vigorous trade movement which began at that time to be felt throughout the civilised world. The most significant part of this movement is to be found in the rapid growth of the iron industry in the basin of the river Don. Preparation had been made for this by the opening, in 1884, of a network of railways in the region, and especially by the construction of the Ekaterēnēnsky Railway, which connected the iron mines at Krivoy Rog with the coal mines of the Don. Up till 1887, the iron mines of the Urals had been the principal sources of supply ; but from that year they lost ground steadily. In 1887 there were

---

[1] Tugan-Baranovsky, p. 332.
[2] The agricultural incidents of these periods are considered elsewhere.
[3] Prēklonsky, S., in *Delo*, 1883 ; cited by Tugan-Baranovsky, p. 332.

only two ironworks in the Don region—those of Hughes and Pastukhov. Other ironworks followed, until in 1889 there were seventeen large smelting works and twenty-nine active blast furnaces. Each of these works employed about 10,000 men. The price of coal lands doubled in a very few years.[1] " The industrial mood has infected all classes of the inhabitants of South Russia. . . . In two years the south of Russia has changed its physiognomy."[2] The principal products of South Russia at this time were rails and other materials for railway construction and maintenance. Between 1866 and 1899 the production of pig iron in Russia multiplied five times ; at the former date Russia produced less than 3 per cent. of the world's production ; at the latter date nearly 7 per cent. In 1899 Russia came third in the list of producers of pig iron, England and Germany leading.[3]

Between 1887 and 1893 the number of workmen in the Russian factories increased by 264,856, and the value of the production by 400 million rubles ; between the years 1893 and 1897 the number of workmen increased by 515,358, and the value of the production by 1104 million rubles.[4] This tremendous growth was too rapid. The arrest came in 1899–1900.[5] The movement was a complicated one. The rush of working men from the small towns to the great industrial centres, which began from positive causes in the early part of the period of inflation, proceeded in the later part of it from negative causes. The small towns in the Dnieper valley, for example, were drawn upon heavily by Warsaw, Lodz, Minsk, and other large industrial towns. The small river towns had slender manufacture for export. They were dependent mainly upon the local trade. Thus the drawing-off of large numbers of their working population disturbed the local conditions, reduced demand, and induced flight to the industrial centres. Meanwhile the villages which relied upon the towns in their locality for the marketing of their produce found their market diminishing, excepting for wheat, which was, in any case, sold chiefly for export. The diminished purchasing power of the villages reacted upon the

---

[1] Tugan-Baranovsky, p. 339.
[2] *Vyestnik Fēnansov*, No. 33, 1897, p. 474 ; cited by Tugan-Baranovsky, p. 339.
[3] Tugan-Baranovsky, p. 340. [4] *Ibid.*, p. 340.
[5] Professor Tugan-Baranovsky in March 1898 foretold the approaching crisis. See *op. cit.*, 1st ed. (St. Petersburg, 1898), p. 325.

towns and intensified the depression there.[1] Diminution of purchasing power throughout the country was also caused by the inferior harvests of 1898 and 1899. The two causes acting together produced the depression in so far as it was due to domestic causes. In so far as the large manufacturing cities were dependent upon the domestic market, they were thus encountered by collapse of the previously increasing demand, and those industries which were created to meet this demand were inevitably the first to feel the depression.

Stagnation in the cotton industry began to manifest itself in Ivanovo in the autumn of 1899 ; in the spring of 1900, the same condition affected Moscow, and also Tula, which is a centre for the manufacture of *samovars* and other household articles in universal use. So also at Belostok, the cotton industry suffered heavily, and at Lodz, the iron industry. These economic disturbances affected credit all over Russia, and at Baku there was a financial crisis in November 1899. In the region of the Don, eighteen Belgian enterprises stopped payment, with liabilities of 4½ million rubles. In Kiev in December 1899, there was a crisis in the sugar industry.[2] At the same time an advance in the price of coal increased the cost of metallurgical processes[3] and contributed to the diminution of the production of metallurgical works. The crisis in credit occurred in the spring of 1900, when there were many failures of industrial, commercial, and financial houses with large liabilities. Following upon these there came a sharp fall of prices.

While the influence of deficient harvests upon the general situation must not be ignored, the details which have been given seem to prove decisively that Russia was no longer a purely agricultural country, and that she had entered upon the capitalistic field to a very large extent and with very great rapidity. This rapidity had been indeed so great that she had not only been drawn into the network of international commercial relations, and had thus become subject to the fluctuations of these, but her own

[1] These conclusions are from observations made by the writer in Poland in the late summer of 1899.
[2] Arising probably from over-production.
[3] This advance in the price of coal in the teeth of the fall of other prices, seems to have been due to the increase in the customs duties on foreign coal, and to the fact that the Russian mines could not immediately replace with their own production the quantity which would have been imported.

industry and commerce had their own important domestic fluctuations. While, no doubt, like America, Russia was still predominantly agricultural, her industries now constituted a formidable factor; and in the present phase of her development, the economic equilibrium, which was formerly dependent almost exclusively upon agriculture, had become largely dependent as well upon industry.

What were the causes of this transformation, so rapid and on so vast a scale? There can be no single answer to this complicated question. Many causes co-operated to produce the result. *First*, there-may be put the Emancipation of the peasants in 1861. Prior to Emancipation, peasant labour may be regarded as having been relatively inefficient, and as having become rather more than less so as the period of emancipation approached. It is possible that in the eighteenth century, under the pressure of the whip, the produce of a bonded peasant was not less than that of a free man; but it is scarcely possible that it was as great in the nineteenth century, when, after all is said that may be said on the subject, the lot of the peasant was, on the whole, better, and his treatment by his *pomyetschĕk* milder, than it had been in the eighteenth century. For this reason the number of peasants upon a given area of land was greater than was necessary to cultivate the land under skilful administration. When Emancipation took place, and when, as they did, the landowners proceeded to cultivate large areas by means of hired labourers under the control of skilled persons, the number of peasants necessary for the operations was naturally smaller than formerly. So also when the peasants were liberated from compulsory labour in the *votchinal* and possessional factories, a smaller number of hired labourers sufficed to take their places and to do the work which they formerly did. Emancipation thus set free for employment a vast surplus of labourers accustomed to a low standard of comfort. The majority of these, as we know, had land, but they had no agricultural capital, and although the large majority of the peasants who had formerly been engaged in agriculture remained in that occupation, considerable numbers of them offered themselves for employment in the towns. *Second*, interior changes in peasant life have contributed to increase the supply of labour since Emancipation. Among these may be observed the abolition of the method of taxation by " mutual guarantee " which had contributed to hold the village population in the villages, and to prevent them from going into the industrial centres. The abolition of the "mutual guarantee" rendered "separations" more easy by increasing the mobility of the peasant, and enabled him readily to become a workman. The same change tended to obviate the previous necessity for the working man to go back to his village from the factory where he was employed, in order to take his share in field labour in his village. As this practice diminished, which it was doing in the nineties, the factories found that it was not necessary to employ quite so many hands in order to obtain the same amount of work. Counting upon a month as a minimum period of absence from the factory of each workman, the factory, in order to maintain a full working force would require to employ on the average about 8 per cent. more men than they would have had to employ had all their workmen worked all of the time. As the practice diminished, so would this percentage, and thus a certain surplus of labour would be gradually created, directly and indirectly through the abolition of the "mutual guarantee." *Third*, the promotion of education by the Zemstvo authorities, especially prior to the so-called "righting of the Zemstvos," had an important influence in diverting peasant lads from agriculture to industry. The same cause also probably rendered them less obedient to parental discipline, especially when it was exercised tactlessly by uneducated parents, and thus the youths became less inclined to adopt the parental occupation. *Fourth*, there were the attractions which Russia offered to foreign capital through her vast resources, coupled with a supply of labour, ample and low in price for the reasons which have been explained. This capital was largely supplied by French and Belgian investors. Some of these had been previously investing heavily in the United States, but they had suffered in the crisis in that country in 1873, they suffered again heavily in the crisis of 1893, and they were, therefore, disposed to look for other fields for investment. On the whole. Russia offered the most favourable field at that time.

These causes, the first two relating to the supply of labour, the third to the education of the labourer, and the fourth to the equally necessary supply of capital, seem to account for the possibility of an industrial movement of magnitude in Russia, although they do not account for the oscillations of that movement. These causes might not, however, have been operative but for a *fifth*, which gave all of them opportunity for action. This cause was the development of the Russian railway system.[1]

The conditions out of which the first three causes mentioned arose are considered elsewhere; the fourth cause of the expansion of Russian industry may be illustrated briefly. Foreign capital and foreign management had played a considerable rôle in Russian industry since the time of Peter the Great, but they became highly important in the forties of the nineteenth century.[2]

The establishment of the cotton-spinning and weaving factory industry in Russia owes its beginning to a German immigrant, Ludwig Knoop, who was a clerk in a Manchester house. He persuaded his employers to give him an agency for the sale of cotton-manufacturing machinery in Russia. By dexterous financial and diplomatic management, he succeeded in establishing a large number of cotton-spinning and weaving mills and factories; in fact, nearly all of the cotton mills in Central Russia were founded by Knoop.[3] The great mill of Krengolmsk (Kränholm), near Narva, which he established, had more than 400,000 spindles, and it was regarded as the largest cotton-spinning mill in the world.[4] Knoop took many English managers from Lancashire, who reproduced " a corner of England on Russian soil."[5] The firm of Knoop became enormously influential, not only with the Government, but also with the banking and financial houses. For a time it practically controlled the cotton-factory industry of Russia.

> " No church without a pop
> No mill without a Knop."[6]

Knoop's method of procedure was as follows : When a manufac-

---

[1] Professor Tugan-Baranovsky (*op. cit.*, p. 365) regards this as the main cause. Unless, however, the other causes mentioned above, or causes making in a similar direction, had been previously in action, the building of railways could not of itself have created any but temporary expansion.

[2] There are at present living in Russia, several English and Scotch families whose ancestors went to Russia to engage in industrial enterprises in the middle of the eighteenth century, and many whose grandfathers or fathers went at subsequent periods. For early English settlers in Russia, see Gamela, I., *English in Russia in the Sixteenth and Seventeenth Centuries*, (St. Petersburg, 1865).

[3] For accounts of Knoop, see *The Firm of Knoop and its Meaning* (St. Petersburg, 1895), and Schulze-Gävernitz, G. von, *Volkswirtschaftliche Studien aus Russland* (Leipzig, 1899), pp. 91 *et seq.* Knoop died in 1894.

[4] *Ibid.*, p. 97. [5] *Ibid.*

[6] A popular couplet of the " forties." *Ibid.*, p. 92.

turer desired to build a factory, he was obliged to call reverentially at Knoop's office and inquire whether the officials would receive his name and would consider the expediency of permitting him to engage in his proposed enterprise. The officials thereupon made independent inquiries as to the standing of the applicant, whether he or his wife had any capital, and in what form it existed. If he were already in business, it was necessary to know if he had been successful, whether or not he was indebted to the firm, or otherwise, and the like. Should these inquiries result in a satisfactory report, the manufacturer was required to repeat his visit. He then met, probably after several preliminary calls, the mighty Baron Romanovich, the superintendent of the office, by whom he was informed loftily, "Well! We shall build a factory for thee." Sometimes a manufacturer ventured to remark that he had heard of some improvement which he would like to have adopted in the factory which was to be built for him, and for which, of course, he was to be responsible; but he was always told severely, "That is not your affair; in England they know better than you."

The manufacturer was entered by a number on the office lists, and the firm (of Jersey) in Manchester was ordered to supply a factory for this number. Detailed drawings for the factory buildings were then sent out from England, and these were sent down to the factory site, provided English managers were in charge; if such were not the case, the office of Knoop appointed an English manager to look after the erection of the factory. When the buildings were completed, a full installation of machinery came out from England, together with English workmen to erect it. The workmen so sent out were independent both of the office of Knoop, and of the owner of the factory. They were in correspondence with the firm in England by whom they had been sent out (the firm of Jersey acting only as agents).[1]

In addition to the factories which it financed and in which it retained shares, sometimes to a large extent, the firm of Knoop had also mills and weaving factories in its own exclusive possession, the largest of which, near Narva on the Baltic, has already been mentioned.

During recent years a very large number of French, Belgian,

[1] *The Firm of Knoop and its Meaning* (St. Petersburg, 1895), pp. 35, 36, and 39; cited by Tugan-Baranovsky, p. 371.

and some American enterprises have been established. Probably the largest individual establishments in Russia were in the hands of English and French capitalists. Examples of the former were the woollen mills of the Thorntons on the Neva, and of the latter were the Nobel works at Baku, largely financed by English and French capital. The Krivoy Rog iron ores on the Dnieper, and the coal of the Don basin, were both exploited by foreign capital and by foreign (the latter by English) [1] management.

Schulze-Gävernitz concludes his very interesting account of Knoop by what Tugan-Baranovsky calls facetiously " a dithyramb," in which he says that the emergence in these days of men like "Rocke-feller and Knoop, Stumm and John Burns," proves conclusively the fallacy of the pessimistic philosophy of Nietzsche and of the doctrine that the human race is degenerating.[2] Even from the less enthusiastic point of view of Tugan-Baranovsky, the rôle of Knoop in " Europeanizing " the crude capitalism of the Russia of his time was extremely important. He thinks, moreover, that the same process may with advantage be carried yet farther. " The more energetically international capital flows to Russia, the sooner will cease the present condition of excess of demand over supply of the products of capitalistic industry. The Russian market is not yet sufficiently used by capitalism, and therefore there is no reason to fear that chronic over-production which at one time appeared as a threatening monster upon the Western European horizon." [3]

The growth of Russian capital sufficient to check the flow of foreign investments can only begin when Russia recovers from the disease which Rosa Luxembourg called " hypertrophy of profit." [4]

It might also be held that in Russia the market is more compact than it is in the West. The small area and the isolation of England compels her to seek for her markets in Asia, in Africa, in America, and elsewhere at a great distance from her shores. In Russia there is an immense population within a strictly continuous land area ; and, given means of communication, there ought to be an immense interior market. In England the opening of a new line of railway

---

[1] The pioneer in the iron industry in Southern Russia was Mr. J. Hughes, an Englishman. See Tugan-Baranovsky, p. 372, and Schulze-Gävernitz, op. cit., p. 298.

[2] Schulze-Gävernitz, op. cit., pp. 100–101.

[3] Tugan-Baranovsky, op. cit., p. 373.   [4] Quoted by ibid.

brings into the mercantile circle a comparatively small number of additional persons. In Russia the opening of a new line of communication brings into relation an enormous number of persons, and opens up at once new markets. In America the railway is usually in advance of population ; in Russia the railway drags behind population, and when it comes, it at once gives a fresh direction to previously latent productive powers.

It is to be remarked that Professor Tugan-Baranovsky rejects the suggestion that the protective tariff was an important general cause of the growth of Russian industry. For this reason the discussion of it as a doubtful *sixth* cause of the sudden expansion of Russian trade has been relegated to this place. In the first instance, those cases in which its influence is admitted by Professor Tugan-Baranovsky may be considered. Chief among these he places the rapid growth of the iron trade following upon the increase of the customs duties upon iron in 1887. Up till that date the development of iron manufacture was weak. Under the tariff of 1868 iron was charged a small duty of 5 kopeks per *pùd*, but a large quantity of imported iron entered Russia without duty, since the railways were permitted to import duty free all iron required for railway, and even for some other purposes. From 1881 these exemptions were abolished, and the duties upon iron gradually increased. In 1887 these duties were 25 kopeks, and in 1891 30 kopeks in gold per *pùd* at the sea board ; and 35 kopeks per *pùd* on the western land frontier.[1] The sharp increase in iron-smelting in the Russian furnaces which began in 1887 was undoubtedly connected with the increase in customs duties. So also in respect to coal.[2] The duties upon foreign coal were advanced in 1886 and in 1887, and the production of Russian coal was increased considerably, although the price was advanced[3] and the state of trade was depressed.

In reference to the development of the iron trade in Russia, Professor Tugan-Baranovsky remarks that in such a complicated question as the connection between the tariff system and the condition of industry, it must first of all be recognized that *post hoc* is not *propter hoc*. He points out that iron-smelting was practised in Russia on a large scale in early times,[4] and that from the begin-

[1] *Cf.* Tugan-Baranovsky, pp. 363–4. [2] *Ibid.*, p. 364.
[3] Cf. *supra*, p. 375. [4] Cf. *supra*, vol. i. p. 434 *et seq.*

ning it was above all other industries supported and encouraged by the Government. Prior to Emancipation, the importation of iron was prohibited, and the Government expended enormous sums in maintaining ironworks in private hands. Nevertheless this industry was in a state of complete stagnation until the Emancipation of the peasants. The protective policy, he argues, not only did not develop, but rather killed, the Russian iron industry. It led to the increase of the price of iron and to the complete stagnation of technical effort.[1] During the period between the liberation of the peasants and the imposition of a protective tariff, while there was no material impediment to importation, the production of iron developed, although very slowly. In this slow development the Russian protectionists thought they recognized the influence of the absence of protection through the customs. They thought that if Russia had not yielded to the representations of liberal free-traders, she should have become a second America. Professor Tugan-Baranovsky argues, however, that the free importation of iron for railways had enabled the network of lines to be constructed which was, he thinks, by far the most important cause of the development of Russian industry.[2] Moreover, he believes that further growth in Russian manufactures in general must depend upon the relatively low price of iron. Only by cheap iron and by cheap coal can capitalistic industry be stimulated. The price of iron fell somewhat in the nineties, and the southern iron manufacturers began to speak of over-production and the necessity of some action by the Government in the direction of standardizing iron after the manner of the sugar industry, and of giving premiums upon exports. He considers that either of these measures must be injurious to industry in general, and that an essential condition of prosperous manufacturing is competition in raw materials, so that they may be obtained at a price so low that demand is stimulated. Moreover, the Government is the largest user of iron, and the general interests of the State thus demand that it should be supplied without adventitious additions to the price.[3]

[1] It may be observed in this connection that, in spite of the magnitude of the steel trade in the United States, the important improvements in the manufacture have not been American, but have been English, German, or French. Witness, e.g., the Thomas, Siemens-Martin, and Bessemer processes. This is due, no doubt, to a series of complicated causes other than protection.

[2] Tugan-Baranovsky, p. 365.

[3] Cf. ibid., p. 373.

In regard to cotton manufacture, Professor Tugan-Baranovsky points out that while the increase of the customs duty upon raw cotton increased the cultivation of cotton in Russian Middle Asia it could only impede the development of cotton-spinning and weaving. Similarly the increase of the duty upon cotton yarn constricted the weaving industry.

The special interest in the study of the effect of customs duties in Russia lies in the fact that the reactions of these may be observed in relation to a lower scale of general prices than in any other country with so high a customs tariff. It may be observed also that, owing to historical causes, an account of which has been attempted in preceding chapters, the effective demand of the Russian people is so slender, notwithstanding the enormous population, that the productive powers of a comparatively small proportion of that population, when efficiently directed, easily outruns this demand. Thus on the principle of domestic commercial exchange of product for product, there must be inevitably great over-production on one hand, and great want on the other, at frequent intervals. That the idea of communism as a final solution of the *impasse* should so frequently arise in Russian speculation is, therefore, not surprising. On the other hand, Marxism and all that it implies has taken so formidable a hold of so many Russian economists that it seems necessary at this stage to notice the view of the capitalistic process which was held by Professor Tugan-Baranovsky while he was still a convinced Marxist. According to the theory promulgated in his *Commercial Crises*,[1] capitalistic production creates for itself a market. The sole condition which is necessary for the creation of a new market is the justly proportional division of products. It is true, he says, that this condition constitutes an important obstacle to the growth of capitalistic production, because complete equilibrium of production is impossible within the limits of capitalistic production, and the attainment of that approximate equilibrium which is required in order to avoid the complete arrest of capitalistic production involves many hardships. In one case, however, these hardships

---

[1] Tugan-Baranovsky, M. *Commercial Crises in Contemporary England.* St. Petersburg (*c.* 1896).

are much diminished. This case occurs when the capitalistic growth takes place in an atmosphere of natural economy. Let us imagine, for example, he says, that the whole social production consists of two branches only—the production of cloth, and the production of bread. If the products of each are designed exclusively for exchange, in that case the equality of demand and supply—that is to say, the stability of their prices—is possible only if the quantities of the products are strictly proportional. In other words, the prices do not vary, if the exact quantity of cloth is produced which is wanted by the persons who produce a specific and unvarying quantity of bread. If the amount of cloth which is produced is doubled, in order to maintain the equilibrium of prices, the quantity of bread must be doubled also. If, however, there is no correspondent increase in the quantity of bread, the phenomenon of over-production of cloth would at once make its appearance, and the price of cloth in terms of bread would be diminished. Since under existing conditions there is no necessary accordance between those who produce cloth and those who produce bread, and since neither can control the production of their respective goods, there is no foundation for the belief that the increase of the production of cloth would lead to the increase in the production of bread. It is true that price regulates capitalistic production, and establishes eventually a certain rough proportion in capitalistic economics ; but price is an imperfect regulator, and equilibrium is often reached only through the limitation of production. The disorganization of production which thus results is a direct drag upon its growth. If we suppose that cloth is subject to capitalistic production and bread to production under " natural economy," in such a case the growth of the production of cloth does not require a corresponding growth in the preparation of agricultural products. In order that, under these circumstances, the sale or exchange of cloth should be increased, it is necessary that agriculture should exchange a greater proportion than formerly of its bread for cloth. This necessity, continues Professor Tugan-Baranovsky, may arise from various reasons. For example, the industry of the home, which usually furnishes dress or the materials for dress, may decline. Yet the quantity of cloth may increase even although the total sum of agricultural production may diminish. The two forces, the possibility of the increase of the exchange of goods, notwithstanding there being on one side a stationary or even declining production, and the facility of the enlargement of production by the force of purely natural conditions, constitute the fundamental factors of capitalistic industry in young countries, where natural economy predominates. In old countries, on the other hand, capitalistic industry already predominates, and for that reason the conditions of the market are incomparably more favourable for the growth of capitalistic industry in Russia than in the old capitalistic countries of the West.[1]

In brief, Professor Tugan-Baranovsky's argument seems to be susceptible of expression in the following terms : Interior trade is subject to the law of comparative costs in approximately the same degree as international trade is subject to this law. An impediment introduced into the system will, therefore, produce effects similar to those produced by similar impediments introduced into international exchange. The equilibrium of prices will be disturbed by an alteration in the tariff, and the proportions between the supply of domestic and the supply of foreign products may be altered ; but the eventual equilibrium will be the result of reactions supervening upon the original cause of disturbance. The process of readjustment of the equilibrium of prices is too complicated to justify the statement that the tariff by itself determines prices. If the tariff does not exercise an exclusive influence over prices, it cannot do so over either demand or supply, therefore it cannot do so over trade. In proportion, however, as its influence predominates, and it may, sometimes, over prices, it exercises an influence over trade in general, acting through those forces which determine prices and trade at all times.[2]

From the details which have been given above, it is evident that the great growth of Russian industry was very recent and that it was very fluctuating. It is also observable that it was to a large extent exotic. The explanations of these important facts imply previous examination of the Russian character as it has emerged from the past history of the Russian people. Attachment to the land and reluctance to engage in mechanical occupations seem to be still deeply rooted, although the abolition of bondage right modified both to a great extent.

[1] Tugan-Baranovsky, p. 368.
[2] Cf. *ibid.*, pp. 366 and 367.

In the early nineties, critics of factory enterprise who leaned to what they regarded as the characteristic form of Russian industry— *e.g.* " V.V." (Vasili Vorontsev) ; Nikolaï-On (Nicholas Danielson), Nicholas Karisheff, and N. Khablukov [1] developed the thesis that, as industrial development in Russia increased, the numbers of persons engaged in it, in proportion to the total number of the population, must diminish. Khablukov even asserted that this number must diminish absolutely as well as relatively.[2] The theory upon which this thesis was based was simply that machinery replaced human labour and that the universal adoption of machinery would enable labour to be wholly dispensed with. " If shuttles could throw themselves, there would be no use for slaves."

The polemics of these writers were, however, supported by statistics which did not bear the test of examination. In his counter-blast, Professor Tugan-Baranovsky was easily able to show that both relatively and absolutely there was a great increase. The following are his statistics, supplemented by the corresponding figures for 1900, and by the numbers of factories, &c.

	No. of Establishments.	Total Number of Miners and Factory Workers.	Total Number of Persons Employed on the Railways.	Total.
1887	...	1,318,048	218,077	1,536,125 [3]
1897	39,029	2,098,262 [4]	414,152	2,512,414
1900	38,141	2,373,419 [5]	450,000 [6]	2,823,419

These figures represent an increase of 64 per cent. between 1887 and 1897, while the increase of population was not greater during the decennial period than 15 per cent. But these few categories, although the numbers are large, do not exhaust the numbers of workmen engaged in or connected with mechanical industry. Pro-

[1] All of the *Narodněk* group.   [2] *Cf.* Tugan-Baranovsky, p. 374.
[3] *Ibid.*, p. 375.
[4] *Statistical Return of Factories and Works, &c., Ministry of Finance, Dept. of Industry, for* 1900.   Compiled by V. E. Varzar (St. Petersburg, 1903), p. ix.
[5] *Ibid.*, p. xi.   [6] Estimated.

fessor Tugan-Baranovsky considers that it would be legitimate to add one million to the totals for 1897 on this account, and a somewhat smaller figure to the total for 1887. Not less significant is the concentration of factories which went on in Russia. What are known in America as " mergers " were formed vigorously immediately after Emancipation in 1861; and the same process went on afterwards with varying vigour.

The relative statistics of 1897 and 1900 would seem to indicate a considerable amount of concentration, since the number of workmen employed increased while the number of factories diminished; but whether or not there was any concentration during this period cannot be ascertained from the figures in the table, because they are not strictly comparable. In the collection of the statistics for 1897, all factories which had an annual output of the value of 1000 rubles were included. There were in this number many very small shops, even *kustarni* workshops, while in the figures for 1900, these were all excluded, and only those factories which were under the jurisdiction of the factory inspectors were taken into account. Such factories were not segregated upon any definite principle, but in general had ten as a minimum number of employees, and 5000 rubles as a minimum value of their annual production.[1]

It is thus necessary to examine the categories of which the gross figures are composed, in order to ascertain the extent to which concentration went on. This need not be attempted for recent years, in this place, but a few particulars regarding certain trades and for certain periods may usefully be given. In the cotton factories, the number of workmen employed in the large establishments increased by 300 per cent. between 1866 and 1894, while the number of such factories increased by only 50 per cent. At the same time the number of working men in small factories increased by about 16 per cent., and the number of factories diminished about 6 per cent., while the number of working men in factories of intermediate size increased more than 250 per cent., and the number of factories by 200 per cent. The tendency towards intermediate and large factories is unmistakable.[2]

The concentration of commercial capital had, as we have seen, antedated in Russia the concentration of industrial capital. This

---

[1] Cf. *Statistical Return*, &c., p. ix.
[2] *Cf.* Tugan-Baranovsky, p. 377.

process of concentration in commerce proceeded rapidly. The circulation of great commercial firms formed, in 1886, 47 per cent. of the total circulation of the firms enrolled in the merchants' guilds; in 1888, this figure was 55 per cent. The firms which did more than one-half of the business carried on by the members of the guilds as a whole did not form more than one-half per cent. of the membership.

CHAPTER II

WAGES

During the first year after Emancipation, 1861-1862, in spite of the great increase in the supply of labour which that event produced, wages rose. The reason for this appears to have been that there was a tendency for the workmen who had been bonded to a factory to leave it in order to return to their villages. Some of these workmen had saved money during their employment in the factories, and returned to their villages to engage in light agricultural labour ; others returned to the villages with a knowledge of a craft and with the intention of exercising it in *kustarni* industry.[1] The peasants of the industrial regions had smaller land allotments than those of the regions where there was no industry, consequently, returning peasant workmen had to take into account the necessity of making their living otherwise than by cultivation exclusively. The cities and industrial towns were thus temporarily partially denuded of their industrial population. Within a few years the stream turned back towards the factories, and wages fell.[2] Meanwhile, however, the urban prices of food and clothing had advanced, so that when the stream of workmen set in for the factory again, real wages had fallen, and, moreover, the machine had, to a large extent, taken their places. The situation is well described by Garelēn, who was a large manufacturer in the village of Ivanovo.

" The beautiful times of high wages for the Ivanovo working men were concluded by the introduction of machinery. So long as there was no machinery, or only a few rare and new machines, it can be said that the working men ruled the factory. It depended upon himself—if he worked well he could receive large wages and he could, at the same time, yield the owner large profits. If he were

---

[1] Golubev, A., *Historico-Statistical Review of Industry in Russia : The Weaving and Spinning of Cotton*, p. 98 ; cited by Tugan-Baranovsky, p. 143.
[2] *Ibid.*

offended at the owner he might spoil his goods, and, without any disadvantage to himself, he could go over to a competitor and perhaps contribute to give an advantage to the latter over his previous employer. . . . In a word, the owner was dependent upon the workman. But the machine made its appearance, and gradually took possession of the whole affair. The workman could rule no more, but became dependent upon the soulless machine. A new epoch in the life of the workman then began." [1]

According to Garelēn, wages in all branches of labour were higher in the beginning of the eighties than in the fifties by from 15 to 50 per cent. On the other hand, the price of rye flour in Ivanovo advanced during the same period 100 per cent., butter 83 per cent., and beef 220 per cent. In 1858 the weavers made from 10 to 16 rubles per month ; in 1882–1883 the same weaver made from 12 to 18 rubles per month. That is to say, while wages increased about 20 per cent., bread doubled in price.[2] The period of the early eighties was, as we have seen, a period of industrial stagnation. In the Moscow district the industrial crisis resulted in a return of many peasant workmen to the land. In the later half of the eighties the stream poured back to the factory.

The existence of a great labour reservoir in the land undoubtedly gave the workman a great advantage, but the extent to which he could make real use of it depended upon the extent to which he kept in touch with agricultural labour, and at the same time kept in touch with his craft, whatever it was. It was possible for him to do this when he could go annually in the summer to his village and return annually to the factory in the winter. So long as the operations of the factory were conducted exclusively by hand labour, and so long as there was an insignificant amount of capital employed in the enterprise, it was not inconvenient for the factory to arrange its management in accordance with these conditions. It was possible, and even advantageous, to work in winter, when wages were relatively low, and to close down in summer, when, owing to the demand for outdoor labour, wages were relatively high. But when expensive machinery was installed, the case was altogether different. In order to justify its installation, the machine

[1] Golubev, A., *Historico-Statistical Review of Industry in Russia : The Weaving and Spinning of Cotton*, p. 432.
[2] *Ibid.*, p. 433.

had to be kept at work continuously, and in order to obtain the best results, the workman had to work continuously. The machine thus acted as a separator between the workman and his land. The change came about gradually, but in the cotton-weaving trade especially it came about effectively.[1]

From inquiries made in 1884–1885 by Dementiev, at the instance of the Zemstvo of Moskovskaya *gub.*, it appears that in the three districts of Serpukhov, Kolomna, and Bronnits, only 14.1 per cent. of all workmen at that time left the factory periodically for field work. The proportion varied in different forms and kinds of factory industry. For example, among the hand-loom cotton-weavers, only 18 per cent. worked in the factory all the year round, the smaller factories ceasing work altogether in the summer ; while in the steam-power spinning and weaving factories from 93 to 96 per cent. of the workers worked all the year round, and so did the factories. The silk-weavers who worked altogether by hand customarily went to their villages in the summer. The leather and sheep-skin furriers left the factories for the villages to the extent of 53.7 per cent. of the workers ; and in the crockery factories about one-half. In the woollen cloth factories, the hand-loom weavers left the factory for the field to the extent of 37 per cent., while of the weavers who work self-acting looms, " no one went away " for field work. In dyeing and chintz-printing factories, the hand workers went away to the extent of 36 per cent., while the machine workers went away to the extent of only 8 per cent. Among factory artisans, moulders, painters, roofers, plumbers, &c., only 3.3 per cent. went away for field work in the summer. The conclusions which Dementiev draws from these data and others of a similar character are that in those factories where mechanical power is employed, there is found the alienation of the workman from the land, and that this alienation varies with the specialization of industry.[2]

While there were natural economic causes for this phenomenon of alienation from the land, these were sometimes reinforced by

[1] Yet up till 1899 the workmen of even the largest cotton mills went to the villages in the summer, and sometimes even at other times when they had fits of nostalgia. (From information from mill managers received by the writer in Russia in 1899.)

[2] Dementiev, *The Factory, What it gives the Inhabitants and what it takes away from them* (Moscow, 1897), pp. 1–11 and p. 26.

interior factory regulations. It was clearly in the interests of factory management to have workmen who could be relied upon for constant labour or, at all events, for labour when the exigencies of the factory, and not the exigencies of the field, were in question. It was also to the interests of the factory industry that there should be created a group of factory operatives who would be economically dependent upon the factory alone for their employment, and who would not be able to withdraw themselves from it whenever they chose to do so. Thus at many factories the working man who left the factory during summer-time was subjected to a heavy fine, sometimes reaching a month's wages or more.

Prior to the issue of the law respecting the hiring of working men of 3rd June 1886, the customary contract between the workmen and their employers divided the year into two periods—usually 1st October till Easter, and Easter till 1st October. During the former period, the workman might, on giving proper notice, leave the factory at any time before Easter ; but during the latter period the right of the workman to leave the factory was not recognized anywhere. If he left he was liable to reduction in his wages. For example, in the cotton factory of Konshin at Serpukhov, a workman who desired to leave in the winter-time was obliged to give ten days' notice, otherwise he was fined twelve days' pay. Those who went away after Easter were fined twelve days' pay whether they gave notice or not. In the print works of the same company the fine for leaving in the summer was one month's wages.[1]

As for those peasant workmen who oscillated between the factory and the field, it is not surprising to learn that they were looked upon by their fellow-workmen in the factory as peasants, and by their fellow-peasants in the village as factory workers. They thus occupied an anomalous social position. It is true that they had the legal right to possess land, but frequently they had allowed the right to possess particular pieces of land to pass from them ; they had often no economical relations with the village, for in those cases in which they had transferred their families to the town, they had sold their houses, and in those cases in which they were unencumbered they had had no houses to sell. In either case they were looked upon as strangers by the village population.

[1] Dementiev, p. 38.

Such peasant workmen had, therefore, a tendency to abandon the village altogether, even although they might continue to be responsible for, and even to pay, their taxes as nominal village inhabitants, and even although they held passports from the village authorities and changed that passport periodically. But, as we have seen, the great majority of the factory hands had in the last two decades of the nineteenth century formed a class quite separate from the peasantry in all essential relations—a real proletariat already even beginning to appear in its third generation.[1]

Out of 18,576 working men catechized by Dementiev, 55 per cent. were the sons of factory workers—that is to say, of workers who habitually worked in the factory, and who did not supplement their factory wages by *kustarni* industry or by any other occupation. The greater proportion of these, or 70 per cent., were employed in the textile trades, and the smaller proportion, 15 per cent., were general labourers—that is to say, the mechanical employments exhibited a tendency to recruit from a hereditary class of factory workers, while the hand occupations drew from the villages.[2]

So also from an examination of the factory workers of Moskovskaya *gub.*, Professor Erisman found that only 9 per cent. of the workers entered the factory after they reached twenty-five years of age, while 63 per cent., or nearly two-thirds, entered under the age of sixteen years.

The investigations of Dementiev were made in 1884–1885, and it is clear that even at that period Russia had already gone far in adopting the capitalistic factory system, in detaching her people from the land, and in creating a proletariat class similar in its constitution, if dissimilar in respect to education, to the proletariat of Western Europe. Afterwards Russia went farther in the same direction. If in 1884–85 only about one-fifth of the factory workers retained even a nominal connection with the land, it is certain that those who did so on the eve of the Revolution formed an insignificant fraction of the total of factory workers.

It has been remarked, however, that even after the factory workers ceased to go to their villages for the purpose of engaging in periodical field labour, they continued to pay their taxes as village inhabitants, and thus it may now be observed they retained a certain relation to the economy of the village. This relation

[1] Cf. Dementiev, p. 46.   [2] *Ibid.*

was, no doubt, amplified by the subsidies of money which they sent to their relatives, and sometimes also by retiral to the village in declining years with their small savings. Living in the village was cheaper, and for them also, no doubt, more pleasant than living in the town. In this connection, an investigator remarks that " the return for field work is not a sufficient criterion of the degree of the solidity of the connection between the factory workman and the land. This connection might be expressed, and is really expressed, in different ways, by sending money to the village, by maintaining families there, and finally by returning to the village during temporary unemployment, or during sickness or old age." [1] Thus although owing to the development of machinery and the effect of this development upon factory conditions, the connection of the workman with the land has become feeble, it is nevertheless even now greater in Russia than it is in any other country.[2] The reason why this connection has survived lies in the low wages of the Russian workman. If the agriculture of the peasant was ineconomical because he was obliged to supplement it with industry, the industry of the factory worker was ineconomical because he was able to supplement it with agriculture. Yet the very facts that the peasant was able to do the one and the workman the other, contributed to the depression of the earnings of each from his appropriate occupation, and probably contributed also to the diminution of his total efficiency. Thus the connection with the land is at once the cause and the consequence of inferior wages, and is also one of the causes of the inferior productivity of Russian labour. The maintenance of two economies, one in the village for his family, and one, however meagre, in the town for himself, involves inevitably some waste. Moreover, the moral effects of this separation are not to be ignored. Apart from its injurious influence upon sexual morals, the weakening of the family tie, and its reduction to a merely economical bond contribute to retard the development of the working man and to depress his moral dignity. From the side of the factory and from the side of the village, he finds

---

[1] *Collection of Statistical Reports* (Moscow), Sanitary Part iv., part i. p. 289; cited by Tugan-Baranovsky, p. 447.

[2] It is, however, very great in Japan, and for the same reason, viz. that it is not practicable within any short period to convert farmers into skilled artisans.

himself looked upon as a working animal from whom, on the one hand, as much work and, on the other hand, as much money as may be, must be procured.[1] Professor Tugan-Baranovsky goes so far as to say, "Complete rupture between the factory and the village is inevitable, and the sooner it occurs the better."[2]

Schulze-Gävernitz has thrown the process of the separation of the proletarian factory worker from the land into the following schematic form. In the *first* phase of the process, the connection between the factory and the land is intimate. The factory workmen, especially those belonging to small factories, have no separate sleeping-places; they sleep anywhere in or near the places where they work, and food is brought to them from home. This contingent of workmen is composed of the peasants of factories near the village. Such are in the fullest sense of the word *mujìki*, cultivators who go to the factory because to go is an economical necessity, although the factory is repugnant to them, and who leave it whenever they can. In the *second* phase, the connection with the factory is more intimate, and that with the land weaker. The working men live in factory barracks, they eat in messes, and it often happens that they go away for field work. Their families remain in the village. In the *third* phase, family life makes its appearance at the factory, the working men become segregated from the peasants, they organize messes at which they may feed together along with their wives and families, bedrooms make their appearance. Yet the connection with the land is not dropped completely—the workmen send money to the village, and they have there their economical interests; sometimes they go to the village, or sometimes they send their children. Finally, in the *fourth* phase, the working man is a full proletarian who lives continuously at the factory, in a hired house, or in a factory chamber with his family. All these four phases exist simultaneously in various factories and branches of industry, and the larger the factory and

[1] On the above points, compare the instructive observations of Tugan-Baranovsky, p. 449.
[2] *Ibid.* It is to be remarked, however, that when Professor Tugan-Baranovsky wrote the first edition of his book on the Russian factory system, he was an ardent Marxist. His views on general questions have altered since 1897; but his view of the factory-village question, so far as the writer is aware, has not altered.

the greater the rôle of the machine, the nearer it comes to the fourth phase.[1]

According to Professor Tugan-Baranovsky, until very recent times Russia has been passing through the *third* phase; and although the preceding decade had seen great changes in industrial life, it is possible that Russian industry is not yet wholly in the *fourth* phase. The affair, he remarks, is in a vicious circle. The connection of the factory with the land cannot be broken, and the workman and his family cannot be brought together without an advance of wages, and an advance of wages cannot be brought about without the rupture of connection with the land. The contradiction can alone be solved by further industrial development.[2]

[1] Schulze-Gävernitz, G. von, *Volkswirtschaftliche Studien aus Russland* (Leipzig, 1899), pp. 146–164; cited by Tugan-Baranovsky, p. 447.

[2] Tugan-Baranovsky, p. 449. The contradiction was, however, at least temporarily solved in another manner by the Revolution. See *infra*.

CHAPTER III

THE HOUSING OF THE WORKING PEOPLE

THE first general census of the Russian Empire, which was taken on 28th January 1897, showed that the city population, especially in the capitals, had increased greatly during the preceding thirty-three years. The population of St. Petersburg in 1864 was about 540,000 ; in 1897 it was 1,330,000. In the suburbs there were, in addition, in 1889, 80,000, and in 1897, 134,000. The greater part of this increase appears to have been in the later years. In 1890, out of 142,523 lodgings (that is, *apartements*) in St. Petersburg, 7374 were underground. This condition is still more unfavourably revealed in Moscow, where, in 1882, there were 7253 underground lodgings out of 89,765 lodgings altogether, or about 5 per cent. and 8 per cent. respectively. In these vaults or underground lodgings in St. Petersburg there lived in 1890, 49,669 persons ; while in Moscow there lived in 1882, under the same conditions, 58,850 persons, or nearly seven and more than eight per lodging respectively. The predominant type of house in St. Petersburg is a two-storey dwelling. Such dwellings form 42 per cent. of the total ; one storey 19 per cent. ; three storeys 21 per cent. ; four storeys 14 per cent., and five storeys or more 4 per cent.[1] The buildings are frequently arranged in courts. In each court there are, on the average, sixteen lodgings, with 107 inhabitants. Where the dwellings are isolated, in each dwelling or tenement there are on the average eight lodgings, and in each lodging five inhabitants.

[1] Jarotsky, V., " The Housing Question," in *Brockhaus and Ephron's Encyclopædia*, ed. completed 1904, vol. xiv. p. 853.

The inferior lodgings in St. Petersburg may be enumerated as follows, according to the St. Petersburg census of 1890 :

1. Underground lodgings 7,374
   Number of rooms in these 12,217
   Number of inhabitants 49,569
2. Lodgings in garrets 3,499
   Number of rooms in these . . . 5,813
   Number of inhabitants 21,804
3. Percentage of total number of lodgings in St.
   Petersburg with windows in the courtyard . . 55.3 per cent.
   Percentage of houses of 1 room having windows in
   the courtyard . . . . 70.8 „
   Percentage of houses of 2 rooms having windows in
   the courtyard . . . . 68.7 „
   Percentage of houses of 3–5 rooms having windows
   in the courtyard . . . . 50 „
   Percentage of houses of 7–10 rooms having windows
   in the courtyard . . . . 14.8 „
   Percentage of houses of 11 rooms and over having
   windows in the courtyard . . . . . 6.3 „

Only 48 per cent. of the lodgings in St. Petersburg have separate kitchens, and 14 per cent. are kitchens only. The average lodging in St. Petersburg accommodated in 1890 seven persons ; but in the vaults the people were crowded together in the proportion of four to one room. Sanitary conveniences exist in less than one-half of the St. Petersburg lodgings, and baths in only 10 per cent. The average rents in 1890 were, for underground lodgings, 125 rubles per year ; for first floor, 263 rubles ; second floor, 375 rubles ; third floor, 463 rubles ; fourth, 450 rubles ; fifth and sixth floors, 380 rubles ; garrets, 112 rubles.

The poorest people at this time paid, on the average, 112 rubles a year.[1] The official sanitary reports of 1897 reveal a seriously insanitary condition. Dr. Pokrovsky, who described the housing conditions of St. Petersburg at this time, says that in many working men's lodgings there are less than 86 cubic feet of air space per person. The police reports are to a similar effect. The underground rooms are sometimes divided by small cages for the inhabitants of the corners, there being a stove in the middle of the room. It must be realized that St. Petersburg is built upon a swamp—it is impossible to conceive of a city where underground dwellings are

---

[1] That is to say, about 4s. 4d. per week per lodging.

less desirable. The building regulations of the city forbid the erection of such buildings in places liable to inundation ; but these regulations are habitually disregarded. The overflowing of the waters of the Neva in 1895, resulted in the flooding of great numbers of St. Petersburg workmen's cellars. In the construction of houses little care is taken to avoid sewers and cesspools whose contents during inundations flow into living cellars, and as well into those in which food products are stored. These, when dried out, are sold. Thus on all sides there are more or less ample facilities for the spreading of epidemics. The overcrowding of these cellars, which is at once a cause and a consequence of high rents, and the scarcity of house accommodation, produced between 1899 and 1901 a lodging crisis in St. Petersburg.

In Moscow the situation was, in some respects, worse. There the practice of migration from village to town, and from town to village, lingered much longer than in St. Petersburg. The peasant is accustomed to overcrowding in his *ēzba*. Round the single apartment of the *ēzba* there is usually a wide bench, and on this the peasant reclines.[1] In Russia, as everywhere else, when peasants migrate to the town, they continue their practice of huddling together, partly from absence of means to do anything else, and partly from habit, failing to realize that in their native villages there were compensations for the interior unhygienic conditions of the *ēzba* in the fresh and wholesome air surrounding it, in which they customarily spent, at all events in the summer, the greater part of the day. The poorer lodgings of Moscow are more overcrowded than those of St. Petersburg. When the revival of trade of 1894 had been in progress for about a year, the demand for labour in Moscow had brought an influx from the villages, and housing conditions became rapidly worse. An inquiry was instituted in 1895 by the Moscow City Council, and was conducted by Professor M. Duchovskoy. A very detailed investigation was undertaken into the conditions of life in Prechēstensky, one of the quarters of Moscow. The general conclusion of the report is that " the condition of the poorest class of inhabitants in vaults and in corners of rooms in Moscow is most unsatisfactory. These people live in more or less unsupportable hygienic conditions, and often in outrageous moral surroundings." The details are almost in-

---

[1] Sometimes these are expanded into what are really box beds.

credible. The stairs which lead down to the dens which the people inhabit are covered with all kinds of filth ; the dens themselves are almost filled with dirty boards, upon which there is equally foul bedding, and in the corners there is only dirt. The smell is close and heavy. There is hardly any light, because the dens are half underground and little light obtains entrance through the dirty windows. Beneath the windows it is absolutely dark ; the walls are damp and covered with mould.[1] Yet these loathsome habitations realized a handsome profit to their owners.

The case was even worse in those places where the people not only slept, but also worked. The total number of lodgings which formed the subject of investigation was 16,478. In these there lived 180,919 persons, or 17 per cent. of the population of Moscow. Of these 49 per cent. were men, 33.2 per cent. women, and 17.8 per cent. children under fourteen years of age ; or 141,215 adults, and 39,704 children. The investigators add that these children constitute the future candidates for admission to the prisons, and the future applicants for social charity. The poorer among these people cannot afford more than a share of a bed, the richer have a single room in which they sleep along with their family.

In Nijni-Novgorod the conditions were similar, although on a smaller scale.[2] So also in the Little Russian towns, like Chernigov, whose underground dwellings have often been made the subject of investigation. Such dwellings were occupied largely by Jews. Some of these dens were even under buildings belonging to the Government and to ecclesiastical foundations.

It is thus evident from numerous statistical inquiries that up till the year 1900 the conditions of large numbers of the working population of the cities was almost incredibly bad. At the mining villages and at those occupied by ironworkers in the Ural Mountains, the case was no better. The condition of these people was first investigated in 1870 by Dr. Portugalov. Speaking of the gold mines on the river Salda, near Kuvshēnsky, in an article on

---

[1] " Some Data about Moscow Bedroom Lodgings," in *Collection of Articles on Questions relating to the Life of Russian and Foreign Cities* (Moscow, 1899) (reprinted from the Reports of the Moscow City Council, February–September 1899) ; cited by V. V. Svyatlovsky. *Housing Question* (St. Petersburg, 1902), p. 52.

[2] See *Materials for Valuation of Immovable Property in Nijigorodskaya Gub.* (Nijni Novgorod, 1901), i. p. 15 ; cited by Svyatlovsky, *op. cit.*, pp. 81–2.

" Work in the Mines," he says : " The work is carried on in a wooded marshy locality. . . . Many of the workmen are casual labourers, who are housed in temporary erections. These barracks are, in most cases, low, close, and dirty. . . . The men lie in them like herrings in a barrel." [1] Another investigation was made in the same regions in 1892, and very similar conditions were found to exist. " In almost all the mines, the dwelling-places for workmen are clearly the nurseries for all kinds of diseases." . . . " In summer the workmen do not use the covered places, which are infested by vermin ; they sleep out of doors. In winter the barracks are overcrowded to an incredible extent. At nightfall these barracks rapidly fill up with wet and cold men, the fire is re-inforced in the stove, and round it are hung wet clothing, boots, and leg wrappers. The upper strata of air are filled with vapour from the wet garments and from the perspiration of the men. The air is further penetrated with thick tobacco smoke and the heavy odour of petroleum from the lamps. When to all these is added the specific aroma of the Tartar, there is produced an atmosphere so impossible that even a healthy but unaccustomed man can with great difficulty support it for more than a few minutes." [2]

In 1895 another inquiry in the metallurgical works of the Moscow and Middle Volga regions disclosed a state of affairs as insanitary but varying in detail. In these regions separate dwellings for workmen were unusual. In most cases the workmen either find very insanitary accommodation in the villages or they live in so-called *balagani*.[3] A *balagan* is a hole, usually square in shape, and several feet deep, roofed over with a frame of wood covered with turf. A window is occasionally made in the angle of the roof. Even then the window is not glazed. There is a stove in the middle of the hole. Such dwellings are, of course, dark, damp, smoky, and narrow.[4]

In 1892 the district engineer, Jordan, inspected the engineering and rail-rolling mills of Briansk, and reported : " These places

[1] Cited by Svyatlovsky, *op. cit.*, p. 179.
[2] Bertenson, L., *Sanitary-medical Affairs at the Mountain Works and Trades of the Ural* (St. Petersburg, 1892) ; cited by Svyatlovsky, *op. cit.*, p. 180.
[3] Svyatlovsky, *op. cit.*, p. 183.
[4] Galician immigrants frequently house themselves in *balagani* in the north-west of Canada until they earn sufficient money to obtain the materials to build a house.

(where the workmen lived) can only be compared, without exaggeration, to places where cattle are kept ; they do not suggest human dwellings. Even in summer, when the doors and windows are open, the air is stifling ; along the walls and on the sleeping benches traces of mould are to be seen. The floor is invisible because it is covered with dirt." [1]

In Poland the conditions about this period varied. At the Treasury works the conditions were good. Some families live in separate brick houses, others share a house between two families. Some have separate houses built upon their own lots, and in addition to their work at the factory, they cultivate their land. The Strakhovitsky Company give lots without payment to those who have not land of their own. In the Polish towns the overcrowding was excessive, both among the workmen and among the Jewish shopkeepers.[2] Yet the superiority of the intelligence, manners, and habits of the Polish workmen, when compared with those of the Russian workmen, is undoubted. The Polish workman would not tolerate the conditions under which the Russian workmen very customarily live.

The fishermen of Russia form a large group. They are, for the most part, to be found in regions otherwise unpopulated, and although their calling offers certain invigorating compensations, their domestic conditions are, in general, very unhygienic. The bulk of the fishing population inhabit the estuaries of the great rivers. An interesting study of the fishermen of the Volga was made in 1895 by Dr. N. Schmidt.[3] According to him, the form of dwelling used by the greater part of the fishermen is the reed hut. The reed hut is really a portable house, exceedingly cheap, because the material of which it is built can always be obtained on the spot. Each hut serves for the gang of a " draw-net," which consists of from twelve to eighteen persons. The hut is convenient though primitive. It is usually round ; in the centre hangs the kettle, in which all food is prepared, the fire being fed by reeds.

---

[1] Svyatlovsky, op. cit., pp. 184–5.
[2] The writer found in Minsk, in 1899, large numbers of Jewish shops which were only 3 ft. wide extending to the rear for about 40 ft. In the front of these shops the business was done largely in the middle of the narrow street, while the family lived in the narrow interior.
[3] Schmidt, Dr. N., The Hygiene of the Fishing Trade at the Mouth of the Volga (Moscow, 1895) ; cited by V. V. Svyatlovsky, op. cit., pp. 204–5.

The earthen floor is covered with reeds. At night the men sleep with their heads towards the circle, and their feet towards the fire in the centre. Another form of dwelling affected by the Volga fishermen is the " cold-earth hut." A square hole, from two to three feet deep and of an area of from 750 to 1000 square feet, is dug at a distance of about 40 feet from the edge of the water, and in this depression, a turf house is built. Wooden barracks are very rare. The fishermen of the Volga are, in general, well off, but they appear to prefer to live as they do. Those of the Caspian shore and of the Dnieper, the Dniester, and the Murman coast of the White Sea live in a similar manner.

The immense migration of Russian harvesters has already been noticed. Every year upwards of a million peasants move south-wards for the early harvests and northwards for the later. They tramp along the roads and sleep where they can. No provision of any kind is made for them. The few who travel by rail, of course, escape the hardships of travelling hundreds of miles under such con-ditions. Only iron types can survive the exposure to which, especi-ally late in the season, they must be subjected. In the height of the summer the peasants think no more of these industrial pilgrimages than they do of the pilgrimages which in large numbers they cus-tomarily undertake to the holy places at Solovietsky, Sergei Passad, or Kiev. The tramping harvesters are to be found sleeping in the market squares, on the unoccupied banks of rivers, or in the neigh-bourhood of grain elevators or warehouses, where they may hope to find employment. Some sleep anywhere in the open, others carry with them small tents.[1] When the harvesters arrive at the place where they are to be employed, their condition is not improved. According to the results of the investigations of the Sanitary Bureau of the Zemstvo of Samara, " there are no dwellings for temporary labourers anywhere." The labourers are always kept in the field, and even in bad weather they are not allowed to find shelter in the farm buildings.[2] The harvesters customarily hire themselves until 1st October in the south, and towards the north, where the harvests

[1] Varb, E., *The Village of Rovnoë : Hired Agricultural Labourers in Life and Legislation* (Moscow, 1899), p. 156 ; cited by V. V. Svyatlovsky, p. 211. See also Prince N. Shakhovskoy, *Agricultural Work far away from Home* (Moscow, 1896), *e.g.* p. 75.

[2] Svyatlovsky, *ibid.*, p. 214.

are later, until 15th November. The conditions which have been described are barely endurable at any time ; but when the cold weather sets in, which it does, even in the south, early in the autumn, they become intolerable. Even the agricultural labourers permanently employed are inadequately housed. In some places in the Samara region, for example, the men were expected to sleep in " the cattle huts in the backyards, while the women live in cleaner houses, together with the clerks of the estate." [1]

In the cities the cost of shelter for the workmen led in Russia, as elsewhere, to the provision, by charitable means, and sometimes by commercial enterprise, of night refuges, where homeless persons might find lodging at a minimum price. In Russia the formation of Societies for Night Refuges dates from the period immediately succeeding Emancipation, when, as has been narrated in another chapter, there was a stream of peasants from the country to the towns The movement began in Moscow in 1864. It was initiated by the Governor-General of Moscow, who suggested to the City Council that night refuges should be established under proper hygienic conditions, so that honest and poor working men should have " a clean, warm, and harmless shelter." The city government was very apathetic on the subject. It proposed to erect four night refuges, but made no steps to do so. Fifteen years later, when the plague was at hand, steps were taken, and a house was adapted for the purpose of providing a night refuge for about 500 persons. From the beginning this house was excessively overcrowded ; it was sometimes occupied by 700 persons. This refuge was enlarged in the eighties, but it was still always overcrowded, sometimes to the extent of having in it from 10 per cent. to 25 per cent. more than it should have had. There were in addition many night refuges founded by private charity or by private enterprise. These were even more seriously overcrowded. The atmosphere is described as having been so stifling that only persons in a drunken stupor could pass the entire night in these places. Their moral condition is represented as being correspondent to their physical loathsomeness. The Moscow branch of the Russian Technical Society appointed a Commission of Inquiry into the condition of the night refuges. This

[1] *Collection of the Sanitary Bureau of the Zemstov of Samara ;* cited by Svyatlovsky, p. 212.

commission found that the city refuges were quite unsuitable for the purpose to which they were applied, and that the private refuges were worse, the regulations which had been imposed upon them being persistently violated.

In 1881 Dr. N. Dvoryashēn brought before the Ministry of the Interior a project of a " Society of Brotherly Help." The project was not sanctioned, and the author changed it into a project of a " Society of Night Refuge Homes in St. Petersburg." This project was sanctioned on 20th February 1883.[1] In 1884 three night refuges were opened ; one more was added in 1886, and one was closed in 1899. About 500 or 600 people were accommodated in them nightly. The night shelters provided by the city were of about the same dimensions. In St. Petersburg, as elsewhere, the greater number of homeless persons were received in shelters provided by private enterprise. From an examination of all night shelters, &c., made by the St. Petersburg police on the night of 16th November 1900, it appears that there were at that time in St. Petersburg 10,000 homeless people. The places of shelter were all overcrowded ; those which were organized by private enterprise were, as a rule, of better type than the customary lodging of the poorer working men, although they left much to be desired.[2]

In Russia, as in Western Europe, some enlightened employers grappled with the difficult question of housing, and provided accommodation for their workmen. For example, in Moscow, the chintz-printing factories of Emil Zundel erected spacious dwellings of barrack-room type for their bachelor workmen, with separate rooms for workmen with families.[3] On these measures the factories invested a capital of nearly one million rubles. So also the paper factory on the foundation of the Empress Maria organized for its working men suitable houses, with gardens and orchards, at a rent of from 2 to 6½ rubles per month. The Kolomensky Car-building Company built a workmen's settlement. The town is well planned and organized. The Ramenskaya manufac-

[1] *Report of the Society of Night Refuges in St. Petersburg for* 1901 (St. Petersburg, 1902) ; cited by V. V. Svyatlovsky, pp. 234-5.
[2] Svyatlovsky, *op. cit.*, p. 245.
[3] Shestakov, P. M., *Working Men at the Factory of Emil Zundel in Moscow. Statistical Inquiry* (1900), p. 7 ; cited by V. V. Svyatlovsky, p. 245. See also *Manufacturing Company of Emile Zundel*, 1874-1908 (Moscow, 1908).

tory of P. Malyotēn, the Marēēnsky Sugar Refinery at Balasheva, in Kievskaya *gub.*, the Nikolskoë Factories of Morozov, Son, & Co., and the cotton-weaving factory of Morgunov & Co., are a few of the numerous examples of intelligent administration, serious desire to improve the conditions of working men, and of ability to organize an effective plan.[1]

[1] For these and other examples, see V. V. Svyatlovsky, *op. cit.*, pp. 245–75.

CHAPTER IV

FACTORY LEGISLATION

PRIOR to Emancipation the question of child labour in factories began to occupy the attention of the " higher spheres." A special commission appointed by the Governor-General of St. Petersburg in 1859 collected information about child labour in the workshops and factories of St. Petersburg, and elaborated " A Project of Rules for Factories and Workshops in St. Petersburg and in the Districts surrounding the City." The rules set forth in this project forbade the employment of children under twelve years of age, and limited the working day for persons under the age of fourteen to ten hours. No person under sixteen was permitted to work at night. Three of the large St. Petersburg manufacturers were members of this commission, and they are understood to have supported the project. The Moscow and the provincial manufacturers were, however, very hostile. The commission discovered in the course of its inquiries that the St. Petersburg cotton mills, employing 8200 workmen, had in them 616 children of from four to eight years of age. At six of the mills work was continued night and day, at other six work was carried on by day only for fourteen hours, children as well as adults working for this period. The project was submitted to the cotton manufacturers and, as a rule, was approved by them. There were, however, some exceptions. For example, the Khludov Brothers, owners of one of the largest cotton mills in Russia,[1] objected to dispense with child labour because it would be necessary to replace it with the labour of adults. When the same commission issued a protocol recommending a system of factory inspection, the opposition of the manufacturers was much more active. The labours of this commission were followed by those of another appointed by the Ministry of Finance. This commission accepted the principle of excluding children under

---

[1] In Egoryevsky district of Ryazanskaya *gub.*

twelve years of age from the factory wholly, and extended the age limit from sixteen to eighteen in the limitation of working hours.[1] A Government inspectorate of factories was also recommended, as well as the establishment of courts for the settlement of industrial disputes.[2] The commission did not recommend any alteration in the law respecting strikes, which provided a penalty of imprisonment for from three weeks to three months for the leaders and for from one week to three weeks for others ; but it recommended that in case of strikes, the employers should reduce the wages of striking workmen on their return to the factory.[3] The industrial court which was to be established was recommended to be composed of an equal number of working men and of employers,[4] and suggested that it should be entirely independent of the administration. All factories in which hired labour was employed were to be placed under the jurisdiction of the inspectors. This, on the whole, enlightened project of factory legislation was not carried into effect. In 1866 an epidemic of cholera aroused the Government to take steps to enforce the adoption of sanitary measures in the factories by issuing an ukase on 26th August of that year. This ukase was intended as a temporary measure, but as it has not yet been superseded, this ukase remains in force. Under it all factories in which one thousand workmen and upwards are employed are required to build a hospital with ten beds for the first thousand workmen, and five beds each additional thousand. Factories employing less than one thousand were to provide hospital accommodation at the rate of one bed per hundred workpeople. The factories are forbidden to take payment from the workmen for medical assistance, drugs, nursing, or food during sickness. This law was not, however, rigidly carried out. At many of the factories hospital accommodation was merely fictitious. In the absence of proper governmental inspection and organization the law remained in practical abeyance excepting in the case of some of the larger factories. In Moskovskaya *gub.* between 1880 and 1890, of 150,000 working men, only 67,000 enjoyed real, and not fictitious,

---

[1] Sections 112–14 of the revised project ; cited by Tugan-Baranovsky, p. 392.

[2] Sections 116–21. *Ibid.*   [3] Section 269. *Ibid.,* p. 393.

[4] Imitating the French *Conseils des Prudhommes,* but providing that the chairman of the court should be elected by the members, not appointed by the Emperor, as in France. *Cf.* Tugan-Baranovsky, p. 393.

medical assistance.[1] In the Kharkov factory region at the same time, out of 658 workshops, employing 30,000 men, only four provided medical attendance in accordance with the provisions of the Act of 1866. The factory inspectors frequently reported deficiencies and violations of the law in this connection. Many of the large factories in Warsaw, for example, had no hospitals, no medical men, and no nurses.[2] Even at works in the Ural Mountains belonging to the Treasury, the organization of medical assistance is very defective. It is little wonder that this neglect also affected the private works in the same region. So also in the region of the Vistula and in the Caucasus, where medical attendance in the petroleum enterprises was badly organized.[3] The same was generally true of all outlying regions. Even at large factories and mines there was no hospital, no resident physician, and medical assistance was in general woefully deficient.

Several times during the period from 1866 to 1880, the Government attempted to introduce factory legislation more or less of the character of the projects of 1859, but always without success. The manufacturers were always able to bring their united forces against every project which was advanced by commission after commission. In 1867 Kolbe, director of the great cotton mills at Kränholm, proposed to the Government to limit the working day. In spite of his influence, the project came to nothing. In 1870 General Ignatiev was appointed chairman of a commission to investigate and report upon the subject ; in 1872 the Minister of the Interior recommended legislation ; in 1874 another commission was appointed under the presidency of Valnev. All of these measures were without avail. In 1875 a congress of mechanical engineers was held in St. Petersburg. One of the members, a large manufacturer called Golubev, drew attention to the excessive number of hours which were habitually worked, and urged that, in the interest of the manufacturers themselves, an eight-hour working day should be established, and that the total number of working days in the year should be limited to 300. The congress eventually passed an unanimous resolution in favour of a ten-hour working day. In 1874 the Imperial Russian Technical

---

[1] Professor F. F. Erisman, quoted in *Russia in the Past and in the Present*, Brockhaus and Ephron (St. Petersburg, 1900), p. 216.
[2] V. V. Svyatlovsky ; cited *ibid*.　　　　[3] L. Bertenson, *ibid*.

Society of St. Petersburg began to take a deep interest in the question. The president of the society, E. Andreyev, drew the attention of the commission of 1874 to the fact that the two fundamental obstacles to the promotion of technical education were the great length of the working day and the employment of children.[1]

The Imperial Technical Society undertook an inquiry into the question. Interrogatories were sent to manufacturers, and 135 replies were received. These replies showed that at a majority of the factories, children under ten years of age were frequently employed. Their hours of labour were the same as those of adults, usually fifteen hours per day ; and in one factory, seventeen hours per day. In consequence of this investigation a committee, composed partly of members of the society, partly of manufacturers, and partly of Government officials, was appointed to draft a project of a law. This committee agreed on the following principles : The employment of children under twelve years of age was to be forbidden. Between the ages of twelve and fifteen children might be employed for five hours per day, excepting in dangerous or harmful employments, where seventeen years was the age limit.[2] Still there was no result.

Finally, on 1st June 1882, during the reaction which ensued after the assassination of Alexander II, and after a long series of commissions and projects for nearly twenty-five years, a law was issued under the Ministry of Bunge. The age limit was fixed at twelve years. Between twelve and fifteen young persons might work eight hours per day; night work being prohibited for them, as also work on Sundays and holidays. Opportunity was to be given them by their employers to continue their education, and a system of Government inspection of factories was instituted. Thus at last, after a long interval of *laisser faire* between the rigorous control of the eighteenth century and modern factory legislation, the first Russian factory law came into being.

The usual division of interests and opinions was immediately manifested. The St. Petersburg manufacturers were in favour of the law; the Moscow manufacturers were, as formerly, opposed to any factory legislation. The latter protested against the measure,

---

[1] E. Andreyev, *The Work of Children in Russia and Western Europe*, p. 43 ; cited by Tugan-Baranovsky, p. 400.

[2] Andreyev, *op. cit.*, pp. 51 and 54 ; cited by Tugan-Baranovsky, p. 400.

and clamoured for the " liberty of labour." When factory inspection was instituted, there were many conflicts with the manufacturers, who were very reluctant to obey the law. The law of 1882 was only the beginning. Amendments followed quickly. On 12th June 1884 a law was issued relating to the education of persons under age who were working in factories, and dealing with hours of labour and the regulation of factory inspection. On 19th December 1884 another law dealing with the last-mentioned subject was issued. On 3rd June 1885 night work at textile factories was forbidden to persons of either sex under seventeen years of age. On 3rd June 1886 an act generally regulating work in factories was also issued. It is clear that the depression in industry which was experienced during this period had not only diminished the spirit of resistance on the part of the manufacturers, but the factories were generally, in any case, working on short time, and many workmen had been discharged. The St. Petersburg manufacturers even took the initiative in making proposals, which were negatived by the Moscow manufacturers ; but disturbances in some of the large Moscow factories in 1884 and 1885, and the St. Petersburg proposition about prohibiting night work for women and young persons was embodied in the law of 3rd June 1885. The law of 3rd June 1886, which was passed on the initiative of Count D. Tolstoy, went further than any of its predecessors. Wages were required to be paid at least once a month. What is known in England as *truck*, or payment in kind, was prohibited. Payments for medical attendance and for lighting of workshops, &c., were forbidden to be exacted from workmen.[1] At the same time, owing to the disturbances of the two previous years, the punishment of strikers was made more severe, and the duties of the factory inspectors were made more ample. The Government had now fully stepped back upon the path of control and regulation which, under the influence of the liberalism of the thirties and forties of the nineteenth century, it had largely abandoned.

As trade began to improve, the factory-owners became restive. They struggled against factory inspection. They accused the Government of legislating in a spirit of antipathy to the capitalist class

---

[1] For explanation of this provision, see extract from official commentaries upon Act of 1886 in *Bulletin of the International Labour Office* (London, 1908), vol. iii. No. 2, p. 219.

and in a spirit of partial protection to the employed " low class."
The agitation became more vigorous as the improvement of trade
continued. Upon the great factories, conducted on a high technical
plane, the law pressed lightly.[1] Those who felt it most severely
were struggling in deep financial waters resulting from the prolonged
depression. The manufacturing interests turned upon the Minister,
Bunge, who had been responsible for the legislation, and accused
him of failing to understand Russian conditions, and of being carried
away by the theories of Western European doctrinaires. Bunge
resigned, and the Moscow manufacturers approached his successor,
Vyshnegradsky, with some hope of inducing him to alter or modify
the factory policy of the Government. They were not immediately
successful ; but in 1890 the Government capitulated. Glass factories were permitted to employ young persons of twelve to fifteen
years at night, and the factory inspectors were allowed to permit
the employment of children on Sundays and holidays, and also in
some cases to allow night work by young persons of fifteen to seventeen years. The Minister of Finance, with the consent of the Minister
of the Interior, might sanction the employment of children of ten to
twelve years of age.[2]

Seven years later, on 3rd June 1897, the Government once more
made a step in the direction of further regulation. By this Act the
working day for all factories and workshops was limited to 11½ hours
for adults as well as for persons under age. If night work was adopted,
the period must not be more than 10 hours. Work on Sundays
and holidays was forbidden. Naval and military establishments
were exempted from the operations of the law. But the law of
14th March 1898 altered the regulations about overtime to such an
extent as almost to nullify the Act of 1897 so far as concerned this
matter.

Apart from factory legislation, a large number of the factories
in Central Russia, of their own motion, reduced their working
hours. In 1896 the St. Petersburg factory-owners proposed that
the working day should be compulsorily reduced to 11 hours, or
half an hour shorter than was provided by the Act of 1897.[3]

---

[1] Repeating the provision of the law of 26th August 1866 (cf. *supra*,
p. 408).

[2] *F.C.L.*, coll. iii. vol. x. 6743.

[3] The above account has been drawn chiefly from Tugan-Baranovsky,
op. cit., pp. 385–429.

CHAPTER V

THE LABOUR MOVEMENT SINCE EMANCIPATION

THE abolition of " bondage right," which was involved in the Emancipation of the serfs, transformed the working men and women of the *possessions-fabriken* from serfs owned or hired by the proprietors of these, into wage-paid artisans. The Emancipation, the tendency towards separations, the system of recruiting and short service in the army, and the highly protective fiscal policy, combined to promote the migration from the country to the town which, commencing in the pre-Emancipation period, proceeded at an accelerated rate in the epoch immediately succeeding Emancipation. Increase in the numbers of urban workmen due to these causes, and due importantly to the migration from the rural districts of *dvorovie lyudē*, now liberated without land, brought about greatly increased competition for employment, together with low wages. Scarcity of agricultural capital in the country had its counterpart in scarcity of industrial and of commercial capital in the town, and thus, in spite of the superabundance of labour, there was for a time a slender amount of industrial enterprise. The traditions of bondage still remained to keep wage employment in inferior conditions. The factories, which were frequently in buildings not specially designed or adapted for factory purposes, were often exceedingly insanitary ; the practice of search [1] was universally carried on, and beating of workmen by foremen was very frequent—in flagrant violation of the feelings of human dignity which had been aroused by the mere act of Emancipation.

These incidents led to great strike activity, not immediately, but within ten years after the date of Emancipation. In 1870 there was a strike in the tailors' shops of St. Petersburg, and in the same year the workers in the Nevsky Cotton-spinning Mills struck. While the

---

[1] Up till 1905 each workman was searched on leaving the factory for tools or goods which he was presumed to be desirous of stealing. The writer witnessed the process in St. Petersburg in 1899.

latter strike was in progress, the strikers elected from among themselves, deputies for the purpose of conducting negotiations with the factory-owners. These deputies were afterwards accused of leading the strikers, and, after trial, were sent to prison for a week. In 1870 also there were a strike at Warsaw and labour difficulties at Kronstadt. In 1871 the cabmen at Odessa struck, and in 1872 the workmen in the building trades at Kronstadt and those in the Kränholm Factory at Narva struck. In the latter case the strikers followed the example of those at the Nevsky Mills in the previous year, and elected deputies. The deputies were arrested by the officer of *gens d'armerie*, to whom they had gone to ask for protection for the strikers. These proceedings irritated the factory workers, discontent and disaffection grew rapidly, and troops were called out to " pacify " the industrial centres.[1]

The workers in the Lazarev Clothing Factory in Moscow struck in 1874 ; in 1875 there were strikes at Usovka (Hughesville) among workers in railway construction and among weavers at Serpukhov (70 miles south of Moscow). In 1876 there began the period of industrial stagnation during which there was a long series of strikes. Among these were the strikes of the cotton-spinners in the factory of Morozov (Vladimirsk. *gub.*) in 1876. In 1878 there took place the strike in the New Cotton-spinning Mills on Obvodni Canal, St. Petersburg, in which about 2000 workers participated. This strike was occasioned by the reduction of wages. The strikers appealed to the Crown Prince (afterwards Alexander III), and invited his interference. The petition was expressed in naïve terms : " We apply to you as children to a father ; if our just requirements are not satisfied, we shall then know that we have no one to whom to appeal, that nobody will defend us, and that we must rely upon ourselves and upon our own hands." [2]

No answer was given to this petition, but the strike was shortly afterwards settled. In November 1878 the cotton-spinners in the König Cotton-spinning Mills, St. Petersburg, struck. These also

---

[1] Svyatlovsky, V. V., *The Labour Movement in Russia* (St. Petersburg, 1907), p. 7.

[2] For the details of this strike, see *Natchalo* (The Beginning), No. 1 (underground newspaper); also *The Revolutionary Journalism of the Seventies*, 2nd Appendix to the magazine, *State Crimes in Russia*, ed. by V. Bachilevsky (V. Bugocharsky), published by *Donskaya Retch* (1906), pp. 19–23 ; G. V. Plekhanov, in *Russian Workers in the Revolutionary Movement* (St. Petersburg, 1906), pp. 39–53 ; and V. V. Svyatlovsky, *op. cit.*, p. 8.

appealed to the Crown Prince, and with similar results.[1]   In January 1879 the strike at the New Cotton-spinning Mills began again. This renewed strike marks an important development of the Russian labour movement, for it induced sympathetic strikes in allied industries, and thus initiated a general instead of an individual factory movement ; although as yet the scattered groups were not formally united into a definite organization.   Moreover, collections to aid the strikers were made in nearly all St. Petersburg industrial establishments.   The first to formulate demands sympathetically with the cotton-spinners at the New Cotton Mills were the weavers of the Schau Factory at St. Petersburg.   Both bodies of workmen demanded that persons elected by them respectively should be present when material was given out to the workers and finished goods received from them.   The spirit of resistance soon became infectious, and the workmen of numerous diversified trades joined in making similar demands upon their employers.

Under the influence of this rising spirit of determination to alter the conditions of labour by spontaneous organization and collective action of the working groups, there came the idea of forming a general organization which should include all the trades and all the factories.   This idea had its rise in one of the Socialist groups.   The intention of the General Russian Workers' Union was to unite the forces of the rural and the urban working population.   The first step which was taken was the organization, in 1878, of the North Russian Working Union.   Although primarily organized as a political association—it was, indeed, intended to be the purely working-class wing of the " Social Democratic Party of the West "—this union was also organized for the purpose of reinforcing the economical demands of striking workmen.   Its formation constituted the first effort of the Social Democratic Party to assume the leadership and to direct the policy of the Russian working class.   While the name of the union apparently confined its activities to North Russia, it was intended to form

[1] These appeals to the Crown Prince (afterwards the Tsar Alexander III) are susceptible of two explanations.   Either the strikers and their revolutionary allies (who were cognizant of the appeals, and perhaps even sometimes instigated them) desired to distinguish sharply between the reactionary tendencies under whose influence the Tsar Alexander II was understood to have fallen and the supposititious zeal for reform of the Crown Prince ; or they knew that their appeals would receive no answer, and that this fact would contribute to the discredit of the autocracy in the eyes of the people.

the nucleus of an ultimate Pan-Russian working-class organization.[1]

There were even international ideals in the minds of the leading spirits of the new union. For example, in reply to the greetings of Warsaw working men who urged the avoidance of national hostility and the pursuit of the general interests of humanity, the union declared that it did not regard its interests as separate from those " of the workers of the whole world." [2] The union was, however, permitted to pursue its aims for a very short time. Its newspaper, *Natchalo*, achieved only one number, when it was suppressed, and the union came to an end.

In 1875 there had been formed the " South Russian Workers' Union." This union was founded, not by working men, but by *intelligenti* under the leadership of one Zaslavsky. The leader and some of his followers were arrested, and the union collapsed.[3] In 1880 another organization bearing the same name made its appearance, founded also by *intelligenti*—E. Kovalskaya and Schedrin, both of anarchist leanings. They entered into relations with the working men in the arsenal at Kiev where an agitation for increased wages was then going on. The union issued a manifesto embodying the demands of the working men, and threatening the chief of the arsenal with death in case of non-compliance. The authorities of the arsenal capitulated.[4] The terroristic activities of this union were brought to a conclusion by the arrest in 1881 of nearly all of its members. Among those who were arrested, there were no working men.[5]

Meanwhile the conditions of the factory system attracted the attention of the members of the Council of State. This body resolved, in 1880, to request the Ministers to bring before it such measures [6] " as experience might suggest to alter the laws respecting

---

[1] Plekhanov, G. V., *Russian Workers in the Revolutionary Movement*, p. 71 ; and Svyatlovsky, V. V., *op. cit.*, p. 10.
[2] Plekhanov, G. V., *loc. cit.*
[3] See Martov, L., *Proletarian Struggle in Russia*, p. 42.
[4] See Memoirs of E. Kovalskaya in *Biloye*, No. 2, p. 152 ; quoted by Svyatlovsky, *op. cit.*, p. 11.
[5] Svyatlovsky, *loc. cit.*
[6] Under the then existing constitution of the State Council, the Ministers were permitted to submit to it *projets de loi* ; if they were approved they passed to the Tsar with the recommendation of the Council. The Council could not initiate legislation, but, as in the above case, it might suggest that legislation was expedient.

labour." Following upon this step, there came several legislative Acts which took effect between 1880 and 1882. Under these Acts, the labour of children under twelve years of age was prohibited in metal and leather and clothing factories. The hours of labour of persons from twelve to fifteen years of age were limited to eight hours per day ; young persons were prohibited from working in the night and on Sundays and holidays ; and a system of factory inspectorship was instituted.

During the period of reaction after the assassination of the Tsar Alexander II, all open labour organization disappeared under the pressure of the coercive measures applied by the police. By these means the Government succeeded in crushing labour unions, whether they were being utilized for political or for purely economical purposes ; but two consequences followed. Labour organization was driven underground, and hostility to employers on account of low wages and long hours of labour was transferred to the Government, which was held to be responsible, because it prevented the working men from improving their position by means of combination, a method which was permitted in Great Britain and tolerated elsewhere in Western Europe. Although the Government either prevented trade unions from being formed or crushed them when they were formed, strikes in individual establishments could not be prevented. In 1882 strikes took place in the railway workshops at Brest against reduction in the number of men employed, and in Borisoglebsk against reduction of wages. A small strike which occurred in December 1882 in Bielostok against reduction of wages is remarkable, because it revealed the existence, in spite of laws and police action, of a purely working-class trade union.[1] In 1882, also, the workers of Kränholm Factory, at Narva, struck against reduction in wages ; in 1883, 3000 workers in Voznesenskya Factory, near Moscow, struck against a simultaneous reduction of working hours and of wages. In the same year 10,000 workers employed in Girardovsky Factory struck ; and in 1884 strikes took place in railway workshops at Moscow. The most notable strike of this period occurred in 1885 at Nikolsky Factory, in Orekhovo-Zyevo (Vladimirsk. gub.). The significance of the strike lay in

---

[1] The first trade union properly so called in Russia, according to S. Prokopovich in *Toward the Labour Question in Russia*, p. 62 ; quoted by Svyatlovsky, *op. cit.*, p. 12.

the demand for freedom of election of a " headman," whose functions were to comprise negotiations with the employers, attention to the interests of the workers, &c.   The leaders appear to have endeavoured to deter the strikers from damaging property and to give the strike a regular and orderly character.[1]   This strike was brought to a conclusion by the arrival of troops ; over thirty working men were arrested and imprisoned and 800 persons were banished.   In the autumn of 1885 simultaneous strikes occurred in five cotton dye works in Ivanovo-Voznesensk, involving 6000 persons.

Fresh legislation was devised to meet these conditions.   In 1884 the system of factory inspectorship was extended, and the instruction of young persons in industrial employments was provided for.   In 1885[2] night work in cotton, woollen, and linen factories by young persons under seventeen and by women was prohibited.   In 1886 contracts between employers and their workpeople were subjected to regulation ;[3] and their mutual relations during the currency of these contracts were placed under the supervision of the factory inspectors.[4]   In 1888 the workers in *all* the factories in the Schuysko-Ivanovsky region struck against night work, with the result that night work was abolished.

Thus throughout the early eighties, while trade was stagnant and profits were low, the beginnings of the labour movement properly so called took place in Russia.   The strikes were almost altogether of a defensive character—against reduction in wages, or against deductions or alleged ill-treatment by foremen and others.   The movement had not as yet assumed an aggressive character.   The wave of trade revival after the " long depression " made its appearance in Russia in 1888 or 1889, and for a short interval there were few labour difficulties.

Up till this period the labour movement, so far as is indicated by the causes of individual strikes, wears a purely economical complexion.   From about this time political forces begin definitively to act upon the labour movement and to give it an aggressive character.   The history of the political parties which have from time to time influenced the labour movement is sketched elsewhere.[5]   It is necessary, however, in this place to notice the

---

[1] Svyatlovsky, *loc. cit.*   [2] Law of 3rd June 1885.
[3] Law of 3rd June 1886.   [4] Law of 1st October 1886.
[5] See Books V, VI, and VII.

effects of the propagandas from the point of view of the labour movement itself.

Probably the first attempt on the part of political agitators to influence labour organization since 1880, was the formation in the winter of 1886-1887 of " The Union of St. Petersburg Workers." This union was formed in the Franco-Russian Metal Works by workmen, assisted by a *simplified intelligent*—that is, an educated person who had joined the ranks of the working class for the purpose of arousing the working men to assert themselves in the interests of their class. This union was crushed in 1887.[1]   In 1889 St. Petersburg working men who had belonged to isolated Social Democratic circles or clubs united themselves into a committee, which called itself " The Group Assembly of Factory Representatives."   During its life of about three years, this small organization, which consisted of about eight working men and one " intelligent," aided several strikes by making assessments upon its adherents and contributing the amounts so collected to strike funds, and by issuing manifestoes.[2]

Organization of the labour movement on the part of the Social Democrats had its effective beginning in the late eighties.   By 1890 working men's " circles " had been formed not alone in St. Petersburg, but also in Vladimir, Tula, Kazan, Kharkov, Kiev, Rostov-on-Don, Vilna, and Minsk.[3]   Within another year there were circles also in Moscow, Warsaw, Lodz, Odessa, Samara, Saratov, and other cities.[4]   The characteristic of these " circles " at this time seems to have been increased reliance on the part of the working men upon their Social Democratic allies.   " Their theoretical studies fell more and more into the background." [5]   The reason for this is obvious : the workmen had neither sufficient education, nor had they sufficient leisure of mind to pursue recondite studies in socialist dogma.   It was inevitable that they should refrain from working out the economico-philosophical basis of their movement for themselves, and should lean more and more upon those

[1] " This organization initiated the observance of Labour Day (1st May) in Russia."   " Memoirs on the Dawn of Russian Social Democracy," in *Biloye* (Paris, 1907), quoted by Svyatlovsky, V. V., *op. cit.*, p. 15.
[2] *Ibid.*   [3] Martov, L., *The Proletarian Struggle*, p. 82.
[4] Svyatlovsky, *op. cit.*, p. 16.
[5] Lyadov, M., *History of the Russian Social Democratic Working Men's Party* (St. Petersburg, 1906), part i. p. 68.

whose equipment rendered the process of study easier, or whose pretensions made it appear that this was the case. The Social Democratic *intelligentsia* were thus able to secure a great hold upon the working men, and they were constituted their leaders by a natural process.

Up till this period the Social Democratic Party had existed in scattered small groups. The strikes of January 1895 in St. Petersburg,[1] which were the first really large strikes in that region, prepared the way for definite organization of the working men of Social Democratic leanings. The result was the formation of the " St. Petersburg Union for the Struggle for the Emancipation of the Working Class." This union formed the nucleus of what afterwards became the Russian Social Democratic Working Men's Party. The union was formed out of several Social Democratic circles in St. Petersburg. It began at once a policy of agitation, attacking one factory after another by means of leaflets specially prepared for each factory. These leaflets encouraged the working men to strike, and many strikes occurred at the instigation of the union. In many cases the strikers secured concessions, and the result of these was a great stimulus to the labour movement. The working men awoke to the advantages of concerted action. The St. Petersburg union began also to feel its power, and openly announced its existence in a leaflet in which it put the question to which its existence was the answer : " Does the economical struggle of the St. Petersburg proletariat receive leadership in ideas and in the formulation of its necessities ? "[2]

On 27th May 1896 there began a series of strikes of an aggressive character, in which the working men demanded improvement of their condition. This series of strikes was partly promoted and partly assisted by the " Union for Struggle." In the end of May the workmen in the largest factories in the St. Petersburg district were on strike. It was the first simultaneous mass movement of the Russian working class. At this time a hundred strikers met, formulated their demands, and handed them to the union. These demands were forthwith printed and circulated. In the beginning of June the strike became a general strike of St. Petersburg workers

[1] For an account of these strikes, see Tarr, K. M., *Outline of the St. Petersburg Labour Movement of the Nineties* (St. Petersburg, 1906), pp. 14–17.
[2] Svyatlovsky, *op. cit.*, p. 17.

employed in the textile industry. The interference of the police and the refusal of the factory-owners to yield caused the collapse of the strike, and the working men resumed work under the former conditions ; but the strike was an important incident in the labour movement, because it gave an object-lesson in organization. The fighting union with its strike treasury from that moment became an object of interest to the St. Petersburg working men. " The Union for Struggle " now printed model constitutions, and also constitutions prepared by the members of individual unions ; and the Russian trade-union movement properly so called may be said to have begun.

Although no important material successes had been achieved by the Social Democrats in their guidance of the labour movement up till 1896, the advantage of organization had been deeply impressed upon the working men by them, and the methods of accomplishing this organization, the hostility of the Government and the action of the police notwithstanding, had been demonstrated. Moreover, the ideas of Social Democracy had so penetrated the " Union for Struggle," and the latter had so much increased, that it was now possible to develop it into a definite political party. This was carried into effect in 1897, when the Russian Social Democratic Working Men's Party was formed. From that period until the Revolution the history of this party is the history of the working-class movement in Russia. The questions which have been raised by the party in the course of its history and the causes of the strikes which it has promoted or aided, have been sometimes predominantly political and sometimes predominantly economical. Sometimes also the methods which have been employed have been revolutionary—that is, existing authority, whether of the factory, of the police, or of the Government, has been simply disregarded; and sometimes the methods have been diplomatic. The economical grievances formed the ostensible basis of union, and the union was then used for political agitation.

While the labour movement was thus practically absorbed into the Social Democratic movement and became insusceptible of discrimination from it, there nevertheless remained unabsorbed certain groups of working men whose leanings were not towards socialism. These groups formed societies of mutual assistance, with treasuries for the receipt of contributions and for the payment of benefits of various kinds. In so far as the labour movement was absorbed into the Social Democratic movement, it falls to be considered in relation to the contemporary political and social revolutionary movements ; [1] the mutual assistance or friendly societies of working men alone fall properly to be considered in this place.

The friendly society movement, though of ancient date in Western Europe, is quite recent in Russia. Probably owing to the absence in Russia of the guild organization, [2] which played so large a part in the history of the towns in Germany and in Italy in the Middle Ages, and to the formal character of the structure of society in the Russian towns, the growth of spontaneous social groups for mutual assistance was retarded. It is not surprising that when such spontaneously organized groups make their appearance they do so, in the first instance, in those regions of European Russia which came more immediately under the influence of Western Europe. So far back as the sixteenth century there were friendly societies in Poland and in the Baltic Provinces. [3] These appear to have been copied from the societies of journeymen which sprang up during the guild ages. They furnished benefits for sickness, unemployment, travelling to obtain work, and the like. In addition to strictly class organizations, there were societies for funeral benefits, to which members were admitted irrespective of class.

These and similar societies remained until the Revolution, their limited aims having enabled them to acquire a legal status, which was denied to societies whose objects were more aggressive. Their importance lies in the fact that they habituated large groups of the working class to act together for mutual advantage, and prepared the way for the trade union properly so called, which was to follow.

In the friendly society movement of the north-western provinces of European Russia, an important place must be assigned to the Jewish societies. [4] Friendly societies known as *Hevra* have existed in every trade and in many cities. The *Hevra* seem to have had their origin in the end of the eighteenth century. In their early

[1] See Books IV and VII.
[2] For other social effects of the absence of guild organization, see p. 588.
[3] Svyatlovsky, *op. cit.*, p. 22.
[4] An account of these societies is given by S. Prokopovich in his *Towards the Labour Question in Russia* (St. Petersburg, 1900), by Sara Rabinovitch in her *Organization der Judischen Proletariats in Russland* (Carlsruhe, 1903), and by V. V. Svyatlovsky in *op. cit.*, pp. 22 *et seq.*

stages the *Hevra* had a religious character, but latterly the religious features have become less important, and even the purely friendly society features have in many cases been subordinated to the prosecution of the interests of the trade by trade union methods.[1] While some of the *Hevra* thus underwent development towards trade unionism, others became the nucleus of employers' organizations.

In their internal structure the *Hevras* were similar to the old Polish Jewish craft guilds. Each *Hevra* had its constitution inscribed upon a parchment roll. The executive committee of the *Hevra* was elected by a double ballot. Electors were in the first instance selected by lot, and these again, by direct ballot, elected the committee. In their earlier phases, some examples of which still survive, the *Hevra* contained in its membership both employers and employed. In the later phases the working members leave the old *Hevra* and organize a purely working-class *Hevra* on a similar plan. The occasion of the secession was usually an attempt on the part of the employers who were members of the *Hevra* to utilize their power in the *Hevra* to deny benefits to the working members unless they submitted to the labour contracts proposed by the employers. The result of the schism was, in some cases, improvement in the terms of the wage contract, reduction of the number of working hours, and the like.[2] The old *Hevra* usually continues to exist as an employers' association ; " in rare cases does it become a fighting employers' union." [3] About 1890 there began to appear among the *Hevras* some whose structure and policy were very similar to those of the English trade union.[4]

As the trade union movement developed, the *Hevras*, in spite of the services they had rendered in early organization for trade interests, lost their influence until in the revolutionary years they practically disappeared.

In addition to the *Hevra* there began also to appear at this time, numerous strike treasuries. The first of these, the strike treasury of the stocking-knitters of Vilna, was established in 1888. By 1894 there were very numerous organizations of this character

---

[1] *E.g.* in Mohilev there are such *Hevra* among shoemakers, watchmakers, and tinsmiths.

[2] As in the case of the cabinetmakers of Mohilev, narrated by Sara Rabinovitch, *op. cit.*, pp. 63, 64.

[3] *Ibid.*, pp. 66–7.   [4] Svyatlovsky, *op. cit.*, p. 25.

all over Poland and the north-west *guberni*.[1] In Vilna alone there were in 1895 about 850 organized workers in twenty-seven trades.[2]

In this year, 1895, there was formed what is said to have been the first trade union in Russia which was not limited to one locality. This was " The Universal Union of Bristle Workers in Russian Poland." The union was wholly composed of Jews, who have a practical monopoly of the bristle trade of the world. This new type of union seems to have been looked upon with some hostility by the *Hevra*.

The most extensive group of friendly societies in Russia was the group of such societies formed by merchants' salesmen or commercial travellers and salesmen. The first of these societies was established in Riga in 1859. Later, in 1863, a similar society was founded in Moscow, and in 1865 one was formed in St. Petersburg. In 1898 in European Russia alone, exclusive of Poland, the Baltic Provinces, and Finland, there were seventy-four such societies.[3] In 1896, at the first assembly of these societies held in Nijni Novgorod, the number of members was stated as 5000 ; in the second assembly held at Moscow in 1898, the number was 20,000. Many of these societies were patronized by the employers, and they included in their membership higher administrative officers—managers and the like.[4] This condition was quite inevitable for two reasons. The retail and even the wholesale business of Russia, excepting in the great commercial and industrial centres, was carried on by small firms, the salesmen of which frequently live with the families of their employers, and did not form a social class separate from them, and thus the solidarity of the salesmen as a group was impeded. The second reason is that the salesmen belong to the layer of *intelligentsia* or *semi-intelligentsia* which was necessarily in more immediate personal contact with the employing class and therefore trade-union methods of organization were not readily adopted by them. Moreover, the restrictions

[1] *Materials toward the History of the Jewish Labour Movement* (St. Petersburg, 1906), p. 44.
[2] *Ibid.*, p. 50. [3] Svyatlovsky, *op. cit.*, p. 28.
[4] According to V. I. Grachov, quoted by V. V. Svyatlovsky (*ibid.*), benefactor members—employers and others—numbered 13 per cent. of the total membership in 1895. Jews were expressly excluded from some of these societies, *e.g.* that of Yaroslav. (*Ibid.*, p. 30.)

which were imposed by the police rendered activity in trade-union organization impracticable. The salesmen's societies were thus limited to the exercise of benevolent and social functions, alike by internal disposition and by external control. Towards the year 1900, however, the character of these societies began to change. The Odessa Society of Salesmen appealed in 1902 to M. Wittë, then Minister of Finance, to make an inquiry into the question of working hours. In the course of this inquiry the salesmen's societies everywhere began to formulate demands, some of which previously had not been publicly expressed. These demands included limitation of the working day to ten hours, full holiday rest, and the right to organize trade unions. In 1903 the salesmen of Kutais (Caucasus) went out on strike, demanding holiday and Sunday rest. The newer salesmen's societies, in which young men predominated, became practically trade unions, while the older societies adhered to their traditional attitude. The change in the character of the salesmen's societies became manifest in the third assembly, which took place in Moscow in the end of June 1906. In addition to the old type of salesmen's friendly society, there was present also the new type of salesmen's trade union. Societies of the latter type were sufficiently influential to secure the passing of a resolution recommending the transformation of the mutual assistance societies into fighting organizations, or the subordination of the friendly society to the trade-union element.[1]

The next most important group of societies which underwent a similar gradual transformation from mutual assistance to trade unionism, were the societies of the metal workers. The first friendly societies composed of workers in the group of metal trades, were formed in Poland under the title of " Brotherhood Offices " in the year 1821. Membership in these " Offices " was made compulsory for all workers employed in working in metal in establishments belonging to the Government, the contributions being compulsorily deducted from their wages. The funds provided by the deductions having been found to be insufficient after the scheme had been in existence for some years, the State was obliged to

---

[1] Cf. Bellin, A., *Professional Movement of Trade Selling Employees in Russia* (St. Petersburg, 1906); Goodvon, A., *Salesman Question* (Life and Labour of Salesmen) (Odessa, 1905); Prokopovich, *op. cit.*, and Svyatlovsky. *op. cit.* The latter contains brief bibliography (p. 32).

give supplementary funds which, up till 1894, amounted to an annual average of about 20,000 rubles.[1]

Similar funds were established for the miners in Poland. They were definitively subjected to governmental control in 1900. Originally established spontaneously, they fell into financial disorder.

Similar societies were formed in private concerns engaged in metal industries in Poland.[2]   The growth of such schemes in Poland is attributed by Professor Svyatlovsky[3] to the circumstance that the operation of the Code Napoléon, which was the law in effect in Poland, imposed liability for accidents upon employers.[4]   In order to diminish this liability, the employers encouraged the formation of mutual assistance societies among their workmen. Since most of the mineral and metal enterprises in Poland were working on leases from the State, and since they took over the State establishments during the currency of their leases, they continued the mutual assistance funds which were already in existence, and sometimes contributed to them, sometimes managing them wholly, and sometimes permitting the employees to participate in the management.

In 1892 (9th March) the law compelled the employers to defray the cost of medical attendance for their employees, and thereupon the employers who had previously made contributions to the funds ceased to do so.   In 1900 a further change took place, when the management of the mutual assistance funds was taken out of the hands of the employers and entrusted to the factory inspectors.

The organization of mutual assistance societies in connection with mining and metallurgical industries in the Ural Mountains began in 1861 (8th March), immediately after the State peasants who had been employed in these undertakings were emancipated from bondage.   The avowed object of the new law was to bind by a tie, other than that of bondage, the workers to the undertakings

---

[1] Tigranov, I., *The Cash Offices of Metallurgical Workers;* quoted by V. V. Svyatlovsky, *op. cit.,* p. 34.

[2] According to Prokopovich, 59 per cent. of the total number of workers in these enterprises were organized in benefit societies.

[3] *Op. cit.,* p. 35.

[4] By articles 1382 and following.   For discussion of these, see, *e.g.,* M. Bellom, *De la responsabilité en matière d'accidents du travail* (Paris, 1899), p. 8.

to which they had been assigned as serfs.[1] Under this law deductions, unreturnable, of from two to three per cent. were made from wages, and benefits for sickness and for old age, &c., were granted. The funds derived from the contributions of the workers were supplemented by equivalent contributions from the administration and by fines which might be exacted. In addition to the funds of individual State establishments, there was also a general fund of " metallurgical partnerships," which might be drawn upon in case of necessity. Pensions were granted after thirty-five years' service, varying according to the character of the work which the pensioner had performed. In injurious occupations, the pensions were greater proportionately than in others. The metallurgical partnership funds also accepted savings on deposit at 3 per cent. interest. The savings plan did not, however, work out satisfactorily, because the workers feared that if they deposited their savings the amount of these would be known to the administration, and might have the effect of reducing the benefits which would otherwise be payable to them.[2]

In the privately-owned establishments, the factory-owners sometimes receive financial assistance from the " partnership " funds, i.e. from the funds of the benefit societies. In addition to the friendly society functions of these metallurgical partnerships, they were charged by law with the settlement of disputes between the workers and the employers. This function was rarely exercised, and was practically abolished by the law of 10th March 1898.

The general effect of the institution of metallurgical partnerships has been to intensify administrative control over the workers in the Ural Mountains, to diminish their mobility, and to prevent them from engaging in spontaneous organizations of a trade-union type.

The organization of societies of railway servants in Russia began in 1858 in the workshops of the Nikolaiskaya, the Warsaw-Vienna, and the Warsaw-Bromberg Railways ; but up till 1885 there were few societies of importance. The real beginning of such organization was in 1888, when, under the law of 30th May of that year,

---

[1] See Tigranov, *Review of the Activity of Metallurgical Partnerships in State Industrial Undertakings and Mines during the Period* 1881–1893, p. 1 ; quoted by V. V. Svyatlovsky, *op. cit.*, p. 37.

[2] In 1904, *e.g.* the amount of loans to members was over half a million rubles, and the amount of deposits by members was only 2000 rubles.

the Council of State required all railways in private hands to establish mutual assistance societies, the constitutions of these being approved, according to certain general principles, by the Minister of Ways of Communication. The law relating to this matter in the railways of the State is contained in the law of 3rd June 1894, and in that of 2nd June 1903. Under all these laws employers were obliged to contribute to the funds; deductions were made of 6 per cent. from wages and of 10 per cent. from bonuses. The State contributed an amount equal to one-half of the amount of the deductions. The funds also benefit by the sales of unclaimed baggage, &c., and from fines. At the age of fifty-five the interest of a contributory ceased, because at that age he became eligible for a State pension, and a double pension was not permitted.

The details which have been given above illustrate sufficiently the methods by which the Government attempted systematically to control the relations between the workers in public employment and the individual administrations, as well as to control the relations between the workers in private employment and their employers. Steps were taken to provide, through deduction from wages for the most part, for medical attendance, for sick allowances, for pensions, &c., and the workers were so far as possible bound by these arrangements to the particular field in which they were employed. They could move only with difficulty. The principle of binding to the soil which had been regarded as the chief desiderata in an agrarian policy was applied also to industry. In addition, combination among workmen for any other purpose than work and mutual assistance in a friendly society manner, was definitively discouraged, and so far as possible stringently forbidden.

CHAPTER VI

EMPLOYERS' ASSOCIATIONS

THE rapid development of the spontaneous trade union movement had the inevitable result of alarming the employers of labour. Dismissal of men who were known to belong to the unions was the first measure adopted by individual employers ; but this expedient had no effect in retarding the growth of the movement. The next inevitable step was counter-organization. This naturally began in those industries in which the employers were accustomed to association for purposes other than mere opposition to trade unions.[1] The " syndicate " or " trust " movement, which began in the eighties, had already trained the employers in certain trades in the art of combination. Master printers, master tailors, as well as manufacturers and millers who had " syndicate " experience, began, towards the end of 1905, to form associations for the purpose of fighting the trade unions. In many cases the masters' associations came into existence almost contemporaneously with the trade unions. For example, when the Union of Clerks began to introduce the system of " holiday rests " in certain branches of commerce, the traders who employed these clerks began to discuss the expediency of forming a Traders' Association, with the object of resisting these " holiday rests." So also the master tailors in Warsaw, Dvinsk, Moscow, and St. Petersburg associated themselves together. The strike in St. Petersburg of the bakers caused also a temporary organization of the owners of bakeries, and the growth of the tanners' union in Vilna caused the master tanners there to form an association.

These masters' associations followed in many ways the example of the trade unions. Nor was this movement on the part of the

[1] Most of the details in this connection are derived from V. V. Svyatlovsky, *Trade Union Movement in Russia* (St. Petersburg, 1907), pp. 324 *et seq*. See also Ozerov, Professor E. Kh., *Politics of the Labour Question in Russia in Recent Years* (Moscow, 1906).

429

masters unconnected with the political situation. As the reactionary movement of 1906 developed, the activity of the masters
in checking the growth of trade unionism by counter-unionism
increased. They were now able to adopt measures by the aid of
the police, to which measures the administration had formerly
denied support. Thus the counter-labour movement came to have
political significance, and to form a part of the general system of
repression. The counterpart of the trade union strike is the employers' "lock-out." From the period immediately succeeding
the dissolution of the First Duma, this English word was incorporated into the Russian language, and the lock-out became a
frequent expedient. The master printers of Kiev and the master
tanners and shoe manufacturers of Warsaw, the master bristle-
brush makers of Meziëvich, in Siedletskaya *gub.*, the flour millers
in Ekaterinoslav, the tobacco and the metal manufacturers and the
shipowners in St. Petersburg, the metal manufacturers in Lodz,
the naphtha manufacturers in Terek, and many other employers
in different parts of Russia, decided in their associations to resist
the demands of the workmen. In Lodz this attitude led to a great
lock-out involving 40,000 workmen. The working men of Lodz
were not, however, united upon the question. The "nationalist"[1]
workmen declared that the demands of the unions were formulated
by a comparatively small group of socialists who were engaged in
politics, and that they did not think it proper that all working
men should suffer on this account. They therefore ranged themselves on the side of the manufacturers, and threw themselves into
the struggle against the revolutionary elements. The result was
a series of murders and disturbances. Similarly at Dvinsk, in
January 1906, the masters, aided by the support of the skilled
workmen, decided to oppose the demands of the less skilled and of
unskilled labourers. Within a short time eighteen employers'
associations were formed in rapid succession : tailors, ladies' tailors,
dressmakers, shoemakers, dealers in furnishings, painters, carpenters, printers, photographers, barbers, cab-proprietors, carting
contractors, tanners, cigarette-filler manufacturers, paper-box
makers, and paint manufacturers.

At St. Petersburg also the masters' union of metal manufacturers of the northern region formed a special fund for fighting

[1] Polish " nationalists."

the unions. Each member of the association was obliged to pay into the fund 3 per cent. of his annual profits.

At Moscow there was formed early in 1906 the Association of the Manufacturers and Mill-owners of the Central Industrial Region. This association extended its operations over ten *guberni* round Moscow. Its programme was as follows : *first*, to provide temporary support to, and co-operation among, its members in their struggle against demands for increase of wages and diminution of working hours ; *second*, support of the members in strikes, including financial, judicial, and other assistance ; *third*, acceptance of universal compulsory measures, applicable to the whole region, alike in the prevention of strikes and in combating them.

In Lodz, in the woollen industry, the association of masters required a deposit of 15,000 to 20,000 rubles, which might be forfeited in case of failure of a member to comply with the regulations of the association. One of these regulations was to the effect that when the committee decided to oppose a concession to the workmen, the factory in which the concession was demanded must be closed. A similar regulation was in force in the Warsaw Association of Manufacturers.

In Vitebsk a conference of employers was held in December 1906. This conference adopted the following resolutions, which were characteristic of such conferences : (1) To support one another in case of a conflict between the manufacturers and the employees ; (2) not to receive workmen from one another except when they present letters from their former employers ; (3) bristlers from Poland who are locked out are not to be employed ; (4) when a lock-out exists, the factories of members must be closed until the men compromise ; (5) manufacturers who do not enter into the union are not permitted to do business in Leipzig ; (6) manufacturers who suffer from strikes are to be supported by the union. The manufacturers agreed not to maintain any relations with the Bristlers' Trade Union, and they also agreed to introduce piece-work wages where such wages did not exist, and to reduce the scale of piece-work where they did exist.

The regulations were frequently imitated from those of similar associations in Germany, such regulations having been translated and circulated among the manufacturers. In general the associations were ostentatiously protective against the trade unions; in only one case—that of the St. Petersburg printers—was disclaimer made of special antagonism to the unions.[1]

The working men's unions, in so far as the repressive attitude of the Government permitted, sought to meet this form of counter-agitation by increasing the effectiveness of their own organization. For instance, the textile workers of the Moscow region held a conference and issued an appeal to all those engaged in textile manufacture, urging them :

" 1. To organize energetically, in order to counteract the organized strength of capital.

" 2. To secure harmony in political and economic action among the working class.

" 3. To promote closer union for a more successful political struggle and a quicker introduction of socialism.

" 4. To afford greater pecuniary aid to the comrades in Lodz who were suffering from a lock-out."

So also at the first conference of the unions of the working men engaged in the metal industry, passed the following resolution :

" Taking into consideration that the result of the revolutionary struggle of the working class, which brought about the whole series of political and economic conquests and a mighty growth of labour organizations, there is to be observed the considerable growth of the fighting unions of the employers. The object of these unions is to take away the result of the conquests and to put an end to the trade unions. The principal means of their struggle is the dismissal of the working men in masses (lock-outs). In this struggle the employers profit by the fullest co-operation of the authority of the Government. The conference finds that the fundamental conditions of successful struggle against the organized capitalists, with their tactics of lock-outs, appear to be : *first*, the creation of strong craft organizations and their union into provincial and All-Russian unions ; *second*, the full accord of the actions of the economic and political organization of the working class. At the same time the

---

[1] *Cf.* Svyatlovsky, *op. cit.*, p. 328, and V. E., " Lock-outs in Russia," *Trade and Industry Gazette*, No. 27, for the year 1907. " In the same Gazette it was reported that the Warsaw manufacturers of beds and washstands demanded the diminution of wages, the increase of working hours, and the signing of a special declaration of incontestable obedience. The Union of the Polish Sugar Manufacturers declared that it would put an end to the new order of things introduced by the working men in the course of the last year." Svyatlovsky, *loc. cit.*

conference proposes that the local unions existing at the present time should undertake the following immediate measures : (*a*) To secure the best possible information about the general state of affairs in the given branch of industry, about the strength, means, and immediate plans of the employers' associations ; (*b*) to all their action against employers, and especially to all their aggressive strikes, to give the best prepared and organized character ; (*c*) to weigh carefully the demands which are presented, to guide themselves thereby, in the interests of the union as a whole, and to secure for the union a decisive voice ; (*d*) in case of a lock-out, to carry out the strictest boycott on all works and orders from those establishments from which working men had been dismissed, and to try to prevent the influx of workmen into those establishments ; (*e*) to endeavour to utilize the conflict of interests between different cliques of capitalists who organize a lock-out. The conference realizes that only by means of the solidarity of all classes of working men can a struggle against a lock-out be successful. . . . The conference at the same time expresses itself decisively against response to a single lock-out by a wide strike. Strikes of this kind, breaking out under conditions more favourable to employers than to working men, are almost invariably doomed to inevitable defeat, and those unorganized masses which are involved in them become afterwards, for a long time, incapable of any kind of organization."

Finally, some unions adopt special measures in respect to a lock-out. Thus the Moscow Union of Employees in the Printing Industry decided not to respond to a lock-out by a general strike, which might cause an undesirable street movement, and it projected a special organization, " The Council of the Striking Printing Shops." " The Council " was a department of the management of the union, and undertook a series of extraordinary measures according to a specially worked out programme.

BOOK VII

THE REVOLUTIONARY MOVEMENT
IN RUSSIA, 1903–1907

INTRODUCTION

So long as the powers of the central authority of the Russian State were preoccupied in repelling invasion, and, even when the risk of invasion was diminished, in keeping the Tartars on the south, the Poles on the west, and the Swedes on the north-west, in sufficient subjection, or at a sufficient distance, it was impossible to deal drastically with interior affairs. These affairs tended, indeed, to drift in directions unfavourable to the maintenance of the central power. The appanage princes being enlisted by the Moscow Sovereigns, or crushed by them, and the " free towns " being deprived of their autonomy, the permanent interest of the central authority could not be served by the growth of a new and powerful class of serf-owners, who were removing from the tax-rolls large bodies of men, and who were by this means compromising the recruiting system. The serf-owner was, moreover, industrial entrepreneur as well as exploiter of agricultural labour and tax-collector. There were certain conveniences, in an age of crude administrative methods, in thus farming out the taxes and the working force of the country ; but the tax-farming nobility acquired a degree of political power much stronger than their predecessors of the appanage ages. This political power was sufficiently firmly established in an economic sense to thwart efforts towards reform, whether these were made from above or from beneath. Indeed, the serf-owning *pomyetschēk* was more of an autocrat than the Tsar, because he was less amenable to discipline and more skilful in his methods in dealing with his master than the peasants could possibly be in dealing with him. Yet the interests of the serf-owners were best served by supporting the throne, and by exacting from it in return privileges and immunities. The land- and serf-owners formed, indeed, the only effective support of the throne ; and, as already has been shown, the throne was at many junctures obliged to recognize this fact, and to acknowledge the political importance of the land-owners by safeguarding their economical interests. The liberation of the serfs was thus delayed and the political enfranchisement of the whole people prevented by the desire of the Government to liberate the serfs without curtailing the privileges of the landowners. While the landowning gentry had thus during certain epochs a considerable degree of political influence, they never enjoyed during the period of the development of the Moscow State any legal political status so far as concerned the central authority of the State. They were the serfs of the Tsar, not his advisers. The council of the Sovereign was not necessarily drawn from their ranks and, moreover, the influence of its decisions upon legislative or executive measures for long periods was insignificant. The will of the Tsar was nominally supreme. While, however, the central authority lay in the hands of the Tsar, the local authority lay largely in the hands of the landowners. They occupied the local seats of justice, and they administered in their own favour laws formulated for the purpose of safeguarding their interests. It is, therefore, not surprising that the peasants should have identified the interests of the landowner with the interests of the autocracy, and that each should suffer for the sins of the other as well as for their separate offences. The structure of Russian society did not permit the growth of a middle class, and the autocratic system prevented the development of open criticism of public administration by economically and socially independent and intelligent groups. Criticism of the Government, therefore, inevitably consisted in more or less violent attacks upon it. There was no helpful and effective discussion of advisable changes, because all initiative was presumed to come from above, and because there was no political machinery for the estimation of popular desires or for the continuous study of popular needs. Commissions and committees performed these functions spasmodically; but even when their recommendations were ostensibly adopted, the fitting machinery for carrying them out was wanting.

Grievances thus tended to accumulate, and political and social changes became long overdue. The autocracy assumed the exclusive right to legislate and to direct the administrative mechanism.

In previous chapters we have seen these grievances converging upon a catastrophe—a dramatic climax—in the rebellion known by the name—insignificant of itself—of Pugachev. This outburst of the rage of the sheep, when it turns upon its tormentors after immense endurance, was eventually crushed. The accumulation of grievances continued, scarcely affected by the temporary explosion of pent-up ferocity.

Complications in the order of succession offered an opportunity at the close of the first quarter of the nineteenth century for a fresh contract with the throne ; but the force behind the liberal elements was inadequate, and the principle of autocracy was established more firmly than ever during the reaction which followed the *Dekabrist* movement. The political and social movements, which in Russia followed the political and social evolution of Western Europe during the second quarter of the nineteenth century, were submerged by the movement for Emancipation.

Disillusion supervened after the Great Reform ; the prosperity of the peasant was compromised by the debt dependency which had been one of the causes of his previous legal bondage. The peasant had acquired a certain mobility, but this was qualified by the *mutual guarantee* for the payment of taxes and by the consequent authority of the *mir* over the individual peasant. Agriculture was improving on the large and efficiently managed estates, and rents were increasing, while among the peasantry the lack of agricultural skill and capital prevented improvement and kept the peasant at the margin of subsistence. Meanwhile the industrial progress of the towns was attracting the peasants to them. A proletarian artisan population was gradually arising, and was acquiring ideas previously foreign to the peasant mind.

The changes in the form of social structure which resulted from the abolition of bondage right had brought into relief the gulf between the peasant and the gentleman ; and an instinctive desire to cross this gulf began on the side of the more ardent and humane among the educated gentry, especially in the capitals. The *V Narod*, or " To the People " movement was the outcome of this desire. The movement, innocuous as it certainly was in the beginning, awoke suspicion in the minds of the Government. Suppression of the movement was followed by the development of a revolutionary spirit of a conspirative character. From 1872 till 1881 the Government found itself under the necessity of fighting for its life against a terror that was maintained by a small but extraordinarily active group of revolutionaries.

The instinct of self-preservation impelled the Government to decide to grant a constitution. It delayed too long. A final stroke came before the intention was announced. The price of procrastination was the assassination of the Tsar Emancipator, Alexander II. The assassination was followed by negotiations with the revolutionary elements and by a promise that executions in reprisal should be stayed. The promise was kept to a certain extent, but the Government set itself with renewed vigour to eliminate the revolutionary groups. Under Alexander III this policy was temporarily successful. But in 1885, and up till 1896, the struggle was renewed, and the Government had once more to fight for its life. Meanwhile two formidable economic changes were in progress. The peasantry was becoming more and more impoverished, and the city proletariat was becoming more and more numerous. The incompetence and shortsightedness of the landowners, the ignorance of the peasants, and the enormous increase of the deteriorated population, combined to bring about an insoluble agrarian problem, and the protective policy of the Government had not merely encouraged industry, but had prepared and fertilized an appropriate and ample soil for the growth of revolutionary ideas. The social revolutionary elements had been crushed out of existence by 1885, but the ideas represented by them were not extinguished. They went at once deeper and higher. As in the twenties of the nineteenth century, they began to affect the *intelligentsia* and they began to fructify amongst the impoverished peasantry. In the cities the Social Democratic movement began at the same time to make itself felt. By 1900 both of these processes had made a considerable headway. The movement among the peasants in 1902 and 1903, and the movement among the city proletariat of the latter year, were the signs of the renewed activity of the revolutionary spirit.

Before the Russo-Japanese War these activities were chiefly noticeable among the peasants and the working men; the professional and merchant classes were scarcely affected. But as the war proceeded, and as it became evident that the Government was unable to defend itself against a minor Power, even the moderate elements began to express dissatisfaction—the *intelligentsia*,[1] the merchants, and the nobility alike became disaffected. When the

---

[1] On the constituents of this group see *infra*, pp. 585 *et seq.*

war closed, practically the whole of Russian society was opposed to the Government. Three forces were, indeed, definitely arrayed against it. First, the city proletariat, led by the Social Democrats ; second, the impoverished peasantry, led by the Social Revolutionists ; and third, the newly arising middle class, disaffected but not united, and not led by any one. The Government met the crisis by a display of force. The Grand Ducal Party round the throne openly urged violent repression—the usual remedy. " Let us hang one or two hundred of these revolutionists, and then they will be satisfied," one of the Grand Dukes is reported to have said. Whether or not any of them committed himself to language so blunt, the temper of the group is not unfairly indicated by this expression. The episode of Bloody Sunday showed that some such idea was in their minds. Terror seemed to be the only remedy for terror.

But an effective Governmental terror meant complete reliance upon the army, and the army was everywhere exhibiting signs of disaffection. An entirely new spirit was manifesting itself among the people. Ideas and movements hitherto confined to small groups now began to affect large masses. Liberties long withheld, through fear of dreadful things to follow, were now seized by people in such numbers that it was impossible either to punish those who seized them or to ignore their seizure. For a time the Government was powerless. Autocracy had come to an end, and only the instinct of order, which is very strong in Russia, intervened between society and mere barbaric anarchy. Thus, a century and a quarter after Pugachev, there came a second catastrophe or anti-climax. When the Government emerged from the panic into which it had been thrown, it offered a long-delayed constitution of a kind.

The association and the conflict of economical and political ideas has rendered an extended account of the revolutionary movement necessary. This movement cannot be understood without a knowledge of the economic background and of the economical struggles with which it was accompanied, and by which it was to a large extent compromised. A political idea may lead to some distant end, and may therefore unite masses of people for an indefinite period ; but an economical question may be settled, and the settlement of it usually results in the automatic disbanding of the forces which accomplished the settlement. The crumbling of the revolution to powder and the subsequent reaction may both be debited against the oppositional forces which failed to arrive at, or, having arrived at, to maintain, their unanimity. The autocracy, backed by the inertia of the mass of the people, was too strong to be overthrown by divided, undisciplined, and even mutually hostile forces.

CHAPTER I

THE GENERAL STRIKE IN SOUTH RUSSIA IN 1903

THE first indications of turbulence in South Russia appeared among the workmen of the railway workshops at Tĕkhoryetsk Station on the Vladikavkas Railway. This turbulence was occasioned by a minor though deplorable incident arising out of the misconduct of an official and the death of a girl named Zolotova, whom he had disgracefully maltreated. The workmen of the shops became infuriated with the narrative of the sufferings of the girl, and wrecked the station buildings, beating the police and the Cossacks who had been implicated in the transactions.[1] Although a Government investigation was held into the affair, and although the Cossacks were found to have been guilty, the apparent intention on the part of the authorities to screen the major offender left a disagreeable impression, and contributed to the state of feeling which resulted in the strike of 2nd November 1902 in the railway shops at Vladikavkas and at Rostov-on-Don.

This strike was instigated by the Donskoë Committee of the Russian Social Democratic Party, which issued a manifesto formulating the strikers' demands. These demands related exclusively to questions of wages and conditions of employment. About 4000 workmen were involved at the beginning of the strike; but this number was soon increased by strikes in the ironworks of Pastuhov, Tokorov, and Dutikov, and in other factories in the neighbourhood, as well as in bakeries and tobacco shops. The Social Democrats began at once to utilize the meetings which the strikers held daily in the outskirts of Rostov. Sometimes these meetings were attended by upwards of 30,000 persons, including not only strikers, but also numbers of merchants, officials, ladies with lorgnettes in their hands

[1] Details of this deplorable case are given by F. Dan, *The History of the Labour Movement and Social Democracy in Russia*, 2nd edition (St. Petersburg, 1905), pp. 27 *et seq.* The official account is contained in a volume of evidence taken at the investigation instituted on behalf of the Government.

in carriages—in fact, the population of Rostov.[1] These meetings were addressed by agitators belonging to the Social Democratic Party, who delivered denunciations of the autocracy to the assembled crowds. During a whole week, from 4th November till 11th November, the meetings went on. To begin with, it appears that there was some disapprobation of the tone of the addresses, but later the crowds appeared to sympathize fully with the denunciations, on the one hand of the Government, and on the other of the capitalists. During the week the authorities seemed to have been in a state of perplexity, and for a time took no action, although on the outskirts of the crowd each day there was a force of police and Cossacks. On 11th November, while the usual meeting was dispersing, some stones were thrown (by children, it is alleged), and thereupon the Cossacks fired a fusillade, killing six and wounding severely twelve persons, and then galloped off immediately. This action did not put an end to the meetings, which continued, with the obvious sympathy of the inhabitants of Rostov, until 23rd November, when the strikers returned to work. Then wholesale arrests began to be made. Although the strike was unsuccessful, yet the facts that enormous meetings were held in spite of the authorities, and that revolutionary addresses were delivered to sympathetic audiences, were of great importance at this juncture. In the following March (1903) meetings were held, although no strike was in progress, at which again all Rostov made its appearance. At one of these meetings where shouts were raised, " *Vive* the eight-hour day ! " " *Vive* political freedom ! " a skirmish with the police took place, in which a police inspector was killed by a blow from a stick.[2]

In Kostroma also there were demonstrations, although these appear to have been organized by the working men spontaneously. Troops were called out, barricades were erected by the working men, and an unknown number of persons were killed and wounded.[3]

These minor events served as the prelude to the general strike of the summer of 1903 which affected nearly the whole of South Russia. From April onwards there were numerous small strikes in factories and many demonstrations by social democratic organizations. Throughout April and May a general spirit of unrest was

[1] The population of Rostov is about 120,000.
[2] Dan, *op. cit.*, p. 31.   [3] *Ibid.*

manifest. Discontent seemed to spread by an irresistible impulse. On 1st July the working men employed in the mineral oil trade at Baku went on strike, and in four or five days the whole city was involved. On 1st July also, at Tiflis, there was a demonstration to protest against the banishment to Siberia of four " politicals," and on 14th July the railway workers and the salesmen in shops went on strike, and they were shortly joined by practically all the working men in Tiflis. In Batùm, also, a sympathetic strike broke out, and by 17th July the whole city was involved. On 1st July the strike began in Odessa with the working men at the docks and railway shops (numbering 2000) ; by 22nd July the working men of the city were involved. In Kiev the strike was general on 24th July. In Elisavetgrad the strike began on 28th July. At Ekaterinoslav and Kertch work was suspended on 7th August, although by that date the strike in other places had already come to an end.

In all of these cities the strikers marched throughout the streets in crowds, went into the factories where work was still going on, had the whistles blown to cease work, and stopped the street railway cars. Every trade was involved in the movement, even porters (concierges) and (in two of the municipal districts of Kiev) policemen. In Batùm, Tiflis, and Baku, the number of strikers is stated to have been upwards of 100,000 ; in Odessa, 50,000 ; in Kiev, 30,000 ; in Nikolaiëv, 10,000 ; in Ekaterinoslav, between 20,000 and 30,000 ; in Elizavetgrad, 20,000. The total number is placed at 225,000.[1]

The aspect of the cities affected by the strike was strange. All shops, including bakeries, were closed ; horse and electric cars, as well as cabs, had disappeared from the streets ; trains were standing in the stations ; great quantities of goods littered the platforms ; steamers and sailing vessels lay idle in the harbours ; there were no newspapers. Provisions became scarce and more and more expensive. There was no bread and no meat. In the streets there were no lights, and the cities were in inky darkness. In the houses there were only candles, and these were not lighted in rooms with windows on the street in order to avoid attracting attention. The streets were not swept. All industrial life was in a state of complete stagnation. Throughout the day, however,

---

[1] Dan, *op. cit.*, pp. 31 and 33.

crowds of men marched through the streets, and the city seethed with excitement. Revolutionary songs and addresses were heard everywhere, and everywhere also were patrols of police and of soldiers.[1]

The demands of the strikers were almost identical in the different cities. They were, as a rule, formulated by the Social Democratic organizations. The chief points were : an eight-hour working day (in some cases nine hours), increases of wages of from 20 per cent. to 70 per cent., fixation of a minimum wage, the abolition of fines, and demands for civil treatment and improvement in the conditions of labour.

In addition to the manifestoes of industrial demands, there were extensively circulated manifestoes of a political character demanding the convocation of an All-Russia National Assembly, liberty of striking, of the formation of trade unions, and of public meetings, liberty of speech and of the press, liberty of conscience, and inviolability of the person.

In Odessa, in the early stages, a conspicuous rôle in the initiation of the strike movement was played by Zubàtov's agents. Zubàtov's ally, Shaëvich, had succeeded in forming some so-called " Independents " into societies analogous to trade unions, but at a very early stage these societies seem to have broken off from the leadership of Shaëvich. Almost at once the societies so formed expelled the police organizers from their meetings.[2] For example, when at one meeting Shaëvich, in evident despair, asked the working men " What do you want ? To run your heads against a wall, or to bore the wall ? " he was answered by shouts, " To run our heads against the wall ! " Leaflets were also circulated among the workmen with the phrases " Down with fraud ! Down with small demands ! We want more."

In Baku, also, meetings very numerously attended took place—sometimes 3000 persons, and sometimes with bystanders, the meetings numbered 20,000 to 30,000 persons.[3] These meetings were addressed by Social Democrats, and leaflets in Russian, Armenian, Georgian, and Tartar were circulated. The demonstrations reached such dimensions that the Government was evidently reluctant to employ troops to disperse the gatherings. The difficulty of dealing with a population *en masse* was obvious. When comparatively

[1] Dan, *op. cit.*, p. 34.   [2] *Ibid.*   [3] *Ibid.*

small numbers were collected, these were dispersed by the
nagaïkas of the Cossacks. When the excitement had somewhat
subsided, workmen were thus driven to work by whips, and were
compelled to perform their industrial duties under the guard
of soldiers.[1]

In Tiflis and Batum, where the strike did not assume proportionately such dimensions, the workmen who were arrested were
compelled to pass through ranks of Cossacks armed with *nagaïkas*.

In Odessa, Kiev, and Ekaterinoslav, there were meetings of
40,000 to 50,000 persons, with marches of working men singing
revolutionary songs. These processions were attacked by Cossacks,
and the working men defended themselves by using sticks and
stones. Sometimes arrested workmen were rescued by the crowd,
yet hundreds of workmen were arrested and beaten. Many of
these died in the hospitals.

In Kiev, on 23rd July, 2000 railway employees laid themselves
prone upon the rails, in order to stop the movement of trains. After
a sanguinary conflict, in which many were wounded on both sides,
and in which there were fired three fusillades, four working men
were killed at once, and twenty wounded, some of the latter
mortally. So far from pacifying the strikers, this attack added
fuel to the flame, and the strike became general. The workmen
said among themselves : " Yesterday they shot some of us at the
station ; to-day we will not work. In the factories there is oppression, and everywhere rascality." In Podol (a part of Kiev) similar
scenes took place. Here also *nagaïkas* were employed, and later
fire-arms. The fury of the Cossacks was responded to by the
crowd with similar fury. On one occasion the infantry poured
four fusillades into the rear ranks of the crowd, killing three and
wounding very many more.[2] Altogether in Kiev in these days of
the general strike there were fifteen killed and two hundred
wounded. Fifteen police and Cossacks were wounded also.

In Ekaterinoslav, during one of the skirmishes, a woman struck
an officer, and thereupon he ordered his men to fire—result, eleven
killed at once and thirteen mortally wounded. At the Cher-
nomorsky works the working men met a company of soldiers ready
for action, but a working man succeeded in convincing the officer
in charge that the people would disperse quietly if they were given

---

[1] Dan, *op. cit.*, p. 35.　　　　　　　　[2] *Ibid.*, p. 36.

an opportunity of doing so ; this was agreed to, and the people dispersed.

Exaggerated rumours spread everywhere. Reports were current that two hundred working men had been killed at Kiev. The workmen at Elizavetgrad, for example, were inflamed by this rumour. They made a demonstration, and succeeded in repulsing infantry who attacked them.

In Kertch an attempt was made to release prisoners, and several persons were killed and wounded.

This state of tension could not last indefinitely. Everything was at a standstill, and this circumstance of itself wore out the strikers.

By the date of the Feast of the Assumption (15th August), a great festival in Russia, the general strike had come to an end.

Of definite concrete aims it is difficult to find much trace in the movements of the working men which have been described.[1]   At all costs they were determined to make a demonstration of their power, such as it was. The Government displayed spasmodic energy— at one moment aiding them in their strikes, and at another moment abandoning them to the fury of the Cossacks or banishing them to Arkhangel or Siberia. The Government had power to do much, but the working men also had power. What would happen in the cities when they folded their hands ? Much suffering to the working men and their families, no doubt, but also complete paralysis of the governmental machinery, as well as of industrial and commercial life.

The economic effect of a general strike of workmen in Russia is different from that of a similar strike in Western Europe. The absence in the Russian manufactory towns, up almost to the present time, of an urban proletariat of any considerable dimensions means also the absence of that reserve of labour from which necessary workmen may immediately be drawn even during strikes by promises of high pay and other inducements.

The days of the general strike meant also to the working men increased bitterness over their " rightlessness " ; each fusillade and each attack of Cossacks left dead and wounded upon the ground, and bitter memories in the minds of the people. The merely industrial grievances faded into the background before the deep

[1] *Cf.* Dan, *op. cit.*, p. 36.

feeling of resentment against a Government that played fast and loose with the labour question, and in the end always shot down the workers.   The use which the Social Democrats and Social Revolutionists made of the general strike for propagation of their doctrines must not be ignored.   The publication and circulation of propagandist literature, previously rigidly prohibited, came like a flood. Liberties sternly denied were simply seized, the censorship was ignored, and the " right " of public meeting was vindicated by the simple process of meeting in such numbers that dispersal was impossible.   *L'action directe* [1] became the order of the day.

The strike also brought out sharply the distinction between the two parties—the Social Democrats and the Social Revolutionists.   The former took credit to themselves for confining the strike agitation within peaceful limits, and thus for preventing " that useless slaughter of working men which might so easily have occurred in these days, and which might have drowned in a sea of blood the proletarian movement at its very beginning." [2] On the other hand, the Social Revolutionists derided what they regarded as the restricted aims of the Social Democrats, and advocated the adoption of violent measures of defence against the attacks of the authorities.   It does not appear, however, that the influence of the latter party was dominant, or even very influential, in the South Russian movement of 1903.

In so far as the movement was influenced by propaganda, it appears to have been influenced chiefly by the Social Democrats, who provided a large proportion of the speakers at the meetings. But indeed the movement was mainly spontaneous.   Industrial discontent due to lower wages and more unfavourable conditions of employment than those reported to be enjoyed by workmen elsewhere, combined with aspirations for political action and indignation aroused by the misconduct of local functionaries in some cases, and in many others by the accounts, sometimes exaggerated, of attacks upon working men and the forcible dispersal of meetings by the authorities, and perhaps also irritation at the tactics of the " Black Hundred " [3] in different centres—these appear to have been the really influential causes.

[1] Cf. *infra*, pp. 515–17 and 521.
[2] Dan, *op. cit.*, p. 37.
[3] For explanation of this expression, see *infra*, p. 499.

While the strike was accompanied by demands of an industrial character, and while the conditions of employment had much to do with the state of discontent into which working men had fallen, yet the substantial reason for the strike was a political rather than an economical one. The idea came to be prevalent that the Government would suffer by the strike to a greater extent than anyone else—the Government railways, post, telegraphs, the Government factories, &c., would yield no revenue during the strike, taxes would not be paid, and the financial credit of the Government would be shaken.

CHAPTER II

THE MOVEMENT OF FATHER GAPON

OBSCURE as are some of the motives in the movement known as the " Zubàtovshina," they are luminous compared with the as yet unfathomed mysteries of the " Gaponovshina " with its tragic sequel in the " Gaponiade." Perhaps one day light may be shed upon the dark places by the memoirs of Ministers of State, some of whom are alleged to have been involved in the events immediately preceding the end of Gapon. As yet the literature on the subject is scanty. Gapon's own articles in the popular magazines tell us practically nothing of the inner history of his propaganda. Father Georg Gapon[1] was in 1904, chaplain in one of the gaols of St.

[1] Georg Gapon was of Little Russian origin. He was the son of a peasant of a village in the district of Bielyaki, in Poltavskaya *gub.*, where he was born about 1873. Until the age of seventeen he attended an elementary school in Poltava. His teacher in this school was Ivan Trégubov, for many years well known afterwards among the Russian exiles in Paris as a Tolstoyist and writer upon Russian social subjects. Trégubov (in *L'Ere Nouvelle*, Paris, 3me Series, 2me vol., No. 33, 10 Février 1905, p. 47) describes Gapon as he was at the age of fifteen to seventeen as " an intelligent, serious, meditative, but very vivacious young man. His studious habits enabled him to take always his place among the first of his class. Extremely desirous of instructing himself, he read much. I (Trégubov) gave him some books, among others the works of Leo Tolstoy, which, interdicted in Russia, circulated then clandestinely in manuscript. I allowed, with much zeal, these manuscripts to fall into the hands of my pupils and of young priests. They produced upon them the same lively impression which they did upon me. Simultaneously with my departure from the elementary school, Gapon went to pursue his studies in the High School of Poltava." [This is an error. He went to the Theological Seminary (or intermediate school for theological students).] " Afterwards he went to the Faculty of Theology at St. Petersburg." [This also is an error. He went to the Theological College.] " I (Trégubov) know that he maintained relations with the Tolstoyans at Poltava. The strike and the pacific manifestations of the workers at St. Petersburg show that he remains faithful to the ideas which we had in common these fifteen years, and which find lodgment more and more in the minds of the Russian people. . . . Sooner or later there will occur the declaration of a general strike which will cause to disappear from the face of the earth this survival of barbarous times—the autocracy." (Ivan Trégubov in *L'Ere Nouvelle*, loc. cit.) Gapon is also described by others who knew him as

Petersburg, where, on account of his influence over the prisoners, he was *persona grata* with the authorities.

It appears that about 1902, Gapon conceived the idea of effecting an organization of the working men of St. Petersburg upon a purely industrial basis, and of leading them collectively to demand improved conditions of work and increased wages. He apparently thought that if it were possible to show that his organization was of a non-political character, and was not intended in any way to engage in political agitation, it might be possible to obtain official sanction. By these means, meetings of working men might be held openly and legally and the economical interests of the working men might be freely discussed. Gapon was, no doubt, aware of Zubàtov's activity in Moscow, and of that of his agents in St. Petersburg in 1902 and 1903.[1] This knowledge must, however, have convinced him that such plans as those of Zubàtov must be very

being of an attractive personality and as being a good public speaker. He paid a visit to America in 1901.

After the procession of Bloody Sunday, 9th January 1905 (O.S.), Gapon was searched for by the police, partly because they held him responsible for the procession at the head of which he was marching, and partly on account of his denunciation of the Tsar which followed the tragedy of 9th January. (See Appendix to this chapter.) Through the assistance of Social Democrats he contrived to make his escape. Within a few days he made his appearance in Paris, and afterwards in London. In these cities he was not only lionized by sympathizers with the Russian revolutionary movement, but he was also surrounded by editors clamouring for accounts of his propaganda. Suddenly, for the first time in his life, he found himself of pecuniary value. This unfortunate circumstance seems to have demoralized him, overstrained as his nerves must have been by his St. Petersburg experiences in December and the first days of January. In this condition he appears to have gone to Monte Carlo, probably to work off his abnormal nervous excitation. On the granting of the amnesty of 21st October 1905 (O.S.), Gapon returned to St. Petersburg an altered man. From this time until his death his proceedings are shrouded in mystery. It is conjectured that he entered into relations with Ministers of State (specifically with Count Witte and M. Durnovo), but to what end he did so, if he did so at all, remains unexplained. On or about 28th March 1906 (O.S.) he was killed in a cottage at Ozerky, a summer resort on the St. Petersburg-Viborg Railway. It was alleged at the time that he was hanged by revolutionists who accused him of treachery ; and circumstantial details of his end were given in the newspapers ; but the rooted conviction remained in the minds of the working men of St. Petersburg that he was actually killed by agents of the police (cf. *infra*, pp. 464 and 578). His body was found by the police about 28th April. An investigation into the circumstances was ordered, but it was mysteriously blocked, and nothing came of it. See, however, an account by Rutenberg in *Biloye* (The Past), No. 12. Paris, 1909.

[1] Opinions differ about the relations between Zubàtov and Gapon. There is as yet no definite proof that they were known to one another.

difficult to carry out in St. Petersburg, for the reasons that the
working men of the northern capital were more alert and intelligent
and more accustomed to political action and to police interference
than were the working men of Moscow. They were therefore less
easily deceived. If there were in their minds the faintest suspicion
that the police had anything to do with Gapon's movement, that
movement was doomed at the outset. Yet there seems little reason
to doubt that, since Gapon's plans made in the same direction as
those of Zubàtov, namely, in the direction of separating the industrial from the political issues, the police from the beginning were
willing to facilitate his attempt to organize the working man in a
peaceful organization. Even if the police of St. Petersburg had
not been influenced by the temporary success of Zubàtov in Moscow,
this would have been an obviously reasonable policy ; and there
were grounds for believing that the police department might be
able to exercise a more stringent control over the Gapon movement
than experience had shown they were able to do in the case of
Zubàtov. The higher officials were, moreover, distracted by the
events in Manchuria and by the discontent among the working men
nearer home, and, moreover, before Gapon's movement became
conspicuous the "Spring" of Prince Svyatopolk-Mirsky—the period
of amiability—brief and illusory as it was, had begun. Towards
the end of 1903, Gapon formulated a project for an "Assembly
of Russian Factory and Mill Workers of St. Petersburg." In order
to obtain legal sanction, it was necessary to submit a draft constitution to the police, and also to the Minister of the Interior.
The draft of the constitution of the first police trade union in
Moscow was, as we have seen, prepared and preserved by Professor
Ozerov ;[1] but no such preliminary document relating to Gapon's
organization is at present available.

The principal clauses of the constitution of the society, as ultimately adopted, were as follows :

1. The Assembly of Russian Factory and Mill Workers of St.
Petersburg is established : (*a*) for sober and rational passing of
leisure time by the members with actual benefit for them in spiritual
and moral, as well as in material respects ; (*b*) for exciting and
strengthening among the members of Russian national self-con-

---

[1] Cf. *supra*, p. 192.

sciousness ; (c) for forming and developing among the members prudent views upon the duties and rights of workers ; (d) for the exercise by members of self-activity making for the legal improvement of the conditions of labour and of the life of the workers.

2. The means for attaining the above purposes are : (a) the absolute prohibition in the premises of the Assembly of games for money, of the use of intoxicating drinks, and of persons, whether members or guests, in a state of intoxication; (b) the purchasing of useful publications of Russian newspapers and magazines, the foundation of a library, the institution of a reading-room, the formation from among the members of a church and secular choir and of musical clubs, the institution in permanent premises of the Assembly, and in hired premises of concerts, family and literary vocal soirees ; (c) weekly club and general meetings of members for prudent discussion from all points of view of their necessities and for self-education ; (d) the institution of religious and moral discussions and also of lectures with discussions ; (e) the organiza-tion, with proper permission, of lectures on subjects of common education, especially on knowledge of the Fatherland, and parti-cularly on labour questions which would point out and explain to the worker his judicial status and the legal ways of emerging from ignorance and dirt into the light ; (f) the institution of a mutual assistance fund for cases of illness, unemployment, and special necessity among the members.

Other clauses provided that in case of strikes, benefits were not to be given from the mutual assistance funds, that a tea and lunch room should be provided for the use of the members, also that meetings might be held for the purpose of discussing questions such as demands for the increase of wages ; but that special per-mission must be obtained from the proper authorities on each occa-sion. The subordination of the Union to the St. Petersburg police is made quite clear. " The chief leader and controller of the whole activity of the Assembly " and " the chief person responsible to the Government, must be approved of by the Chief of the St. Petersburg police " (Par. 16).[1]

" The Assembly of Russian Factory and Mill Workers " was

[1] The police are mentioned nineteen times in fifteen clauses of the con-stitution. See V. V. Svyatlovsky, op. cit., pp. 76-8.

solemnly inaugurated on 11th April 1904,[1] with Father Gapon as patron and president of the council. For some time Gapon failed to attract any considerable number of adherents to his society. The fact of his being a priest was a grave disadvantage. The intelligent and progressive working men were indifferent or hostile to the Church, and the wave of "class-consciousness," though rising slowly, was even then sufficiently powerful to cause the progressive working men to look with some suspicion upon all movements which did not arise within their own ranks.[2] Thus the indifference of the progressive elements sufficed to prevent any considerable adhesion to the society from the mass of the working men of St. Petersburg.

By some means Gapon became acquainted with a small group of "influential working men." [3] He held secret meetings with this group, and the result of these meetings was an agreement on their part to assist Gapon, and on his part to endeavour to obtain through his organization the satisfaction of their demands. This group frankly informed Gapon that they were aware that he had some connection with the police, and that they would only consent to join his organization upon his entering into this agreement. The demands were then formulated, and they formed the basis of the petition which some months afterwards was prepared for

---

[1] The following passages are extracted from the report of the inaugural meeting appearing in the *St. Petersburg Gazette* (No. 100, of 14th April 1904); cited by Svyatlovsky, *op. cit.*, p. 78:
" . . . It became clear that the constitution of the Assembly granted on 15th February 1904, by the Minister of the Interior, gave for the first time in Russia the possibility of actual union without any interference of the administration. All is based upon profound trust, and upon idealistic, unselfish, and sound service to the interests of the workers. The first steps of the new society afford ample grounds for belief that the working men will fully justify the hopes entertained about them. At the close of the session, by unanimous resolution, a despatch was sent to the Minister of the Interior, requesting respectfully that he lay before the feet of his Imperial Majesty, the adored monarch, the most humble feelings of the workers, animated as they were by zealous love towards the Throne and the Fatherland." The whole Assembly sang three times with "enormous enthusiasm"—"God Save the Tsar!" and shouted "Hurrah!" After the close of the session Mr. Litvonov-Falinsky, factory inspector, delivered an address upon the relation of the factory inspectors towards the workers.
[2] It was by playing skilfully upon this "class-conscious" feeling that Zubàtov acquired his first influence upon his selected working men. Cf. *supra*, p. 190, and F. Dan, *op. cit.*, p. 41.
[3] Four in number. For the details of these proceedings I am indebted to a correspondent who had exceptional opportunities of knowing what took place.

presentation to the Tsar on the day which came to be known as Bloody Sunday.[1]

There thus came to be *four* elements in Gapon's movement : (1) the enthusiastic Gapon himself, apparently disinterested in the early stages, afterwards torn by conflicting interests and unable to pursue an independent course ; (2) the police, participating partly overtly through the control provided by the constitution of Gapon's society, and partly covertly through spies, and probably also, consciously or unconsciously on his part, through Gapon ; (3) the small group of working men whose influence Gapon had found it necessary to enlist in order to secure adherents to his movement, and who afterwards forced Gapon into a position from which he would gladly have escaped ; and (4) the mass of working men and working women members and strikers joining the society at the last moment, who, on the one hand, were depressed by low wages and by conditions of employment which they regarded as oppressive, and, on the other, were inflated with the promises of liberty and of improved conditions of life which were recklessly made to them by the progressive parties, and whose views about Gapon, as well as their adhesion to him, fluctuated from time to time.

As soon as the agreement with the influential group of working men was concluded, adherents began to pour into the society in great numbers. During the year 1904 eleven sections of the Union were formed in rapid succession.[2]

Large groups of workmen, especially from the large industrial establishments, became members. Many meetings, debates, lectures, dances, &c., took place. Such gatherings of the people had hitherto been sternly suppressed by the police, now they were held without hindrance. It is not necessary to suppose that the

---

[1] See Appendix to this chapter for text of petition.

[2] The number of members who actually paid their subscriptions in the early phases of Gapon's society was very small. Up till 1st May 1904, there were only 170 members who had done so. By 21st September the number of paying members had increased, under the influence of the new elements, to 1200. From this time onwards it is impossible to distinguish the actual members from the enormous number of adherents who attended the meetings, and who paid their subscriptions in small instalments of 5 and 10 kopeks (1¼d. to 2½d.). (*Cf.* Svyatlovsky, *op. cit.*, p. 79.) By the end of 1904, the number of members may be put down as nominally 100,000, of which number about 74,000 belonged to the mechanical trades, *i.e.* practically the whole of the workmen engaged in these trades in St. Petersburg and its outskirts.

police were ignorant of the compromising position of Gapon, standing as he did between the revolutionists on the one hand and the police on the other, each, as he must have realized, most likely to be acutely watching for any slip on his part. It is more reasonable to believe that they permitted the movement to go on, understanding it up to a certain point, but not realizing fully whither it was drifting.

On 19th September 1904 there took place, in a hall hired for the purpose, an enormous general meeting. Here it was decided to expand the organization by the formation of numerous branches in St. Petersburg and its environs. Prior to the official granting of the constitution the work of the society had been carried on by thirty " responsible " persons. This circle was now largely increased until it comprised several hundreds (in Vasilyevsky Ostrov, an island in the Neva, and an important working-class district, 100, and in Narvsky Ward, 300). The important decisions regarding the policy of the organization were taken at the meetings of these " responsible " persons, and the decisions were carried into effect by the executive committee elected by and from these persons.[1] On Saturdays the " responsible " persons met, and on Sundays the members of the branches met, originally at ten in the morning, but later at two in the afternoon, the meetings in each case lasting throughout the remainder of the day, usually until midnight. The time was passed in listening to lectures and addresses, and in dances, teas, &c. From April 1904 lectures were also delivered on Wednesday evenings, by Mr. Malinin (editor of the *Prison Messenger*) on Russian history, and by others on geology and general literature, and on economic and other questions of current moment. Discussions took place at these lectures. In the earlier stages there was much freedom of speech at the meetings—several of the more " class conscious " working men speaking their minds very freely. In the autumn of 1904, however, it began to be apparent that, although the branches were numerously attended, there was an absence of *intelligentsia*, and an obvious presence of some who came for the purpose of wrecking the organization. This condition led to inner meetings of the more serious propagandists. These meetings were secret, and were held at Gapon's house. Some sixty or seventy enthusiasts continued to meet there for purposes of study.

[1] Svyatlovsky, *op. cit.*, p. 80.

Their studies appear to have been carried on with some degree of system, and to have included not merely economical questions, but even larger political issues. They studied, for example, the political constitutions of Germany and England, as well as economical questions—wages, co-operation, trade unionism, &c. The history of the labour movement in Russia was expounded to them and discussed. Among those propagandists there was a small group of Social Democrats, who necessarily gave a certain direction to the debates.[1]

Women became members of the branches in considerable numbers. In the late autumn they numbered nearly a thousand in all the branches.[2] At first the presence of women was resented by the working men, and even by Gapon himself. The women's meetings were fairly successful, although attempts to interest women of the *intelligentsia* in the movement conspicuously failed.

Meanwhile, in the autumn of 1904, there occurred the " Spring " of Prince Svyatopolk-Mirsky, and the influence of the mild régime of this Minister began to be felt in the branches. When, for example, someone shouted at a meeting,[3] " Down with the autocracy ! " the shout was received with " great indignation." [4] In the phase through which the working men's minds were passing at that time, much importance was attached to the " providential rôle of the autocracy." The autocracy was to put everything in order. It would be wiser, after all, to trust to the autocracy than to a democracy of a pattern which might give predominance to wealth and capital, and in which the working masses might be no better off than before. The Tsar, when he knew the situation of affairs, would take prompt measures to redress the grievances of the working men and the peasants. The faith of the people in the Tsar had not yet been broken, although the measure of their continued faith in him would be determined by the extent to which he accepted their views concerning what ought to be done.

In November 1904 the newspapers published the petition to the Tsar of the Saratovsky Zemstvo. Like the petitions of other Zemstvos, the Sarotovskaya petition asked for the convocation of a Representative Assembly. This document was read at the meet-

---

[1] Svyatlovsky, *op. cit.*, p. 80.
[2] The leader among the women was an intelligent working woman known as V. M. K. (Svyatlovsky, *loc. cit.*).
[3] In the beginning of November 1904.   [4] Svyatlovsky, *op. cit.*, p. 83.

ings, and almost immediately there arose a desire to present a similar petition to the Tsar.

Gapon now found himself in a difficult position. His society had been founded upon a non-political basis, and it had been sanctioned by the Minister of the Interior on that explicit understanding. If it came to be transformed into a group for political propaganda, Gapon must either leave the society or run the risk of involving himself as well as the society in conflicts with the police, who must soon come to learn of the radical change in policy. While there were, as we have seen, socialist elements in Gapon's society, the pressure to introduce politics into its activity did not come exclusively from them. The general Social Democratic and Social Revolutionary propagandas among the working men had made so far in that direction before the society was formed, that Gapon realized early that without the help of persons known to be in sympathy with the political propaganda he could not succeed in forming a society of any magnitude. Thus the larger his society became the greater was the risk of it being converted into a group for political propaganda.

When the desire to present a petition to the Tsar was formulated, Gapon opposed it energetically.[1] He said that such a petition would be extremely untimely, and that those who proposed it desired to wreck the organization. The strength of the desire to present the petition was, however, overwhelming, and Gapon had to give way, the only concession which he was able to extort being that the general mass of the members should be consulted.

This resolution was the turning-point of the movement. From this moment it is clear that Gapon ceased to lead, and that he was driven by his former followers. That his influence did not altogether cease is, however, suggested by the essentially pacific character of the movement throughout its course.

The feeling of the branches was found to be unanimously in favour of the presentation of a petition, and the central committee, headed, of course, by Gapon, was charged with the composition of the petition and the arrangements for its presentation. It was decided to write to the representatives of other " parties " to invite their co-operation. Thus the Social Democrats and the Social Revolutionists were invited to consider the expediency of presenting

---

[1] Svyatlovsky, *op. cit.*, p. 84.

a joint petition. This meant, of course, that Gapon's society regarded itself as having emerged on a platform similar to that of the revolutionary groups.

The " influential group " of working men who had made the success of Gapon's movement possible were now in a position to compel him to implement his agreement. The movement had become political in spite of Gapon.

The circumstances of the time seemed, on the whole, favourable to the presentation of a petition. During the later months of 1904 the war had resulted in a series of disastrous blows to the military prestige of Russia, and events were hastening towards the fall of Port Arthur.[1] The administration was preoccupied and little inclined to force conclusions in internal affairs, while the flower of the army, upon which the autocracy must in the last event rely, was barely holding its own in Manchuria.

Moreover, the idea was at this time widely prevalent among the working men that the Tsar was not implicated in the mis-government of the country. They thought that the blame of this misgovernment should be laid entirely on the shoulders of the bureaucracy, and that they had only to bring the state of matters to the notice of the Tsar to have a new system inaugurated which would speedily result in a great improvement of their economical position.

The Social Democrats and the Social Revolutionists were alike eager to take advantage of the circumstances and of the optimistic attitude of the working men as it appeared in Gapon's organiza-tion. Still, working men who were actively engaged in these parties as a rule, and *intelligentsia* almost wholly, held aloof from Gapon. During the discussions upon the policy of presenting a petition to the Tsar, which were held by Gapon's adherents, some of the private meetings were attended by a " semi-party group." [2] This group, which possessed no definite political colour, was composed of journalists who were merely educating themselves by " looking into " the labour movement. Five of these journalists and five working-men adherents of Gapon met secretly in Gapon's house. Gapon, who presided, declared that the working men must compose

---

[1] Port Arthur fell on 20th December (O.S.).

[2] Svyatlovsky, *op. cit.*, p. 85. A " semi-party " group is a group whose claim to be regarded as a party is not generally recognized.

a protest in such a form as " to astonish the whole world." After the constitution of the organization had been shown to the journalists, they urged Gapon's adherents to enlist a large number of people in a movement for a protest to the Government. At the same time they told them that the Government was always deceiving the Liberals, and that the Liberal current which arose in the " Spring " of Svyatopolk-Mirsky would inevitably result in " a new fraud." This view was not accepted by the working men, and they determined to compose their petition and to present it in their own way, without the assistance of anyone. The " clubbing of *intelligentsia* " by the police during a demonstration opposite the Kazan Cathedral in the Nevski Prospekt [1] confirmed this resolution, and largely attended meetings [2] were held in December on the subject of the petition. In December also there took place the strike of metal-workers in the Putilovsky works, and excited meetings were held daily. Gapon appears to have pleaded for delay until a larger number of members could be obtained in order to make the numbers presenting the petition more formidable. On the 27th December (O.S.) the employees of all the St. Petersburg factories went on strike and decisive meetings were held on the following day, the 28th December, in Vasilyevsky Ostrov and other places.

On 2nd January 1905 (O.S.) there met in Gapon's house a hundred of the most influential of his adherents. Gapon again urgently pleaded for delay, but the working men " in the most categorical manner " insisted " that the fire of the excitement might die out," and that the strike at the Putilovsky Works presented an opportunity such as was not likely soon to occur again. They told Gapon also that if he did not lead them they would leave him. " We have been branded," some of them said, " as Zubàtov's men, and as provocators, and here is the chance to wash out this detestable stain." This appeal was received sympathetically, and those present unanimously resolved upon going with the largest possible crowd to the Winter Palace with a petition on the following Sunday.

" So let it be ! " Gapon said at last, worn out by the opposition

---

[1] On the occasion of the suicide in prison of Vetrova, a girl student.
[2] Meetings attended by 800 persons, *e.g.*

to his appeals for delay.[1] From this time Gapon concealed himself from the police. They had been watching the proceedings at the branches, and it was evident that they had realized the change in the tendencies of the movement.

Troops were hurried into the city on the night of the 8th,[2] and preparations were made to receive the petitioners. The mode of dealing with the crisis which was adopted is said to have been suggested by the late Grand Duke Vladimir,[3] while the military dispositions were placed in the hands of Prince Vasilchikov, Commander-in-Chief of the Corps of the Guard. The Tsar and the Imperial Family had gone to Tsarskoë Selo some days earlier.

At the height of the movement of Gapon, the actual number of registered members of the branches did not exceed 9000, but the number of persons who attended the meetings of the branches was much greater—" some scores of thousands." [4] The number of persons who took part in the procession of " Bloody Sunday " is difficult to estimate owing to the fact that many fractions of the procession were dispersed soon after they started. The usual estimate of the total number of those who set out upon the procession is 200,000.

Early in the morning of the 9th January, red-cross arm-bands were distributed to the women and to some men. The object of this is rather difficult to explain, unless we realize that in so great a concourse, consisting of many widely separated groups, there were many different and even conflicting ideas. These red-cross bands may have been assumed to indicate that their wearers were not militant participants in the procession or they may have been

---

[1] The subsequent accusations of Petrov (see *infra*) suggest that had Gapon not acquiesced in the demands of the majority at that time, he might then have been denounced as a police spy, or at least as a defender of the autocracy rather than of the liberties of the people.

[2] 8th January 1905 (O.S.). [3] Uncle of Nicholas II.

[4] *Cf.* Svyatlovsky, *op. cit.*, p. 92. The organization of Gapon corresponds to the general Labour Unions familiar in the early stages of Trade Unions in England and in the United States. (*Cf.* Webb, *History of Trade Unionism* (London, 1894), p. 199, and Hollander and Barnett, *Studies in American Trade Unionism* (New York, 1907), p. 353.) Conflict of trades soon began to develop in Gapon's organization, and it came to be divided into three sections—one of the mechanical trades, another of the weavers, and the third of lithographers. These met as separate trade groups. Yet these groups appear to have been rather social clubs than trade unions. The only strike in which they took part was that at the Putilovsky Ironworks on the eve of the demonstration of 9th January.

assumed for the practical purpose of calling upon their wearers to act as nurses to the wounded in an anticipated sanguinary struggle. While it is not impossible that arms were carried by some, it is also true that in some of the groups, those who came to the rendezvous with arms were deprived of them by their fellow-workers before the procession started on its way.   The more " class conscious " working men seem to have marched in front of the different processions with their arms linked, thus forming chains across the line of the procession.

The early morning of Sunday, 9th January, was " bitterly cold, with a piercing wind and fine driving snow." [1] People went to church as usual.   There were no troops in the great square opposite the Winter Palace.   Traffic across the Neva by the bridges was unimpeded.   At ten o'clock in the forenoon the movements of troops began.   It was the evident intention of the military authorities to deal with the crowd in detachments, and to hold the constituent elements of the procession at or near their respective starting-points.   At the same time the bridges were strongly held, and the Palace square was occupied by troops, which early in the forenoon debouched from the courtyards of the Winter Palace.

The attacks by the troops upon the processions took place at many different points, and for that reason a connected statement of the occurrences is difficult.   The procedure appears, however, to have been generally the same at all the points where the military came into collision with the crowd—a summons to disperse—followed speedily by a volley of blank cartridge and then a volley of bullets.   The official account admits firing in the Schlüsselburg Chaussée, at the Narva Gate, where the crowd was led by Gapon, in the Troitsky Square, in Vasilevsky Ostrov, in the Alexander Gardens, near the Winter Palace, and in the Nevsky Prospekt, especially at the Kazan Cathedral.   The official account also says that three barricades were erected.[2]   Accounts of the number of killed and wounded vary widely.   The estimate from the side of the working men,[3] of 500 killed and 3000 wounded, is probably an exaggeration, while the official figures, which are much lower, probably minimize

[1] Correspondent of *Daily Mail*, London, 23rd January 1905.
[2] These were probably the first barricades erected in St. Petersburg. Barricades had been erected in South Russia in 1903.   Cf. *supra*, p. 444.
[3] See *History of the Council of Labour Deputies*, Section by Khrustalov-Nosar (St. Petersburg, 1910), p. 46.

the losses. The official account of the events which led up to "Bloody Sunday" is not ingenuous. Nothing is said of the encouragement given to the movement of Gapon in its early stages by the police, and even by the Minister of the Interior. The allegation in the official account that the working men's association was "soon" reinforced by the "agitation of revolutionary circles" is not consistent with the narrative given above, and is probably inaccurate. The influential working men who joined Gapon, as described, were not at that time revolutionists, although they were the originators of the political side of the propaganda, while the terms of the protest were no more revolutionary than were the Zemstvo petitions upon which, indeed, Gapon's petition was founded.

The history of the Gapon labour movement, or "Gaponovshina," closed with 9th January 1905. It is true that some of the branches lingered for some months, but the movement had wholly collapsed. In the autumn of 1905 there occurred the short-lived so-called "Gaponiade." This episode began with a letter by a working man, Nicolaï Petrov, which was published in the St. Petersburg newspaper *Russ*.[1] Petrov accused Gapon of having been bribed by the Government. Upon this accusation there began "a violent polemic"—ten chairmen of branches bringing a counter-accusation of embezzlement against Petrov. Gapon had returned to St. Petersburg after the amnesty of 21st October 1905. He is reported to have entered into relations with Count Witté and with Prince Androvidov, with the apparent design of rehabilitating himself in the opinion of the authorities. His influence with the working class was, however, wholly destroyed, and in a summer house at Ozerky, near St. Petersburg, he passed from the scene on or about 28th March 1906.[2] Even the "Gaponiade" has had its sequel. Among the disclosures of the Lopukhin-Azef case, in January 1909, was the statement that Gapon had been killed by the order of Azef, a member of the militant organization of the Socialist Revolutionary Party, and at the same time an agent of the political police.[3]

It is necessary now to examine the evidence which throws light

---

[1] *Russ.*, No. 32, 8th February 1906. *Cf*. Svyatlovsky, *op. cit.*, p. 93.

[2] Gapon's body was found hanged in a summer cottage. An inquiry was ordered into the circumstances of his death, but it was mysteriously blocked. Cf. *supra*, p. 452*n*.

[3] See *Novoë Vremya* (St. Petersburg), 19th January 1909, and cf. *infra*, p. 578.

upon the frame of mind of the working men who engaged in the demonstration. So far as those working men are concerned who were most active in the movement, and probably so far as Gapon himself was concerned, it seems possible, though it is not certain, that they realized the imminent risk of a conflict with the troops. As regards the working men in question, they may have felt that the situation was such that bloodshed must be risked. Yet there is no evidence that they intended to attack the troops or to commit any violence. The moral effect of their demonstration would have been lost if they had so intended. Gapon, reluctant as he was to lead the procession, may have realized the risk he was running, and he may have been made aware of the military and police measures which were about to be taken ; but his actions suggest that he thought the procession might be permitted to carry out its programme. As regards the rank and file of the procession, the mere fact that they brought with them their women and children, and that they sang as they marched along, " God Save the Tsar," is sufficient to dispose of the suggestion that the bulk of the procession either intended to commit violence, or anticipated that violence would be committed upon them.

Yet there can be no doubt that there were revolutionary elements in the procession, as there were among the members of Gapon's union. When the authorities made it plain that they intended to resist the passage of the processions, the peaceable elements naturally fell back, and the revolutionary elements then became conspicuous. These elements indeed gained in strength, and continued to engage in conflicts with the police and the military for three days after Bloody Sunday. In the processions of that day, however, there is no evidence that the turbulent elements were numerically important, and therefore the merciless severity of the military operations seems to have been devoid of sufficient reason.

Even if the procession had been wholly revolutionary in its character (and there is no evidence to that effect) there was ample available military force to adopt the policy of refraining from action until after the crowd had committed itself to a revolutionary act. To attack a crowd which comes ostensibly with peaceable intent, can be justified only, even on administrative grounds, if there is reason to believe that the ostensible aims are not the real ones, and that the real aim is the overthrowal of the Government. There is no evidence to show that this was the aim of Gapon's movement, or that the influence of the revolutionary elements was sufficient to make it so at any stage of the movement. To assume a state of revolution is an act of wisdom only in a Government which finds itself on the edge of destruction. Even then, the disaster which the Government wishes to avoid may be precipitated. Prior to Bloody Sunday the dynasty was in no peril. The traditional veneration for the Tsar had not been seriously impaired by the disasters of the war, for which he was not held personally responsible.

From the point of view of the working men, inside of and outside of Gapon's union, the appeal of 9th January was an appeal to the Tsar direct. Whether or not his Ministry, headed by Prince Svyatopolk-Mirsky, was chiefly to blame for the issue of events must be determined by the historian of the future, when the memoirs of the principal actors make their appearance and the archives of the ministries are available. In the minds of the working men of St. Petersburg, however, the blame was laid upon the Tsar himself. They wished to see him, to speak to him, and he received them with bullets.

So far as appears from the available evidence, and in the light of subsequent events, it would seem that the wise course, even from the point of view of the autocracy, would have been to admit some of the petitioners into the Palace Square, and for some responsible officer to undertake at least to hand the petition to the Tsar. Undoubtedly the Tsar had already the petition in his hands.

The issue could hardly have been more unfavourable for the dynasty and for the autocracy than the actual course of events proved. The volleys of the Tsar's regiments swept away the last shred of respect for the Tsar, showed him demonstratively as panic-stricken, and definitively removed from the sphere of political influence the whole of the Grand Ducal party. Thus, in a sense, the victims of Bloody Sunday did not perish in vain. Some change was, in any case, inevitable ; but the tragical incidents of that day must be regarded as having been an important factor in the train of causes which led to the revolutionary crisis of a few months later. A situation which demanded tact and delicacy rather than bullets was met with an Asiatic barbarity which shocked the world. Yet this very barbarity rendered inevitable concessions which might otherwise not have been granted so speedily, or which might not have been granted at all.

Powerful as it was, the autocracy was nervously sensitive of Western European opinion, and rehabilitation of the Russian Government before the eyes of the world was a necessity of the months succeeding the events of 9th January 1905.

The first attempt to effect this rehabilitation was carried out, it appears, by order of General Trepov, who had been appointed Chief of Police. He required the factory-owners to find fourteen "loyal and decently dressed working men," in order that they might be presented to the Tsar at Tsarskoë Selo. What happened may be gathered from the description of one of these men.

" They took me to the Winter Palace, searched me, and when we were all collected there, we were taken to Tsarskoë Selo. We were told by General Trepov that we must bow to the Tsar in the Russian manner " (that is, not merely with the head, but with the whole body). "We were to bow, and then to listen to what the Tsar might tell us. We were not to enter into conversation with him. If we did, we should afterwards be banished from St. Petersburg." The working men, according to this narrative, were taken in imperial carriages to the railway station, and thence by first-class carriages to Tsarskoë Selo. When they arrived, " We were bowing all the time ; and the Tsar was speaking. We had to walk back to the station, and to return in third-class carriages." [1] The fourteen loyal working men were treated afterwards with hostility by their fellows, and some of them were obliged to leave the factories where they were employed. In addition to organizing this somewhat farcical deputation, the Government thought it well to bestow a sum of 50,000 rubles upon the families of those who were killed or wounded.

The significance of the Gapon movement must be estimated altogether apart from the personality of Gapon. Excepting in the feeble initiation of his society, his influence was not predominant. The importance of the movement is to be judged by three circumstances: (1) It was the first large legal trade union in Russia, and it was the means of giving the St. Petersburg working men an idea of combination on a large scale and experience of the

[1] *History of the Council of Labour Deputies* (St. Petersburg, 1910), p. 47.

external danger and internal difficulties as well as of the possibilities of such combination. (2) Its issue destroyed at a blow the faith of the common people in the Tsar. The childlike character of this faith had led the great bulk of the concourse of people who formed the procession to believe implicitly in the Dear Father whose paternal care would ultimately provide for everyone. (3) It marked the beginning of " the year of liberties," when, by a concurrence of causes, the autocracy, confused and dismayed, suffered many liberties to be " grasped " that it had previously tenaciously withheld.

The movement may, for these reasons, be regarded as the manifestation of a " state of mind " so widely diffused among the people as to be practically universal. While such manifestations of themselves may be very crude, and may be put down with or without violence, and while those who engage in them may be wholly exterminated, the " state of mind," of which the manifestations are merely some of the overt signs, is unaffected or even intensified.

APPENDIX TO CHAPTER II

A

Letter of Gapon to the Tsar, dated 8th January 1905, the day before the Demonstration.

SIRE,—Do not believe the Ministers; they are cheating Thee in regard to the real state of affairs. The people believe in Thee. They have made up their minds to gather at the Winter Palace to-morrow, at 2 P.M., to lay their wants before Thee. If Thou wilt not stand before them, Thou wilt break that spiritual connection which unites Thee with them. Their belief in Thee will disappear. The shed blood will separate Thee from them. Do not fear anything. Stand to-morrow before the people and accept our humblest petition. I, the representative of the working men, and my comrades guarantee the inviolability of Thy person.   GAPON.

B

*Letter of Gapon to the Minister of the Interior,
dated 8th January 1905.*

YOUR EXCELLENCY,—Working men and St. Petersburg inhabitants of various classes desire to see, and they must see, the Tsar on 9th January at 2 P.M. in the Place of the Winter Palace, in order personally to explain to him their wants and the wants of all the people. The Tsar has nothing to apprehend. I, as the representative of the Union of Russian Working Men, our co-workers and comrades, and even so-called revolutionary groups of all tendencies—we guarantee His inviolability. Let him as the real Tsar with an open heart come out to His people. Let Him accept from our hands the petition ! All this is necessary for His welfare and for that of all the inhabitants of St. Petersburg and of the Fatherland, otherwise the moral connection uniting up till now the Russian Tsar with the Russian people may be broken.

Your great moral duty, both before the Tsar and before all the Russian people, is to present immediately to the Tsar these lines as well as the Petition to which they relate.

Say to the Tsar that I, the working men, and many thousands of people have made up our minds, peacefully and with entire trust, but with irresistible firmness, to appear at the Palace. Let him in deeds, and not in manifestoes, prove his trust in the people.   GAPON.

[*Revolutionary Russia*, No. 58, 20th January 1905.]

C

*Text of Gapon's Petition to the Tsar, which was intended
to be presented on 9th January 1905.*

SIRE,—We, working men and inhabitants of St. Petersburg of various classes, our wives and our children and our helpless old parents, come to Thee, Sire, to seek for truth and defence. We have become beggars ; we have been oppressed ; we are burdened by toil beyond our powers ; we are scoffed at ; we are not recognized as human beings ; we are treated as slaves who must suffer their bitter fate and who must keep silence. We suffered, but we are pushed farther into the den of beggary, lawlessness, and ignorance. We are choked by despotism and irresponsibility, and we are breathless. We have no more power, Sire, the limit of patience has been reached. There has arrived for us that tremendous moment when death is better than the continuation of intolerable tortures. We have left off working, and we have declared to the masters that we shall not begin to work until they comply with our demands. We beg but little; we desire only that without which life is not life, but hard labour and eternal torture. The first request which we made was that our masters should discuss our needs with us; but this they refused, on the ground that no right to make this request is recognized by law. They also declared to be illegal our requests to diminish the working hours to eight hours daily, to agree with us about the prices for our work, to consider our misunderstandings with the inferior administration of the mills, to increase the wages for the labour of women and of general labourers, so that the minimum daily wage should be one ruble per day, to abolish overtime work, to give us medical attention without insulting us, to arrange the workshops so that it might be possible to work there, and not find in them death from awful draughts and from rain and snow. All these requests appeared to be, in the opinion of our masters and of the factory and mill administrations, illegal. Everyone of our requests was a crime, and the desire to improve our condition was regarded by them as impertinence, and as offensive to them.

Sire, here are many thousands of us, and all are human beings only in appearance. In reality in us, as in all Russian people, there is not recognized any human right, not even the right of speaking, thinking, meeting, discussing our needs, taking measures for the improvement of our condition. We have been enslaved, and enslaved under the auspices of Thy officials, with their assistance, and with their co-operation. Everyone of us who dares to raise a voice in defence of working-class and popular interests is thrown into jail or is sent into banishment. For the possession of good hearts and sensitive souls we are punished as for crimes. Even to pity a beaten man —a man tortured and without rights—means to commit a heavy crime. All the people—working men as well as peasants—are handed over to the discretion of the officials of the Government, who are thieves of the property of the State—robbers who not only take no care of the interests of the people, but who trample these interests under their feet. The Government officials have brought the country to complete destruction, have involved it in a detestable war, and have further and further led it to ruin. We working men have no voice in the expenditure of the enormous amounts raised from us in taxes. We do not know even where and for what is spent the money collected from a beggared people. The people are deprived of the possibility of expressing their desires, and they now demand that they be allowed to take part in the introduction of taxes and in the expenditure of them.

The working men are deprived of the possibility of organizing themselves in unions for the defence of their interests.

Sire, is it in accordance with divine law, by grace of which Thou reignest ? Is it not better to die, better for all of us toiling people of Russia, and to let the capitalist exploiters of the working class, officials, "grafters," and robbers of the Russian people live ? This is before us, Sire, and this has brought us to the walls of Thy Palace. We are seeking here the last salvation. Do not refuse assistance to Thy people. Bring them from the grave of rightlessness, beggary, and ignorance. Give their destiny into their own hands. Cast away from them the intolerable oppression of officials. Destroy the wall between Thyself and Thy people, and let them rule the country together with Thyself. Art Thou not placed there for the happiness of Thy people ? But this happiness the officials snatch from our hands. It does not come to us. We get only distress and humiliation. Look without anger, attentively upon our requests. They are directed, not to evil, but to good for us as well as for Thee. Sire ! not impudence, but consciousness of needs, of emerging from a situation intolerable for us all, becomes articulate in us.

Russia is too great. Its necessities are too various and numerous for officials alone to rule it. National representation is indispensable. It is indispensable that people should assist and should rule themselves. To them only are known their real necessities. Do not reject their assistance, accept it, order immediately the convocation of representatives of the Russian land from all ranks, including representatives from the working men. Let there be capitalists as well as working men—official and priest, doctor and teacher—let all, whatever they may be, elect their representatives. Let everyone be equal and free in the right of election, and for this purpose order that the elections for the Constitutional Assembly be carried on under the condition of universal, equal, and secret voting. This is the most capital of our requests. In it and upon it everything is based. This is the principal and only plaister for our painful wounds, without which our wounds will fester and will bring us rapidly near to death. Yet one measure alone cannot heal our wounds. Other measures are also indispensable. Directly and openly as to a Father, we speak to Thee, Sire, about them in person, for all the toiling classes of Russia. The following are indispensable :

I. Measures against the ignorance and rightlessness of the Russian people :

1. The immediate release and return of all who have suffered for political and religious convictions, for strikes, and national peasant disorders.

2. The immediate declaration of freedom and of the inviolability of the person—freedom of speech and press, freedom of meetings, and freedom of conscience in religion.

3. Universal and compulsory elementary education of the people at the charge of the State.

4. Responsibility of the Ministers before the people and guarantee that the Government will be law-abiding.

5. Equality before the law of all without exception.

6. Separation of the Church from the State.

II. Measures against the poverty of the people:

1. Abolition of indirect taxes and the substitution of a progressive income tax.

2. Abolition of the Redemption Instalments,[1] cheap credit, and gradual transference of the land to the people.

3. The orders for the military and naval ministries should be fulfilled in Russia, and not abroad.

4. The cessation of the war by the will of the people.

III. Measures against the oppression of labour:

1. Abolition of the factory inspectorships.[2]

2. Institution at factories and mills of permanent committees of elected workers, which, together with the administration (of the factories) would consider the complaints of individual workers. Discharge of working men should not take place otherwise than by resolution of this committee.

3. Freedom of organization of co-operative societies of consumers and of labour trade unions immediately.

4. Eight-hours working day and regulation of overtime working.

5. Freedom of the struggle of labour against capital immediately.

6. Normal wages immediately.

7. Participation of working-class representatives in the working out of projects of law upon workmen's State insurance immediately.

Here, Sire, are our principal necessities with which we come to Thee! Only by the satisfaction of these the release of our native land from slavery and beggary is possible; only by this means is possible the flourishing of our native land, and is it possible for working men to organize themselves for the defence of their interests against impudent exploitation of capitalists and of the officials' government which is plundering and choking the people. Order and take an oath to comply with these requests, and Thou wilt make Russia happy and famous and Thou wilt impress Thy name in our hearts and in the hearts of our

[1] The Redemption Instalments were abolished 3rd November 1905.
[2] On the ground that the factory inspectors favoured the employers.

posterity to all eternity. If Thou wilt not order and wilt not answer our prayer—we shall die here on this Place before Thy Palace.

We have nowhere to go farther and nothing for which to go. We have only two ways—either towards liberty and happiness or into the grave. . . . Let our life be a sacrifice for Russia which has suffered to the extreme limit. We do not regret this sacrifice. We willingly offer it.[1]

D

Letter sent by Gapon to the Tsar after the Demonstration of 9th January 1905.

Letter to Nikolas Romanov, formerly Tsar and at present soul destroyer of the Russian Empire.

With naïve belief in thee as father of thy people, I was going peacefully to thee with the children of these very people. Thou must have known, thou didst know, this. The innocent blood of workers, their wives and children, lies forever between thee, O soul destroyer, and the Russian people. Moral connection between thee and them may never be any more. The mighty river during its overflowing thou art already unable to stem by any half measures, even by a Zemsky Sobor (Popular Assembly). Bombs and dynamite, the terror by individuals and by masses, against thy breed and against the robbers of rightless people— all this must be and shall absolutely be. A sea of blood—unexampled— will be shed. Because of thee, because of thy whole family, Russia may perish. Once for all, understand this and remember, better soon with all thy family abdicate the throne of Russia and give thyself up to the Russian people for trial. Pity thy children and the Russian lands, O thou offerer of peace for other countries and blood drunkard for thine own!

Otherwise let all blood which has to be shed fall upon thee, Hangman, and thy kindred!   GEORGE GAPON.

Postscriptum.—Know that this letter is the justifying document of the coming revolutionary terroristic occurrences in Russia.

20th March—7th February 1905.   G. G.

Supplement to *Revolutionary Russia*, No. 59, 10th February 1905. [Printed in Geneva.]

[1] Svyatlovsky, V. V., *The Labour Movement in Russia* (St. Petersburg, 1907), pp. 389–91.

E

Open Letter to the Socialist Parties of Russia.

The bloody January days in St. Petersburg and the rest of Russia brought the oppressed working class face to face with the autocratic régime, the blood drunkard Tsar at its head, and the great Russian Revolution began. Everybody for whom national liberty is really dear is under the necessity of winning or dying. Conscious as I am of the importance of the historical moment through which we are living under the present situation of affairs, and being first of all a revolutionist and a man of action, I summon all the socialist parties of Russia to enter immediately into agreement among themselves and to begin the business of armed uprising against Tsarism. All the forces of every party should be mobilized. The technical plan of conflict should be a common one for all. Bombs and dynamite, terror by individuals and by masses—everything which may contribute to the national uprising. The first purpose is the overwhelming of the autocracy. The provisional revolutionary government immediately proclaims amnesty for all fighters for political and religious freedom, immediately arms the people, and immediately convokes a constituent assembly on the basis of an universal, equal, secret, and direct electoral law. To work, comrades ! Ahead, for the fight ! Let us repeat the cry of the St. Petersburg working men on 9th January, "Liberty or death ! " Every delay or dispute is a crime against the people whose interests you are defending. Having given all my powers for service to the people, from the depths of whom I myself originated, having irrevocably connected my fate with the struggle against the oppressors and exploiters of the working class, I naturally with all my heart and all my soul will be with those who are undertaking the task of the real emancipation of the proletariat and of the whole toiling mass from capitalistic oppression and political slavery.

GEORGE GAPON.

Revolutionary Russia, No. 59, 10th February 1905.

CHAPTER III

THE STRIKE MOVEMENT IN RUSSIA IN 1905

GENERAL SKETCH

A SKETCH of the rise of labour unions in Russia has already been given,[1] and the close connection between the industrial and the political movements has been noticed.

Industrial strikes organized by temporary unions were by no means unknown in Russia even in the eighteenth century,[2] and when continuous or permanent unions came to be formed, such strikes increased in frequency. Yet compared with the industrial strike movement in other countries, the industrial strike movement in Russia up till the year 1905 was insignificant. In the decade ending in the year 1904, the average number of workers annually involved in strikes was only 43,000, or rather less than 2.75 per cent. of the total number of workers employed in industrial establishments.[3] The year 1905 witnessed not only the greatest strike movement in Russia, but the Russian strike movement of that year was by far the greatest in point of numbers involved, and in the proportion of these numbers to the total number of workers employed, of any strike movement in modern times.[4] The motives which induced these strikes were not purely industrial, as may be seen from the following official analysis :

---

[1] In Book VI, chap. v.   [2] Cf. *supra*, p. 442 *et seq.*

[3] Calculated from data given by V. E. Varzar in *Statistics of Labour Strikes in Factories, &c., in* 1905 (Report to the Ministry of Trade and Commerce) (St. Petersburg, 1908), diagram facing p. 4. From this diagram it appears that the number given above is about double the similar average for Belgium, about one-half that for Germany, and about one-third that for Great Britain. See also *Statistics of Labour Strikes, &c.*, 1895–1904, by same author (St. Petersburg, 1905). It is to be observed that these statistics do not include the numbers of strikers in the employment of railways, tramways, gasworks, banks, wholesale and retail merchants, or in the employment of the Telegraph Service. There were even strikes among the police.

[4] *Cf.* the instructive diagram in Varzar, *op. cit.*

475

STRIKES IN RUSSIA IN 1905.[1]

Causes of Strikes.	Numbers of Establishments Involved.	Proportion of Establishments in which Strikes Occurred to Total Number of Establishments.	Number of Workers Involved.	Proportion of Workers Involved to Total Number Employed.
		Per Cent.		Per Cent.
Disputes about Wages . .	2,679	...	620,145	...
Disputes about hours of labour . .	1,317	...	306,269	...
Grievances about factory conditions .	193	...	92,085	...
Definitive industrial causes	4,189	...	1,018,499	...
Political and miscellaneous causes . . .	8,915	...	1,691,012	...
Unknown causes . . .	6	...	184	...
Total . .	13,110	93	2,709,695	163.8

The following table exhibits the distribution of strikes throughout the year 1905 : [2]

	Establishments.	Strikers.
January	1,989	414,438
February	1,034	291,210
March	225	72,472
April	454	80,568
May	1,048	219,990
June	848	142,641
July	582	150,059
August	539	78,343
September	261	36,629
October	2,628	481,364
November	1,327	323,549
December	2,172	418,215
Date uncertain	3	217
	13,110	2,709,695

[1] Compiled from data given by Varzar, *op. cit.*, pp. 44 and 61. [2] *Ibid.*, p. 6.

The diagram on page 601 exhibits the ebb and flow of the strike movement throughout the year. It is clear that the political ferment, in so far as it was expressed by strikes, died down after the ebullition in January, and that although, during the summer, strikes, both from economical and from political causes were frequent, not until October did the strike fever rise again to boiling-point, to abate slightly in November, and to rise to white heat during the Moscow upheaval in December.

The proportion of strikes induced by political causes to those induced by industrial causes was about eight to five. The loss in working time amounted to the enormous total of 23,609,387 days.[1] Practically every worker struck at least once during the year.

The strike epidemic became widespread immediately after " Bloody Sunday." [2] In January 1905, throughout the Empire, more than four hundred thousand workers struck in nearly two thousand establishments. The regions principally and most speedily affected were St. Petersburg, the Baltic Provinces, Poland, Nijni Novgorod, Ekaterinoslav, and the Caucasus. The Government became alarmed, and a committee, under Senator Shidlovsky, was appointed to inquire into the grievances of the working men of the St. Petersburg district. This committee began by inviting the working men to elect delegates, intimating that those who were elected might engage freely in " business discussions " without fear of punishment. The representatives of the working men insisted upon further preliminary concessions. These were refused, and the workers then declined to elect delegates. Early in March the committee was brought to an abrupt conclusion, and some of the working-men electors were arrested. At the same moment the last serious defeat sustained by the Russian arms took place at Mukden.[3] The illusion of the military impregnability of the autocracy was dispelled in Manchuria, and the illusion of its benevolence was rudely shaken by the recollection of " Bloody Sunday " and by the arrest of the working men in the early days of March. The failure of the Government to grapple with the industrial discontent, together with the vanishing of these illusions, acted as a signal for the general uprising of the working class.[4] This uprising did not take place im-

---

[1] Varzar, *op. cit.*   [2] 9th January 1905.   [3] 10th March 1905.
[4] These incidents are associated by Khrustalov, the leader of the working men's Deputies. See *History of the Council of Working Men's Deputies*, (St. Petersburg, 1910), p. 47.

mediately, but it soon became apparent that the revolution which began in January had entered upon a new phase.

The arrest of the working-men electors was followed by a strike by way of protest. This strike was not of long duration, and when it was over there began a period of external calm during which, beneath the surface, there were gathered the forces that in the autumn of 1905 carried the revolution another step forward.

The details which follow show how inevitable such fluctuations are. A very prolonged general strike is an impossibility. During its continuance the life of the community affected by it is arrested, and with it even the progress which has been the design of the strike. Apart from the physical and mental strain which such a condition involves, the necessities of life must tend to bring the strike to an end, and the more general the strike, the sooner it must arrive at this issue. Not long-continued but frequently repeated strikes might appear to be advisable ; but the frequent use of a weapon blunts it, and for this reason the industrio-political strike became too blunt for effective employment against a still powerful Government, and in the presence of a peasantry whose self-contained life rendered it immune to inconveniences intolerable to an urban population. When the supply of food, water, news, light, and means of communication are shut off from dwellers in towns, their speedy capitulation is inevitable. During the general strike the towns, indeed, placed themselves voluntarily in a state of siege. It is true that the revenue of the Government was temporarily cut off, and that it suffered a serious loss of prestige both in Russia and out of it ; but taken by itself, perhaps the major force exerted in the general strike spent itself in recoil.[1]

The significance of the widespread strike movement of 1905, spasmodic as it was, lies in the fact which the statistics disclose, viz. that it affected the mass of the working people. " Up till the 9th January there were movements *in* the working class ; from the 9th January there began the movement *of* the whole working class." [2]

One immediate result of this general movement, by which practically the mass of the population in the capitals and the large in-

[1] Although the political strategy of the Moscow uprising in December (cf. *infra*, pp. 563-4) may be viewed adversely, it is scarcely open to doubt that an active revolutionary movement may be less injurious to the people, whether it fails or succeeds, than a peaceful general strike.

[2] Khrustalov, *op. cit.*, p. 48.

dustrial towns threw itself into the revolutionary struggle, was the immensely increased accessibility of the mass of artisans to the socialist propaganda. This propaganda had been indifferently successful. The working men had not embraced its doctrines save to a slender extent. Now the whole situation was changed, and the socialist parties found themselves called upon to supply guidance and leaders for people who had suddenly experienced a kind of Pentecost. Although the parties as parties did not sustain an uniform or important rôle in the leadership of the working class, yet the working men's representatives were undoubtedly inoculated with socialist ideas, and were in constant relations with the party leaders. Probably, on account of this fact, the working men's deputies acquired speedily after the collapse of the Shidlovsky committee an extraordinarily authoritative influence over the mass of the working men.[1]

The propaganda of revolution thus became immensely more active in the spring of 1905. Meetings were held in many places in St. Petersburg, posters were displayed in the factories, socialist literature was widely distributed, reading and debating clubs were formed. Ideas wholly new to them began to ferment in the minds of working men and women of all industrial ranks. " Working women from liquor shops and from factories, women cloth-pressers, working men in very small shops,"[2] of which there are a great many in St. Petersburg, as well as the workmen in the large industrial enterprises, became saturated with the idea that some kind of popular government must insistently be demanded. At this time their chief watchword was " A Constituent Assembly."[3] " This idea for the first time found its way into the working man's psychology."[4] " The revolution brings new impressions. In response to these, the social conscience boils as in a kettle, and without delay passes from one ideal to another; yesterday's unknown to-day is acknowledged, and to-morrow people will be ready to sacrifice their lives for it."[5]

While this fermentation was going on in the minds of the industrial classes, the peasantry were in a state of open revolt. Beginning in Orlovskaya *gub.*, the agrarian movement passed rapidly

---

[1] *Cf.* Khrustalov, *History of the Council of Working Men's Deputies*, p. 48.
[2] Khrustalov, *op. cit.*, p. 49.   [3] *Ibid.*   [4] *Ibid.*
[5] *Vestnik Evropy*, January 1906, p. 113.

through Kurskaya and Chernigovskaya *gub*. *Zemlya ē Vola*, " Land and freedom," proved to be a more exciting watchword than "Constituent Assembly." Everywhere there were destruction of property and seizure of estates.[1]

Legislation upon Strikes.—During the reign of Alexander II, and up till 1905, when the law was suspended by special circular, strikes having for their object the increase of wages or the change of conditions before the expiry of contracts between workmen and their employers, were forbidden on pain of imprisonment for from four to eight months. Strikers who employed violence or threats to force non-strikers to join them were liable to double the imprisonment mentioned. On 29th November 1905 an ordinance was issued prohibiting strikes of employees on railways, whether in private hands or in the hands of the State, public telephone services, and in general on all undertakings the cessation of whose activities might endanger the safety of the State and of the public, the penalty for infringement of the law being from four to sixteen months' imprisonment. Those who incite others to strike were liable to from sixteen months' to four years' imprisonment in a fortress, and to deprivation of some civil rights.

On 13th April 1906 strikes of agricultural labourers were prohibited by law.

In actual operation these laws have been enforced only against the leaders of strike movements, and even in these cases the full penalty was not usually imposed. In some cases offenders were simply fined; in others they were sent to prison for three months without hard labour. Owing, however, to the courts being blocked with cases of all kinds, the sentences were generally imposed by administrative order.[2]

---

[1] An account of these movements is given in Book III.
[2] At Lodz (Poland) a singular instance of arbitrary rule was afforded by the General Governor of Petrokovskaya *gub*., who announced in 1908 that manufacturers in whose establishments strikes occurred should be fined. *Russ*, May 1908.

CHAPTER IV

THE GENERAL STRIKE OF OCTOBER 1905

TOWARDS the end of September 1905 the strike movement had somewhat abated, but labour struggles were still in progress in Moscow, in Lodz, and in other industrial towns. Early in October the period of relative calm came to an end, and the first rumblings of the new storm began. On the 5th October newspaper despatches from Moscow reported, " The strike is over ; complete quietness reigns in the streets." On the 7th October the engine-drivers on the Moscow-Kazan Railway struck, and the drivers of goods trains followed. On the 8th October the movement of all trains ceased on the Moscow-Archangel, on the Moscow-Kursk, on the Moscow-Nijni-Novgorod, and on the Moscow-Riazan lines. On the 9th October the employees on the Moscow-Kiev-Voronej Railway struck. On the 10th the strike extended southward and eastward over the whole network of railways, and in the north on the 12th St. Petersburg was isolated, excepting for the Finnish Railway. On the 16th St. Petersburg was totally isolated. On the 14th the Trans-Caucasian Railways joined the strike, as well as the Middle Asiatic and Siberian Railways.[1] In ten days the strike involved about 26,000 miles of line and 750,000 employees.[2] That this series of strikes was produced by nervous tension from long-continued expectation is evident from the rapidity with which it spread from centre to centre ; but this is also shown from the circumstances which attended its initiation. On the 20th September the pension committee of the railway union met in St. Petersburg, having been called thither by the Minister of Railways in order to discuss the grievances of the railway employees. Although this committee

---

[1] Khrustalov, *op. cit.*, p. 57. *Cf.* Mievsky in *The Social Movement in Russia in the Beginning of the Twentieth Century* (St. Petersburg, 1910), vol. ii. p. 79.
[2] Khrustalov, *op. cit.*, p. 57.

was primarily designed for the discussion of the scale of pensions for railway servants, it appeared that the Minister (Prince Khilkov) thought that he might use it as a lightning-conductor to draw off the irritation of the men.[1] The pension committee of the railway union, under the influence of a stream of telegrams from its constituents, formulated a series of demands, including a Constituent Assembly, political freedom, an eight hours' working day, complete amnesty for political offenders, autonomy of nationalities and of institutions, and the formation of a militia.

The bold way in which the pension committee advocated its sweeping programme induced among its constituents the fear that the members of it might be arrested, and on the 7th October a rumour obtained circulation in Moscow that they had actually been put in prison. Although the members of the committee themselves telephoned to Moscow that the rumour was without foundation, " the lower layers of the employees of the Moscow-Kazan Railway broke the dam of expectation " [2] and declared a strike, in spite of the efforts of the committee to prevent them from doing so. It would appear that the committee thought that the fear of a railway strike would be more potent than the fact of it, and that the threat of a strike should be used as a means of extorting concessions.[3]

But the strike began, and its rapid extension proved that the Moscow engine-drivers had seized the psychological moment, although, so far as the promotion of a general strike was concerned, they did so rather by accident than design. On technical grounds the moment was not ill chosen. The movement of grain from the great grain-growing regions of Eastern and Southern Russia was nearing its height. Vessels were waiting in the harbours of Odessa, Nikolaev, and Rostov for cargoes for England, Germany, and Holland.

The railway has entered so fully into the structure of life in

---

[1] After the railway strikes of February and March the Minister had promised certain improvements, which had not been carried into effect. Khrustalov, *op. cit.*, p. 56.

[2] Khrustalov, *op. cit.*, p. 57.

[3] The majority of the committee consisted of higher officials of the railways and the minority of working men. The committee was elected by double ballot. For each 12,000 electors there was one delegate. The delegates were drawn from every part of Russia, and the reports of the proceedings of the committee were transmitted daily to each voting centre, as though by an " enormous megaphone." Khrustalov, *op. cit.*, p. 56.

urban communities that the sudden cessation of its functions is like the sudden stoppage of the circulation in an organic body. Either as inevitable result, or by way of sympathetic action, steel-works, factories, and industrial establishments everywhere closed their doors.

On the 10th October the electric railways in Moscow, Kharkov, and Reval ceased to work. On the 12th October, at St. Petersburg, work ceased in many of the great industrial establishments along the Schlusselburg Road—in the Aleksandrovsky Locomotive Works, the Nevsky Shipbuilding Yard, the Atlas, the Imperial Card Factory, and in the factories and workshops of Pali, Maxwell, Aristov, and Newmann. Although the Government had stopped the traffic by the Neva ferries, in order to isolate the north bank of the river, signals were made between the two banks, and work was discontinued at Thornton's and at Vargunin's. On the 13th October there were further accessions to the ranks of the strikers from the Putilovsky Ironworks, the New Admiralty Works, and many others. On the afternoon of this day movement on the horse-power railways, with one exception, ceased, as well as on the electric railways, and in the electric-lighting stations. On the 13th also the inferior function-aries of the railways, of the St. Petersburg provincial Zemstvo offices, and of the office of the Department of Ways and Communications, and the employees of banks, of the law courts, and even the clerks in the central office of the Union of Unions, ceased to work ; and scholars of gymnasium and *real schule* ceased attendance.

On the 11th October all trade and industry ceased in Smolensk, Kozlov, Ekaterinoslav, Minsk, and Lodz ; and on the 12th at Kursk, Belgorod, Poltava, Samara, and Saratov. On the 11th October a St. Petersburg agency received the following despatch from Ekaterinoslav : " The city is in darkness, the shops are closed, the streets are empty. Patrols of soldiers pass occasionally. The railway station is closed. Some of the telegraph wires are injured." [1] Here also six barricades were built, and nine persons were killed in the streets.[2] At Kharkov, barricades were built, red flags made their appearance, and fourteen persons were killed.[3] Banks and municipal and Government offices closed their doors.

---

[1] *Nasha Jézn*, No. 307, quoted by Khrustalov, *op. cit.*, p. 57.
[2] Mievsky, *op. cit.*, ii. p. 81.   [3] *Ibid.*, p. 82.

At Kharkov, also, at four o'clock in the afternoon, the telegraph service was suspended, because the telegraph clerks joined the strikers.[1] On the 13th October the telegraph clerks struck at Chelyabinsk and at Irkutsk, on the 14th at Moscow, and on the 15th at St. Petersburg. The whole telegraph system of the country, as well as the postal system, was paralyzed; and the telephone service was impeded, although it was not wholly suspended. There ceased to be any certain means of communication. Even the wireless telegraph installation between the Imperial Palace at Tsarskoë Selo and St. Petersburg was inactive.[2] On the 11th October a part of Moscow was without water, because the waterworks were damaged and repairs were impossible. There was no milk throughout the city, and there was no delivery of letters, because no trains had arrived. The price of beef advanced seriously.[3]

Immense meetings of strikers and of the public took place in many cities, and collisions occurred between the people and the troops. On the 14th October the strike began at Riga. The employees at the electric-lighting stations struck, and on that night the city was in darkness. Crowds of strikers filled the streets. They broke into shops where arms were sold, and into the Government liquor shops. Encounters between the crowds and the soldiers continued throughout the night. The demands of the strikers at Riga were of an exclusively political character. They involved the liberation of political prisoners and the removal of the soldiers from the streets. The civic administration met and decided to support the demand that political prisoners be liberated forthwith. The Governor of Estland (Lopoukhin) was forced into submission, and on the following day (15th October) the political prisoners were set free. The civic administration gave the representatives of the working men 750 rubles per day for the organization of a guard and the maintenance of order.[4] At Riga on the 16th a collision took place between the crowds and the troops, and sixty persons were killed.[5] Even children were drawn into the uprising. In Odessa, for instance, on the 14th October, a demonstrative band of schoolboys was beaten by the police. Immediately afterwards a crowd of a thousand children held a political meeting

[1] Khrustalov, *op. cit.*, p. 58.   [2] *Ibid.*, *op. cit.*, p. 59.
[3] *Ibid.*, *op. cit.*, p. 58.   [4] Mievsky, *op. cit.*, ii. p. 83.   [5] *Ibid.*

at which revolutionary speeches were made by boys of fourteen years of age.[1] Nor was the movement confined to the working class. The unions of professional men everywhere passed resolutions of a character similar to those passed at the working men's meetings, demanding a representative assembly and the release of political prisoners. On the 14th October, at St. Petersburg, a meeting was held in the University attended by eight hundred civil servants, guarded by an organized group of students. At this meeting a resolution was passed demanding a representative assembly with full powers, to be elected by equal, direct, and secret vote. The financiers and manufacturers whose business was paralyzed by the general strike joined in reproaching the Government, and protested against the use of troops, excepting in extreme cases in which waterworks, light, &c., were interfered with violently by strikers.[2]

The arrest of the movement of goods in the interior of the country reacted upon its foreign trade. Grain for export was arrested in transport ; imports intended for the interior remained in the ships or on the wharves at the ports. The disorganization of the postal service even delayed the delivery of goods already shipped. Cargoes of grain sent from St. Petersburg, Libau, and Windawa remained unloaded in the ports of London, Hull, Hamburg, and Rotterdam, because the shipping documents could not be forwarded to the consignees. The expenses attending these delays were enormous. The exporters appealed to the Government ; but the Government was powerless. On the 11th October the foreign exchange houses and the banks were in a state of panic. No transactions took place in St. Petersburg Bourse on that day because there were neither buyers nor sellers.[3] The Committee of the St. Petersburg Bourse and the leading bankers appealed to the Government to extend the term of obligations. The Moscow factory owners sent a memorandum to the General Governor of Moscow to the effect that the movement was really a social revolution which they were powerless to struggle against. The president of the beef market in St. Petersburg declared before the Duma of that city on the 12th October : " We are now just the same

---

[1] Mievsky, *op. cit.*, ii. p. 83.
[2] In Moscow, *e.g.* Mievsky, *op. cit.*, ii. p. 84.
[3] *Russ.*, No. 246, 1905.

as in Port Arthur. . . . The working men appear in the beef markets and say ' sell us beef as cheaply as before, otherwise to-morrow we will take it ourselves ' ; and they will take it." The answer of the Duma to this appeal was a resolution calling upon the Government to make concessions.[1] The Committee of the Moscow Grain Trade warned the Government that the impossibility of moving grain meant famine in the cities within a short time. Perishable goods arrested in transit rotted in the railway wagons and in the yards and stations of the railways. Credit was at an end. The Central Government was cut off from the provincial governments ; the Ministers even found it difficult to maintain communications with their Imperial master. Even funerals were impeded. The strike of the engine drivers of the Moscow-Kazan Railway had become a general political strike throughout industrial Russia. Although, as frequently has happened in important strike movements, the actual outbreak of the strike of October was occasioned by an accidental and unfounded rumour, the materials for a serious conflagration were ready for the spark which was to set them ablaze. The passing of the railway strike into a general political strike was no accident ; this contingency had already been widely discussed, and the inevitability of a widespread political strike had been recognized. Nothing but a complete capitulation by the Government at an early stage could have prevented it. Yet it occurred without immediate premeditation. It was not organized by any central body of working men or of revolutionists. It was the product, as it were, of spontaneous combustion. It lasted for only nine days, but the political effect of it was enormous. When the general strike was actually in being, as it became between the 10th and the 13th October, all was chaos. The general strike had been brought about partly by innumerable large and small striking groups and partly by the inevitable cessation of work of complementary industries and services. If the general strike were to have any definite result, there must be some definite guidance. The working men fell back after all upon authority. " Authority as constituted by law " having been reduced to inaction by the mere cessation of the exercise of their functions by its servants, a new authority was conceived to be necessary. Thus out of the chaos

[1] Mievsky, *op. cit.*, p. 85.

there rose a quaint species of provisional government, " The Council of Working Men's Deputies." For a short time this singular body was the real government of Russia, issuing its decrees, permitting and prohibiting, commanding and being obeyed, performing the functions of sovereignty.

Remarking upon all these occurrences, Menshikov, one of the writers of the *Novoe Vremya* of St. Petersburg, by no means predisposed to such a view, said, " If this is not a revolution, I should like to know by what name to call it." [1]

With the discontinuance of work in the factories and workshops, there arose the need of organization of the striking masses and of " calling off " those who had not yet ceased to work. At a meeting held in the Technological Institute on the 12th October, it was decided to form a Council of Working Men's Deputies. These deputies were to be elected by the working men, and a number were elected on the 13th. On the same day the first meeting of the Council took place, also in this institute. On this day, also, " the St. Petersburg group of the Russian Social Democratic Working Men's Party instructed its agitators to obtain election to the council " [2] On the night of the 13th the newly formed nucleus of the Council issued a manifesto : " The Russian general strike has begun. The working class urgently demands a constituent assembly and universal suffrage. These have been denied, and it now has recourse to the last forcible means—a universal working-class movement and a general strike. Before the class-conscious power and solidarity of the proletariat, the blind strength of the autocracy is shaken. The president of the Committee of Ministers, Count Witté, openly acknowledged before the railway deputies that the Government might fall.[3] . . . One more attack, and there fall from the people the chains of long-continued slavery. But for this attack the working class must unite strongly . . . as one organized power. It is not permissible that strikes in separate factories and workshops should begin and discontinue, therefore we have decided to unite the leadership of the movement in the

---

[1] Quoted by Khrustalov, *op. cit.*, p. 58.   [2] Khrustalov, *op. cit.*, p. 61.
[3] What Count Witté appears to have said on this occasion was : " Remember under such conditions, the Government can fall ; but you will destroy all the best forces of the nation. In this way you will play into the hands of the very bourgeoisie against whom you are struggling." Quoted by Khrustalov, *op. cit.*, p. 59.

hands of a general working men's committee. We invite every workshop and every factory and trade to elect deputies, one for each 500 men. . . . This committee having united our movement, will give to it organization, unity, and strength. It will appear as the representative of the needs of the St. Petersburg working men before the rest of society. It will define what we should do during the strike. It will declare when it should be discontinued. . . . In the next few days decisive events will take place in Russia. Upon these events will depend for years the fate of the working class. We should meet these events in complete readiness, and in full consciousness, united by our general working men's committee under the glorious red flag of the proletariat of all countries." [1]

This manifesto, which is evidently inspired by social democratic ideas, and which is couched in social democratic phraseology, was widely circulated on the 14th October.[2] Khrustalov, the president of the Council of Working Men's Deputies, says that the majority of the working men who joined the strike up till the 13th October " did not realize its political character. The development of the political demands was left to the Council." [3] Some of the deputies, however, were sent to the Council with explicit instructions to make political as well as economical demands. One group of deputies, for example, was instructed to demand : " (1) freedom of speech and of the press, freedom of union and of meeting, freedom to strike, safety of person and home ; (2) complete amnesty for political offenders ; (3) eight hours' working day." [4] Another group demanded : " (1) Eight hours' working day ; (2) creation of city militia ; and (3) a constituent assembly for the establishment of a democratic republic." [5] The working men of the printing business sent their deputies with the resolution " That the general political strike announced by the Russian Social Democratic Work-

[1] Khrustalov, op. cit., p. 62.
[2] Khrustalov says that the Manifesto was composed by the St. Petersburg group (i.e. of the Russian Social Democratic Working Men's Party). It was published in the first issue of the Bulletin of the Council of the Working Men's Deputies. The first meeting of the Council of the Working Men's Deputies was attended exclusively by " official representatives " of the Russian Social Democratic Working Men's Party (St. Petersburg group). " This group was the nurse of the forthcoming council." Khrustalov, op. cit., p. 72.
[3] Ibid., p. 62.
[4] The Working men of Gesler's. Ibid., p. 63.
[5] The General Assembly of the Council of Salesmen. Ibid.

ing Men's Party appears to be the first step from which the working class will go farther along the road of the decisive struggle with the autocracy of the Tsar. Realizing the inadequacy of a merely pacific struggle—that is, merely the discontinuance of work—we decide to form a working-class army—that is, to organize immediately military *drujini*.[1] These militant groups should proceed to arm the rest of the working masses, even by means of pillage of armories, and by taking arms from the police and the military where this is possible. Hurrah for the Constituent Assembly! Hurrah for the Democratic Republic! Hurrah for the Great Russian Revolution! " [2] The working men of the electrical stations and water works also demanded a constituent assembly on the basis of a universal, equal, direct, and secret vote, and a democratic republic, and concluded, " we declare before the whole working class our readiness with arms in our hands to struggle for complete popular emancipation." [3]

One deputy from an engineering establishment, whose owner was not a Russian, put vividly what was, at all events, in his own mind. Khrustalov remarks upon it as typical :

" We cannot continue to live longer in such a way. Remembering all our struggle since 1884, all the strikes of 1885, 1888, and 1896,[4] and the endless struggle during 1905, all the working men of our factory felt in their bones that our position was deteriorating day by day. We have no other issue than to take into our hands a stick and to crush all that prevents us from living. Our struggle for life has been impeded by the autocracy. The employers' oppression is multiplied ten times by the double-headed eagle. Having carried all on our humps (*sic*), for the first time we have learned that it is necessary to wipe out the autocracy." [5]

These and similar declarations show that the one point which united the working men who took part in the strike and who elected the deputies to the council was the single negative point that the autocracy should be abolished. The positive demands were varied, and for the most part were left wholly to the discretion of the Council.[6]

The first act of the Council was the sending of a deputation to

---

[1] Cf. *supra*, vol. i. p. 20, and *infra*, p. 503.
[2] Khrustalov, *op. cit.*, p. 63.
[3] *Ibid.*, p. 64.
[4] These dates apply to the factory in question.
[5] Khrustalov, *loc. cit.*, p. 65.
[6] *Cf.* Khrustalov, *loc. cit.*

the St. Petersburg City Duma (or Council). The deputation demanded that the Duma take immediate measures to support the striking workers, to give the use of city property for meetings of working men, to discontinue the use of city property for police purposes, and to give money to the Council of Working Men's Deputies for the purchase of arms. The deputation from the Council was reinforced by elected representatives of the Social Democratic Party, by those of the Union of Unions, by those of the Council of the Professors of the Technological Institute, and by those of the students of the same institute. The Duma received the deputation on the 16th. The city buildings were occupied by police and by infantry, but no arrests were made. The Duma deferred its answer, and afterwards decided to refuse all the demands.

The speech of one of the deputies is instructive. " We come to you in order to learn with whom you are : with the people against Asiatism or with absolutism against freedom. We did not come to ask you to accept our militant watchwords, or to struggle side by side with us. We know very well that owing to your social position you will never struggle under our watchwords. . . . The change which is taking place in Russia is a bourgeois change ; it is also in the interests of the bourgeoisie. It is to your interest that it should be soon over, and if you want to be to any extent far-sighted, if you really understand the interest of your class, you should with all your power assist the people in the conquest of absolutism. . . . We want places for our meetings—open our city buildings. We want means for the continuance of the strike—assign the means of the city for this and not for the support of the *gens d'armerie*. We want arms for taking and keeping freedom—assign means for the organization of a proletariat militia." [1]

The Russian Social Democratic Working Men's Party had taken the leading part in the organization of the Council, and a representative of the Menshiviki or minority faction of that party had presided at its earlier sessions. At the *third* session of the Council held on 15th October, the representatives of the Bolshiviki or majority faction of the Russian Social Democratic Working Men's Party proposed to recognise the revolutionary parties by admitting to it specially elected deputies—three from each of the factions of the R.S.D.W.P. and three from the S.R.P. or Socialist Revolu-

[1] Khrustalov, *op. cit.*, pp. 70, 71.

tionary Party.[1] There were, at this time, twenty-six deputies representing ninety-six industrial establishments and five trade unions. Of these, four out of fifteen deputies from the union of printing trades and five out of eleven deputies from the union of salesmen, two watch-makers, and many of the deputies from other trades, the total number being unstated, were members of the R.S.D.W.P. ; while a smaller number were members of the S.R.P.[2] Thus nearly all the deputies of the Council on the 15th October belonged to one or other of the revolutionary parties. On this date the Council decided to send some of its deputies to " call off " non-strikers, to visit the employers of non-striking workshops, and to threaten both workmen and employers with " violence " and " plunder " of workshops unless work was immediately suspended.[3]

Khrustalov says that the mere appearance of bodies of strikers at the gates of the works was sufficient, and that there was no need for violence.[4] It was otherwise with the retail shops, especially those in which food was sold. On the 13th many were closed by persuasion. On the 14th it was difficult to close them even by force. The Council had ordered provision shops to be closed excepting during the hours of 8 and 11 in the morning and on holidays between 1 and 3 in the afternoon. But the number of striking salesmen was not great, and the proprietors found themselves between two fires. They were threatened with pillage by the Council if they opened their shops, and they were threatened with banishment by the Chief of Police (M. Trepov) if they closed them. The Council issued a manifesto to the shopkeepers, telling them, " All Russia is on strike. The people are emancipating themselves. Masters, upon you the autocratic organization has laid its heavy hand. You are pillaged by the police, ruined by unjust law-courts, skinned (sic) by the higher officials. Masters ! if you want a better life, if you want to cease being slaves and to become people and citizens, you should join the general Russian strike. It is better to endure for a short while than to suffer oppression and humiliation for a lifetime. . . . If you will not fulfil this demand, your stores will be broken, your machines will be destroyed." [5]

[1] These parties will be referred to henceforward as the R.S.D.W.P. and the S.R.P.
[2] Cf. Khrustalov, op. cit., p. 72.
[3] Khrustalov quoting text of decision of Council, op. cit., p. 72.
[4] Ibid., p. 73.   [5] Ibid.

This appeal was not generally effective, nor even generally circulated ;[1] but in the working-class quarters the shops were all closed. Cossacks sent to the Putilovsky works on guard duty were unable to obtain food in the neighbourhood.

The Technological Institute, where the Council had been holding its sessions, was surrounded by troops on the 16th October. The Council was unable to find a suitable place of meeting, and no session took place on that day. Large meetings were held in many open places by strikers because the schools where they had previously met were converted into " bivouacs " by the troops. On the 16th large numbers of Government employees joined the strike—officials from the State Bank and the Ministry of Finance. So also did officers of insurance companies. On the 17th there were further accessions from the same classes of officials. The Commercial Court ceased to sit on the 16th, and on the 17th the courts of the city judges were discontinued. On the same night, the *corps de ballet* of the Marinsky Theatre struck. At the waterworks the men were immured and compelled to work under military supervision. The only light in the capital was " a blinding ray " from a huge projector on the tower of the admiralty buildings which swept the Nevsky Prospekt. On the 15th, 16th, and 17th St. Petersburg was without neswpapers.[2]

The Council of Working Men's Deputies had found on the morning of the 17th a place in which to hold their meetings. Their hosts were the Imperial Free Economical Society.[3] At this meeting an Executive Committee of thirty-one deputies was appointed, the representatives of the revolutionary parties [4] who were placed upon this committee had, however, only an advisory voice.[5] This business had just been transacted when the Council was dispersed by the police, to meet again, however, elsewhere shortly afterwards.[6] The " material condition of the striking working men having become grave," the Council recommended the suspension of payment for rent and for supplies of food by strikers, and recommended the

---

[1] The printers being on strike, this appeal appeared only in the *Bulletin* of the Council. " It did not reach the hands of those for whom it was intended. It remained a literary memorial." Khrustalov, *op. cit.*, p. 74.
[2] There were two exceptions. Cf. *infra*.
[3] For the history of this society, see *supra*, vol. i. pp. 312–4.
[4] Nine in number.   [5] Khrustalov, p. 76.
[6] They met in a private popular institution for higher education.

shopkeepers not to institute suits against them.[1] On the 17th the central organ of the strike came to be known as the Council of Working Men's Deputies, and its first *Bulletin*, with one exception the only newspaper published in St. Petersburg on that day,[2] was issued. Immediately afterwards similar bodies in " Moscow, Ekaterinoslav, Odessa, Rostov, Kiev, Kremenchug, and elsewhere " adopted the title, and peasants' organizations came to be known as councils of peasants' deputies. Similarly soldiers' groups called themselves councils of soldiers' deputies.

It has been remarked that for three days St. Petersburg had been without newspapers. The public knew nothing of what was going on. The mere absence of journals indicated that the strike was still in being, otherwise nothing was known excepting what was to be seen in the streets. Placards might have been posted, but the working-men leaders were too busy " calling off " non-strikers, compelling factory owners to close their gates, appointing committees, and discussing programmes, to heed the public demand for information. The journalists were the first to bring the question to an issue. They represented to the Council that all newspapers should be exempt from the general suspension of labour. But the printers' union strongly objected. If, they said, newspapers are printed, the printing of books cannot be prevented ; bookbinding, paper-making, and the supply of paper from warehouses must follow, and the general strike will gradually come to an end. This view was taken by the Council, and it was then decided that the Council should publish its own newspaper. The first number of the *Bulletin* was printed by a " legal " printing office ; afterwards it was printed " arbitrarily," [3] *i.e.* in printing offices by printers who appropriated from their employers the necessary materials.

The strike reached its zenith on the night of the 17th October.[4] On the same night the Tsar signed the celebrated manifesto which granted a constitution. It appeared to the world as though, after all, he had capitulated in time. To the revolutionists the manifesto meant that the autocracy thought to save itself by issuing

[1] Khrustalov, *op. cit.*, p. 76. These recommendations were probably quite unnecessary. The payment of rent had undoubtedly been already suspended and the courts of law had been closed.

[2] The exception was the *Pravětelstvennie Vestnik* (Government Gazette). No other newspapers were published on the 15th and 16th October.

[3] Khrustalov, *op. cit.*, p. 78.   [4] *Ibid.*, p. 75.

an irredeemable obligation—a note of hand promising to pay that which was never meant to be paid.

The Manifesto of the Tsar was issued on the night of the 17th. On the morning of the following day a crowd which had collected round the Technological Institute was attacked with *nagaiki* by the police.[1] On the night of the 18th Colonel Min attacked a crowd in Gorokhovaya, and cossacks fired volleys at a crowd at Putilovsky Iron Works.

These proceedings were so contradictory to the letter and apparent spirit of the manifesto of the Tsar, that they neutralized its effect very seriously. They also gave rise to suspicions of most sinister designs on the part of the Government.[2]

The Council of Working Men's Deputies met on the 18th.[3] The resolution which was passed exhibited fully at least the social democratic view of the manifesto:

" Pressed in the iron vice of the general political strike of the Russian proletariat, the Russian autocratic government has arrived at concessions. It has made an announcement about liberties, about the legislative power of the future Imperial Duma, and about the intention to introduce into the Duma representatives of the working men and of the intelligent layers of the people. But the struggling revolutionary proletariat cannot lay down its arms until the political rights of the Russian people are established upon solid foundations, until there shall be established a demo-

[1] In St. Petersburg the mounted police used *nagaiki* (whips) tipped with lead at the end of the lash for the purpose of beating the people. During the later phases of the revolutionary movement, the people assailed the police with stones and other missiles and the *nagaiki* went almost altogether out of use. They can only be used effectively against an unarmed crowd. The *knut* is used exclusively as a horse whip. The handle of the *knut* is 2½ ft. to 3 ft. long ; that of the *nagaika* is only 9 to 10 inches long, the lash of the latter is proportionately to the handle much longer than the lash of the *knut*.

[2] A suspicion, for example, was prevalent among the working men and even among certain groups of *intelligenti*, that the Government had made public announcement of coming liberties in order that demonstrations should take place in the streets and that the " political elements " might be destroyed in the *pogroms* which would occur, or in the course of the police and military measures which might be taken to put them down. This suspicion affected the reputation of the Government in the minds of the working men most seriously. True or false, it was plausible enough for credence at a moment of extreme tension.

[3] There were present 248 deputies from 111 establishments. Khrustalov, *op. cit.*, p. 80.

cratic republic, the best method for the advancement of the struggle of the proletariat for socialism. Therefore the working men's council declares : (1) that until freedom is substantially guaranteed, there must be complete elimination of the powers by means of which the autocratic government has oppressed and kept down the people, viz. the whole police system from top to bottom . . . and in its place a popular militia must be created, and for this purpose arms must be given to the proletariat ; (2) that in spite of the liberties announced by the government thousands of our brother fighters for freedom continue up till the present time to be kept in prisons and in banishment, therefore we demand complete amnesty for all persons convicted by the courts or convicted administratively for political and religious convictions, for strikes, peasant movements, &c." The third and fourth clauses in the resolution demand the abolition of martial law and the convening of a Constituent Assembly. In order that the struggle might be continued the Council decided " to carry on the strike until the moment when conditions indicate the necessity of a change in tactics." [1]

During the day of the 18th the question of amnesty for political prisoners and exiles seemed to take the first place. The meeting of the Council was interrupted by a noisy crowd demanding immediate liberation of the prisoners in St. Petersburg. The Council elected three commanders and these went off with the crowd, which speedily assumed formidable dimensions. The crowd proceeded towards the Kazan Cathedral in the Nevsky Prospekt singing the *Marseillaise*, *Varshavyanka* (the song of the Polish Social Democrats), *Vechnya Pamat* (Eternal Memory), and *Vy jértvoýu pali* (the funeral march of the proletariat). The crowd was organized after a fashion. A chain of men with locked arms went in front, behind them a mass of men, behind these another chain, and so on. They passed along the Nevsky Prospekt and debouched into the square of the Winter Palace. Here the crowd appears to have exhibited symptoms of nervousness. They remembered the record of the place, and they feared that troops might have been secreted in the palace. The mob passed through the square and proceeded to cross the river. When the front ranks had reached the Academy of Arts, the rear ranks were still on the English Quay, near the

[1] Khrustalov, *op. cit.*, p. 80.

Winter Palace. At the buildings of the University a troop of infantry with an officer made its way through the densely-packed crowd, which opened its ranks to allow the troop to pass with pale faces through a narrow passage. The troop might easily have been disarmed. The mob was good-natured, and moreover it had no definite objective. The commanders appointed by the Working Men's Council led the crowd to the Naval Barracks of the 14th and 17th equipages. They hoped to enlist the sailors ; but the sailors did not emerge. After some time of fruitless persuasion and expectation the crowd, now dispirited, passed on through streets from which the traffic and almost all the police had disappeared. No attempt was made by the authorities to interfere with the crowd, until at the corner of Serghievskya Street the commanders were told that Predvaritelnaya Prison was filled with soldiers whose instructions were to fire at the crowd. The commanders were about to ascertain whether or not this was the case, when at that moment another message was brought to the effect that the amnesty had been signed by the Tsar, that the object of the demonstration had been attained. The messengers who came from the Union of Engineers urged the commanders to disperse the crowd and thus to save useless bloodshed in Predvaritelnaya Prison. The crowd dissolved, and another serious moment in the history of Russia passed. The event showed that the authorities were wise in allowing the demonstration to take place. No harm came of it ; nor in the temper of the crowd at that moment was there any element of danger.[1]

On the 17th October the Council of Working Men's Deputies had resolved to continue the strike in St. Petersburg until the conditions should indicate the expediency of a change in tactics— the conditions in question including importantly the continuation of the strike movement in Moscow and elsewhere. On the 19th October the conditions changed. On that day the general strike at Moscow ceased, and the strike movement on various sides was suffering disintegration. Under these circumstances, to continue the struggle in St. Petersburg was, from the point of view of the strike as a political movement, quite futile. On that day, therefore, the Council issued a manifesto declaring that the general political

---

[1] Khrustalov very properly says that such a crowd would never have stormed the Bastille. It was nervous and frightened almost from the beginning. *Op. cit.*, p. 83.

strike should come to an end on the 21st October.[1] According to Khrustalov, the only strikers who disobeyed the mandate of the Council were the druggists, who resumed work on the 20th.

In discontinuing the strike in this way, the Council evidently meant to demonstrate its power over the 200,000 people who are said to have composed the ranks of the strikers ;[2] and in discontinuing the strike it evidently did not mean to suggest either that it trusted the Government or that it intended to discontinue the struggle. Upon the announcement of the close of the strike, the bulletin of the Council remarks : " The proletariat knows what it wants, and knows what it does not want. It wants neither Police-hooligan[3]-Trepov nor Liberal-broker[4]-Wittë, neither a wolf's mouth nor a fox's tail. It does not want a *nagaïka* wrapped up in a constitution." [5]

In discontinuing the strike, the Council explicitly announced that " leaning upon the victories already obtained, it was necessary for the working class to arm itself for the final struggle." [6]

Although the political strike was at an end for the time, the economical strikes, which were included in the general strike movement, did not necessarily come to an end. The strikes upon the St. Petersburg horse-power tramway, in an ironworks, and in a telephone instrument factory continued. Indeed, in order to continue these strikes the Council recommended that those strikers who joined the movement on political grounds should demand of their employers payment of wages for the nine days of the strike, and that the funds so obtained should be paid into the treasury of the Council as a strike fund for the support of those still on strike on economical grounds. It does not appear that any large sum was paid in this connection. The employers who had suffered from the strike made no attempt to lock out the workmen when the political strike came to a conclusion ; but the Government refused to reopen the Baltisky engineering works. A deputation from the Council to the manage-

---

[1] Thursday, 21st October (O.S.). The resolution to discontinue the strike was carried with one dissentient voice—that of a railway delegate.
[2] Khrustalov, *op. cit.*, p. 85.
[3] Referring to M. Trepov's reputed connection with the Black Hundred bands.
[4] Referring to M. Wittë's reputed speculations on the Stock Exchange.
[5] Bulletin No. 3 ; quoted by Khrustalov, *op. cit.*, p. 85.
[6] Khrustalov, *loc. cit.*

ment of the works went on its own initiative to M. Wittë, who told them, " The works will be open to-morrow." [1]

It had been arranged that the funerals of the victims of 18th October were to take place on the 23rd, and there were rumours that the occasion was to be utilized by the revolutionary parties in the promotion of a great popular demonstration.   The St. Petersburg City Duma appealed to the people " to forget political quarrels," and urged them not to attempt " to square political accounts in the streets.   The street is not the place, and the day of the funerals is not the time when and where such accounts can be settled.   Citizens !   Before every one of you stands the large problem of building up a free country.   Let us do all that is possible for pacification, in order that innocent blood may not again be shed."   On the day before the date fixed for the funerals, the Duma also appealed to M. Trepov to the effect that " he must not impede the organization of the funerals, and that he should withdraw the troops."   M. Trepov, however, took his own course.   In spite of this appeal, he issued a notice intimating that " in the present troublous times, when one part of the population is ready with arms in its hands to rise against the action of another part, no political demonstration could be permitted."   He advised those who had intended to take part in a demonstration on the occasion of the funerals to desist, otherwise decisive measures would be taken.

The Council of the Working Men's Deputies arrived at the conclusion that Trepov's intention was to allow armed Black Hundred bands to attack the procession, and then, " under the mask of pacification, to shoot down " those who took part in the funeral demonstration.   It therefore decided not to accept the challenge of Trepov at that moment, but to choose its own time and method of attack ;   and by way of preparation for that, to devote itself to arming the working men.   With that end in view it advised the holding of " formidable meetings " at various centres rather than a single march with the funeral procession.

[1] Khrustalov, *op. cit.*. p. 86.

CHAPTER V

COUNTER-REVOLUTION IN 1905-1906

THE chaos into which the Russian administration fell in 1905, and the evident impotence of the Government before the widespread spirit of revolt, led inevitably to attempts to promote a counter-revolution. The explanation by the members of the Extreme Right of this phenomenon is that the movement was due to a spontaneous rising of the loyal Russian people against the revolutionists. This rising was intended to assist the autocracy by taking advantage of the existing lawlessness to inflict damage upon the revolutionaries, even though this damage should be committed without reference to the ordinary observance of law, this observance being by common consent suspended.

These counter-revolutionary groups came to be known as Black Hundreds. How far these were organized by the Union of Russian People, how far they were organized by the police, or how far they were organized at all, has not yet been fully disclosed, for an impartial account of the counter-revolutionary movement remains to be written.

The discovery, however, in 1906, in the recesses of the Ministry of the Interior of a secret printing office, in which a newspaper was printed at the instance of two officers of *gens d'armerie*,[1] disclosed a certain connection between the police and the operations of the Black Hundred groups. The printing office was suppressed, the two officers were punished by the Government, and a statement in connection with the affair was made in the Duma by M. Stolypin. The information given by him places in effect the Black Hundred incident in the same category as the provocative activities of Zubàtov in 1903, and of Azef at a later period ; although there is also evident the participation in it of the Union of Russian People.

[1] Their names were Komissarov and Bugadosky. See interpellation in First Duma. *Stenographic Reports*, vol. ii., 8th June 1906.

Prince Urusov, previously Deputy-Minister of Interior, in the debate in the First Duma on the occasion of an interpellation to M. Stolypin àpropos of the " underground printing office," described the methods of the Black Hundred bands and of the promoters of the *pogroms*, or riotous attacks, perpetrated by them.

" The *pogrom* is always preceded by rumours about it, proclamations are spread widely to excite the population, a kind of ' stormy petrel ' makes its appearance in the form of people belonging to little-known scum of the inhabitants. . . . The actions of the *pogromshēkē* (or promoters of *pogroms*) exhibit a kind of system. They appear to be conscious of some right (to do what they do) and of some immunity (from official disfavour), and they continue to act only so long as this consciousness is not shaken among them. When they are no longer confident, the *pogrom* ceases with extraordinary rapidity and ease. There is, on the contrary, no uniformity in the actions of the police. While in some police districts, even where there is a considerable force of police, the *pogroms* result in heavy disasters, in other districts individual officers, acting with firmness and courage, and in conscientious performance of their duties, stop the *pogroms* at the beginning." Prince Urusov went on to say that in January 1906 there was received by a functionary of the Ministry of Interior (not himself) who was " an opponent of the *pogrom* policy," evidence of " preparation of *pogroms* in Belostok, Kiev, Wilna, Nikolaiev, Aleksandrovsk, and other cities. This revelation led to inquiries, with the following result : A patriotic society [1] had organized a fighting detachment [2] for the purpose of carrying on a struggle against the revolution. The society thought that the sedition which existed was to be found chiefly among the non-Russian races—among Poles, Armenians, and Jews. By means of manifestoes the Russian population was incited to lynch the offenders, and thus to fight the enemies of the Fatherland with their own weapons. These manifestoes were circulated " by hundreds of thousands " ; but they were not distributed quite indiscriminately. Many officials in the service of the Government received them, and many police officers, but not all. The result of this circulation of the

[1] The Union of Russian People was hinted at, though it was not mentioned by name.

[2] Corresponding to the *drujēnē*, or fighting companies of the revolutionary parties.

manifestoes was the prevalence of alarming rumours. Fearful of disturbances, people left their homes ; others complained to the Governors. These sometimes did not know whether or not it would be possible to maintain order. The rumours reached the Ministry of Interior. Orders were sent to the local authorities that disturbances were to be suppressed. Sometimes the police did not believe that the orders from headquarters were intended to be obeyed. They supposed that the orders had been given merely " for the sake of form," and that the real intentions of the Government were quite otherwise. The result was complete disorganization and demoralization of authority. These manifestoes, according to Prince Urusov, were printed upon the " underground press " in the Ministry of Interior. The work was done so secretly that neither in the Ministry nor even in the Department of Police did any but a small number of persons know anything about it. When the existence of this printing office was discovered, and Komissarov was asked by a person who was supposed by him to be in sympathy with the *pogrom* policy, whether or not this policy was successful, he answered, " A *pogrom* may be arranged as you like ; if you like, for ten persons ; or if you like, for ten thousand." [1] Sometimes, however, the *pogrom* did not take place as arranged. A *pogrom* was arranged for a certain date in Kiev, for example, to involve ten thousand persons ; but someone succeeded in rendering the attempt abortive.[2] The existence of this printing office having been discovered by M. Goremykin, President of the Council of Ministers, Komissarov was summoned, and within " three hours " the printing office and its contents disappeared. "That is why neither the Minister of the Interior nor any one of us will ever learn about those persons who controlled the actions of this wide organization, secured impunity for the participants in it, influenced, as if by magic, the minds of the police and other officers, and even had such power that " they controlled rewards and promotions.[3] Prince Urusov said further, that peace and order could not be restored until an end was put to these " criminal semi-governmental organizations," or so long as " dark forces standing behind an untouchable fence has the power of grasping with rough hands the mechanism of the State, and of exercising their

---

[1] Quoted by Prince Urusov in the Duma, 8th June 1906. *Stenographic Reports* (1906), ii. p. 1131.
[2] *Ibid.*
[3] *Ibid.*

political ignorance in experiments upon living people, performing a kind of political vivisection." He argued that the Duma was endeavouring loyally to place the Tsar beyond the field of political conflict, and to relieve him of responsibility for political blunders, but that these efforts were rendered nugatory by the " dark forces " which were depriving the Duma of the confidence of the Throne and submerging national welfare in class struggles and in the pursuit of personal interests.[1]

The Union of the Russian People was composed of high officials, clergy, large landowners, and merchants.

The constituents of the Black Hundred bands are represented as : (a) those who did not realize what the movement meant, but who were drawn into it because they were told that the real authors of the state of affairs under which they were suffering were the *intelligentsia ;* and (b) those of doubtful past who were desirous of rehabilitating themselves in the eyes of the police and of the authorities by playing the rôle of patriots, the profits of the pillage, in which they were to engage being an additional inducement.[2] Some of the first of the two classes above mentioned were drawn out of the ranks of the Black Hundreds by the revolutionary parties, while these ranks were recruited from the landowners, who found themselves ruined by the agrarian disorders, and from the " less conscious elements " in the army.

The activities of the Black Hundred bands were less in St. Petersburg than elsewhere, yet on the 18th October an attack was made by one of them " in the presence of the police," upon a member of the Council of Working Men's Deputies. This member, whose name was Khakharov, defended himself, and found himself immediately placed under arrest by the police.[3] Assaults upon the deputies took place every day. It was proposed in the Council that groups of militant *drujēnē* should be formed under its auspices ; but this proposal was not carried into effect. There was, however, available for defensive purposes, a small number of " party *drujēnē*" —that is, armed members of the Social Democratic and Social Revolutionary parties.

The arming of the St. Petersburg working men on a considerable scale began on 29th October 1905. In the factories workmen

---

[1] *Stenographic Reports of the Duma* (1906), ii. p. 1131.
[2] Khrustalov, *op. cit.,* p. 92.   [3] *Ibid.,* p. 93.

made stilettos, bayonets, and metallic whips.[1]   On that day the workmen of the Putilovsky, Semanykovsky, Rasteriev, Lesnya, and other works forged " cold arms " of various descriptions—pikes and *castyeti* [2] in addition to those mentioned.[3]   Firearms were purchased in the gun shops.   Arms were sold openly, for the population generally was arming itself.   In three factories 8500 rubles were collected and expended upon Browning's and Smith's pistols. The working men in some of the printing offices demanded money from their employers for the purchase of arms ; and in some cases money was given to them.   The revolutionary parties supplied arms to workmen, and from the 29th October the Council of Working Men's Deputies did so also.   During the meetings of the Council in the rooms of the Free Economical Society the surrounding streets were kept under observation and the courtyard was occupied by armed working men, in order to ward off a threatened attack by Black Hundreds.   Armed *drujēnē* patrolled the streets and assumed the functions of the police.   According to one statement, there was a force of about 6000 armed working men.[4]   The immediate occasion for the arming of the working men is alleged to have been the rumours of Black Hundred attacks ; but self-defence was not the only motive.   There is no doubt that an armed uprising against the Government was contemplated.[5]   " Against force there is only one means—force." [6]   Moreover, the *drujēnēkē* meanwhile guarded the printing offices where the revolutionary newspapers were printed, and carried on a struggle with " strike-breakers," especially with those whom the Government were employing in the post-telegraph service.   In November the process of disarming these armed bands was seriously undertaken by the Government, and they were gradually hunted down.   It is probable that the comparative immunity of St. Petersburg from *pogroms* was due to the presence of these *drujēnēkē*.   Later in Moscow, when the " armed uprising " took place in December, a formidable organization of the same kind appears to have driven the Black Hundred bands from the streets.[7]

---

[1] Khrustalov, *op. cit.*, p. 94.

[2] A corruption of *casse tête*, tomahawk, head splitter.   [3] *Ibid.*

[4] Some had revolvers, pistols, and hunting rifles, and some had " cold weapons." *Pravitelstvennsie Vestnik* (Government Gazette), 8th November 1905 ; quoted by Khrustalov, p. 96.

[5] *Ibid.*, p. 97.   [6] *Ibid.*   [7] See *infra*, p. 562.

CHAPTER VI

DISCONTENT AND MUTINY IN THE ARMY AND THE NAVY

THE military discontent which had been growing during the confusion of the war broke out in open revolt on 23rd October 1905, in the form of a riot of sailors in Kronstadt.[1] On 26th October there was a second riot there. On 5th November the sailors in the port of Sevastopol held an open-air meeting to discuss their grievances. On the 11th several thousand sailors revolted in Sevastopol, and Admiral Pisarevsky was wounded. On 12th November the Breski Regiment and part of the Belochtosky Regiment joined the mutinous sailors at Sevastopol. On the same day the commandant of the port and his officers were disarmed by the mutineers, and many of the inhabitants of Sevastopol fled from the city. On the 13th the mutineers raised the red flag on the battleship *Potyemkin*, and the sailors of the battleship *Ochakov* joined the mutiny. On 14th November Sevastopol was declared to be in a state of siege, and the remaining inhabitants were panic-stricken. Troops were hurried to the city from the neighbouring military districts. On the same day at St. Petersburg 106 mutinous soldiers of the Electro-Technic company were thrown into the fortress of Peter and Paul. On 15th November at Sevastopol the mutinous sailors of the battleship *Ochakov*, having acquired complete control of the vessel, offered the command to Lieutenant Schmitt, who

---

[1] The organization of the revolutionary elements among the sailors at Kronstadt in October 1905, resulting as it did in two riotous outbreaks, was nevertheless by no means so considerable as it became afterwards. By the month of May 1906 this organization had become very formidable. The revolutionary groups had organized, among soldiers and sailors alike, squad and " equipage " committees, two Garrison Assemblies, and an executive committee of ten members, five from the Social Democratic and five from the Social Revolutionist Garrison Assembly. The executive committee met every day. They occupied themselves with working out the plan for a general uprising. Nikolai Yegorov's narrative, *Biloye*, No. 8, 1908, p. 70 (Paris, 1908).

accepted the dangerous rôle. On 16th November five vessels of the Black Sea Squadron joined the *Ochakov*, and the gunners of some of the batteries of the port of Sevastopol gave their adhesion to the revolt. On 17th November sedition broke out among the troops at Warsaw. On 18th November the sailors' barracks at Sevastopol was stormed by infantry. At Kiev there were simultaneously a military riot and a Jewish *pogrom*. At Voronej there were also military disorders. On 19th November the frontier guard at Sosnovitsi and at Karovitsi broke into open revolt. On 20th November Kiev was declared under martial law, a portion of the garrison being in revolt. On 21st November a meeting of 16,000 persons was held in the Polytechnic, guarded by the mutinous soldiers. On 24th November a sailors' barracks occupied by mutinous sailors was surrounded by troops. On 28th November all the garrison troops in Irkutsk (Siberia) held a meeting to decide upon their attitude towards the situation. On 29th November the 1st Battalion of the Preobrajensky Regiment of the Imperial Body Guards, excited by the repressions of military disorders, refused to perform the service of the guard.[1] On 1st December meetings of the troops in the garrison of Moscow were held. On 2nd December sedition broke out in the Rostovski 2nd Grenadier Regiment at Moscow, and commotion among the other troops of the garrison increased.

The foregoing details show that, especially during the month of November 1905, the commotions among the troops spread all over European and Asiatic Russia. Not merely in the cities, but also in the rural districts, troops were being employed upon police service, and they were becoming restive under the pressure of disagreeable duties. The military authorities took care to employ troops belonging to one *gubernie* for the suppression of revolts in another, in order to avoid the risk of their fraternizing with the mobs.[2] They even used, where such an arrangement was possible, troops of one race to put down disorders among people of another. They used also rural troops in towns and urban troops in the country. The utmost advantage was thus taken of natural antagonisms. Yet, excited by the mismanagement of the war, and

---

[1] They were banished to Novgorodskaya *gub.*

[2] The policy of garrisoning one part of the country with natives of another part was definitively adopted in 1882, and it has been pursued ever since.

by the continual repressions and punitive expeditions, and even more by their own military grievances about incompetent commissariat arrangements, inadequacy of allowances, extremely low pay, and ill-treatment by their officers, meetings of the garrison troops were held at many military centres. The army and the navy alike were in a state of dangerous fermentation.

In spite of the difficulties which they encountered, the Social Democratic and Social Revolutionary groups were carrying on an active propaganda among the garrison troops in the towns. These troops, already disaffected on purely military grounds, readily lent their ears to such propaganda, and for a time hopes that the coming revolutionary attempt might be aided by the troops ran high, especially among the Social Democrats. The isolated outbreaks which occurred were not, however, countenanced by them.[1] They wished to postpone active measures until the " state of mind " of the troops was ripe for common action, and until the association between the troops and the organizing bodies of working men should be more decisive. Reports [2] from some centres seemed to encourage the belief that the troops were " nearing " the working men, as the phrase ran.

Reports of this kind engendered the belief, especially in Moscow, that the troops were seriously affected by sedition for reasons of their own, and that they would not only refrain from taking an active part against the working men when they should rise, but that they would actively participate in their favour. Indeed the agitation among the troops seemed likely to precipitate a general conflict prematurely.

The Moscow committee of the Russian Social Democratic Party seems even to have been prepared to declare a general strike if the Government should attempt to put down these military disorders by armed force.[3]

The soldiers returning from Manchuria were also supposed to be in full sympathy with the working men, and to be prepared to give them active assistance. In Moscow, soldiers and officers appeared on the platform at revolutionary meetings.[4]

The idea of a general political strike thus gradually came to

[1] See *Moscow in December* 1905, edited by " Kokhmansky " (Moscow, 1906), p. 3.
[2] For details, see next chapter.
[3] *Moscow in December*, 1905, p. 4.   [4] *Ibid.*

be uppermost in the minds of some portion of the troops, of some portion of Government employees, and of a large portion of the working men. Their economical grievances appeared to be beyond their power to remedy unless the political situation was radically altered. They seem to have thought that the Cabinet should be dismissed and a new group of Ministers appointed. Probably had this been done in the early days of December, the armed uprising, with its disastrous national consequences, might not have taken place. The growing discontent among the troops in face of the highly disturbed state of the people alarmed the Government. On 6th December a manifesto by the Tsar announced a series of concessions to the army. Increased pay and allowances and special rewards for those who were employed upon police duties were promised to private soldiers.[1] These concessions were made just in time to enable the authorities to use the troops, with some measure of confidence in their fidelity, for the suppression of the still more serious disturbances which everyone recognized were now imminent.

The specific reasons for the loyalty of the army, in spite of the active propaganda of the revolutionary parties, were these :

1. The development by the military administration of the policy of utilizing racial antipathies. Thus in the Moscow garrison there were no Great Russians. The garrison was composed largely of Little Russians, who have a traditional dislike of the inhabitants of Moscow. They speak of them as foreigners and enemies of the Tsar. The Little Russians do not wear beards, and do not like people who do.[2] There were also many Poles, whose strong national prejudice against the Great Russian can always be relied upon. The remainder of the garrison were Lithuanians, whose general mental level is not high, and Cossacks of the Don, whose mental level is also low, and whose interests are exclusively military. Antipathies other than racial were also utilized. Thus peasant troops were employed to garrison cities, and city-bred troops to garrison rural districts. The majority of the non-commissioned

---

[1] Prior to this date private soldiers were obliged to provide for themselves tea, sugar, and soap. Now these articles were to be given to them. They were also to receive 15 kopeks (3¾d.) per day extra pay for police service. The officers were not affected.

[2] The Little Russians speak of the *Muskali* (Little Russian for Muscovites) as *Katzapi* (goats), because they wear beards.

officers and of the private soldiers are peasants, and their attitude towards the working men in cities is, in general, antagonistic.[1]

2. The grievances of the troops in respect to insufficient pay and allowances, and in respect to treatment by their officers, were met in a conciliatory spirit by the authorities in the height of the crisis. Increased pay and allowances were given and conditions were improved.

3. The young troops were drawn off to Manchuria, and the older troops were left behind in the garrisons. These latter were less likely to be stampeded into a widely extended insurrection than young troops might have been.

4. The officers, being exclusively drawn from the nobility, were as a rule beyond suspicion of disloyalty, and a military revolt would for this reason have been one exclusively of the rank and file, and would, therefore, not have been really a revolt of the army as a whole.

5. The influence of the habit of discipline is very strong among the Russian troops. Thus although there were several serious outbreaks, these were in no case determined by political motives, but were exclusively determined by the economical situation. The troops wanted more pay. They were not clamouring for the " overwhelming of the autocracy."

6. The severity of the authorities when propaganda in the ranks of the army was discovered prevented any considerable preparation for a revolt in so far as a propaganda could have contributed to such preparation.

7. The bulk of the army being drawn from the peasant class, the troops shared the general absence of preparation of their class. They did not know what they wanted. While the soldiers were rioting they frequently shouted, " Vive the Tsar ! " and " Vive the Tsar and the Duma." [2]

---

[1] In the villages, especially in those which are situated at a distance from industrial centres, the peasants do not drink tea, nor do they eat white bread, excepting on holidays. In cities the working men usually have tea and white bread at least twice a day. The peasant soldier thinks that the city working men engage in rioting because they are fat and overfed, and because they do not work long enough or hard enough.

[2] An exception might perhaps be made in the case of Kronstadt. Being near St. Petersburg, propaganda had always been going on in that fortress. During and after the riots, the soldiers there were very resolute. The rioters who were shot sang revolutionary songs until within a few minutes before their execution.

CHAPTER VII

THE COUNCIL OF WORKING MEN'S DEPUTIES AT ST. PETERSBURG AND THE SECOND GENERAL POLITICAL STRIKE, 2ND TILL 7TH NOVEMBER 1905

ALTHOUGH the first political strike had come to an end on 21st October, the Council of Working Men's Deputies which had been brought into existence in the course of the preparation for the strike had continued its meetings and had preserved its influence over its constituents. The disappointing incidents which followed the issue of the manifesto of 17th October, the Black Hundred *pogroms*, the stern suppression of the revolutionary movement in Poland, and the affair of Kronstadt, brought up the question of the expediency of subjecting the Government to another general political strike, the immediate object being the " saving of the lives " of the mutinous Kronstadt sailors. The sound interpretation of the political strike of 2nd November is with high probability that it was a strategic manœuvre with the purpose of connecting demonstratively the proletarian revolutionary movement with the mutiny in the army. The leaders of the strike had undoubtedly in their minds the idea that a strike would at that moment contribute importantly towards establishing an *entente cordiale* between the revolutionary working men and the mutinous soldiers and sailors. This *entente* might be calculated upon to facilitate subsequent revolutionary propaganda in the army and the navy, and might also have some effect in increasing the lack of confidence entertained by the Government in the fidelity of the troops, and thus in diminishing the use of them for police purposes. The revolutionary circles even began to dream of the transference of the army and the navy from the service of the autocracy to the service of the revolution.[1] Nor was the dream without a certain

[1] *Cf.* Khrustalov, *op. cit.*, p. 106.

509

basis of fact. Compulsory military service had really brought into existence a popular army. "The army is but a splinter of the whole people, and it cannot but experience the popular movement." [1] The employment of troops on guard duty at factories, &c., had contributed at once to their knowledge of the character of the revolutionary movement and to their dissatisfaction. Guard duty was arduous and unpleasant. Even veteran troops soon became demoralized by street fighting ; and they began to censure the Government rather than the revolutionaries. It was an obvious opportunity for the revolutionaries to declare that "the affair of the sailors was the affair of the working men," [2] and to endeavour to recruit for the revolution the discontented in army and navy alike.

These larger views were not, of course, entertained by the working men generally. The decision on the part of the Government to try the sailors by a special tribunal was looked upon by the working men as presaging their certain condemnation to death. "This tribunal is not a court; it is an abattoir." [3] Some of the groups of working men demanded a public inquiry into the circumstances which led up to the revolt at Kronstadt. They alleged, for example, that the men had suffered from the "profanation of human dignity and the abuse of authority." [4] Even the question of the eight-hours day was relegated into the background. "How can we present economical demands when so many people are about to be shot ? We must stand up for the sailors." [5] Many of the groups passed resolutions calling upon the Council of Working Men's Deputies to organize a general political strike with the demand that at least the sailors should be tried by a civil rather than by a military court. In the communications to the Council of Working Men's Deputies only one voice appears to have been raised against the proposal to strike. "We have not finished the struggle for the eight-hour day. A new strike will break our strength. . . . Protest should be made in the form of meetings, demonstrations, &c." [6] Yet the Executive Committee of the Council of Working Men's

---

[1] Khrustalov, op. cit., p. 107.　　　　　　　　　　　　　　　　[2] Ibid.
[3] The employees of the steel-tempering works of Tillman & Co. in the pages of Novaya Jēzn, quoted by Khrustalov, op. cit., p. 108.
[4] Ibid., p. 108.
[5] The working men of the Baltic Foundry, quoted ibid., p. 109.
[6] Deputy from Rasteriev Metal Foundry, ibid., p. 111.

Deputies was unanimously opposed to a strike at that moment, even the representatives of the revolutionary parties in the committee acquiescing. But when the proposal to strike was brought before the Council as a whole by the Social Democratic and Socialist Revolutionary delegates, the resolution was carried by a large majority, and a general political strike was declared for the following day, the 2nd November, at noon.

The declaration of the strike was accompanied by an appeal to the army, narrating its cause, viz. the situation of the mutinous sailors at Kronstadt, and demanding their liberation. " The Government wants to torture them to death. Let us give one another a hand and save our sailor brothers." [1]

In the early days of the first political strike, a large part of the time of the members of the Council of Working Men's Deputies was occupied in " calling off " reluctant adherents from their customary work. The second strike was otherwise characterized. The working men struck spontaneously even before the hour fixed for the commencement of the strike. During the forenoon of the 2nd, thousands of working men from the foundries and factories paraded the streets. At twelve o'clock the working men of the factories of Keppel, Semanyekov, Alexandrov, Obukhov, Pal, Maxwell, Pintsch, Nobel, Lessner, Rasteriev, Putilov, and the Belgian Corporation, the Baltisky Works and other large establishments were on strike. The smaller industrial groups joined the strike on the following day. Resolutions which indicate the state of mind of the working men poured into the Council.

" We do not believe in the curtailed constitution of Witté. We do not believe in the assurances of liberals, capitalists, landowners, and fat *intelligentsia*. We see up till now only thousands of dead bodies, thousands of beaten and wounded people. We hear the sorrowful cries of prisoners in the cells, and we continue our struggle for immediate improvement of our condition, for transference of all the land into the hands of the toilers, for freedom of personality and complete popular government. To this struggle we invite our brothers, the toiling peasantry. Give bread to working men ! Give land to peasants ! Give freedom to the people ! Away with the autocracy ! To the comrades, sailors and soldiers, who raised the flag of freedom, we express our sympathy, and send our hearty

[1] Khrustalov, *op. cit.*, p. 113.

greetings. Now for the happiness of our Fatherland, not a single drop of the blood of our comrades will be left unavenged." [1]

This resolution was forwarded by a group of piano-makers. Other resolutions mentioned " black hundreds " and martial law in towns, and condemned the " treacherous policy of the usurper Wittë." While the second political strike was general among St. Petersburg workmen, the professional groups, which constituted an important part of the first strike, were absent in the second. Civil servants were reluctant to join the ranks of the strikers. Some groups naïvely suggested to the Council to induce other groups to strike, in order that they might be locked out. [2]

The post and telegraph employees did not join the strikers because they were at that moment negotiating with the Government about an improvement in the conditions of their employment, and they considered that their economical interests would be imperilled if they engaged in a political demonstration. Moreover, they were guarded from any interference on the part of the strikers by troops with machine guns. The latter course was probably unnecessary, since the Council had apparently arrived at the conclusion that any violence directed against civil servants might have the effect of driving them into the arms of the " Black Hundred." [3]

The horse tramways continued to run. A violent attempt to prevent their operation was followed by fusillades from Cossacks. The majority of the retail shops were open, as was the case in the first strike, and for the same reasons.

The Council set itself immediately to the promotion of an active agitation among the troops. Thousands of copies of manifestoes were distributed in barracks and in the marine " equipages." On the 3rd November the meeting of the Council was attended by 417 deputies ; at this meeting there was read Count Wittë's appeal to the working men to resume work on the ground that the Government needed time to deal with the labour question. " Give us time, and then all that is possible will be done for you. Pay heed to a man who is favourably disposed towards you, and who wishes

[1] Resolution of the employees of the Schroeder Piano Factory. Khrustalov, *op. cit.*, pp. 113–14.

[2] The drivers of the Post Office delivery waggons suggested that the sorters should be called out. *Ibid.*, p. 116.

[3] Khrustalov, *op. cit.*, p. 116.

you well." [1] The Council answered this communication of Count Witë by saying, " The working class does not need the favours of the usurper. It demands popular government on the basis of general, equal, direct, and secret suffrage."

Nevertheless, the appeal of Count Witë placed the Council in a quandary. The strike was practically universal so far as the working men in the St. Petersburg factories were concerned ; but owing to the absence of the participation of the employees of the Government, the mechanism of life was by no means arrested as it had been in October. The successful continuance of it was therefore very problematical. From the point of view of the strike as a demonstration of the power of the Council, and of the sympathy of the working people with the mutiny in the army and navy, one day was as efficacious as a week. The strike might therefore have been declared at an end on the 3rd November ; but if this decision were arrived at on that date, the cessation would appear to have been brought about by Count Witë's telegram. The question of the discontinuance of the strike was thus postponed. On the following day, however, the executive of the Council decided to discontinue the strike by a majority of nine votes to six. This decision was, however, negatived on the same day (4th November) by an overwhelming vote in the Council as a whole.[2] There was a heated discussion, in which the executive committee was roundly denounced. It was reminded that it ordered a strike for a definite object, and that that object had not been attained. Nevertheless, either the executive was better informed than the Council, or it was in a position to make a sounder diagnosis of the situation. Although the strike had been unprecedentedly widespread on its first day, and although it had been in progress for three days only, it was already abating ; and the committee knew that the striking mass could not be held together. On the 5th November this fact became evident to everyone, and a resolution was passed to bring the strike to an end on the 7th November.

Meanwhile the Government had conceded something. The case of the sailors at Kronstadt was handed over, not to a court martial,

---

[1] *Ibid.*, p. 168. Count Witë's telegram began with the familiar phrase, " Little brothers ! " A group of electrical workmen reported upon it laconically: " Read and struck."

[2] A hundred votes to four.

but to the military circuit court, which, unlike a court martial, is a permanent military-judicial tribunal.

The speech made by the member of the executive committee of the Council of Working Men's Deputies who moved the resolution that the strike should come to an end, put the whole position very clearly. He pointed out that to sustain the strike until the sailors were handed over to a civil tribunal and until martial law was abrogated in Poland, meant that it must be sustained until the complete downfall of the autocracy. He did not deceive himself so far as to suppose that that event was imminent. It was better then to cease the existing strike, and to resume the attack later when occasion seemed opportune. A series of assaults was necessary. The strike had not been unsuccessful. Something had been gained. The sailors had been saved from the summary jurisdiction of a court martial. The Government had capitulated so far. Besides, the Government had been frightened, and its credit had been injured, by the collapse in the price of Russian securities on the foreign exchanges. Again, the elections for the Duma were soon to take place. These must be organized, and through them a further blow might be struck against the Government. Beneath this optimism, however, there was in the speech an undercurrent of despondency. The speaker avowed, what in the later days of 1905 was becoming obvious, that the nation was no longer united against the autocracy—that the struggle was becoming more and more a class struggle. Even the *intelligentsia*, who had joined heartily in the first political strike, were less sympathetic in the second. They were saying, " Do you hope to defeat the enemy with your strength only ; your strikes are setting society against you." [1]

The second political strike in St. Petersburg showed conclusively that the general strike as a political weapon had become perceptibly blunter. The effect upon the Government was by no means so great as the effect of the first strike, and in the end it was not apparent that any impression had been made upon the army and the navy, in spite of the fact that the strike was an attempt to enlist both on the side of the revolution.

[1] Khrustalov, *op. cit.*, p. 124.

CHAPTER VIII

THE AGITATION FOR AN EIGHT-HOURS WORKING DAY

THE Council of Working Men's Deputies, at its meeting on 29th October 1905, " decreed " the establishment of an eight-hours working day.[1] Khrustalov, who was the president of the Council, quotes from the report of the Geneva Congress (1866) of the International Working Men's Association : " The shortening of the working time appears to be the necessary condition without which all the aspirations of the proletariat towards its emancipation must fail." [2] To secure a universal eight-hours working day, one or other of three methods may obviously be employed : a law may be passed by the State, an agreement may be arrived at between workmen and their employers, or the workmen may simply leave their work on the expiry of a daily period of eight hours. Khrustalov points out that the Council of Working Men's Deputies was not averse from availing itself of the powers of the State. The large influence of the Social Democrats would naturally be exerted in that direction. " If," he says, " the working class did not ask the old authority for the shortening of the working day, that was because the police-autocratic State, in terms of its own existence, was unable to solve the working men's question." [3] The intermediate method offered no prospect of immediate success. The final method seemed to be the only one. Historically, Khrustalov says that the idea belongs to French syndicalism. At the congress of *La Confédération Générale du Travail* held at Bourges in March 1905, a resolution was adopted calling upon working men to obtain the eight-hours working day by " encroachment," or by " *l'action directe* "—that is, by taking it.[4] The method commended itself to the " state of mind " of the Russian proletariat at the time. The " right of striking," the " right of public meeting," the " right of free speech," had all been obtained by " encroachment—by *l'action*

---

[1] Khrustalov, *op. cit.*, p. 103.   [2] *Ibid.*, p. 100.   [3] *Ibid.*

[4] Cf. *Mouvemente Socialiste*, 15 mars 1905, and Pouget, Émile, *La Confédération Générale du Travail* (Paris, *c.* 1911), p. 58.

directe. If the " right " of an eight-hours working day were universally vindicated by all working men simply refusing to work for a
longer period daily than eight hours, the battle was won.   It would
be impossible to bring sufficient force to bear upon the working mass
to compel them to work longer than they chose to work.   Hundreds
and even thousands of people might be sent to prison,[1] but millions
could not be dealt with in this way.

The " decree" was passed by the Council on the night of 29th
October, and it was carried into effect on the 31st.   The manifesto
announcing this " decree " required all working men to introduce
the eight-hour day into their factories "in the revolutionary way "
—that is, by refraining from working longer than eight hours.
The Council also " considered " that an increase of hourly and piece-
work wages must be demanded, so that the wages should remain at
their former level, the shortening of working hours notwithstanding.
Khrustalov says that the Council insisted upon this because, although
in some industries a diminution of working hours might enable
labour to be intensified, and thus to avoid net reduction in wages,
there were other industries in which the machinery was so automatic
that it was beyond the power of the workman to increase his output
per unit of time.[2]

On Wednesday, 31st October, in a large number of the St. Petersburg foundries and factories,[3] the workmen, having worked for eight
hours, marched out of their respective places of employment, with
red flags, singing the " Marseillaise," and " taking off " workmen
in the smaller establishments who were still working.[4]   In one
factory, the management agreed to accept the eight-hour day, and
agreed also to increase wages.   In that case it was possible to increase the prices of goods by from one-half to one per cent.   In
general, however, the employers, while powerless to prevent the
workmen from leaving their work at the expiry of eight hours
labour, did not encourage them to do so by agreeing to an advance
of wages.

On the 2nd November the second political strike began, and the
eight-hour question was submerged for the five days during which

[1] As they might be under the code, for participation in strikes.
[2] Khrustalov, *op. cit.*, pp. 103–4.
[3] A long list of them is given by Khrustalov, *op. cit.*, p. 105.
[4] The printers, however, refused to be " taken off," on the ground that
they wished time to consider the question.

that strike lasted, to come to the surface again as a cardinal factor in the whole revolutionary situation. When work was resumed on the 7th November, some of the working men's deputies raised the question whether the " decree " of the 29th October upon the eight-hours day question ought to be rescinded. The employers had meanwhile met the difficult pass in which they had found themselves, by organizing employers' associations for the purpose of resisting the demands of the working men by their united strength. Some of these associations had already announced that their members would not agree to the eight hour day, and that a wholesale lock-out of working men would follow any attempt to impose it by *l'action directe*. The Government also agreed to support such a movement by refusing to reopen its industrial establishments. The moment was not ill chosen. The working men of St. Petersburg were exhausted by repeated strikes. Their wives and children were suffering want. If in striking they desired to relieve themselves of the burden of labour, they should have more relief in that kind than perhaps they desired. The Council of Working Men's Deputies had carried affairs with a high hand for a time, but during this time the Government had been able to recover its nerve, and the moment was now opportune for inaction. All that was necessary to break the revolutionary spirit was to keep the factory doors closed ; the military situation was no longer embarrassing, for most of the workmen had been relieved of their arms. As for the employers, they had probably gained as much potential advantage out of the revolutionary movement as they were likely to gain. A certain amount of freedom for them had been secured at comparatively slight cost and without compromising themselves with the Government. It was time now to draw the line. Khrustalov not inaptly compares the position at this moment of the St. Petersburg manufacturers with that of neutral states which step in when peace agreements are being made, to gain as much advantage as they can from both the previously contending parties. While the struggle was going on, the employers, as fully admitted by the representatives of the working men, had sustained well the rôle of neutrals. In the October strike some of them had even exhibited a certain sympathy with the working men's movement, because they recognized its predominantly political character. They did not seek to prevent the strikers from holding meetings in their works while the strike was in progress, and "the majority of the strikers" [1] received from their employers half wages during the strike ; some of them even received their wages in full. No working man was dismissed because he went on strike. The management of the Putilovsky Ironworks, for example, paid in full the wages of the deputies of their workmen who were members of the Council of the Working Men's Deputies, and who were, therefore, absent from work not only during the strike, but afterwards. The administration of the Obukhovsky Foundry offered the Council the use of a steamboat.

These amenities undoubtedly tended to diminish the friction between working men and their employers, and tended at the same time to give the strike more and more of a political character. But the insistence upon a universal eight-hours day after the two political strikes were over brought up again the economical features which, after all, lay at the root of the working men's movement.

If Count Witté had granted an eight-hours day, he might for the time have captured the working men, much as they distrusted him ; but he would have made mortal enemies of the St. Petersburg manufacturers ; and unless he had extended it to all the industrial centres of Russia, he would have imperilled the industrial interests of the capital. He may well be supposed to have shrunk from this course, and thus the employers and the Government were drawn together, the city proletariat was isolated, and the revolution, notwithstanding important changes in the methods of administration and in the forms of government, was rendered abortive.

On the 7th November the Government workshops remained closed, and numerous private establishments followed this example.[2] The manager of the Semyavikovsky Foundry posted the following notice: "If the work of the foundry is not performed according to the existing rules for interior management, all working men will be dismissed, and the foundry will be closed. Owing to the rumours that have reached me, working men, in spite of the decision of the administration (of the foundry) have the intention of working only eight hours per day. I regard it as my moral duty to convey to the knowledge of the working men that in seventy private foundries in St. Petersburg—and in this number

---

[1] Khrustalov, *op. cit.*, p. 127.
[2] A long list is given by Khrustalov, *op. cit.*, p. 128.

are all the large establishments—the former working day of ten to ten and a half hours is re-established." [1]

Soldiers were despatched to the factories, and meetings were forbidden. In one factory the employer, on being asked to give a room for a meeting, answered, " There shall not be any more meetings. You aim at too high political purposes, thus forcibly to introduce an eight-hour day." [2] The entrance of affairs upon this new path became known on 6th November, the day before the period fixed for the cessation of the strike. On that date a meeting of the Executive Council was held.[3] At this meeting the Council found itself confronted by the fact that there was no unanimity upon the question of the eight-hour day. Some employers were willing to agree to it upon condition that others did so also. Others agreed to reduce the number of working hours from ten to nine ; others from ten to nine and a half. It became apparent that a universal eight-hour day could not be arbitrarily imposed. The Council of Working Men's Deputies had not force enough to do it. The eight-hours day without increase of wages was likely to impoverish the working men, already exhausted by two political strikes in addition to a whole year of frequent and prolonged strikes on economical grounds. The majority of the working men were threatened with dismissal unless they abandoned their attempt to force the eight-hour day upon the employers.

The Council then decided upon an inevitable but fatal step. They left the question to the decision of the groups of workmen in the factories and foundries separately. The deputy of the printers very pertinently observed that the whole meaning of the Council was that it united the working men ; now it was dissolving the movement once more into mere party skirmishes. Moreover, if there must be division, it should be by industries, and not by regions. The fact of competition must not be ignored.[4] This argument showed, however, wherein the weakness of the Council lay at that moment. Insensibly but rapidly the Council of the Working Men's Deputies of St. Petersburg had acquired the hegemony of the Russian revolutionary movement. During the first political strike this was very evident. The second political strike occurred too soon after the first, and was too indecisive. Repres-

---

[1] Khrustalov, *op. cit.*, p. 128.   [2] *Ibid.*, p. 129.
[3] *Ibid.*, p. 130,   [4] *Ibid.*, p. 133.

sions were going on in the provinces, in spite of the critical state of affairs in the capital. Gradually the influence of the Council waned, and although, as will be shown later, there were attempts to mobilize the revolutionary forces under the leadership of the St. Petersburg Council, these attempts failed. Thus the Council was quite unable to deal with the eight-hour question in any wide way. The protest of the printers' deputy was unheeded, and the resolution, in which the struggle for the eight-hour day was practically abandoned, was passed.

The Government factories were reopened under the former conditions; but 19,000 men were locked out of thirteen factories, &c., on the 12th November, " because they insisted on the eight-hour day and because they went ' too far in politics.' " [1]

On the 13th November the Council discussed the expediency of answering the lock-out by declaring a general strike; the majority decided against any such course, unless a general Russian strike could be proclaimed.

The defeat upon the eight-hours day was a serious blow to the labour movement. It showed the working class the comparatively narrow limits of their power, and it reinvigorated both the employers and the Government.

[1] Khrustalov, *op. cit.*, p. 133.

CHAPTER IX

THE RELATION OF THE PRESS TO THE REVOLUTION

THE " Censure " in Russia is a formidable institution. Everyone is familiar with the " caviare " which obliterates objectionable passages in otherwise innocuous publications, and with the suspension of newspapers by administrative order. Under the pre-revolution régime no issue could be made from any printing-press until after it had passed the department of the " censure," and no printed matter could be delivered by the Post Office without passing through the ordeal of examination. There were three separate branches of this department for foreign books and journals: one at St. Petersburg, one at Moscow, and one at Kiev. These, as well as the numerous offices for the censure of domestic publications, were under the control of the committee of the censure in the Bureau of Press Affairs at St. Petersburg. For about six weeks, from 23rd October until 2nd December 1905, the Russian censure-ship was paralyzed by the " seizure of liberty " by the press. Practically all the newspapers simply disregarded the censor, and began freely to print criticisms of the Government. Police visits followed, and confiscations in some cases; but the revolt of the press was too widespread to deal with otherwise than in detail. There is no doubt that this " seizure of freedom " was due to the general situation ; but it was also due, undoubtedly, to the action of the printers. The printers established a censureship of their own. They refused to print anti-revolutionary writings. For example, when the so-called " righting of the Zemstvos " [1] took place the meeting of representatives of the Zemstvos at Moscow passed a manifesto which the compositors refused to set in type. M. Guchkov (in 1910, President of the State Duma) in intimating this circumstance to the meeting, used the following remarkable expressions :

" Apparently the new Bureau of Printing Affairs has distributed circulars to this effect : ' Here we have freedom of the

[1] Orientation towards the Right. Cf. *supra*, p. 281.

Press !' But this is the old régime, only from another end. There remains to us to use the methods of this régime, to print abroad or to start an underground printing office." [1]

The " righted Zemstvos " and the newspapers were obliged to surrender to the typesetters. The leading newspapers in the capitals, even the *Novoë Vremya*, were obliged to send their issues to the revolutionary censor. One newspaper only, *Slovo*, the organ of the Oktabrist party, obtained a special exemption. M. Guchkov's reference to the new Bureau of Printing Affairs was, of course, meant for the Council of Working Men's Deputies. At the meeting of the Council on 19th October it " decreed " the freedom of the press ; but no newspapers were permitted to be published excepting the *Bulletin* of the Council. While the strike lasted this " decree " was necessarily inoperative, because no newspapers were printed.[2] At the conclusion of the strike the question assumed a new aspect.

Simultaneously with the outbreak of the October strike and the formation of the Council of Working Men's Deputies, an union was formed of the publishers of newspapers and periodicals for the purpose of securing the freedom of the press from the arbitrary pencil of the censor. The first meeting of this new organization took place on 13th October, in the offices of *Nasha Jëzn*.[3] To this meeting working men were not invited ; but at the second meeting, which was held shortly after, there appeared together representatives of conservative journals like *Novoë Vremya*, of liberal journals like *Russ*, of radical journals like *Sën Otechestva*, and representatives of the working printers. All without doubt desired to secure the same end, namely, the freedom of the press, but in some cases this end was final, and in others it was only a means to remoter ends. The points of view were irreconcilable, and the working men withdrew, leaving the publishers and the men of letters to adopt their own methods. Strangely enough, the method upon which they finally agreed was not dissimilar from that which had been adopted by working men in the cities and the peasants in the provinces—they proposed to achieve the freedom of the press by taking it—that is, by *l'action directe*. The method was modified

---

[1] Khrustalov, *op. cit.*, p. 99.   [2] Cf. *supra*, p. 493.
[3] A. Simonovsky in *The History of the Council of Working Men's Deputies* (St. Petersburg, 1910), p. 219.

subsequently, but in the first instance it involved the policy of refraining from appealing to the Government for legislation and of ignoring the department of the censure. The resolution of the union that the censor be ignored was to be printed in every issue, and, in addition, news and comments upon public affairs, which would most probably have attracted the notice of the censor under the existing system, were to be printed in exactly the same form by all the newspapers in the union. This uniformity was adopted so that if any newspaper was suspended by the police, all would have to be dealt with. The newspapers also agreed that, should any of them be attacked, all would voluntarily suspend publication—a form of " peaceful boycott."

This union of the newspapers was organized while no newspapers were being published during the currency of the first political strike. No conflict between the Government and the newspapers was thus possible at that moment. During the strike the Council of Working Men's Deputies had made the freedom of the press— so far as its liberation from the department of the censure was concerned—an actual fact. Not only was the *Bulletin* of the Council issued and sold publicly in the streets of St. Petersburg in great numbers—it possessed a monopoly, for no other newspaper excepting the official gazette was published—but large numbers of other issues were made from the revolutionary press, now no longer underground, but openly established in " legal " printing offices.

Affairs were in this posture when the manifesto, the authorship of which is attributed to Count Wittë, was issued on 17th October. While freedom of speech was certainly mentioned in it, there was no mention of the freedom of the press. On the night of the 17th Count Wittë received a deputation from the Union of Unions, and gave an assurance that the expression " freedom of speech " included freedom of the press.[1] During the night of the 17th, the printers being still on strike, the question arose whether or not newspapers containing the manifesto should be printed on that evening or on the following morning. The staffs of various newspapers, notably that of the *Novoë Vremya*, pled with the printers to set up the paper, because of the change in the situation pro-

---

[1] Simonovsky, *op. cit.*, p. 220. At a subsequent " pilgrimage " to him, Count Wittë is reported to have said, " During his term the printed word will enjoy real freedom ; but we want to continue the laws about the censure " (*Russ*, 20th October 1905 ; quoted by Simonovsky, *op. cit.*, p. 222).

duced by the promise of representative government contained in
the manifesto of the Tsar. The printers replied that to do so
would be " to break " the strike and to break faith with their
union. The executive of the union met, and decided that the
promises of the manifesto could not be relied upon, and that the
strike should not be discontinued. The manifesto had already
been set up in type, but the type was distributed. On the night
of the 17th October the text of the manifesto was published by
one newspaper only, the *Pravitelstvennie Vestnik* (official gazette).
Delegates from the printers went to the office of this paper in order
to endeavour to dissuade the printers from setting up the document, but they were too late—the manifesto had been set up in
type and was being printed, not by printers, but by troops. *Novoë
Vremya* adopted the expedient of printing the manifesto on a
Remington typewriter and exposing a copy in a window lighted by
electricity. On the 18th the *Svyet* newspaper published the manifesto, the printing having been done by deserting strikers among
their own workmen. The printing office was afterwards pillaged
by " foundry workers." While the publication of the manifesto
of the Tsar was thus impeded by the revolutionists, as if to show
that they were masters of the situation, " enormous quantities " of
a revolutionary manifesto issued by the Social Democratic and
Social Revolutionist Parties were printed and distributed openly on
the 18th October.

When, on the 20th October, the Council of Working Men's
Deputies announced the discontinuance of the general political
strike, it also announced that the strike of newspaper printers
should continue in respect to those newspapers whose management
recognized the department of the censure by submitting their issues
to it in conformity with the existing law. Those printers who were
compelled to remain on strike because their employers did not
adopt this course were to receive full wages from the funds of the
Council. The resolution of the Council is as follows. " The ukase
of the Tsar promulgates freedom of speech, yet the head office for
press affairs is preserved. The Council, starting from the position
that the working class carries on its shoulders all or almost all of
the burden of the struggle, should say its word also about freedom
of the press. The freedom of the press should be conquered by
the workers themselves. The Council decides that only those news-

papers may be circulated, the editors of which ignore the committee of the censure, do not send their issues to the censor, and in general conduct themselves in the same manner as the Council does in the publication of its newspaper (the *Bulletin*). Therefore typesetters and other workers in the printing business who take part in the publication of newspapers, begin their work only when editors announce and effect the freedom of the press. . . . Newspapers which do not act in conformity with this resolution will be confiscated, their printing machines and printing offices will be destroyed, and working men who do not subject themselves to the council will be boycotted." [1] The Council also passed, on the same day, another resolution calling upon the Union for the Defence of the Press, in the event of the Government continuing to exercise repressive measures, not to adopt the means of the pacific boycott, as had been proposed by it, but to continue to disregard the department of the censure. In the latter case the Council promised to give its assistance to the Union for the Defence of the Press.

The newspapers were thus left still under embargo, the manifesto of the Tsar and the cessation of the general political strike notwithstanding. Moreover, they were on the horns of a double dilemma. If they did not accept the terms of the Council of Working Men's Deputies, their newspapers were not printed ; if they did accept them they ran the risk of having the publication of their newspapers suspended by Government. If they printed by means of strike-breakers their offices might be pillaged by the Council ; if they printed by means of the strikers, they might be raided by the police. Under these circumstances the newly formed Union for the Defence of the Press determined to send a memorandum to the Government demanding a new press law. In this memorandum [2] the publishers required the abolition of the system of preliminary censorship—that is, the system by which they were obliged to send to the censor everything that was intended to be published before issue. They also demanded that the practice of dealing with alleged offences against the press

---

[1] Simonovsky, *op. cit.*, p. 223. The book printers urged the Council to deal with them in the same manner as the newspaper printers had been dealt with ; but the Council refused. Their refusal was not quite consistent with their previous position, viz. that the newspaper printers could not be isolated, partly because books and newspapers were frequently printed in the same offices. (See Simonovsky, *loc. cit.*, and *cf.* Khrustalov, *op. cit.*, p. 77).

[2] Printed in full in *Russ*, 22nd October ; quoted in Simonovsky, *op. cit.*, p. 222.

law by administrative order should be discontinued, and that a new formal press law should be anticipated by immediate assurances of immunity from prosecution under the existing law.

Meanwhile the newspapers tacitly accepted the agreement proposed to them by the Council of Working Men's Deputies, the printing offices were opened, the printers resumed work, and the censure was ignored.   A stereotyped notice appeared in the newspapers to the effect that the issue in question had not been submitted to the censor.   On the first day of this new order, the 22nd October, *Russ*, the organ of the Constitutional Democrats, announced " with a certain risk we call this issue the first number of a new era—the era of the freedom of the Russian press."

The newspapers of more radical tendency—as, for example, the *Sēn Otechestva*—proclaimed themselves more vigorously.   " We are told that in the expression, ' freedom of speech,' there is included freedom of the press, but the censure remains unabolished ; and the press is obliged by its own efforts to throw off the chains of the censure." [1]   The press may have thought that its valorous action was due to its own initiative, but the Council of Working Men's Deputies entertained a quite different view.[2]   The distribution of credit, which is difficult at any time, is impossible during a revolution ; nor is it important now to assess precisely from which side came the initial, and from which the effective impulse.   The general state of mind was already making for the disintegration of the various elements of society which had been temporarily fused together in a negative attitude towards the autocracy.   The morrow of a revolution usually witnesses the dissolution of the combination by which it was effected.   The relations of the Union for the Defence of the Press with the Council of the Working Men's Deputies had never been cordial.   Such an attitude on both sides arose out of deep-seated prejudices, and contributed with similarly discordant points of view on the part of other revolutionary elements " to bring the revolution to dust."

---

[1] *Sēn Otechestva*, 1905, No. 210.

[2] This is very caustically put by Simonovsky, *op. cit.*, p. 224.   " The silence of the liberal marionettes (about the initiative of the Council of Working Men's Deputies) was not due to casual editorial oversight ; it arose out of the very substance of the liberal bourgeoisie spirit to register for themselves credit not only for the victories of others, but for the initiative."

CHAPTER X

THE RÔLE OF THE ST. PETERSBURG COUNCIL OF WORKING MEN'S DEPUTIES IN THE REVOLUTIONARY MOVEMENT

THE significance of the movement which began on the 13th October 1905 seems to lie in the fact that the Russian revolution passed from the hands of small isolated conspirative groups into the hands of an avowedly revolutionary body, which carried on its operations openly, entering into the struggle with the autocracy without disguise and without fear. This body was the St. Petersburg Council of Working Men's Deputies. The traditions of the revolution centre round it. There were similar councils of working men's deputies in other cities ; but the Russian working man of revolutionary sympathies who is invited to give his opinion about the driving force of the revolution unhesitatingly speaks of the St. Petersburg Council. Although at the height of its influence there were over four hundred members, the dominating voice in the Council was that of the president, G. Khrustalov-Nosar.

This remarkable man, under happier circumstances, might have served his country as the leader of an important party, recognized by the constitution and taking its share in the conduct of public affairs. His history of the events of October and November is the record of a calm, clear-headed man who thoroughly understood an unprecedented situation, and whose powerful brain appeared to grasp instantly the implications of the projects with which the Council was inundated and the wily snares with which its path was beset. Complete success of the revolution at that moment was, as the event proved, impossible ; but he guided it with cool and energetic hands at the critical moments, and at least contributed to prevent it from resulting in merely futile anarchy.

The " state of mind " of the professional classes, of the army, of the navy, of no inconsiderable proportion of the moneyed classes, of the urban proletariat, and of the peasantry in the early days of October was such as to suggest that a general and simultaneous Russian revolutionary movement was not only possible, but was inevitable. Whenever the St. Petersburg Council of Working Men's Deputies was formed, its executive committee was instructed to enter into relations with the Post-Telegraph Union, the Railway Union, the Peasant Union, and the working men of the industrial centres. It soon appeared that all these wide and widely scattered organizations were at once in need of guidance, and anxious to entrust this guidance to the working men deputies of St. Petersburg, which was at the same time a great industrial centre and the nearest to the central authority. So early as the 13th October the working men of Riga appealed to the St. Petersburg working men to send delegates there in order to be made aware of the moment of action. The working men of Reval, Ribinsk, Schlüsselberg, and Kharkov did the same thing. On the 6th November the Polish Socialist Party appeared in the Council by deputies ; on the 12th 35,000 working men of Narva sent their deputies, and on the same day those of Kiev and Rostov telegraphed their adhesion. In consequence of the affiliation of these widely scattered groups, it seemed advisable to convene a conference by means of which a formal central body might be elected to manage the revolutionary movement. But time did not permit of this. The first political strike pressed on, as described above ; then came the manifesto with its consequences, and later the second political strike. These brought labours enough to the Council, and it was not until after the eight-hour day struggle was over that it was possible to consider a consolidation of the All-Russian movement. Towards the middle of November the St. Petersburg Council of Working Men's Deputies sent delegates to Moscow, to the south of Russia, and to the Ad-Volga region. In Moscow these delegates stimulated the working men towards the re-establishment of the council of working men's deputies, which had fallen into abeyance in that city. At the same time they organized closer relations with the Jewish Bund in the north-western provinces, as well as with the Post-Telegraph and the Peasants' Unions.

Meanwhile in many towns, councils of working men's deputies had been formed, especially during the early days of October. The idea seems to have occurred to the Kharkov Society of Mutual

Assistance to Working Men [1] that a conference of representatives from these councils should be held, and in accordance with this suggestion a preliminary conference had been held in Moscow. The intention of this conference was, to begin with, simply to bring the newly organized labour movement to a focus, and to unite the various societies of the Kharkov type with the trade unions. But the debates of the conference went far beyond this comparatively narrow aim. They embraced the large questions of the relation between the trade union movement and the political agitation for constitutional government, and the relation of the labour movement in general to the prospective State Duma. The conference was attended not merely by the representatives of the councils of working men's deputies and of the mutual assistance societies, but also by those of the socialist parties. In the general revolutionary atmosphere of the time it was impossible to restrict either the membership of the conference or the debates which took place in it. At this preliminary conference it had been decided to have another conference, to which delegates were to be specifically elected, and to convene this conference for the 15th November. The preoccupation of the St. Petersburg Council, first in the October strike and later in the November strike and in the eight-hours day struggle, prevented any elections from being held under its auspices, nor had it leisure during these weeks, full of revolutionary activity, to formulate the business for a conference. Therefore on 10th November the St. Petersburg Council telegraphed to Moscow, proposing to postpone the conference until the end of December. This proposal was, however, not adopted, and the conference was held as previously arranged. Nevertheless, by means of this conference and otherwise, the St. Petersburg Council stimulated and organized the working men all over Russia. The machinery of organization was provided by the Council. The strike of the Post-Telegraph Union, which had been postponed, as above related, took place on its urgent demand. The Council also organized the union of wood-workers, port labourers, electric and gas-lighting workers, tobacco factory employees, shoemakers, and tailors. They also initiated the organization of weavers and spinners, workers in the metal industries, and others. All these

---

[1] This society had no political affiliations, and had confined itself to an educational propaganda among workmen and to a certain extent among peasants.

unions, thus formed and united by the St. Petersburg Council, were fighting unions which threw themselves vigorously into the revolutionary struggle. Some of them in their frequent resolutions made demands of a character quite alien to their own specific economical interests. Thus, the electric and gas-lighting union demanded a Constituent Assembly and the transference of the ownership of land into the hands of the peasants without payment by them.

Towards the end of November the unions acquired and exercised a great deal of power. The Government was forced into concessions. When, for example, the engineer Sokolov, together with other employees upon the railways, were brought before a court martial and sentenced to death, the railway unions threatened to strike again unless the death sentence was commuted by eight o'clock in the evening of 23rd November. This ultimatum was sent to the Ministry at St. Petersburg. The sentence was commuted by telegram, which was sent through the railway unions, the Ministry declaring that, owing to the post-telegraph strike, they knew nothing of the circumstances, and could not get into communication with the local authorities.[1]

In the last week of November the psychological moment arrived when the Government might, without risk to its own safety, assume an attitude of energetic hostility against the Council. On the 26th November Khrustalov, the president, was arrested. This action marked the end of the effective activity of the St. Petersburg Council of Working Men's Deputies. When its leader was arrested several courses presented themselves to the executive. The expedient of another general strike might be resorted to ; the executive might appear to dissolve in order to carry on conspirative activity " underground," or its members might consult their own safety by capitulation or flight.

The first-mentioned course, viz. the calling of another general strike, was clearly a risky one. The conclusion of the strike which had just been brought to an end had been confused, and the advantage which had been gained was very dubious. So far as St. Petersburg was concerned, the general strike, considered as a weapon in the revolutionary duel, was already blunt. The second course did not commend itself. The moral influence, such as it was, which the Council exercised over the working mass in St. Petersburg was due

[1] Khrustalov, *op. cit.*, p. 141.

to the fact that the proceedings of the Council were open. Its hostility to the Government as a whole was not disguised, and it was not engaged in conspirative attacks upon individuals. To abandon this position was to destroy its influence and in effect to cease to exist. The third course was a last resort. There remained the rather lame proceeding of continuing to carry on their routine business and to await events.[1]

The arrest of Khrustalov was thus not followed by any reprisals in St. Petersburg ; but the working men of Moscow were still unexhausted, and the centre of interest was removed to that city, where the professional classes and the working class were alike in a state of fermentation.

It should be observed that, although the St. Petersburg working men are generally reputed to be more intelligent than those of Moscow, the working men of Moscow have been more accustomed to discussion. Even during reactionary phases the atmosphere of Moscow has always been freer than that of St. Petersburg. This circumstance has been due partly to jealousy on the part of the bureaucrats of Moscow of their superiors at the centre of the bureaucratic mechanism at St. Petersburg, and partly to the civic rivalry of the general population of the two cities—one the seat of Slavophilism and all that that implies, and the other the seat of Western European influence.

On the 2nd December the revolutionary groups joined in issuing a manifesto which was in effect an indictment of the Government. This manifesto is not couched in the rhetorical terms customary in such documents, but is a forcible statement the general truth of which it was impossible to contest. Eight newspapers published the manifesto.[2] They were all suspended, and the issues in which

---

[1] These alternatives were recognized at the time by the executive. See Zvesdin, V., in *Hist. of the Council of Working Men's Deputies of St. Petersburg ;* cited, pp. 170 *et seq.*

[2] The eight newspapers were *Nachalo, Nasha Jezn, Novoya Jêzn, Russkaya Gazetta, Russ, Svobodny Narod,* and *Sên Otechestva.* The manifesto was issued by the following groups : The Council of Working Men's Deputies, the Main Committee of the All-Russian Peasant Union, the Central Committee and Organizational Committee of the Russian Social Democratic Working Men's Party, the Central Committee of the Socialist Revolutionary Party, and the Central Committee of the Polish Socialist Party.

The following is the text of the manifesto : " The Government is on the edge of bankruptcy. It has converted the country into a ruin and strewn it with corpses. The exhausted and starving peasant is unable to pay his

the manifesto appeared were confiscated. Immediately afterwards " The Union for the Defence of the Liberty of the Press " decided to publish the manifesto as a protest against what was considered to be an infringement upon the freedom of the press. One hundred

quit rents. The Government opened with the money of the people a means of credit for landowners ; now the estates are encumbered with mortgages. Factories and mills stand idle. There is no work, and there is general stagnation of trade. By means of capital derived from foreign loans the Government has built railways, has built a navy and fortresses, and has accumulated reserves of arms ; but the foreign loans are now exhausted, and orders to the State and private industrial establishments have ceased. Merchants, purveyors, contractors, mill-owners, who used to get rich through the orders of the State have closed their offices and works. One bankruptcy is followed by another. The banks are ruined. All the circulation of trade is contracted to the last point. The struggle of the Government against the revolution creates continual agitation. No one is sure of to-morrow. Foreign capital is returning abroad, and even Russian capital is swimming away. The rich are selling their property and escaping to other countries. Plunderers are running away from Russia and carrying off the property of the people. For a long time the Government has been spending all the income of the State on the army and the navy. There are no schools. The roads are in disorder. Notwithstanding this, there are not sufficient means to provide for the soldiers. The war was lost partly because the military ammunition was insufficient. All over the country there have been uprisings of the distressed and starving army. The railway economy is in disorder. The treasuries of the railways are ransacked by the Government. To replenish the railway economy, many hundreds of millions of rubles are necessary. The Government has despoiled the Savings Banks and has given the money deposited in them to support the private banks and industrial enterprises—the latter sometimes inflated. Government is speculating on the Exchanges with the capital of the small depositor, risking this capital every day. The gold fund of the bank is insignificant compared with the demands on account of State loans and the requirements of the trade balance. This fund will be converted into dust if for all dealings payments in gold are required. Profiting by the circumstance that the State finances are not disclosed, the Government has long ago concluded loans far in excess of the means of payment by the country. By means of fresh loans it is defraying the interest upon the old ones. Year after year the Government compiles fraudulent estimates of income and expenditure, showing both in less than the actual amounts in order to present a false excess instead of a real deficit each year. The uncontrolled officials peculate the already exhausted fisc. Only a Constituent Assembly following after the overwhelmed autocracy can put a stop to this financial destruction. The Assembly will occupy itself with a strict investigation of the State finances and will procure detailed, clear, and exact estimates of State income and expenditure. The fear that the control of the people will reveal before the whole world the insolvency of the Government compels the latter to delay the convocation of a representative national assembly. The financial bankruptcy of the State has been brought about by the autocracy as well as its military bankruptcy. Before the national representatives there lies, possibly quite soon, to settle the debts (incurred by the autocracy). In defence of its rapacity the Government compels the people to carry on against it a life-and-death struggle. In this struggle hundreds of thousands of citizens are perishing

newspapers published the manifesto ; the Government refrained from further prosecutions. The immediate effect of the manifesto was a run upon the Government Savings Banks, which resulted in the withdrawal of over a hundred millions of rubles of deposits.

and are being ruined ; and the foundations of production, trade, and transportation are being ruined also. There is only one outcome—to overwhelm the Government, to take away from it its last remaining power. The ultimate source of its existence, its financial income, must be cut off. This is necessary not only for the political and economical emancipation of the country, but also for the reformation of the financial economy of the State.

" Therefore we decide :

" To refuse payment of redemption instalments and all other fiscal payments.

" To demand in all payments of wages and salaries payments in gold, and for amounts of less than five rubles full weight of hard coin.

" To withdraw the deposits from the Savings Banks and from the State Bank, demanding payment of all amounts in gold.

" The autocracy has never enjoyed the trust of the people and derives none of its power from them. At the present time the Government is acting within its own frontiers as if it were in a conquered country. Therefore we decide not to acknowledge the debts which, in the form of loans, the Government of the Tsar has contracted while it has been carrying on open war against the whole people." *Russkoë Bogatstvo*, Nos. 11 and 12, pp. 193–5.

CHAPTER XI

THE ARMED UPRISING IN MOSCOW FROM DECEMBER 9TH TILL 19TH, 1905

THE project of a third general political strike was discussed from the beginning of December not only in the revolutionary party organizations, but in the working men's unions and in the councils of their deputies. The " state of mind " of the party organizers and of the working men at this time seems to suggest that they were impelled towards aggressive action by an irresistible impulse. The disastrous events of the Russo-Japanese War, the obvious confusion of the bureaucratic administration, evidently at its wits' end, and the activity of the revolutionary parties had combined to excite the hopes of the city industrial population. They felt that " events were terribly nearing " ; they thought that the time to strike had arrived, and that a few bold strokes would " overwhelm " the autocracy. What was to come after ? First of all a Constituent Assembly, widely representative ; and out of that would emerge some kind of constitution. This " state of mind " was certainly not wholly due to the revolutionary propaganda of the Social Democratic and Social Revolutionary Parties, but it was undoubtedly fomented by this propaganda. The psychology of the revolutionary party leaders at this time is not hard to understand. Their campaign had been conducted for at least fifteen years with skill and courage. They had circulated hundreds of thousands of pamphlets and newspapers. They had conducted numerous demonstrations. Yet they felt uncertain about the next step. If the Tsar refused or delayed to convene a Constituent Assembly, what was to be done ?

Two " peaceful " general strikes had failed. The boycott had cost the Government much, but it had cost the people more. Fresh tactics must be employed. The working men who had declared their adherence to the revolution were impatient. They had lost all faith in the promises of the Government, and they might be calculated upon speedily to lose faith in the promises of the revolutionary leaders unless they led them somewhere. Something decisive must be done, or the results of the ardent propaganda of past years, and especially of the past months, would go for nothing. There seemed no choice but acquiescence in the demand of the working men for an armed movement. If it were possible to get the military to " come over to their side," a sudden and successful revolution might be accomplished, or, at all events, a weakening blow might be struck at the tottering autocracy. If the military did not join them, the revolutionary leaders did not disguise from themselves that an " armed uprising " must fail. Their orators and pamphleteers were not military leaders. Many of the *intelligentsia* who were with them in the propaganda, and who enjoyed evasion of the police and contempt of authority, could not be relied upon for real revolutionary business when that business meant fighting in the streets against disciplined troops. Their own prophets[1] had told them indeed that in any case revolutionary movements involving barricades and street fighting were hopelessly archaic, and that the machine gun and the magazine rifle had rendered the old type of revolution now impossible of realization. Very few of them were armed with any weapons, and still fewer knew how to use arms even if they had had them. Above all, they had no artillery and no military leaders. They were well aware of all these facts, yet the working men, excited by the various influences of which mention has been made, and daily further excited by reports of fresh repressive actions on the part of the Government, were urging the party organizations to take some decided action. Were they to refuse to obey this summons which came from all quarters, the party leaders would undoubtedly be accused of cowardice, and the influence of their propaganda would be absolutely at an end. The leaders of the revolutionary parties thus found themselves in a horrible dilemma. On one side, the blood of themselves and others, death by shrapnel shells or bullets, with inevitable failure to obtain any material advantage excepting their doubtful enrolment on the roll of martyrs for liberty; on the other side, ignominious confession of defeat, not in the field, which they would have refused, but in a hopeless *impasse* into which they had led their unfortunate followers. Besides, at that moment any faltering in attack might have been even more fatal than an

---

[1] Friedrich Engels, and later August Bebel, had written in this sense.

aggressive advance, and might retard the whole movement for liberty and compromise the future.   They might continue to harass the Government by repeated strikes and boycotts, because these were the only weapons which they had at their hands and which they knew how to use.   To cut off the public revenues by stoppage of industry and of transportation, and by consequent paralysis of commerce—in short, to use every means to bring the machinery of the country to a standstill—all these had been tried and, to a large extent, effected without decisive result.   What remained to do was to strike once more and, with the army of workers thus relieved from industry, to take up arms in open rebellion.   In so far as there was a plan, this seems to have been the plan, but no evidence has come to light of any definite conspiracy, or of any design to seize upon any strategic position or to attack any specified person.   The movement was blind, and, being blind, was all the more formidable.

The people were apparently ripe for a serious rising, yet they were not ready for it.   To deliver incendiary speeches against the Government was one matter, to devise military measures to attack and overthrow an established military autocracy with disciplined troops at its absolute disposal was quite a different affair.

Clear as the hopelessness of the struggle must have been to some, it was by no means so to all.   The minds of most appear, indeed, to have been in a state of confusion.   Neither those who threw themselves upon the Government nor even the Government itself seem to have thoroughly realized the situation.   Each side alike miscalculated the power of the other, and each miscalculated its own power.   The fighting organizations upon whom the brunt of the fighting eventually fell found themselves in the centre of a noisy, garrulous, and unreliable mob instead of an army, and, on the other hand, the Government found its troops more loyal than it had suspected.

Yet the Moscow " armed uprising " had a certain influence upon the political and even more upon the financial situation.   Its influence upon the former was not favourable to the revolution, because it contributed to the reaction,[1] but its influence upon the financial situation was much more serious than the influence of the disasters of the war in respect to the injury which its occurrence

[1] Although reaction might have taken place in any event.

inflicted upon the credit of the Russian Government both in Russia and abroad.[1]

From the beginning the chief question, apart from the question of the general strike, was, Will the army remain loyal to the Tsar ? Meeting after meeting was held in the last days of November and in the early days of December in the various Moscow districts, and it was reported at these meetings that there was grave disaffection among the troops. It was said that in some places the working men and the soldiers had, in fact, already fraternized.[2]

A meeting of the council of working men's deputies of Presnya and Hamovniki districts of Moscow, in which there were forty-three deputies from eleven factories, was held on 2nd December. At this meeting the representative of the Moscow group of the " minority faction " of the Social Democratic Party intimated that a premature uprising among the troops was possible, in spite of the efforts of the " military organization " of the Social Democratic Party to prevent such uprising until " a closer connection between regiments might be arranged." [3] The meeting then discussed the desirability of supporting such an outbreak, even though it might be premature.

So also at a meeting of workers in the electrical industry held on 4th December, at which 280 persons were present, similar statements were made. These were followed by exclamations, " We shall not give up our fellow-soldiers. We shall pour for them our blood." A declaration was also made at this meeting that the Moscow Committee of the Russian Social Democratic Working Men's Party was prepared to announce a general strike if the Government made up its mind to check the strike of the soldiers by armed force, and also that the railway men had decided not to allow to pass any trains carrying soldiers returning from Manchuria unless the soldiers undertook " to assist the proletariat." These declarations seem to

[1] See *infra*, Appendix to Book VII, Prices of Russian 4 per cent. State Debt on the Paris Bourse in 1904 and 1905.

[2] At Kharkov and Novorossiesk, for instance. *Moscow in December* 1905 (Moscow, 1906), p. 3.

[3] *Moscow in December* 1905, p. 4. Speeches showing " the state of mind " of the soldiers were made at this meeting. The deputy from the silk factory of Girot, *e.g.* reported that the dragoons and grenadiers who were on guard at that factory were drilling the working men in using weapons, saying, " Don't be afraid of us ! When you will rise up, we will too ; and we will open the arsenals for you."

represent fairly the views of the Moscow working men at that time· They did not feel themselves prepared for an armed uprising on their own account, but they were prepared to support a military rebellion, even if it were premature.

At the same meeting there were shouts to the following effect : " Let us overwhelm the autocracy. Let us struggle until the end ! We may perish, but we will not leave to our children shackles for their inheritance. They must not have to call their fathers traitors to the proletariat." [1]

Officers and private soldiers frequently appeared on the platforms of the meetings.[2] There was even on 3rd December some practical evidence of the sympathy of the troops with the working men. On this date a meeting of post-telegraph employees was to be held in the Aquarium. When the hour arrived, the entrance to the building was found to be closed and to be guarded by police. A crowd of about 3000 persons having collected, a detachment of Cossacks was sent to disperse the crowd. This, however, the Cossacks did not do ; and after an open-air meeting, at which several speeches were delivered, had gone on for some time, the doors were opened and the crowd was admitted to the building.

On 3rd December there was held a meeting of railway employees called primarily to discuss their economical grievances. On the proposal that the railway men should support the post-telegraph workers' strike then in progress, the meeting decided not to arrange partial strikes in view of the " imminence " of a " general strike." [3]

There appears thus to have grown gradually in the minds of the working men the idea of a general political strike, in which the military would refuse to act against the working men, and by means of which the autocracy might be brought to terms. The Moscow Council of Working Men's Deputies had sent one of its members to St. Petersburg to report upon the " state of mind " there after the arrest on 26th November of the president of the Council of Working Men Deputies in that city (Khrustalov). On Sunday, 4th December, a meeting was held to receive the report of this delegate. He said that " it was worth enormous efforts on the part of the St. Petersburg Council to avert a general strike as a reply to the arrest

---

[1] *Moscow in December* 1905, p. 4.
[2] As, for example, at a meeting at the Aquarium on 4th December.
[3] *Moscow in December* 1905, p. 5.

of its president " ; yet the " state of mind " of the St. Petersburg working men might lead to such a strike at any moment, and that " the Moscow proletariat must be ready for an active outbreak." This meeting considered the manifesto formulated in St. Petersburg, and adhered to by various groups, urging the people to refrain from paying taxes, quit rents, &c., to the Government, and agreed to adhere to it. Then the meeting " ardently discussed the question of a general political strike." Nearly all the speakers declared that everywhere—in factories, mills, &c.—the working men were *ready to begin the strike immediately*. After prolonged and eager debate between the opponents and adherents of an immediate declaration of the strike, it was decided to devote the following day to agitation in the factories and mills, and afterwards to meet for final decision on the question.[1] On the ground that the " Black Hundred " was preparing for a *pogrom*, it was also agreed that on the following day " cold weapons " (steel weapons of various kinds) should be forged in the factories, and that patrols of *drujēnēkē* (or fighting companies) should be organized in order to oppose any attacks by Black Hundred groups.

At the close of the meeting the following resolutions were passed :

" 1. The Moscow Council of Working Men's Deputies points out to the comrades that the Government is making a new desperate attempt to retain power in its hands. In St. Petersburg the Council of Working Men's Deputies is arrested, papers are suppressed and confiscated, and meetings are dispersed. Working men comrades should be ready. The Council of Working Men's Deputies points out to the working men deputies that *many of the Moscow regiments are ready to go over to the side of the uprisen people*. Applauding the movement among the soldiers, the Council of Working Men's Deputies summons the soldier comrades to compel the chiefs to arrange a revolutionary self-government, and by a given signal to go over to the side of the people. Taking into consideration all these circumstances, the Council of Working Men's Deputies *decides that the Moscow workers must be ready at any given moment for a general political strike and armed uprising*.

" 2. Taking into consideration the communication about Black Hundred *pogroms* under preparation, and about their manifestations, the Moscow Council of Working Men's Deputies declares that

[1] *Moscow in December* 1905, p. 6.

the Moscow proletariat will offer the most decisive resistance to the Black Hundred actions of the Government and its detestable agents." [1]

On the same day (4th December 1905) a meeting was held of the General City Inter-District Conference of the Moscow group of the Russian Social Democratic Working Men's Party, 250 persons being present. Here also reports were given of "the state of mind" of the working men in St. Petersburg and in Moscow. From St. Petersburg it was reported that the working men were eager for a general political strike, but that their leaders had succeeded in preventing them from premature actions. Still the arrest of Khrustalov and of the executive committee of the Council of Working Men's Deputies, the dispersal of working men's meetings, and the repression of the organizations of the railway employees, had "overfilled the cup of patience of the St. Petersburg proletariat, and *one of these days we have to expect decisive actions on its part. Occurrences are coming terribly near, and Moscow must be ready.*" [2] Then followed statements about the "fermentation" among the soldiers of the Moscow garrison. The sappers had been the first to advance their demands for increase of pay and for additional allowances. These demands had been complied with, and then other parts of the garrison had made similar demands, the Rostovsky Regiment "being particularly prominent." On the 4th December, after numerous arrests, this regiment surrendered, and a reactionary meeting of the regiment had been arranged. Nevertheless, among the other regiments the fermentation was increasing ; and "the organizations *have to take care of the preparations of the Moscow proletariat for the day of outbreak of the troops.*" There had already been formed among the troops a "Council of Soldiers' Deputies," and delegates from that council came to the working men's meetings.

The reports from the various districts of Moscow declared that some of the factories and mills were ready for the outbreak, and that in others "fermentation" was going on. In order to keep up this "fermentation," there must be "increased agitation." The declaration of the representative of the printers' union to the effect

[1] From *Borba*, No. 8 ; quoted in *Moscow in December* 1905, p. 7.
[2] *Moscow in December* 1905, p. 7.

that all the printing offices would stop work at an hour's notice was loudly applauded.

A resolution to the following effect was passed—preparation must be made in Moscow for "a general outbreak" according to the summons of the St. Petersburg proletariat. This preparation was to consist in spreading the manifestoes of the revolutionary organizations, in the "revolutionization of the troops," and in the "exposure of the provocative and reactionary policy of the Government." One of the participants in this conference stated that one of the delegates to St. Petersburg reported that the "state of mind" there was not the same in all districts, but that he believed that the arrest of the Council of Working Men's Deputies would affect an increasing number. It was clear from the speeches at the conference that although "*the proletariat was not ready for the uprising,* yet, owing to the action of the Government in depriving them of the liberties which had been seized, there was nothing to be done by the proletariat but to respond to this provocation by a general strike, which under present conditions, by the objective current of events, *may and must pass into an armed uprising.*" [1]

On 5th December, at seven o'clock in the evening, there was a meeting of the *Bolshevēkē* faction of the Social Democratic Party. About 400 persons were present. The two following questions were put to the meeting, working men delegates alone being permitted to make declarations.

1. Does Moscow agree to go on strike in response to the summons of St. Petersburg?

2. Does Moscow agree to go on strike independently if necessary?

The replies to these questions by the representatives of different districts were nearly uniform—the working men were ready "long ago," and were "angry" with the organizers because they had not summoned the working men to strike. The representative of the military organization said that connections had been established with "nearly all the infantry regiments," and that the "state of mind" among the soldiers was such that "one may hope, if not on their actively joining, at any rate on sympathy upon their part." As for Cossacks and dragoons, the "state of mind" was indefinite. The speaker did not, however, touch the question as to *what* the

[1] *Moscow in December* 1905, p. 8.

troops would join, although he seemed to regard the strike and the armed uprising as inseparable. It was announced that the railway men were ready for a general strike, but that they did not think it expedient to declare their intention publicly.

At this juncture a warning voice came from a working girl belonging to the Social Democratic Party.

"Comrades," she said, "think it over! What are you doing? We have no weapons, and the troops will not come over to our side." She was supported by one railway worker. The chairman also pointed out that the "state of mind of the troops was *the* indefinite factor," and that while some of the soldiers might sympathize with the working men, they were unlikely to turn out to support them. If the strike were to be declared, "it must not be made dependent upon the state of mind of the troops." [1]

Notwithstanding these warnings, the meeting decided nearly unanimously to begin "a general political strike." By a majority it was decided to begin it upon 7th December. It was decided also to prepare "cold weapons" in case of attack by the Black Hundred; and each communicated a statement of what weapons were available in the various districts.[2] The meeting dispersed about one o'clock in the morning.

Simultaneously with the meeting of the *Bolshevēkē* on 5th December, there was held a conference of representatives from twenty-nine railways. This meeting was convoked for the consideration of professional demands connected with recognition of their trade union, formalities of dismissal from employment, wages and allowances, and the like. These demands had been formulated during the previous month. At this meeting there appears to have been a "consultation" with a group of members of the executive committee of the Moscow organization of the Russian Social Democratic Working Men's Party. The question of a political strike was broached, in the course of the consultation, by the group in question, and the representative of the group who spoke upon the subject "expressed his conviction that the political strike should pass over into an armed uprising." Another speaker said that "the people could not be detained longer," that the "unorganized mass was pressing from below on the Council of Working Men's Deputies," and that the latter "was being compelled to take decisive measures."

[1] *Moscow in December* 1905, p. 9.   [2] *Ibid.*, p. 10.

Only one speaker, a railroad man, spoke out for declaring an economical, and not a political strike.

" An unorganized mass is rushing into conflict," he said. " Those who are organized know the uselessness of this. There is no power for such a struggle." He was supported by only two or three voices, and his motion was not put to the vote.

The majority of the meeting seemed to entertain the view that in any case the Government would break up the Union of Railway Men, and that nothing could be gained by Fabian tactics. " If so, it is better to make up our minds to fight." [1] One person who was present narrates that in the early hours of the meeting it was apparent that the railway men were not ready for a political strike, and also that the speeches disclosed that everyone felt that a political strike at that moment must inevitably pass into an armed uprising. Moreover, the speeches also disclosed that those who attended the meeting had in their minds the idea that the Government might try to provoke a premature uprising, knowing that the working men were not prepared for a trial of strength. Notwithstanding this unanimous opinion, the statement by the representatives of the Social Democratic Party to the effect that the factory and mills working men would engage in a political strike with or without the support of the railway men, led the meeting to decide to engage in the general strike. While this decision was being arrived at, " there was no animation among the members of the conference. All were in a melancholy state of mind. All were conscious that they were submitting to bitter necessity, and were going to unavoidable ruin." [2]

The conference decided—(1) to begin a general political strike, and (2) to leave to the Council of Working Men's Deputies to declare, by agreement with the various parties, the day and hour when the strike should begin. The representatives of the Social Democratic Party went from the railway conference, which closed at eleven o'clock, to the meeting of the *Bolshevēkē*, which was still sitting, and intimated the decision which had been reached.

On 6th December, in the daytime, there was held a regular meeting of the *Bolshevēkē* faction of the Social Democratic Party. A member of the Moscow Committee of the Russian Social Democratic Working Men's Party, who was present at this meeting, communicated the resolution of that committee summoning the

---

[1] *Moscow in December* 1905, pp. 10–11. [2] *Ibid.*, p. 11.

working men " to a general strike and uprising in such a form that the strike might pass over into an armed uprising." A member of the *Bolshevēkē* objected that to summon to an uprising at that moment was impossible, because the opportunity for such a movement had passed. The Rostovsky Regiment, upon which reliance had been placed, had changed its attitude, and now it could not be expected to be otherwise than hostile. The same speaker refused to accept the formula " might pass over into an armed uprising," on the ground that it did not show clearly where " we are leading the masses." Although there seems to have been a good deal of confusion at this meeting, and lack of unanimity, some speakers insisting that the moment was not opportune for an uprising,[1] resolutions were passed to the effect that " the proletariat were ready for the struggle," and that the coming " political outbreak " should be supported.[2]

While the party meetings were going on, numerous meetings of working men in various groups were being held. On 5th December, at a meeting of delegates of city working men, a resolution was passed, " to join the general political strike with the object of attaining the emancipation of the nation." [3]

On 5th December the printers of the printing office of Kushnerov [4] passed the following resolution : " We are ready to respond to the provocation of the Government by a general strike, hoping that it *may and must pass into an armed uprising*." [5] On the same day, 5th December, the employees of the Yaroslave Railway, after discussing the circular of the Minister of Ways of Communication about strikes, passed a resolution, the close of which is as follows : " We summon our comrades, and also those on all railroads, to accept the fighting challenge of the Government and to be ready at the first summons of the conference of the Railroad Union to begin the final and decisive fight." The Over-Moscow River district of the Moscow group of the Social Democratic Party decided on 6th December that the Council of Working Men's Deputies should " take upon itself the initiative in declaring the strike." On 6th December, at a meeting of electrical workers, it was intimated that the building locksmiths had decided to obey the

---

[1] *Moscow in December* 1905, p. 12.   [2] *Ibid.*   [3] *Ibid.*
[4] The second largest printing office in Moscow.
[5] *Moscow in December* 1905, p. 13.

summons to go on strike.[1] On the evening of 6th December it was reported in Moscow that the Council of Working Men's Deputies in St. Petersburg was in favour of the strike. On the same evening a " proclamation " [2] was posted in the streets of Moscow, signed by " The Council of Deputies of the Working Men of Moscow." This proclamation contained the bold statement : " The Council declares a General Political Strike, which it will endeavour to transform into an armed uprising."

Thus was initiated the third general strike.

On 7th December the morning papers of Moscow announced that the Moscow Council of Working Men's Deputies had decided to summon all working men to a general strike from noon of that day. Throughout the morning the whole city was in a state of feverish excitement. The inhabitants were in the shops making extensive purchases in order to accumulate provisions, and numerous meetings of working men were held in different parts of the city. In the forenoon some of the railways entering the city and some of the tramways ceased to run. A huge meeting of railway men was held, at which one of the speakers shouted amid thunders of applause, " It begins—not a strike, but a Great Russian Revolution." At noon almost all the railways stopped running trains into Moscow ; only those trains carrying soldiers returning from the theatre of war were allowed to enter the city. On the Yaroslav line, trains carrying the children of employees to school were also permitted to pass.[3] On the Nikolai Railway (St. Petersburg-Moscow), part of the shops stopped on the 7th and the remainder on the 8th. The trains between the two capitals continued, however, to run.[4] In the telegraph offices only the chief employees were working. On some railway lines [5] conflicts took place between the strikers and the employees who refused to join them ; several

---

[1] *Moscow in December* 1905, p. 12.

[2] 6th December being a holiday (the day of St. Nicholas the Miracle-worker and the name-day of the Tsar), the strike was announced to begin at noon the following day.

[3] *Moscow in December* 1905, p. 19.

[4] From the date of the first general strike the administration had been gradually concentrating men upon whom it could rely upon this railway, the most important from a strategic point of view. It was thus impossible for the railway organizations to draw them from their allegiance. The Railroad Battalion was also employed on the line when the strike took place.

[5] Kiev-Voronej, for instance.

persons were wounded, and on the Kazan Railway two engine-drivers were killed. At the station of this railway in Moscow, weapons were distributed.

In the factories and mills the workers went on strike almost quite unanimously. By noon of the 7th the largest industrial enterprises were closed.[1] All the printers (the best-organized trade in Moscow, numbering 10,000), went on strike at once.

By the afternoon of 7th December there were probably 50,000 men on strike from the factories and mills, and approximately an equal number from railways and miscellaneous employments.[2]

The morning of the 7th seems to have been occupied in some of the larger works, especially the engineering shops, in the forging of " cold weapons " for the coming conflict.[3] On this day also a meeting of the employees in banks and other credit institutions in Moscow was held, and a representative of the Council of Working Men's Deputies who was present suggested that the employees should agree to work until 10th December, in order that those who desired to do so might withdraw their savings. But the employees did not approve of this. They pointed out that such a measure must lead to a run upon the private banks and consequent bankruptcy. Finally it was agreed that Savings Banks employees should continue to work during the strike on the ground that the " most materially depressed masses of the population had their savings there." [4]

In the majority of the State and municipal offices work ceased at noon on the 7th. Although the expression " armed uprising " was continually repeated in resolutions and was found later in manifestoes, there is no evidence that at this time the general mass of working men had any clear idea of the meaning of the phrase. The working men seemed indeed to think that the soldiers of the Moscow garrison would either refrain from firing upon them or would take their part actively in sufficient numbers to form a fighting force on the side of the strike. Both of these anticipations were wholly illusory. Some, however, of the sympathetic *intelli-*

---

[1] *Moscow in December* 1905, p. 20.   [2] *Ibid.*

[3] *Moscow in December* 1905, p. 21. Weapons appear to have been forged in the following factories : Prokharov's (where the last stand of the revolutionists took place later) ; Singel's, Sion Factory ; Block's, Bromléy, Michaelov, Riabov, Deal Winter, &c.

[4] *Ibid.*, p. 21.

gentsi entertained more serious views. Forced as they felt themselves to be into a conflict which was due to the impact upon the immature minds of the working mass of ideas which they had had some share in spreading—a conflict which they regarded as premature—they nevertheless decided to organize a fighting force, and to use as a nucleus of this the *drujinnēkē* or fighting companies. These had been organized for the purpose of meeting the " Black Hundred " groups, whose outrages had rendered the streets of Moscow unsafe. Even the *drujinnēkē* appear to have had somewhat naïve views upon the conduct of so serious a campaign as an " armed uprising " against the Russian Government.

On the morning of the 7th, before the actual commencement of the strike, a small body of *drujinnēkē* seized the printing office of Setin and mounted guard, while, in the presence of the Chief of the District Police, whom they had arrested, the first number of *Izvestia Savetta Rabotchich Deputatov* was printed. This was the revolutionary bulletin which was issued daily during the strike.

The burthen of the conduct of the strike fell upon the executive committee of the Council of Working Men's Deputies. This committee mapped out for itself, on the evening of 7th December, the following programme for the succeeding days : General and special meetings were to be held daily. The newspaper *Izvestia* was to be issued daily. Caretakers of factories and mills were to remain at their posts in order to protect the property of their employers. Guards were to be organized for the further protection of property. Tea-shops were to be permitted to carry on their business, but without the sale of liquors, on condition that the shops might be freely used for the purpose of holding meetings. Co-operative stores were to be permitted to carry on business on condition of giving credit. Payment of rent during the strike was suspended. While steam-heating was stopped in factories, &c., where the workmen were on strike, the heating of residential premises must not be suspended.

In all these regulations it is tacitly assumed that the Council of Working Men's Deputies had succeeded the legally constituted authorities in the administration of at least a portion of Moscow, and this before any blow had been struck.

At two o'clock in the afternoon of 7th December, Moscow was

declared by the General Governor of the Moscow district, Vice-Admiral Dubassov, to be under extraordinary guard.[1]

The theatres did not open their doors on the evening of the 7th. " The streets were quiet and deserted." In Tverskaya, one of the great avenues of traffic, there was no light. Now and again one of the mounted *gendarmes* passed by and a frightened pedestrian ran for shelter. The police were not at their usual posts ; only here and there a group of policemen stood together. There were no patrols, and troops were not to be seen. Yet domiciliary visits were being made, and many persons whose activity in the movements in progress was suspected were arrested. Probably the first actual conflict took place in Chisty Proody, where two *drujinnēkē* were attacked by several policemen, and one of them was slightly wounded.

The inaction of the authorities during the 7th, in spite of the declaration of " extraordinary guard " requires explanation. The military commanders were not sure of their men. The Moscow garrison had been decidedly disaffected ; and although on the 6th steps had been taken to remove this disaffection by concessions, sufficient time had not elapsed for the effect of these concessions to become evident. It seemed wise, therefore, to confine the troops to barracks. While the police do not appear to have been disaffected, there were many resignations immediately on the eve of the strike, and although some of these had not been accepted, the feeling of the authorities was evidently uneasy. The police information seems to have been defective and the civil and military administration confused and vacillating.

It has been alleged that the inaction of the authorities in the early days of December was due to Macchiavellian design, and

[1] There are three phases of special or exceptional law: (*a*) Stronger guard, (*b*) extraordinary guard, and (*c*) martial law. From 1882 Moscow was at all times under " stronger guard." Although from a military point of view the city is not a position of importance, it was always occupied by about 10,000 troops—consisting usually of eight regiments of grenadiers, six batteries of artillery, one Cossack and one dragoon regiment. Extraordinary guard was really equivalent to a minor state of siege, but it was not officially so described on account of the adverse effect which a declaration of martial law in one of the imperial capitals would have upon Russian funds on the foreign exchanges. The laws regulating these combined military and police measures date from 1881, when they are believed to have been suggested by M. von Plehvë, who was at that time Director of the Department of Political Police.

that Admiral Dubassov deliberately allowed the insurrection to attain a certain height in order the more effectually and thoroughly to crush it, and in the crushing of it to contribute to the reaction which must follow. There is no available evidence that any such design was in the mind of the authorities. If it was, the game was a dangerous one to play, for the capital remained practically in the hands of the revolutionists for ten days, all business was suspended, the insurrection was only put down at a great cost in blood, and in consequence of it there occurred a most serious collapse in Russian credit, both at home and abroad.

On the 7th December numerous meetings of strikers were held, and conflicts between them and the troops took place; but no firing occurred on either side.[1]

On the 8th December a meeting, attended by about 12,000 persons, was held in the Summer Theatre (which at that time was unused otherwise). Troops, *gendarmes*, police, and Cossacks surrounded the building and did not allow anyone to leave without search for and surrender of arms. The authorities seemed at this time to be anxious rather to show that they were prepared for eventualities than to proceed to extremities, for it would appear that the search was perfunctory, and that many persons who carried revolvers did not give them up.[2] At three o'clock in the morning of 8th December eleven *drujinnēkē* broke into a gunsmith's shop and took a quantity of fire-arms.[3]

On the morning of the 8th most of the shops in Moscow remained closed, the windows being freshly protected by wooden boards. Bakers' and grocers' shops were to some extent open, the pro-

---

[1] The Tver Dragoons rode through the streets and beat the people with long poles.

[2] From the date of the manifesto of 17th October 1905, there developed in Moscow the suspicion that the " privateers " of the " reaction," the so-called Black Hundred, would engage in *pogroms* against *intelligentsia* and non-Russians, *e.g.* Poles and Jews (although there are very few Jews in Moscow). Such *pogroms* had indeed taken place in very many other cities immediately after the publication of the manifesto. For this reason the people of Moscow, irrespective of their political opinions, determined to carry weapons for self-defence, and before the beginning of December had done so quite openly, purchasing revolvers in large numbers in the gun shops of Moscow. Thus the circumstance that some of the people who attended this meeting were armed did not necessarily mean that they harboured revolutionary designs.

[3] The shop was that of Bitkov in Bolshaya Lubanka. The arms taken were twenty-five revolvers, nine carbines, one rifle, and one Browning automatic magazine gun. *Moscow in December* 1905, p. 24.

prietors having obtained permits from the Council of Working Men's Deputies. Here and there Cossacks swept through the streets dispersing the mobs. Many meetings were held in public halls [1] and in the open air.[2]

A characteristic scene, vividly described by a Zemstvo physician, occurred in Strastnya Place. A Cossack patrol went into the Place and dismounted. They were immediately surrounded by a crowd drawn there by curiosity. Although the crowd pressed upon the Cossacks, these showed no disposition to disperse the people. They began indeed to argue with them, saying, " Please go away ! " Excited persons in the crowd addressed the Cossacks. " Brothers ! Comrades ! you will come over to the side of the people," &c.

Meanwhile another crowd was heard marching along the Tverskaya Boulevard, singing the Russian Marseillaise. The two crowds mingled together and surrounded the Cossacks, who ultimately mounted their horses and disappeared without any conflict.[3]

At Lobanskaya Place, about half-past two in the afternoon of the 8th, a detachment of dragoons had a somewhat similar experience. Here, however, the soldiers were upbraided by the crowd with shouts of " Rascals ! Outcasts ! " but they stood silently, and again no conflict took place. About the same time a body of workers in the metal trades were marching to a meeting in the Polytechnic Museum when they found their way blocked by police. The policemen were ordered to draw their swords and to disperse the crowd ; but some of the workmen went to the police inspector and told him that they were going to a meeting, whereupon he ordered that they be allowed to pass. The ranks of the police opened, and the workmen passed through.

Meanwhile, the strike spread from railway to railway. The employees " dismissed the higher officials and elected others to take their places." [4] Reservists and pupils of the railway school were forwarded to their destinations by order of the Council of Working Men's Deputies.

Most of the factories and mills had either been closed because

---

[1] In the Polytechnic Museum and at the street railway car depots, *Ibid.*, p. 25.
[2] On Taganskaya Place, Trubnaya Place, &c. *Ibid.*, p. 26.
[3] *Moscow in December* 1905, pp. 26–8. [4] *Ibid.*, p. 29.

the workers had gone on strike, or because the owners thought well to close them. Still there were some which held out. To these there went groups of strikers to " take off " the workpeople. These groups marched with red banners and sang revolutionary songs. Some of these crowds were attacked by Cossacks and dragoons, and beaten by *nagaïki*.[1] In one case (at the Danielovsky factory) shots were fired from a house and from the crowd, wounding twelve persons. Similarly, owing to a misunderstanding, a permitted train was received with revolver shots, and the engine-driver was killed.[2]

The day passed with marches of groups of working men from the factories. " The state of mind everywhere increased. Everybody asked what further steps were to be taken. The young men were eager to take up arms."[3] In Presnya, a large industrial district, the strike was complete.

Yet the Council of the Working Men's Deputies seemed not to know what to do next. The excitement among the mass of the workmen was tremendous, yet there was apparent no plan of action —no definite objective—everything was vague and confused. Contradictory speeches were everywhere made—the very meaning of the strike was not clear. It was a strike against the Moscow police. It was a strike against the bureaucracy. It was a strike for a republic.

The inferior officials in the Government offices held meetings on the 8th. Some declared themselves in sympathy with the strike, and some declared that " the army would not direct its bayonets against the struggling nation."[4] The officials at the law courts were " taken off," but the judges continued to sit.[5]

The accessions to the ranks of the strikers on the 8th were about 50,000, so that the total number on strike on that date was about 150,000.[6]

On the 8th there were some conflicts with the members of the " Black Hundred " ; but when the real conflict began this group disappeared. Letters continued to be delivered, although three-fourths of the Post Office employees and one-half of the telegraph

---

[1] Cossack whips.
[2] *Moscow in December* 1905, p. 29.
[3] *Ibid.*, p. 31.
[4] *Ibid.*, p. 32.
[5] *Ibid.*, p. 33.
[6] *Ibid.*

employees were on strike. In spite of the exertions of the Council of Working Men's Deputies to isolate Moscow from St. Petersburg, communication by rail, post, and telegraph continued.

Up till the evening of the 8th the authorities seemed to be taking the rising storm very coolly. No serious efforts were taken to prevent the strike from assuming grave political importance. The demands of the strikers were nowhere specifically formulated, and no step had been taken on either side of an expressly aggressive character. Yet the industry and commerce of Moscow stood still. From the point of view of Western European administration, there is little doubt that it would be generally held that the authorities should have acted purely on the defensive, that the demonstrations, in so far as they were peaceful, might well have been permitted, as, indeed, up till this time they were as a rule, that the mere vagueness of the demands of the strikers would have caused their ranks to thin in a day or two, and that the strike might thus die a natural death.

However, this was not the point of view of Admiral Dubassov. A mass meeting of strikers was to be held on the night of the 8th at the Summer Theatre, in the grounds of the Aquarium, and he appears to have conceived the idea of allowing this meeting to take place, and then of surrounding the building with troops, and of frightening everybody who attended it. The meeting in the Aquarium took place at eight o'clock in the evening, and at nine o'clock the chairman intimated that the place was invested by troops. At ten o'clock the meeting was closed, and the audience were left to deal with the situation as best they might. No concerted action was suggested or taken. When the people left the building in which the meeting had been held, they found themselves to the number of about 4000 in a courtyard, of which all the gates were closed, and from which there was no apparent exit. They were caught like rats in a trap.

Some who knew the locality contrived to escape by climbing fences; among these were many who had taken a prominent part in the meeting; others managed somehow to get into neighbouring houses. It became very cold in the courtyard, and many returned to the theatre. There all was darkness. A candle was found, and the remainder of the audience, now reduced to about 1000, discussed the situation. The upshot of the affair was that, for some reason, the authorities did not take full advantage of their *coup*. The audience was searched for weapons, some forty or fifty were arrested, many were beaten, and allowed to escape. It was apparent that the affair had not yet become acute enough for decisive action on the part of the authorities.

Although the meeting at the Aquarium had passed without serious consequences, the display of troops in force did not have a tranquillizing effect. The general population became nervous. The appearance of Cossacks in the streets, which on the 8th created no excitement, now resulted in panic. The *drujinnēkē* also began to make themselves felt. Wherever policemen were found by them, they were disarmed. At the meetings collections were made for the purchase of weapons. Prices of provisions began to advance, and demands came to the Council of Working Men's Deputies that trains conveying flour should be allowed to enter the city. The working men in some groups called upon the Council to act more energetically. Among some of the groups there were shouts for a " Constituent Assembly." Inscriptions containing these words were placed on the flags carried by marching workmen. In one factory the workmen demanded of their employers the payment in cash of the fine fund, in order that the money might be handed to the Council. Meanwhile the working men and their leaders seem to have been hoping against hope that the troops would at least refuse to shoot at them. Nor were reasons altogether wanting for such hope. The infantry especially seem to have been at this time a rather unstable factor. One detachment had left its barracks with its band playing marches, apparently with the intention of joining the strikers. The detachment was surrounded by Cossacks and dragoons and compelled to return. Afterwards the detachment was promised additional allowances and was confined to barracks. There appears even to have been some doubt about the loyalty of the Cossacks. A conflict was even said to have taken place between a troop of dragoons and 500 Cossacks, who refused to fire on a mob. The truth about these stories is difficult to discover ; but their mere circulation had an effect at the time in maintaining the belief that the troops might side with the strikers.

By the evening of the 9th the " state of mind " of the strikers had become very " intense." The situation was critical, and a slight matter might easily produce grave results. On this evening a crowd of some 300 or 400 persons collected in Strassnaya Place.

This Place has become celebrated in the street disturbances of,
Moscow. It contains the statue of the Russian poet, Pushkin,[1]
and round this statue throughout the year 1905 many scenes
occurred. On this occasion some orators were addressing the
crowd, when suddenly from two sides, dragoons made their appearance. They were greeted with shouts : " Brothers, don't touch
us ! come over to us ! " The troop passed by ; but " a quarter
of an hour after " the dragoons reappeared reinforced, and at once
attacked the mob, which dispersed. In the Place there was a
pavilion which served as a waiting-room for passengers by the
tramways, and in this building some fifty persons took refuge.
The dragoons demanded that they should surrender. On their
refusal, " several fusillades " were fired into the building and then
the troops galloped off. One boy of sixteen or seventeen years of
age, a pupil in an intermediate technical school, was killed, and
several persons were wounded.[2] The mob, which was composed of
workmen, shop clerks, and youths, now returned, and, infuriated
at the action of the dragoons, sprinkled the pavilion with petroleum
and set fire to it. It was now seven o'clock, and the night was
pitch dark, only feeble lights appearing in the windows of the houses
in Tverskaya Street.[3] The sudden blaze of the burning building
lit up the surrounding region, and soon the bells of the firemen
were heard approaching the Place. The mob did not seek to prevent the firemen from discharging their duty, and immediately
began to stream towards the Old Triumphal Gates. Opposite the
house of Hirschman (a wealthy Jew) the movement was arrested.
There the mob dragged barrels, boards, and odds and ends of
various sorts from obscure corners, and in a short time the first
barricade was built. When this obstacle was hastily constructed,
the crowd surged on to the Triumphal Place, where they cut down
telegraph poles, stretched wires across the streets, and built a second
and more formidable obstacle.

These first barricades seem to have been built spontaneously
by this mob, on the suggestion of some unknown person and without
any instructions from the Council of Working Men's Deputies.[4]

[1] The name was changed from Strastnaya to Pushkin Ploshet (Place)
in 1899, but the new name has never passed current.
[2] *Moscow in December* 1905, p. 44.
[3] Account of an eye-witness. *Ibid.*
[4] *Moscow in December* 1905, p. 45.

A physician who passed near this place late on the evening of the 9th describes the scene as follows :

" The aspect of affairs was quite unusual. Some new atmosphere is felt. People are dragging fences and signs, pulling down posts and cutting off wire. All over the place groups of fifty to a hundred persons are standing. One group of thirty or forty men is singing— the men taking off their caps—' You fell as victims in the fatal struggle.' [1] In the centre of the group a man was standing upon a chair, leading the singing. Not far away stood a policeman with his cap in his hand. He either shared or made pretence to share the general state of mind." [2]

The troops did not interfere with the construction of these barricades, but when they were finished they opened fire upon them, and for two hours fusillades were heard, and several persons were killed and wounded. Rare revolver shots answered the fusillades of the troops. About eleven o'clock in the night, a military wagon with an electric searchlight was driven up to the barricades. Behind this carriage came dragoons, who fired as they went. Shots came also from the houses in the neighbourhood, where it appeared troops had been placed in ambush.[3]

There are not wanting charges to the effect that the first barricades were not erected by insurgents, but were erected by *agents provocateurs*, acting under the orders of the police.[4] The stories about previously arranged ambuscades, if true, would appear to lend some colour to these charges ; but the truth is probably now quite impossible to ascertain.

The first barricades were easily destroyed by the dragoons, who thereupon began to fire indiscriminately along the dark streets. This firing lasted until two o'clock in the morning, when at last all was quiet.

Meanwhile elsewhere another significant scene was happening.

On the night of the 9th a meeting not specifically connected with the " uprising," convened for the purpose of discussing the strike then in progress on the Kazan Railway, was held at a private school belonging to one Fiedler. Many young men and some young women were present at this meeting, and some of these were, no

---

[1] " The Funeral March of the Proletariat," a very popular air at this time.
[2] *Moscow in December* 1905, p. 45. [3] *Ibid.*, p. 46. [4] *Ibid.*, pp. 47-8.

doubt, carrying weapons.[1] This meeting was raided by the police, troops were summoned, and the building was surrounded. Those within were called upon to surrender. They refused to do so, and the building was at once bombarded.[2] Two bombs were thrown from the house; but very speedily resistance ceased, and those who remained within surrendered.[3]

The police reported that the leaders of the " uprising " had been captured; but the subsequent course of events showed that this could not have been the case. The trial of the persons who were arrested in Fiedler's also showed afterwards that they were not of importance in the movement.

On the afternoon of the 10th (Saturday) the first fusillades by troops on the central streets took place, and artillery fire swept the main street of Moscow—the Tverskaya. On this afternoon and evening barricades were erected in many different parts of the city. They were constructed of overturned vehicles, including street railway cars, gates of houses and yards, sign-boards, telegraph and telephone poles, timber, and generally whatever was available. Snow and water were thrown upon the mass, and in the night the materials were frozen together. Wire entanglements were also used in front of the barricades. The height of the barricades, and the fact that they were not pierced for rifle fire, rendered them unsuitable for use in actual fighting. Their principal object was to impede the movement of troops. Each barricade had at either side a passage, so that fugitives might pass in the event of flight, and so that the people of the district might move about. These openings permitted the passage of only one person at a time, so that in the mornings there was sometimes a long *queue* of persons waiting to pass through the barricades in important streets. During the ten days of " uprising " the authorities and the people fell into the habit of regarding the forenoon as a period of truce. People moved about on necessary affairs until eleven o'clock in all districts; and then firing began, to last until darkness set in. From eleven o'clock

[1] For the reason explained above.

[2] Fiedler's was bombarded by two three-inch field artillery Krupp guns (1866 pattern). There was no modern artillery in the Moscow military district at the time.

[3] It is reported by one of those who attended the meeting that those who remained in the school surrendered on condition that they should be allowed to leave without molestation. They gave up their arms, and were then beaten by the Cossacks, some of them being severely wounded.

in the forenoon until three o'clock in the afternoon, shells shrieked through the air. Each day the cannonade was directed against a different quarter of the city.

It is an extraordinary fact that of about five hundred barricades erected altogether, only about twenty were destroyed by the troops. Some of these were demolished by the fire of the artillery, and some were pulled to pieces by firemen. The reason for this meagre result of ten days' fighting was that the guns could not get near to the barricades, partly owing to the involutions of the streets, and partly owing to the shooting of the gunners by sharp-shooters from the houses. When the serious bombardment began, the guns were posted at a distance, and the industrial quarter was shelled indiscriminately at long range.

The barricades were almost all erected on the afternoon of the 10th. They were for the most part erected by the inhabitants of the immediate locality, who acted partly from sympathy with the " uprising," although they may have taken no further part in it, and partly from an instinct of self-preservation. The barricades formed a measure of protection against the indiscriminate firing along the streets. Labouring together upon their construction were frequently to be seen well-dressed people side by side with *sans-culottes*. It was dangerous to go out into the street at any time. Very few persons appeared after noon, and at night no one, for although the troops were withdrawn at dusk, the city was in pitch darkness. There was no electric light and there was no gas. Even oil lamps were not used in windows in the fronts of houses.

From the afternoon of the 10th the trade of Moscow was wholly suspended. Factories and shops alike were closed. The bakers only were ordered by the " Council of Working Men's Deputies " to bake bread ; but they baked black (or rye) bread alone, so that in all parts of the city the inhabitants were obliged to eat " the bread of the proletariat." The public services, with the exception of the waterworks, were at a standstill. No newspapers were published. The General Governor issued daily bulletins, but these circulated only in those portions of the city not in the hands of the insurgents.

A " Provisional Government " was installed in Presnya, and bulletins containing " instructions " and news were issued by it daily, and were circulated in the revolutionary quarters. Courts were held with some formality, and the inhabitants of the quarter fully recognized the authority of the workmen's committee.

On the 11th (Sunday) the People's Theatre, in which the " Council " had its headquarters at that time, the approaches being strongly barricaded, was bombarded by artillery fire.

In spite of the free use of shells upon their positions, the insurgents held a large part of Moscow.[1]

The system of barricades nearly encircled the heart of the city. The stronghold of the insurrection was, however, the large industrial quarter in the north-west of Moscow, called Presnya, and this quarter was subjected to daily firing from rifles, from a low hill near the police station, which is situated on the borders of the quarter, and from a cemetery a short distance to the north-west.

Fighting having been going on continuously from the 10th to the 14th, and many persons having been killed and wounded, private ambulances were used to convey the wounded from the streets to the hospitals and to private houses. On the 14th General Governor Dubassov forbade private ambulance corps to assist the wounded. On this day also the celebrated Semenovsky Regiment arrived at Moscow from St. Petersburg. Up till this time, and for three days afterwards, the troops of the Moscow garrison were strictly confined to barracks. The authorities were still uncertain about the attitude of the troops. They feared that the troops might join the insurgents. This fear corresponded with a hope which was entertained by some of the insurgent leaders, that the troops might join them. The force of military discipline was, however, strong enough to prevent fear and hope alike from being realized.

On the 15th a group of 300 revolutionists invested the house of the chief of the secret police of Moscow (Voiloshnikov), who lived on the border of Presnenskaya quarter. He was permitted to take leave of his family and to arrange his affairs, and was then brought into the street and shot.

During the " uprising " passers-by were shot from police stations, and sometimes from houses occupied by the so-called " Black

---

[1] It appears that General Governor Dubassov asked for additional troops to be sent from St. Petersburg. The military authorities, apprehensive of a similar rising in that city, refused. It was only when Admiral Dubassov assured the Tsar personally by telephone that the city was in absolute danger of falling wholly into the hands of the insurgents, that the Semenovsky Regiment was despatched to Moscow.

Hundred." Sometimes such houses were entered by the revolutionists, and the occupants were dragged out and killed in the streets. Large quantities of provisions were looted by insurgents from the railway yards.[1] At an early stage in the " uprising " the insurgents discovered that " reservists " returning from Manchuria were added to the troops already in the city, or were drafted into the police force, from which there had been many resignations on the eve of the " uprising." The insurgents therefore seized the trains containing " reservists " and forced them to give up their rifles.[2] Two unsuccessful attempts were made by the insurgents to capture railway stations, one of them being the station of the Nikolaevskaya Railway. There was also a skirmish between the troops and the insurgents in front of the City Hall. Wherever the troops came within the range of the positions occupied by the insurgents there was firing from the windows and the balconies of houses. In order to check this practice, the General Governor (Admiral Dubassov) ordered that all houses from which firing proceeded should be cannonaded.

On the 16th the insurgents reluctantly realized that there was now no possibility of the Moscow garrison joining their ranks, and the expediency of abandoning the struggle was discussed. The Social Democratic groups proposed that hostilities should cease on that day ; but the Social Revolutionaries refused to submit. They agreed, however, to abandon the outlying positions, many of which were hardly tenable, and to concentrate their remaining forces in the Presnenskaya quarter.

On this day, the 16th, the " Council of the Working Men's Deputies "—in other words, the Revolutionary Committee—issued the following proclamation : " The Uprising should be considered as not successful, therefore the Council dissolves the fighting de-

---

[1] Two gunsmiths' shops were also looted.

[2] Apart from the few rifles thus and otherwise secured, the insurgents used about 200 Mauser ten-shot automatic pistols. This arm is admirably adapted for street warfare. Its range is 1000 metres, calibre 7.63 millimetres. The cartridges contain " dum-dum " bullets. The weapon is fitted in a wooden case, which is convertible into a shoulder piece, so that the arm becomes a short rifle. There were also a few Winchester 44 calibre ten-charge repeating rifles and a few " Browning " pistols. As a rule, however, the insurgents carried only pocket revolvers. Bombs were used only in attacks upon buildings and in repelling such attacks. They were not used against troops in the streets. Probably not more than one-tenth of those who possessed fire-arms were accustomed to the use of them.

tachments, adjourns the struggle until a more convenient moment, and invites the people of Moscow to remove the barricades and other defences erected during the Uprising." Though after this proclamation the ranks of the insurgents were without doubt considerably reduced, the " Uprising " was by no means at an end. The barricades round the Presnenskaya Quarter were retained, and behind them were concentrated the more desperate spirits of the insurrection, while the non-combatants among the inhabitants of the quarter withdrew from it.

On the afternoon of the 17th the troops attempted to penetrate the quarter ; but they were repulsed by the insurgents. Colonel Min,[1] commander of the Semenovsky Regiment, was ordered to surround the quarter and to shell its defenders into submission. During the two following days (the 18th and the 19th) Presnya was heavily bombarded,[2] especially the Prokhorov Works,[3] which had now become the headquarters of the insurgents, and Schmitt's Factory, which was eventually levelled to the ground by shells. During this investment of the quarter, ordinary siege tactics were employed ; all arms of the service were engaged, and artillery, cavalry, and infantry attacked the positions from several points. The bombardment began at 5.30 in the morning (before sunrise) of the 17th, and it continued without intermission until one o'clock the same day. The range was about 2000 yards.[4] By the evening of the 17th the quarter was on fire. The bombardment was renewed on the 18th, and on the afternoon of that day a white flag was hoisted on the Prokhorov Works, and the " uprising " was at last at an end. During the two days' sharp bombardment of Presnenskaya Quarter upwards of 600 grenade and shrapnel shells were fired. The numbers of killed and wounded in this quarter are wholly unascertainable. There can be no doubt that indiscriminate fusillades from rifles and bombardment by shrapnel shells killed and wounded many non-combatants, although on the

---

[1] General Min was shot dead at Peterhof by a girl, Zenaïda Konoplanikova, on 13th August 1906.

[2] By means of shrapnel from 3-inch quick-firing field artillery guns which had been brought from St. Petersburg.

[3] Calico-printing works, employing about 10,000 persons, the largest factory in Moscow.

[4] The factory is commanded by high ground immediately to the north ; but this position was exposed to the fire of the insurgents.

17th, before the final sharp bombardment took place, many of the inhabitants had left the district.

After the surrender and the subsequent entry of the Semenovsky Regiment into the Presnenskaya Quarter, many were executed, *e.g.* twelve were shot in the courtyard of the Prokhorov Factory. Some girls who were found attending to the wounded were whipped by Cossacks. After the surrender many persons were searched for weapons, and robberies by Cossacks and troops were frequent.

The number of persons killed during the "uprising" is not ascertainable with any precision. The estimated number is about 670. The wounded were very numerous ; but so many had their wounds dressed secretly in private houses that it is impossible to ascertain the total. This number is, however, provisionally stated at 2000. About 10,000 persons were arrested at the close of hostilities; many of them were released after a detention of from two weeks to four months. A considerable but unknown number were shot without trial; many were banished from Moscow to their native villages or to Siberia. The destruction of property from shells and from fires to which the shells gave rise, was very great, especially in the Presnenskaya Quarter.

Two series of prosecutions arose out of the Moscow "uprising." One of these was the prosecution of those who were arrested at Fiedler's school, and the other was the prosecution of those who were arrested after the resistance in the Presnenskaya Quarter was overcome. These prosecutions were both conducted by Zolotarev, Deputy Prosecutor in Moscow. It became obvious almost from the first that the Prosecutor and the police realized that the persons who had been arrested had not been materially concerned in the organization of the "uprising," and that the real leaders had escaped or had been killed. It became clear from the evidence that the police had failed to secure not only their persons, but even their names. As has been the case in the history of nearly all similar movements, the leaders sprang from unknown quarters, they assumed or were given pseudonyms by which alone they were known.[1] After the rising they disappeared.

While large numbers of persons assisted in building the barricades, the actual number of combatant insurgents was very small.

---

[1] The pseudonyms of the three conspicuous leaders in the Presnenskaya Quarter were " The Bear," " The Buckled " (or Belted) man, and " Andrew."

Their great activity, by means of which they defended a position until the last moment and then, instead of surrendering, disappeared in the tortuous byways or through houses, to reappear at another point some distance away, contributed to the illusion that the insurgent force was much more numerous than it really was. From all the information available, it seems unlikely that the " uprising " was conducted by more than 3000 actively engaged combatants.[1]

The relative shares of the two revolutionary parties principally concerned in the " uprising " and in the series of movements which led to it—the Social Democratic Party and the Social Revolutionary Party—are not very easy to discriminate. There was a good deal of jealousy between them, and they frequently refused to co-operate together or even to support each other. " When one group went out to fight, the other refused to go." [2] The Social Democrats were undoubtedly largely in the majority, and probably had a commanding influence upon the " uprising." [3] The military leaders, whoever they were, came most probably from other cities or from abroad. It is unlikely that they belonged to Moscow.

During the early days of the " uprising," the troops of the Moscow garrison were not employed owing to the fear that they might refuse to fire upon the crowd, or might even fraternize with the insurgents. This fear proved to be groundless. The peasant soldier has little feeling about suppressing a revolt in a city where he thinks everyone earns high wages and enjoys an amusing and agreeable life with which he ought to be content. Only in the villages do people suffer. Yet the general commotion among the troops which has already been noticed caused the military authorities to proceed carefully. Thus the first days of the " uprising " were characterized by comparative inaction. Only in the last days, when this fear was no longer present, and when the insurgents were being worn out, did the military operations assume a seriously aggressive character.

[1] The above particulars, excepting where published material is quoted, have been derived verbally from well-informed persons who were residing in the disturbed districts at the time of the " uprising." Varying accounts will, no doubt, be forthcoming. The same incident has different complexions from different points of view.

[2] Writes a correspondent.

[3] It was, however, commonly understood in Moscow that the Social Revolutionists, though relatively few in number, made up for this by extreme activity.

On the suppression of the " uprising," the General Governor of Moscow, Vice-Admiral Dubassov, received the thanks of the Tsar, promotion to the rank of Admiral, and one million rubles for the " pacification " of Moscow.

It is now necessary to examine the affair critically, basing the criticism upon the above statement of the facts.

From the point of view of the revolution, the " uprising " was ineffectively planned or not planned at all. The available active force was scattered over an area wide enough no doubt to engage the troops in many different quarters at the same moment, but so wide that the insurgents were unable to co-operate together effectively. The troops, which outnumbered the insurgents several times,[1] were in a compact mass in the central area of the city, while the small number of insurgents was scattered round the outskirts. Until the last two days (18th and 19th December) the larger body was really almost surrounded and invested by the smaller. Disagreements among the active participants militated against the prolongation of the struggle. It may be observed that the Moscow " uprising " is the first revolt of magnitude in a city population since the rising of the Commune of Paris in 1871. It has, therefore, a great interest because of what it discloses with reference, not to the possibility of a successful revolution, but with reference to the capacity of a comparatively small number of intelligent, courageous, and self-regardless men to hold authorities at bay for so great a length of time as to produce by this mere fact a change in the political situation.

The only sense in which the Moscow " uprising " can fairly be called " non-successful " within the limits of the possibility of such attempts, is in the sense that the period of ten days was, under the then political circumstances, not quite long enough to produce of itself a manifest effect upon the general situation. Yet a period of ten days is a long time for a city of over a million inhabitants to have its normal course completely arrested. When it is considered also that this city was a military camp occupied by a formidable force, which was equipped with ample material of war, was ready at all times for engaging in a civil if not in a foreign campaign, and was accustomed to treat resistance with merciless severity,

[1] More than five times, if the figures given above are to be accepted, and if the Moscow garrison is taken into account.

it is surprising that a small number of men, inadequately armed and practically unled, should have been able to hold the troops at bay even for ten days, and should have been able to offer so obstinate a resistance that the quarter of the city in which they entrenched themselves should have had to be practically destroyed by shells and fire before they were defeated. The explanation seems to lie in the construction of the enormous number of barricades, and in the fact that these were constructed not wholly by insurgents, but even chiefly by the general population. The people who constructed the barricades were evidently more afraid of the troops than of the insurgents, and were especially afraid of stray bullets from long-range rifles and of shells.

The utilization of this probably quite unforeseen but effective ally—the natural instinct of the population to defend itself, even though its defence may result in the prolongation of the state of insurrection—is a new factor in armed revolutionary movements. The reasons apparent for the delay in decisive action on the part of the military authorities were, no doubt, sufficient, yet the springing up of barricades in all directions on the second day of the conflict made subsequent movements of cavalry and infantry impossible, and rendered an artillery attack at long range upon established positions the only means of reducing them. It would appear that in opening fire upon the crowds of people in the streets on the 10th, General Governor Dubassov was acting either prematurely or too late. The immediate reply to his attack was the erection of innumerable barricades, and this he was powerless to prevent. So also when, on the 17th, the resistance was prolonged by a comparatively small number of insurgents, the colonel in command, Colonel Min, failed to occupy the Presnenskaya Quarter, although it was defended by a force insignificant in numbers and inadequately armed.[1] On the other hand, it must be allowed that numerous barricades rendered guerilla warfare possible, and that the troops were confronted by wholly novel conditions. The military authorities were obviously startled and perplexed by the new problems in city warfare—a kind of campaigning in which hitherto

---

[1] The writer is informed that during many of the conflicts in Moscow, the troops, supplied *ad libitum* with liquor from the Government liquor shops, were drunk, and that their firing was quite haphazard. The frequent defeats of troops by small bodies of insurgents may thus be accounted for.

they had had everything their own way—in which the *nagaïka* was the customary weapon, and in which, up till the beginning of 1905, the rifle had not played an important rôle. In Moscow even important streets are narrow and tortuous, and in the greater part of the city there are winding lanes, *culs de sac*, and obscure passages. Few cities in Russia present the opportunities of prolonged resistance upon an extensive scale which Moscow offers, least of all St. Petersburg, where the streets are wide and straight, where there are many large open spaces, and where the number of troops in garrison is always overwhelming.

The injury to the prestige of the autocracy became increasingly serious with every hour in which its capital city of Moscow remained in the hands of the insurgents. Fatality seemed to dog the arms of Russia, even in civil war.

After the " uprising " had begun, and still more after it had been suppressed, suggestions were not wanting that, as in the Zubàtov-shina and the Gaponovshina, the hand of the police might be detected, and that the " uprising " was the result of provocative action. Certain considerations, no doubt, tend towards the justification of such a charge, which was made chiefly by the Social Democrats.[1] This charge is based principally upon the fact that the " uprising " was likely to lead, as it did lead, to a reaction similar to that which followed the Polish revolt in 1863 [2] and that which succeeded the assassination of Alexander II in 1881. Although this outcome has been for the time favourable to the autocracy, as it was in the two former historical cases, and although it was wholly in the interest of the " old régime " " to transfer the struggle to the field of immediate physical action before it was too late to do so," [3] it is not clear that it was to the interest of the autocracy to familiarize the people with the idea and the practice of revolution. There has always been a temptation in such cases to find the subtle hand of the Russian Government behind every movement, luring it on to its destruction. In the case of Zubàtov,[4] the policy is public and confessed ; in the case of Gapon [5] it is less clear, although the evidence affords some proof of complicity of the Government in the earlier stages ; in the

[1] As, for instance, by V. Gorn in his *Peasantry in the Russian Revolution* (Moscow, 1907), p. 153.
[2] For the reaction following the Polish insurrection, see the lively account by Prince Kropotkin in his *Memoirs* (Boston, 1899), p. 174.
[3] Gorn, *op. cit.*, p. 153.   [4] Cf. *supra*, p. 188.   [5] Cf. *supra*, p. 451.

case of the Moscow " uprising " it is not clear at all. The presumptions are almost altogether against the supposition that the " uprising " was brought about by provocative measures. The risk, under the conditions of general conflagration, which characterized the close of 1905, was too great for any responsíble authority to trifle with worn-out schemes of " provocation." The army, the navy, and the fortresses were all in a temper of highly uncertain loyalty, the peasantry were in a state bordering upon widespread insurrection, the city working men were, to say the least of it, highly disturbed, and in little need of " provocation." Nothing but the extreme of folly could have driven the autocracy upon a path with which it was already familiar, but in which it had already met with repeated defeats. " Provocation " had had its day in Odessa,[1] and had been attended with unanticipated results. Moreover, the expense of the frequent punitive expeditions, of the policing of the towns, of strikes, and of other incidents of the revolution, was becoming enormous, and the credit of Russia was suffering on the foreign exchanges.[2] The country needed a period of quiet rather than one of disturbance. It is, moreover, now quite certain that the administration was better informed than any of the extreme party groups of the state of mind of the peasantry, and that it was well aware of the futility of an attempt on the part of the city proletariat alone to force the revolution in a direction determined by its own interests without the support of the mass of the peasant population.

It is more reasonable to regard the " uprising," as well as the incidents at Kronstadt, at Sevastopol, and those of the agrarian disorders, as springing from causes which were beyond the power of the autocracy, within the terms of its own existence, to prevent, rather than to suppose that any one of them sprang from deliberate playing with fire.

In March 1906 [3] there arose in official circles fears of a repetition

---

[1] Cf. *supra*, p. 203.

[2] For the effect of the Moscow uprising upon Russian securities, see *infra*, Appendix to Book VII.

[3] Between the suppression of the " uprising " in December 1905 and March 1906, many irregularities occurred in which soldiers and police were alike implicated. For example, both sold back to the revolutionists, at high prices, arms which had been confiscated in the course of their duty and purchased at low prices inferior weapons which they reported and delivered to their superior officers. In the end of February 1906, the Minister of Interior issued a circular intended to put a stop to this practice.

of the "armed uprising" in Moscow. The rank and file of the police were to some extent affected by panic, and they began to send in their resignations in considerable numbers. Under these circumstances a police circular was issued intimating that any policeman who sent in his resignation without sufficient reason would be subjected to three months imprisonment and subsequent banishment. The moment passed, however, without any recurrence of the resort to arms.

In St. Petersburg also, throughout the early months of 1906, the authorities feared an outbreak similar to that of Moscow, but the presence of an immense garrison, and the hopelessness of relying upon disaffection among the troops prevented further disturbances there also.

The Moscow uprising of December 1905, serious as it was, lasted only for a few days. It ultimately collapsed, partly through inherent weakness and partly through the military measures which were taken to suppress it. One of its consequences was the proof that risings in cities under modern conditions are much more easily suppressed than risings in the rural districts. During the previous ten years the policy of the Government had been directed towards strengthening the city garrisons. The city had become an armed camp. Although Moscow is not an important military centre, the garrison is never less than 10,000, while St. Petersburg has usually a garrison of 30,000. A revolutionary movement in any of the great cities may disturb the Government, or may even seriously discredit it, but so long as the army is loyal, it cannot overthrow the Government. A peasant rising, on the other hand, when it is widespread, may keep expedition after expedition moving for an indefinite period. The rising may be crushed in one region only to reappear in another. It is conceivable that guerila warfare of this kind might go on indefinitely. The fear expressed by some of the Social Democrats,[1] that the peasantry would betray the revolution by accepting concessions before the city proletariat was prepared to lay down its arms, showed that account was not taken of the actual conditions. The city proletariat must for the reasons stated lay down its arms within a few days ; the peasant revolt, when it exists widely, may not be compelled to do so until after repeated expeditions.

[1] *Cf.* Gorn, *op. cit.*, p. 139.

CHAPTER XII

THE DISTURBANCES IN THE URALS IN 1907

SPORADIC disturbances continued to take place in the year 1907. One of the principal areas affected by these disturbances was the region of the Ural Mountains, where the exploitation and manufacture of iron are the principal means of employment. This region is situated in Permskaya *gub*. One of the largest of the companies which carried on operations in the iron region was the Bogoslovsky Mountain Foundry Joint-Stock Company, to which the whole of the Bogoslovsky Mountain district belonged. In one of the foundries of the company—Nadejdinsky—rails were manufactured, and from 3000 to 3500 men were employed. Most of these men belonged to the surrounding peasant population, and for the most part they retained their connection with their former villages, although they lived in a large village in the immediate neighbourhood of the foundry. The population of this village (12,000 to 15,000) was occupied almost exclusively in labour in the foundry proper or in subsidiary enterprises connected with it—charcoal-burning, saw-milling, &c. The wages of this considerable group of working people were relatively high (40 to 70 rubles per month), and the general level of comfort, relatively to that of the mass of the Russian artisans and peasants, was also high. Situated as they are, remote from centres of cultivated life, and inevitably to some extent separated even from their own former villages, the population, in spite of their material comfort, are seriously addicted to drink, and their level of culture is very low. The lowest of these are said to be the permanent workers in the foundry, those having the best wages and the best positions, who have to a large extent severed their connection with their native villages, and who have thus ceased to be affected even by their rudimentary culture. There was not, moreover, according to report, any *intelligentsia* element either in the foundry or in the village. In 1905 a small group of Social Democrats attempted to form an organization of such elements as they could find ; but they were speedily " frozen out." So also the Social Revolutionary Party attempted to form an organization. The organizers only succeeded in attracting to themselves working men who were not influenced by revolutionary doctrines so much as by the prospect of disturbance. This group thus became involved in a militant organization, in small *terror* and expropriations. These actions led to the hostility of the authorities and eventually to the breaking up of the party group. *Intelligentsia* belonging to the Social Revolutionary Party attempted to revive the organization. This had little direct effect ; but the existence of the agitation prepared the way for the events of August 1907, which culminated in the closing of the foundry and the dismissal of all the workmen. The most effective factor in these events was, however, the arrival at the foundry of a working man called Lvov. Lvov had worked in another foundry in the same *guberni,* and had served as an artillery man in the Russo-Japanese war. After his return from Manchuria he was decorated for gallantry ; but during the period of military disaffection in 1905 he had organized means for preventing the dispersal of soldiers' meetings, and in this way he had been brought into conflict with the authorities. He had escaped arrest ; but from thenceforward he was not " a legal man." He now threw himself into the revolutionary movement, and determined to organize bands of men with the object of carrying on the struggle against the Government. He began by making raids with a small number of spirits like himself. These raids resulted in " expropriations," and with the funds so derived, arms for larger groups were purchased. These " expropriation " exploits were so frequently conducted with great skill, audacity, and success, that everywhere in the *gubernie* people began to look upon Lvov as a hero who possessed extraordinary courage and ingenious organizing ability. Legends about him grew up, and the people aided him, concealed him when necessary, and gave him information about the movements of the police and of troops. " Soon the name of Lvov was thundering over the whole of the Urals, and even the metropolitan newspapers began to give him attention." [1] His

---

[1] *Znamya Truda*, No. 8, December 1907. Lvov was regarded by the peasants as a worthy successor of Stenka Razēn and Pugachev (cf. *supra*, p. 21 *et seq.*). He and his companions were known as the " Forest Brothers."

activities gave rise to tales so obviously exaggerated that it is almost impossible to discover beneath these tales the truth about his activities. The one fact about which there is no manner of doubt is his extraordinary popularity. Youths of all sorts crowded to his standard—some attracted by the opportunity he afforded for revolutionary activity, others by a mere love of adventure. Nearly all were destitute of the moral discipline necessary for a sincere revolutionary movement.

The arrival of Lvov at Nadejdinsky Foundry with about twenty of his comrades resulted in his obtaining a large number of recruits of various sorts, and arms were distributed to this heterogeneous mob. Lvov's plan was to seize the office of the mines and the sub-post office, and to get what money was held there, and at the same time to capture the store of dynamite at the mines. This plan was almost openly discussed ; and the people of the village were in a general state of sympathetic expectancy. In the night of the 13th August 1907 the village was aroused by a series of explosions of bombs, which were found to have destroyed a newly built sawmill. At the same time the railway line was cut and communication by telephone was interrupted. The movement of troops into the district was thus prevented for a time.[1] The administration of the mine had, however, taken advantage of the publicity which had been given to Lvov's movements and had removed all but a trifling amount of money, so that the " expropriations " amounted to very little. A number of arsons took place, however, and the engineer of the foundry was killed, together with another member of the administration. Immediately after these murders the foundry was closed and all the workmen were dismissed. The local authorities now concentrated two companies of soldiers, eighty mounted Ingushi, and thirty constables, and instituted a hunt for Lvov. A number of his followers were arrested, but the leader escaped. Simultaneously with his flight, and therefore his acknowledgment of defeat, the reputation of Lvov among the people collapsed. They had believed him to be invincible, and now he was defeated, and the sole result of his agitation for them was the closing of the works and the cessation of their means of livelihood. They turned,

---

[1] There had, however, been brought into the region a small force of Ingushi (cf. *supra*, vol. i. p. 577), who had been brought from the Caucasus to protect the mines against attack.

indeed, with much fury upon one of the followers of Lvov, and they were with difficulty prevented from permitting him to be burned alive in a house from which the police succeeded in rescuing him.

Lvov established a kind of " Seych "[1] in the mountains, where he gathered about him a number of adventurous spirits, some of them Social Revolutionists, a few Social Democrats, and many mere adventurers. Lvov and his bands continued to appear suddenly in different places. So many police were killed by them that the police became victims of panic and resigned " by scores." The Governor, Bolatov, was ordered at all costs to effect the capture of Lvov; and reinforcements of troops, Cossacks, and Ingushi were sent into the district. The region was declared under Extra-ordinary Guard.[2] Then began a kind of battue ; everybody who came within the net was punished by arrest or by being shot without trial. Many persons wholly out of sympathy with Lvov suffered with the guilty. The fashion of going into " Seych " gradually ceased, and the agitation subsided. Eventually in the winter of 1907–1908, Lvov was captured.

The disturbances as a whole disclose the existence of a crudely revolutionary " state of mind " among the population of the Urals. The youth were evidently ready for any desperate enterprise, grievance or no grievance, and without any fixed aim either for themselves or for the country at large. Such elements disappeared with the capture of Lvov, only, no doubt, to reappear whenever a similar personality emerges to take the leadership of the revolutionists by instinct. " Any Ataman will find hundreds or even thousands of young men of the Ural Ushkunēkē "[3] ready to follow them.

[1] The " Seych " was an island in the Dnieper, the resort of the Cossacks. For a lively description of this singular republic of adventurers, see Sienkiewicz, H., *With Fire and Sword*, chap. xi. See also *supra*, p. 22.

[2] Cf. *supra*, p. 548.

[3] *Znamya Truda*, Nos. 10 and 11, February-March 1908. The Ush-kunēkē were the pillaging parties of old Novgorod. Cf. *supra*, vol. i. p. 32.

CHAPTER XIII

THE POLITICAL POLICE, AZEFSHINA, AND THE
COLLAPSE OF THE TERROR

THE ambiguous rôle played by the Russian police departments
in the political and revolutionary movements of recent years has
already been illustrated in the cases of Zubàtov and Gapon, both
of whom attempted to organize the city working men upon a
non-political basis. The first of these was a police officer, the
second was under the suspicion of being, consciously or unconsciously, a police agent. But the rôle of the police in the organization of ostensibly pure trade unionism is unimportant beside their
alleged rôle as masters of the autocracy and of the revolution
alike. The disclosures of January 1909, connected with the case
of A. A. Lopukhin, formerly Director of the Police Department,
and with that of Yevno Azef, formerly head of the " Militant
Organization of the Central Committee of the Socialist Revolutionary
Party," and at the same time police spy and *agent provocateur*,
suggest that the political police spy system had reached, in 1905
and 1906, " perfection " in its kind. When the spy acquires complete control of the situation, and in his own person unites the
functions of the autocrat and revolutionist, no further development in that kind is possible.

The statements of the Government and of the officials concerned,
and similar statements made by the Central Committee of the
Socialist Revolutionary Party, may all be open to suspicion. Conspiracy and counter-conspiracy are indeed public and confessed ;
and both are alike excused on the ground of inevitability. Only in
so far as the Government and the Revolutionary Party can both be
regarded as sitting, under the strain of these revelations, upon the
stool of repentance, can their statements carry conviction.

It is first of all necessary to explain the official organization of
the Russian police. It has been described as " a terribly and extraordinarily complicated organized army, that possesses its general

staff, its soldiers, its spies, and its effective instruments of annihilation." [1] At the head of this formidable institution there was the Minister of the Interior. He was responsible to the Tsar for the conduct of its various departments: the Detective Department and the Department of Political Police, as well as the department charged with the police administration in the capitals and in the provinces. Alongside every general governor and every governor there stood a police functionary who was responsible to the Minister of the Interior.

The ambitions of members of the Police Department have frequently been commensurate with the extraordinary powers which they exercised. In 1881, for example, Sudeikin [2] appears to have acted deliberately in imposing upon the Tsar Alexander a régime of terror. He frightened him by continuous disclosures of conspiracy, and endeavoured to induce him to dismiss Count Dmitri Tolstoy for incompetence, and to appoint himself (Sudeikin) as practical dictator, the Tsar being only an ornamental head of the State. [3]

Apart from the recognized officials of the Police Department, every *concierge* (dvornik) was licensed by the police, and might be compelled to exercise surveillance over every person who resided in

---

[1] Von Moskwitsch, " Die Polizei," in *Russen über Russland, Ein Sammelwerk*, ed. by Josef Melnik (Frankfurt-am-Main, 1906), p. 420.

[2] Sudeikin was Chief of the Detective Department in St. Petersburg in 1881. In one of his domiciliary visits he arrested, along with others, a sous-captain of artillery called Dugaiëv, who was evidently acquainted with some of the active members of the *Narodnaya Volya*. Sudeikin noticed this young man in the crowd of arrested persons and determined to make use of him. He visited him in the prison in which he was confined and came to an understanding with him. He obtained for Dugaiëv a position as draughtsman in one of the Government offices, and began to utilize him as a secret detective agent. By means of Dugaiëv's acquaintance with the members of the *Narodnaya Volya* party many of these were arrested and many " underground printing offices " were disclosed and suppressed. The rôle of Dugaiëv in these transactions was discovered, and the *Narodnaya Volya* party sentenced him to death. Feeling that so long as he remained in St. Petersburg the life of Dugaiëv was in danger, Sudeikin sent him to Paris. There, however, Dugaiëv soon became aware that his movements were under observation by his former allies. Convinced that his assassination was inevitable, Dugaiëv entered into negotiation with the members of the *Narodnaya Volya*, and in exchange for his life undertook to commit any revolutionary act which they might require. The act prescribed by them was the assassination of Sudeikin. Dugaiëv assisted in the accomplishment of this deed and escaped. The Government offered a reward of 10,000 rubles for the capture of Dugaiëv, but the reward was never claimed. After the deed was done the *Narodnaya Volya* announced its disapproval on principle of such a method of carrying on its war as the deed involved, and declared its intention not to repeat it.

[3] Cf. *supra*, pp. 130 and 132.

the premises of which he was caretaker. In addition to these, there were besides innumerable regular and occasional spies, who were paid by the police to keep them informed of the personal activities of suspects and others.

The functions of the Russian Police Department were not confined to Russia. In every foreign country where there were Russian emigrants there were police agents whose business it was to worm themselves into the confidence of the emigrants, and to make reports upon their activities. The operations of these agents were directed by the Superintendent of Russian Political Police Abroad, whose office in St. Petersburg was a branch of the Department of Political Police. The agents of the Russian police abroad were no doubt, as a rule, obscure persons who played the part of common spies; but occasionally disclosures have been made which leave little doubt of espionage having been carried on by persons who occupied more or less conspicuous positions in one or other of the Western European capitals.

The *rationale* of this system is undoubtedly the necessity under which an autocratic government lies to make itself aware of oppositional movements in time to counteract them, whether these movements are intended to have a violent issue or not. The police system, with its espionage, is thus an incident inseparable from autocracy;[1] but like autocracy, its development in Russia has shown that it contains within itself the seeds of its own destruction. The spy system appears to tend to develop, upon its fundamentally unsound ethical basis, until it brings down the system to which it is attached. In Russia the pecuniary gains of the first-class spy have evidently been so considerable as to induce him first to organize and then to betray—the outcome of this process being widespread " provocation," the implication of enthusiastic but weak people, and their subsequent destruction.[2] The transition from espionage to " provocation " is inevitable ; for the spy who has gained admis-

---

[1] It may even be argued that the system of espionage is inseparable from Government *per se*, the chronic condition of crisis through which the Russian Government has been passing for upwards of a century merely accounting for its special manifestation in Russia. A case analogous to the conspicuous Russian case of Azef, is that of Major le Caron, who was instructed by the British Government in 1875 to join the Fenian United Brotherhood for the purpose of espionage. See Le Caron's evidence before the Special Commission, 1888, 5th February 1889.

[2] This process was illustrated in the case of Zubátov, *supra*, pp. 188-9n.

sion to the centre of a revolutionary organization must act as a revolutionist, or he would be immediately suspected of treachery. The "perfect spy" must not betray continuously, therefore, but only occasionally, in order to prepare for a magnificent *coup* in which the revolutionary movement should be altogether crushed. In the process, however, many attempts must be permitted to succeed, and must even be instigated by the spy in order to convince the revolutionists of his loyalty. This discloses to the spy who is not "perfect" immense possibilities for the exercise of private vengeance and for the removal, under cover of his unique position— one of immunity from the authorities and of extreme danger from the revolutionists—of a Minister who might stand in the way of the promotion of his patron, of a Grand Duke who might have exhibited hostility to his race, or even of the Sovereign, by whose removal a chaos, in which he might profit, would ensue.

To the spy as such, the crushing of a revolutionary movement is the end of his business ; it is therefore to his interest to keep the state of revolutionary agitation going, in order that he may continue to profit by it. In the same way the party of reaction profits by revolutionary agitation, because it frightens the ordinary peace-loving citizen, who forms the bulk of all communities, and who is in general quite willing to entrust the suppression of such agitations to any strong and determined authority which offers itself.

It appears from the extraordinary case of Azef and Lopukhin that the course of development thus sketched in the abstract had, especially in 1905 and 1906, concrete reality.

The perplexing part of the Russian situation in this particular is that, in presence of a genuine revolutionary movement, produced by deep-seated causes, the Government should allow itself to be embarrassed and compromised by remorseless and unscrupulous agents, who were at all times evidently willing to sacrifice, even in the most terrible way, either the Government or the party to which they had attached themselves. There is no more ghastly episode, either in the political or in the criminal history of modern times, than the career of the spy Azef, who, according to the statements of the Socialist Revolutionary Party, took a leading part in organizing the murders of M. Plehvë, M. Sipiaghin, and the Grand Duke Sergey, at the very moments when, according to the admissions of the Government, he was acting as its paid agent. It is not alleged that members of the Government were aware of the extreme development of the double rôle of their employée, but they were undoubtedly aware of the double rôle itself, and, therefore, their continued employment of so dangerous an agent is not creditable to their sagacity. The incident, with its terrible consequences, reflects no credit upon the wisdom either of the Government or of the Socialist Revolutionary Party, and indeed places them both on the same plane in being both deceived by the same unusually able criminal.

In 1892 Yevno Azef, a Jew, then about twenty-four years of age, an engineer, was living in Ekaterinoslav. He was at that time a member of the Social Democratic organization there. Shortly after this date he went to Carlsruhe, where he became a student of engineering in the Polytechnic.[1] " In the second half of the nineties," while he was in Germany, " he joined the Russian revolutionary group abroad, known as ' The Union of Russian Socialist Revolutionaries,' and published a paper called *Russki Rabochi* (Russian Worker). In July 1899 Azef returned to Russia, and through the recommendation of the above-mentioned union, entered in Moscow ' The Northern Union of Socialist Revolutionaries ' " (founded by Argunov, Pavlov, Seluk, and others). " This organization issued the first two numbers of the paper, which afterwards became the organ of the Socialist Revolutionary Party, *Revolutsionnaya Rossiya*. When the printing office of the union at Tomsk was seized by the police, the leaders of the union, apprehensive of arrest, handed over to Azef all connections and powers." [2] That is to say, they gave him lists of the members of the group, correspondence and other party documents ; and they entrusted him with power to negotiate with the southern groups of Socialist Revolutionaries, with a view to the union of the north and south groups.

In December 1901 [3] Azef, George A. Gershuni,[4] and another

---

[1] These details were given by M. Stolypin in his speech to the Duma on 11th February 1909.

[2] From the Circular of the Central Committee of the Socialist Revolutionary Party (Paris, 7–20th January 1909).

[3] Socialist Revolutionary Circular, 7–20th January 1909. M. Stolypin said that Azef became acquainted with Gershuni in 1902.

[4] Gershuni played at this time, and for several years afterwards, a very conspicuous part in revolutionary and terroristic organization. See *Mémoires de G. Gerchouni* (in Russian) (Paris, 1908). According to M. Stolypin (speech in Duma, 11th February 1909), " the chief rôle in the revolution " was played by Gershuni and Gotz. These two men with Victor Chernov formed the revolutionary centre. According to the same authority, quoting the infor-

member of the Northern Union, succeeded in uniting these groups into one Socialist Revolutionary Party. He took also the closest part in the resumption of the publication of *Revolutsionnaya Rossiya* as the recognized organ of the new party.[1] He also interested himself in attempting to form a Federal Union between the Socialist Revolutionary Party and the " Agrarian Socialist League." At the same time Azef took part in the elaboration of the plan of campaign of organized terror, the beginning of which was signalized by the assassination of Sipiaghin.

At this time Azef seems to have exhibited extraordinary energy.[2]

mation in the hands of the police, Gershuni organized *all* the terroristic acts, while Gotz acted as instructor. Gershuni is said by M. Stolypin to have been present when Sipiaghin was killed ; so also he was in Ufa when General Bogdonovich was killed ; he was present during the unsuccessful attempt upon M. Pobyedonostsev in the Nevsky Prospekt in St. Petersburg, and he sat in the Tivoli Garden at Kharkov while the equally unsuccessful attempt was made upon Prince Obolensky. He was found guilty of complicity in these terroristic acts, and was sentenced to death. His sentence was commuted to banishment to Siberia for life. Escaping from Siberia, he found his way to France, where he died in 1908.

[1] The first seven numbers of *Revolutsionnaya Rossiya* were printed in Russia ; Nos. 8–76 were printed in Paris and elsewhere. On the publication of the manifesto of 17th October 1905 by the Tsar the Russian press abroad was suspended and the staffs of the various newspapers and magazines returned to Russia. Disappointment upon the non-fulfilment of their hopes and the activity of the police drove them once more abroad.

[2] The prime authority for the activity of Azef and for the rôle which he played in the terroristic acts of the Militant Organization of the Central Committee of the Socialist Revolutionary Party is to be found in the Circulars issued by the Central Committee at Paris on 26th December 1908, 7th January and 1st February 1909 (all O.S.). The central fact of Azef's employment by the Government is admitted in the *Official Communiqué* issued through the Information Bureau of the Russian Government and published in the semi-official *Novoë Vremya* (St. Petersburg), 19th January 1909. Many of the details are confirmed by well-informed articles in that newspaper on this and on immediately succeeding dates.

Details, with sinister interpretations, are also given in the formal " interpellations " in the State Duma on 20th January 1909 by the Constitutional Democratic Party and by the Social Democrats and the Toil Groups. These " interpellations " are to be found in the *Stenographic Reports of the Duma* and in M. Milyukov's newspaper, *Ryech* (St. Petersburg), 21st January 1909. The speech of the Deputy Pokrovsky repeats in effect the circular of the Central Committee of the Socialist Revolutionary Party. Additional details are to be found in the letter of M. Lopukhin, formerly Chief of the Department of Police, addressed to M. Stolypin, Prime Minister, and to M. Sheglovitov, Minister of Justice, dated 19th November 1908, and read in the Duma on 20th January 1909 as part of the " interpellation " of the Social Democratic and Toil Groups. Further details of Azef's career are also given in the speech of the Prime Minister, M. Stolypin, in the Duma on 11th February 1909, and in *Znamya Truda* (The Banner of Labour), the organ of the Socialist Revolutionary Party, published in Paris, No. 15, 28th February 1909.

He travelled in many different parts of Russia, as well as abroad, and established secret revolutionary groups in several places. He supervised the preparation of explosive chemicals in the revolutionary workshops, organized the transportation of these explosives across the frontier, compiled and circulated revolutionary leaflets and pamphlets, and smuggled these into Russia by most ingenious methods. He was the soul of many conspiracies, some of which succeeded in their aim, and then concluded through his agency with the arrest of the majority of the conspirators.[1] " He frequently accused his party comrades of treason, and endeavoured to get them sentenced to death by the revolutionary tribunals. Among these was Gapon, whose death (in 1906) was the outcome of an accusation by Azef that he had sold himself to M. Wittë." From June 1902 " Azef worked in St. Petersburg, simultaneously as a member of the Central Committee (whose headquarters were in Paris) and of the St. Petersburg Committee. He organized the transportation of propagandist literature through Finland, and together with Gershuni discussed the plans of terroristic enterprises. . . . But Azef's principal efforts were directed towards the solution of the question how to use explosive materials as a new technical basis for the terroristic struggle. From 1904 onwards Azef was at the head of the enlarged Militant Organization, which was entered by Kalyaev,[2] Sozonov,[3] Schweitzer,[4] and others. *He arranged the terroristic work against Plehvë.* . . . At the same time he took part in the general party work, and organized in Russia dynamite laboratories." In January 1905 Azef further recruited the " Militant Organization " and divided it into three detachments. " The first detachment was sent to Moscow to assassinate the Grand Duke Sergey—the attempt succeeded ; the second to St. Petersburg (against Trepov) ; and the third to Kiev (against Klegels[5]). In the summer of 1905 Azef took part in the shipment

[1] *Novoë Vremya*, 19th January 1909.
[2] Kalyaev killed the Grand Duke Sergey. Accounts of him, very interesting from a psychological point of view, are given in *Biloye* (Paris), No. 7, pp. 20 and 43.
[3] Sozonov killed M. de Plehvë.
[4] Schweitzer was for a time the technical expert of the " Militant Organization." He took no part in the actual performance of terroristic acts ; but confined himself to the manufacture of explosives. He was killed by an accidental explosion in his own workshop.
[5] Russianized form of Clayhills, the name of a Russo-Scottish family.

of arms in quantity by steamer from England. In January 1906 Azef organized an attempt upon M. Durnovo, Minister of the Interior, superintending one part personally, the other part being taken by his nearest comrade. . . . Azef then went to Moscow to superintend further terroristic actions. . . . Shortly before the dissolution of the First Duma, Azef organized an attempt upon the life of the Minister of the Interior (M. Stolypin). This attempt failed ; but soon after, on the urgent demands of the Central Committee, he worked out a plan of activity which led to the assassinations of Launitz (Chief of the Police of St. Petersburg), Pavlov (Chief Military Prosecutor), and others." [1]

This startling catalogue of crimes is given in a document sent by the Central Committee of the Socialist Revolutionary Party in Paris to M. Pokrovsky II, and read by him to the State Duma. The Central Committee seem to have made up its mind to make a general confession. The fact, otherwise unknown, that Azef was the head of the " Militant Organization " leaves no doubt of his complicity in all of the crimes, even if instigation is left out of account. The other side of the story, the detail of his functions as spy, has not yet been fully published ; but on the main point the official *communiqué* leaves no doubt.

" The engineer, Yevno Azef," says the *communiqué*, " who was a member of the Secret Association, called the party of Socialist Revolutionaries, and who delivered to the detective organs of police information about the criminal contemplations of the said group, has been convicted by the members of it of relations with the police ; in this exposure of the activity of Azef, the former Director of the Department of Police, the retired Actual State Councillor, A. A. Lopukhin, took part. From the investigation made into this matter, it appears that Lopukhin really had delivered to the said Revolutionary Party the evidences against Azef, which evidences were known to Lopukhin, exclusively through his previous service in the said position, the above-mentioned action of Lopukhin having directly resulted in the exclusion of Azef from the ' Party,' and the cessation by Azef of the possibility of informing beforehand the police about the criminal plans of the

---

[1] Speech in the State Duma by Poktrovsky II, reported in *Ryech* (St. Petersburg), 21st January 1909. See also *Stenographic Report of the State Duma*, 20th January 1909.

association, which had as its purpose the accomplishment of terror-istic acts of first-rate importance. The material collected on the subject served as a basis for beginning the preliminary investiga-tion to which Lopukhin, as accused, after a domiciliary search, has been submitted and has been taken into custody." [1]

Some of the details of the activity of Azef, both as revolutionist and as spy, were given in the interpellations to the State Duma, introduced on behalf of the Constitutional Democratic Party and of the Social Democratic and Toil Groups. These interpellations bluntly accused Azef of complicity in practically all the important assassinations and attempts at assassination during the past six years, and the Social Democratic and Toil Group interpellation further explicitly accused Rachkovsky, Superintendent of the Rus-sian Political Police Abroad, of complicity with Azef, and of having been fully aware beforehand of the preparations for the various terroristic acts, and demanded his prosecution. The complicity of Rachkovsky was further insisted upon by Pokrovsky II in his speech to the Duma, proofs and evidence of witnesses being offered by him to the Government.

The figure of Azef looms up through all the documents as a man of extraordinary activity and capacity for organization, as well as of a man whose motives for the commission of his colossal crimes, apart from merely pecuniary motives, are very obscure. The sketch of him given by an evidently well-informed writer in *Novoë Vremya*, shows him to be a man tall and stout,[2] of swarthy complexion, calm features of Kalmuk Tartar type, broad nose, pendent lower lip, and slightly outstanding ears.[3] His practice was to dress elegantly; in the summer he was to be seen in St. Petersburg in white lawn-tennis costume; and he was in the habit of frequenting theatres and concert gardens, where he spent money freely, and where he is represented as conducting himself with un-restrained joviality. There is a touch of the sensation novel in the fact that he appears to have had a double, who possessed or took his name, and by means of whom he managed to concoct *alibi*, which

---

[1] Issued by the Information Bureau (Official). Printed in *Ryech*, 20th January 1909.

[2] He was known as Azef the Great, one of his soubriquets, or as *Tolstyak =* Fat Man.

[3] Azef was born about 1871.

baffled for long the ingenuity of those among his fellow-conspirators who entertained suspicions about him.

From time to time such suspicions inevitably arose. Movements of conspirators, known to him alone, led to their arrest. Attempts were sometimes frustrated by the arrest of all the persons engaged in the preparations. Yet his skill in organizing the major operations, which were successfully accomplished—the assassination of Plehvë and of the Grand Duke Sergey, for example—convinced at least some of the doubters of his good faith. Yet two men seem for long to have entertained suspicions and to have patiently woven the coils about him. These were Bakay, a former police spy, who had become a genuine revolutionist, and Burtsev, editor of the Socialist Revolutionary review, published in Paris, *Biloye* (The Past). But Azef had so carefully obliterated his traces that sufficient evidence against him was not forthcoming. Meanwhile the Central Committee, on their own showing,[1] were urging Azef to fresh proofs of his loyalty to them, and the result was a fresh series of assassinations planned by him. His activity as spy went on concurrently with his activity as revolutionist. By slow degrees he was hunted down by Bakay and Burtsev. When called upon to make explanations before the Central Committee, he suddenly made his appearance, " unannounced," in the working cabinet of Lopukhin, his former chief, and former Director of the Department of Police, in his house at St. Petersburg.[2] He told Lopukhin that he had been accused of treachery by the Central Committee, which intended to call as a witness before its tribunal Lopukhin himself. Azef's life, therefore, depended upon Lopukhin's denial of his employment by the police during Lopukhin's period of office. Two days after Azef's interview, Lopukhin received a similarly " unannounced " and mysterious visit from General Gerasimov, Chief of the Detective Department, who said that any communication which might be made by Lopukhin to

---

[1] " By the persistent demands of the Central Committee, he (Azef) worked out a plan of activity which soon led to a series of assassinations, Launitz, Pavlov, &c." From the *Document of the Central Committee*, read by Pokrovsky II in the State Duma, 20th January 1909.

[2] Azef's visit to Lopukhin is described by the latter in a letter to M. Stolypin, Prime Minister and Minister of the Interior, dated 21st November 1908, and published in the (semi-official) *Novoë Vremya* on 19th January 1909. The visit of Azef to Lopukhin took place at 9 P.M. on 19th November 1908.

the revolutionary tribunal would be well known to him. This implied threat Lopukhin on the same day communicated to the Prime Minister, M. Stolypin, and to the Minister of Justice, M. Sheglovitov. In his communication, which was published later, he does not indicate the course which he was going to pursue ; but clearly he met the demand of the revolutionary tribunal with proofs of Azef's treachery.[1] On becoming aware of Lopukhin's action, Azef, who was at the time in Paris, disappeared. The tribunal, no doubt, sentenced him to death, although nothing has been disclosed on this subject. All the indications point to the extraordinary rôle played by Azef on the one hand and, on the other, to the as yet unexplained rôle of Lopukhin, Rachkovsky, and Gerasimov, all high officials of the police. The precise attitude of the Government is far from clear. On the one hand, it seems to be sincere in declaring that it desires to expose to full publicity the details of this terrible embroglio ; on the other, the terms of the *communiqué* suggest that the Government was disturbed chiefly by the cessation of Azef's services as spy through the action of Lopukhin.

The net result of the episode was that, at a terrible cost of life, liberty, and prestige, the air was cleared somewhat. Although M. Stolypin's statement on the subject in the Duma was very full and apparently extremely candid, it is difficult to reconcile his insistence upon the position that while Azef played the rôle of spy he did not play the rôle of " provocator " with the transparent fact that in Azef's case the separation of the rôles is quite inconceivable. Azef's position in the councils of the Socialist

---

[1] See the official *communiqué*, quoted above; and see also M. Stolypin's speech in the Duma, 11th February 1909, where he says that Lopukhin went to Germany and met Burtsev, and to London, where he met Savenkov, Argunov, and Victor Chernov, who represented the revolutionary tribunal. M. Stolypin said that Lopukhin told these representatives of the revolutionary party that Azef had assuredly acted as a police spy. See *Russki Viedomosti*, No. 34, 12th February 1909. The rôle of Lopukhin appears to be intelligible only on one or other of two grounds. Either he suddenly discovered the double rôle of Azef and honestly denounced him immediately, or, more probably, he was fully aware of Azef's actions, and fearing that he might himself become one of Azef's victims, was impelled to save himself by denouncing Azef, while purchasing immunity from revolutionary attack by the manner of the denunciation.

Revolutionary Party, which is fully admitted by the Government, rendered it quite indispensable that he should take a more or less active part in the organization of acts of terror. It is impossible to believe that the other members of the Central Committee, not to speak of the other members of the " Militant Organization," should have allowed him to be a mere spectator in the tragedies which they were consummating. Even if due weight is attached to the supposition that the leaders of the Socialist Revolutionaries find it to be in their interest now to lay a large share of the blame of their proceedings upon the shoulders of Azef, it is not credible that they should, for at least five years, have allowed him to share their councils without any active service whatever. As matter of fact, however, they fully acknowledged their own complicity by the course which they adopted of accusing Azef. It is quite true, as M. Stolypin states, that the source of the attack upon Azef was the former police agent, Bakay, whose career does not entitle him to credence; but the accusations against Azef do not rest upon his evidence alone. The information in the hands of the police, as disclosed by M. Stolypin in the Duma, is of itself sufficient to show that Azef could not, in the nature of things, have pursued the career of spy for so many years without taking some share in the acts of the organization of which he was a member. The revelations by the Socialist Revolutionary Committee of Azef's activity may be fantastic exaggerations, but the central fact of his activity as organizer of assassinations is most difficult to disprove. Further, the action of Lopukhin in betraying Azef to the revolutionaries is unintelligible unless he at least was convinced of the reality of the double rôle which Azef was playing.

M. Stolypin admitted that there had been acts of " provocation " by police agents, although he denied that " provocation " had been reduced to a system. He cited several cases in which " provocation " had been practised and in which the provocators had been handed over to the courts for punishment ;[1] and he intimated that a commission of

[1] The cases were an officer of *gendarmes* arrested for " provocation," and spies at Kaluga and Penza. *Russki Viedomosti*, 12th February 1909.

inquiry into the police system had been ordered with a view to reform.

The Azef affair marks the close of the terror which preceded and accompanied the revolutionary movement of 1905 and 1906.

CHAPTER XIV

THE *INTELLIGENTSIA* AND THE REVOLUTION [1]

THE expression *intelligentsia* [2] is used in current phraseology in Russian in a double sense. It is used to designate the " general *intelligentsia* " or those who in all classes of society are engaged in the pursuit of intellectual interests, whether they earn their living by this pursuit or not ; and it is also used to designate those who obtain their living exclusively by mental labour. [3] In the former sense the expression includes those who adopt a certain critical attitude towards life, [4] whatever their economical and social status may be ; in the latter sense, it is possible to separate from the social mass a specific group and to regard this group as *intelligentsia*. In this sense the *intelligentsia* appears as an integral social layer intermediate between the exploited and the exploiting classes, to use the phraseology of the Social Democrats. In its upper and more specifically professional layers this class naturally allies itself with the class of capitalist employers or " proprietary bourgeoisie," while the lower and less secure layers naturally ally themselves with the proletariat or labouring mass. The upper layers of the *intelligentsia* are composed of the managers and the superior technical experts of industrial and similar enterprises, and the lower layers of the clerks and foremen of these. The *intelligentsia*, considered as a class, is thus less uniform in its economical status than other classes of society, and its different layers must therefore gravitate both politically and socially to those different classes of

---

[1] This chapter was published in the *University Magazine* (Canada). The writer is indebted to the editor for permission to print it here.

[2] The introduction of this word into the Russian language is said to be due to P. D. Boborēkin. See Tugan-Baranovsky, " *Intelligentsia* and Socialism," in *Intelligentsia in Russia* (St. Petersburg, 1910), p. 248.

[3] *Cf.* Cherevanēn, N., " *Intelligentsia* Movement " in *Social Movements in Russia in the Beginning of the Twentieth Century* (St. Petersburg, 1909), vol. i. p. 259.

[4] Tugan-Baranovsky, *loc. cit.*

society with which they are more or less nearly allied. While the absence of education and culture among the peasants, on the one hand, and the comparatively slender development of higher education among the gentry and the merchant classes on the other, prevents in Russia so complete an identification of the *intelligentsia* with one or other of the classes mentioned as might be shown to exist in Germany and in England, for instance, there was in Russia prior to the revolution a certain amount of this identification. For example, in the Zemstvos the *intelligentsia* allied themselves with the more intelligent of the Zemstvo gentry. For a time during the last ten years of the nineteenth century and the first five years of the twentieth, the *intelligentsia* succeeded, by means of this alliance, in directing the activities of the Zemstvos. During these years the *intelligentsia* attempted to make the Zemstvos the " crowbar " of the movement against the Government.[1] Simultaneously the more revolutionary of the *intelligentsia* went among the peasantry as similar enthusiasts went in the *V Narod* movement of the seventies. They tried to identify themselves with the peasant points of view and to stimulate the peasants into political action. Yet in neither case did the *intelligentsia* succeed in leavening the masses on the one hand of the landowning gentry or on the other of the peasantry. In the first case the landowning gentry became frightened at the prospect of the goal to which the *intelligentsia* were leading them, and began to lose faith in the efficacy of the educational and other movements into which they had been drawn by the *intelligentsia*. The result of this state of mind made itself evident in the so-called " righting of the Zemstvos," and in the expulsion from them of the *intelligentsia*. This proceeding had the ulterior effects of the voluntary exclusion from the Zemstvos of numbers of intelligent gentry who disapproved of the return to reaction, and of the definite alliance of these with certain of the *intelligentsia* in the formation of a new political party, viz. the party of Constitutional Democrats. Thus the city professional men and the more liberal landowners were for the first time united in their political aims. Although the numbers of the gentry who united themselves in this manner with the *intelligentsia* was not great in proportion to the total number of landowning gentry, it was nevertheless considerable. The *intelli-*

---

[1] Cherevanēn, *loc. cit.*, p. 260.

gentsia who had been at work among the peasants were not able to draw from them any similar group, nor were they able to endow the peasant movement with any such definite political character. They did not represent the peasant masses, and the peasant masses did not as a whole absorb their political doctrines. This was true of Social Democrat, Social Revolutionary, and non-party *intelligentsia* alike. Yet undoubtedly the professional *intelligentsia* constituted the backbone of the revolutionary movement. They seized liberties when these could be seized, and they directed against the Government all the forces they could muster. Yet their influence over the classes with which they had allied themselves was inadequate to effect a political and social union sufficiently powerful to overthrow the autocracy.

The reason for this failure may probably be fairly regarded as twofold. First, the masses of the people were not ready for such action as might lead to the overthrowal of the autocracy, and second, the *intelligentsia* were divided into two main factions. These factions were, on the one hand, the groups who trusted in revolutionary methods pure and simple, and, on the other hand, those who believed in political action, properly so called. The first faction were not numerically powerful, and perhaps were not skilful enough in the special kind of skill which was necessary to create a situation in which the autocracy must collapse, while the second faction were not sufficiently experienced in political methods to turn to the best advantage the universal discontent. This division into two factions, while quite inevitable in certain phases of all such movements, must have been fatal to the complete realization of the revolution, even although each faction had been more widely supported than was the case.

Much importance must also, however, be attached to the fact that the overthrowal of the autocracy was a political measure, while the advocacy and the struggle of both factions were not merely political, but were also social. The aims of the *intelligentsia*, as a whole, were twofold. They desired a political revolution and they desired a drastic social change. The origins of this double aim must be sought for in the historical circumstances which gave the Russian *intelligentsia* its special character.

Professor Tugan-Baranovsky finds the chief mark of distinction between the development of Western Europe and the development of Russia to lie in the presence in the former and the absence in the latter of the guild organization of industry.[1] This organization, in Professor Tugan-Baranovsky's view, was largely instrumental in the creation in Western Europe of a class of cultivated bourgeoisie, which not merely acquired predominant political power, but represented the intellectual force of its time. The greater bourgeoisie had no monopoly of culture, for culture was also shared by the smaller bourgeoisie, who played a leading social and political rôle for several centuries. In Russia the greater bourgeoisie or trading-capitalist class was not cultivated, and the small bourgeois class did not exist. In Western Europe the professions were chiefly recruited from the small bourgeoisie. Sons of the small manufacturers became statesmen, lawyers, clergy, and men of letters, and gave to society such intellectual and cultivated tone as it possessed. Moreover, they acted as a connecting link between the upper and lower layers of society. Out of this condition there arose in Western Europe the sense of citizenship which was common to all classes and which served to bind society together. Such a state of mind did not exist in Russia, because that country did not possess the class in whose minds it could take root.

Peter the Great was one of the first to recognize that Russia could never become a powerful empire without the aid of educated men. He therefore encouraged and required the nobility to devote themselves to education in order to provide the State with the instruments necessary for administration. The duty thus laid upon the nobility and the gentry, and the practical exclusion from the higher service of the State of all but these, resulted in the exclusion from the ranks of the *intelligentsia* up till the middle of the nineteenth century of all but members of the nobility and gentry, and among these officers of the army and civil officials predominated. The type of educated men thus formed was essentially different from the type produced in Western Europe by continual accessions to the ranks of the educated classes from the ranks of the small bourgeoisie. The *intelligentsia* of Western Europe, derived from and sympathizing with the bourgeoisie, shared its interests,

---

[1] See Tugan-Baranovsky, " *Intelligentsia* and Socialism," in *Intelligentsia in Russia* (St. Petersburg, 1910), pp. 235 *et seq*. There were guilds in the Free Towns, but they do not appear to have been influential after the absorption of the towns by the Moscow State. Cf. *supra*, pp. 28 and 33.

and therefore not only threw itself as a class into the political struggles of the eighteenth century which early in the nineteenth century resulted in the victory of the bourgeoisie and in their capture of political power, but when that phase of political struggle was over and the proletariat attempted to displace the bourgeoisie and to seize the reins of power, the *intelligentsia* in general was ranged, not on the side of the proletariat, but against it. The origin and history of the *intelligentsia* of Western Europe thus account for the antagonism of the *intelligentsia* to socialism. The origin and history of the *intelligentsia* in Russia, on the other hand, predispose the *intelligentsia* of that country towards socialism. Their sympathies and interest do not incline them towards the bourgeoisie, and since the smaller bourgeoisie does not as a class exist in Russia, the advent of socialism would produce by no means so great an economic disturbance in Russia as must inevitably be the case elsewhere. It must be acknowledged, moreover, that the *intelligentsia* are perhaps the only socialists in Russia. The peasant masses cannot be transformed into Social Democrats, and the working men of the industrial centres are not sufficiently well educated to entertain any but crude ideas of socialism, even when they are in general well affected towards socialist ideas as presented to them by the Social Democrats.

The Russian *intelligentsia* have, moreover, by origin and tradition, a profound lack of faith in the autocratic State. Russian evolution has for them meant the development of absolutism, therefore they are opposed to the Russian State in its present form. Under the pre-revolution conditions, Russian men of letters and jurists exercised no influence upon the Government. This exclusion from political power, for the exercise of which they conceived themselves to be well fitted, was the chief cause of their oppositional activity. They threw themselves into the struggle against the autocracy, and in this struggle the *intelligentsia* naturally allied themselves with the parties which devoted themselves to "active resistance."

The attitude towards life and towards the evolution of society which is adopted by the Russian *intelligentsia*, is thus quite different from that adopted by analogous groups in Western Europe. From the beginning of the nineteenth century, the class in Russia was growing in numbers, its education was frequently of the highest order, yet its influence upon the conduct of affairs was *nil ;* under these circumstances the *intelligentsia* threw themselves with ardour into the struggle for a change. The *Dekabristi* were among the first to be influenced by Western European thought ; and each successive group of *intelligentsia* was more and more influenced by it. Whether or not Pestèl was inspired by contemporary French writers like Saint Simon, for example, or whether he arrived spontaneously at doctrines very similar to those of that writer, may not be susceptible of determination, but later groups were undoubtedly influenced by their French and German contemporaries. The current of ideas which is vaguely known as Socialism swept the Russian *intelligentsia* along in numbers proportionately much greater than was the case in any other country. These doctrines won their way very slowly in Western Europe, and they have never been accepted with any ardour by the first-rate minds, although in one or another form they have been embraced by writers of enthusiastic and impulsive temperament.[1] Probably the causes of Russian enthusiasm for Socialist doctrines may be found in two characteristics of Russian life : (1) in the detachment of the intellectual Russian from the sordid materialism of the peasant and the merchant ; and (2) in the detachment, in an intellectual and moral sense, which arose out of the existence of political despotism and ecclesiastical stagnation, and the consequent diversion of his mind from the political and ecclesiastical spheres to purely intellectual and moral spheres. This detachment on two important sides of his life has endowed the intellectual Russian with a sense of freedom[2] and an indifference to tradition which have marked him off especially from Frenchmen and Englishmen of the same degree of ability and education, in whose minds political interests have assumed a large place, and have served, as it were, to adulterate their intellectual products. The Western European is thus by no means so free from intellectual and moral prejudgments as the Russian. The purely intellectual and critical attitude of mind of the Russian may be held to have exposed him in an especial manner to socialist convictions, because, prevented as the intellectual Russian was from entering the political field, he was not accustomed to regard that field as enclosing any but a part of the national

---

[1] As, for example, by John Ruskin and William Morris.
[2] *Cf.* Tugan-Baranovsky, *op. cit.*, p. 239.

life; and, finding in the national life much to condemn and much to reform, he proposed to seek the direction of reform, not within the field of politics, but altogether outside of the contemporary political conventions. He was thus led to consider a complete social change as the indispensable condition of progress. For these reasons he was most likely to embrace socialism, whose offers of regeneration were the most generous in the intellectual market.[1]

The ideals offered by Liberalism sufficed to stimulate the intellectuals of Western Europe ; but for the Russian they paled before more ample promises. A constitutional monarchical State, firmly based upon the support of the capitalist and landowning classes, had no attraction for the Russian *intelligent*. The historical moment for embracing an ideal of that kind had passed long since. For him the State did not require to be strengthened—it was already too strong. The development of the Russian State had brought its power to the utmost limits, so far as concerned its relations with the Russian people ; nothing more could be hoped from that development. It was necessary to go outside the field of Russian political and social thought to discover a new ideal. The selection of this ideal might be accomplished by abstract methods and in a disinterested manner. The change must be a drastic one in any case—why not at once aim at the result most highly desirable within the range of contemporary human vision ?

Moreover, in Russia the struggle between classes was of an essentially different character from that which obtained in Western Europe. In the latter region the classes were engaged for centuries in a series of contests for the mastery of political power. In Russia no such contests took place. No class had any political power ; there was thus little class solidarity either for defensive or for offensive purposes. From the beginning of the Moscow State the power of its princes had been directed towards the organization of the community into officers and rankers. Every nobleman had his functions—military or civil—to perform, and every peasant had his place and his obligations. There were no others, excepting the clergy, and these also had their rights and duties. All were under the control of the great " leveller " the Tsar. Thus in Russia the building up of self-conscious classes has yet to begin. In no case have the classes of which society is composed acted together for any

[1] *Cf.* Tugan-Baranovsky, *op. cit.*, p. 240.

length of time, nor have they even acted separately with any degree of interior cohesion. The mere existence in Russia of the *intelligentsia*, belonging as it does to various classes, is a proof of the absence in that country of class solidarity.

Up till the period of Emancipation the Russian *intelligentsia* comprised chiefly members of aristocratic families, with a few sons of the clergy and a few sons of professional men, these being connected directly or indirectly either with the aristocracy or with the Church. The wealthier bourgeoisie also contributed to the *intelligentsia*, but to a slender extent. After Emancipation the *intelligentsia* was subjected to an invasion, and its character was altered. This was the invasion by *raznochintsi*, or plebeians, who now, undeterred by legal barriers, came out from the people. The *intelligentsia* was thus, as it were, democratized, and the consequence is apparent in the facile adoption by the new elements of the socialist ideas of that period.[1] Thus the *intelligentsia*, recruited by new, active, and highly articulate groups, came to be regarded by the world at large as consisting wholly of these groups, and the forms of socialism which they had accepted came to be looked upon as representing the attitude of the *intelligentsia* as a whole.[2] The new members of the *intelligentsia*, teachers, physicians, Zemstvo clerks, journalists, &c.[3] belonged to the people by birth and early training, and belonged to the intellectual group by higher education. They had the faults of their qualities, and the strength and weakness of the class from which they sprang. They were full of hope and enthusiasm, yet their social and mental equilibrium was not secure. They felt themselves at war with the peasant conditions which they had abandoned, and they disliked the vulgar ostentation of the more conspicuous of the superior classes, while they had little opportunity of knowing the charm of the simplicity and refinement of mature social types. Their view of society thus lacked perspective. Their criteria of relative values were imperfect, and they thus attached to certain phases of life exaggerated importance. The outcome of all this was a certain fanatical enthusiasm—in extreme cases tending to merely futile visions or to violent action with intent to produce immediate results.

This group has been defined by a recent writer as " a number

[1] Largely the ideas of Marx.
[2] *Cf*. Tugan-Baranovsky, *op. cit.*, p. 242.   [3] *Ibid.*, p. 243.

of militant monks of the nihilist religion of earthly well-being. This group, so strange to the monastic system, declares war against the world in order forcibly to benefit it and (as it were in spite of itself) to satisfy its material needs. The whole energy of this monkish army is directed towards the material interests and needs, for the creation of a terrestrial paradise of abundance and security. Everything that is transcendental, every faith in absolute values, is a hateful enemy." [1] This view of the Russian *intelligentsia*, or rather of that large portion of it which has been recruited from the inferior social layers, is contained in one of the essays which compose a singular volume entitled, *Vyekhē*.[2] These essays offer in general the same interpretation of the relation to the revolution of the *intelligentsia*. According to this interpretation, the rôle of the *intelligentsia* in the revolution failed because of the fundamentally erroneous ideals of the group. These ideals, being based exclusively upon material needs, lacked the spiritual character which alone can stimulate people to heroic deeds. To accomplish the overthrowal of the autocracy, such deeds were indispensable, but the spiritual force being lacking, they were not accomplished. This criticism involves the postulate that spiritual life is supreme, both " theoretically and practically, over the external forms of social life." [3] The exaggerated importance which was attached to these external forms led the *intelligentsia* to neglect the interior life of society, and thus to its inability to act as guide towards the emancipation of the people.

This critical attack upon the *intelligentsia* in the pages of *Vyekhē* is not conducted by reactionaries, but by writers who may fairly be regarded as themselves belonging to the *intelligentsia ;* many of them are Constitutional Democrats. " We do not," they say, " judge the past, because its historical inevitability is clear, but we do point out that the path which Russian society has trodden has brought it to this *impasse.*" [4]

The state of mind which *Vyekhē* and the literature which has

[1] S. L. Frank in " The Ethics of Nihilism," in *Vyekhē* (Moscow, 1910).
[2] Moscow (first edition), 1909 ; fifth edition, 1910. The contributors are N. A. Berdyayev, S. N. Bulgakov, M. O. Gershenzon, A. S. Izgoyev, B. A. Kēstyakovskie, P. B. Struvē, and S. L. Frank. The fifth edition contains a bibliography of the very considerable mass of literature which has sprung up round the book. The word *Vyekhē* means the tall posts which are set up in the winter to indicate the road while the country is covered with deep snow.
[3] *Ibid.*, Preface, p. ii.   [4] *Ibid., loc. cit.*

sprung up round it reveals is evidently due to reaction after the revolution. That this reaction should assume a semblance of pietism is no novelty. Outbursts of religious fervour after great emotional strain are common alike in individual and in national life. The authors of *Vyekhē* make their position quite plain in a casual phrase in their preface. " This very point " (the main point they urge, viz. the supremacy of the spiritual over the material forces) " has been untiringly repeated from Chaadayev to Soloviev and Tolstoy, by all our profound thinkers. They were not listened to. The *intelligentsia* went past them. Perhaps now awakened, as by an earthquake, they will listen to weaker voices." [1] That is to say, that after the turmoil of the revolution is over the exhausted spirit turns to the seers or to the confessional, and the stool of repentance.[2]

In his very able and interesting criticism of *Vyekhē*, Professor Tugan-Baranovsky observes that the opposition which the authors of that volume have discovered between external social reforms and the interior improvement of personality is not at all fundamental, but, on the contrary, the elements of this alleged opposition are indissolubly connected with one another. Social forms, he says, and human personality do not represent two distinct social categories. It is equally right to say that personality creates social forms as to say that social forms create personality. Each limits and determines the other.[3]

The authors of *Vyekhē* regard the *intelligentsia* as a separate social group, and they attribute to this social group the principal rôle in the revolution. There is much to be said for this view, but their continuation is more doubtful. This group, they say, is making for the disintegration of the Russian Empire; it is, therefore, their duty to dissolve themselves and to fall back into the classes to which they respectively belong ; because, says Struvë, the foundations of politics are to be discovered, not in the organization of society, but in the " internal self-development of the man." It is true that a bad man cannot make a good citizen, but it is not advisable, even if it were possible, to hold society as dissolved until each person in it is improved to the desired pitch.

[1] *Vyekhē*, Preface, p. ii.
[2] It is to be noticed also that at the close of the revolutionary period there were other concomitants of reaction after nervous strain, *e.g.* an outburst of licentiousness and greatly increased circulation of obscene books.
[3] Tugan-Baranovsky, *op. cit.*, p. 245.

The *intelligentsia*, with all its faults, is clearly a present fact of Russian social life. It has been the inevitable result of the conditions of Russian society of the past hundred years. Moreover, for the reasons explained above, the *intelligentsia* is to be regarded " rather as a social-ethical than as a social-economic category," [1] that it is not a social class, but a group in a certain scheme of social classification. Although a large number, perhaps the majority, of the Russian *intelligentsia* have been swept along by the socialist wave, as Social Democrats or Socialist Revolutionists, yet it would not be safe to suppose that there was only an insignificant minority. This minority may be held to be composed of those of more placid temperament, who are not readily carried away by the currents of fashion, and who are disposed to look at social progress as the result of the interaction of many forces.

In Germany, France, England, and in the United States, there has undoubtedly appeared during recent years a social phenomenon which corresponds more or less to the description of it given by Kautsky.[2]

The development of capitalism, he says in effect, has resulted in the appearance of a special class, hired by the capitalist. This class is necessary to perform operations for which high mental ability and scientific education are necessary. One of the frequent, though not invariable, concomitants of this high mental ability and specialized education is capacity to think abstractly, and another is detachment from special class interests. There is thus a new class within a class which possesses a " wider spiritual horizon " than any other. This new class has, therefore, before it, not class interests, but the wider interests of society as a whole. The aims of this class, to begin with, are likely to be of an ethical character. They thus tend towards *Katheder Sozialism*, the co-operative movement, arbitration, and the like.

Jaurès, the French Revisionist, notices also the rise of this class and predicts that, " insulted by a society based on coarse mercantile interests and disappointed with bourgeois domination," this class will become socialist.[3] The consequence to socialism is not

---

[1] Tugan-Baranovsky, *op. cit.*, p. 248.
[2] In a long series of articles in *Die Neue Zeit.* The passage in the text is quoted by Tugan-Baranovsky, *op. cit.*, p. 249.
[3] Quoted by Tugan-Baranovsky, *op. cit.*, p. 251.

regarded with equanimity by orthodox Marxists,[1] who consider that the socialist party is in the throes of a crisis owing to the influx into its ranks of large numbers of " bourgeois intelligents."

From these and other considerations, Tugan-Baranovsky arrives at the conclusion that the *intelligent* is drifting away from the bourgeoisie to which he belongs by birth and training, and is approaching the proletariat. Assuming that this means an approach towards socialism, he meets the argument that it means also the *debâcle* of socialism by expressing the opinion that while it may involve the passing of Marxism, it need not involve the passing of socialism, " which existed before Marx and is likely to exist after him." [2]

In any case he thinks that the democratization of Western Europe is probably making in this direction, and that in this respect Russia is likely to follow the West.[3]

It must be observed, however, that the great change which occurred in Russian public life, the institution of the Duma, and the greater freedom of the press, altered materially the conditions which promoted the influence of socialism upon the minds of the *intelligentsia*.[4] There was a tendency to draw at all events the milder types into the current of political discussion and to the expenditure of their energies in that direction, rather than in the direction of discussions of social change of a drastic order. Besides, socialism denuded of Marxism so altered in character and in political and social aims as to demand a new name. For Marxism, after all, afforded a certain fixed *credo*, to which appeal could be made from the heretics; and the abandonment of this fixity was not unlikely to result in vague and fluctuating positions, useless for purposes of propaganda.

Necessary as " revision " had come to be, it meant the inclusion in the socialist ranks of many who were not in the older sense fairly to be regarded as socialists. Therefore the new ranks, useful and progressive as they may have been, were, strictly speaking, other than socialist, however convenient the retention of the traditional name might be and however difficult it was for the public to learn any other.[5]

[1] As *e.g.* by Lafargue.   [2] Tugan-Baranovsky, *op. cit.*, p. 254.
[3] *Ibid.*, p. 256.
[4] This is recognized by Tugan-Baranovsky. Cf. *op. cit.*, p. 256.
[5] Cf. *supra*, pp. 77–102.

EPILOGUE

THE account of the economic history of Russia closes appropriately with the revolutionary movement of 1905-07 and its immediately related consequences. Although reaction followed this, the first stage of the Russian Revolution, the economic and political history of Russia entered upon a new phase.

The causes of the Revolution have already been indicated. They may now be summarized. So far as the peasantry were concerned, the causes may be traced to accumulation of grievances resulting chiefly from conditions arising out of the method of Emancipation in 1861. The transference of the votchinal power from the *pomyetschëkë* to the *mir*, the retention by the former of a considerable degree of local control, the absence of mobility, the rise of rent, and the need of land, together with the absence of agricultural capital and the recurrence of deep depression with every deficient harvest, were the principal causes of the accumulation of grievances. The peasants were in general unskilful farmers; but their education was impeded by ecclesiastical influences, as well as by their own deep reluctance to alter the methods to which they had been accustomed. Their education was also impeded spasmodically by the local authorities. These authorities were at times enthusiastic advocates of rural education. They established rural schools and encouraged dissemination of knowledge of agricultural improvements, as well as the adoption of agricultural implements of an improved character. At other times the same authorities became nervous about the effects upon the peasants of education in inducing discontent with their economic and political conditions. This fear was undoubtedly well grounded; but the *V Narod* propagandists were right in believing that discontent was a necessary incident in the improvement of these conditions. The rapid growth and the racially diversified character of the population rendered the adoption of a uniform policy and the task of co-ordinating local with central administration very difficult. The people had never been permitted to act for themselves, and therefore there had rarely grown up among them any groups of persons to whom the

597

tasks of local government could wisely be confided in the interests of the people. They had been assiduously taught to look to the classes above them for direction, and the duties of that direction became with the increasing peasant population more and more arduous. Meanwhile the growth of industry had brought about a great increase of the urban population, and the decline of the habit which induced working men to return at frequent periodical intervals to the villages to which they belonged had brought about an increase of the urban proletariat. At the same time the breaking up of the large peasant households had begun to result in a partially or wholly nomadic peasant proletariat. In the absence of adequate educational measures of an official order, rendered difficult because of the rapid increase of the population and because of the inferiority of its capacity for industrial production, the artisan readily accepted the ideas of the educated sympathisers in the Social Democratic groups of the *intelligentsia*. The prosecution of working men of a socialistic frame of mind led to their dispersal to the villages and to diffusion of the doctrines which they had absorbed.

Exclusion of the educated classes from participation in government, active measures against the Jews, who were in general eager for education and social advancement, provoking retaliation on their part, and dissociation of the comparatively small and inefficient governing groups from the general social mass, prepared the way for active measures against the autocracy.

The Russo-Japanese War may be held to have delayed the outbreak of the Revolution, but to have contributed to the revolutionary state of mind by the exposure of the military incompetence of the autocracy. For a short time the oppositional groups acted simultaneously, although not definitely in concert. The unanimity, such as it was, was merely negative. When positive action came to be necessary, the oppositional groups dissolved into factions. The extreme groups were irreconcilable. They demanded a democracy, but they required that the democracy should share and act upon their sectarian doctrines. It was in effect this condition which brought the Revolution of 1905–07 "to dust," and gave time for the autocracy to collect its demoralized forces and to overcome the extreme factions. The grounds of disagreement among the oppositional groups were partly racial and partly economical. The liberal elements among the landowners came to be afraid of peasant control and even of peasant vengeance, especially among the non-Russian peasant populations. The excessive demands of the working men frightened the rising manufacturing and employing class, and the officials, among whom there were many moderate liberals, saw in democratic control only confusion. In all the groups there seemed to arise a lust for power. There is no evidence of any widespread desire for popular representative government, with all its possibilities and all its risks. Although there was a clamour for an assembly convened for the purpose of formulating a constitution, few realized what such an assembly meant, and probably very few would have been disposed to accept the compromises which any constitution formulated by such an assembly would have involved.

Russia paid during the Revolution a high price for the banishment, imprisonment and execution of many of her best men. The class that should have formulated her constitution had been dispersed and reduced to impotence. Some of them returned from abroad, but even these had lost touch with the currents of Russian life, and their influence in many cases disappeared.

The numerous strikes and riots produced in the people a certain neurasthenic condition. They were wearied, and they desired merely a rest. This was the real reaction—the reaction of the people; and this made possible the reaction of the Government. In spite of this undoubted fact, it must be realized that Russia had changed abruptly from a country in which criticism was sternly suppressed to one in which criticism abounded. The Duma, with all its defects, became a school in which a new generation of competent rulers might be trained. Without some such school as that —outside of the bureaucratic field—it was impossible for Russia to aim at an effective democracy.

Fate has determined that Russia should experience no such gradual process. The autocracy fell suddenly and hopelessly because of its inherent weakness. There was a revolutionary state of mind among the people; but the autocracy fell not by a revolutionary onslaught, it crumbled to pieces. In the chaos which supervened the Revolution revived, and that which was begun in 1905–07 was carried a stage farther. A new and perplexing volume of the economic history of Russia and of Europe was opened in 1917.

APPENDIX TO BOOK VII

Prices of Russian 4 per cent. State Debt on the Paris Bourse[1]

18/31 Dec. 1903.[2]	98	Before the outbreak of war.
19 Jan./1 Feb. 1904.	99	Before the outbreak of war.
26 Jan./8 Feb. 1904.	98	First attack on Port Arthur.
2/15 June 1904.	91.05	Defeat at Va-fang-hu.
12/25 July 1904.	93.40	Defeat at Ta-shih-kiao.
29 July/10 Aug. 1904.	93.70	Naval disaster at Port Arthur.
23 Aug./5 Sept. 1904.	91.60	Defeat at Liao-yang.
22 Dec. 1904/4 Jan. 1905.	89	Fall of Port Arthur.
9/22 Jan. 1905.	85	"Bloody Sunday."
25 Feb./10 March 1905.	81	Fall of Mukden.
19 May/1 June 1905.	87.25	Battle of Tsu-shima.
8/15 July 1905.	85.80	Mutiny on *Kniaz-Potyemkin*.
30 Aug./12 Sept. 1905.	88.85	Peace of Portsmouth.
7/20 Sept. 1905.	94	Before the Baku Strike.
30 Oct./12 Nov. 1905.8	88.50	First General Strike.
5/18 Nov. 1905.	89.80	Mutiny at Kronstadt.
27 Nov./10 Dec. 1905.	86.25	Insurrection at Sevastopol.
8/21 Dec. 1905.	77	Third General Strike and Uprising in Moscow.
10/23 Dec. 1905.	80.50	Rumours of close of Strike.

· *Journal des Economistes*, 6e série, tome 5 (Paris, 1905), p. 19, and *ibid.*, tome 9 (1906), p. 27.

[2] The first-mentioned dates are according to the Russian or old style, the second according to the West European or new style.

INDEX

DIAGRAM OF THE STRIKE MOVEMENT

(See page 477)

Showing the proportions of the numbers officially recognized as engaged in economical and political strikes in Russia during the year 1905.[1]

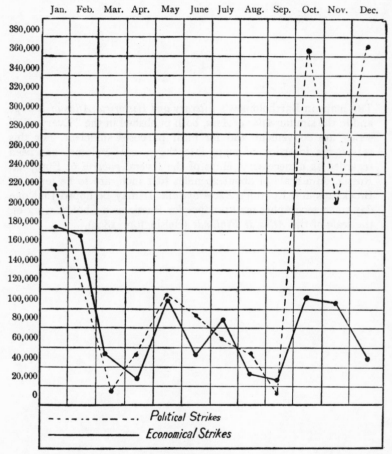

¹ Constructed from data in Varzar, *op. cit.*, pp. 101, 102. According to the same authority, the total number of strikers on economical grounds during 1905 was 1,018,620 in 4192 establishments, and of those on political grounds was 1,691,075 in 8918 establishments, the gross total being 2,709,695 in 13,110 establishments.

THE maps in Bartholomew's *Literary and Historical Atlas of Europe* and in the similar *Atlas of Asia*, both published in the "Everyman" series, are convenient and for most purposes sufficient. For this reason the insertion of maps into the present volumes has been regarded as unnecessary. Maps of the several *guberni* of European Russia, on a scale of about 20 miles to 1 inch, are to be found in Brockhaus and Ephron's *Encyclopædia*. It may be hoped that one day some geographer may produce for Russia as a whole a work on the scale of the *Atlas de Finlande* (Helsingfors, 1899).

GLOSSARY

Arshin, 2.33 feet.

Barin, master.
Bartschina, labour rendered by a bondman for his master without wages.
Bobyeli, landless peasants.
Boyarstvo, nobility.

Chetvert, 5.77 bushels.
Chinovnik, civil functionary, bureaucrat.

Dessyatin, 2.70 acres.
Dvorovie lyudē, household serfs.
Dvoryanstvo, gentry.

Gubernie, state, *department*.

Ispravnēk, local chief of police.

Jetnetsa, rye-growing regions.

Kabala, document binding to service.
Karasea, serge.
Kazachikh, labouring woman.
Kazakov, labouring man.
Kholop, bondman, serf.
Krestyanie, peasantry.
Krugoviya peruka, mutual guarantee.

Meshanie, small householding class.
Mir, world, village or group of villages constituting a local administrative unit.
Mujìk, peasant.

Obrŏk, payment in kind or in money in lieu of *bartschina*.

Obtschina, community.
Obyazannyeya, obligative possessional factories.
Osmak, unit of taxation in Baltic provinces.

Peryelojnoë, ten-year cultivation system.
Polonianichnikh, bond money.
Polovnēkē, metayer tenants.
Pomyestneye, estates.
Pomyetschēk, proprietor of an estate.
Posàd, suburb.
Pozemelneya obtschina, agrarian community.
Pozrednēk, chief of the *mir*.
Prekaz, bureau.
Pùd, 36.11 lbs. avoirdupois.

Raba, bondwoman.
Ratusha, town-hall.
Ruble, 308.5806 grains gross 900 fine, or 277.7221 grains pure silver. Par value 38$\frac{3}{64}$d. English.

Sajen, 7 feet English.
Selo, village.
Selskiya obtschestva, village community.
Skhod, village meeting.
Sobor, assembly.
Sobranie, assembly of the nobility.
Sokha, modern Russian plough.
Sotsky, chiefs of village groups of 100 men.
Stàrosta, village headman.
Starshinà, chief of the *volost*.
Streltsi, bowmen.
Streltskaya, adjectival form of *streltsi*.

Tyaglo, unit of taxation.

603

Udeli, appanage.
Udelnye, estate of Imperial Family.
Ukase, decree, legislative act.
Uyezd, district.

Verst, .66 English mile.
Volost, group of villages for purposes of local administration.
Votchina, heritable property.
Votchinĕk, owner of a heritable estate.

Voyevoda, military governor.
Vyvodnye, payment by peasant bride for leave to marry.

Yamskikh, carrier tax.

Zapadnĕk, Westerner.
Zemsky Sobor, popular assembly.
Zemstvo, area of local administration.

INDEX

Equerries' quarter, Moscow, 66
L'Ere Nouvelle, 451 *n.*
Erfurt programme (Social Democratic), 150
Erisman, Professor, 409
Espionage, 188 *n.*
Excess of candidates for employment, 364
Executive Committee (1877–81), 109 ; (1879), 117, 125, 131, 133
Exile of notable men, consequences of, 73, 73 *n.*
Expansion of Russia eastwards, 211–243
Explosion near Moscow (Nov. 19, 1879), 127, 127 *n.*
Expropriation of land, 301, 301 *n.*
" Expropriations," 569
Extraordinary growth of Russian industry (1893–8), 374
Extraordinary guard, 548, 548 *n.*
Extravagance of the Zemstvos, 281
Ezymovskoë province, 36

FACTORIES and mill administration of Moscow district, 194
— obliged to provide hospital accommodation for their workers, 408
Factory inspection, 365, 408
— — manufacturers' struggle against, 411
Factory inspectors' reports, 195
— law of Aug. 26, 1866, 412
— — of June 9, 1882, 410
— — of June 3, 1885, 418, 418 *n.*
— — of June 3, 1886, 411, 418, 418 *n.*
— — of Oct. 1, 1886, 418
— — of June 3, 1897, 412
— — of March 14, 1898, 412
— legislation, 85, 407
— — imperfect administration of, 408
— owners obliged to provide medical attendance to sick workmen, 408
— system after 1861, 368
False decrees, 53 *n.*
— tsars, 139
Family, the undivided or joint, 264–266
Famine of 1891, the, 174
Famines, political utilization of, 147
Far East, Russia in the, 211–43
Fashoda affair, 236
Fatalism in Russian character, 19

Federation of the Jura, 102
Feminist terrorism, 4 *n.*
" Fermentation " among the troops at Moscow, 540
Fērsov, N. N., 25 *n.*, 53 *n.*
Fertilizers, 284
Feuerbach, 80 *n.*, 83
Fiedler's school, meeting at, 555
Fighting organization of the Socialist Revolutionaries, 184
Figuer, Vera, 132
Finlanders, 246
Finland, Russification of, 139
Finlay, George, 204 *n.*
Finnish literature, growth of, 248
— Party, 5 *n.*
Fishing population on the Volga, 402
Fleet of Russia in Chinese waters (1895), 230
Flights of peasants, 9, 21
Fluctuations of opinion in oppositional groups, 144–7
Foochow, 221
Foreign capital in Russia, 156, 156 *n.*
Forest regulations, 277 *n.*
Fourier, 65, 66 *n.*, 82, 82 *n.*, 88 *n.*
France, 15, 47, 53, 53 *n.*; influence of, on Russia, 63, 83, 221, 222
Franco-Belgian syndicate (China), 235 *n.*
Franco-Prussian War, 97
Franco-Russian *entente*, 236, 240
Frank, S. L., 593 *n.*
Freedom of Cossack life, 24
— of the press restricted by the C.W.M.D., 524, 525
Free Economical Society, 503
Freeman, Professor, 100 *n.*
Freemasonry, 63 *n.*
Freiman, Major-General, 35, 36, 53
French Ambassador and the Goujon strike at Moscow, 196
— capital in Russia, 155
— encyclopedists, 66
— fleet before Petropavlovsk (1854), 220
— Revolution, 4 *n.*, 13, 15, 62, 62 *n.*, 77
— — (1830), 82
— — (1848), 82, 161
Frēsh, V. I., Chief of Police of St. Petersburg, 201
Friendly society movement in Russia, 422, 424
Frolenko, 123
Fur trade, 211, 227